The Conceptual Worlds of the Fourth Gospel

The Conceptual Worlds of the Fourth Gospel

Intertextuality and Early Reception

Charles B. Puskas
and
C. Michael Robbins

CASCADE *Books* · Eugene, Oregon

THE CONCEPTUAL WORLDS OF THE FOURTH GOSPEL
Intertextuality and Early Reception

Copyright © 2021 Charles B. Puskas and C. Michael Robbins. All rights reserved. Except for brief quotations in critical publications or reviews, no part of this book may be reproduced in any manner without prior written permission from the publisher. Write: Permissions, Wipf and Stock Publishers, 199 W. 8th Ave., Suite 3, Eugene, OR 97401.

Cascade Books
An Imprint of Wipf and Stock Publishers
199 W. 8th Ave., Suite 3
Eugene, OR 97401

www.wipfandstock.com

PAPERBACK ISBN: 978-1-5326-8171-4
HARDCOVER ISBN: 978-1-5326-8172-1
EBOOK ISBN: 978-1-5326-8173-8

Cataloguing-in-Publication data:

Names: Puskas, Charles B., author. | Robbins, C. Michael, author.

Title: The conceptual worlds of the fourth gospel : intertextuality and early reception / by Charles B. Puskas and C. Michael Robbins.

Description: Eugene, OR: Cascade Books, 2021 | Includes bibliographical references and index.

Identifiers: ISBN 978-1-5326-8171-4 (paperback) | ISBN 978-1-5326-8172-1 (hardcover) | ISBN 978-1-5326-8173-8 (ebook)

Subjects: LCSH: Bible. John—Criticism, interpretation, etc. | Intertextuality in the Bible.

Classification: LCC BS2615.52 C66 2021 (print) | LCC BS2615.52 (ebook)

01/05/21

*Dedicated to our wives, Susan Puskas and Annette Robbins,
for their patience and support.*

We extend also our sincere gratitude to our teachers for their learning and insight: Benny C. Aker, Merrill C. Tenney, Frederick W. Danker, Robert F. O'Toole, SJ, Charles W. Hedrick (Charles), Valdis Leinieks, Ray Bystrom, James M. Robinson, Dennis R. MacDonald, and Gregory J. Riley (Michael).

Contents

Credit Lines | ix
List of Tables | xi
Abbreviations | xiv
Preface | xxiii

Introduction | 1

Map of the Mediterranean World | 15

I. New Testament Intertextualities: Synoptic and Johannine traditions | 16

II. Jewish Scriptures (Septuagint) | 35

III. Jewish Wisdom and Angelology | 45

IV. Philo | 56

V. The Dead Sea Scrolls | 69

VI. Rabbinica and Targumim | 83

VII. Greco-Roman Cults and Philosophies: Isis, Plato, Hermetica | 103

VIII. The Dionysian Gospel | 126

IX. Odes of Solomon, Samaritan Traditions, and Mandaean Writings | 148

X. Nag Hammadi Library | 168

XI. Gospel of Thomas | 180

XII. Early Reception of the Fourth Gospel | 206

Conclusion | 232

Bibliography | 239
Index | 285

Credit Lines

Scripture quotations are from the New Revised Standard Version of the Bible, including the Apocryphal/Deuterocanonical Books of the Old Testament © 1989, by the Division of Christian Education of the National Council of the Churches of Christ in the USA, and used by permission.

Permission to cite Targumic parallels to the Fourth Gospel are granted by the author who holds the copyright to following work: John Ronning, *The Jewish Targums and John's Logos Theology*. Hendrickson, 2010. Grand Rapids: Baker Academic, 2011.

Scripture quotations of the Greek Old Testament are from Pietersma, Albert, and Benjamin G. Wright, eds. *A New English Translation of the Septuagint* © 2007 by the International Organization for Septuagint and Cognate Studies, Inc.

Brown, Raymond E. "The Gospel of Thomas and Saint John's Gospel" *NTS* 9 (1962–1963) 155–77.

Permission from its author to cite from: James R. Davila, "The Perils of Parallelism." https://www.st-andrews.ac.uk/divinity/rt/dss/abstracts/parallels/ with bibliography.

Evans, Craig A. *Word of Glory: On the Exegetical and Theological Background of John's Prologue*. New York and London: Bloomsbury Academic Press, 1993.

Foerster, Werner. *Gnosis: A Selection of Gnostic Texts*. 2 vols. Trans. R. McL. Wilson. Oxford: Clarendon, 1972–1974. Permission grant by original publisher, Artemis Verlag of Zürich.

Garcia Martinez, Florentino, and Eibert J. C. Tigchelaar, eds. *The Dead Sea Scrolls: Study Edition*. 2nd ed. 2 vols. Leiden: Brill, 1997. Grand Rapids: Eerdmans, 1999.

Hays, Richard B. *Echoes of Scripture in the Gospels*. Waco, TX: Baylor University Press, 2016.
———. *Echoes of Scripture in the Letters of Paul*. New Haven, CT: Yale University Press, 1989.

Litwa, David A. "'I Will Become Him': Homology and deification in the Gospel of Thomas," *JBL* 133 (2015) 427–47.

MacDonald, Dennis R., *The Dionysian Gospel: The Fourth Gospel and Euripides*. Minneapolis: Fortress, 2017. Used by permission.

Nock, A. D. and A. J. Festugière, *Corpus Hermeticum*. Vols. 1–4. 2nd–4th eds. Collection des Universités de France. Repr. Paris: Les Belles Lettres, 1972–1974. Permission granted by Publisher.

Philo, Works of. Trans. C. D. Yonge, 1854. Foreword by David M. Scholer. New updated version. Peabody, MA: Hendrickson, 1993. Public domain.

Richardson, Kurt A. *James*. New American Commentary 36. Nashville, TN: Broadman & Holman, 1997 (Map of Mediterranean World, p. 50).

Robinson, James M., gen. ed. *The Nag Hammadi Library*. Rev. ed. New York: HarperCollins, 1990. Permission granted by HarperCollins, NY.

List of Tables

1. A. Similar Sequence of Events in Mark and John with Verbal Similarities | 24
1. B. Mark and John: Double Cycle Tradition | 25
1. C. Mark and John: Lexical and Thematic Parallels | 25
1. D. Verbal Parallels of Mark and John | 26
1. E. Similar Themes of 1 John and the Gospel of John | 32
2. John and Jewish Scriptures (LXX) | 37
3. A. The Fourth Gospel and Jewish Wisdom (LXX) | 46
3. B. The Fourth Gospel and Jewish Angelogy | 53
4. The Fourth Gospel and Philo | 57
5. A. The Fourth Gospel and the Dead Sea Scrolls | 72
5. B. Tests for Evaluating Alleged Parallels | 79
6. A. The Fourth Gospel and Rabbinic Literature | 85
6. B. The Fourth Gospel and Aramaic Targumim | 92
6. C. Tests for Evaluating Alleged Parallels | 98
6. D. Responses to Critics of a Targumic Context | 100
7. A. Isis and the Fourth Gospel | 106
    1. Isis (Cyme-Memphis) and FG | 106
    2. Isis (Metamorphoses) and FG | 107
    3. Isis (Diodorus Siculus) and FG | 108
7. B. Tests for Evaluating Alleged Parallels | 109
7. C. The Fourth Gospel and Plato, Platonism | 115
7. D. Tests for Evaluating Alleged Parallels | 119
7. E. Hermetic Writings and the Fourth Gospel | 122
7. F. Tests for Evaluating Alleged Parallels | 124
8. A. The Fourth Gospel and *The Bacchae* (Mark Stibbe) | 131
8. B. List of Proposed Imitations (Dennis MacDonald) | 133

8. C. Intertextual Commentary (Dennis MacDonald) | 134

8. D. The Seven Criteria of Mimesis Criticism (Dennis MacDonald) | 142

9. A. The Odes of Solomon and the Fourth Gospel | 149

9. B. Assessing the Literary Relationship | 154

9. C. The Fourth Gospel and the Samaritans | 156

9. D. Mandaean Writings and the Fourth Gospel | 162

9. E. Mandaean and Related Writings in Bultmann's *Gospel of John* Commentary | 165

10. A. The Gospel of Truth, Apocryphon of John, and the Fourth Gospel | 172

10. B. The Gospel of Thomas and the Fourth Gospel | 174

10. C. The Gospel of Philip and the Fourth Gospel | 175

10. D. The Gospel of Truth, The Apocryphon of John, and FG (Redux) | 176

10. E. Trimorphic Protennoia (Three Forms) and the Fourth Gospel | 176

11. A. FG and GTh: Assessing the Relationship | 184

11. B. The Gospels of John and Thomas (Raymond E. Brown) | 187

11. C. The Gospels of John and Thomas (Helmut Koester) | 191

    1. Sayings about Life-Giving Power | 193

    2. Abiding by and Ingesting Jesus' Words | 193

    3. Sayings about the Light | 193

    4. Sayings about "the all" and one's origin | 194

    5. Jesus as paradigm for the Gnostic; Salvation through Jesus | 194

    6. Miscellaneous | 195

11. D. The Gospels of John and Thomas on Mystical Themes (April D. DeConick) | 199

    1. Ascent | 199

    2. Vision | 199

    3. Way | 199

    4. Agent | 199

11. E. The Gospels of John and Thomas (M. David Litwa) | 201

    1. Divine Nature | 201

    2. Divine Destiny | 202

12. A. The Fourth Gospel and Ignatius of Antioch | 208

12. B. The Fourth Gospel and Justin Martyr | 211

12. C. The Fourth Gospel, 1 John, and the Epistle to the Apostles | 213
12. D. The Fourth Gospel and Hippolytus of Rome | 216
12. E. The Fourth Gospel and Heracleon (in Origen's Commentary) | 218
12. F. The Fourth Gospel and Melito, *On the Pascha* | 222
12. G. The Fourth Gospel and the Egerton Papyrus 2 | 224

Abbreviations

Abbreviations for journals (*JBL*, *NTS*), periodicals (BA), major reference works (*NIDB*), and series (LCL, NIGTC) follow those of *The SBL Handbook of Style: for Biblical Studies and Related Disciplines*, 2nd ed., B. J. Collins, Project Director, et al. Atlanta, GA: SBL Press, 2014, and also *The Chicago Manual of Style*. 15th ed. Chicago: Univ. of Chicago Press, 2003. Note: we cite the abbreviations below that are most frequently used in our book.

Modern Publications and Series

ACG	Helmut Koester, *Ancient Christian Gospels* (Philadelphia: TPI, 1990)
ABG	Arbeiten zur Bibel und ihrer Geschichte
ACW	Ancient Christian Writers
ANCL	Ante-Nicene Christian Library. Edited by A. Roberts, J. Donaldson, et al. 10 vols., 1864–1885; repr.
ANET	*Ancient Near Eastern Texts*. Ed., James B. Pritchard (3rd ed., Princeton, 1969).
ANF	*The Ante-Nicene Fathers*. Edited by Alexander Roberts and James Donaldson. 1885–1887. 10 vols. Repr. Peabody, MA: Hendrickson, 1994.
ANRW	*Aufstieg uns Niedergang der römischen Welt* (Berline: de Gruyter, 1972—)
AYB	Anchor Yale Bible. Edited by William F. Albright and David N. Freedman. 90 vols. New York: Doubleday, 1974–2016; New Haven, CT: Yale University Press.
AYBD	*Anchor Yale Bible Dictionary*. Edited by David N. Freedman. 6 vols. New York: Doubleday, 1992; New Haven, CT: Yale University Press.

BDAG	Bauer, Walter, Frederick William Danker, W. F. Arndt, and F. W. Gingrich, eds. *A Greek-English Lexicon of the New Testament and Other Early Christian Literature.* Rev. and ed. by F. W. Danker. 3rd ed. Chicago: Univ. of Chicago Press, 2000.
BDF	Blass, Friedrich W. and Albert Debrunner. *A Greek Grammar of the New Testament and Other Early Christian Literature.* Trans. and rev. by Robert. W. Funk with supplementary notes of A. Debrunner. Chicago: University of Chicago Press, 1961.
CBQ	*Catholic Biblical Quarterly*
CC	Continental Commentary (series)
CPG	*Clavis Patrum Graecorum.* M. Geerard, ed., 5 vols. Turnhout: Brepols, 1974–1987.
CTJ	*Canadian Theological Journal*
DM	Dennis MacDonald, author of *The Dionysian Gospel* (Fortress Press, 2018)
DNTB	*Dictionary of New Testament Backgrounds.* Edited by Craig Evans and Stanley E. Porter Jr, eds., Downers Grove, IL: IVP Academic, 2000.
DSD	*Dead Sea Discoveries*
DSS	Dead Sea Scrolls
DSS:SE	García Martínez, Florentino and Eibert J. C. Tigchelaar, eds. *The Dead Sea Scrolls: Study Edition.* 2nd ed. 2 vols. Leiden: Brill, 1997. Grand Rapids: Eerdmans, 1999.
EncJud	*Encyclopedia Judaica.* 16 vols. Edited by Cecil Roth. Jerusalem, 1972
EKK	Evangelisch-katholischer Kommentar
ESV	English Standard Version
ICC	International Critical Commentary
IDBS	*The Interpreter's Dictionary of the Bible, Supplementary Volume.* Keith Crim, ed. Nashville: Abingdon, 1976
ISBE	*International Standard Bible Encyclopedia.* Rev. ed. 4 Vols. Edited by G. W. Bromiley et al. Grand Rapids: Eerdmans, 1979–1988

IVP	Inter-Varsity Press (Downers Grove, IL)
JAC	*Jahrbuch für Antike und Christentum*
JBL	*Journal of Biblical Literature*
JETS	*Journal of the Evangelical Theological Society*
JSNT	*Journal for the Study of the New Testament*
JTS	*Journal of Theological Studies*
LCL	Loeb Classical Library (Cambridge, MA: Harvard University Press)
LF	Library of the Fathers (43 vols., Oxford, 1838–74)
LSJ	Liddell, George Henry, et al., eds. *A Greek-English Lexicon.* Rev. and augmented by H. S. Jones, et al. Oxford: Clarendon, 1996.
NA[28]	Aland, Barbara, et al., eds. *Novum Testamentum Graece.* 28th rev. ed. Stuttgart: Bibelgesellschaft, 2012.
NETS	*A New English Translation of the Septuagint.* Edited by Albert Pietersma and Benjamin G. Wright. New York: Oxford University Press, 2007.
NHL(E)	Nag Hammadi Library (in English)
NIB	*New Interpreter's Bible.* 12 vols. Edited by L. E. Keck et al. Nashville: Abingdon, 1994—2004.
NICNT	New International Commentary of the New Testament
NIV	New International Version
NIDB	*New Interpreter's Dictionary of the Bible.* 5 vols. Edited by Katherine Doob Sakenfeld et al. Nashville: Abingdon, 2006
NJB	New Jerusalem Bible
NovT	*Novum Testamentum*
NRSV	New Revised Standard Version
NTS	*New Testament Studies*
OCD	*Oxford Classical Dictionary.* Edited by Simon Hornblower et al. (Oxford University Press, 1996)
ODCC	*Oxford Dictionary of the Christian Church* (Oxford, 20005)
PG	Patrologiae Graece (Patrologiae Cursus Completus) J.-P. Migne, ed., 162 vols. 1857–1886.

PNTC	Pillar NT Commentary (Eerdmans)
PRSt	*Perspectives in Religious Studies*
RB	*Revue biblique*
RBL	*Review of Biblical Literature*
RGRW	Religions in the Greco-Roman World
RevQ	*Revue de Qumran*
RSV	Revised Standard Version
SBLDS	Society of Biblical Literature Dissertation Series
SBT	Studies in Biblical Theology
SC	Sources chrétiennes, (Grk. , Lat., 600 vols. Eds., J. Daniélou, et al. Lyon, 1942–)
SD	Studies and Documents
SNTMS	Society of New Testament Monograph Series
SPhilo	*Studia Philonica*
SUNT	Studien zur Umwelt des Neuen Testaments
SVF	*Stoicorum Veterem Fragmenta*, 4 vols., ed. Hans von Arnim (Leipzig: Teubner, 1902–1904).
TBT	*The Bible Today*
TDNT	*Theological Dictionary of the New Testament.* Edited by Gerhard Kittel et al. 10 vols. ET. Grand Rapids: Eerdmans, 1964–76
TPI	Trinity Press International
WBC	Word Biblical Commentary
WJK	Westminster John Knox
WUNT	Wissenschaftliche Untersuchungen zum Neuen Testament
ZNW	Zeitschrift für die neutestamentliche Wissenschaft

Books of the Bible

Col	Colossians
1–2 Cor	1–2 Corinthians
Dan	Daniel

Deut	Deuteronomy
Eccl	Ecclesiastes
Eph	Ephesians
Exod	Exodus
Ezek	Ezekiel
Gal	Galatians
Gen	Genesis
Heb	Hebrews
Hos	Hosea
Isa	Isaiah
Jas	James
Jer	Jeremiah
John	Gospel of John (The Fourth Gospel)
Josh	Joshua
Judg	Judge
1–2 Kgs	1–2 Kings
Luke	Gospel of Luke
Mark	Gospel of Mark
Matt	Gospel of Matthew
Mic	Micah
1–2 Pet	1–2 Peter
Phil	Philippians
Prov	Proverbs
Ps(s)	Psalms
Qoh (or Eccl)	Qoheleth (or Ecclesiastes)
Rev	Revelation (Apocalypse of St. John)
Rom	Romans
1–2 Sam	1–2 Samuel
1–2 Thess	1–2 Thessalonians
1–2 Tim	1–2 Timothy
Zech	Zechariah

Apocrypha and Old Testament Pseudepigrapha

2 Bar.	2 Baruch (Syriac Apocalypse)
3 Bar.	2 Baruch (Greek Apocalpse)
1 En	1 Enoch (Ethiopic Enoch)
2 En	2 Enoch (Slavonic Apocalypse)
3 En	3 Enoch (Hebrew Apocalypse)
2 Esdr.	2 Esdras (composite of 4–6 Ezra; NRSV)
1–2 Macc	1–2 Maccabees
Odes	Odes of Solomon
Pss. Sol.	Psalms of Solomon
Sir	Sirach/Ecclesiasticus
T. Adam	Testament of Adam
Wis	Wisdom of Solomon

Rabbinica and Targumim

'Abot R. Nat.	'Abot de Rabbi Nathan
b.	Babylonian Talmud
Ber.	Berakot
Ketub.	Ketubbot
m.	Mishnah
Meg.	Megillah
Mek.	Mekilta
Pesaḥ.	Pesaḥim
Sifre	Sifra or Sipre
Tanḥ	Tanḥuma
Tg. Ket.	Targum Ketubim (Targum Writings)
Tg. Neb.	Targum Nebiim (Targum Prophets)
Tg. Onq.	Targum Onqelos
Tg. Ps.-J.	Targum Pseudo-Jonahtan
y.	Jerusalem Talmud
Yad.	Yadayim
Zebaḥ.	Zebaḥim

Dead Sea Scrolls (DSS)

CD	The Damascus Document (4Q265–73)
1QpHab	Pesher Habakkuk
1QM	Milḥamah or War Scroll
1QS	Serek Hayaḥad, or Rule of the Community
1QS^a	Rule of the Congregation (Appendix a to 1QS)
4QFlor	Florilegium, or Midrash on Eschatology
4Q254	Commentary on Genesis

Other Writings of Antiquity

Ap. John	Apocryphon of John (Secret Book of John)
Apoc. Adam	Apocalypse of Adam
Corp. herm.	Corpus hermeticum
Euripides, *Bacch.*	*Bacchae* (*Bacchanals*)
Eusebius, *Hist. eccl.*	*Historia ecclesiastica*
GTh (Gos. Thom.)	Gospel of Thomas
Herm. *Man.*	Shepherd of Hermas, Mandates (older numbering: 7.1)
Herm. *Sim.*	Shepherd of Hermas, Similitudes (8.7.6)
Hippolytus, *Haer.*	*Refutatio omium haeresium*
Hyp. Arch.	Nature of the Rulers
Ign. *Magn.*	Ignatius, *To the Magnesians*
Ign. *Pol.*	Ignatius, *To Polycarp*
Ign. *Smyrn.*	Ignatius, *To the Smyrnaeans*
Ign. *Trall.*	Ignatius, *To the Trallians*
Josephus, *Ant.*	*Jewish Antiquities*
Josephus, *J.W.*	*Jewish War*
Justin, *1 Apol.*	Justin Martyr, *First Apology*
LAB	Liber antiquitatum biblicarum (Pseudo-Philo)
Origen, *Cels.*	*Contra Celsum*
Origen, *Comm. Jo.*	*Commentarii in evangelium Joannis*

Philo, *Opif.*	*De opificio mundo* (On the Creation of the World)
Plato, *Symp.*	Plato, *Symposium*
Protr.	*Protrepticus* (Exhortation to the Greeks) by Clement of Alexandria
Three Forms	Three Forms of First Thought (Trimorphic Protennoia)

General Abbreviations

adv.	*adversus*
Aram.	Aramaic
AT	author translation
BCE	before the Common Era
BD	Beloved Disciple
bk(s)	book(s)
CE	Common Era
cent.	century
cf.	*confer*, compare
ch(s).	chapter(s)
ed(s).	editor(s); edition; edited by
Eng.	English
ET	English translation
ep.	epistula
e.g.	*exempli gratia*, for example
esp.	especially
et al.	*et alii*, and others
FE	The Fourth Evangelist
FG	The Fourth Gospel (The Gospel of John)
fr.	fragmentum, fragmenta
Ger.	German
Gk.	Greek
Heb.	Hebrew
HT	Hebrew text
i.e.	*id est*, that is

Intro.	Introduction
JBap	John the Baptist
Lat.	Latin
LXX	Septuagint, Greek Old Testament
ms(s)	manuscript(s)
MT	Masoretic Text of Hebrew Bible
n.	note
n.s.	new series
NT	New Testament
OT	Old Testament
p(p)	page(s)
par(r).	parallel(s)
passim	scattered (throughout)
re.	regarding
repr.	reprinted
rev.	revised
SP	Samaritan Pentateuch
tbl(s).	table(s)
trans.	translated by
vs.	versus
v(v).	verse(s)
vol(s).	volume(s)

Preface

INSPIRED BY THE WRITINGS of Rudolf Bultmann, C. H. Dodd, C. K. Barrett, Raymond Brown, and Rudolf Schnackenburg, who compared John's Gospel with other relevant literature, I, Charles, began my research for this book in the 1980s when I was working on *An Introduction to the New Testament* for Hendrickson Publishers. In order to make the textbook more concise and marketable, it was not included, so this study (revised and expanded) is now published by Cascade Books of Wipf and Stock Publishers, thanks to Dr. D. Christopher Spinks, our editor.

My co-author, Michael, whose primary contributions to this book are chapters 8 ("The Dionysian Gospel") and 11 ("Gospel of Thomas"), had also joined me on the revision of my New Testament introduction (also with Cascade Books). Michael studied the Gospel of Thomas under James M. Robinson and Gregory J. Riley at Claremont Graduate University and was privileged to also have Dennis R. MacDonald on his dissertation committee (*The Testing of Jesus in* Q, Peter Lang, 2007). Michael has taught Advanced Hellenistic Greek at CGU, and numerous courses on the Gospels at Asuza Pacific University.

The current research of Harold Attridge, Jörg Frey, Craig Evans, and Craig Keener has shown me that comparisons of the Fourth Gospel (FG) with other relevant writings (e.g., Dead Sea Scrolls, Philo) are still pertinent to our understanding of (1) the themes and concepts used in this Gospel and (2) why they were used in this particular manner by the author.

One need only consult Greek words in a lexicon to discover the importance of words in their context, and how they are used elsewhere in the New Testament, the Greek Septuagint, Philo, and other ancient writings. Although it is important to understand the Gospel of John on its own terms, we cannot neglect the meaning of its words and its distinctive themes in the context of its own world, both Hellenistic and Jewish in a Greco-Roman milieu.

In our study, we will compare FG with the Synoptic Gospels and the Old Testament (OT). Are these the only documents that can provide compelling parallels to FG? Did FG draw *only* on them for its composition, and no others? Was FG's selection and use of the OT, for example, influenced, in some way, by other ancient writings? Were there any *other* influences on FG, direct or indirect, to explain its creative approach to the OT and especially its distinctive portrayal of the life and teachings of Jesus? If so, how and why? What can explain FG's *particular* tendencies, views, and nuances of expression (if explanations can be found)? Our goal here is to locate what Michael Fishbane calls a "common word field" or a "shared stream of linguistic tradition" that provides a thesaurus of terms and images for each set of comparisons, observing differences, as well as similarities.[1]

The numerous parallel charts that we have compiled will provide many opportunities for the reader to compare and contemplate. In some chapters, we have offered criteria for evaluation that may prove helpful. It is noteworthy that Raymond E. Brown, Mark Allan Powell (Colossians and Ephesians), and Craig S. Keener (Luke and Acts) have made use of parallel charts that I have compiled in my other works: *The Letters of Paul* (Liturgical Press, 1993, 2013) and *The Conclusion of Luke-Acts* (Pickwick, 2009).

The Conceptual Worlds of the Fourth Gospel will be useful in the classroom for courses on the four Gospels and especially the Fourth Gospel. It will be a helpful, contextual resource, in one accessible volume, a "must have" for scholars and serious students of John's Gospel.

---

1. Fishbane, *Biblical Interpretation*, 288.

Introduction

"It is the essence of genius to make use of the simplest ideas."

—Charles Peguy

"The ability to express an idea is just as important as the idea itself."

—Bernard Baruch

"There is one thing stronger than all the armies in the world, and that is an idea whose time has come."

—Victor Hugo[1]

Related to our comparisons of ideas in the Fourth Gospel (FG), Professor H. H. Price of Oxford University makes this astute observation. It concerns how conceptualizing is derived from the perception of repeatable and recurring phenomena.

> When we consider the world around us, we cannot help noticing that there is a great deal of recurrence or repetition in it.... These constant recurrences or repetitions, whether separate or conjoint ones, are what make the world a dull or stale or boring place... Nevertheless, this perpetual repetition, this dullness or staleness, is also immensely important, because it is what makes conceptual cognition possible. In a world of incessant novelty, where there was no recurrence at all and no tedious repetitions, no concepts could ever be acquired; and thinking, even

---

1. The above quotations are from the website http://www.ideachampions.com/weblogs/archives/2010/11/50_very_awesome.shtml.

of the crudest and most primitive kind, could never begin. For example, in such a world nothing could ever be recognizable.[2]

Regarding conceptual understanding by means of analogy or comparison, George Lakoff and Mark Johnson state the matter more succinctly.

> We claim that most of our normal conceptual system is metaphorically structured; that is, most concepts are partially understood in terms of other concepts.[3]

Over, under, and through John's story of Jesus are unforgettable ideas and concepts, profoundly simple and simply profound,[4] for his own audience and beyond.[5] These ideas did not originate in a vacuum. They have recurred and been repeated before and after the writing of FG. Roland Barthes observes,

> every text is an intertext: other texts can be perceived within it at various levels, in various forms which may be more or less

---

2. Price, *Thinking and Experience*, 7–8. In this classic survey of ideas, concepts, and conceptualization, Prof. Price examines the content and concept of cognition, its relation to sense-experience and to symbols (verbal and non-verbal), and our ability to classify correctly concepts, ideas, or words (adj., nouns, verbs) according to P. Butchvarov, "Conceptualism," in Audi, ed., *Cambridge Dictionary of Philosophy*, 170. See also Krell, *Martin Heidegger*, 366–67 (Krell's introduction to *What is Called Thinking?*); and the essays in Goodman and Fisher, *Rethinking Knowledge*. On different responses to post-modern skepticism here, see the essays in Patton and Ray, *Magic Still Dwells*.

3. Lakoff and Johnson, *Metaphors We Live By*, 56. See also the helpful discussion on "Parable" (Gk, *parabolē*; Lat. *similitudo*) in Aune, *Westminster Dictionary*, 329–34.

4. Most of the enigmas of the Fourth Gospel (FG) occur with regard to certain characters (Nicodemus, Pharisees, the crowd), but with his readers, FG usually aims at clarity in his essential message (John 1:41–42; 4:2; 14:26; 20:30–31), see Engberg-Pedersen, *John and Philosophy*, 35, 345–57.

5. We resist the view that FG's language is coded exclusively for his "in group." Malina and Rohrbaugh, *Social Science*, 4–7, e.g., employ three linguistic modes from Halliday, *Language as Social Semiotic*. They write that FG focuses on *how* something is said (textual) and with *whom* something is said (interpersonal, with FG's readers) over *what* is being said (ideational mode, including logical and/or experiential) to explain the way FG over-lexicalizes, i.e., having many words for one central concern, e.g., "believe, come, abide, follow, love, keep, have, see" so that FG can implement for his "in group" new values (not new structures as with Paul and the Synoptic Gospels). The above view of FG presupposes a particular view of FG and his ("in group") community (Meeks, "Man from Heaven," 191–94; Petersen, *John and Sociology*), a position that has met with strong criticism. See Lamb, *Text, Context, and the Johannine Community*, 56–144 (conceding that language has a social function and texts have a social context, 102). We hope that our study will show that FG envisioned a broader audience and was just as concerned with ideas, as he was with textual and interpersonal concerns. T. L. Brodie, e.g., analyzes seven different attempts at reconstructing the Johannine communities and concludes that the Evangelist was an integrated member of a large, world-oriented church, in *Quest for Origins*, 15–21, 144–52. For more discussion, see our n56 of this chapter, p. 14.

clearly discerned: the text of earlier culture and those of its contemporary context. Every text is a new construction of past quotations.[6]

FG is no exception here, and its intertextual relationships, include, for example, interpretations of the "Word" (Gk. *logos*) in its first chapter,[7] as well as favorite vocabulary: light and darkness, life, Spirit, glory, descent and ascent.

The **conceptual or thought worlds**[8] of the Fourth Gospel (FG), reflect diverse and complex Hellenistic and Jewish intertextual relationships.[9] They are so diverse and complex that Robert Kysar wrote "nearly

---

6. R. Barthes, "Text (théorie du)," cited in Jean Zumstein, "Intratextuality and Intertextuality," 121.

7. See Kleinknecht, "Logos in the Greek and Hellenistic World"; on the diverse views regarding the origins of FG's Logos (John 1; from, e.g., a special revelation to a gnostic or other Hellenistic context), see also Keener, *John*, 1:339-50, 375-79. Many of the proposed religio-historical influences we will examine in our chs. that follow.

8. Let us define our language and approaches here. (1) What we mean by "conceptual worlds" or "thought worlds" (Ger. *die Gedankenwelten*) is "concepts and their formation" (Lat. *concipere* "to conceive"; Ger. *konzeptionellen, begriffliche*) in their given "context, (Ger. *Umwelt*), background, environment," (Fr. *milieu*) as in "intellectual milieu", or "setting in life" (Ger. *Kontext, Sitz im Leben*), see Brown, *Gospel according to John*, 1:lii-lxvi; Kysar, *Fourth Evangelist*, 102-46. We use "worlds" (pl.) to accurately describe the diverse comparative phenomena of our book. (2) The approach of our book is related to the religio-historical method or history of religions (Ger. *Religionsgeschichte*) and also "tradition history"(Ger. *Traditionsgeschichte*), "theological worldview" (*theologische Weltanschauung*), and "comparative religious studies," see Frey, "Between Torah and Stoa," 190-95; Frey and Schnelle, *Kontexte*, 3-4, 35n156; see Odeberg, *Fourth Gospel*; for a critical assessment see Colpe, *Die religionsgeschichtliche Schule*; for a more recent review and assessment, see Seelig, *Religionsgeschichte Methode*, 260-335; our goal here is to locate a "common word field" or a "shared stream of linguistic tradition" that provides a thesaurus of terms and images, for each set of comparisons, see Fishbane, *Biblical Interpretation*, 288; Middleton, *Liberating Image*, 62-64; and finally (3) "history of interpretation" (*Auslegungsgeschichte*), and "history of effects" (*Wirkungsgeschichte*) of the earlier work upon the later, see R. Evans, *Reception History*, 1-50; Rasimus, *Legacy of John*; Frey, "Between Torah and Stoa"; C. E. Hill, *Johannine Corpus in the Early Church*.

9. We use the phrase "conceptual worlds of FG," to describe the diverse comparisons within this book. Although the thought-worlds of FG are complex and diverse, our underlying concern is what best represents the conceptual worlds of both the implied author and his implied readers, based on our prior understanding of the text and the likelihood that both knew or assumed such at that given time in late antiquity.

We use the phrase "Hellenistic and Jewish" not to imply distinct, separate entities, because both Judaism and Christianity developed in the Hellenism of the Roman era and are even regarded by some as "Greco-Roman cults." See Hengel, *Judaism and Hellenism*, 1:255-314 and Hengel, *Hellenization of Judea*; Gruen, *Heritage and Hellenism*; see also Fitzmyer, *Semitic Backgrounds*, especially "Languages of Palestine" 2:29-56; Boring et al., *Hellenistic Commentary*; Horsley et al., *New Documents*; S. E. Porter prefers "Judaism within Hellenism," in his "The Context of Jesus," in Holmén and Porter, *Handbook for the Study of the Historical Jesus*, 2:1461, see also 1441-63; and M. Pucci Ben Zeev, "Jews, Greeks, Romans," in Collins and Harlow, *Dictionary of Early Judaism*, 237-55.

every conceivable religious and/or philosophical movement in the Roman world has been proposed as the intellectual setting of the Fourth Gospel," and concluded that "there has never been (in recent years) anything like a consensus of scholars on the history of religions background of the gospel."[10] Nevertheless, as a corollary of reading FG as narrative theology, Charles H. Talbert states,

> It is inappropriate to focus on only one background for understanding the narrative (e.g., Qumran, rabbinic Judaism, mystical Judaism, Hellenistic Judaism, Greco-Roman philosophy, Hermetica, Gnosticism, etc.) since it will likely take knowledge of most or all to comprehend a tradition that developed not only through time but also moved geographically.[11]

Udo Schnelle programmatically states that any one-sided explanation of FG (e.g., within an inner-Jewish context) is insufficient.[12] Hans-Josef Klauck adds that "understanding a text only reaches its goal when the whole circle of its context has been measured off."[13] Martin Hengel writes, "the richness of the traditions developed in the Fourth Gospel demonstrates the richness of the spiritual climate in Palestine during the first century CE."[14]

Much of our understanding of the conceptual worlds of FG will be derived from "parallels."[15] **Parallels** involve similar or analogous vocabulary,

---

10. Kysar, "Fourth Gospel," 2413 (see also 2389–480). On the history of religion studies, beginning in nineteenth- and early twentieth-century Germany, with e.g., Herman Gunkel, Richard Reitzenstein, Wilhelm Bousset, Rudolf Bultmann, see Boers, "Religionsgeschichte School," in Hayes, *Dictionary of Biblical Interpretation*, 2:383–87; Baird, *History*, 2:238–53, 280–87.

11. Talbert, *Reading John*, 66, noting the Johannine history of tradition from 30–95 CE, and from Judea-Galilee to Ephesus.

12. From "kann nicht monocausal erklärt werden," in Schnelle, *Das Evangelium nach Johannes*, 40. ET quotation from Frey, "Between Torah and Stoa," 194. M. Becker firmly agrees with Schnelle's statement (above), see his "Zeichen," in Frey and Schnelle, *Kontexte*, 235–36.

13. Our translation of "Das Verstehen eines Textes gelangt erst zu seinem Ziel, wenn der ganze Zirkel seiner Kontexte abgeschritten ist" in Klauck, *Herrenmahl und helleistischer Kult*, 4. Klauck's definition of context is also noteworthy here "in a broad sense the entire spiritual or intellectual space of an expression, taking into account its history" our trans. of "Kontext im weitesten Sinn ist der gesamte geistige Raum, in dem eine Äußerung steht, unter Einbezug seiner Geschichte" (4).

14. Hengel, *Johannine Question*, 113, favoring a strong Hellenistic Jewish piety.

15. (Gk., *parállēlos*, παράλληλος, from παρά + ἄλληλος, "along or beside each other"). Plutarch (46–120 CE) arranged his "parallel lives" with the working assumption that some divine plan was at work in them (Appian, *Hist. rom.* 7.8.53; Plutarch, *Demosthenes* 3.2 (*Lives* LCL VII)). Comparing different authors provided a way to locate their strongest and weakest points, e.g., their best and worst speeches (Dionysius of

phrases, and sentences (linguistic and verbal), as well as parallel themes, concepts, images, forms, structural patterns, or social and cultural contexts. Such parallels may help to determine the meaning of a word or expression, the translation of a particular language, direct literary influence (e.g., quotations), the influence of ideas (whether a body of work, teaching, shared context, or similar historical trajectory), shared membership in a social group (e.g., Essene) or cross-cultural type (e.g., prophet, king) or phenomenological pattern (e.g., agent, intermediary).[16]

The examination of parallels employs **the comparative method**, used profitably in the natural sciences, as well as comparative linguistics, comparative mythology, comparative literature, and especially (for our study) comparative religious research. The data and the focus, of course, will vary in each field of study, determining also the kinds of comparative methodology to be employed. All fields of study benefit by observing the differences as well as the similarities of the phenomena that are compared and contrasted.[17]

One example of the "shared phenomenological (cross-cultural) pattern that helps to order the parallel data" (J. R. Davila) is from Adele Reinhartz. She argues for a **cosmological tale** (similar to theological story) told by the FG narrator alongside two other tales: the historical (Jesus confronts Jewish leaders in Judea), and the ecclesiological (church vs. synagogue in the diaspora).[18] This cosmological tale of the Word in the world confronting

---

Halicarnassus, *Pomp.* 1–2, 6; *Thuc.* 35; late first century BCE) from Keener, *John*, 2:917, 967, 1183. On resemblances, recognition, sign-cognition, concepts and their manifestations, see Price, *Thinking and Experience*, also mentioned in note 2 of this chapter.

16. Derived from Davila, "Perils of Parallelism." Prof. Davila (a Dead Sea Scrolls [DSS] scholar) also cites the works of Sandmel, "Parallelomania," 1–13; and Smith, *Drudgery Divine*, esp. 51–52. With his permission, we will also cite from Prof. Davila's article, regarding some criteria for evaluating parallels, e.g., "what is being compared to what and how," analogy is not always genealogy, note *differences* and similarities, context, find patterns of parallels, widely shared parallels are less significant, avoid preconceived evolutionary goals (e.g., from pristine Christ-followers to early catholic assimilation), and formulate parallels in such a way that they are subject to falsification when new or better evidence can prove them wrong.

17. See the helpful discussion on comparative methodology in these diverse fields of study (with criticisms) in Seelig, *Religionsgeschichtliche*, 265–76, see also 296–331. See also Patton and Ray, *Magic Still Dwells*, esp. the prologue, "In Comparison, A Magic Dwells," by J. Z. Smith (23–44) for a critique of faulty methodological assumptions, and ch. 11 "Methodology, Comparisons, and Truth" (172–81) by Huston Smith for a powerful defense of the comparative study of religion.

18. Reinhartz, *Word in the World*, 2–6, 26, 100. The ecclesiastical tale of the Johannine community is probably the most speculative level, see Porter and Fay, *Gospel of John in Modern Interpretation*, esp. the article on R. E. Brown's reconstruction of John's community (Jipp, "Raymond E. Brown and the Fourth Gospel," 173–96).

forces that oppose his divine mission is developed not only by the intrinsic data supplied by the narrative (pre-existence, earthly descent, ascent to the Father)[19] but "the extrinsic data which the implied readers or intended audience brought to their reading of the text."[20] This extrinsic data includes biblical and post-biblical allusions as well as ancient near eastern and Greco-Roman backgrounds (classical and early Christian).[21] The cosmological tale of the Word's descent to the world and ascent to the Father, "constitutes the larger frame of reference for the temporal, spatial, and theological aspects of the other two tales and provides the interpretative key for discrete symbols and pericopes of the narrative text."[22]

Understanding the metaphors, images,[23] religious ideology, themes, and theological vocabulary[24] of this dramatic gospel story of biographical narrative[25] in its given context, is not without its historical and literary challenges.[26] Nevertheless, the interaction of related texts in context, we

19. Reinhartz, *Word in the World*, 18–25.

20. Reinhartz, *Word in the World*, 107; we can only surmise what external data these implied readers bring to the text. See also "History of Religions Background," 107–31 (focusing on the imagery of John 10:1–5, as a test case).

21. Her investigative approach supports D. E. Aune's claim: "The Christianity of the New Testament is a creative combination of Jewish and Hellenistic traditions . . . a reality related to two known things but transcending them both," in his *New Testament in its Literary Environment*, 12.

22. Reinhartz, *Word in the World*, 100; see also 100–104. See her chart on 93 which clarifies some of the problems encountered by both the historical and ecclesiological readings of John 10:1–5. For explanation of "Interpretative Key," see 42–44.

23. For "unpacking" FG's numerous metaphors, see Frey et al., *Imagery in the Gospel of John*; Howe, *Because You Bear the Name*; Koester, *Symbolism*; Lakoff and Johnson, *Metaphors We Live By*; Ricœur, *Interpretation Theory* and *Rule of Metaphor*; Van der Watt, *Family of the King*.

24. For titles that focus on the theological message of the FG, see, e.g., Koester, *The Word of Life*; Köstenberger, *Theology of John's Gospel*; Bauckham and Mosser, *Gospel of John and Christian Theology*; Smith, *Theology of the Gospel of John*. For history of discussion, see Olson, "Biblical Theology," 1:461–65; Claassens, "Biblical Theology as Dialogue," 127–44.

25. For discussion on the composite genre of FG, e.g., ancient biography in dramatic form, cited in Burridge, *What are the Gospels?*, 279–81 (as a dramatic mode); Puskas and Robbins, *Introduction to the NT*, 123–33 (FG as ancient drama); Brant, *Dialogue and Drama*, ch. 1; and surveys of genre comparisons in Keener, *Gospel of John*, 1:3–34 and Carter, *John*, 3–20. On the narrative of FG, see Culpepper, *Anatomy of the Fourth Gospel*; the essays in Thatcher and Moore, *Anatomies of Narrative Criticism*. For overview, see Rhoads, "Narrative Criticism," 4:222–23.

26. On diachronic and synchronic approaches, we concur with Moloney, "Although traditional historical criticism must go on (cf. Painter, *Quest*; Schnelle, *Antidocetic Christology*), the narrative of the Gospel of John must be appreciated as a whole, as a unified, coherent utterance, and not be dissected into its constituent parts to be left,

hope, will make some significant contribution to our understanding of the Johannine conceptual worldview for a better and broader understanding of the FG narrative. These challenges also include how certain similarities of language and expression (e.g., "spirit of truth" in FG and DSS) and common images ("living water, shepherd") relate to the different conceptual worlds of FG. Are the literary-contextual development of similar expressions in each of the *documents to be compared* adequately distinguished in our efforts to understand the conceptual worlds of FG? Also, regarding the identity of the parallels: are they analogical *and* genealogical? Was FG influenced by the specific document with which it is compared, the influencer of the other parallel document, or were both influenced by a source common to both? Are there any compelling reasons for presenting a particular comparison?[27] We will seek to address some of these challenges with a few suggestions for further investigation.

Some of the **proposed influences** on the thought world of John are readily discernible (e.g., early Christian traditions, Jewish Scriptures of the Septuagint), some might be plausible (Jewish wisdom and angel speculations including apocrypha and pseudepigrapha, Dead Sea Scrolls, Philo), others are possible,[28] reflecting similar language (Euripides, Plato) or world view (rabbinica and targumim), many might indicate early reception of FG or parallel traditions (Nag Hammadi, Mandaean, early church "fathers").[29]

---

in pieces, on the scholar's table," see the balanced discussion in his *Gospel of John*, 13, and 11–20. See also Nissen and Pedersen, *New Readings in John*, 12–17; Fortna and Thatcher, *Jesus in Johannine Tradition*, 354–55; Frei, *Eclipse of Biblical Narrative*, 160; and Reinhartz (cited earlier) who advocates a cosmological tale (the Word in the world), in addition to the historical (Jesus) tale, and the eccesiological (Johannine) tale, in her *Word in the World*, 2–6, 100. See our ch. 3, pp. 50–51, for more discussion of Reinhartz's three-tale perspective.

27. Concerns expressed via personal correspondence with Craig Koester (May 24, 2019) after his reading an earlier draft of two of our chapters. Analogical and genealogical comparisons are discussed in Smith, *Drudgery Divine*, 46–53, esp. 51–52.

28. "Is it analogy or genealogy? . . . similarities or points of agreement that we discover between two different religions . . . or are they dependent one on the other, demonstrable borrowings?" Deissmann, *Light from the Ancient East*, 265. See also Smith, *Drudgery Divine*, 48–50.

29. There has been considerable resistance concerning comparative studies of FG and non-Jewish writings, e.g.: "Moreover since all Jews, even to some extent Palestinian Jews, had long been exposed to Hellenistic influences there seems no need to search outside the world of first-century Judaism for such Greek traits as are exhibited by the Fourth Gospel," Ashton, *Understanding Fourth Gospel*, 97 (Ashton, 96–97, is also critical of MacRae's Isis-FG analogy cited later in this ch.). See also Smith, "John," in Barclay and Sweet, *Early Christian Thought*, 96–111. We conclude, however, that because of the *pervasive* influence of Hellenism upon Judaism, the evidence of *a break* with torah-focused Judaism in FG (despite DSS and rabbinic parallels), and the unknown

Important factors to consider when attempting to make any causal connections are: similar contexts, chronological proximity to FG, availability to author and readers, common viewpoints, and verbal/thematic coherence of FG and the writings in question.[30] There are numerous tests and criteria that make use of these factors, although the results vary in significance.[31] As far

---

identities of the author and final editor, FG's exposure to non-Jewish Greco-Roman influence (Heraclitus, Euripides, Plato) should not, therefore, be ruled out of consideration. J. Z. Smith argues that the (*mostly* Protestant) preference for Jewish origins of the NT was often embraced as an insulating device against later syncretistic tendencies of Christendom beginning in the fourth century (suspected as a Roman Catholic tendency), *Drudgery Divine*, 46–48. Later (80–81), Smith includes in this "Jewish origins" camp, the more sophisticated Semitic work of the Catholic R. E. Brown, which displays *no* Protestant bias (although he accuses Catholic H. Rahner of this bias, 114). In Fr. Brown's case, it might be his preference for Jewish origins over that of pagan that Smith highlights here (45–48). He even compares Brown's preference to that of Herodotus (ca. 440 BCE) who had favored Egyptian influence over that of the more syncretistic Persians (*Histories* 1.135; 2.43–50, 57–58, 79).

30. See the following works that advocate the importance of comparing contexts, determining accessibility, and thematic coherence, not merely "juxtaposing excerpts," see Sandmel, "Parallelomania," 1–13; H. Ringgren, "Qumran and Gnosticism," in Bianchi, *Origins of Gnosticism*, 379–84; "The Theological Vocabulary of the Fourth Gospel and the Gospel of Truth," in Barrett, *Essays on John*; "Criticisms of Methodology," in Yamauchi, *Pre-Christian Gnosticism*, 170–86; Fitzmyer, *Impact of the Dead Sea Scrolls*, 90–96; Smith offers keen insights on the nature and limits of comparative religious studies, *Drudgery Divine*, 46–53; see our overview of source criticism in Puskas and Robbins, *Introduction to the NT*, 83–85. Note also the caution expressed by James Barr on the contrast of Hebrew and Greek thought, as well as determining ideology from linguistic analysis alone in isolation from contextual study, *Biblical Words for Time* and "Common Sense and Biblical Language"; and his *Semantics of Biblical Language*, especially his focus on syntactical relations and the groupings of words at the sentence level, 222, 249–50, 69–70; note also Anthony Thiselton, "Semantics and Biblical Interpretation" in Marshall, *New Testament Interpretation*, 75–104; and Silva, *Biblical Words and Their Meaning*.

31. On tests for discerning scriptural echoes, see Hays, *Echoes in the Letters of Paul*, 29–33 and his *Echoes in the Gospels*, 7–14, 291–344; on the four criteria of evaluating intertextual comparisons with compositions that *postdate* the NT period, see Evans, *Word of Glory*, 18–28. See also (from n16 of this ch.) Davila, "Perils of Parallelism"; Sandmel, "Parallelomania," 1–13; Fishbane, *Biblical Interpretation*; and Smith, *Drudgery Divine*. The tests and criteria from these works will be developed as we explore specific intertextualities and alleged parallels (see, e.g., ch. 5, pp. 79–81; ch. 7, pp. 119–21, 124–25). See the following work that evaluates the application of these criteria in the search for the counter-imperial subtexts of Paul's letters, Heilig, *Hidden Criticism?*, 21–49. Heilig argues for the use of Baye's probability theorem (e.g., the probability of event A, given that event B is true, equals the relationship of the two multiplied by specific data demonstrating A as true, divided by the event B). Baye's theorem works best with sufficient amounts of measurable data to make statistical projections with percentages of probability. It is less effective, however, when applied to our "fragmentary data from two millennia ago, almost always open to multiple interpretations," M. D. Given, review of

as it can be established, the degree of authorial intention or FG's conscious use of texts and traditions will determine if we are examining a direct allusion or an echo that is unconscious or incidental.[32]

Let us now define and describe our use of the following terms: intertextuality, allusion, echo, and reception history. **Intertextuality** was first introduced by Julia Kristeva, building on the work of Mikhail Bakhtin. Kristeva used the term *intertextualité* to suggest a dialogical relationship between texts broadly conceived of as a system of codes or signs.[33] Intertextuality has had broad meanings, but some controls were established when the concept made its way into biblical studies with the publication of Richard B. Hays's *Echoes of Scripture in the Letters of Paul* and *Echoes of Scripture in the Gospels*.[34] Intertextuality represents, for us, the rubric of all interaction between texts in general, whereas allusions represent the specific occurrences of an *intentional appropriation* of an earlier text for a particular purpose. A quotation cites the source, usually with an introductory formula, e.g., "Isaiah says . . . " Allusions and quotations are both *intentional appropriations*. **Echoes** are "faint traces of texts that are often unconscious but emerge from minds soaked in the scriptural heritage of Israel" and related traditions of the Greco-Roman world.[35] Some echoes

---

C. Heilig, *Hidden Criticism?* at http://www.bookreviews.org/subscribe.asp. See Heilig's response, "What Bayesian Reasoning Can and Can't Do for Biblical Research," posted in Zürich NT blog (Mar 27, 2019): https://www.uzh.ch/blog/theologie-nt/2019/03/27.

32. On the plausibility of determining authorial intention, see Hirsch, *Validity in Interpretation*, 1–23, 207; for a survey of views with a "reconstructive proposal" (246–48), see Vanhoozer, *Is There a Meaning in This Text?*, 201–65. On, e.g., direct allusions and embedded echoes, see also Köstenberger and Patterson, *Invitation to Biblical Interpretation*, 538–48.

33. Kristeva, *Desire and Language*, 66, see also 64–91; Bakhtin, *Dialogic Imagination*. "In the Word Become Flesh, we perceive the carnate, material grounding of the utterance," Clark and Holquist, *Mikhail Bakhtin*, 86. On FG, see also Anderson, "Bakhtin's Dialogism," 133–59.

34. Hays, *Echoes of Scripture*, 14–24; and his *Echoes of Scripture in the Gospels*, 1–14; see also Manning, *Echoes of a Prophet*, 3–15. Intratextuality in biblical studies usually refers to the relationship of texts within a single book (e.g., FG's parallel scenes, chiasms, framing devices). The intratextuality of FG is unavoidable in our study (e.g., repeated texts or themes) but it will not be our main focus. See Zumstein, "Intratextuality and Intertextuality," Thatcher and Moore, *Anatomies of Narrative Criticism*, 121–35, esp. 122. For examples of intratextuality in FG, see Thompson, *John: A Commentary*, 114, 129, 422, 432–33, 442; Brown, *Gospel according to John*, 1:84–85; Neyrey, *John*, 337–41, 448–49.

35. Moyise, "Intertextuality and the Study of the OT in the NT," 18–19. See also Porter, "Use of the OT in the NT," 92; MacDonald, *Mimesis and Intertextuality in Antiquity and Christianity*.

are firmly embedded in the text, linguistically, thematically, and structurally, others are implied or incidental.[36]

Reception history or "history of effects" (Ger. *Wirkungsgeschichte*) was best articulated by Hans Robert Jauss, a former pupil of Hans-Georg Gadamer.[37] The text may live on after its production, but readers change and bring new horizons of experience, which change the readers' perceptions from age to age. A text can change our horizons. It can satisfy, surpass, disappoint, or refute old expectations. Reconstructing the actual horizons of expectation enables the critic or reader to pose new questions of the text and to discover how the reader *might* have *understood* the work.[38] Jörg Frey proposed a study of the early reception of FG to point us to some aspects of the intellectual world in which the gospel was received.[39] Ulrich Luz has applied reception theory to the Gospel of Matthew, in the *Evangelisch-katholischer Kommentar zum Neuen Testament*.[40] See especially reception theory (applied to FG) in the works of Mark Edwards, Titus Nagle, and Charles E. Hill.[41]

The many generic similarities that John's Gospel (FG) shares with different writings of late antiquity, however, may point to **a common type of intellectual milieu** that had developed then: a complex, Greco-Roman, universalizing Jewish, and mystical ("gnostic-like") context. [42]

36. Köstenberger and Patterson, *Invitation to Biblical Interpretation*, 541–47. We try to focus on both the "quotations" and "citations" that we identify as "intentional allusions to discernable sources," to some degree and in some manner.

37. See, e.g., where H. R. Jauss discusses the history and development (in subsequent contexts) of the short, pithy Jesus sayings identified by R. Bultmann as *apophthegmata*, in his *Aesthetic of Reception*, 100–101. On the merging of horizons between reader and the text, see Gadamer, *Truth and Method*; Evans, *Reception History, Tradition*, 1–50; discussion with examples, in Thiselton, *Hermeneutics*, 316–26. See essays in Rasimus, *Legacy of John*; and also Hill, *Johannine Corpus*.

38. The Centre for Reception History of the Bible at Oxford University has organized conferences, publication series, and an academic journal; as well as a projected multi-volume work, *The Encyclopedia of the Bible and Its Reception* (Berlin: De Gruyter, 2009—).

39. Frey, "Between Torah and Stoa," 197.

40. EKK series, 1989—2005; ET, Hermeneia, 3 vols; Fortress. For his criteria of selection regarding *Wirkungsgeschichte*, Luz preferred interpretations that: determine our own preunderstanding of the text, had an impact on Protestant and Catholic confessional traditions, came close to the original meaning of the text in a changed situation and can have corrective functions for us, and (finally) the earliest and most effective ones (e.g., Irenaeus), in his *Matthew 1–7*, 62.

41. Edwards, *John through the Centuries*; Nagel, *Die Rezeption des Johannesevangeliums*; Hill, *Johannine Corpus*.

42. See Jonas, *Gnosis und spätaniker Geist*, vol. 1. Martin Hengel concedes that *if* gnosis is broadly defined to include, e.g., the dualism of Qumran, Philo, Jewish apocalypticism, Hermetica, and Neoplatonism, then FG shares some of these characteristics,

George W. MacRae, SJ, observes that "the process of Johannine theology according to John's intention corresponds to a process of 'Hellenization' that is paralleled elsewhere in the history of ancient religion" (e.g., Isis aretalogy).[43] Robert Kysar ironically adds "It is the accomplishment of current Johannine scholarship that the evidence for the syncretistic, heterodox Jewish milieu of the gospel has become irresistible."[44] Pursuing these observations may be helpful in providing some insights regarding the FG's origins (broadly defined), as well as its message and purpose.

We favor a late first-century **date** of FG, with a **location** in Syria-Palestine, and eventually, Ephesus (90–100 CE).[45] The final **author** seems to have been a member of a "Johannine community" that identified with the "Beloved Disciple" (BD, John 13:23–25; 19:26–27; 20:2–8) who had provided eyewitness testimony and was a key source for FG (John 19:35; 21:24–25). BD may have founded the community.[46] Regarding the final author of FG, perhaps it was John the Elder (2 John 1; 3 John 1).[47] It may explain the parallels between FG and 1–3 John (see our ch. 1, pp. 32–33). The identity of BD is uncertain (John the son of Zebedee, John "the Baptist," Nathanael, Lazarus, Thomas, or someone else).[48] We also assume at least a three-stage development of FG: (1) historical Jesus, (2) post-resurrection perspective, and (3) writing of FG (in first and second editions).[49] We are

---

in his *Johannine Question*, 113. See also our ch. 7: Greco-Roman Cults and Philosophies, pp. 103–25; ch. 10: Nag Hammadi Library, and ch. 11: Gospel of Thomas.

43. MacRae, *Studies*, 30–31 (from "The Fourth Gospel and Religionsgeschichte," *CBQ* 32 [1970] 13–24). MacRae emphasizes here how a local, near eastern cult was transformed into a universal symbol of worship, as a result of Hellenization.

44. Kysar, *Fourth Evangelist*, 270 (heading C). For a succinct history of modern FG scholarship, see Edwards, *John*, 7–14.

45. See discussion in Barrett, *Essays on John*, 123–34; Keener, *John*, 1:142–49. On external tradition for "John" in Ephesus, see Eusebius, *Hist. eccl.* 3.23.1–4; 3:28.6, citing second-century sources, Irenaeus of Lyons and Clement of Alexandria.

46. On the diverse views of school or community, see Culpepper, *Johannine School*, 34–38. See the influential Brown, *Community*. See esp. Brian Stock's "textual communities" organized around a common script, in his *Listening for the Text*, 23, 150, cited favorably by Lamb, *Text, Context and the Johannine Community*, 70–71, 202–5.

47. For discussion of John the apostle and John the elder, see Irenaeus, *Haer.* 3.1.1; 3.3.4; especially, Eusebius, *Hist. eccl.* 3.39.1–4; 5.8.4; 7.25.

48. On FG authorship, see Keener, *John*, 1:82–115 (Apostle John is BD and FG author, with some qualification); J. H. Charlesworth, *Jesus as Mirrored in John*, 61–77 (BD as unknown eyewitness); Hengel, *Johannine Question*, 102–13 (John the Elder as final author); Bauckham agrees with Hengel here in his *Testimony of the Beloved Disciple*; and *Jesus and the Eyewitnesses*. Michaels discusses the different possibilities of BD's identity in his *John*, 16–17.

49. Talbert writes that "multiple life situations, past and present, likely have their

aware also of the challenges of historical reconstruction, i.e., distinguishing each stage consistently and coherently, as well as the problems with maintaining this perspective as an exclusive interpretive grid.[50]

The **chronological challenges** that so many of these other writings present might also contribute to an understanding of the early reception of the FG. The important issue is how the intersection and interaction of these diverse writings help us to understand FG, even when source-critical questions become matters of early reception.[51] For example, even if the Mandaean and much of Nag Hammadi and rabbinic literature[52] are chronologically suspect, the interaction of these ancient texts with FG might shed some insights on how FG was understood in late antiquity and beyond.

Starting with plausible influences and then moving to early receptions, noting also the differences,[53] we will examine similar texts, concepts, images, forms, and other modes of expression in the following:

---

echoes in the text," in his *Reading John*, 66. Ancient Hellenistic biographers and historians also wrote from a two-level perspective (back then and now): Isocrates, *Nicoles* 35; *To Demonicus* 34; Polybius 1.1.2; Livy 1, pref. 10–11; Plutarch, *Aem.* 1.1 (*Lives*, LCL VI); Lucian, *Demonax* 2, from Aune, *New Testament in its Literary Environment*, 62. J. H. Charlesworth argues for a pre-70 CE date for the *first* edition of FG, in his *Jesus as Mirrored in John*), 48–51. Mark Stibbe, who combines diachronic with synchronic approaches, cites with approval Prof. Brown's modified 3-stage development in Brown and Moloney, *Introduction to John*, 2–6, 62–89 (intended for the second edition of Brown's commentary); see Stibbe, "Magnificent but Flawed," and Zumstein, "Intratextuality and Intertextuality," in Thatcher and Moore, *Anatomies of Narrative Criticism*, 152–55.

50. See recent surveys and analyses by Carter, *John*, 158–70; Skinner, *Reading John*, 35–46. On the nature of the Johannine community, T. L. Brodie, e.g., analyzes 7 different attempts at reconstruction and concludes that the Evangelist was an integrated member of a large world-oriented church, in *Quest for Origins* (Oxford, 1993), 15–21, 144–52; see also Bauckham, *Gospels for All Christians*; Porter and Fay, *Gospel of John in Modern Interpretation*, esp. the article on R. E. Brown by J. W. Jipp, 173–96; Reinhartz, *Word in World*, 8–9, 101, 104: she combines both stages of post-resurrectional and the writing of FG under "ecclesiological tale," 3–5, 37, 67–68. See also our n26 of this ch., pp. 6–7, on diachronic and synchronic approaches.

51. Following Umberto Eco's three levels of intention regarding the work, the reader, and the author, in Eco, *Limits of Interpretation*, 50–54, see Utzschneider, "Text—Reader—Author," 1–22. Such an approach includes diachronic and synchronic intepretations, reader-response criticism (similar to reception history) and composition criticism (Ger. *Kompositionsgeschichte*). See also Tate, *Handbook for Biblical Interpretation*, 81, 365–66.

52. See especially Neusner, *Rabbinic Literature and the New Testament*, 21–40.

53. Much can be learned from differences, e.g., the message of FG as *distinct from* the Synoptic Gospels, when redaction and composition criticisms are employed, noted by Davila, "Perils of Parallelism" (see n16 of this ch., p. 5); on redaction criticism, see Puskas and Robbins, *Introduction to the NT*, 97–101.

I. New Testament Intertextualities: Synoptic and Johannine traditions

II. Jewish Scriptures (Septuagint)

III. Wisdom and Angelology

IV. Philo

V. The Dead Sea Scrolls

VI. Rabbinica and Targumim

VII. Greco-Roman Cults and Philosophies: Isis, Plato, Hermetica

VIII. The Dionysian Gospel

IX. Odes of Solomon, Samaritan Traditions, and Mandaean Writings

X. Nag Hammadi Library

XI. Gospel of Thomas

XII. Early Reception of the Fourth Gospel

The above categories are not rigid, since we detect neo-Platonic influences in both Philo and Hermetica, some type of "gnosis" at Qumran, hellenistic rhetoric in rabbinics, Jewish influences in so-called Gnosticism (Apocalypse of Adam), and the Palestinian origin of some Jewish-influenced gnostic writings (e.g., Gospel of Thomas, Apocryphon of John, Paraphrase of Shem). The Mandaeans are neither Jewish nor Christian. Some early Christian writings outside the New Testament are Jewish-Christian, and others are not. Nevertheless, such categories are helpful in the organization of this book for distinguishing direct intertextual allusions (LXX) from implicit echoes and early FG reception (echoes and reception relate well to much of chs. 7–12).[54]

Despite all of the suggested tests of verifiable relations that we present along with the cautionary notations, our most important efforts will be to supply you the reader with parallel tables of the comparisons. We will briefly introduce the material to be compared (e.g., date, location, literary focus) and certainly comment on the differing literary and cultural contexts with FG, but these efforts will only function as a starting point for you the reader to further analyze and draw conclusions about the relationship of FG and the given document or tradition to be compared. We will supply you with

---

54. The following work by Chrys C. Caragounis is insightful, but it addresses the natural world as the NT authors supposedly perceived it to be (e.g., regarding astronomy, geography, physics, medicine), whereas our work focuses on the conceptual religio-theological world of FG, see Caragounis, "*Weltanschauung* of the NT Authors," 46–66.

some **criteria of discernment or tests of verifiability** (although NT studies are more aesthetic than scientific) but space will not permit us to run every comparison that we do through a six or seven-point test. On certain chapters, we have gone through this procedure, (e.g., ch. 5, FG and DSS). In other chapters, we will allude to these tests, stressing a relevant two or three points. The focus of our study is to present the tables of parallel data with some introductory discussion and analysis, but to let you, the reader, make the final decision on their validity, relevance, and applicability.

Professor George W. MacRae, SJ, observed that the milieu of FG was varied deliberately so as to make the universality and transcendence of the divine son appealing to a wide audience.[55] If Professor MacRae's observation holds true, our efforts to investigate the conceptual worlds of FG, may also disclose the broad readership[56] that FG envisioned and sought to address with its universal and transcendent Christologies.

---

55. MacRae, *Studies*, 15–31, esp. 18, 28, 30–31. We hope to support this statement by MacRae in our book. On similar reflections, see Frey and Schnelle, *Kontexte*, 35–45. C. R. Koester writes that FG's symbols have a range of meanings accessible to a "spectrum of readers" from different cultural backgrounds, in his *Symbolism of the Fourth Gospel*, 235. R. Kysar concludes his *John, the Maverick Gospel* (1976) with a reflection on FG's universal appeal, for its first and subsequent readers (111).

56. On the broad FG readership, not simply written for the specific needs of a particular Johannine community, see S. C. Barton, "Gospel Audience?" in Bauckham, *Gospels for All Christians*, 189–94. "It is important to note, however, that the gospel in general, and 20:30-31 in particular, do not explicitly limit their intended audience to a specific community," says Reinhartz, *Word in World*, 9, and 8–9, 101, 104; see also her "Building Skyscrapers on Toothpicks," in Thatcher and Moore, *Anatomies of Narrative Criticism*, 55–76 (questions Johannine sectarianism and the FG relevance of *Birkat haminim*). In Frey and Schnelle, *Kontexte*, Frey cites Bauckham on audience, 39n178 and 132n68; and see the following work, with essays supporting, qualifying, or contesting Bauckham's position, Klink, *Audience of the Gospels*. After critical reviews of scholarly constructs regarding a Johannine sectarian community (1–28), D. A. Lamb finds essential agreement with Bauckham, Klink, and Koester in Lamb, *Text, Context, and the Johannine Community*, 203–4; see the criticisms of a specific John community, in Kysar, "Whence and Whither," 65–81. See also our n5 of this ch., p. 2, where we resist the view of FG as a sectarian writing.

Map of Mediterranean World

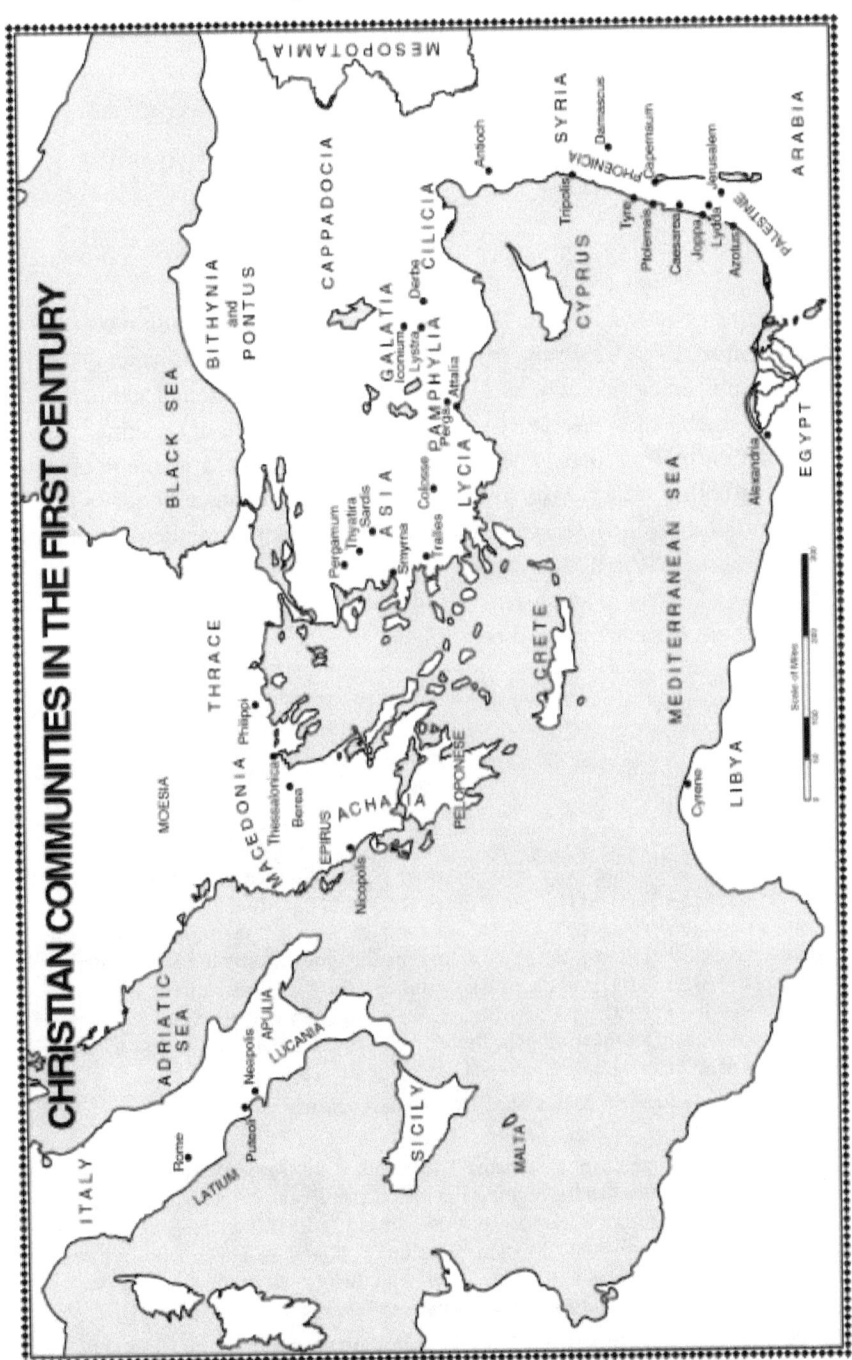

I. New Testament Intertextualities: Synoptic and Johannine Traditions[1]

IN MAKING COMPARISONS OF FG with other early Christian traditions of the first century CE, we have the advantage of working within similar contexts, establishing some accessibility to similar traditions, chronological proximity, and establishing thematic coherence in similar worlds of meaning.[2] The circulation of Paul's letters, the missional activities noted in the book of Acts and other related writings indicate that there was an early network of communication and interaction among the early mission-minded Christian communities of the Roman world.[3] The challenges we face here are in determining the nature and extent of these parallels and their significance in positing any dependence or direct influence.[4]

---

1. Comparisons have been made between FG and Revelation or with other NT books (e.g., Eph). These will be briefly noted at certain points in this ch. when relevant. Some have argued also that the Odes of Solomon (ca. 140 CE?) shares a common traditions with FG. Early second century dating for the Odes is disputed and its identity uncertain: Jewish-Christian or a Jewish document that was Christianized? What similarities does it share with gnostic writings? Was it originally written in Greek or Syriac? See Lattke, *Odes of Solomon*, vii–viii. Therefore, the intertextual relationships of FG and the Odes of Solomon will be discussed later in our ch. 9, pp. 148–55.

2. See the four criteria of evaluating intertextual comparisons in Evans, *Word of Glory*, 18–20.

3. See the arguments in Bauckham, "For Whom Were Gospels Written," *Gospel for All Christians*, 30–49; Brodie, arguing for FG's dependence on the Synoptic Gospels concludes that the author of FG was not sectarian, but "primarily an integrated member of the larger world-oriented Christian community" (*Quest for the Origin*, 144). M. F. Bird finds evidence of broad circulation even with the non-canonical Gospels, "Sectarian Gospels," in Klink, *Audience of the Gospels*, 27–48.

4. Frey discusses the description and classification of parallels in his "Impact of the DSS on NT Interpretation," in *Bible and the Dead Sea Scrolls*, 3:441–42.

I. NEW TESTAMENT INTERTEXTUALITIES

A. The Synoptic Gospels and John's Gospel

Although the Fourth Gospel (FG) tells its own story, having a distinct literary style and thematic concerns (with a vocabulary of about 540 words) one cannot overlook its relationship to the Synoptic Gospels. Despite its distinct material, FG has sayings and stories similar to those also found in the Synoptic Gospels. Before looking at these similarities, we will look at some of those noteworthy differences.

When we read FG, we seem to enter a different narrative world than that of **the Synoptic Gospels**.[5] In contrast to the Synoptics, FG introduces us to a distinctly different Jesus who is not only the promised Messiah (*Messias*), King of the Jews/Israel, Savior of the world, and Son of Man, but also the preexistent Word (λόγος; *logos*),[6] who "pitched his tent among us" (*skēnoō*) as God's only Son (μονογενής; *monogenēs*),[7] and the Lamb of God who removes the sin of the world (John 1).[8] If the Synoptic Gospels advocate the *imitating* of Jesus (Matt 16:24-28; parr.), FG advocates an *experiencing* of Jesus (John 1:4, 14; 3:36; 14:18-21; 15:1-11; 20:31; cf. 1 John 1:1-3; 5:12).[9] Sir Edwyn Hoskyns reflects on Clement of Alexandria's quotation that FG, compared with the earlier gospels, "composed a spiritual gospel" (Eusebius, *Eccl. hist.* 6.14.7). He writes that FG has so presented the history of Jesus that his readers are confronted with what is beyond time and beyond visible occurrence—with the Word of God and the life of eternity.[10]

---

5. See discussion in Anderson, *Riddles of the Fourth Gospel*, 50-59; see also Smith, *John among the Gospels*.

6. See the helpful survey of different explanations regarding the origins of FG's Logos (in the Greco-Roman world) by Keener, *John*, 1:339-50; and also Theobald, *Die Fleischwerdung des Logos*, chs. 1-2. Many of them we will examine in our chs. that follow.

7. LXX Judg 11:34, i.e., Jephthah's "only child," uses the Gk. *monogenēs* for the MT Heb. *yaḥid*, "only." On the odd use of *monogenēs theos* (μονογενὴς θεός) in John 1:18, see Metzger, *Textual Commentary*, 169-70.

8. On the function of John 1, see Anderson, "Johannine Logos-Hymn," 219-42 (a christological hymn introducing FG); Theobald, *Die Fleischwerdung des Logos*, ch. 6; and Zumstein, "Intratextuality and Intertextuality," 123-24 (John 1 provides the hermeneutical framework for interpreting FG). On the intratexutal parallels between John 1 and the rest of FG, see Carson, *Gospel according to John*, 110-111; J. F. O'Grady, "Prologue and John 17," Thatcher, *What We Have Heard from the Beginning*, 217-21; Theobald, *Die Fleischwerdung des Logos*, 296-399.

9. Kysar, *John, the Maverick Gospel* (2007 ed), 95, 173. R. A. Burridge notes, however, that the disciples are exhorted also to follow Jesus in footwashing and observing his love command, John 13:14-15, 34-35 (*Imitating Jesus*, 343-45).

10. Hoskyns, *Fourth Gospel*, 17. Jesus is called "The Word of God" in Rev 19:13, and "the word of life" in 1 John 1:1.

FG and Mark do not include a birth story as do Matthew and Luke. There is no baptismal scene of Jesus (although it may be assumed: John saw "the Spirit [τὸ πνεῦμα; *to pneuma*] descend as a dove from heaven" on him, John 1:32-33; cf. Luke 3:22).[11] FG does not mention the forty-day sojourn of Jesus in the wilderness, nor his temptation there (cf. Mark 1:9-13; Matt 3:13—4:11; Luke par.).[12] In Mark 1:14 Jesus's ministry begins when John ("the Baptist," Mark 1:4)[13] is imprisoned, whereas in John 3:22-24 and 4:1-3 the two ministries, both involving baptism, are concurrent at the beginning.[14] FG has no mention of Jesus's associations with tax collectors (*telōnēs*) or Sadducees.

In FG, we find not the pithy parables or parabolic stories of the Synoptics, but we encounter metaphorical and revelatory pronouncements.[15] The concise Synoptic aphorisms have become extended discourses in the form of dramatic dialogues and lengthy monologues (chs. 3-6, 9-10).[16] The

---

11. "Being born of water and spirit" (John 3:5) recalls John's baptizing statements in John 1:33 (cf. Ezek 36:25-27).

12. Epiphanius of Salamis (ca. 390) mentions this omission and other distinctive features (wedding of Cana) to explain why some (he calls them *Alogoi*, "senseless") reject FG, see Epiphanius, *Pan.* 51.18.6; 21.15-16, cited in Hill, *Johannine Corpus*, 176. This unknown group also rejected Revelation for its difficult sayings and even attributed it (and FG) to the controversial Cerinthus (ca. 100; *Pan.* 51.3.1-6; cf. on Cerinthus, Irenaeus, *Haer.* 3.3.4). We will discuss this issue further in our ch. 12.

13. Nowhere does FG call John "the Baptist," (JBp). John is not the light, nor the Messiah, and has not done any miracles (John 1:8-9, 20, 30; 3:28; 4:1-2; 10:41). Evidence is insufficient to delcare him the mentor of Jesus. Citing data for a "JBap following" (Acts 18:24—19:7; Pseudo-Clem. *Recog.* 1.54.8; *Sib. Or.* 4.165), some scholars have argued that FG seeks to win over followers of JBap after his death, but see the analysis and criticism in Brown and Moloney, *Introduction to the Gospel of John*, 153-56.

14. Eusebius (ca. 330) explained here that FG supplied information about the ministry of Jesus *before* the arrest of John the Baptist (John 3:24) in his *Eccl. hist.* 3.24.11-12.

15. R. E. Brown describes John 10 as a "parabolic comparison" (vv. 1-5) with explanation (vv. 11-16 cf. Mark 4:13-20; LXX Ezek 17:2; 1 En 1:3) that FG refers to as "figure of speech" or "veiled saying" (*paroimia*, John 10:6; cf. 16:25, 29; LXX Sir 39:3; 47:17) "parable" (Gk., *parabolē*) does *not* occur in FG (Brown, *Gospel according to John*, 1:390-98). In his second vol., Fr. Brown in John 15 prefers using *mashal* (Heb.) to convey the similar idea (as in John 10) of "metaphorical comparison" or "similitude," see Brown, *Gospel according to John*, 2:668-84; see also Carson, *John*, 511-13; Moloney, *John*, 422. See also Bultmann, *John*, 343, 358.

16. The longest sayings groups in Matthew are the Sermon on the Mount (ca. 2435 words; NRSV count) and the sayings group of 23:1—25:46 (ca. 2900). The collected sayings group of Matthew look noticeably different from the long discourses in FG (with, e.g., interruptions, structural markers); John 5:19-47 (ca. 641 words); 6:37-70 (ca. 597 words); 8:34-58 (ca. 648 words); 10:7-38 (ca. 611 words); 14:1-11 (ca. 711 words); 15:1-27 (ca. 615 words); 16:1-33 (ca. 704 words); 17:1-26 (ca. 656 words). The last four discourses in FG are somewhat continuous making them almost 2,700 words,

kingdom of God, mentioned in John 3:3, 5; (kingdom of Jesus) 18:36, is not of this world,[17] and one must be born anew or born from above (ἄνωθεν; *anōthen*) to enter it.[18] The miracle stories are limited to seven "signs" (σημεῖα; *sēmeia*), symbolically-loaded enactments, that reveal God's glory in the mission of Jesus and vindicate him as God's son and emissary.[19]

Unlike the Synoptic Gospels, FG focuses on seeing (*horaō*) God's glory (*doxa*) in the life and ministry of Jesus (1:14; 2:11; 11:4; 17:24), God's glorifying (*doxazō*) his Son (and the Son glorifying the Father), and Jesus's being glorified in his death, resurrection, and return to the Father (13:31-32; 14:13; 17:1, 5).[20] FG has no exorcisms (cf. Mark 1:21-28; 3:11; 5:1-17),[21] no healing of lepers (cf. Mark 1:40; Luke 17:12-13) and there is no messianic secret as in Mark (e.g., Mark 1:34; 3:11-12; 5:42-43; 8:29-30). FG's emphasis on the Judean ministry of Jesus is evident by the five trips Jesus makes to Jerusalem (2:13; 5:1; 7:10; 10:22-23; 12:12), in contrast to one visit as an adult in the Synoptic Gospels (Mark 11:11; Matt 21:10; Luke 19:45; with a few, odd exceptions, e.g., temptation scene, Matt 4:5; Luke 4:9 and "in the synagogues of Judea," Luke 4:44).[22]

---

or comparable to the collections in Matthew. It is the ways that these speech complexes are used that create the significant differences, see Puskas and Robbins, *Introduction to the NT*, 175n19; Keener, *John*, 1:68-80.

17. In FG, the world (*kosmos*) is often a negative spatial entity associated with death and darkness, resistance to Jesus, and believers must depart from it in order to be saved (1:9-10; 7:7; 8:23; 9:4-5; 12:31; 14:17; 16:11; 17:14). It sometimes is used in a neutral sense (3:16-17; 4:42; 6:14, 33; 8;12; 12:47; even positive, cf. 1:1-5; Gen 1;), and of human habitants of the world (3:16-17; 4:42; 12:47; the public, 7:4; 8:26; 12:19), see Reinhartz, *Word in the World*, 38-41, 79-80.

18. On double meanings in FG (e.g., *anōthen*), see Wead, *Literary Devices*, 38-39. Barnabas Lindars argues that John 3:3-5 is an expansion of a Synoptic saying (Mark 10:15; par.), in his "John and the Synoptic Gospels." Read also John 1:12-13 with 3:3-5.

19. For example: (1) the changing of water into wine (2:1-11); (2) the healing of the nobleman's son (4:46-54); (3) the healing of the lame man (5:1-15); (4) the feeding of the multitude (6:1-15); (5) walking on water (6:16-21), (6) the healing of the blind man (9:1-41) and (7) the raising of Lazarus (11:1-54). For various reasons the number of the signs in FG is disputed (6, 7, or 8? Include 6:16-21?), some also include the resurrection appearances (20:11-31), see Thompson, *John: A Commentary*, 66, 429; Puskas and Crump, *Gospels and Acts*, 168 (table 7.2).

20. See Frey, *Glory of the Crucified One*, ch. 7.

21. In FG, Judas is described as a devil (6:70) whom the devil or Satan enters to betray Jesus (*diabolos*, 13:2; *Satanas*, v. 27). When Jesus is glorified the "ruler of this world" will be driven out (12:31) and Jesus prays that his disciples be protected from the evil one (17:15; cf. 18:8-9).

22. The surprising Judean reference in Luke 4:44 is determined to be "almost certain [B]," in Metzger, *Textual Commentary*, 114-15.

According to the Synoptic Gospels, the temple was cleansed at the close of Jesus's ministry (Mark 11:15-19; Matt 21:12-13; Luke 19:45-46), in FG's longer account it occurs at the beginning (2:13-22) and the words of Jesus on the temple's destruction and (christological) restoration is identified with his death and resurrection (vv. 19-22; cf. Rev 21:22-23). Although FG writes of, e.g., God's love, Jesus's love for the Father, and Jesus's commandment to his disciples to "love one another" (*agapō, agapē*, ca. 45 times), nowhere in FG does Jesus tell them to "love your enemies" (*echthros*, Matt 5:44; Luke 6:35).[23]

The Synoptic words of institution at the Last Supper (Mark 14:22-25; parr.) are missing in FG, replaced by Jesus's foot washing of the disciples (John 13:1-16).[24] Only in FG is the "Beloved Disciple" mentioned (John 13:23; 19:26; 20:2, 8; 21:7, 20) and his identity is uncertain here (John, the son of Zebedee? Nathanael? John 1:47; or Lazarus? 11:3). The discourse on the eating of flesh and drinking of blood (John 6), betrays only *some* acquaintance with the words of institution.[25] FG also includes a long Farewell Discourse of the resolute Jesus (chs. 13-17), replacing the Synoptic prayer for strength at Gethsemane (e.g., Mark 14:32-42; contra John 12:27). In the Synoptic Gospels, Simon of Cyrene was compelled to bear the cross (Mark 15:20-21; parr.), but in FG Jesus is "bearing his own cross" without assistance (John 19:17).

At his arrest, Jesus boldly identifies himself in FG with "I am he" (*egō eimi*) and the arresting party "step back and fall to the ground" (18:4-6). Jesus also tells his captors to let (*aphiēmi*, imperative) his disciples go free, in order to fulfill what he had spoken regarding his not losing any of those followers entrusted to his care (18:8-9; cf. 6:39; 10:28; 17:12, except Judas). The Synoptic Gospels agree that the crucifixion of Jesus took place on the Passover (Nisan 15), shortly after the Last Supper, arrest, and trial. In FG, Jesus is crucified on the eve of Passover (and before Sabbath) to coincide with the sacrifice of lambs (John 1:29, 36; 19:30-37; cf. b.Sanh. 43a).[26] Finally,

---

23. On love in the Johannine tradition (and also: love of enemies), see Furnish, *Love Command*, 132-58 (love of enemies, 45-62); Perkins, *Love Commands*, 104-22 (love of enemies, 27-41); Kristeva, *Tales of Love*, 147-49 (Johannine love).

24. I. Dunderberg explores this omission in his "How Far Can We Go? in Iricinschi et al., *Beyond the Gnostic Gospels*, 347-66, esp. 360-62.

25. Although FG does include sacramental language (1:35-36; 6:53-58; 19:34), "the 'bread' which Jesus gives is his flesh—given for the life of the world on the cross (6:51)," from P. N. Anderson's "Naming Stars," in Bauckham and Mosser, *Gospel of John and Theology*, 316; for other points of tension, e.g., humanity and divinity, gnosis and pathos, present and future eschatology, see 314-17, 327-28.

26. M. A. Matson finds some early Christian support for FG's death of Jesus on the eve of Passover in the fourteenth of Nisan observance of Jesus's death in Asian churches (late second century) that prompted the "Quartodeciman controversy"

the length of Jesus's ministry in FG is at least three years (more plausible), whereas in the Synoptic tradition it appears to be only one.

It becomes evident from a comparison of FG with the Synoptic Gospels that much of the structural arrangement and thematic emphases of the former is distinctive. John 1:19–12:50 seems to be built around the theme of signs (2:11; 4:54; 12:37); chapters 13–17 are thematic discourses and a prayer,[27] and chapters 18–20 are a passion-resurrection narrative (with *some* Synoptic similarities). In distinction from the Synoptic tradition, we find in FG (1) a very high Christology (e.g., the preexistent Word, who has "come down" from heaven),[28] (2) both a moral dualism (light/darkness, life/death, lost/saved), and a cosmic dualism (above/below, heaven/earth) of binary opposites,[29] (3) an emphasis on faith or belief (e.g., *pisteuō*, 1:7; 3:12–18; ca. 98 times), (4) the gift and pneumatic instruction of the Paraclete (chs. 14–16),[30] and (5) "realized" eschatology (e.g., *echō aiōnos zōē*, 3:15–16, 36; 5:24–25; 11:25–26). "Life" and "eternal life" are often linked to "the age to come" (Mark 10:29–30; cf., 2 Esdr. 7:113; 8:46, 52; 1 En 37:4; 58:3; 71:15), but in FG are a present possession for those who believe (John 3:36; 6:47).[31] Many of these distinct emphases of FG are held in "both-and" ten-

---

(Eusebius, *Hist. eccl.* 5.23–25), in his "John's Passion Dating," in Anderson et al., *John, Jesus, and History*, 2:302–6.

27. See Segovia, *Farewell of the Word*, 5–20; Moloney, *Glory Not Dishonor*, 1–127. See comparisons of Eph 1:1—3:13 with John 17:20–26; Eph 3:14–21 with John 17:1–5; and Eph 4–6 with John 17:20–26 in Brodie, *Quest for Origins*, 128–34.

28. J. R. D. Kirk writes, "Divine and preexistent Christologies can be found in ... John's Gospel, the Christ hymn of Colossians 1, and the opening salvo of Hebrews ... but they are not (significantly) constitutive of the Christologies that empower the narratives of Matthew, Mark, and Luke" (*Man Attested by God*, 16). We would also include Phil 2:5–11 and 1 Tim 3:16 along with Col 1:15–20 and Heb 1:1–4 (mentioned above), see discussed in Anderson, "Johannine Logos-Hymn," 233–38. On FG's Christology, see also R. A. Culpepper, "Christology," in Powell and Bauer, *Who Do You Say?*, 66–87; Loader, *Jesus in John's Gospel*; Thatcher, "Remembering Jesus," 165–89; M. M. Thompson, "Learning the Identity of Jesus from the Gospel of John," in Gaventa and Hays, *Seeking the Identity of Jesus*, 166–79.

29. "In B67, 88, and 11, Heraclitus [of Ephesus ca. 500 BCE] places the following pairs of opposites together: day/night, winter/summer ... life/death, wakefulness/sleep, youth/old age. In contrast to Anaximander's opposites [ca. 570, Miletus] these pertain to experience. Experience encompasses human beings and their world and combines them into a unity" (Ricken, *Philosophy of the Ancients*, 26, we added [brackets]). G. W. F. Hegel seems to have applied this insight of Heraclitus to his dialectical concept of history, "World History," §342—60 in his *Philosophy of Right*. For more discussion on dualism, see our pp. 71–72, 111.

30. On the roles and functions of the Spirit (*pneuma*) in FG, see Johnston, *Spirit-Paraclete*; Koester, *Word of Life*, 133–60; Windisch, *Spirit-Paraclete*.

31. Thompson, *John: A Commentary*, 88. John 3:13; 5:47; 12:34–35 may reflect a

sion, e.g., the humanity and divinity of Jesus, universalism and exclusion, predestination and free will, present and future eschatology.[32]

FG also contains stories and discourses not found in the Synoptic Gospels: the wedding at Cana (2:1–11); the narratives concerning Nicodemus (3:1–21) and the Samaritan woman (4:7–42); the healing at the pool of Beth-zatha (5:1–9); the healing of the man born blind (9:1–12); the raising of Lazarus (11:1–44); Jesus's washing of the disciples' feet (13:1–17; cf. Mark 9:35); the Farewell Discourse (13:18—16:33); the so-called high priestly prayer (ch. 17); and on the cross, the guards cast lots for his garments, and the side of Jesus is pierced with a spear (ch. 19). In FG, Jesus appears to Mary Magdalene in a scene where she mistook him for a gardener (*kēpouros*), Jesus also appears to his disciples with Thomas absent and then present (ch. 20). Although the miraculous catch on the sea of Galilee (Tiberius) and the encounter of Peter with Jesus in John 21 (editorial edition?)[33] recalls the narrative of Luke 5:1–11, Jesus, in FG, renews his commission to Peter, foretells Peter's death, and comments on the life span of the Beloved Disciple who "has written these things" (John 21:15–25).

FG, however, omits teaching and stories crucial to all three Synoptic story lines: Jesus's baptism (Mark 1:9–11; and parr.), the temptation in the wilderness (Mark 1:12–13), the exorcisms (e.g., Mark 1:21–28), the transfiguration (Mark 9:2–8), warnings about the destruction of Jerusalem (Mark 13), the Last Supper with the words of institution (Mark 14:22–25; parr.), Jesus's

---

polemic against apocalyptic traditions exalting Enoch as the Son of Man who ascended to heaven and obtained special knowledge of the divine (1 En 19:3; 71:14; 103:2), see Charlesworth, *Jesus as Mirrored in John*, 295–306.

32. P. N. Anderson, "Naming Stars," in Bauckham and Mosser, *Gospel of John and Theology*, 314–17, 327–28.

33. Some maintain that ch. 21 is originally part of FG (e.g., Carson, Hoskyns, O'Day), others regard it as a later editorial addition, which we favor (e.g., Bultmann, Barrett, Beasley-Murray, R. Brown), See discussion in Georg, *Reading the Tapestry*, 1–36; Thompson, *John: A Commentary*, 431–34. John 1–20 "introduces Christ into the narrative, the epilogue introduces the narrative into the church" (Zumstein, "Intratextuality and Intertextuality," 125); John 21 has an intratextual relationship to FG although it is a later addition.

Note the similarities regarding Luke 5:1–11 and John 21:1–13, 19. Both accounts take place on a boat (*ploion*) in the sea of Galilee (Gennesaret, Tiberius) with Jesus, "Simon Peter," the sons of Zebedee, and "two other disciples" (John 21:2). Nothing was caught all night, after Jesus's directive, their nets (*diktyon*) seized a great haul of many fish (*plēthus ichthus*), the disciples are awestruck and "Simon Peter" (Luke 5:8; John 21:7) reacts in fear. It concludes with an invitation from Jesus with the compliance of the disciples. There are differences, but it seems likely that "they represent a piece of gospel tradition that has come independently to the two evangelists" (Fitzmyer, *Gospel According to Luke I–IX*, 1:561, see also 559–69; Brown, *Gospel according to John*, 1:1089–92.

prayer in Gethsemane (Mark 14:32-42), his being derided on the cross, and his cry of agony "on the ninth hour" (Mark 15:27-39; parr.). FG omits them.

After noting the differences between FG and the Synoptics, D. Moody Smith concludes,

> Attempts to interpret John on the basis of its specific differences from the Synoptics tend to break down precisely because on major theological points John stands in general agreement with them.[34]

In support of this general agreement, we find that FG has sayings and stories in common with the Synoptic Gospels. For example:

- The appearing of Jesus as a light (*phōs*) for the people (John 1:9; 8:12; Matt 4:16; Luke 1:79; 2:32 cf. LXX Isa 9:1; 42:6; 49:6; 60:1-3); and the phrase "light of the world" (*to phōs tou kosmou*; John 8:12/Matt 5:14).[35]
- John is not worthy to untie the coming one's sandals (John 1:26-27; Mark 1:7-8, parr.), John baptized with water, but Jesus will baptize with the Holy Spirit (John 1:32-33; Luke 3:16); John saw "the Spirit descend as a dove from heaven" on him (John 1:32-33; cf. Luke 3:22).
- There is a call of the disciples (1:35-51; Mark 1:16-20; Luke 5:1-11, although FG has Andrew finding Simon, then Philip and Nathanael);
- Jesus is compared to a bridegroom (John 3:29; Mark 2:19-20; parr.), and there is the healing of the official's son (John 4:46-53; similar to Luke 7:1-10, centurion's servant);
- The feeding of the multitude, followed by a sea-crossing miracle, controversy, and bread/food discourse (John 6:1-51; Mark 6:30—7:43; see table 1.B., p. 25)
- Peter's confession (6:66-69); the entry into Jerusalem (12:12-15); the cleansing of the temple (2:13-22, transposed); the full humanity of Jesus (2:12; 4:6-7; 6:42; 11:33-38; 19:1-3)[36]
- The shortcomings of the disciples, especially Simon Peter (18:10, 17, 27), the anointing at Bethany (12:1-8); the "Last Supper," with a prophecy of betrayal (13:1-11);

---

34. Smith, *Theology of the Gospel of John*, 64.

35. Wead has noted the similar use of the light metaphor in Matt 5:14-15 and FG, in his *Literary Devices*, 102-4.

36. See Thompson, *Humanity of Jesus*, 3, 8, 14-15, 128.

- Basic features of arrest, passion, and resurrection (John 18–20; cf. Mark 14–15; parr.).[37] All of the above similarities are dominated by Johannine literary style and thematic concerns.

Events in FG that appear to follow Mark's sequence[38] are the following:

A. Similar Sequence of Events in Mark and John with Verbal Similarities

1. The work and witness of John: Mark 1:3, 7–8, 10–11; John 1:23, 26–27, 32–33

2. Jesus's departure to Galilee: Mark 1:16; John 1:43

3. The feeding of a multitude: Mark 6:37–38, 43–44; John 6:7, 9–10, 13

4. Walking on water: Mark 6:49–50; John 6:19–20

5. Peter's confession: Mark 8:29; John 6:69

6. The departure to Jerusalem: Mark 10:1, 32–33; John 7:10–14

7. Entry into Jerusalem and the anointing: Mark 11:9–10; John 12:13; Mark 14:3,5, 7–8; John 12:3, 5, 7–8 John 12:3, 5, 7–8

8. The Last Supper, with predictions of betrayal and denial: Mark 14:18; John 13:21

9. The arrest, passion, and resurrection: Mark 14:47; John 18:10; Mark 15:26; John 19:19

The Fourth Gospel, as Matthew and Luke had done, appears to follow Mark's general outline and it is difficult to conceive of FG's development of this nine-point outline, independent of Mark. It is unlikely, to us, that FG's "life of Jesus" was derived only from the brief outlines of apostolic preaching (e.g., 1 Cor 15:3–7; Acts 10:36–43)[39] or even a similar life-of-Jesus tradition that Mark had also used.

FG has parallels with a double-cycle tradition in Mark: the feedings (Mark 6:30–44; 8:1–10; and John 6:1–14), lake crossings (Mark 6:45–52; 8:10; and John 6:16–21), and controversies (Mark 7:1–13; 8:11–13; and John 6:15) followed by a discourse on bread (Mark 7:14–23; 8:14–21; and

---

37. On John 18–19 and the Synoptic accounts of the passion narratives, see comparisons in Brown, *Gospel according to John*, 2:787–802.

38. Both Matthew and Luke appear to follow Mark's general outline of Jesus's ministry, with each Gospel altering, inserting material, and expanding upon it for their own literary and thematic purposes, see Puskas and Crump, *Gospels and Acts*, 89–93, 106–7. FG *also* appears to follow Mark's general outline.

39. Dodd, *Apostolic Preaching and Its Development*.

John 6:22–51). Even though there are verbal differences in the accounts, the similar order and themes seem to indicate a common cycle of tradition.[40]

B. Mark and John: Double Cycle Tradition

Event	Mark	John
1. Feeding	6:30–44 (5,000); 8:1–10 (4,000)	6:1–14 (5,000)
2. Lake crossing on boat	6:45–52; 8:10	6:16–21 (*ploion, mē phobeō*)
3. Controversy	7:1–13; 8:11–13	6:15 (make him a king)
4. Bread/food discourse	7:14–23; 8:14–21 (*artos*) (no food, *brōma*)	6:22–51 (bread, *artos*)

A synopsis of the Four Gospels show significant similarities between the Markan and Johannine passion narratives, both in actions and in wording.[41] See also the verbal and thematic similarities in the next two sets of parallels (tables C and D, below).

C. Mark and John: Lexical and Thematic Parallels

Action Parallels	Mark	John
1. The anointing of Jesus for burial, with similar vocabulary	14:3–9	12:3–8
2. Prediction of betrayal and denial	14:18–21, 27–31	13:21–30, 36–38
3. Trial before the high priest, in the context of Peter's denial	14:54 [55–65] 66–72	18:15–18[19–24] 25–27

40. Chart on the double cycle from Puskas and Crump, *Gospels and Acts*, 75; see also P. N. Anderson, "Passion Narrative," in Frey, *Imagery*, 172n26; Schnelle, *Antidocetic Christology*, 105–15.

On FG and the Synoptic tradition, see Anderson, *Riddles of the Fourth Gospel*, 79–80, 163–66; Brown, *Gospel according to John* 1:236–44; Carter, *John* (2006), 141–45; Thompson, *John: A Commentary*, 2–8.

41. See Aland, *Synopsis of the Four Gospels*, 299–324. On John 18–19 and the Synoptic accounts of the passion narratives, see Brown, *Gospel according to John* 2:787–802. Some similarities are noted in our table A.9, on p. 24. The arrest, passion, and resurrection.

4. Pilate and the "king of the Jews ('*Ioudaioi*)"	15:2–15	18:33–40
5. Certain aspects of the crucifixion (e.g., "Hail King of the Jews")	15:18, 22, 27, 36, 40, 43	19:3, 17, 18, 25, 29, 38

D. Verbal Parallels	Mark	John
1. "Stand up," *egeire* "take your mat," *aron ton krabatton* "and go/walk" *kai peripatei* (different settings; Mark specifies "paralytic")	2:11	5:8
2. bread worth two hundred denarii	6:37	6:7
3. "an alabaster jar of very costly ointment of nard" ... "a pound of costly perfume made of pure nard"	14:3	12:3
4. "losing one's life" (*tēn pyschē autou apoluei/apolesei autēn*)	8:35	12:25
5. My soul is greatly distressed/troubled ... the hour (*hōra*) has come	14:33–34, 41	12:27–28
6. The "cup" (*potērion*) of suffering given from the Father that Jesus is to drink (more resolute[42] in John's Gospel)	14:36	18:11

FG also shares some of the traditions also found in the Gospel of Luke.[43] For instance, John baptized with water, but Jesus will baptize with the Holy Spirit (John 1:32–33; Luke 3:16). In addition, we note that John saw "the Spirit descend as a dove from heaven" on him (John 1:32–33; cf. Luke 3:22), and "Satan" enters Judas to betray Jesus (John 13:27; cf. Luke 22:3).

---

42. Aside from certain "impressions" of grief (John 11:35–38), Attridge finds FG's Jesus portrayed as serene and measured even in the face of death, a noble Stoic ideal, "Jesus and Stoic Tradition," in his *Essays*, 125–26.

43. See Fitzmyer, *Luke*, 1:87–89; and Brown, *Gospel according to John*, 1:xlvi–xlvii.

In FG and Luke, compare also the two stories of Jesus's anointing (John 12:3–8; Luke 7:36–50). In John 12 the two unusual actions of Mary are explainable if FG knew Luke's simpler version. In FG she *first* anoints the feet of Jesus (with "costly ointment") then dries them with her hair (!), whereas in Luke the woman wipes Jesus's feet with her hair before anointing them. FG's version seems more complicated and unusual.[44] Luke's account is simpler and less problematic. Luke is also the earliest gospel to include the two ritualistic acts. In Mark 14:3–9, for example, the woman only anoints Jesus's head; there is *no* mention of her wiping his feet with her hair. Therefore, a plausible case can be made that the author of FG derived *both* acts of foot washing and anointing from Luke's source (or a parallel tradition) and added his *own* curious changes, which we read in John 12:3–8.

Furthermore, only in FG and Luke do the two sisters Mary and Martha appear together (John 11:1–44; 12:1–8; Luke 10:38–42). To his frightened disciples on a boat, Jesus says "fear not!" (*mē phobeomai*, John 6:20; Luke 5:10). Only in FG and Luke does Pilate pronounce Jesus innocent three times (John 18:38; 19:4, 6; Luke 23:4, 14–15, 22). Finally, when the risen Jesus appears to his disciples, he greeted them with "peace to you" (*eirēnē humin*) and "showed (*deiknumi*) them his hands (*cheiros*) and side/feet" (John 20:19–20 "side"; Luke 24:36, 40, "feet").[45]

We list below three sets of Synoptic-type parallel traditions, oral and written, that may have been selectively used in the composition of FG.[46] Raymond E. Brown wrote that

> In addition to the material drawn from this independent tradition, John has a few elements that seem to suggest a more direct cross-influence from the Synoptic tradition.[47]

---

44. W. E. S. North makes a similar observation in her *Journey Round John*, 216–19.

45. Both Luke 24:36 and 40 are omitted in certain Western witnesses. The semitic greeting "peace to you" (*eirēnē humin*), might be expected on this occasion (cf. Tob 12:17). It might even reflect a common tradition rather than an interpolation of a later copyist. If Luke 24:40 had been interpolated directly from FG, copyists would have left more traces of its FG origin by, e.g., retaining FG's "side" (*pleura*) in place of "feet" (*podos*, Luke 24:40). See Metzger, *Textual Commentary*, 160–61.

46. On Rudolf Bultmann's source theory (Bultmann, *John*) and an alternative (Synoptic-like) theory, see Puskas and Crump, *Gospels and Acts*, 158–64; on Bultmann, see also Nigel Turner's comments in Moulton and Turner, *Grammar of New Testament Greek*, 4:64–67; and esp. Smith, *Composition and Order of the Fourth Gospel*. For other source theories see Martyn, *History and Theology*; a "signs sources," in Fortna, *Fourth Gospel and Its Predecessors*; and Synoptic sources according to Brodie, *Quest for Origins*; for discussion, see Keener, *John*, 1:37–39 (with ancient analogies to narrative incongruities); and Skinner, *Reading John*, 35–46 (on J. Louis Martyn's two-level drama).

47. Brown and Moloney, *Introduction to the Gospel of John*, 104. Although Bultmann

Many of the examples below may reflect independent engagement with parallel traditions, and not direct dependency.[48]

Synoptic-Type Sayings Sources

Synoptic-type sayings are Jesus-sayings that probably originated independently and later became the nuclei of Johannine discourses and dialogues. Many of them are brief maxims, aphorisms (e.g., 3:6, 8), and sayings of Jesus prefaced by formulas like "very truly [amēn amēn], I tell you . . ." (3:3, 5, 11). There are also sayings that find some parallel in the Synoptic tradition, both Markan and Q: John 1:51/Mark 14:62; John 10:15/Matt 11:27/Luke 10:22; John 12:25/Matt 10:39; John 13:20/Matt 10:40. In fact, the portion of Jesus's Synoptic (Q) prayer found in Matt 11:27/Luke 10:22, "no one knows (epiginōskō/ginōskō) [who is] the Son except the Father, no one knows [who is] the Father except the Son," has famously been described as "a lightning bolt fallen from the Johannine heaven" (cf. John 1:18; 3:35; 7:29; 10:15a; 13:3; 17:25–26).[49]

Synoptic-Type Stories Source

The Synoptic-type stories source includes the narratives that John has in common with the other gospels (e.g., cleansing of the temple, the anointing of Jesus) and Markan or pre-Markan material in FG (e.g., feeding of multitude connected to sea-crossing miracles, controversy, and discourse on bread/food, Peter's denial in the context of Jesus's trial before the high priest).[50] As we discussed earlier, the wording and sequence of these narratives in FG presuppose some acquaintance with traditions used by the Synoptic Gospels.

---

claims that FG's sources for the passion narrative "are not the Synoptic Gospels" (635), he concedes in the narrative on John "the Baptist" that a final editor has inserted "parallel sayings in the Synoptic tradition," (e.g., John 1:27; p. 97) in Bultmann, *John*.

48. See Paul N. Anderson's examination of the "interfluential, formative, and dialectical relationships" of FG and the Synoptic Gospels, in his *Fourth Gospel and the Quest for Jesus*, 102–26.

49. This much-repeated phrase was first coined by Karl von Hase, *Geschichte Jesu*, 422; see also Sabbe, "Can Mt 11,25–27 and Lc 10, 22 Be Called a Johannine Logion?", 263–71. On the knowledge of God in FG, Thompson, *God of the Gospel of John*, 140–43.

50. In support of FG's use of Mark, see Barrett, *John*, 42–54; Brodie, *Quest for Origins*. The following favor independent dialogue with parallel traditions, not dependency, see Smith, *John among Gospels*, 139–76; P. N. Anderson, "John and Mark," in Fortna and Thatcher, *Jesus in the Johannine Tradition*, 175–88.

Synoptic-Type Concepts

Although FG is distinctive in its emphasis on the immediacy of realized eschatology (e.g., in John 3:16, 18, 36; 5:24; 11:24-25, eternal life and the final judgment occur here and now), the author also preserves some of the "already/not yet" tension more typical of the Synoptic Gospels (e.g., in John 5:28-29; 6:39-40; 12:25, 48, resurrection, eternal life, and final judgment are delayed until the future). Although it does not include a Gethsemane scene, FG seems to interact with it, portraying the *confident resolve* of Jesus (John 12:27-28; 17:11; 18:11) in contrast to his *sustaining faith* in the Markan scene (Mark 14:34-36, 41). In addition, while FG develops an elaborate, noteworthy series of "I am" statements, identified by the awkward Greek phrase *egō eimi*,[51] the identical construction, complete with christological overtones, appears less frequently but just as significantly in the Synoptic Gospels (Mark 13:6/Luke 21:8; Mark 14:62). In fact, the absolute "I am" statement in John 6:20 is similar to Jesus's words in Mark 6:50/Matt 14:27.

B. The Johannine Letters and the Fourth Gospel

What is the intertextual relationship between **the Johannine letters** and the FG? We will first look at the differences of the two works (especially 1 John and FG) before examining some of the thematic and structural similarities.

There are noteworthy differences to suggest separate authors for 1 John and FG. First and most obvious are the differences in genre. FG is a narrative of the life and teaching of Jesus and First John is an exposition of Johannine teaching, probably circulated with the other Johannine letters. Secondly, there are specific grammatical differences. The grammar of the gospel is explicit (e.g., John 1; 15), whereas that of 1 John is often obscure (e.g., 1 John 1:1-4; 3:19-20; 5:6-7). Also, some grammatical features frequent in FG (e.g., "for" *gar*, "therefore," *oun*) rarely occur in 1 John. Fourth, certain key words in the gospel never occur in 1 John: e.g., "Lord" (*kurios*, e.g., John 1:23; 6:68; 9:38; 20:28), "judge/judgment" (*krinō, krisis*, John 3:17-19; 5:22-30; 8:16; except *krisis* in 1 John 4:17), "to seek" (*zēteō*, John 1:38; 7:18; 13:33; 20:15),[52] "to send" (*apostellō*, John 3:17; 11:42; 17:3,18-25). The fifth set of differences between 1 John and FG concern their distinct theologies. (a) First John, for example, refrains from using some christological titles or attributes. In fact, what is often attributed to Jesus in FG (Jesus is the light, Jesus's commandments) is ascribed only to God in 1 John.[53] Also, 1 John emphasizes the reality and

---

51. See our ch. 2 n33, pp. 42-43, for more discussion of the "I am" statements in FG.
52. See "Search for Jesus," in Collins, *These Things Have Been Written*, 94-127.
53. The FG epithets of Jesus the Christ, the Word with God, the source of Life, the

tranquility of the Son of God who came in the flesh, whereas FG speaks of the Word of God made flesh who reveals God's glory (*doxa*).[54] (b) The sacrificial and atoning character of Jesus's death is more explicit in 1 John (1:7; 2:2; 3:16; 4:10) than in FG, where Jesus's death is viewed as a triumph and glorification (*doxazō*, 12:27-32: 13:31-32; 14:30-31; 16:14, 33; 17:1). (c) First John gives less attention to the Spirit (3:24; 4:2, 13; 5:6,8) than FG (John 1:33; 3:3-8; 7:39; 14:17, 26; 15:26; 16:13; 20:22). (d) FG seems to offer some present effects of future expectation or realized eschatology, e.g., "may have eternal life," John 3:16-19, 35-36; 5:24; "I am the resurrection," 11:25, 26; "now is the judgment of this world" 12:31; 17:3, whereas 1 John envisions a future judgment and final revelation of the Son of God (1 John 2:28; 3:2).[55] (e) There are only a few allusions to the LXX Scriptures in 1 John although there are many in FG. These are even used in John 13-17 which has the most parallels to 1 John.[56] The final set of differences between 1 John and FG concern their life settings.[57] (a) First John lacks the Jewish-Christian context of FG with its many citations and allusions to the LXX Scriptures. (b) in FG there are critics, seekers, and followers of Jesus

---

glory of the Son, and Light of the world (John 1:1-2,4, 14b; 2:11; 8:12; 9:5; 12:41, 46; 20:31) may have been *misinterpreted* in a docetic manner by the opponents of 1 John, this *misinterpretation* may be what 1 John is seeking to correct. See Brown, *Epistles of John*, 73-79.

54. The words, "glory" (*doxa*, 19 times in FG) or "glorify" (*doxazō*, 23 times in FG) do not occur in the Johannine Letters. Note also "self-glory" or "the glory of other people" (human acclaim) portrayed in a negative manner (John 5:41, 44; 7:18; 12:43; *doxazō*, 8:54a), the opposite of glory that is from or directed to God (1:14; 2:11; 11:4, 12:41; 17:5,22, 24; *doxazō*, 7:39; 11:4; 12:16, 23, 28; 13:31-32; 17:1, 4-5, 10; 21:19). See Köstenberger, "Glory of God in John's Gospel," 108, see also 107-26; and Frey, *Glory of the Crucified One*, ch. 7.

55. FG's realized eschatology where the future promises of the eschaton are available in the present, through the coming of Jesus, presupposes and anticipates a future eschatology (e.g., 5:28-29; 6:39-40,44; 12:48b). See A. R. Culpepper, "Realized Eschatology," in Koester and Bieringer, *Resurrection of Jesus*, 253-76; Frey, *Die johanneische Eschatologie*, 1:119-50; Attridge, "Resurrection Motifs," in his *Essays*, 160-76. In 1 John, some statements could be interpreted as future hopes realized in the present in, e.g., 1 John 2:5, 8, 13-14; 5:4. Nevertheless, FG's thought is more conjunctive and dialectical than the Johannine Letters with their disjunctive threats and corrective Christology, see P. N. Anderson's "Naming Stars," in Bauckham and Mosser, *Gospel of John and Theology*, 325n20. For J. H. Charlesworth, FG reflects a polemic against apocalyptic traditions in 1 Enoch that exalt Enoch as Son of Man (1 En 71:14), *Jesus as Mirrored in John*, 295-306.

56. Some OT phraseology (e.g., Isa 6:10; Jer 31:34; Gen 4:8) are found in 1 John 2:11, 18, 27; 3:12. See D. A. Carson, "1—3 John," in Beale and Carson, *Commentary*, 1063-67. See also chart of common themes in 1 John and John 13-17, in Smalley, *1, 2, and 3 John*, xxx. See John 13:18; 15:25; 16:22 for OT quotations to be discussed in our ch. 2, p. 38.

57. Brown, *Epistles of John*, 28-30; On John's worldview and use of the OT, see Köstenberger, *Theology of John's Gospel and Letters*, 275-310.

with whom the author (and his community) has entered into debate (e.g., Jewish critics,[58] followers of John, Jewish and Hellenistic seekers, Jewish followers of Jesus) whereas in 1 John the debate seems to be carried on with insiders who have now left the community (i.e., secessionists). (c) none of the opponents in FG (e.g., John 5:18, *hoi 'Ioudaioi*) seemed to have had so high a Christology as those in 1 John (e.g., contra Docetism, 1 John 1:1-4; 4:2-3; 5:6; cf. 2 John 7).

Looking now at the similarities between 1 John and FG, both were written in the late first century and may have originated from the same location.[59] Both can be outlined in broad chiastic patterns.[60] It has been argued that 1 John is an exposition of FG to refute the secessionists (1 John 2:19, 26) who also revered the book.[61] The question has also been raised: is FG the source of the letters, or vice versa?[62] Extensive lists of parallels[63] of 1 John and FG can be drawn up:

---

58. On the issue of *hoi 'Ioudaioi* as, e.g., "Judeans (7:14-15), Jewish leaders (1:19; 5:15-18), Jewish people (5:1; 6:4; 19:19)," see North, *Journey Round John*, 148-67; Thompson, *John: A Commentary*, 199-204; Skinner, *Reading John*, 56-67. See also helpful essays by A. Reinhartz (213-27) and other major FG interpreters in R. Bieringer and Vandcasteele-Vanneuville, *Anti-Judaism and the Fourth Gospel*.

59. We favor a late first-century date, with a location in the Syria-Palestine area, but possibly Ephesus, see Puskas, *Hebrews, General Letters*, 125-28. See our Intro. p. 11 for date and location of FG.

60. In FG we have a plot structure of: A complication (1:19—12:19); B crisis (12:20—26); A' denouement (12:27—20:31), see Puskas and Crump, *Introduction*, 166-71. In 1 John, we also have: A complication (1:1—3:7-12), B crisis (3:13-17); and A' denouement (3:18—5:21), see Heil, *1-3 John*, 25, 202-3.

61. Brown, *Epistles of John*, 90-100. The example of the *pesharim* of the Dead Sea Scrolls is provided, i.e., the haggadic, midrashic (non-halakic) commentary of Scripture (e.g., on Habbakkuk, 1QpHab, Nahum, 4QpNah, Isaiah, 1QpIsa). A commentary on John by the Valentinian gnostic Heracleon, and the gnostic *Gospel of Truth* (both discussed later) may also serve as parallel examples because both seek to update and apply the Fourth Gospel to their own situation, but the author of 1 John is not as speculative or mythological. See also Puskas, *Hebrews, General Letters*, 131-32.

62. Udo Schnelle argues for the following order of composition: 2 John, 3 John, 1 John, and then FG, in his *Die Johannesbrief*, 9-19. According to Urban von Wahlde, 1 John modified FG (second ed.) and then FG (third ed.) incorporated the modified views of 1 John into this final ed. of FG, idem, *Gnosticism, Docetism*, 1-23; See survey of different views in Brown, *Epistles of John*, 30-35; and Keener, *John* (2003) 1:122-26.

63. Some of the following parallels are derived from the following: Brown, *Epistles of John*, 757-58; Painter, *1, 2, and 3 John*, 61-72; Köstenberger, *Theology of John's Gospel and Letters*, 129-35; and Parsenios, *First, Second, and Third John*, 8; and Theobald, *Die Fleischwerdung des Logos*, 400-437. To be sure, 2 and 3 John also include themes from FG: e.g., unity of Father and Son (2 John 9), truth (2 John 1; 3 John 3, 8), in the flesh (2 John 7), new commandment (2 John 5), love one another (2 John 5), fulfilled joy (2 John 12). Our table 1.E is derived from Puskas, *Hebrews, General Letters*, 118-21.

E. Similar Themes	1 John	Gospel of John
Beginning word, life revealed/made flesh, in the Father's (God's) presence	1:1–3	1:1, 2, 4, 14 (Rev 19:13)
We have seen and testify	1:2	3:11
Unity of Father and Son	1:3; 2:24	5:20; 10:30, 38; 14:10
Joy filled/fulfilled	1:4	15:11; 16:24; 17:13
God is light; I am the light	1:5	8:12; 9:5
Walking (abiding) in darkness/light	1:5–7; 2:9–11	8:12; 11:9–10; 12:35, 46
Know, do, act in truth	1:6; 2:21; 3:19	3:21; 8:32; 18:37
Have no sin	1:8	9:41
Indwelling truth	1:8; 2:4	8:44
Jesus/Holy Spirit as Paraclete[64]	2:1	14:16, 26; 15:26; 16:7
"Little children" (*teknia*)	2:1, 12, 28; 3:7, 18; 4:4; 5:21	13:33
Keep (God's/Jesus's) commandments	2:3, 4; 3:22, 24; 5:3	14:15, 21; 15:10
Abide in God/Jesus	2:6, 27–28; 3:6, 24; 4:15–16	6:56; 15:4, 6–7
A new commandment	2:7–8	13:34
Conquered Evil One (Prince of the World [system])	2:13, 14, 4:4; 5:18	12:31; 16:11; 17:15
Love one another	3:11, 23; 4:7, 11 FG love command assumed here?	13:34; 15:12, 17
Born of God	2:29; 3:9	1:13; 3:3–8
Children of God (*tekna theou*)	3:1, 2, 10	1:12; 11:52
Everyone who does sin	3:4, 8–9	8:34
Hated by the world (system hostile to God)	3:13	15:18–19; 17:14

64. In John 14:16, Jesus refers to the Holy Spirit as "another Paraclete," but *no one else* is called Paraclete in the Gospel. 1 John 2:1, however, refers to *Jesus* as the Paraclete. Does FG presuppose 1 John here? See Parsenios, *First, Second, and Third John*, 13; Johnston, *Spirit-Paraclete*, 73–78.

I. NEW TESTAMENT INTERTEXTUALITIES

E. Similar Themes	1 John	Gospel of John
Passed from death into life	3:14	5:24
Laying down his life for others	3:16	10:11, 15, 17–18; 15:13
Ask and you will receive	3:22; 5:14	11:22; 14:13–14; 15:7, 16; 16:23–24
Divine indwelling and Spirit	3:24	14:17
Confess Jesus Christ/Jesus as Messiah	4:2	9:22
Jesus coming in the flesh	4:2	1:14
Spirit of truth	4:6	14:17; 15:26; 16:13
God's love in sending His only Son	4:9–10	3:16–17
We have known and believed	4:16	6:69
Believe Jesus is messiah/the Christ	5:1	20:31
Conquers (*nikaō*) the world	5:4	16:33
Water and blood	5:6–8	19:34–35
The witness (*martyria*) of men	5:9	3:33; 5:34
Purpose of writing	5:13	20:31
To know the true one "Jesus Christ"	5:20	17:3

The above parallels range from embedded thematic allusions to implied conceptual echoes. Each parallel will need to be examined separately to determine where each similarity lands on the scale of allusion probability.[65] The challenge is to discern intentionality and the question of causality (source criticism). Is First John an exposition of FG (cf. R. E. Brown) to refute the secessionists and their own interpretation of FG?[66] Do both re-

---

65. See Köstenberger and Patterson, *Invitation to Biblical Interpretation*, 541–44.

66. Prof. Brown has argued that 1 John is a midrash (commentary) of FG, providing a "right way" for the church to read FG, perhaps in reaction to gnostic interpretations, Brown, *Community*, 149–50. See our ch. 12 that examines the gnostic use of FG, pp. 217–21, and orthodox responses, pp. 225–31. J. Zumstein, in some agreement with R. Brown, views 1 John as the reception text (or hypotext) of FG that provides a correct

flect common (eyewitness) tradition within a Johannine community? Did FG make use of traditions from First John (cf. Udo Schnelle)? Perhaps John the Elder (2 John 1; 3 John 1), who probably wrote 1 John, was also the final author of FG?[67] This view might find support with some of the parallels that we have provided above.

Much is presupposed regarding introductory matters (date, place of writing, authorship, purpose) and the creditability of the answers is found in the type of data employed, how it is used, and the forcefulness of the stated argumentation. How compelling is it? "All the proof of a pudding is in the eating."[68] In a similar manner, Gerald Seelig, in the field of biblical studies, writes that "the intention behind the comparison determines its outcome." What are we attempting to accomplish in our historical-religious comparisons? He later concludes, "Everything he [the exegete] does is to ensure a proper interpretation of the New Testament: All paths and necessary detours only make sense if he can bring something from it that contributes to this goal."[69] It is a worthy goal for us to pursue in all of our comparative studies.

---

understanding of FG the reference text (or hypertext) according to the *relecture* (re-reading) model, in his "Intratextuality and Intertextuality," 132.

67. We have argued for the common authorship of 1–3 John in Puskas, *Hebrews, General Letters*, 116–18. The view that John the Elder is author of FG is supported by M. Hengel, *Johannine Question*, 102–13, and R. Bauckham in his *Testimony of the Beloved Disciple*; and *Jesus and the Eyewitnesses*.

68. Proverb used in the English translation of Miguel de Cervantes's *Don Quixote* (Modern Library) pt. I, bk IV, p. 322, by P. A. Motteux (1700–1703), first attributed to William Camden's *Remaines of a Greater Worke Concerning Britaine*, 1605, see Bartlett, *Bartlett's Familiar Quotations*, 195b.

69. Our trans. of the first quote "die hinter dem Vergleich stehende Intention sein Ergebnis bestimmt," in Seelig, *Religionsgeschichtliche*, 262, and our trans. of Seelig's concluding remark: "alles, was er tut, um einer sachgemäßen Auslegung des Neuen Testaments willen tut: Alle Wege und notwendigen Umwege bekommen erst dann einen Sinne, wenn er davon etwas mitbringen kann, das zu diesem Ziel beiträgt" (335).

II. The Jewish Scriptures (Septuagint)

IN FG WE NOTE: (1) a discernible influence of **the Jewish Scriptures (Septuagint)**, (2) a plausible acquaintance with Jewish wisdom and angelology (mostly Septuagint), (3) noteworthy similarities with the themes and thought-world of the Dead Sea Scrolls, rabbinic thought and argumentation, and also the writings of Philo.[1] In this chapter we will discuss FG's use of the Jewish Scriptures (OT) mostly derived from the Septuagint.[2]

When we mention the Old Testament (OT) we refer to the books of the Jewish and Protestant canon based on the MT (the Hebrew Masoretic text).[3] The Septuagint, a Greek translation of the OT, also includes books outside post-70 Jewish canon (e.g., 1–4 Maccabees, Sirach, Tobit, Wisdom of Solomon, Ps 151), called the OT Apocrypha or deutero-canonical writings (latter phrase for those books that are in the Roman Catholic and

---

1. The writings of the Septuagint (third century BCE) and Philo (ca. 20 BCE–50 CE) both originate from Alexandria, Egypt. The Dead Sea Scrolls (third century BCE–first century CE) are from Judea, and the rabbinic writings are from Judea/Palestine (e.g., Mishna, Palestinian Talmud, third to fifth centuries CE) and Babylon (Babylonian Talmud, seventh century CE). See Collins and Harlow, *Early Judaism*; and Tov, "Textual Criticism: OT," 6:393–411. Other Greek versions (e.g., Old Greek, Theodotion) will be noted when pertinent to our study.

2. See Tov, "Septuagint," Mulder and Sysling, *Mikra*, 161–88; L. Greenspoon, "Septuagint," *NIDB* 5:170–77; Müller, *First Bible of Church*, 25–45. Some OT references depart from the LXX and appear to reflect a source closer to the Hebrew text of the MT (tenth century CE), see M. J. J. Menken, *Old Testament Quotations*, 205–6; Beale and Carson, *Commentary*, 415–21. B. G. Schuchard is sympathetic to the idea that FG knew Aramaic and could understand Hebrew, but is suspicious that FG made direct use of the Hebrew Bible ("Form versus Function," in Myers and Schuchard, *Abiding Words*, 35). On the problem of Greek equivalents of the Hebrew Bible, see Tov, *Greek and Hebrew Bible*, 101–5, equivalents, 131–52. FG echoes (not quotations) of LXX writings that are *outside* the Jewish canon (e.g., Bar, Sir, Tob, Wis) are also detected, see NA[28] loci citati vel allegati, pp. 869–77; these apocryphal and deutero-canonical references will be discussed later in ch. 3 under "FG and Wisdom" pp. 46–49, and "FG and Angelology" pp. 53–54.

3. On the centrality of the Masoretic text (ca. tenth century CE) in the development of the Hebrew Bible, see Tov, *Textual Criticism of the Hebrew Bible*, 24–26, 155–90, esp. 160–61.

Eastern Orthodox Bibles).[4] Because the OT versification of the NRSV is based on the MT, not the LXX, we add LXX to OT citations that are explicitly from the Septuagint.[5]

In making comparisons of FG with the LXX, we have the advantage of working within similar linguistic and cultural Hellenistic Jewish contexts (Koine Greek, eastern Mediterranean), establishing the accessibility to the LXX (OT in NT), the chronological antiquity of the LXX to FG, and establishing some thematic coherence in similar worlds of meaning.[6] The challenges that we face here are determining the nature and extent of these parallels, their thematic coherence or lack of coherence, and their significance in positing any dependence or direct influence.[7]

Although in FG we find about twenty-three scriptural references, much less than in the Synoptic Gospels (Mark 70, Matt 124, Luke 109), FG is saturated with OT themes and imagery.[8] These references, with only few exceptions, are from a Greek translation of the OT, the Septuagint (LXX).[9] We use the phrase "scriptural references" as a generic phrase that could imply either cited quotation or intentional allusion here.

---

4. The origins of Jewish canon are uncertain, but sometime after the destruction of the Temple (70 CE), and perhaps at Jabneh (90 CE), what came to be know as the Tanak began to take shape. See Trebolle, "Canon of the OT," 1:548-63 and L. T. Stuckenbruck, "Apocrypha and Pseudepigrapha," in Collins and Harlow, *Early Judaism*, 143-62. For LXX we follow and include as LXX, all of the books in Rahlfs, *Septuaginta*; and Wevers and Fraenkel, *Göttingen Septuagint*.

5. See helpful comparison chart highlighting these differences in Appendix B: English/Hebrew/Greek Versification in Collins et al., *SBL Handbook of Style*, 265-68.

6. See the four criteria of evaluating intertextual comparisons in Evans, *Word of Glory*, 18-20; also the seven tests of discerning scriptural echoes, in Hays, *Echoes in the Letters of Paul*, 29-33; and *Echoes in the Gospels*, 7-14, 291-344. These are mentioned also in our Introduction, n31, pp. 8-9.

7. Frey discusses the description and classification of parallels in his "Impact of the DSS on NT Interpretation," in *Bible and the Dead Sea Scrolls*, 3:441-42.

8. Our chart of 23 references (mostly allusions) is derived from NA[28] *loci citati vel allegati*. See also Barrett, "Old Testament in the Fourth Gospel," 155 (counts 27 from Westcott and Hort Greek New Testament); Bratcher, *Old Testament Quotations*, 22-24 (19 refs.). See also Menken, *Old Testament Quotations*, 11-12 (17 refs.); Daly-Denton, *David in the Fourth Gospel*, 33-34 (16 refs.); Burney, *Aramaic Origins of the Fourth Gospel*, 114-25 (20 refs.); Freed, *Old Testament Quotations in John's Gospel*, 126 (18 refs.); A. J. Köstenberger, "John," in Beale and Carson, *Commentary*, 415-21 (14 refs.); Schuchard, *Scripture within Scripture*, xiii-xiv (13 refs.); listings of most of the above references are from Hays, *Echoes of Scripture in the Gospels*, 424nn3-4.

9. For LXX, we consulted Rahlfs, *Septuaginta*; Wevers and Fraenkel, *Göttingen Septuagint*; and Pietersma and Wright, *NETS*. In the chart, we follow the LXX numberings (that differ in places from the MT, on which the NRSV is based). See also Greenspoon, "Septuagint," 170-77; Jobes and Silva, *Septuagint*; McLay, *Use of the Septuagint*; Hengel, *Septuagint as Christian Scripture*.

II. THE JEWISH SCRIPTURES (SEPTUAGINT)

Citations, Quotations, and Allusions

In the references below, FG usually (1) follows the Greek Septuagint (LXX), but in a few cases, (2) he *favors* the same wording that is also found in the Masoretic Hebrew text (MT) over the Greek, (3) sometimes he happens to agree with both (LXX, MT), or (4) paraphrases the LXX or something like the MT (p = paraphrase).[10] The following are most of the primary OT references (LXX) identified in FG (following FG's order):

Theme Text (LXX)	*John*	OT/LXX
In the beginning	1:1–5	Gen 1:1–5, *en archē*; *legō*, *phōs*, *skotos*; cf. *tō logō kyriou hoi ouranoi*; Ps 32:6 LXX[11]
voice in desert	1:23	Isa 40:3 (LXX, p); cf. Matt 3:3; Mark 1:3; Luke 3:4
ascent/descent	1:51	Gen 28:12 (allusion)
zeal for house	2:17	Ps 68:10 (LXX over MT Ps 69:9)
serpent lifted up	3:14	Num 21:8–9, *ophin*; cf. Isa 52:13, *hypsoō*; John 12:32–34
bread from heaven	6:31	Ps 77:24 LXX; Exod 16:4 (p); cf. 1 Cor 10:3; Rev 2:17
taught by God	6:45	Isa 54:13; cites "written in the prophets"
seed of David	7:42	Mic 5:2; Ps 88:4–5 (p)

10. Writing to a Greek-speaking audience, FG uses the LXX, but he also, as does Revelation, make use of the MT text type or a common tradition, Hengel, "Prologue," 269n16; "the Fourth Gospel, the Johannine Epistles, and John's Apocalypse lie much closer to the Hebrew," L. T. Stuckenbruck, "Semitic Influence on Greek," in Keith and Donne, *Jesus, Criteria*, 88, see also 73–94; Beale, *Revelation*, 76–99, esp. 77–78; Beale and Carson, *Commentary*, 417–18. See also G. H. R. Horsley, "The Fiction of 'Jewish Greek,'" in his *New Documents*, 19–40. The above comments might also connect FG to Jewish Palestine.

11. On FG's rereading of Gen, see "Earth Made Whole," in Painter et al., *Word, Theology, and Community*, 65–84. The association of John 1:3 and Ps 32:6 LXX (Ps 33:6 MT) was first made in Irenaeus, *Haer.* 3.83 (ca. 180 CE). For more reception history of the Pss, see Gillingham, *Psalms through the Centuries* and esp. involving FG, Edwards, *John through the Centuries* and Daly-Denton, *David in the Fourth Gospel*.

Theme Text (LXX)	John	OT/LXX
Shepherd/sheep	10:16	Ezk 34:23; 37:24 (LXX, some MT?); Zech 11:17
you are gods	10:34	Ps 81:6 LXX (MT Ps 82:6)
Blessed coming	12:13	Ps 117:25–26 LXX (Ps 118), cf. Matt 21:9; Mark 11:9–10
Fear not behold	12:15	Isa 40:9; Zec 9:9 (p); cf. Matt 21:5
Troubled save me	12:27	Ps 6:4–5; 41:6 (LXX; allusion)
who has believed	12:38	Isa 53:1 (LXX, some MT); cites "Isaiah" twice, vv. 38–39; cf. Rom 10:16
spiritual blindness	12:40–41	Isa 6:10 (LXX, p); cf. Matt 13:15; Mark 4:12; Acts 28:27 "Isaiah said this" (John 12:41)
the betrayer	13:18	Ps 41:9 (MT) favors MT over LXX; cf. Matt 26:23; Mark 14:18; Luke 22:21; John 17:12; Acts 1:16
hated me without cause	15:25	Ps 34:19 LXX; Ps 68:5 LXX; cites "the law"
heart to rejoice	16:22	Isa 66:14 (LXX, some MT?)
parted garments	19:24	Ps 21:19 (LXX, some MT); Ps 22:1 MT in Matt 27:46; Mark 15:34
vinegar for thirst	19:28–29	Ps 68:22 LXX
take down the body	19:31	Deut 21:22–23, *sōma*; cf. Gal 3:13; Josh 10:26b LXX
bone not broken	19:36	Exod 12:10, 46; Num 9:12; see Ps 33:21 LXX (MT Ps 34)
look on pierced	19:37	Zec 12:10 (LXX; "pierce" MT); cf. Matt 24:30; Rev 1:7

II. THE JEWISH SCRIPTURES (SEPTUAGINT)

There are (at least) five references to the Pentateuch (Gen, Ex, Num, Deut),[12] nine to the Prophets (4 from Deutero-Isaiah),[13] and nine to the Psalms (four in John 13–19). Some passages are explicitly cited, e.g., "that the word spoken by the prophet Isaiah might be fulfilled" (twice in the climactic John 12:38–40), some are quoted without citing the source, e.g., "Hosanna! Blessed is he who comes in the name of the Lord" (John 12:13; Ps 118 MT), others are embedded allusions, e.g., "the angels of God ascending and descending" (John 1:51/Gen 28:12).[14]

Some of these references to OT texts are also used elsewhere in the NT (e.g., Exod 16:4; Pss 22; 41:9; 78:24 [Ps 77:24 LXX]; 118:25–26 [117:25–26 LXX]; Isa 6:10; 40:3; 49:6; 53:1; Zech 12:10 [MT]).[15] It has been proposed by some that these texts may have been part of an early Christian *testimonia*, a collection of Israel's Scripture used to support Jesus as the Messiah.[16] There are also Jewish examples of *testimonia* from the Dead Sea Scrolls (e.g., 4Q175) and Isa 40:3 was also a favorite text (1QS VIII, 14; 4Q176, 1–21, 6–7; 4Q259III, 4–5), but the literary contexts of the two works are distinct.[17] See later in chapter 5 (pp. 77–81) for our discussion of FG and the DSS.

---

12. T. L. Brodie compares Exod 1–4 with John 4 (121–27) and shows how FG follows the general sequence of the Pentateuch, from Gen to Deut (162–67) in his *Quest for Origins*.

13. A. T. Lincoln has found many more allusions to Isa 40–55, especially the lawsuit motif, in his *Truth on Trial*, 38–51, 518. See also Day, *Jesus the Isaianic Servant*. Other Deutero-Isa allusions will be noted in this ch. (e.g., *egō eimi* and Isa 43:10; 45:3).

14. Augustine first saw this allusion to Gen 28 in his *Tract. ev. Jo.* 7.23.3, ca. 417 CE. It is noteworthy that FG has no quotations or citations from the so-called apocrypha or pseudepigrapha only embedded allusions as we shall find in ch. 3 on wisdom and angelology.

15. On Zech 12:10 cited in John 19:37, it is not implausible that FG (or the final redactor) knew Hebrew and used Hebrew sources here, Sheridan, "One They Have Pierced," 208. "Some measure of influence from a Hebrew textual tradition is undeniable," Bynum, *Fourth Gospel and Scriptures*, 167. See also Burney, *Aramaic Origins of the Fourth Gospel*, 122–24. The text is also quoted in Rev 1:7 (with "pierced," *ekkenteō* as in John 19:37). A. Schlatter cites Lam. Rab. 1, 5 as a similar rabbinic text on "piercing" (Heb. *dāqar* as in MT Zech 12:10) related to the escape of R. Yohanan ben Zakkai from Roman-occupied Jerusalem in a coffin (his disciples prevented his body from being "pierced" by a suspicious guard), in his *Johannes*, 355. J. Neusner regards it as a late legend, however, in his *Development of a Legend*, 228. See also Justin Martyr on Zech 12:10 in our ch. 12, tbl.B, p. 212.

16. Dodd, *According to the Scriptures*. For a history of discussion on the *testimonia* hypothesis, see Albl, "And Scripture Cannot Be Broken."

17. Brooke, "Isaiah 40:3 and the Wilderness Community," 117–32 and *Dead Sea Scrolls and the NT*, 92, 128n41.

Themes, Images, and Phrases

These are numerous in FG.[18] Even though intentional allusion is less certain with some of the following examples, some verbal connection or embedded echo seems evident in many of them. As Martin Hengel stated, FG "prefers the bare terse clue, the use of a metaphor or motif more than the full citation."[19] Recent attention has been paid to determining the sources and forms of FG's references to Scripture, using social and rhetorical perspectives, and understanding FG's use of Scripture for constructing memory images for its anticipated readers.[20]

The opening hymn in John 1 recalls both the Gen 1 creation story (e.g., *en archē; legō/logos*,[21] *phōs, zosan/zoē*) and the account of personified Wisdom (e.g., *sophia, en archē, dikaiosunē, alētheia, phōs*, Prov 8:1-8, 22-31; 9:1-6; Sir 1:1-4; 24:1-12; Wis 7:28-30; 9:1-4). The theme of divine glory (*doxa*, John 1:14; 11:40; 13:31; 17:22) also has OT roots (Exod 24:16-17; 33:18-19; Isa 35:2; 40:5; Ezek 43:2,4). Images derived from the OT are those of divine light (*phōs*, John 1:4-5, 9; 3:19; 8:12; 9:5; 12:35, 46; Pss 27:1; 119:105, 130 [LXX 26:1; 118:105, 130]; Isa 9:2; 42:6-7; 49:6; 60:1-3; Bar 4:2; Wis 7:28-29), life (*zoē, zaō*, John 1:4; 5:26, 40; 6:51, 63; 8:12; 10:10; 11:25; 14:6; 20:31; Gen 2:7; Deut 5:16; 6:2; 28:11; 30:16-20; Pss 16:10-11; 119:77,144 [LXX 15:10-11; 118:77,144] Hos 6:2),[22] living water (*hydōr zōn*, John 4:10, 14; 7:37-38; Prov

---

18. See Beutler, "Use of 'Scripture,'" 147-62; Daly-Denton, *David in the Fourth Gospel*; Hays, *Echoes of Scripture in the Gospels*, 281-366; Hengel, "Old Testament in the Fourth Gospel," 380-95; A. J. Köstenberger, "John," in Beale and Carson, *Commentary*, 415-512; Menken, *Old Testament Quotations*; Schuchard, *Scripture within Scripture*. See, e.g., J. T. Nielsen, "Lamb of God," in Frey, *Imagery in the Gospel of John*, 217-56; Koester, *Symbolism in the Fourth Gospel*; Evans, *Word of Glory*; Evans and Sanders, *Early Christian Interpretation*. Note: there will be more discussion on the imagery of FG (e.g., wisdom, word, life, truth) in this and subsequent chs. of our book.

19. Hengel, "Old Testament in the Fourth Gospel," 31-32.

20. See survey of scholarship by B. G. Schuchard, "Conclusion," in Myers and Schuchard, *Abiding Words*, 237-46, and introduction by A. D. Myers, 1-20.

21. In the LXX, λόγος, *logos* is primarily a translation of the Heb. דָּבָר, *dabar* ("word"); See Procksch, "Divine Word of Creation," 4:99-100. Both have a wide range of meanings: e.g., speech, dialogue, narrative, oracle, (even "matter" or "thing"). The Heb. אָמַר, *'āmar* "say, answer, declare," e.g., "and God said," (Gen 1:3) is also closely related (LXX, has Gk. *legō*). In the LXX, *logos* can have a dynamic meaning as "the word of the Lord" (Ps 32:4, 6 LXX), sometimes ῥῆμα, *rhēma* ("word, utterance") is used (Isa 40:8 LXX; MT, Heb. *dabar*); see BDAG, *logos*, 598-601; *rhēma*, 905; LSJ, 1057-59, 1569. On *dabar* see Koehler and Baumgartner, *Hebrew and Aramaic Lexicon*, 211-12 and for *'āmar*, see 65-67. See our discussion of the related Aramaic words, *dibbera* (cf. Heb. *dabar*) and *mēmra* (Heb. *'āmar*), in our ch. 6, FG, Rabbinica, and Targumim, pp. 91-92.

22. On life (*zoē*; BDAG 430-31) and eternal life (*zōēn aiōnion*; BDAG 33) in John, see Thompson, *John: A Commentary*, 87-91.

II. THE JEWISH SCRIPTURES (SEPTUAGINT)

18:4; Isa 44:3-4; 55:1; Zech 14:8), and vine imagery (*ampelos,* John 15:1, 5; Ps 80:8-9 [79:9-10 LXX]; Isa 5:7; Jer 2:21; Ezek 15:1-8).

Mentioned also are the patriarchs, Abraham (John 8:33-40, 52-58, "before Abraham was, I am" *egō eimi,* v. 58) and Jacob (4:5-6). Notice furthermore the comparison of Nathanael as a "a true Israelite in whom there is no deceit (*dolos;* 1:47; Gen 27:35 LXX)," who identifies Jesus as the "King of Israel" (v. 49; Jacob-Israel, Gen 32:28-30) and who will see "the angels of God ascending and descending" (John 1:51; Gen 28:12).

Jesus is compared to Moses (John 1:17; 5:46-47; 6:14-15; Deut 34:10-12) and his "signs" recall those that Moses did in Egypt (e.g., John 4:48; 6:30; Exod 4:8-9, 28-31).[23] In FG, Jesus is often portrayed as "the prophet" (1:21) of whom Moses wrote in Deut 18:15-22 (e.g., John 1:11,17-18; 5:19-23; Deut 18:18-20; cf. Num 12:5-8). As the children of Israel saw the face of Moses "charged with glory" when he descended from Mt. Sinai, in FG "we beheld his glory" (*doxa,* John 1:14; *doxazō,* Exod 34:29 LXX).[24] The Word "dwelt/pitched a tent" among us (*skēnoō,* John 1:14) recalls the "tent," of witness that was filled with the glory of the Lord (*skēnē,* Exod 40:28-29 LXX; MT 40:34, *mishkan,* "tabernacle," MT; see also Ezek 37:27; Zech 2:10 MT; Rev 21:3).[25] The events of the wilderness wanderings are also alluded to: manna (6:31-32; Deut 8:3), bread from heaven (John 6:51; Exod 16:4; Ps 78:23-25 [77:24 LXX]),[26] murmurings (*gogguzō,* John 6:41, 43, 61; *diagogguzō, goggusmos,* Exod 16:2, 4, 8; Num 11),[27] "Just as Moses lifted up the serpent in the wilderness" (John 3:14; Num 21:8-9), so must the Son of Man be lifted up (cf. John 8:28; 12:32, 34; Isa 52:13).[28]

---

23. Smith, "Exodus Typology in the Fourth Gospel," 329-42; Meeks, *Prophet-King,* xi-xxx.

24. See themes common to John 1:14-18 and Exod 33-34 (e.g., presence, glory, *chesed* and truth, no one can see God) in Keener, "'We Beheld His Glory,'" 2:24.

25. On "pitched a tent" see MT Josh 18:1; Ps 78:60 (*shakan,* Hiphil) in Koehler et al., *Hebrew and Aramaic Lexicon,* 1499. See "Shekinah" (deriv. Heb. root *shakan*) denoting God's "pitching a tent" or "tabernacling" (Exod 25:8; 40:34) with the Israelites in the wilderness in *NIDB* 5:222-23. In the LXX, the Greek verb *kataskēnoō* denotes the same expression, see LXX Ps 77:60; Josh 18:1; Sir 24:8-12. See also *skēnoō,* "God's tenting with Israel," *BDAG* 929. In John 7:2, "festival of Booths," *skēnopēgia* is based on *skēnopēgeomai* "pitch a tent" *BDAG* 928; *TDNT* 7:390. See Collins, *These Things Have Been Written,* 198-216; and Koester, *Dwelling of God,* esp. 19-20, 100-15.

26. Borgen, *Bread from Heaven,* 33-43. J. Zumstein observes that the use of Scripture (hypotext A) in John 6 (hypertext B) generates new horizons of meaning for both texts (A & B), in his "Intratextuality and Intertextuality," 133-34.

27. R. E. Brown has found numerous parallels between Num 11 and John 6, in his *Gospel according to John,* 1:233.

28. The Son of Man lifted up (*hypsoō*) has multiple meanings: (1) lifted up on a cross, (2) exalted and glorified by God in his death *and* resurrection, (3) lifted up to the

The feasts of Israel,[29] the occasion for many key episodes of FG, are referenced: Passover/Pesach (Gk. *pascha*, John 2:13,23; 6:4; 11:55; 12:1; 13:1; cf. Exod 12:1–20; Deut 16:1–8); Booths/Tabernacles/Sukkoth (*skēnopēgia*, 7:2; cf. LXX *heortē skēnos*, LXX Lev 23:33–36; Deut 16:13–14; MT *hag sukkōth*); Dedication/Hanukkah (*egkainia*, 10:22; cf. 1 Macc 4:52–59; 2 Macc 10:6–7).[30]

The following Johannine titles have a rich OT context: prophet (John 7:40,52; Deut 18:15, 18); shepherd (John 10:11–14; Ps 78:70–72; 95:7; Isa 40:11; Jer 23:2; Ezek 34:23; Zech 11:17);[31] Messiah (John 1:41; 4:45; "the Christ," 6:69; 7:26–27, 42; 9:22; 20:31);[32] and "I am" (*egō eimi*, John 8:12, 58; 9:5; Gen 17:1; Exod 3:14; Lev 26:13; Deut 32:39; Isa 41:4; 43:10; 45:3; 48:12; cf. Rev 1:8; 21:6).[33] Prophetic and apocalyptic themes from Daniel are also

---

Father in heaven by way of the cross, see Keener, *John*, 1:565–66.

29. See B. D. Johnson, "Jewish Feasts," in Anderson et al., *John, Jesus, and History*, 117–29; Wheaton, *Role of Jewish Feasts in John's Gospel*; Yee, *Jewish Feasts*.

30. Many of the intertextual connections that we have established (above) create "a poetic effect of metalepsis" that recall a chain of associations (similar to metonymy). "Metalepsis is a literary technique of citing or echoing a small bit of precursor text in such a way that the reader can grasp the significance of the echo only by recalling or recovering the original context from which the fragmentary echo came and then reading the two texts in dialogical juxtaposition" (Hays, *Echoes of Scripture*, 11, citing J. Hollander, *Figure of Echo* (1981), 65. See p. 8n31 of our Introduction for the various tests and criteria (e.g., context, accessibility, thematic coherence) that we will employ in this intertextual dialogue to determine the extent or limits of intentional allusion or embedded echo.

On FG's interpretation of OT texts, see also our ch. 5 (p. 77) where we compare similar exegetical methods of both FG and DSS, and ch. 6 (pp. 88–90) on FG and the rabbinic methods of interpretation.

31. See biblical and post-biblical allusions to sheep and shepherds in Reinhartz, *Word in the World*, 107–112. J. D. Turner also explores the rich shepherd imagery in the ancient Near Eastern and Greco-Roman worlds, in Beutler and Fortna, *Shepherd Discourse*, 33–52. W. Meeks sees the faithful shepherd patterned after Moses (311–12), noting also that David is called a good shepherd (308), in *Prophet-King*. See also R. Zimmerman, "Jesus im Bild Gottes," in Frey and Schnelle, *Kontexte*, 81–116, who compares FG with the OT shepherd imagery to substantiate the claim of Jesus in John 14:9, "whoever has seen me has seen the Father" (cf. John 12:45).

32. In John 7:42, the Messiah must be a descendant of David and come from Bethlehem, David's town (John 7:42; cf. 1 Sam 16:1; 2 Sam 7:12; Jer 23:2; Mic 5:2; Pss Sol 17:21; Matt 1:20; 2:1; Luke 2:4). R. Zimmerman explores "Messiah" and other christological titles in his *Christologie der Bilder* (Tübingen, 2004).

33. There are seven "I am" statements with predicates that affirm something about the subject ("bread of life," 6:35; "light of the world," 8:12; 9:5; "door," 10:7, 9; "shepherd," 11, 14; "resurrection and life," 11:25; "way, truth, life," 14:6; "vine," 15:1). At least four "I am" statements without the predicate are used as the object of what one believes (8:24, 28, 58; 13:19), these four have the closest association with God's self-identification in Exod 3:14; Deut 32:39; esp. Isa 43:10–11; 45:3, challenging the reader/listener to reflect

evident: authority given to the "Son of Man" (John 5:27; Ezek 3:17; Dan 7:13–14);[34] the appropriate time or "hour" (*hōra*, John 2:4; 4:23; 7:6, 8, 30; 8:20; 12:23; 13:1; 16:2; Dan 8:17, 19; 10:14; 11:14; 12:1–4);[35] and a final resurrection of the just and unjust (John 5:28–29; Isa 26:19; Dan 12:2).

In addition to themes and images, there are phrases in FG that seem to be lifted from OT texts: e.g., "what have I to do with you" John 2:4; 1 Kgs (3 Reigns) 17:18 LXX (cf. Mark 5:7);[36] "your son lives" John 4:50; 1 Kgs (3 Reigns) 17:23 LXX; "to open the eyes of the blind" (John 9:17, 30; Isa 42:7 LXX; Ps 146:8 MT), "now my soul is troubled" (John 12:27; Ps 6:4 LXX); "your word is truth" (John 17:17; Ps 118:160 LXX);[37] "I have given my cheeks to blows" (John 18:22; 19:3; Isa 50:6); "It is finished" (*tetelestain*, John 19:30; *syntetelesthai*, Job 19:26 LXX);[38] "he breathed on them and said "receive the Holy Spirit," (John 20:22; *emphysaō*; *pnoē/pneuma*, Gen 2:7; Ezek 37:9 LXX).

Richard B. Hays observes that although the author of FG focuses on fewer scriptural texts than the Synoptic writers

> John reads the entirety of the Old Testament as a vast web of symbols that are to be read as figural signifiers for Jesus and the life that he offers. The temple is a proleptic sign for Jesus' body. Israel's cultic practices and the great feasts of Israel's liturgical calendar encode numerous latent signs and symbols of Jesus: the pouring of water and kindling of lights at the Feast of Tabernacles (*Sukkoth*); the rededication of the temple by the good shepherd who truly feeds and heals God's people; the Passover

---

upon all the "I am" sayings of Jesus (at least 20). See Thompson, *John: A Commentary*, 156–60. C. R. Koester notes that the "I am" statements in Revelation (Rev 1:8, 17; 21:6; 22:13) are closer to that of Deutero-Isaiah (41:4) than in FG, see Koester, *Revelation*, 81, for further comparisons, see also 81–83. These scriptural motifs, common to both Rev and FG, Koester sees as parallel, but *independent* developments.

34. Robert Rhea favors a prophetic (pre-apocalyptic) context (Ezek 2–3; T. Ab. A 13:2–3) for FG's Son of Man sayings, in his *Johannine Son of Man*, 38–39, 71. M. M. Pazdan provides a concise history of discussion in her *Son of Man*, 21–29.

35. See Mihalios, *Danielic Eschatological Hour in the Johannine Literature*. See Pietersma and Wright, NETS (2007) 991–94 on the old Greek (OG) and Theodotion (TH) versions of Dan in Greek. On *hōra* "a point in time as an occasion for an event," see BDAG 1103.

36. A similar expression (*kai ti pros eme?*) appears in the diatribes of Epictetus, *Disc.* 4.5.33.

37. The LXX has "The beginning of your words (*logoi*) is truth" Ps 118:160 LXX, whereas the MT has "the sum (Heb. *rosh*, "head, chief, best") of your word (sing.) is truth" MT Ps 119:160 (NRSV).

38. There may also be an allusion here to LXX Gen 2:1 *sunetelesthēsan*. Does not FG have Jesus here completing the "restoration" of creation?

lamb whose bones are not broken; the bread that comes down from heaven to Israel in the wilderness. All these events and symbols point insistently to Jesus, who embodies that which they signified. When we read the story of Moses lifting up the serpent on a staff in the wilderness, we are to understand that we are reading a prefiguration of the lifting up of the Son of Man on the cross.[39]

FG is replete with echoes of and allusions to OT themes, phrases, and imagery.[40] How confounding would be our reading of FG without an intertextual engagement with the Scripture of Israel. We agree that "without the basis of the Old Testament ... the Gospel of St. John is an insoluble riddle."[41]

In our first chapter, we have compared FG with other NT writings (Synoptic Gospels, Letters of John) and in chapter 2, the OT (LXX, MT). Do these documents alone provide compelling parallels to FG? Did FG draw *only* on these sources for its composition, and no others? We have shown that FG has made creative and distinctive use of these sources (oral and written). Was FG's selection and use of the LXX, for example, influenced, in some way, by the DSS, Philo, and other ancient writings? How or why did FG interpret the LXX in this particular way? Were there any other influences on FG, direct or indirect, to explain its creative and distinctive approach to the OT and especially the life and teachings of Jesus? If so, how and why? What can explain FG's particular tendencies, views, and nuances of expression (if explanations can be found)? We hope to pursue some of these significant questions and others in the chapters that follow.

---

39. Hays, *Echoes of Scripture in the Gospels*, 354–55. This figural interpretation of Israel's Scripture in FG is not unlike the christologically-infused cosmological tale of the preexistent Word who becomes flesh, and is sent by God into the world to bring salvation, see Reinhartz, *Word in the World*, 4. Both are synchronic presentations based on diachronic analyses of sources and traditions.

40. In addition to our note on p. 41n25, see, e.g., Coloe, *God Dwells with Us*; Kerr, *Temple of Jesus' Body*; Koester, *Dwelling of God*; Manning, *Echoes of a Prophet*; Meeks, *Prophet-King*; Van der Watt, *Family of the King*; Jones, *Symbol of Water*; Thompson, "'They Bear Witness of Me,'" 267–83. On identifying echoes and allusions, see Köstenberger and Patterson, *Invitation to Biblical Interpretation*, 541–47.

41. Westcott, *St. John*, 1:111. J. Zumstein writes that FG's use of the Jewish Scriptures is the "paradigmatic example" of FG as a "networked text" or intertext that "presumes the existence of other writings" ("Intratextuality and Intertextuality," 121–22).

III. Jewish Wisdom and Angelology

IN THIS CHAPTER WE will observe FG acquaintance with Jewish wisdom and angelology (found mostly in the Greek Septuagint).[1] First, we will examine FG's interaction with wisdom writings before viewing its intertextual relations with angel speculations.

Jewish Wisdom

Although our sources for **wisdom** will include some texts of the Jewish canon (e.g., Job 28; Prov 1-9) and some apocalyptic texts (e.g., 1 En 42:1-2; 48:4),[2] our chief sources are the Hellenistic Jewish writings of Baruch (Bar 3:9—4:4), Sirach (Sir 1; 4:11-19; 6:18-31; 14:20—15:10; 24), the Wisdom of Solomon (6-10), and Joseph and Aseneth (16).[3] Why have we focused on these wis-

---

1. As mentioned earlier, FG echoes LXX writings that are *outside* the post-70 Jewish canon (e.g., Sir, Wis, Bar), see NA[28] loci citati vel allegati, 869-77; many of them are concerned with wisdom or angel speculations. For LXX, we consulted Rahlfs, *Septuaginta*; and Wevers and Fraenkel, *Göttingen Septuagint*.

For trans. we consulted Pietersma and Wright, *NETS*; and the NRSV Apocrypha. In the chart, we follow the LXX numberings. Discussed elsewhere in our book, see wisdom in Philo (pp. 57, 60) and in Targumic writings (92.); see also angels representing God (Samaritans, p. 160) and in cosmic conflict (71n17, 74, 177).

2. The pseudepigraphic Book of Enoch (1 En) is probably a composite of different genres (testament, oracle, wisdom, apoc), dating from the third century BCE (1 En 72-82) to the first century CE (1 En 37-71). It is extant in an Ethiopic translation of a Greek translation, probably from Aramaic originals, see Nickelsburg, "Enoch," 265-68; Collins and Harlow, *Early Judaism*, 579-87. We use the text from Charlesworth, *Old Testament Pseudepigrapha*, 1:5-89. G. von Rad had suggested that speculative wisdom (Qoheleth) may have given birth to apocalypticism in his *Wisdom in Israel*, 277-28 and Hans-Martin Schenke sees this pessimistic wisdom on a continuum toward gnosticism, in his "Die Tenenz der Weisheit zur Gnosis." Hans Conzelmann outlines a diversity of views in his "Mother of Wisdom," 230-33. For current discussion by different authors on wisdom's origins, see Longman and Enns, *Dictionary of Wisdom*, 139-40, 562-66, 852-53, 914-15.

3. Plausible dates and locations: Bar or 1 Bar, ca. first century BCE, probably from Palestine, written in Greek with Bar 1:1-5:9 originally in Hebrew; Sir originally written in Heb (ca. 175 BCE) and translated into Greek, sometime after 132 BCE; Wis written

dom texts and not others? In these Jewish texts are examples of personified attributes of God portrayed as his principal agent, especially God's Wisdom and God's Word (*logos*).[4] Along with similar vocabulary, FG shares similar conceptual viewpoints and reflects similar contexts.[5]

David Penchansky makes the following observations of Hokmah (Heb. "Wisdom"):

> I have long been attracted to this divine figure who invites young men back to her house to teach them the proper manner in which to live their lives. I wonder along with Roland Murphy, 'Just who is she, and what is she up to?' (Murphy 1998, 53). I ask further: What is she doing in this monotheist document, the Hebrew canon, if monotheism won out?[6]

The sources for Jewish Wisdom (Gk. *sophia*) are fragmentary, but when pieced together from Proverbs, Job, and other (LXX) wisdom writings, they present a compelling story of her life with God and her activities on earth on behalf of God's people.

A. The Fourth Gospel	Jewish Wisdom (LXX)
Preexistence	
The word (*logos*) was in the beginning with God before "all things came into being" (1:1–3) "before the world existed," 17:2	Wisdom (*sophia*) existed with God from the beginning (*archē*) even before the earth (Prov 8:22–23, 27–30; Sir 1:4; 24:9; Wis 6:22; 9:4, 9; Job 28:12, 20, 23–24; 2 En 24:2).

---

in Greek, between 100 to 50 BCE. Both Sir and Wis are probably from Egypt. Joseph and Aseneth (daughter of Egyptian priest, Gen 41:45), from Egypt, 100 BCE to 100 CE. See Collins, *Between Athens and Jerusalem*; Collins, *Jewish Wisdom in the Hellenistic Age*; Murphy, *Tree of Life*; Collins and Harlow, *Early Judaism*, 425–26 (Bar); Longman and Enns, *Dictionary of Wisdom*, 720–28 (Sir), 885–91 (Wis).

4. See Borgen, "God's Agent," 121–32. See also Hurtado, *One God, One Lord*, 41–50.

5. See Brown, *Gospel according to John*, 1:cxxiii–cxxv; R. Bultmann, "Prologue," in Ashton, *Interpretation of John*, 18–35; Carter, *John*, 136–40; Dodd, *Interpretation*, 274–75; Talbert, *Reading John*, 71–74; Ringe, *Wisdom's Friends*; Willett, *Wisdom Christology*; Witherington, *Jesus the Sage*.

M. Scott notes significant developments in the portrayals of Sophia and Yahweh in Prov (as the giver of life), Sir (Israel's Torah), and Wis (an emanation of God) in his *Sophia and Johannine Jesus*, 50–58, on FG, see 88–91.

6. Penchansky, *Twilight of the Gods*, 51. See also Murphy, *Proverbs*, 53. A. F. Segal also explores these questions in his *Two Powers in Heaven*, 23–24, 79, 185–86.

III. JEWISH WISDOM AND ANGELOLOGY

A. The Fourth Gospel	Jewish Wisdom (LXX)
	With God
The Word was "with God" (*pros ton theon*, 1:1)	"I was beside him" (*egō eimi para autos* Prov 8:30; "sits by you" Wis 9:4); a place for wisdom was found for her in the heavens, 1 En 42:1.[7]
	The agent of creation
"All things came into being through him"(the Word, 1:3)	"Who made all things by your word" and formed humans by your wisdom, Wis 9:1–2; cf. 7:22; Prov 3:19; 8:29–30; ("by word of the Lord," Ps 32:6 LXX; cf. Jub 3:1)
	Shares divine glory
Jesus has the Father's glory which he manifested to people (1:14, 18; 8:50; 11:4; 17:5, 22, 24)	a pure emanation of the glory (*doxa*) of the Almighty (Wis 7:25–26; cf. 7:22)
	Light (*phōs*)
God is light (1 John 1:5), Jesus who is from God is the light of the world and people will have the light of life who follow him (1:4–5; 8:12; 9:5); "the light has come into the world" (3:19)	a reflection of eternal light of God (Wis 7:26); more radiant than light and never ceases (Wis 7:10, 29); toward the shining in the presence of her light (Bar 4:2), they kindle right deeds like the light, those who fear God (Sir 32:16); "a light for the gentiles" (1 En 48:4; LXX Isa 42:6; 49:6); "Now you shall shine like the lights of heaven" (1 En 104:2–3).
	Cannot be overcome by darkness/evil
"the darkness did not overcome it [the light]" (*katalambanō* 1:5; cf. 12:31, 35)	"against wisdom [a superior light]" evil did not prevail" (*katischuō*, Wis 7:29–30); "For the sun has shined upon the earth and darkness is over" (1 En 58:5)
	Source of life (*zoē*)
"in him was life and the life was the light of all people" 1:4 "I am the resurrection and the life" 11:25.	"my goings out (*exodus*) are the goings out of life" Prov 8:35; 3:16–18; "all who take hold of her are for life," Bar 4:1b.

---

7. See Charlesworth, *Jesus as Mirrored in John*, 298–99, where the following parallels are suggested: (1) "the elect shall be in the light/children of light," 1 En 58:2; John 12:36; (2) speaking of heavenly matters, 1 En 19:3; John 3:12; (3) knowledge of what is written in the holy tablets, 1 En 103:2; John 5:47; (4) the Lord of the sheep/good shepherd 1 En 89:42; John 10:7, 11; (5) revealing of the Son of Man, 1 En 69:27; John 13:31; (6) "he shall proclaim peace to you," 1 En 71:15; cf. John 20:19, 21.

A. The Fourth Gospel	Jewish Wisdom (LXX)
Descent/Dwell	
Jesus is the Son of Man who has descended from heaven to earth to dwell with people (*skēnoō*, 1:14; 3:13; 6:38; 16:28)	Wisdom's descent from heaven to dwell with people (Prov 8:31; 30:4; *skēnē*, Sir 24:8, 11–12;[8] Bar 3:29, 37–38; Wis 9:10, 16–18; 1 En 42:1–2; cf. John 1:10); the "Son of Man" was revealed to them and appeared to them (1 En 69:27–29).[9]
Teacher/Revealer	
Jesus teaches about heavenly things (3:12; 7:16; 8:26) speaks the truth (1:17–18; 8:45; 18:37), reveals God's will (4:34; 5:30; 6:38) lead people to eternal life (1:4; 3:15–16, 36; 5:24–26; 10:10, 28; 11:25)	Wisdom is to teach people of the things that are above (Job 11:6–7; Wis 9:16–18) to speak truth (Prov 8:6–9; Wis 6:22) reveal God's works (Wis 8:4; 9:9–10), to lead people to life (Prov 4:10; 8:32–35; Sir 4:12; Bar 4:1) and immortality (Wis 6:18–19).[10]
Rejected by people	
"the world did not know him … his own people did not accept him," 1:10–11; cf. 3:19; 8:24, 46; 10:25.	"The Wisdom went out to dwell with the children of people but she found no dwelling place," 1 En 42:1–2; "they have not learned the way to wisdom," Bar 3:23 (vv. 12, 20–23); Prov 1:20–24, 28–30; Job 28:12–13, 20–21.
Help the receptive to receive God	
"to all who received him … he gave power to become children of God" 1:12; 5:24; 13:20.	"In every generation she passes into holy souls and makes them friends of God …" Wis 7:27; cf. 6:12; 9:18; wisdom rescued, guided, gave knowledge, 10:9–10.

8. The verb *eskēnōsen* in the wisdom tradition, especially Sir 24, contains a "plethora of terminological and material parallels" to John 1:14, according to Frey, *Glory of the Crucified One*, 276.

9. As we mentioned (n2), 1 En is a composite of different genres (testament, oracle, wisdom, apocalyptic), and "Son of Man" is a favorite title for the messiah (1 En 48:2–3, 10; 46:3–4; 52:4; 62:5, 7, 14; 63:11; 69:29). FG, also a composite of different genres, often uses the Son of Man title for Jesus (John 1:51; 3:13–14; 5:27; 6:27, 62; 8:28; 12:23, 34; 13:31). On composite genres of FG, e.g., see Keener, *John*, 3–28 (who favors a bios component in the mix).

10. "He who considers absolutely the highest cause of the whole universe, namely God, is most of all called wise" (Aquinas, *Summa* 1.6) cited in M. Csikszentmihalyi, "Evolutionary Hermeneutics," in Goodman and Fisher, *Rethinking Knowledge*, 129.

III. JEWISH WISDOM AND ANGELOLOGY

A. The Fourth Gospel	Jewish Wisdom (LXX)

Seeking people

Jesus calls together disciples (1:35–51) seeks out people (5:14; 9:35) and extends public invitations (7:28, 37–38; 12:44–46).	Wisdom roams the streets seeking people and calling out to them (Prov 1:20–21; 8:1–4; Wis 6:16; 1 En 4:1–3).

Disciple Formation

Jesus instructs his disciples (chs. 14–16) and calls them little children (19) who are her children (Prov 8:32; 13:33); Jesus sanctifies his disciples with his word and truth (15:3; 17:17) and tests them (6:67) until he can call them his beloved friends (15:15; 16:17).	Wisdom instructs disciples (Wis 6:17–20; 9:11–12; Sir 4:11); wisdom tests her disciples and forms them until they love her (Prov 8:17; Sir 4:17–18; 6:20–26) and they become friends of God (Wis 7:14, 22–23, 27).

Symbols of food and drink

Jesus employs the symbols of food and drink in his teaching and invites people to eat and drink (4:13–14; 6:10–14, 35, 51–58; cf. Luke 14:7–24; Matt 22:1–4). See Maritz and Van Belle, "Imagery of Eating and Drinking," 333–52.	For instruction, Wisdom uses the symbols of food and drink, and invites people to eat and drink (Prov 9:2–5; Sir 24:17, 19–21; Jos. Asen. 16:8–9; Wis 16:20; 19:21; cf. Isa 55:1–3)

Indwelling presence

After the resurrection Jesus dwells within those who believe in him (14:21, 23; 15:1–11; 17:23)	Wisdom pervades and penetrates all things, including "holy souls" (Wis 7:24, 27; "she entered into the soul of the attendant," 10:16; cf. Sir 6:27; 24:12).

The above wisdom motifs are used in FG to assert the identity of Jesus as the revealer of God's life-giving purposes and to interpret the significance of human response to his ministry. As wisdom, Jesus originates with God as the self-revelation of God, coming from God in close relation with God, and committed to God's purposes and will, Jesus is God's agent among humans. In Jesus, those who receive him encounter God's life, presence, nourishment, and gifts, which challenge the status quo.[11] FG's prologue happens to use Word (*logos*) instead of Wisdom (*sophia*), while retaining these wisdom motifs, perhaps because both it and the LXX of Gen 1 begin alike (*en archē*, "in the beginning;" *legō*, and God "said"), and because a masculine term (*logos*) seemed more appropriate for the man Jesus than the feminine wisdom

---

11. Carter, *John*, 139.

(*sophia*).[12] Martin Scott argues that while the title Logos is used to present Jesus as "the immanent Son who makes the transcendent Father visible" (quoting Dunn, *Christology in the Making*, 250), "the Prologue is at the same time an introduction to Jesus as Sophia, the feminine face of God."[13]

We had mentioned in our introduction the three-level drama advocated by Adele Reinhartz: (1) historical tale of Jesus and his disciples, (2) ecclesiological tale of the Johannine community of FG, and (3) the cosmological tale of the Word in the world.[14] There is much in our comparison of Jesus as Word and Wisdom for developing a cosmological tale of the one who existed with God from the beginning as God's agent of creation, sharing divine glory as a light shining in the dark, teaching and revealing wisdom to people who would receive it, and welcoming them to come and dine as disciples and friends.[15] This view certainly coincides with and is informed by the literary imagination of the implied author and his implied audience as presented in narrative criticism.[16] Adele Reinhartz makes the following conclusion in her discussion of the implied reader:

> In conclusion, the cosmological tale provides the temporal and spatial framework for the historical and ecclesiological tales, and through its open-ended conclusion allows room for the implied reader in the history of salvation. In doing so, the tale encourages readers to locate themselves within the temporal and spatial framework . . . It is therefore by universalizing the specific temporal and spatial boundaries of the historical and

---

12. C. H. Talbert also mentions here that this interchangeability of names is in line with other early Christian usage: e.g., the use of Wisdom in Odes of Solomon 41:9, 15 (cf. Prov 8:22-23) with the use of Word in 41:11, 14 (cf. John 1:1) and 41:12 (cf. Phil 2:6-9) where Wisdom becomes the Word, in his *Reading John*, 74. See also (for different reasons) the gnostic Three Forms, where the heavenly redeemer, Barbelo, is identified as Father, Mother, Son, Word, and Wisdom, see Layton, *Gnostic Scriptures*, 86-100; discussed in our ch. 10, p. 177.

13. Scott, *Sophia and the Johannine Jesus*, 170, see discussion in 170-73. See also on John 1:1-18, Dunn, *Christology in the Making*, 239-50.

14. Reinhartz, *Word in the World*, 2-6. As noted earlier, the ecclesiastical tale of the Johannine community is probably the most speculative level (e.g., the John community expelled from the Jewish synagogue).

15. We will see similar themes as those above surface in our forthcoming comparisons of FG and angelology in this ch. 3, pp. 53-54.

16. See, e.g., Genette, *Narrative Discourse*, 33-35; Chatman, *Story and Discourse*, 146-51; Iser, *Implied Reader*; Culpepper, *Anatomy of the Fourth Gospel*, 53-75. The cosmological tale of Reinhartz relies on narrative criticism for its synchronic presentation, as does R. B. Hays in developing the narrative substructure behind his figural interpretation of Israel's Scripture. Both approaches, nevertheless, derive from a diachronic analysis of FG's sources and traditions.

eccesiological tales that the cosmological tales allows and encourages reader to situate themselves within the gospel and to see themselves as its addressees. In reading themselves into the time and place of the cosmological tales, readers must confront the Johannine understanding of the "world" into which Jesus came, in which the readers also find themselves. It is in the process of such confrontation that the implied readers are given the opportunity to rethink their self-understanding and their stance towards both the Word and world.[17]

Jewish Angelology

Closely related to Wisdom theology is discussion on **angels** (Heb. *mal'āk*; Gk. *angelos*, "messenger").[18] Wisdom served not only as a figure of reconciliation between creation theology and salvation history (Wis 10–11; Sir 24; Bar 3),[19] but also as a figure of mediation between a transcendent God and the world God created. These intermediary beings included angels, the spirit, the Word, and Wisdom.[20] The appearance of intermediary beings sent by God to act and speak on God's behalf to the world is most prevalent in literature after the Babylonian Exile (587/6 BCE), especially the Hellenistic period (beginning 330 BCE).

As early as 135 CE, Justin Martyr had argued in Ephesus with his Jewish critic, Trypho, that the angel of the Lord (e.g., Gen 22:11; Exod 14:19) was the pre-incarnate Christ.[21] Although "angel, angels" (*angelos, angeloi*)

---

17. Reinhartz, *Word in the World*, 38. Something greater than church and synagogue is here. We can see how this third-level approach, moving beyond the historical analyses of both Jesus of Nazareth and FG's community, to the (synchronic) cosmological tale of the implied author's visionary imagination, has potential for confronting the reader with FG's truth claims. Much that is said here of FG and Wisdom also relates well to our comparison of FG and angelology.

18. On angels, see J. M. Wilson, "Angel," 1:124–27.

19. The view of Whybray in his *Wisdom in Proverbs*, 11. The wisdom writings of the Jewish canon do *not* contain salvation theology. I am grateful to Prof. David Penchansky of St. Thomas University for this observation. See also K. Schifferdecker, "Creation Theology," in Longman and Enns, *Dictionary of Wisdom*, 63. On the creation of the angels by the word (Heb. *dibber*) of God, see 3 En 40:4.

20. Willett, *Wisdom Christology*, 27, citing Hengel, *Judaism and Hellenism*, 1:155 and Rankin, *Israel's Wisdom*, 229. For additional views of wisdom and the divine, see M. Heiser, "Divine Council," 112–16, and J. M. Hamilton, "Divine Presence," 116–20 in Longman and Enns, *Dictionary of Wisdom*. See also Collins, *Jewish Wisdom*; on the functions of divine agency, see Borgen, "God's Agent," 67–78.

21. Justin, *Dial.* 56, 58–61, 76, 86, 126, 128, written later in Rome, 155 CE; see Gieschen, *Angelomorphic Christology*, 187–200.

are mentioned only four times in FG (John 1:51; 5:4; 12:29; 20:12),[22] the so-called fallen angels are also mentioned. See, for example, regarding Judas, "one of you is a devil" (*diabolos*, John 6:70; 13:2; cf. 1 Chr 21:1; Job 1–2; Wis 2:24); Satan entered Judas (*ho Satanos*, 13:27); Jesus is accused of having a demon (*daimonion*, John 7:20; 8:48–49, 52; 10:20–21; cf. Tob 3:8, 17; 6:8, 16–18; 8:3); the ruler of this world (*ho archōn tou kosmou toutou*, 12:31; 14:30; 16:11; cf. Eph 2:2); protection from the evil one (*ponēros*, 17:15).[23]

Our sources for discussion of angelology are the Greek Septuagint (Genesis, Exodus, Judges, Daniel), the Testaments of Abraham, Levi, and Job, Joseph and Aseneth, Third Sibylline Oracles, Philo's *On the Confusion of Tongues*, *Life of Abraham*, and *Allegorical Interpretation*, Pseudo-Philo, Tobit, Jubilees, 1 Enoch, 2 Maccabees, and the Wisdom of Solomon.[24] These are texts that we contend have close parallels to FG.

---

22. On John 5:4 as a later gloss, see Metzger, *Textual Commentary*, 179. In the Synoptic Gospels, e.g., "angel, angels" (*angelos, angeloi*) occur 26 times in Luke, 20 times in Matthew, and 6 times in Mark.

23. See discussion in Stuckenbruck, *Myth of Rebellious Angels*, 187–215. On occurrences of *daimonian* in the Synoptics: Matt (11), Mark (13), Luke (22); *diabolos*: Matt (3), Luke (4); *Satanas*: Matt (1), Mark (2), Luke (3); *ponēros* as "evil one": Matt (3); *archōn* as ruler of demons: Matt (2), Mark (1), Luke (1). See also G. J. Riley, "Devil," in Van der Toorn et al., *Dictionary of Deities and Demons*, 244–49; and "The Tempter," in Robbins, *Testing of Jesus in Q*, 60–72.

24. Plausible dates and locations: The Testaments of Abraham, Levi, and Job, Egypt, first century CE. Text from Charlesworth, *Old Testament Pseudepigrapha*, vol. 1. Joseph and Aseneth (daughter of Egyptian priest, Gen 41:45), Egypt, 100 BCE to 100 CE. Third Sibyl (Sib.Orac.3) is from Egypt, ca. 150 BCE (main corpus). Philo of Alexandria wrote sometime after 38 CE (pogrom under Flaccus). Pseudo-Philo, *Liber antiq. biblicarum* (LAB), is a Latin translation of the Greek, but originally in Hebrew, first century CE. Tobit, was written around 200 BCE or earlier, complete in Greek with Hebrew and Aramaic fragments at Qumran. 2 Maccabees was written in Greek, ca. 100 BCE, from Judea. Book of Jubilees, originally in Hebrew, next Greek, then ancient Ethiopic and Latin, ca. 125–100 BCE. See discussion of these titles in Collins and Harlow, *Early Judaism*. For information on Wisdom and 1 Enoch, see notes 1–3 of this ch. Mention of "angelic beings" will also be found in several of our forthcoming chs.

On angels see Bishop, "Angelology," 46:142–54; S. R. Garrett, *No Ordinary Angel*; Gieschen, *Angelomorphic Christology*; Newsom, "Angels," 248–53 and D. F. Watson, "Angels," 253–55; Stuckenbruck, *Angel Veneration*; Welker, "Angels," 367–80.

III. JEWISH WISDOM AND ANGELOLOGY

B. The Fourth Gospel (FG)	Jewish Angelology
Sent from God	
Jesus is sent from the Father to accomplish the Father's will (4:34; 5:30; 6:39–40; 7:16) and is closely identified with the Father (1:1, 14, 18; 5:19–24; 12:45; 17:21–22).	Angels are sent by God (Gen 18:1–3; 19:1, 15) are God in action (22:11–18) and are closely identified with God's name (16:11–13; Exod 23:20–21; Jub 17:11–14; 27:21–23).
Mediator of the vision	
The son, who "has seen" the father, is from the Father, to makes the Father known to the people (1:18; 6:46; 12:45) Jesus is identified by a true Israelite (1:47) as the king of Israel (1:49; Gen 32:28–30). He and others "will see" angels ascend and descend upon the Son of Man (John 1:51; Gen 28:12).	The Word holds the eldership among the angels, and many are his names, the beginning, the name of God, His Word, the Man after his image, "he that sees" Israel, the "vision of God" (Philo, *Conf.* 146; *Leg.* 1.43; see Borgen, "God's Agent," 73–74).
Human appearance	
The Word became flesh and lived among us (1:14, appearing as man, e.g., 29–30; 2:1–2).	Angels appear often as men (Gen 18:1–5, 22; 19:1–3; *anthropomorphos*, Philo *Abra.* 113; 142–43).
Descent/Ascent[25]	
The mission of Jesus is described as a descent from and an ascent to heaven/from above/the Father (John 3:13, 31; 6:62; cf. John 1:51/Gen 28:12)	The coming and going of angels is described as descent and ascent (Gen 28:12; Exod 3:7–8; Judg 13:20–21; Jos. Asen. 14–15; 17:8–10; T. Abr. 7.3–12; 9:1–8, Recension A)
Save/protect from evil	
In a manner similar to, yet exceeding angelic actions, Jesus saves and protects his own from the evil one.	

---

25. In the "life as journey" metaphor, ascent to heaven (and descent to the underworld) are conceptions of death as departure on a journey, Lakoff and Turner, *More Than Cool Reason*, 4.

B. The Fourth Gospel (FG)	Jewish Angelology
God sent God's Son into the world so that it might be saved (3:16–17; 12:47). Jesus transfers people from death to life (5:24), he bears witness to the Father so that people may be saved (v. 34). Jesus heals the man born blind (9:1–11), prays for and seeks the protection of his disciples ("keep them from the evil one," 17:15; 18:8–9), consecrates, commissions, empowers, and imparts life to his disciples (17:17; 20:20–23); "Did I not choose you, the Twelve? Yet one of you is a devil" (*diabolos*; 6:70). On fallen angels, see Stuckenbruck, *Myth of Rebellious Angels*, 187–212.	Angels save Lot (Gen 19:15, 22–25), Isaac (22:11–18), and Joseph (48:15–16). An angel of the Lord protected Israel from the Egyptians (Exod 14:19–20) to guard and lead them into the land (Exod 23:20; 32:34). The archangel, Raphael, restores Tobit's sight, provides for Sarah a husband, Tobias, Tobit's son, who is also protected from the demon Asmodeus (Tob 3:16–17; 5:21–22; 8:3; 11–12). An angel imparts salvation and foresight to Job (T. Job 2–5). An archangel descends and ascends to assist in Aseneth's redemption, marriage to Joseph, and immortality (Jos. Asen. 14–17; 1 En 99:3; Jub 10:3; 12:20).

Life-giving food

"This is the bread that comes down from heaven, so that one may eat of it and not die . . . whoever eats of this bread will live forever" (6:50–51; cf. vv. 33, 58).	"everyone who eats of it (honeycomb) will not die for ever (and) ever" (eaten by angels and sons of the Most High, Jos. Asen. 16:14b) "you have eaten bread of life" (v. 8) "sweet honey from heaven" Sib.Or. 3:746.

Angelic appearance

"Two angels in white (*leukos*) sitting where the body of Jesus had been lying" (John 20: 12; cf. *astraptō*, Luke 24:4, 23; *lampros*, Rev 15:6).	Miriam in a dream sees a man in linen who foretells of the life and mission of Moses (LAB 9:10; cf. Dan 10:5–6; 12:6). Visions of angels in garments of white who reveal what and who is to come (1 En 71:1; cf. T. Levi 8:2; divine intervention, 2 Macc 11:8).

In the Old Testament, angels—especially the angel of the LORD—are portrayed as a means by which God takes up contact with the creaturely world. Biblical authors reflect on divine power, presence, and agency not only by depicting angels, but also by referring to God's word, glory, wisdom, power, spirit, and name. Sometimes their comments on these divine attributes hint that the attributes (e.g., wisdom) are themselves distinct angelic beings separate from God.

Our comparisons (tbl 3.B) regarding descent/ascent and save/protect from evil disclose an underlying narrative framework within which affirmations about the divine revealer are set. FG's prologue ("the darkness did not

III. JEWISH WISDOM AND ANGELOLOGY

overcome [*katalambanō*, 'seize, attack'] it," 1:5; cf. 12:35; "his own people did not accept him," vv. 10-13; and also 3:19; 8:47) can be viewed as a comment on the elements of opposition between the dark forces of the lower world and the light of life, recalling ancient conflicts (Gen 3:14-18; 6:4; 1 En 6-10; Jub 3-7; John 12:31, 35-36; 14:30; Rev 12:1-6).[26] Regarding the divine revealer/mediator, Susan Garrett writes:

> By the late Second Temple era, the various traditions about angels and about personified divine attributes had coalesced for some Jews into the figure of a chief heavenly mediator. Early Christians used these interpretive conventions to make sense of the person and work of Jesus. They identify him with the chief heavenly mediator: Jesus *is* the Son of Man, the one sent from God, the divine logos, the one through whom the world was created, the image of God's very being, the likeness of the glory of the LORD.[27]

Although FG made use of the above imagery in his portrayal of Jesus, he would agree with the author of Hebrews that Jesus is "much superior to the angels as the name he has inherited is more excellent than theirs" (Heb 1:4).

---

26. Perkins, *Gnosticism and the New Testament*, 15-18, especially 118-19. For more contextual support from second temple Judaism (e.g., Jub 10:3-6; 12:19-20), see Stuckenbruck, *Myth of Rebellious Angels*, 187-212. This narrative of cosmic conflict will be revisited in our ch. 10 on Nag Hammadi Library, pp, 177, 179.

27. Garrett, *Celestial Spirits*, 238.

IV. Philo

ALTHOUGH THERE ARE DIFFERENT portraits of Philo of Alexandria (20 BCE to 50 CE), he essentially was an interpreter of the Jewish Scriptures (LXX), an eclectic philosopher of Stoic, Middle-Platonic, and Neo-Pythagorean ideas, and a contemplative mystic (*Spec* 3.1).[1] From a prominent family of Alexandria, Egypt, Philo used allegorical interpretation[2] to find common ground between his Jewish tradition and Hellenistic philosophy. Philo also did some traveling. He had visited Rome (for an appeal to emperor Caligula, 40 CE), Ascalon (north of Gaza), and Jerusalem to "offer up prayers and sacrifices" in the temple (*Prov* 2.64).[3]

His impact on Judaism seemed to end with the Roman destruction of the Alexandrian Jewish community in 115–117 CE, but his writings gained influence with early Christians who preserved them (over 40 volumes) even

---

1. Hans Jonas explores Philo's mystical knowledge of God in his *Gnosis und spätantiker Geist*, 2:70–121, comparing it with gnosis (broadly defined); but see also Winston, "Was Philo A Mystic?" 161–80 and his *Logos and Mystical Theology in Philo of Alexandria*, who interprets Philo in the middle-Platonic mystical tradition.

2. Allegorical interpretation for Philo ascribes hidden, symbolic meaning to various elements in the sacred text that are not the obvious meanings of the words in their normal or plain sense. Although the allegorical interpretation is higher and more important for Philo, he rarely invalidates the literal sense. Allegorical interpretation of Homer and Hesiod were also practiced by the Stoics and the philosophical schools on Pergamum, centuries earlier, J. I. Porter, "Stoic Interpretation," 3:823–26. See Schenck, *Philo of Alexandria*, 31–33; Borgen, "Philo of Alexandria," 5:337–39; Y. Amir, "Scripture in Philo," in Mulder and Sysling, *Mikra*, 421–53. In *Prob.* 28, 121–25, 157, the eclectic Philo also celebrated the Cynic ideal of poverty, citing Antisthenes and Diogenes (ca. 403–323 BCE), see B. Lang, "Jesus among the Philosophers," in Petersen et al., *Religio-Philosophical Discourses*, 190, 212–14.

3. Schenck, *Philo*, 3–14. See also Birnbaum, "Philo of Alexandria," 4:512–13; Borgen, *Philo of Alexandria*, and his "Philo of Alexandria," 5:333–42; Collins, *Between Athens and Jerusalem*; Dodd, *Interpretation*, 54–73, 276–81; Sterling, "Philo," 1063–70; Winston, *Philo of Alexandria*; *Studia Philonica Annual* (Brown, 1989—) and Borgen et al., *Philo Index*. Our citations are from *Works of Philo* (trans. C. D. Yonge, 1854; Hendrickson, 1993) in the public domain and our translation (AT) is from the Greek text in F. H. Colson, et al. *Philo* (10 vols. LCL; Harvard, 1929–1962), citing Greek in, e.g., Philo, *Conf.* (LCL 4:62). Our abbreviations are from Collins, *SBL Handbook*, 8.3.6.

claiming Philo as their own.[4] Philo was a Greek-speaking Jew who lived in the Diaspora (outside Judea), so were—the apostle Paul (of Tarsus, Cilicia), the author of Hebrews (Alexandria or Ephesus), and perhaps FG (Syria-Palestine or Ephesus). All of Philo's writings were written in Hellenistic Greek, but some titles survive in an Armenian translation (*Prob., QG, QE, Anim.*). Numerous parallels have been drawn between the NT and Philo.[5] His references to *logos* ("Word" ca. 300 refs.) as both God's creative agent (cf. Gen 1) and personified Wisdom (Prov 8),[6] along with his use of related titles "God's First-born, the Beginning . . . the Name of God . . . the Man after His image" (*Conf*. 146), provide a good starting point for comparisons with FG.

The Fourth Gospel	Philo
	The Beginning, *Logos* with God
"In the beginning (*archē*) was the Word (*logos*) and the Word was with God (*ho theos*) and the Word was God (*theos*) He was (*ōn*) in the beginning with God" (1:1–2). "He was in the world (*kosmos*) v. 10. "He came to his own, but his own did not receive him" v. 11	"For he is called the Beginning (*archē*), and the Name of God (*theos*) and His Word (*logos*)," *Conf*. 146 (AT). The *logos* is the image of the "Self-existent One (*ho 'ōn*; Exod 3:14 LXX) who is seen in the world (*kosmos*)," *Conf*. 97 (LCL 4:62). Commenting on Gen 31:13, an angel to Jacob: "I am the God (*ho theos*) . . . who was seen by you in the place . . . of God (*theou*)," *Somn*. 1.229 (as in John 1:1, see Schenck, *Philo of Alexandria*, 88). For Philo, word and wisdom are both personifications of God and distinct powers or (divine) agents of God (Schenck, *Philo of Alexandria*, 58–62. Yonge transl. of *Somn*. 1:229.

---

4. Clement of Alexandria (150–215 CE), Origen (185–254 CE), Eusebius (263–339 CE) in his *Hist. eccl.* 2.16–18 (Eusebius had thought that the Therapeutae, reported by Philo, were Egyptian Christians), see Schenck, *Philo*, 73–95; Runia, *Philo in Early Christian Literature*.

5. On the Philonic characteristics of, e.g., 1 Cor 1–4; 15; Col 1:15–20; Heb; and FG, see Schenck, *Philo*, 73–95; on Heb and Philo, see also Puskas, *Hebrews, the General Letters*, 21–23.

6. According to Eusebius, *Praep. Ev.* 13.12.3–4 (ca. 325 CE), Philo's predecessor, Aristobulus (ca. 150 BCE), wrote of the voice of God at creation "not as words spoken but as construction of works . . . the whole creation of the world as words (*logoi*) of God" (*Preparation of the Gospel*, trans. E. H. Gifford).

The Fourth Gospel	Philo
\<td colspan="2" align="center">*Logos* and Creation\</td>	
1:1–3 "In the beginning was (*ēn*) the Word who was with God ... all things were made by him (*panta di' autou*) and without him not one thing came into being (*egeneto*)" 1:1, 3. (The verbs here in "the Word was" *ho logos ēn* and "all things came into being through him" *panta di' egeneto* distinguish the eternal Creator from temporal creation, F. Kermode reflecting on Chrysostom's comments in Alter and Kermode, *Literary Guide*, 443, 445–46).	The Word of God (*ho theou logos*) made the world (*kosmopoieō*), *Opif.* 20–25, 36. "Who then can it [the house of God] be except the Word (*logos*) which is more ancient than all things ... when He [God] was fashioning the world, He employed it [the Word] as His instrument," *Migr.* 6 (Yonge); Logos separates what is created from the Creator, *Her.* 205–6. For Philo, Wisdom is also an agent of creation, *Her.* 199; *Det.* 5; and Wisdom of God is also the Word of God, *Leg.* 1.65.[7]
\<td colspan="2" align="center">We have seen his glory\</td>	
"And the Word (*logos*) ... we have seen his glory, the glory as of a father's only son, full of grace and truth" (John 1:14); "No one has ever seen (*horaō*) God. It is God the only Son ... who has made him known" (v. 18); "Whoever has seen me has seen the Father" (14:9). See Jörg Frey, *The Glory of the Crucified One*, ch. 7.	"whereas the voice of mortal beings is judged by hearing, the sacred oracles intimate that the words (*logoi*) of God are seen as light, for we are told that 'all of the people saw (*horaō*) the Voice' (Exod 20:18), not that they heard it ... virtue shining with intense brilliance ... the voice of God ... as 'visible'" (*Migr.* 47–48). See Boyarin, "Logos," 546.
\<td colspan="2" align="center">God's eternal today\</td>	
\<td colspan="2">This is a life not measured by time, and has neither past nor future, but is lived in "God's eternal To-day" (Dodd, *Interpretation*, 150).\</td>	

---

7. See similar FG language in Zeno the Stoic (ca. 300 BCE) on deity: *theos ... kat' archas* "God ... in the beginning," Diog. Laert. *Lives* 7.135–36; *theos ... logikos*, "God ... reason." *di' hon ta panta*, "by whom are all things," *Lives* 7.147. Philo embraced similar aspects of Stoic thought.

IV. PHILO

The Fourth Gospel	Philo
"Whoever believes in the son has eternal life; whoever disobeys will not see life, but must endure God's wrath" 3:36; cf. 5:24; 6:47, 54; 8:51. "I am the resurrection and the life. Those who believe in me, even though they die, will live" 11:25. "Father the hour has come to glorify your Son so that your Son may glorify you, since you have given him authority . . . to give eternal life (*zōe aiōnios*) to all whom you have given him. And this is eternal life, that you may know the only true God . . . I glorified you on earth . . . now Father glorify me in your own presence with the glory that I had in your presence before the world existed" 17:1–5.	"For God's life is not a time, but eternity, which is the archetype and pattern of time; and in eternity there is no past or future, but only present existence," *Deus* 32; cf. Plato *Tim.* 37D–38A. "For only those who have taken refuge in God and become His supplicants does Moses recognize as living, accounting the rest to be dead men. Indeed he evidently ascribes immortality to the former by adding 'ye are alive *today*'" (Deut 4:4), *Fug.* 57. "And is it not life eternal (*zōe aiōnios*) to take refuge with Him that is (*to on*) and death to flee away from him" (Deut 19:5), *Fug.* 78.

God's appointed guide

"I am the way (*hodos*), and the truth, and the life. No one comes to the Father but by me" 14:6. The "Father loves the Son, and has given all things into his hand" 3:35. "I have not spoken on my own, but the Father who sent me has himself given me a commandment about what to say and what to speak" 12:49.	Reason (*nous*) is the way (*hodos*) to knowledge of God, *Deus* 143. "He has the divine Word as his leader" *Migr.* 174 (AT); "To His Word, His chief messenger (archangel), highest in age and honor, the Father of all has given the special prerogative" to creation, *Her.* 205 (LCL 4:385). "Divine reason which is the helmsman and governor of the universe" *Cher.* 36. [God also directs the world, *Her.* 228; *Somn.* 1.157].

Life and Light

"In him was life (*zōē*) and the life was the light (*phōs*) of people. The light shines in the darkness and the darkness did not overcome it," 1:4–5 (cf. 1 QS 1.9–10). "I am the light of the world. Whoever follows me will never walk in darkness, but will have the light of life," 8:12; 9:5 (cf. "God is light," 1 John 1:5).	"God is light (*phōs*, Ps 26:1 LXX) . . . the archetype of every other light . . . For the model or pattern was the Word (*logos*) which contained all His fullness—light in fact . . . for God said, 'let there be light'" (Gen 1:3), *Somn.* 1.75. "[God] who is the occasion of life (*zaō*) to all . . . and is it not life eternal (*zōē aiōn*) to take refuge with the one who is (*to ʼov*),"

The Fourth Gospel	Philo
	Fug. 77–78. "Wisdom is God's archetypal luminary (*phōtos*) *Migr.* 40 (LCL 4:154). The life-giving breath of God and light [Gen 1–2], *Opif.* 30.

Wine instead of Water

"Jesus said to them, 'Fill the jars with water.' And they filled them up to the brim. He said to them, 'Now draw some out, and take it to the chief steward.' So they took it. When the steward tasted the water that had become wine, and did not know where it came from (though the servants who had drawn the water knew), the steward called the bridegroom and said to him, 'Everyone serves the good wine first, and then the inferior wine after the guests have become drunk. But you have kept the good wine until now.'" (John 2:7–10)	The mysterious figure Melchizedek, a type of the Word shall "bring forth wine instead of water, and shall give your souls to drink, and shall cheer them with unmixed wine, in order that they may be wholly occupied with divine intoxication, more sober than sobriety itself" (*Leg.* 3.82; Yonge). "And who can pour over the happy soul which proffers its own reason as the most sacred cup, the holy goblets of true joy, except the cup-bearer of God, the master of the feast, the Word?" (*Somn.* 2.249; Yonge). From Hoskyns, *Fourth Gospel*, 192, who notes its differences with FG (esp. Philo's allegoricalization).

Living Water

"The water that I will give will become in them a spring (*pēgē*) of water (*hydōr*) gushing up to eternal life (*zōē aiōn*)," 4:14 (10, 13). "Out of his belly shall flow rivers (*potamos*) of living water (*hydōr zaō*)" 7:38.	"The highest word (*logos*) of God, who is the fountain (*pēgē*) of wisdom (*sophia*), in order that by drinking of that stream he may find everlasting life (*zōēn 'aidion*)," *Fug.* 97 (Yonge), "to that everlasting fountain (*pēgē*) of all that is good, from which he has showered forth other virtues, drawing forth at the same time, for our enjoyment, to make those who drink of it immortal" (cf. Deut 8:7; 11:11; LCL 7:276), *Spec.* 1.303 (Yonge). "God is something more than life (*zōē*) ... the ever-flowing spring (*pēgē*) of living (*tou zēn*)," *Fug.* 198 (Yonge). The divine word as a river (*potamos*) of God [Ps 65:10], a full stream of wisdom, an ever-flowing stream (*pēgē*), *Somn.* 2.245 (Yonge).

Knowing God

IV. PHILO

The Fourth Gospel	Philo
"When the Son of Man is lifted up, then you will know (*ginōskō*) that I am (*egō eimi*; Exod 3:14 LXX), 8:28, 58. "You will know (*ginōskō*) the truth and the truth will set you free," 8:32. "I know my own and my own know me," 10:14b. "That you may know and continue to know that the Father is in me and I am in the Father," v. 38b. "If you know me you will know my Father also," 14:7. "I have made known (*gnōrizō*) to you everything that I heard from the Father," 15:15b. "And this is eternal life (*zōē aiōn*), that they may know (*ginōskō*) you, the only true God," 17:3.	"Knowledge (*epistēmi*) of Him who is (*hos eimi*)," is "the best of human goals," *Decal.* 81. "The knowledge of Him is the consummation of happiness" *Spec.* 1.345. "For the mind is guided by wisdom, while the road is straight and level . . . proceeds along to the end; and the end of this road is the knowledge (*gnōsis*) and understanding (*epistēmi*) of God," *Deus* 143. "Man's highest mystical contact with God, according to Philo, is limited to the Deity's manifestation as Logos" (Winston, "Philo's Mysticism," 82n35).

Belief

"He that believes (*pisteuō*) on the Son has life," 3:36. "Anyone who hears my word and believes him who sent me has eternal life," 5:24. "This is the work of God that you believe in him who he has sent," 6:29. "Those who believe in me even though they die, yet they will live," 11:25b. "Believe in God, believe also in me," 14:1b. "Believe" (*pisteuō*) occurs over 80 times in FG.	"For Abraham also, when he believed (*pisteuō*) is said to have 'come near God' (Gen 18:23)," *Migr.* 132 (Yonge). "Belief (*pistis*) in God is the only true and secure comfort of life, fulfillment of kindly hopes . . . knowledge of piety and possession of happiness" (*Abr.* 268; Yonge). "For though he [Moses] believed (*pisteuō*) God, nevertheless he tried to avoid the office to which God was appointing him," *Mos.* 1.83 (Yonge).

Love

"If God were your Father, you would love (*agapaō*) me," 8:42. "If you love me you will keep my commandments," 14:15. "As the Father has loved me, so I love you, abide in my love (*agapē*)," 15:9. "That they may become completely one, so that the world may know that you have sent me and have loved them even as you have loved me," 17:23. In FG, love for God is directed to Jesus, God's son, but see 1 John 5:2, "when we love God and keep his commandments," 1 John 5:2; cf. 4:16, 21 (reflecting the OT teaching found in Philo).	"All the exhortations to piety in the law refer either to our loving (*agapaō*) or our fearing the Existent. And thus to love Him is most suitable to those (who truly honor Him)," *Deus* 69 (LCL 3:44). God asks nothing from you that is difficult, but only "to love (*agapaō*) Him as a benefactor, or failing this to fear Him as a ruler and lord," *Spec.* 1:300 (Yonge); Moses says to Israel "your life is to love the living God,"(Deut 30:20), *Post.* 69 (Yonge).

Children of God

The Fourth Gospel	Philo
"But to all who received him, who believed on his name, he gave power to become children of God (*tekna tou theou*)," 1:12. Caiaphas the high priest prophesies (inadvertently) that Jesus was about to die for the nation and "to gather into one the dispersed children of God (*tekna tou theou*)," 11:52 (in FG and 1 Jn, the Son of God, *ho his tou theou*, is used exclusively of Jesus. Jesus and the Father are one, 10:30; 14:9, and disciples are to honor the Son as they do the Father, 5:23, and they may ask of the Father in the name of Jesus, 15:16; 16:23).	"You who have enrolled yourselves as children of one and the same Father, who is not mortal, but immortal—God's Man, who being the Word (*logos*) of the Eternal must needs himself be imperishable," *Conf.* 40–41 (LCL 4:32); "But they who live in the knowledge of the One are rightly called 'Sons of God (*huioi theou*),'" *Conf.* 145 (AT). "But the man who has this inheritance from God has advanced beyond the bounds of human happiness; for he alone is nobly born, inasmuch as he has God attributed to him as his father, and being his adopted only son (*monos huios*)," *Sobr.* 56 (Yonge; cf. Wis 2:13; 1 En 42:2), Schenck, *Philo*, 89.

Heavenly Man

"He was in the world, and the world came into being through him yet the world did not know him," 1:11. "No one has ever seen God. It is God the only Son, who is close to the Father's bosom, who has made him known," 1:18. "The one who comes from above is above all; the one who is of the earth belongs to the earth and speaks about earthly things. The one who come s from heaven is above all," 3:31. "He said to them, 'you are from below, I am from above; you are of this world, I am not of the world,'" 8:23 (cf. 1:14, Son of Man, 1:51; 3:13, 6:32–38, 51, 58; 13:1,3; 14:2–3, 6; Meeks, "Man from Heaven," 44–72).	"There are two types of men, the one a heavenly man (*ouranios anthrōpos*) and the other earthly" (Gen 2:7). The heavenly man being made in the image of God (Gen 1:26), *Leg.* 1:31, cf. *Opif.* 69. "So we have two kinds of men, one that of those who live by reason (*logismos*), the divine breathing (Gen 1:27) the other of those who live by blood and the pleasure of the flesh (Gen 2:7) . . . the other is a faithful impress of the divine image," *Her.* 57. "God's First-born, the Word . . . the man after His image (*eikonos*)," *Conf.* 146. "For of the real man (*alētheian anthrōpou*), who is pure reason (*nous*), One, the only God is the maker" (Gen 1:27), *Fug.* 72 (LCL 4:311).

Shepherd and Son

The Fourth Gospel	Philo
"I am the good shepherd. The good shepherd lays down his life for the sheep," 10:11. "I am the good shepherd. I know my sheep and my own know me," v.14. "I have other sheep that do not belong to this fold," v. 16a (FG distinctive: the sacrifice of the shepherd for his sheep, v. 15b). "For whatever the Father does, the Son does likewise," 5:19; "the Father loves the Son and shows him all that he himself is doing," v. 20.	On Ps 23:1, "this hallowed flock [of the world] He [God] leads in accord with right and law, setting over it His true Word (*logos*) and First-born Son who shall take upon Him its government," *Agr.* 51 (Yonge). See also on Ps 23:1, *Names* 115–16; and shepherd as ruler of the irrational flock, *Agr.* 41 *Legat.* 44, cited in *TDNT* 6:490. J. D. Turner explores the rich shepherd imagery of the ancient Near Eastern and Greco-Roman worlds, in Beutler and Fortna, *Shepherd Discourse,* 33–52.

Bread, Manna

"Do not work for food (*brōsis*) that perishes, but for food that endures for eternal life which the Son of Man will give you. For it is on him that God has set his seal," 6:27. "Your ancestors ate manna in the wilderness and died. This is the bread that comes down from heaven, so that one may eat of it and not die. I am the living bread that came down from heaven. Whoever eats of this bread will live forever," 6:48–51a, "for my flesh is the true food," 6:55 (cf. 6:31–40, 48–51, 58)	"The one who extends his vision . . . to look steadfastly for the manna, which is the word of God (*theios logos*), the heavenly incorruptible food (*trophē*) of the soul, which delights in the vision," *Her.* 79, 191. Others derive their food from earth, but "those who have vision receive it from heaven," men in agriculture produce food from earth, "but God the only cause and giver, rains down the food from heaven (Exod 16:4)" *Mut.* 258–59 (Yonge). "The food of the soul is not earthly, but heavenly (Exod 16:4)." And "in the case of manna," let every soul collect what is sufficient for the day to show that God, not itself, is the bountiful guardian of all things, *Leg.* 3.162, 166. See Borgen, *Bread from Heaven,* 29–33, 99–146.

Friends of God

"You are my friends if you do what I command you. I do not call you servants any longer, because the servant does not know what the master is doing; but I have called you friends, because I have made known to you everything that I have heard from my Father," John 15:14–15.	"You must not think that it was said as some unconsidering people suppose, to humiliate the all-wise leader; for indeed it is folly to suppose that the servants of God take precedence of His friends in receiving their portion in the land of virtue," *Migr. Abr.* 45 (to Moses, Deut. 34:4–5; Yonge); Moses as a "friend of God," *Cher.* 49; On Abraham (Gen 18:17–19) *Sobr.* 55–56.

From our comparisons above, Philo's teaching on *logos* as an agent of divine power having its own existence, is a development beyond what we find in, e.g., Proverbs, Sirach, and Wisdom, and may bring us closer to FG's understanding of *logos*.[8] For Philo, the *logos* is the force that holds all things together and lends them their rational coherence.[9] Philo writes of "the second deity, who is the Word of the supreme Being" (*QG* 2.62).[10] As in John 1:1 (*kai theos hēn ho logos*), Philo distinguishes *logos* from God by mentioning the absence of the definite article "in the place of *god*" in his discussion of Gen 31:13 (LXX), emphasizing that "God is one," but that some mistake God's chief governor and agent, God's *logos*, for God (*Somn.* 1.227-30).[11]

"Life" and "eternal life" are linked to "the age to come" (Mark 10:29-30; cf., 2 Esdr. 7:113; 8:46, 52; 1 En 37:4; 58:3; 71:15), but in FG are a present

---

8. *Logos* has a long history in Greek philosophy, beginning with Heraclitus (ca. 500 BCE) who saw it as a universal, structuring principle (*frag.* 1-2, 92), distinguished from matter (as did Aristotle), and associated it with fire, the only constant amid periodic change (*frag.* 20-21, 26). The later Stoics (ca. 300 BCE) followed the distinction made by Heraclitus, and regarded *logos* as the active divine principle that pervades the world. Fire (with Heraclitus) is the superior element over air, water, and earth and is active as *pneuma* (warm breath), and equated with the divine *logos*. See Stoic Seneca on Spirit and Reason, *Helv.* 8:3; Diogenes Laertius, *Lives* 7.147-49 (Zeno); 9.7-8 (Heraclitus); H. Kleinknecht, "λόγος Concept in the Greek World," 4:81-85; Nussbaum, "Heraclitus," 687; Schmeller, "Stoics, Stoicism," 6:210-14; Sedley, *Greek and Roman Philosophy*, 60, 170. Heraclitus citations are from *Fragments* (trans. B. Haxton).

For Philo (and some Middle Platonists) the Stoic conception of God was viewed as too materialistic, but we see, e.g., in the Wisdom of Solomon (2:3; 9:17; 12:1) and Letters of Seneca (a Stoic on Plato, e.g., *Ep.* 58; 65; 102.22) that a Hellenistic Jew (Wis) and a Roman Stoic (Seneca, ca. 50 CE) could incorporate selected ideas from Platonism, in this Transitional period from 100 BCE to 200 CE, see T. Engberg-Pedersen, "Stoicism and Platonism," in Rasimus et al., *Stoicism*, 1-14; Koester, "'Spirit' (*Pneuma*)," in Van der Watt et al., *Prologue*, 240. On FG and Greek philosophy, see also Bultmann, *John*, 24-28, who favors, instead, gnostic influences. Transcending earlier materialistic views, see Stoic conceptions of God as spirit (John 4:24), in Epictetus, *Disc.* 2.8.1 (God is mind, knowledge, right reason, *logos*) and Clement, *Strom.* 5.14 ("For the Stoics say that God is spirit by nature'), cited in Boring et al., *Hellenistic Commentary*, 265.

9. See *Opif.* 43 and *Fug.* 106-8 as noted by Attridge, "Philo and John," in his *Essays*, 47.

10. A. F. Segal views the mention of two gods by Philo as similar to "two powers" in rabbinic debates (*Two Powers*, 159-65). See also, F. Siegert, "Der Logos und zweiter Gott," in Frey and Schnelle, *Kontexte*, 277-94; R. van den Broek, "Jewish and Platonic Speculations in Early Alexandrian Theology," in Pearson and Goehring, *Roots of Egyptian Christianity*, 190-203.

11. See discussion of *theos* without the definite article in Brown, *Gospel according to John* 1:5; BDF (Chicago, 1961) 143, art. 273; Colwell, "Use of the Article," 12-21; Schenck, *Philo*, 61-62, 87-88, 95; Dunn, *Christology*, 241; D. A. Carson contends that the alleged parallels between FG and Philo here are irrelevant with regard to the grammatical concern in John 1:1, *John*, 137.

possession for those who believe (John 3:36; 6:47).¹² C. H. Dodd observes a connection here between FG and Philo.

> For periods of months and years and of time in general are notions of men, who reckon by number; but the true name of eternity is To-day (De Fuga, 57). It is evident that when Philo uses the term ζωὴ αἰώνιος (Ibid., 78), he means by it a life which, like that of God, is 'eternal' in the sense of 'timeless'. The thought of the Fourth Gospel has as we have seen, some affinity with that of Philo. It appears that he too means by ζωὴ αἰώνιος 'eternal life' in the Platonic sense, at least so far, that it is a life not measured by month and years, a life which has properly speaking neither past nor future, but is lived in God's eternal To-day."¹³

Marianne Meye Thompson observes how Philo's use of the divine name (from Exod 3:14 LXX) provides a helpful context for understanding some of the "I am" statements of Jesus in FG:

> Alluding to the LXX, the first-century Jewish exegete Philo repeatedly refers to God as either "the one who is" (*ho ōn*) or more frequently as "that which is" (*to on*). On Exod 3:14, Philo even comments "[God] has no proper name ... for it is not the nature of him that is to be spoken of, but simply to be" (Somn. 1.230-33; Mut. 11-15; Deus 62; Det. 160; Decal. 58). In other words, the LXX and Philo's use of it, show that the revelation of God in Exod 3:14 was understood to emphasize God's sheer existence, the fact that God simply is. There are instances in John where Jesus' "I am" sayings particularly emphasize that he has, and can give, that sort of divine life; that he "is" as God is (e.g., John 8:58).¹⁴

On FG and Philo regarding the feasts of Israel, Kenneth Schenck, makes the following observation:

> Although Philo valued the literal keeping of the Jewish festivals (e.g., *Migr.* 91), both he and John saw their ultimate significance in the symbolic ... Like God, Jesus is always working—even on the Sabbath (John 5:17; cf. *Leg.* 1.5-6).¹⁵

---

12. Thompson, *John: A Commentary*, 88.

13. Dodd, *Interpretation*, 150.

14. Thompson, *John: A Commentary*, 158. On FG, Attridge reminds us that "In contrast to Philo ... the particular is embedded in an individual, Jesus, not in the Torah of Moses" in his *Essays*, 58.

15. Schenck, *Philo*, 76. On symbolic interpretation using temple imagery in both FG and Philo (*Cher.*; Exod 25:19), see Attridge, "Cubist Principle," in Frey, *Imagery*, 51-56.

Even though there are some helpful insights from Philo and noteworthy similarities between FG and Philo, the latter has a different worldview. Philo makes use of Jewish wisdom, but his keen knowledge of Greek philosophy is evident throughout (*Congr.* 78–80; *Aet.* 15–19). For example, Philo understands *Logos* to be an impersonal agent of God identified as the Monad (second level) in the three-story world of Middle Platonism: (1) Uncreated, transcendent God, (2) *Logos*, and (created) Dyad (3) world of senses.[16] Philo agreed with Plato (429–347 BCE) that the world of ideas that we know through our minds is the *real* world, of which the world of our senses only gives us a shadowy picture.[17] For Philo, the *logos* is the ideal image of the one God, God's agent in the creation and governance of the visible world of sense perception.[18] The *logos* is also the archetype of those who live by reason. Those who follow their passions go the way of the earthly man (*Leg.* 1.31; *Opif.* 69; *Her.* 57). To control the passions and live by reason (cf. Stoics) is the noble path that the soul must take (*Leg.* 1.71). Much of Philo's allegorical interpretation, e.g., four branches of rivers from Eden in Gen 2:10–14, pertain to the significance of numbers. The four branches of rivers correspond to the four cardinal virtues (prudence, courage, self-control, and justice), each corresponding to a part of the soul (*Leg.* 1.63–73). By means of allegorical exegesis, Philo sought to show how insights from Greek philosophy originated in the Jewish Scriptures (not the concern of FG):

> Well, therefore, did Heraclitus say this following the doctrine of Moses; for he says, 'we are living according the death of those people and we have died according to their life.' As if he had said, now when we are alive, we are so though our soul is dead and buried in our body, as if in a tomb. But if it we are to die, then our soul would live according to its proper life, being released from the evil and dead body to which it is bound.[19]

---

16. Schenck, *Philo*, 55–56. See also *Praem.* 46 to discern the Uncreated (transcendent God) from the Creator, the monad (the Creator) from the dyad (the thing made), cf. *Somn.* 2.70; *Opif.* 156, where Logos (monad) is tree of life, and dyad is forbidden tree of good and evil (cf. Gen 2:9; 3:3); also similar to first-century BCE Neo-Pythagorean view of monad and dyad, see Diogenes Laertius, *Lives* 8.25; discussion in *Philo VIII* (LCL, 1960), 339, 452–53; *Philo V* (LCL, 1968), 475, 608.

17. Schenck, *Philo*, 54. Although FG is not a Platonic work, see Van Kooten, "Last Days of Socrates and Christ," 219–43; and Steiner, "Two Suppers," 33–61. See also our ch. 7. tbl. C, p. 118.

18. On Logos as a link between creator and created, see R. Williamson, citing and discussing *Her.* 205–6, in his *Jews in the Hellenistic World*, 119–21.

19. *Leg.* 1:108, appears to reflect the Platonic (non-Jewish) view that the soul is entombed in the body until death when it is released from its sepulchre (cf. Plato, *Gorg.* 493 A; *Cratyl.* 400B). Was Philo alluding to Gen 2:7; 35:18a LXX? See text and note in

IV. PHILO

In his argument that the world is created and indestructible, unless its Maker wills otherwise, Philo cites Plato's *Timaeus* 41a–b (*Aet.* 13) and Hesiod (*Aet.* 17) and makes the point that Moses stated that same view years before (*Aet.* 19; cf. Gen 1:1; 8:22).[20] Despite the dissimilarities mentioned above, Eusebius of Caesarea (ca. 330 CE) wrote the following about Philo of Alexandria:

> Philo was rich in language and broad in thought, sublime and elevated in his views of the divine writings.[21]

Jörg Frey makes a noteworthy observation

> Scholarly views vary between the view that Philo leads straight into the core of Johannine Christology and the sober verdict that there is "nothing specific for which Philo is essential to understand it." While the latter may be true for the thought of the Evangelist, we can see in Philo some of the philosophical problems John's readers, or a part of them, might have felt when reading his biblical creation accounts. It it also possible that the same difficulties came up in their reading of the prologue as well.[22]

Although Prof. Frey's observations on the varied views appear to be correct and his comments on FG's readership are noteworthy, we conclude with a statement by Harold W. Attridge that is closer to our view of the matter:

> Philo and the Fourth Gospel are indeed both riffs on a common theme: two intimately related, but distinct articulations of a common exegetical and theological impulse.[23]

Winston, *Philo of Alexandria*, 253, 382. Before Philo, Aristobulus of Alexandria (ca. 150 BCE) claimed that Plato and Pythagoras knew Jewish law and borrowed from it, relying on an earlier Greek translation of some portions of the Hebrew Torah, years before the LXX, according to Eusebius, *Praep. ev.* 13.12.1; on Aristobulus, see Charlesworth, *Old Testament Pseudepigrapha*, 2:831–36.

20. See discussion in Winter, *Philo and Paul*, 72–73. Justin Martyr concurs with Philo's view here, see Justin, *1 Apol.* 59 (ANF 1:182).

21. *Hist. eccl.* 2.18.1, from (K. Lake, trans., LCL 1:157), 89. Clement of Alexandria (ca. 150–212) was also indebted to Middle Platonism, citing both Plato and Philo favorably (*Protr.* 6.60p; *Strom.* 2.4.5).

22. Frey, "Between Torah and Stoa," in Van der Watt et al., *Prologue*, 216. In this article Frey gives examples of strong proponents (e.g., F. Siegert; Hoppe) and critics of the FG and Philo comparisons (L. H. Hurtado; Lleonhardt-Balzer).

23. Attridge, "Philo and John," in his *Essays*, 58.

V. The Dead Sea Scrolls

MANY SCHOLARS HAVE CLAIMED that FG's concepts and expressions seem to echo what we find in **the Dead Sea Scrolls** (DSS).[1] This collection (in its latest redaction) predates FG and no NT fragment has been found among the Dead Sea Scrolls.[2] Not a few make the case that John "the Baptist," perhaps even Jesus, had some acquaintance with the DSS community, near the location of their ministries.[3] John Ashton even argues that the author of FG himself spent time at Qumran.[4] Jörg Frey outlines and criticizes four patterns of development regarding the NT and Qumran, from sensational theories to credible hypotheses.[5] Since almost all of the scrolls are

---

1. Abbreviations for DSS designate: location by Qumran cave number (1Q), title of work, often in Hebrew (1QS, S for *Serek Hayaḥad* or Rule of Community), roman numerals are used for column number, followed by a comma and space, with the line number set as an Arabic numeral (1QS III, 15–17), Brooke, *NIDB* 2:52.

    For DSS citations, we use primarily our own translations (AT) from the Hebrew text of F. García Martínez, et al., *DSS:SE* (2 vols.; Brill/Eerdmans, 2000) *Discoveries in the Judaean Desert* (various editors; 40 vols; Oxford Univ. Press, 1955–2009), and The Leon Levy Dead Sea Scrolls Digital Library at www.deadseascrolls.org.il.; consulting also the ET of Abegg et al., *Dead Sea Scrolls Bible*; Gaster, *Dead Sea Scriptures*; Dupont-Sommer, *Essene Writings from Qumran*, and Vermes, *Complete Dead Sea Scrolls*; but we also consult Wise et al., *Dead Sea Scrolls*; and Charlesworth, *Graphic Concordance*.

2. In 1972, José O'Callaghan published an article in which he claimed to identify 8 of the fragments from cave 7 (7Q4-10, 15) as quotations of NT verses (mostly Mark), but these have been shown to be a Greek trans. of 1 Enoch, see Fitzmyer, *Impact*, 96. On NT in DSS, "In fact, nothing could be further from the truth," Schiffman, *Qumran and Jerusalem*, 36.

3. Jewish NT scholar, S. Sandmel, who was writing when only some of the scrolls were available, is doubtful "without seeing some evidence for it," in his "Parallelomania," 5. Fitzmyer discusses it as an intriguing hypothesis, *Impact*, 91–94; J. C. VanderKam, also entertains the possibility, *Dead Sea Scrolls Today*, 206–9. See also Anderson, "John and Qumran," 20–21. Hartmut Stegemann examines both John the Baptist and Jesus in relation to DSS and finds only general similarities and many key differences in his *Library of Qumran*, 211–57.

4. FG's dualism was so strongly rooted in Qumran that he must have resided there at some time, J. Ashton, *Understanding the Fourth Gospel*, 237, and his argument in 205–37.

5. Frey, "Impact of the DSS on NT Interpretation," 3:419–35; also highlighted in

in Hebrew, the first people to work on them were specialists in Hebrew, not NT scholars, whose expertise only lied elsewhere. Nevertheless, there are noteworthy parallels between the NT and DSS.[6]

This collection of more than 900 manuscripts (MSS) from 11 caves at or near Khirbet Qumran, close to the northwest shore of the Dead Sea, was first discovered in late 1946 or early 1947. The discovery prompted numerous explorations of the caves, the Qumran ruins, and other sites (e.g., Masada, Wadi Murabba'at, Naḥal Ḥever).[7] Most of the DSS are leather scrolls (from goats, sheep, cattle). There are about 150 papyri (made from regional aquatic sedge), one MS is on three sheets of copper, another is on an inscribed piece of pottery (Kh.Q. Ostracon 1), and one is an ink-written stone inscription.[8] A few MSS are well-preserved. Many are fragmentary. Over 740 MSS are written in Hebrew (scriptural, pre-Mishnaic, or regional), 130 in Aramaic, and 27 in Greek (mostly from caves 4 and 7).[9]

The DSS date from the end of the third century, BCE, up to the middle first century CE. About 200 MSS are scriptural texts (Law, Prophets, Writings) including some highly regarded books outside (the post-70 CE) Jewish canon (e.g., Tobit, Sirach, Ps 151, 1 En). Only 200 MSS are sectarian, dealing with liturgy (prayers, worship calendar, poetry), pesher commentaries of Scripture (exclusively applied to the group) that are usually specific fulfillments of prophecy, and rules of the community. The rest (over one half) are reworked paraphrases or reinterpretations of scriptural books (Temple Scroll, Jubilees,

---

Anderson, "John and Qumran," 24-28. See also the critical survey of J. A. Fitzmyer, including his refutation of the so-called pierced Messiah (4Q285) favoring "piercing messiah," in his *Dead Sea Scrolls*, 23-27, 101-3; the following works agree with Fitzmyer: Vermes, "Rule of War (4Q285)"; Schiffman, *Reclaiming the Dead Sea Scrolls*, 344-47. On DSS and modern public, see also Stegemann, *Library of Qumran*, 12-33.

6. See, e.g., H.-W. Kuhn, "Jesus," in Schiffman and VanderKam, *Encyclopedia*, 404-8. Sandmel reminds us that "we can sometimes discover exact parallels, some with, and some devoid of significance," "Parallelomania," 7. J. A. Fitzmyer echoes this same concern in his *Impact of the Dead Sea Scrolls*, 90-91.

7. On the discoveries, see Freedman and Kuhlken, *What are the Dead Sea Scrolls?*, 13-22; Magness, *Archaeology*, 25-31; VanderKam, *Dead Sea Scrolls Today*, 1-46; on survey of explorations 1947-2003, see Vermes, *Complete Dead Sea Scrolls*, 1-12. In 1896, the so-called Damascus Document (CD), later found at Qumran, was discovered among the mss of the Cairo Genizah (synagogue store room), and published by Schechter, *Fragments of a Zadokite Work*, decades before the discovery of the DSS, see Schiffman, *Qumran and Jerusalem*, 16-17.

8. Rendsburg, "Hazon Gabriel Inscription," 107-116.

9. See Brooke, "Dead Sea Scrolls," 2:52-63; Fitzmyer, *Impact of the Dead Sea Scrolls*, 1-14; see also by Fitzmyer, "Languages of Palestine," 2:29-56.

Genesis Apocryphon, Copper Scroll), and documentary texts that relate to business dealings (legal transactions, letters, inventory lists).[10]

Was the community of DSS an Essene group? There are similarities and differences between the Essenes mentioned by Philo (*Good Person* 75-79; *Hypoth.* 11.1-18), Pliny the Elder (*Nat.* 5.15, 73), and Josephus (*J.W.*, 2.119-61), and the DSS sect (DSS: champions of Zadokite priesthood, *no* ties with Jerusalem temple, more insular and reclusive), nevertheless, the DSS sect more nearly resembles the Essenes than any other group.[11] What is the connection between the Dead Sea Scrolls sect and nearby Khirbet Qumran? The community that collected, produced, and preserved the DSS were not the first occupants of Qumran (earliest settlement, seventh-sixth century BCE), but there is sufficient archaeological evidence (many different ritual baths, nearby Jewish cemetery, scriptorium) to support the claim that the DSS sect settled there from the second century BCE until its destruction by the Romans with the First Jewish Revolt (68 CE).[12]

Before a survey of parallels, we will note the differences. First, FG did not share the following with the DSS (especially the sectarian portions): concern for ritual purity (4QMMT), the Zadokite priesthood (more Sadducean than Pharisaic),[13] strict dietary laws, complete detachment from Jerusalem temple worship, strict observance of the weekly Sabbath and the annual feasts in a 360-day solar calendar,[14] disciplinary and organizational

10. The above categories are arbitrary, following Brooke here, "Dead Sea Scrolls," 2:56-61; but VanderKam has biblical, apocryphal/pseudepigraphical, others (mostly sectarian) in his *Dead Sea Scrolls Today*, 47-95; Magness has biblical, sectarian, and non-sectarian, in her *Archaeology*, 32-38; Vermes has rules, poetical and liturgical, wisdom, biblical and apocryphal, and miscellaneous, in *Introduction*, 32-93. It is noteworthy, however, that the library associated with Qumran consisted of more pre-sectarian and non-sectarian writings than those identified as sectarian (e.g., Essene, Qumranic).

11. A. Dupont-Sommer provides most of the above texts in his *Essene Writings*, 21-38. See also VanderKam, "Essenes," 2:315-16; and his *Dead Sea Scrolls Today*, 97-126.

12. Magness, *Archaeology*, 13-18, especially 63-72, sectarian occupancy at Qumran, 100-50 BCE (65). "Archaeological and literary evidence indicates that Qumran was inhabited by the same Jewish sect that deposited the scrolls in the nearby caves" (Idem, "Qumran," *NIDB* 4:708).

13. Schiffman has found in 4QMMT, a number of laws that are directly opposed to those of the Pharisees, yet match those of the Sadducees. Perhaps many in this community had been Sadducean priests who were now under the leadership of the Teacher of Righteousness, *Qumran and Jerusalem*, 33-34.

14. For e.g., CD-A VI, 18-20; see Talmon, *Qumran Calendar in Early Judaism*. A. Jaubert made use of Qumran's solar (old Zadokite) calendar, where Passover, fifteenth of Nisan, always fell on a Tuesday evening/Wednesday, to argue that Jesus ate the "Last Supper" on a *Tuesday* evening, was arrested the same night with the various trials taking place in the next few days, and then crucified on Friday, the official fourteenth of Nisan in the Jewish lunar calendar (as in the Synoptic Gospels); Jaubert, *Date of the Last*

rules, reclusive and insular lifestyle,[15] ascetic communalism (1QS), exclusive application of certain biblical prophecies to their *own* particular situation usually by a Teacher of Righteousness (1QpHab VII, 4),[16] a belief in (at least) two distinct messiahs (of Aaron and Israel or Davidic), and the concept of a post-catastrophic utopia—with or without messiahs (1 QM II,7).[17]

Both DSS and FG assume a modified ethical and cosmological dualism, that is also found in *some* of the Jewish Scriptures (e.g., Job 1:6–12; Ps 89:10–11; Prov 4:10–19).[18] It is modified dualism because in both, God is supreme (e.g., 1QS III, 15–17; John 1:1–3).[19] FG and DSS both criticize the temple, but only the DSS sect detaches from it. There are five kinds of

---

Supper; and her "Jésus et le calendrier de Qumrân," 1–30. However, R. E. Brown does not find sufficient reasons for her reconstruction and her assumption that FG's Jesus observed the Qumran calendar; Brown, *New Testament Essays*, 160–67, 207–17; J. P. Meier also agrees with Brown, in his *Marginal Jew*, 1:391–94.

15. K. S. Fuglseth sees FG's community as cultic rather than sectarian, *Johannine Sectarianism in Perspective*. See further discussion in Anderson, "John and Qumran," 23–24. Culpepper's survey of the "school at Qumran" is also helpful, in his *Johannine School*, 145–70.

16. This contemporizing interpretation, known as pesher (Heb. "interpretation, commentary," Eccl. 8:1 MT; Aram. *pišrā'* in Dan 2:4) is related to the more generic *midrāš*, "study." It begins with a biblical quotation (e.g., prophets, Pss), that is followed by, e.g., "the interpretation of it concerns . . ." which actualizes or contemporizes a person or event, e.g., the Teacher of Righteousness, the Wicked Priest, the Day of Atonement. The mode of interpretation may be historical (referring to an event), allegorical (using symbolism), atomistic (analyzing letters of a word), paraphrastic (saying it in other words), or eschatological (referring to the Essene idea of the end-time). See Fitzmyer, *Impact of Dead Sea Scrolls*, 56–57. On pesher and the Teacher of Righteousness, see Schiffman, *Qumran and Jerusalem*, 59, 197–98, 278. For collection of pesher texts, see Horgan, *Pesharim*. A taxonomy of biblical interpretation at Qumran must allow, though, for several kinds other than that of the pesharim alone.

17. The DSS sectarians were convinced that they had begun to live in what they regarded as the end-time. It still had a future for them. They looked forward to its consummation in a war at the end of days, when God and his angels would come down to do battle along with the sons of light against the sons of darkness (1QM; 4QM; cf. 2 Bar 39–40; Rev 19:11–21). see Fitzmyer, *Impact of Dead Sea Scrolls*, 78. "The War Scroll . . . does not mention the messianic figures," (Schiffman, *Qumran and Jerusalem*, 277–78).

18. Frey reexamines the form and function of the cosmic-ethical dualisms in both FG and DSS, in his "Licht aus den Höhlen?" in Frey and Schnelle, *Kontexte*, 117–203. See also J. Leonhardt-Balzer, "Dualism," in Collins and Harlow, *Early Judaism*, 553–56. Charlesworth traces the Qumran dualism to a specific form of Zoroastrianism, labeled Zurvanism (88–89) in "Critical Comparison," of his *John and Dead Sea Scrolls*, 76–106.

19. See Brown, *Gospel according to John*, 1:lxii; Bauckham, however, observes that, e.g., the contexts of "the Spirit of truth" discourses (John 14:17; 16:13) in contrast to Qumran, are *not* dualistic ("Qumran Community," in Porter and Evans, *Scrolls and the Scriptures*, 113–14. E. E. Popkes observes that both sets of "dualities" are divinely determined, in his "About the Differing Approach," 3:302–4.

scriptural interpretation at Qumran: legal, exhortation, narrative, poetic, and prophetic.[20] We also can find these different scriptural interpretations in FG.

Comparisons will cover, e.g., creation, the work of God, ethical dualism, various topics, and the different kinds of scriptural interpretation.

A. The Fourth Gospel	Dead Sea Scrolls
Creation, the work of God	
"In the beginning was the Word and the Word was with God and the Word was God. He was in the beginning with God. All things came into being through him, and without him not one thing came into being. What has come into being in him was life, and the life was the light of all people. The light shines in the darkness and the darkness did not overcome it," John 1:1–5,10a; cf. Gen 1–2.	"From the God of knowledge comes all there is and all there shall be. Before things were, he determined all their design. And when they were come into being, at their appointed time, they will fulfill all their works according to his glorious design, without changing anything." 1QS III, 15–16; in *DSS:SE*, 1:74. "All things are accomplished by his knowledge; he establishes all things by his plan and without him nothing is done." XI, 11; "without his goodwill nothing is done," line 17. (AT)
Ethical dualism	
The Spirit of Truth (14:17; 15:26; 16:13)	Spirit of Truth (1QS III, 18–19; IV, 21–23)
the Holy Spirit (14:26; 20:22)	the Spirit of holiness (IV, 21) "your holy spirit" 4Q504, frags. 1–2, V, 15)
sons of light (12:36)	sons of light (1QS III, 13, 24, 25)
eternal life (3:15, 16, 36; 5:24, passim)	in perpetual life (IV, 7)
the light of life (8:12)	in the light of life (III, 7) in *DSS:SE*, 1:74
and he who walks in the darkness (12:35)	they walk in the ways of darkness (III, 21)
he will not walk in the darkness (8:12)	to walk in all the ways of darkness (IV, 11)

---

20. From G. J. Brooke, "Biblical Interpretation," in Charlesworth, *Bible and the Dead Sea Scrolls*, 1:304–14. We include Brooke's outline in our tbl. 5. A. p. 78. See also Fishbane, "Use, Authority and Interpretation," 339–77; Mburu, *Qumran and Johannine Language*; and the review in Anderson, "John and Qumran," 37–38.

V. THE DEAD SEA SCROLLS

A. The Fourth Gospel	Dead Sea Scrolls
the wrath of God (3:36)	furious wrath of God's vengeance (IV, 12)
the eyes of the blind (9:32; 10:21; 11:37)	blindness of eyes (IV, 11)
full of grace/fullness of grace (1:14, 16)	the fullness of grace/his grace (IV, 4, 5)
the works of God (6:28; 9:3)	the works of God (IV, 4; CD II, 14–15)
their works (of men) were evil (3:19)	works of abomination/of a man (1QS IV, 10, 20)
human flesh cannot do what the Spirit of God can accomplish (1:13; 3:6; 6:63)	(from Charlesworth, *John and the Dead Sea Scrolls*, 101–2) "your servant is a spirit of flesh . . . you have spread your Holy Spirit" (1QH^a IV, 25–26 in *DSS:SE*, 1:149); God will judge the angel of darkness (1QS IV, 12–15, 18–20)
God will judge the ruler of this world (12:31; 16:11)	

Knowledge of truth

Those who believe will "know the truth" (8:32); the "Spirit of truth" will guide believers "into all truth" (16:13). Jesus is the truth (14:6) and characterized by truth (1:14, 17); the continuation of his work after his death is carried out by the Spirit of truth (14:17; 26); Mburu, *Qumran and Johannine Language*, 184.	The Instructor shall lead the faithful "with knowledge and in this way teach them the mysteries of wonder and of truth in the midst of the men in the community so that they walk perfectly one with another in all that has been revealed to them" 1QS IX, 18–19 (cf. I, 5; V, 3; VIII, 2, 9; 1QHab VII, 11–13).

The works of God

"The works of God," a phrase that a crowd of Judeans use when they ask Jesus how they must conduct themselves to do "the works of God," and Jesus answers, "This is the work of God that you believe in him whom He has sent" (John 6:28–29).	The demands of God: "And now, sons, hear me; I shall open your eyes to see and discern the works [of God], so that you may choose what is pleasing to Him and reject what He hates, so as to walk blameless" CD II, 14–15.

Springs of living water

"Out of his innards shall flow rivers of living water" (John 7:38; cf. Zech 14:8; John 4:10–11).	"But you, my God, you have placed in my mouth . . . a spring of living water [Heb. *meyom ḥayyim*]" 1QH^a XVI, 16 in *DSS:SE*, 1:181.

Eternal life

74 THE CONCEPTUAL WORLDS OF THE FOURTH GOSPEL

A. The Fourth Gospel	Dead Sea Scrolls
The eternal blessing that believers obtain (e.g., John 3:15-16, 36; 4:14; 10:28; cf. 1 John 1:2; 2:25) "eternal life" as the destiny of believers (the reward of "the wise," in Dan 12:2). "Anyone who hears my words . . . has eternal life, and . . . has passed from death to life" John 5:24; cf. 6:58; 10:10.	Promised as "a reward for all who walk in it [i.e., in the spirit of light/truth]: healing, abundance of peace in length of days, fruitful seed with endless blessings, joy forever in life eternal and a crown of glory with a garment of honor in eternal light" (1QS IV, 6-8). "Those who hold fast to him are [destined] for eternal life, and all the glory of Adam will be theirs" (CD III, 20). "He who gives life to the dead of his people," 4Q521 frag 7 +5, II, 6 in *DSS:SE* 2:1046.
The wealth of the temple	
"In the temple he found people selling cattle, sheep, and doves, and money changers seated at their tables . . . Take these things out of here! Stop making my Father's house a marketplace" (*emporion*, John 2:14-16; also vv. 13-22; cf. Mark 11:17, "den of robbers" *lēstēs*; cf. Jer 7:11).	None who have come into the covenant "shall enter the temple [*ha-miqdash*] to light his altar in vain" (Mal 1:10; CD VI, 12-13); "To abstain from wicked wealth [*ma-hōn harisha'*] which defiles, either by promise or by vow and from the wealth of the temple [*be-hōn miqdash*] and from robbing the poor of his people," CD VI, 16. Some Essenes seemed to have retained a connection to the temple (Josephus, *Ant.* 18.19).[21]
The threats of the evil one	
Satan enters Judas to betray Jesus (6:70-71; 13:2, 27); Jesus prays that the disciples be kept from the evil one (17:15); the ruler of this world will be judged (12:31; 16:11)	The angel of darkness misleads the sons of righteousness and opposes the prince of lights (1QS III, 20-IV, 1); God will judge the angel of darkness (IV, 12-15, 18-20)[22]
Messianic expectations	

---

21. The "wealth of the temple" provides a possible context for the business of selling/exchanging in FG (John 2:14-16), but see also: "stealing from the poor" (cf. "den of robbers," Mark 11:17/Jer 7:11). Jesus and his followers also retain a connection to the temple with numerous visits in FG (John 2:13; 5:1; 7:10; 10:22-23; 12:12).

22. On protection from demonic power in DSS relevant to FG (e.g., John 17), see Stuckenbruck, *Myth of Rebellious Angels*, 198-206.

V. THE DEAD SEA SCROLLS

A. The Fourth Gospel	Dead Sea Scrolls
Priests and Levites from Jerusalem question John to learn if he is the Messiah (cf. Ps 18:51; Dan 9:25), Elijah (Mal 3:23), or the Prophet (Deut 18:15), John denies that he is any of them, John 1:19–23. Samaritan woman to Jesus: "'I know that the Messiah is coming (who is called Christ)'" (Gk. *christos*, Heb. *mashiaḥ*, John 1:41). Judean crowd: "'This is really the prophet.' Others said, 'This is the Messiah'" (7:40–41). Some asked: "Has not scripture said that the Messiah is descended from David and comes from Bethlehem?" 7:42.	Only the sons of Aaron will have authority in the community "until the prophet comes and the Messiahs (*mashiaḥ*) of Aaron and Israel." 1QS IX, 7, 11; Deut 18 in 4QTest, 5–8, "until there rises a messiah [*mashiaḥ*] out of Aaron and Israel," CD-B XX, 1 in *DSS:SE*, 1:578; cf. 1Q28a II, 11–15 in *DSS:SE*, 1:103. "Until the messiah of righteousness comes, the branch of David. For to him and his descendants has been given the covenant of kingship of his people for everlasting generations," 4Q252 V, 3–4 in *DSS:SE*,1:504; cf. 4Q285, 5. "And the messenger i[s] the anointed of the spir[it] as Dan[iel] said [about him: *Dan 9:25* "Until an anointed, a prince, it is seven weeks..."* 11QMelch II, 18 in *DSS:SE*, 2:1209.

Love of community members

"This is my commandment that you love one another as I have loved you. No one has greater love than this, to lay down one's life for one's friends." John 15:12–13; cf. 13:34–35; "If the world hates you, be aware that it hated me before it hated you," 15:18. "Holy Father, protect them in your name that you have given me, so that they may be one (Gk. *hen*), as we are one" 17:11, cf. 21, 23.	"... to love [*'ahab*] all the sons of light ... and to hate the sons of darkness" 1QS I, 9–10. "One should reproach one another in truth, in meekness and in compassionate love for one's fellowman." V, 24–25. "For each to love his brother like himself; to strengthen the hand of the poor, the needy and the foreigner," CD-A VI, 20–21. The Rule of the Community is replete with concerns about community [*yaḥad*] cohesiveness and solidarity (e.g., 1QS I, 12,16; II, 24; V, 2; see HT in *DSS:SE*, 1:70, 72, 78).

Faithful Shepherd

"I am the good shepherd. I know my own and my own know me, just as the Father knows me and I know the Father. I lay down my life for the sheep. I have other sheep that do not belong to this fold. I must bring them also ... so there will be one flock, one shepherd," John 10:14–16.	"[You raised up] a faithful shepherd [*rō'eh āmēn*] for them," 1Q34bis frag. 3, II, 8 in *DSS St. Ed.*, 1:147. "[You] established your covenant with David to be like a shepherd [*ke-rō'i*], a prince over your people [*'am*], and sit in your presence on the throne of Israel" 4Q504 frag. 1–2, in *DSS:SE*, 2:1015. IV, 6–8.

A. The Fourth Gospel	Dead Sea Scrolls
	A remnant gathered
"I have other sheep not of this fold. I will bring them also and they will listen to my voice," John 10:16. "To gather into one the dispersed children of God" (11:52).	"He raised up for himself a people called by name [*qiri' shem*], to leave a remnant [*peletah*] for the land," CD-A II, 11 in *DSS:SE*, 1:553. "(Isa 10:21) A remnant [*she'ar*] will return, a remnant of Jacob" 4QpIsa^a frag. 1, I, 22 in *DSS:SE*, 1:312. "Shortly you will raise a survivor among your people, a remnant [*she'ar*] in your inheritance. You will purify them to cleanse them of guilt," 1QH^a XIV, 8 in *DSS:SE*, 1:175. "May you raise us up to be a remnant [*she'ar*] for them," 4Q393, frag. 3, 7 in *DSS:SE*, 2:790; gather into one (*yahad*)," 1QS V, 7 (AT in *DSS:SE*, 1:80).
"I protected them in your name ... they do not belong to the world ... sanctify them in the truth" (John 17:12–17, 23).	
	Expulsion from the community
"For the Jews had already agreed that anyone who confessed Jesus to be the messiah would be put out of the synagogue," John 9:22; 12:42; 16:2; cf. Luke 6:22; Acts 14:19–20; 18:6–7; 19:8–9. See possible grounds for expulsion from the church in 1 John 2:22; 4:2–3; cf. John 17:12.	"Whoever speaks to his fellow with deception or knowingly deceives him, will be punished for six months," 1QS VII, 5; in *DSS:SE*, 1:86–87; cf. VIII, 17–18. Anyone "who breaks a commandment of the Torah of Moses deliberately or by neglect shall be expelled [*shalah*] from the Council of the Community [*yahad*]" VIII, 22–23. Kimelman finds a better precedent for expulsion in DSS than in rabbinic Judaism, see his "Birkat ha-minim," 2:397n59.[23]

---

23. Frey concludes that separation from the synagogue was probably a long process that advanced in different ways in different locations and lasted far into the second century CE and beyond, Frey, *Glory of the Crucified One*, 61. Drawing on materialist evidence (e.g., menorah and Christ symbols), Eric C. Smith shows that boundaries were porous and easily crossed among nonelite groups, in his *Jewish Glass and Christian Stone*.

V. THE DEAD SEA SCROLLS

A. The Fourth Gospel	Dead Sea Scrolls
Scriptural interpretation (from G. J. Brooke)	
(1) Legal interpretation of Sabbath (John 7:16-24), alluding to Gen 17:10-14; Lev 12:3; Num 16:28; 1 Sam 16:7; Ps 91:16 (LXX) to generate new legislation.	(1) Legal interpretation of Sabbath (Deut 5:2), alluding to Deut 15:2; 17:2; 32:47, and Isa 58:13 to generate new legislation, CD X, 14-23.
(2) Exhortatory use of Scripture (Isa 54:13), with allusions to Israel's disobedience in the wilderness, to encourage receptive obedience to God (John 6:43-50).	(2) Exhortatory use of Scripture (Deut 30:1-2) appealing to Moses, the prophets, Israel's history, and David to enjoin the blessings of covenant obedience (4QMMT C, 1-15).
(3) Narrative interpretation of Gen 15:5-6, seen in the expanded discussion echoing Isa 63:16; Sir 44:19-10 of Abraham's true descendants, John 8:39-57.	(3) Narrative interpretation of Gen 14:17-24, seen in the expanded retelling of Abraham's meeting with Melchizedek and the king of Sodom 1QapGen XXII, 12-17 in *DSS:SE* 1:46-48.
(4) Scriptural texts (Isa 6:1, 10; 53:1) are the sources for poetic expressions, John 12:37-41.	(4) Scriptural texts (Isa 52:13—53:12) are the sources for poetic expressions, 1QH^a XII, 22-24 in *DSS:SE*, 1:169.
(5) prophetic interpretations of unfulfilled promises (Isa 40:3) are now taking place, John 1:22-28; see also LXX Ps 33:21 (MT 34:20) and Zech 12:10 in John 19:32-37.	(5) prophetic interpretations of unfulfilled promises (Isa 40:3) are now taking place, 1QS VIII, 13-17; 1QIsa^a; see also Ps 34:20 in 4QPs^a 34, 20 in Abegg, *DSS Bible*, 523 and on Zech 12:10, Abegg, *DSS Bible*, 475.

Samuel Sandmel, writing when only some of the DSS were published, commented on alleged parallels:

> Detailed study is the criterion, and the detailed study ought to respect the context and not be limited to juxtaposing mere excerpts. Two passages may sound the same in splendid isolation from their context, but when seen in context reflect difference rather than similarity.[24]

This concern is noteworthy when we remember the significant differences between FG and DSS. The DSS sectarians are, e.g., more halakic, disciplinary, ascetic, and insular, had different messianic hopes, and are primarily written in Hebrew, not in Greek. FG was more lenient on Torah observance (1:17; 5:1-18, 46), less structured, inclusive in outreach (1:10-12; 3:16-17;

---

24. Sandmel, "Parallelomania," 2.

4:21-24, 10:16; 17:20; 20:21), confessed Jesus as the Messiah,[25] offered admission to all who believe, and was written in Koine Greek.

Shortly before Rabbi Sandmel's comments, Howard Teeple wrote that he had found only three parallels between FG and DSS that were not found in the Jewish scriptures: "sons of light," "Spirit of truth," and the concern for witness to religious truth.[26] Richard Bauckham more recently raised the following concerns, focusing on the light/darkness dualism,

> There is no need to appeal to the Qumran texts in order to demonstrate the Jewishness of the Fourth Gospel's light/darkness imagery. This can be done more convincingly by comparison with other Jewish sources already available long before the discovery of the Dead Sea Scrolls.[27]

"For this reason," Joseph Fitzmyer, SJ, replies "it is necessary to study once again the evidence of the contacts or parallels and not limit them to the 'light/darkness imagery,'" as Bauckham does. Fitzmyer points out that "the dualism is not limited to the opposition of light and darkness, as Bauckham would have the reader believe."[28] Not all of the five points of scriptural interpretation (see our table 5.A, p.77, above), which help to clarify FG's "distinct" scriptural interpretation, are found in the "other Jewish sources available long before the discovery of the Dead Sea Scrolls" (from the Bauckham quote above). It is especially true with regard to "prophetic interpretations of unfulfilled promises" (e.g., John 1:22-28; 19:32-37; 1 QS VIII, 13-17; 1QIsa^a; 4QPs^a 34, 20).

We think it is appropriate at this point to examine briefly FG and the DSS using the seven tests for detecting embedded echoes in the NT, proposed by Richard B. Hays.[29] Because these seven tests deal primarily with

---

25. "Christ" (Gk., *Christos*) occurs 18 times and "Messiah" (*Messias*) twice in FG, but over 500 times in the NT (mostly, *Christos*), whereas "Messiah" or "anointed" (Heb. *mashiaḥ*) occurs only 32 times in the DSS, a much larger collection.

26. H. M. Teeple, "Qumran and FG," *NovT* 4 (1960-1961), 6-25; cited in Orton, *Composition*, 16.

27. Bauckham, "Qumran Community," 115, see also 105-15; and his *Gospel of Glory*, 116-21. Concerning dualisms in FG and DSS, D. E. Aune regards the case for Essene influence on FG and the Odes (J. H. Charlesworth) as astonishingly weak and that of indirect dependence (cf. R. E. Brown; R. Schnackenburg) as a foggy conception, in his "Dualism," *Neotestamentia et Philonica*, 302-3, see also 281-303. These observations are also reported in J. Frey, "Licht aus den Höhlen?" in Frey and Schnelle, *Kontexte*, 132n68, 191-93; Anderson, "John and Qumran," 22-23.

28. Fitzmyer, *Impact of the Dead Sea Scrolls*, 110-111, echoing some of Sandmel's concerns. The challenge with all alleged parallels to FG is to assess them with "sufficient methodological rigor" (Bauckham, "Qumran Community," 106).

29. Our own adaptation for FG and DSS is derived from Hays, *Echoes of Scripture*

echoes (implicit or embedded), and not direct citations, they can be used appropriately here for FG and DSS.

B. Tests for Evaluating Alleged Parallels

1. *Availability.* Was the proposed source of the echo available to the author and/or original readers? The dating of DSS many years before FG pose no chronological problems for positing availability. The DSS date from the end of the third century BCE, up to the mid-first century CE (with most ms. *production* ending *before* the terminus ad quem), many years *before* FG (written late first century CE). Additional support, however, is based on several (somewhat) defensible assumptions: a. The proximity of Jesus and the author of FG (assuming Palestinian origin)[30] to the DSS in Judea. b. If the comments by Philo ("they live in villages," *Prob.* 76), Pliny the Elder (an Essene development south of Engedi, *Nat. Hist.* 5.17.4) and Josephus hold true ("many of them [the Essenes] dwell in every city," *J.W.* 2.124) as, e.g., K. S. Fuglseth contends,[31] contacts (of some sort) with DSS teaching would not be improbable (assuming that the Essenes and DSS community are related). Although, about 80 percent of DSS were written in Hebrew (27 mss. in Greek), and FG was written in Koine Greek, it does not exclude the possibility of FG's "occasional recourse to the Hebrew," and that he was an Aramaic-speaking Judean who "would have had little difficulty either hearing or reading Hebrew with understanding."[32] The discoveries of the Bar Kokhba letters

---

in the Letters of Paul, 29–32. See also Heilig, *Hidden Criticism?*, 35–46. Heilig's concern for proper application of relevant criteria focuses on the use of the Hays criteria to discover counter-imperial subtexts in Paul. Heilig's use of Bayesian probability theory, however, works best "with large and well-circumscribed data sets of various kinds" not with "fragmentary data from two millennia ago," in M. D. Given's review of C. Heilig, *Hidden Criticism? RBL* (Mar 14, 2019). On intentional allusions and embedded echoes, see Köstenberger and Patterson, *Invitation to Biblical Interpretation*, 541–47.

30. When we use "defensible assumptions," we mean that a defense can be made for maintaining certain assumptions, but this defense does not necessarily make these assumptions warranted or undisputed within academic guild. H. M. Teeple, e.g., favored the ideas that FG may have been written by a *gentile* god-fearer, *outside of* Palestine, "Qumran and FG," cited in Orton, *Composition*, 19–20.

31. Fuglseth, *Johannine Sectarianism in Perspective*; and observations by Anderson, "John and Qumran," 23–24.

32. B. G. Schuchard cites here Menken, *Old Testament Quotations*, 205 and Bynum, *Fourth Gospel and the Scriptures*, 171–72, and in his "Form vs Function" in Myers and Schuchard, *Abiding Words*, 35. Schuchard, however, is not convinced that FG made direct use of Hebrew in his biblical citations.

Noteworthy here is E. Tov's study of what Hellenistic Jewish translators preferred as

(132–36 CE), the DSS, and manuscripts found at Masada and nearby wadis (e.g., Naḥal Ḥever) affirm the claim that vernacular (and biblical) Hebrew was used in Roman Judea.[33]

2. *Volume.* This second test has three aspects: a. the degree of explicit repetition of words or syntactical patterns, b. how important was the source text and c. how much the echo was emphasized. For example, "Spirit of truth" is found several times in both FG (14:17; 15:26; 16:13) and DSS (1QS III, 18–19; IV, 21–23) and appears to be an important phrase emphasized in both. Another example is one of a similar syntactical pattern: the prophetic interpretations of unfulfilled promises in FG and DSS (see p. 77).

3. *Recurrence.* How often does FG (here) cite or allude to this same text or phrase? This test is applicable to "Spirit of truth" and the prophetic interpretation of unfulfilled prophecies cited in test 2 (above).

4. *Thematic Coherence.* How well does the alleged echo fit into the line of development that FG is developing? For example, FG personalizes the "Spirit of truth" as a divine agent sent from God to guide the disciples in the right course of thought and action. In DSS, however, it is a force or power within the human members of the group to do good (as opposed to the evil impulse or "spirit of deceit"). So FG's use of the "Spirit of truth" has thematic coherence (intra-textually) and can be seen as a more personalized expression of "Spirit of truth" as a divine agent that is a significant development *beyond* what we find in DSS (intertextually). In FG, "Spirit of truth" is a divine agent from God that is also the source or dispenser of truth. In the DSS it is a positive power from God that resides in the human to know truth. In both it is a positive force sent from God that is the source or dispenser of truth or truthfulness for the benefit of its faithful members. With our second example, different applications of similar texts (e.g., Isa 40:1) can be found in FG and DSS relating to the prophetic interpretation of unfulfilled prophecies.

"Greek equivalents" in their translations of the *Hebrew* Bible, in his *Greek and Hebrew Bible*, 131–52. FG has many of these "Greek equivalents" for Hebrew words found in DSS, as shown in Charlesworth, *John and the Dead Sea Scrolls*, 101–2 (list with Gk. and corresponding Heb., in transliteration). These points might suggest an early ed. of FG composed in Jewish Palestine.

33. See survey in Wise, *Language and Literacy*, 8–13 and his "Bar Kokhba Letters," in Collins and Harlow, *Early Judaism*, 418–21. See also Emerton, "Vernacular Hebrew," 1–23; J. R. Edwards, *Hebrew Gospel*, 166–74; Fitzmyer, "Languages of Palestine" (Latin, Greek, Aramaic, Hebrew), 2:29–56; on the history of biblical and Mishnaic Hebrew, see Segal, *Grammar of Mishnaic Hebrew*, 5–18; Sáenz-Badillos, *History of Hebrew Language*.

5. *Historical Plausibility.* Is it historically plausible that FG would have intended the effect of the echo and that his readers could have understood it? Again we must defer to some of the defensible assumptions of test 1 (above). If FG was written from Palestine and even had contact with the Essenes (or Qumran),[34] and the Essenes inhabited the neighboring towns near Qumran, the echoes would rate high on the probability scale. These assumptions have been defended, but remain disputable claims.

6. *History of interpretation.* Have other readers, both critical and pre-critical, heard the same echoes? In the history of DSS scholarship support from some scholars can be garnered to show the close connection of FG and DSS with regard to similar terms, phrases, and concepts. The descriptions of the Essenes in Philo, Josephus, and Pliny the Elder (assuming a connection to DSS) fill out the picture and provide sufficient precedent for establishing echoes and allusions.

7. *Satisfaction.* To avoid the error of judging or evaluating a text on the basis of its emotional effects on a reader (affective fallacy), this test is expressed with the following questions. With or without clear confirmation from the other criteria listed here, does the proposed reading make sense? Does it illuminate the surrounding discourse? Does it offer a good explanation for the supposed intertextual link? Can we understand FG better with the DSS than without them?

Concerning the intertextuality of DSS and FG, much is presupposed regarding the availability, historical plausibility, and history of interpretation, and (as mentioned at the conclusion of our ch. 1) the creditability is found in the type of data employed, how it is used, and the forcefulness of the stated argumentation. Using some insights from Bayesian reasoning we might ask: based on the prior probability of what we already know about FG and its context, what is the likelihood that FG made use of or was influenced by similar concepts already found in the DSS? How confident are you regarding the influence of DSS on FG?[35]

Although he makes noteworthy connections between DSS and FG, Joseph Fitzmyer, SJ reminds us,

> The Christian message itself, however, has no parallel in those scrolls. There is nothing about Jesus of Nazareth or his story or the interpretation of him, nothing about the Christian

---

34. The position taken in Ashton, *Understanding the Fourth Gospel*, 237, and his argument in 205–37.

35. Heilig, *Hidden Criticism?*, 28. See also our earlier discussion in n29, pp. 78–79.

church, nothing about the vicarious and salvific character of what Jesus accomplished for humanity in his passion, death, and resurrection... For all the light that the Scrolls have shed on the Palestinian Jewish matrix of Christianity and on the ways that early Christians borrowed ideas and phrases in order to formulate their kerygmatic proclamation of the Christian message, there is nothing in the Scrolls that undermines or is detrimental to that message.[36]

Lawrence H. Schiffman writes,

> The proper way to use the scrolls for understanding Christianity is to recognize them as documents illuminating the full spectrum of Jewish groups in the Hellenistic period in Judea.[37]

FInally, Jörg Frey makes the following observation:

> Rediscovery of the common threads binding early Christianity to first-century Judaism, in all its dynamic diversity, is important in theological terms, as well. The message of Jesus and his disciples did not come overnight, and we are bound to understand them within their historical context. We therefore need to realize that the Christian message is essentially linked with the elements of its Jewish mother soil, even in issues like the view of Christ or the Law, where early Christian positions differ markedly from most of the other positions held within contemporary Judaism.[38]

We would add that FG and the DSS both grew in the garden of Jewish mother soil which is part of the vast land of Greco-Roman culture, linguistic modes, and thought. The connection between the two is close (a confluence), but both are influenced differently from other elements in their environment (e.g., Hellenism).[39]

---

36. Fitzmyer, *Dead Sea Scrolls and Christian Origins*, 39–40.
37. Schiffman, *Qumran and Jerusalem*, 36.
38. Jörg Frey, "Impact of the Dead Sea Scrolls," 3:461. Attridge concurs that "The Scrolls do illuminate the Jewish background of the Gospel. They may provide generic examples of the kind of traditions with which the text worked, even if they do not provide the specific stuff of which it was constructed" ("John and DSS," in his *Essays*, 45).
39. Porter writes of "Judaism within Hellenism," noting the spread of Hellenism to the furthest reaches of the Roman empire, in his "Context of Jesus," 2:1461, see also 1441–63.

VI. Rabbinica and Targumim

THE FG BETRAYS SOME acquaintance with rabbinic issues, thought, and methods of argumentation,[1] as well as certain ideas and expressions also found in the Aramaic targums.[2] We have included both in this chapter. Although the rabbinic writings derive mostly from the study house (*beth midrash*) and the Aramaic targums from the liturgy of the synagogue (*beth knesset*), both participate in the same rabbinic interpretative world. Both collections of writings are also diverse (especially the rabbinica) and the dating of the documents range from the first or second centuries CE to the seventh or eighth centuries CE (and later).[3] The challenging problems of dating entire collections (e.g., Mishnah), individual books (m. 'Abot), and specific references (m. 'Abot 3.15) will be addressed later in this one and in subsequent chapters. Determining early traditions in later documents is one of the tasks of the historical methods of criticism.[4]

---

1. See Visotzky, "Rabbi, Rabbinic Interpretation," and "Rabbinic Literature"; Saldarini, "Rabbinic Literature and the NT," 5:602–4; Neusner, *Rabbinic Literature and the New Testament*, 169–90; and his *Rabbinic Judaism*; Sanders, *Jewish Law*. See articles by S. D. Cohen (ch. 6) and I. M. Gafni (ch. 7) in Shanks, *Christianity and Rabbinic Judaism*; Daube, *New Testament and Rabbinic Judaism*; and Steinsaltz, *Reference Guide to the Talmud*. Read with discernment, the following are still helpful resources: Burney, *Aramaic Origin of the Fourth Gospel*; Lightfoot, *Commentary on the New Testament*; Odeberg, *Fourth Gospel*; Schlatter, *Der Evangelist Johannes*; and his *Die Sprache und Heimat des vierten Evangelißten*, esp. 14–144; Smith, *Tannaitic Parallels*; Strack and Billerbeck, *Kommentar zum Neuen Testament*.

2. See Kaufman, "Targums," 5:471–73; Ronning, *Jewish Targums*.

3. See Strack and Stemberger, *Talmud and Midrash*, 1–7, 56–62; Flesher and Chilton, *Targums*, ix–xi, 7–11. Neusner dates the Midrash from the third to the thirteenth centuries CE in his *Rabbinic Literature and the New Testament*, 5, but Mishnah (200 CE) and (Babylonian) Talmud (600 CE), 54; on the dating of other rabbinic works, see Neusner, *Rabbinic Literature*, 3, and his *Midrash Reader*, 9–11. See discussion of pre-70 sages in R. Kalmin, "Rabbis," in Collins and Harlow, *Early Judaism*, 1132–34.

4. On source-, form-, and redaction-critical methods, see Puskas and Robbins, *Introduction*, 77–102. Neusner has applied these methods rigorously to the study of rabbinics, see, e.g., Neusner, *Rabbinic Literature and the New Testament*, 1–17; and his *Rabbinic Traditions about the Pharisees*.

Rabbinica

We begin with the large and diverse collection of rabbinic writings that have a significant number of similarities with FG. Appeals have been made on analogous points of disputation regarding torah observance (e.g., work on Sabbath), the methods of interpretation employed (so-called *Middot* of Hillel), a keen interest in Jewish feasts and customs (John 2:6; 6:4; 10:22; 18:28; 19:31, 40), the Benediction against Heretics (*Birkat ha-minim*) recited in the synagogues involving possible expulsion (John 9:22; 12:42; 16:2),[5] plus various expressions and themes (living water, bread from heaven).

The vast body of **rabbinic writings**, can be broadly divided into *halakah* (*halak*, "walk, behave"),[6] legal discussion mostly in the Mishnah (200 CE) and Talmuds of Israel (400 CE) and Babylon (600 CE), and also *haggadah* ("telling"),[7] expositions of biblical stories and ethical teaching from homilies and maxims, mostly found in the Midrash (100–600 CE, e.g., Gen. Rab., Mek., Sipre). Both Talmuds also contain *haggadah*, with their own biblical stories and legends of the rabbis.

First, we compare similar themes, next, certain topics of legal discussion, then, analogous methods of interpretation.[8]

---

5. Citing as support from rabbinic sources (e.g., y.Ber. 8a; b.Ber. 28b-29a) for the 12th of the 18 Benedictions (the Amidah), see Martyn, *History and Theology*, 56–66; and Horbury, "Benediction of the *Minim*," 19–61 (cautious support). For a negative assessment, e.g., the malediction does *not* clearly include Christians as the *Minim* ("The Nazarenes" was added later) *nor* is "expulsion from the synagogue" mentioned here, even if it was legislation ascribed to "Samuel the Small" at Yavneh, we do not know how influential or binding it was in Palestine and the diaspora, see Kimelman, "*Birkat ha-minim*," 2:226-44; and Katz, "Issues in the Separation," 43–76; Charlesworth, *Jesus as Mirrored in John*, 43–45.

6. Koehler et al., *Hebrew and Aramaic Lexicon*, 246–47. In rabbinica *Halakah* is "practice, adopted opinion," and especially "traditional interpretation of Torah," M. Jastrow, *Dictionary*, 353. On "walk" as the ethical metaphor for behavior: "The life as a journey metaphor is so taken for granted in the Judeo-Christian tradition that we instantly understand God as a guide, and that death [as departure] hangs over us throughout" (Lakoff and Turner, *More than Cool Reason*, 10).

7. "Telling, communication," and especially in rabbinica "homiletic popular lecture" distinguished from "legal interpretation" (*halakah*), Jastrow, *Dictionary*, 330. For a selection of early rabbinic stories, see Martin, *Narrative Parallels*, 81–129.

8. Citations are from the following works: for Mishnah, Danby, *Mishnah*; and Neusner, *Mishnah*; for b. Epstein, *Babylonian Talmud*; for b. and y., we Neusner, *Babylonian and Jerusalem Collection*; for Midr., Freedman and Simon, *Midrash Rabbah*; Neusner, *Genesis Rabbah*; and Townsend, *Midrash Tanḥuma*; for t., Neusner, *Tosefta*; and for Mek., Lauterbach, *Mekhilta de-Rabbi de-Ishmael*; and Nelson, *Mekhilta de-Rabbi Shimon bar Yoḥai*. The former is identified by the trans. Lauterbach. Our abbreviations are from Collins, *SBL Handbook*, 8.3.8–10.

VI. RABBINICA AND TARGUMIM

A. The Fourth Gospel	Rabbinic Literature

Creation

1:1–3, The preexistent (primordial) Logos, with God from the beginning 1:3, "All things came into being through him"	"Seven things were created before the world was created: the Torah, repentance, paradise . . . " (Prov 8:22 cited), b. Pesaḥ 54a; cf. "Torah and throne of glory," Gen. Rab. 1:4. "Before the world was made the Torah was written and lay in the bosom of God," 'Abot R. Nat. 31; cf. "Torah preceded the creation of the world," Gen. Rab. 8.2 (Gen 1:26); cf. m. 'Abot 6:10 (Prov 8:12). "There is no beginning but Torah (Prov 8:22) . . . In the beginning (i.e., in Torah) God created." Midr. Tanḥ. Ber. 1:5, Gen 1:1–2, Townsend, *Midr. Tanḥ*, V, 1:4; cf. Gen. R. Ber. 5.5; "to them was given the precious instrument [Torah] by which the world was created," m. 'Abot. 3:15; "By the word of the Lord the heavens were made" (Ps 33:6) in Mek. Shirata 10 (Exod 15:17–21) in Lauterbach, *Mekhilta*, 218–19; Shirata 36:7A-B in Nelson, *Mekhilta*, 156; cf. "God created the world for the sake of Torah," Gen. Rab. 1.4 (Prov 3:19) and 1:10 (Exod 20:2).

Children of God

1:12, "But to all who received him . . . he gave power to become children of God." 11:52, "to gather into one the dispersed children of God."	"Beloved are Israel, for they were called children of God; still greater was the love in that it was made known to them that they were called children of God" (Deut 14:1), m. 'Abot. 3:15; "But when you stood at Mount Sinai and accepted my Torah, you were called MY PEOPLE (Ps 50:7)," Midr. Tanḥ. Exod. II Wa-'era 2.1 (Exod 6:2–3), Pt. 1 in Townsend, *Midrash Tanḥuma*, 2:27; cf. Midr. Tanḥ. Exod. V Yitro 5.15 (Exod 20:2–3) in Townsend, *Midrash Tanḥuma*, 2:108.

A. The Fourth Gospel	Rabbinic Literature

Life

1:14, "in him was life and the life was the light of people."

5:39, "Scriptures that have eternal life bear witness to Christ who gives life."

"As oil is life for the world, so also are the words of Torah life for the world," Deut. Rab. 7:3; cf. b.'Abot Baraita.

"The Torah gives to them that practice it, life in this age and in the age to come," m. 'Abot 6.7; "Torah is the fountain of life," Pesiq. Rab. 36:1.

Light

1:4, Logos, "the light of all people."

1:5, "The light shines in the darkness."

9:5, "I am the light of the world" (cf. 12:46).

Borgen, "Logos Was the True Light," 107–22.

"As oil is light for the world, so also are the words of Torah light for the world," Deut. Rab. 7.3; cf. Ex. Rab. 36:3 citing Ps 119:105; Sipre Num 6:25; "Whoever makes use of the light of the Torah will revive (after death)," b. Ketub. 111a, b. "Thy words give light," Gen. Rab. 3:1–2 (Ps 119:130). Baba ben Buta said to Herod the Great, who had put to death many rabbis: "you have quenched the light of the world," b. B. Bat. 4a.

Living Water

4:14, "The water that I will give will become in them a spring of water gushing up to eternal life."

7:38, "and let the one who believes in me drink ... out of his belly shall flow rivers of living water."

"As water is life for the world, so also the Torah is life for the world, Sipre Deut 11:22; cf. Midr. Ps 1:18 (Prov 4:22); "The one who learns from the Torah will be like a never-failing stream and a river that flows ever mightily," m. 'Abot 6:1. He who receives his wisdom from the study of the Torah is compared to a tree that spreads out his roots by the river, m. 'Abot 3:18 (cf. Jer 17:8).

Bread from heaven

6:32–34, (Jesus) the true bread from heaven that gives life.

Mek. Vayassa 39:1, 4A-F (Exod 16:4) the Lord brought "bread down from heaven" for his "beloved Israel." Cf. Mek. Vayassa 3 (Exod 16:4–10) in Lauterbach, *Mekhilta*, 234. "If you busy yourself with the words of the Torah, God will provide you with sustenance of this sort [Manna], Mek. Vayassa 9 (Exod 16:28–36) in Lauterbach, *Mekhilta*, 249.

VI. RABBINICA AND TARGUMIM

A. The Fourth Gospel	Rabbinic Literature
6:35, Jesus said to them, "I am the bread of life. Whoever comes to me will never be hungry, and whoever believes in me will never be thirsty."	[Manna] is "Like a word of Aggadah that tugs at man's heart," Mek. Vayassa 42:1, 7D (Exod 16:31). Exod. Rab. 25:8 compares the study of Torah to eating bread and drinking water (Isa 33:16; Ps 136:25); "If there is no meal there is no study of the Torah, if there is no study of the Torah there is no meal," m. 'Abot 3.18. See also Gen Rab. 43:6; Num Rab. 8:9; 13:15-16 (citing Prov 9:5); "you will find it [manna] in the age to come" Mek. Vayassa 41:1, 17B-G (Exod 16:25); also in Mek. Vayassa 6 (Exod 16:16-27) in Lauterbach, *Mekhilta*, 244. See Borgen, *Bread from Heaven*, 55-57, 155-56, where John 6 is viewed as a homiletic midrash.

Commissioned Agent

13:16, "A servant is not great than his master; nor is he who is sent greater than he who sent him" (cf. Matt. 10:24). John 13:20, "He who receives any one whom I send receives me; and he receives me receives him who sent me" (cf. 12:44-45; Luke 10:16). 4:34, "My food is to do the will of him who sent me and to complete his work" (cf. 5:30; 6:39).	"The sender is greater than the sent" (ha-mashalak gedal men ha-mashalak, Gen. Rab. 78,1. "Because a man's agent is like to himself," m. Ber. 5:5; cf. 1 Sam 8:7. The agent representing the householder, b. Qidd. 41a. A man can appoint a messenger for something, b. Naz. 12b. See "John and Hellenism," in Borgen, *Gospel of John*, 82-84.

What the rabbis applied to the Torah, FG applied to Jesus the Word. Although both FG and the rabbis were influenced by older traditions (e.g., wisdom, Prov 8; Job 28), they often share a common interpretation of them. More parallels will be cited later in this chapter with our comparisons of FG and the Targumim.

Some of the discourses of "the Jews" with Jesus betray some familiarity with rabbinic language and argumentation. References to Moses and his relationship to the law (Gk. *nomos*, John 1:17; 7:19, 23) are characteristic of rabbinic language: "blessed be God who gave Torah to Israel through Moses our teacher," (Sipre on Deut 31:4). The Pharisaic disdain for the unlearned crowd (John 7:49) parallels the rabbinic contempt for the "people of the land," (*am ha-eretz*, m. 'Abot 2:6; 3:15; b. Ketub. 111a). The appeal of Nicodemus to the chief priests and Pharisees (John 7:51) also recalls the rabbinic principle: "Flesh and blood if it hears the words of man judges him, if it does not hear it cannot establish his judgment" (Exod. Rab. 21:3).[9] The reasoning in John 9:16 reflects rabbinic argumentation: "Does the All-merciful perform a miracle for liars?" (b. Bera. 58a). Finally, it is argued that the ancients had miracles done for them because they hallowed the Divine Name (b. Bera. 20a [V.3A, E]). If similar thinking was prevalent in the first century, the signs that Jesus performed might have raised concerns that perhaps Jesus was a pious man of God.

Important also are the rabbinic methods of interpretation that FG appears to employ. The three that we will discuss are the Middoth of Hillel ("Measurements of Hillel," seven ascribed to him), although refined later by Akiba (ca. second century CE), they may reflect earlier modes of argumentation (cf. m. 'Abot. 1:5; Aristotle, *Rhet.* 2.23.4-5, 1397b; Seneca the Elder, *Disputes*).[10]

The first method is called *qal vahomer* "light and heavy." It is an inference from a minor to a major point: what can be said of *a* can even more be said of *b* (which is greater than *a*). In John 7:23, this method appears to be used:

> minor *a* "If on the sabbath a man receives circumcision so that the law of Moses may not be broken
>
> major *b* are you angry with me because I healed a man's whole body on the sabbath?"

In this argument the healing of a man's entire body is viewed as a greater deed than the act of circumcising a small part of a man's body (permitted on the Sabbath, m. Ned. 3:11; Šabb. 18:3; 19:1-2; along with, e.g., certain feasts, temple observance). Jesus, however, has done even a greater or more praiseworthy deed on the Sabbath (that certainly should be permitted on the Sabbath). A more stringent case for Sabbath observance was made in a similar mode of argumentation: "If circumcision which affects one of our 248 members, repels the sabbath, how much more must the body repel the sabbath" (b. Yoma 85 a-b; cf. t. Šabb. 15:16 [134]).

Another example of the use of *qal vahomer* appears to be found in John 10:35-36.

---

9. On Pharisees and their relationship to later Rabbinic Judaism, see R. Deines, "Pharisees," in Collins and Harlow, *Early Judaism*, 1061-63; see also Neusner, *Rabbinic Traditions about the Pharisees*.

10. See the history of rabbinic hermeneutics, in Strack and Stemberger, *Talmud and Midrash*, 15-30. On caution regarding first century CE dating, in Visotzky, "Rabbi, Rabbinic Interpretation," 4:719; on some first-century gleanings (citing similar interpretations in DSS), see Longenecker, *Biblical Exegesis*, 19-24; Keener, *John*, 1:187, 717; and E. Earle Ellis, "Biblical Interpretation," in Mulder and Sysling, *Mikra*, 699-702.

VI. RABBINICA AND TARGUMIM

    minor *a* "If those to whom the word of God came were called 'gods'...."

    major *b* how can you say that the one whom the Father has ... sent is blaspheming because I said, 'I am God.'"

In FG, Jesus has argued that if Scripture has referred to some humans as gods (e.g., Moses, Exod 7:1, and certain judges, Ps 82:2-4,6-7),[11] why should they oppose him, who is greater than Moses and judge par excellence (Ps 82), for calling himself God's son?[12]

Qal vahomer is also apparent in John 11:50 (cf. 18:14). Here, Caiaphas the high priest argues for the execution of Jesus, the messianic leader, in order to prevent Judea from following him and thereby arousing the wrath of Rome against his people for their divided allegiance.

    minor *a* "better for one man to die for the nation than to have

    major *b* the whole nation destroyed."

For OT examples, see "let us not perish for this man's life," in Jonah 1:14-15 (cf. 2 Sam 20:21), and parallel passages in the Midrash: "It is better that this man should die, than that everyone be punished on his account," Gen. Rab. 94:9B (Neusner, *Genesis Rabbah*, 3:322); cf. Gen. Rab. 91:10 (Freedman and Simon, *Midrash Rabbah*, 2:846); Midr. Sam. 32.3 (71a); Midr. Qoh. 9.18 (46a).[13]

Recalling our first two examples of *qal vahomer*, if FG was aware of the Torah motifs (cited in our table A., pp. 85-87), the rationale for its Christology might be: if all of these images (e.g., light, life, bread from heaven, living water) can be compared with the Torah (and of Wisdom), *how much more* can they be compared to Christ who is *greater than* the Torah (as the source of all wisdom).

A second rabbinic method is *kayotze' bo memaqom 'aḥer* "equality from one to the other." What can be said of *a* can also be said of *b* because *a* equals *b*. This method seems to be employed in FG's argument for Christ's divine authority: whatever can be said of God can also be said of Jesus (because he also is divine). See John 5:26-27.

    a "For just as the Father has life in himself

---

11. On the exalted view of Moses as prophet and king in the midrashim, see Meeks, *Prophet-King*, 176-215.

12. Keener, *John*, 1:828.

13. Strack and Billerbeck, *Kommentar zum Neuen Testament*, 2:545-46; E. Haenchen, *John 2*, 2:79; Keener, *John*, 2:855n183.

> *b* so he has granted the Son also to have life in himself and he has given him authority to execute judgment because he is the Son of Man."

The above argument is presented in the context of another Sabbath controversy with the Jews. In rabbinic thought it was understood that God does two things on the Sabbath: (1) gives life (e.g., women give birth), and (2) judges (people die on the Sabbath). What the Father does on the Sabbath is also granted to Jesus, FG argues, because he is the Son of Man (5:27; cf. v. 18). This method also seems to be employed in some of the signs that Jesus performed. For example, Jesus walks on the sea (John 6:19) because God walks on the sea (e.g., Job 9:8; 38:16; Ps 77:19). The signs that God does are also granted to Jesus because they are, with regard to divine power, equals.

The third rabbinic method is *gezeira sheva* "similar way" or analogy of expression: what can be said of *a* can also be said of *b*, but *b* is subordinate to *a*. This method appears to be used by FG to define the relationship of the disciples to Jesus. See John 20:21.

> *a* "As the Father has sent me
>
> *b* so I send you."

Jesus is commissioned and the disciples are commissioned. Jesus, however, is commissioned by the Father, and the disciples are commissioned by Jesus, because they are his subordinates. In the same manner, see: (*a*) "because I live, (*b*) you also will live," (John 14:19). A similar state of life everlasting is granted to his disciples by Jesus who initiates and inaugurates for them life everlasting.[14]

From these examples it has therefore been proposed that FG appears to have some acquaintance with rabbinic thought and argumentation. Nevertheless, one can never be certain regarding how many of the rabbinic parallels could actually predate or are even contemporary with FG and the other gospels. The historical and literary contexts of FG and the later, more diverse collection of rabbinic writings need to be discerned, especially for the differences.

---

14. In John 17:6, 26, Jesus describes his mission as revealing the Father's name to the disciples—the same name which the Father also gave to the Son (John 17:11–12), see discussion in Ronning, *Jewish Targums and John's Logos Theology*, 70–83.

Targumim

Targum (sing.), **Targumim** (pl.) constitute the largest body of Scripture translation and interpretation from antiquity.[15] In rabbinic Hebrew the verb *tirgēm* is used for translating the Bible from Hebrew into another language, usually Middle Aramaic, but sometimes also Hellenistic Greek (y. Qidd. 59a; y. Meg. 71c; m. Meg 2:1; b. Šabb. 115a). It normally denotes the Aramaic version of the originally oral renderings of the Hebrew Bible lections read in the synagogue.[16] Middle Aramaic (200 BCE–200 CE) is found in the DSS (1QapGen ar; 11QtgJob), sections of Daniel, words and phrases in the NT and Josephus, and the letters of Simon Bar Kokhba (Kosiba). It was the first language of Jesus, and the common dialect of Palestine (200 BCE–200 CE).[17] Targumim are extant for all the Hebrew Bible, except Ezra, Nehemiah, and Daniel. Although the Aramaic Targums belong more to synagogue liturgy, they participate in the same interpretative world as the rabbinic halakhic and haggadic writings.

It has been argued that FG's use of *logos* may parallel a divine name translation device in the Targums. The Aramaic terms, *mēmra*, *mēmer* "word," are often substituted for "God."[18] "*Memra* of the Lord" is not only a substitution for the tetragrammaton (YHWH), but implies a more thorough theology

---

15. Flesher and Chilton, *Targums*, ix. Our citations are from McNamara et al., *Aramaic Bible*.

16. The Mishnah (*m. Meg.* iv. 4–6, 10) prescribes the proper conduct of the translator during the Scripture reading portion of the service. See Alexander, "Targum, Targumim," 6:320–21. On the Jewish lectionary for the backdrop of FG, see Guilding, *Jewish Worship*, 1–44. The dating of any established lectionary before 200 CE, however, is problematic, see Aageson, "Lectionary," 4:270–71.

17. See Guinan, "Aramaic, Aramaism," 1:228–31; Fitzmyer, *Semitic Background*, 2:29–84 (on the NT and Aramaic); Black finds numerous Aramaic features (grammatical, poetic, and other linguistic data) in his *Aramaic Approach to Gospels and Acts*.

18. See *Mēmer* in Jastrow, *Dictionary of the Targumim*), 775. The Aramaic מֵימְרָא, i.e., *mēmra* is etymologically related to the Hebrew (*'imrah*, "word," e.g., Ps 105:19, "the word of the Lord" or "the Lord" tested Joseph in Egypt). On *Mēmra* as a metonymy for "Lord," see McNamara, *Targum and Testament Revisited*, 439–43. Paul Billerbeck observes: "Sometimes it is God Himself, sometimes it is His Memra who intervenes in the earthly events" (our trans. of "Bald ist es Gott selbst, bald ist es sein Memra, die in das irdische Geschehen eingreifen" in his "Exkurs," in Strack and Billerbeck, *Kommentar zum Neuen Testament*, 2:303).

Mēmra (with cognates, e.g., *Mēmer*) occurs 314 times in Tg. Neof. alone, see Ronning, *Jewish Targums*, 37; see also Boyarin, who argues for a common Jewish midrashic tradition behind FG and the targumim regarding Logos/Memra, in his *Border Lines*, 106–7, 116–19, 125–27.

of the name of God,[19] especially with the more recently discovered Targum Neofiti (1949, Vatican Library), dated earlier from Palestine.[20]

In our comparisons below (e.g., Divine Presence), we will note a combination of the targumic Word with *Shekinah*, glory (*Yegara*), or the glory of the *Shekinah* (cf. John 1:14).[21] Related to *Mēmra* or *Mēmer* (e.g., as Divine Creator) is *Dibbera* (fem. of Hebrew *dabar*, "word,"[22] e.g., used in Seeing God, Descent of the Spirit). Although some of our comparisons may be merely formal or incidental, others may reflect similar language and expressions originating from a common milieu.[23] We provide them for the benefit of the reader to discern (using some of the criteria of evaluation that we have provided, earlier).

B. The Fourth Gospel	Aramaic Targumim
With God in the beginning	
1:1, "In the beginning was the Word and the Word was with God and the Word was God." 8:58, "Before Abraham came into being, I am."	"From the beginning with wisdom the Word (*Mēmra*) of the Lord created and perfected the heavens and the earth" Tg. Neof. Gen 1:1; "The Word (*Mēmra*) of the Lord" revealed as the "I am He who is," Tg. Ps.-J. Deut 32:39.
Divine Creator	
1:3, "All things came into being through him and without him not one thing came into being."	"And the Word (*Mēmra*) of the Lord said to Moses: 'The One who said to the world in the beginning: come into being! And it came into being,'" Frag. Tg. Exod 3:14; "I am the Lord, who made all things; I stretched out the heavens by my Word (*Mēmer*)," Tg. Isa 44:24; cf. Tg. Isa. 45:12 and 48:13.

---

19. Levey, *Targum of Ezekiel*, 15; Levine, *Aramaic Version of the Bible*, 59–60; Frey, "Between Torah and Stoa," 216–17; Hayward, *Divine Name*.

20. On the discovery of Targum Neofiti, see McNamara, *Targum and Testament*, 3–4.

21. Shekinah שְׁכִינָה is an Aramaic word based on the Hebrew שָׁכַן Shakan "dwell," Jastrow, *Dictionary of the Targumim*, 1575. On the glory of the shekinah, see Ronning, *Jewish Targums*, 50–69; his "Targum of Isaiah and Johannine Literature," 247–78; and Chilton, *Glory of Israel*, 56–77 (Isaiah Targum); on *Yegara*, see Jastrow, *Dictionary of the Targumim*, 592–93.

22. Koehler et al., *Hebrew and Aramaic Lexicon*, 211–12.

23. Some of the above parallels were derived from Evans, *Word of Glory*, 114–23; Boyarin, *Border Lines*, 116–19, 125–27; and especially Ronning, *Jewish Targums*, 19, 35, 201, 209, 231, 239, 268.

B. The Fourth Gospel	Aramaic Targumim

The Life and The Way

1:4, "In him was life."	"Better is Torah for the one who attends to it than the fruits of the tree of life: Torah which the Word (*Memra*) of the Lord has prepared in order that it may be kept, so that man may live and walk by the paths of the way of the life of the world to come," Tg. Ps.-J. Gen 3:24; "Torah is a tree of life," Tg. Neof. Gen 3:24.
1:10b, "I came that they may have life, and have it more abundantly."	
14:6, "I am the way, the truth, the life; no one comes to the Father except through me."	

Light

1:4, Logos, "the light of all people"	"And the Word (*Mēmer*) of the Lord said 'Let there be light.' And there was light in his Word (*Mēmer*)," Frag. Tg. Gen 1:3; Neof. Gen 1:3. There was void and darkness "And the Word (*Mēmer*) of the Lord was light and it shone," Tg. Neof. Exod 12:42. "And God said 'Let there be light to lighten the world,'" Tg. Ps.-J. Gen 1:3.
1:5, "The light shines in the darkness."	
1:9, "The true light which lightens everyone."	
9:5, "I am the light of the world" (cf. 12:46).	

Belief

1:12, "But to all who received him, who believed in his name, he gave authority to become children of God."	"They believed in the name of the Word (*Mēmer*) of the Lord," Frag. Tg. Exod. 14:31 and Tg. Ps.-J. Exod. 14:31. "They believed on the name of the Word," Tg. Ps 106:12.
5:24, "Anyone who hears my word and believes him who sent me has eternal life" (cf. 1 John 5:13)	
20:29b, "Blessed are those who have not seen and yet have come to believe."	"Blessed shall be the man who trusts in the name of the Word (*Mēmer*) of the Lord," Frag. Targ. Gen 40:23.

B. The Fourth Gospel	Aramaic Targumim
	Divine presence
1:14, "And the Word became flesh and lived (*skēnoō* 'tabernacled') among us and we have seen his glory (*doxa*) full of grace (*charis*) and truth" (cf. *skēnē*, *skēnoō* Rev 21:3).[24]	"The Word (*Mēmer*) of the Lord our God has shown us the Shekinah of his glory (*Yegara*)," Tg. Ps.-J. Deut. 5:24; cf. Tg. Isa 6:1–8; "You are he, the glory (*Yegara*) of whose Shekinah is in the midst of this people," Tg. Neof. Onq. Num 14:14; "And the Lord made his Shekinah pass by before his face, and he proclaimed, 'the Lord . . . full of kindness (*ḥesed*) and truth,'" Tg. Ps.-J. Exod. 34:5–6; cf. "Does not his Word (*Mēmra*) endure truth and virtue," Tg. Isa. 48:1. "And my Word (*Mēmer*) will be to her [temple] . . . like a wall of fire encircling her round about, and I will make my Shekinah dwell in her midst in honor," Tg. Zech 2:5. "In every place where you remember my name in prayer, I will be revealed in my Word (*Mēmer*) upon you and I will bless you," Tg. Neof. Exod. 20:24. "At the door of the tent of ordinance, we I shall appoint my Word (*Mēmer*) to meet you [and] to speak with you. And there I shall appoint my Word [to meet] with the sons of Israel . . . for my glory (*Yegara*) . . . and my Shekinah shall dwell in the midst of the sons of Israel, and I shall be their God", Tg. Ps.-J. Exod. 29:42b–45; cf. Tg. Zech. 2:10. "My Word (*Mēmer*) will not leave you," Tg. Neof. Gen. 28:15. "My Word (*Mēmra*) will be at your assistance," Tg. Ps.-J. Gen 26:3, 24, 28.
2:19–21, Jesus speaking of his body (*sōma*) as "this temple" (*houtos ho naos*).	
14:18, "I will not leave you orphaned; I am coming to you."	

---

24. Burney, *Aramaic Origin of the Fourth Gospel*, 38–39. For John 1:14 as a unifying theme of FG, see John L. Ronning's article online: https://www.academia.edu/7921022/When_YHWH_Became_Flesh_and_Dwelt_Among_Us_John_1_14_as_Programmatic_for_Johns_Gospel).

| B. The Fourth Gospel | Aramaic Targumim |

Seeing God

1:18, "No one has ever seen God. It is God's only Son who is close to the Father's bosom has made him known (*exēgeomai*)."[25]	"Then he said, 'You will not be able to see the face of my Shekinah; for no man may see me and live.' And the Lord said, 'Here is a place prepared before me . . . when my glory (*Yegara*) passes by, I will . . . shield you with my Word (*Mēmer*) until I have passed by. Then I will remove the word (*Dibbera*) of my glory, and you will perceive that which is behind me, but what is in front of me will not be seen,'" Tg. Onq. Exod. 33:20–23.

Descent of the Spirit

1:32–33, John saw the Spirit descend and remain on Jesus.	"When Moses entered the tent of meeting to speak with him (God), he heard the voice of the Spirit who was speaking with him, *as he descended from the heaven of heavens* over the mercy seat which was upon the ark of the testimony, from between the two cherubim. And from there was the Word (*Dibbera*) speaking with him," Tg. Ps.-J. Num 7:89. On ascent/descent and vision of God, see "John and Hellenism," in Borgen, *Gospel of John*, 84–86.

New temple of God

2:13–21, cleansing the temple of the money changers ("stop making my Father's house a marketplace!" v. 16b), Jesus announcing the temple of his body to be destroyed but raised up in three days (vv. 19, 21). 4:20–24, "the hour is coming when you will worship the Father neither on this mountain nor in Jerusalem . . . the hour is coming . . . when true worshipers will worship the Father in spirit and truth" vv. 21, 23.	"I will make my Shekinah dwell there, in the midst of the children of Israel forever; and the children of Israel shall no longer defile my Holy Name . . . by placing their threshold beside the threshold of my Holy Temple . . . with only a wall of my Holy Temple between my Word (*Mēmer*) and them," Tg. Ezek 43:7b–8. "And he will rebuild the sanctuary which was profaned by our sins," Tg. Isa. 53:5.

---

25. *Memra* represents "an exegesis of the divine name" (cf. John 1:18; 17:6, 26); Chester, *Divine Revelation and Divine Titles*, 115.

B. The Fourth Gospel	Aramaic Targumim
I am the Messiah	
4:25–26, "The woman said to him: 'I know that the Messiah is coming' (who is the Christ) 'when he comes, he will proclaim all things to us.' Jesus said, 'I am he, the one who is speaking to you.'"	"You are witnesses before me," says the LORD, "and my servant the Messiah with whom I am pleased, that you might know and believe before me and understand that I am he. I am he who is from the beginning, even the ages of ages are mine, and there is no God besides me," Tg. Isa. 43:10.
True Witness	
5:32, "There is another who bears witness (*martureō*) of me, and I know that the witness that he bears about me is true (*alēthēs*)."	"May the Word (*Mēmer*) of the Lord be among us as a true and faithful witness," Tg. Jer. 42:5. "Attend to my Word (*Mēmer*) you who pursue truth," Tg. Isa 51:1.
8:14, 16, "My witness (*martyria*) is true ... My judgment (*krisis*) is true (*alēthinos*)"	
I am the Bread of life	
6:35, 48, "I am he, the bread of life"	"And the [Word of the] LORD spoke with Moses, saying '... and in the morning you shall be filled with bread, and you shall *know that I am he*, the LORD your God,'" Tg. Neof. Exod 16:12.
6:41, "I am he, the bread that came down from heaven."	
6:51, "I am he, the living bread that came down from heaven."	
I was before Abraham	
8:58, "Before Abraham came into being, I am."	"I declared to Abraham your father what was about to come, I saved you from Egypt, just as I swore to him between the pieces ... and also from eternity I am He"(Tg. Isa. 43:12–13). "I, even I, by my Mēmra [i.e., Word] decreed a covenant with Abraham your father and exalted him," Tg. Isa 48:15.

B. The Fourth Gospel	Aramaic Targumim

Signs and unbelief

12:37, "Although he had performed so many signs (*semeia*) in their presence, they did not believe in him."

1:11, "He came to what was his own, and his own people did not receive (*paralambanō*) him."

"How long will they not *believe in the name of my Word* (*Tgs. Onq.* and *Ps.-J.*: "believe in my Word"), in spite of all the *signs of my miracles* which I have performed among them?" *Tg. Neof.* Num 14:11. Disobedient Judah, seeking Pharaoh's aid, instead of the Word, to Isaiah, "Remove from before us the Word of the Holy One of Israel," Tg. Isa. 30:11. See M. Becker, "Zeichen," in Frey and Schelle, *Kontexte*, 233–76.

Blood and water

19:34, "One of the soldiers pierced his side with a spear and at once blood and water came out" (cf. 1 John 5:6).

The first time Moses struck the rock, it dripped blood; the second time, abundant water flowed forth, Tg. Ps.-J. Num. 20:11.

Remit and pardon

20:23, "If you forgive the sins of any, they are forgiven them; if you retain the sins of any, they are retained." Cf. Matt 16:19; 18:18; Falk, "Binding and Loosing," 92–100.

The Lord to Cain: "Surely, if you make your work in this world good, you will be remitted and pardoned in the world to come," Tg. Neof. Gen. 4:7. After he kills Abel, Cain to the Lord: "My debts are too numerous to bear, before you there is power to remit and pardon," Tg. Neof. Gen. 4:13.

The purpose of the signs

20:30–31, "Now Jesus did many other signs in the presence of his disciples . . . but these are written so that may come to believe that Jesus is the Messiah, the Son of God, and that through believing you may have life in his name." On the function of "signs" in FG, see Schnackenburg, *St. John*, 1:521–28.

"Thus says the [Word of the] LORD, ' . . . I will do signs and wonders . . . so that you may *know that I am he*, the Lord, whose Word dwells [the glory of whose *Shekinah* dwells] within the land.'" Tg. Neof. Exod 8:20–22. "When the children of Israel saw the signs and wonders which the *Holy One*, blessed be he, had done for them by the shore of the Sea—may his name be blessed forever and ever—they gave glory and praise and exaltation to their God," Tg. Ps.-J. Exod. 15:18.

As stated earlier in our introduction, the following are important factors to consider when making any causal connections: similar contexts, chronological proximity to FG, availability to author and readers, common viewpoints, and verbal/thematic coherence of FG and writings in question.[26] We will briefly reflect on each one.

C. Tests for Evaluating Alleged Parallels

1. **Similar Contexts:** We have seen in previous chapters how Jewish is this Gospel, probably originating in the Palestinian region (geographically), familiar with Jewish feasts and customs (culturally), fluent in the Jewish Septuagint, having some acquaintance with Hebrew and Aramaic, as well as rabbinic forms of argumentation, and images prevalent in the Jewish world. Context, however, extends also to the literary context of meaning (see points 4 and 5, p. 99, below), where intertextuality is most challenging, especially if one is positing a *genetic* relationship in the parallels. Note the following questions. Did the rabbinic writings influence FG? Did the rabbinica and FG have a common source? Or are these rabbinic texts and FG parallel but independent traditions? Did FG have any influence on the rabbinic writings? See footnote 31 of this chapter, p. 99–100, where we mention that the NT or FG may have had only minimal influence on the rabbinica. The questions of a common tradition or parallel but independent traditions raise the fewest problems for us to address.

---

26. We cited earlier (Intro, p. 8n30) the following works that advocate the importance of comparing contexts, determining accessibility, and thematic coherence, not merely "juxtaposing excerpts," see Sandmel, "Parallelomania," 1–13; H. Ringgren, "Qumran and Gnosticism," in Bianchi, *Origins of Gnosticism*, 379–84; C. K. Barrett, "The Theological Vocabulary of the Fourth Gospel and the Gospel of Truth," in Barrett, *Essays on John*; Fitzmyer, *Impact of the Dead Sea Scrolls*, 90–96. See our overview of source criticism in Puskas and Robbins, *Introduction*, 83–85. Smith offers keen insights on the nature and limits of comparative religious studies in *Drudgery Divine*, 46–53.
   On tests for discerning scriptural echoes, see Hays, *Echoes in the Letters of Paul*, 29–33 and his *Echoes in the Gospels*, 7–14, 291–344; see also the four criteria of evaluating intertextual comparisons with compositions that *postdate* the NT period, in Evans, *Word of Glory*, 18–28. See also Davila, "Perils of Parallelism"; Sandmel, "Parallelomania," 1–13; and Smith, *Drudgery Divine*. See the following work that evaluates the application of these criteria in the search for the counter-imperial subtexts of Paul's letters, Heilig, *Hidden Criticism?*, 21–49. Heilig's appeal to Baye's probability theorem is less effective, however, when applied to our "fragmentary data from two millennia ago, almost always open to multiple interpretations," M. D. Given, review of C. Heilig, *Hidden Criticism? RBL* (Mar 14, 2019). Finally, John Ronning responds to objections regarding FG and tgs. in his *Jewish Targums and John's Logos Theology*, 261–69.

2. **Chronological proximity:** This factor is a challenging point, illustrated profoundly by Jacob Neusner in his book subtitled "What We Cannot Show We Do Not Know."[27] He compares the contemporary use of the rabbinic corpus by scholars to studying the writings of early Christendom from (the first century CE) NT to Justin Martyr (second century) and Augustine (early fifth century), treating the diverse collection as one seamless body of work! The dating of rabbinic collections (Tosefta), individual books (m 'Abot) and specific passages (m. 'Abot 3:15) is a problem. It involves the careful use of source, form, and redaction criticisms, whose results achieve little or no scholarly consensus. Rabbinic similarities to earlier works, e.g., LXX, DSS, Philo, are helpful in discerning the antiquity of a phrase or theme,[28] but they can also lessen the *distinct* contribution of the rabbinic parallels to FG. If we can *already* find it in the LXX, what significance does a later, re-emerging theme provide? Is it making any *distinct* contribution to an understanding of FG? If so, what is it?

3. **Availability to FG and his readers:** Concerning the rabbinica, a case can only be made here regarding the antiquity of a particular saying, phrase, image, literary form, or theme and its availability to FG and his readers. The earliest rabbinic collection is 200 CE (Mishnah), and even the Aramaic Targums (second–seventh centuries CE) cannot be dated much earlier. There are certainly some isolated sayings, slogans, and concepts of the rabbinica and targumim with which FG and his readers would have been familiar, perhaps coming from a common cultural milieu.

4. **Common viewpoints:** Although this criterion is easy to comprehend, it is difficult to prove. The different contexts of the word, phrase, concept, directly effects our understanding of "common viewpoint." For example, so much of FG is christological, and both rabbinica and targumim are torah-focused. This basic difference alone qualifies or limits our understanding of "common viewpoint."

5. **Verbal and thematic coherence with FG:** The nature of the parallels as linguistic, verbal, and thematic has been noted earlier.[29] As one of the criterion for determining the authentic sayings of Jesus, it concerns what coheres or is consistent with what we already know about Jesus (e.g., he preached and taught about the kingdom of God),[30] here it includes the coherence of specific wording and similar perspective or emphasis that "point to a genuine and meaningful relationship of language and conceptuality."[31]

---

27. Neusner criticizes the research of biblical scholars for treating early Judaism as a unified entity and the rabbinic corpus as an accessible collection of early traditions from which one can casually draw to present Jewish life "as it was" in the first century CE world; see his *Rabbinic Literature and the New Testament*, 3–7, 21–27, 125–34.

28. A similar argument is also made in Ronning, "Targum of Isaiah and Johannine Literature," 274–77.

29. See especially Davila, "Perils of Parallelism"; but also M. Smith who mentions, e.g., verbal parallels, parallels of idiom, meaning, literary form, and parallels of association, in his *Tannaitic Parallels*, chs. 1–5; and J. Z. Smith who discusses the comparisons of words, stories, and contexts, in his *Drudgery Divine*, chs. 2–5.

30. See Puskas and Robbins, *Introduction*, 179.

31. On this "dictional and thematic coherence," see Chilton, *Galilean Rabbi*, cited in Evans, *Word of Glory*, 19–20. Evans also includes the criterion of contamination (19)

What is the "exegetical payoff"? What insight does it bring to our understanding of FG that we would not have previously had without it? Some of these questions will be answered below by J. Ronning (and in our chapters to follow).

Finally, John Ronning in his *The Jewish Targums and John's Logos Theology* (261–69), evaluates the arguments used against the Targum's background for FG:

D. Responses to Critics of a Targumic Context

1. **Mēmra Is Not Used for Creation**

   George F. Moore in "Intermediaries," 41–85 claimed that in contrast to Philo's Logos, "in the Targums *mēmra* . . . is not the creative word in the cosmogony of Genesis or reminiscences of it." G. F. Moore, however, had overlooked many cases in the Frg. Tgs. of Genesis, Tg. Onq. Deut 33:27, variant readings in Tg. Ps., as well as several passages from Tg. Jon. (Isaiah and Jeremiah). See Ronning's chapter 1 (21–24). Even if Moore's comment had been true when he wrote it, the discovery of Tg. Neof. on Mēmra at creation (1949, Vatican Library) would have overthrown this objection.

2. **Mēmra Is Not a Hypostasis**

   It is misleading to use a term from Christology and apply it to the Jewish concept of *Mēmra*. Like *Mēmra*, *Shekinah* acquires some resemblance of personality by its being a circumlocution for God in contexts where personal states or actions are attributed to him. The targumic Word implies the Tetragrammaton in the sense that it is used to refer to YHWH the God of Israel.

3. **Mēmra Is Not Used in an Absolute Sense**

   This argument assumes that targumic *Dibbera/Dibbura*, which is used in this absolute sense, "the Word," is too late to be of interest. Yet Ronning has argued that FG seems to be illuminated by Targum passages that have this more restrictively used "Word" (*Mēmra*) especially FG's allusions to the revelation of God to Moses in Exod 34, which in the Pal. Tgs. Exod 33:23 (Tg. Neof.) is described beforehand as a revelation of the *Dibbera/Dibbura*, that includes God's self description as "full of grace and truth" (p. 266). Ronning also argued that the isolated use of *Dibbura* in Tg. Jon. (Ezek 1), might be reasonably ascribed to the work of Johanan ben Zakkai, a first-century rabbi.

---

that concerns the question: to what extent has the NT or FG influenced the rabbinic and targumic parallels? Here it is minimal (e.g., b. Sanh. 43a; b.'Abod. Zar. 2.2), but in our comparison of FG with the Nag Hammadi writings (ch. 10), it will be a major concern, especially if a genetic relationship is argued.

4. Mēmra Is Only Used in the Targums

Although *Mēmra* is not found in the Talmudic writings, this view overlooks the fact that the Targums (or at least major portions of them) were meant for public recitation in the synagogue on Sabbaths and feast days. The targums would therefore be "widely used in early Judaism" and are more likely to have been familiar to FG and his readers than material meant primarily for scholars in a house of study.[32]

5. Mēmra in the Targums Is Late

This argument is often made in theory, but it is answered in practice by some pervasive evidence for how FG is illuminated by passages in the Targums that feature the divine Word, that are outlined in our chapter and expounded with more examples in Ronning's work. FG itself constitutes compelling evidence "that *Mēmra* was used in a particular way in the first century" (*Jewish Targums*, 267), the exegetical payoff.[33] See the example below on how the Targums might provide some background on FG's understanding of Num 21:8-9 in John 3:14-15.

Wisdom of Solomon (Wis; between 100 to 50 BCE), commenting on the bronze serpent incident, says, "For the one who turned toward it (the bronze serpent) was saved, not by the thing that was beheld, but by you, the Savior of all.... For neither herb nor poultice cured them, but it was your word [λόγος], O Lord, that heals all people" (16:7, 12). Similar concerns are evident also in Tg. Ps.-J. Num 21, a parallel with John 3:14, especially, the desire to avoid the impression that the Israelites were saved from death by merely looking at the bronze serpent. It is noteworthy that the Targum says that the one who looked would live "if his heart was directed towards the name of the Word of the Lord."[34] This passage can be linked with Tg. Neof. [mg.] and Frg. Tgs. Exod 15:26: "I am the Lord who in my Word heals you." FG might have seen the healing ministry of Jesus as further fulfillment of this promise when the Word became flesh. Wis 18:14-15 describes the death of the Egyptian firstborn, saying that at midnight the Lord's all-powerful "Word" leapt down from the heavenly royal throne carrying the divine command to strike the Egyptian firstborn like a sword (p. 268). In the Targums, when Moses entered the tent of meeting, the Spirit of God descended from heaven over the mercy seat and there was the Word (*Dibbera*) speaking with him," Tg. Ps.-J. Num 7:89.

FG itself provides plenty of clues, beginning with the first verse of the Gospel, that make a targumic origin of the Logos title very possible, along with other expressions and themes. Although the rabbinic writings are later, certain sayings and insights, concepts and forms of argumentation are remarkably similar to those that we find in FG, reflecting some type of

---

32. Culpepper provides a survey of the "house of Hillel," using rabbinic sources, in his *Johannine School*, 171-95.

33. This paragraph (in # 5.) on "exegetical payoff" highlights the rationale and the goal of comparative analysis. We also allude to it in the concluding questions found in our previous table, 2. Chronological Proximity.

34. Cited also in *Tg. Yer. I* on Num 21:4-9, see Martin, *Narrative Parallels*, 64-66.

common milieu. The rabbinic and targumic parallels (as do those from OT, Philo, and DSS) help to explain the Jewish characteristics of this Gospel, likely originating in Palestine, describing (mostly) sympathetic Jewish characters, and having keen familiarity with Jewish feasts and customs, despite its grand portrayal of Jesus as Messiah, the Son of God, and the resulting conflict with leaders of the Jews (*'Ioudaioi*).[35]

---

35. We mentioned in ch. 1 n58, the diverse use of phrase *hoi 'Ioudaioi* as, e.g., "Judeans (7:14-15), Jewish leaders (1:19; 5:15-18), Jewish people (3:1; 4:6, 9, 22; 5:1; 6:4; 11:19, 36, 45; 12:11; 19:19)," in North, *Journey Round John*, 148-67. In Bieringer and Vandcasteele-Vanneuville, *Anti-Judaism and the Fourth Gospel*, P. J. Tomson (183-90) shows that the phrase "Jews" was often used in stories that interacted with "non-Jews" in the Talmud of Israel (e.g., y. Ber. 9:13a-b; y. Sanh. 3:21b; y. Ma'aś. Ś 4:25b-c) and used "Israel" exclusively as inner-Jewish speech (y. Mo 'ed Qaṭ. 3.83b; y. Giṭ. 1:43b; cf. John 1:31; 3:10).

Arguing that FG is "Jew-ish without being Jewish" (62), A. Reinhartz offers the minority view that FG wrote to dissuade those gentiles who were sympathetic with Judaism, by seeking to evict the Jews from their religious heritage and subsume it under the jurisdiction of Jesus, granting all believers Jewish covenantal status without being Jewish, in her *Cast out of the Covenant*, ch. 3. Boyarin, nevertheless, disagrees with the comments that there is "nothing 'Jewish' about John" (supposedly attributed to Bultmann, *John*, 20-29, who favored gnostic influences), in his *Border Lines*, 284n107. Boyarin argues, instead, for the use of common Jewish texts (Gen 1; Wisdom) and midrashic tradition behind FG's Logos and the targumic *Mēmra* (103-7). In FG, it can be argued that the most negative connotation of the *'Ioudaioi* applies to the fiercest opponents of Jesus, "the Judeans" of the southern territory, who resided in or near Jerusalem (5:16, 18; 7:1; 10:22, 31, 33; 11:54; 18:12, 31; 19:7, 12, 38: 20:19).

VII. Greco-Roman Cults and Philosophies: Isis, Plato, Hermetica

ALTHOUGH THESE WRITINGS MAY have influenced Hellenistic Judaism(s) in various ways (e.g., 1 Macc 1:14), this chapter concerns those religious and cultural writings that originated in non-Jewish or gentile contexts. All developed in the Hellenism of the Roman era and all, along with Judaism and Christianity, are regarded as "Greco-Roman cults."[1] Some, e.g., Euripides's *Bacchae* and Plato, originated before the Roman era, but retained influence in later years.

In previous chapters, we examined proposed influences *on* the thought world of John that were readily discernible (e.g., early Christian traditions, Jewish Scriptures of the Septuagint), some that might be plausible (Jewish wisdom and angel speculations including apocrypha and pseudepigrapha, Dead Sea Scrolls, Philo), and others that are possible,[2] reflecting similar language or worldview (rabbinic thought). Many might indicate early influence *from* FG or similar parallel traditions, see our chapters 9–12 (e.g., Nag Hammadi, Mandaean, early Greek and Latin Fathers), pp. 148–231.

There has been considerable resistance concerning comparative studies of FG and non-Jewish writings, e.g., "Moreover since all Jews, even to some extent Palestinian Jews, had long been exposed to Hellenistic influences there seems no need to search outside the world of first-century Judaism for such Greek traits as are exhibited by the Fourth Gospel."[3] We conclude, however, that because of the *pervasive* influence of Hellenism upon Judaism, the evidence of *a break* with torah-focused Judaism in FG,

---

1. See p. 3n9 in our Intro., where we cite the works of M. Hengel and J. A. Fitzmyer, as well as M. Pucci Ben Zeev, "Jews, Greeks, Romans," in Collins; and Harlow, *Early Judaism*, 237–55.

2. See p. 7n28 in our Intro., "Is it analogy or genealogy? . . . similarities or points of agreement that we discover between two different religions . . . or are they dependent one on the other, demonstrable borrowings?" (Deissmann, *Light from Ancient East*, 265). See also Smith, *Drudgery Divine*, 48–50.

3. Ashton, *Understanding the Fourth Gospel*, 97; see also D. Moody Smith, "John," in Barclay and Sweet, *Jewish Context*, 96–111.

and the unknown identities of the author and final editor, FG's exposure to non-Jewish Greco-Roman influence (Heraclitus, Euripides, Plato) should not, therefore, be ruled out of consideration.[4]

As a corollary of reading FG as narrative theology, Charles H. Talbert, states, "It is inappropriate to focus on only one background for understanding the narrative (e.g., Qumran, rabbinic Judaism, mystical Judaism, Hellenistic Judaism, Greco-Roman philosophy, Hermetica, Gnosticism, etc.) since it will likely take knowledge of most or all to comprehend a tradition that developed not only through time but also moved geographically"[5] [e.g., from Palestine to Ephesus]. Udo Schnelle programmatically states that any one-sided explanation of FG (e.g., within an inner-Jewish context) is insufficient.[6] M. David Litwa, for example, who acknowledges Jewish influence, explores the impact that Greek myths had on the formation of the gospels in his *How the Gospels Became History* (2019).

In this chapter 7, we will look at the writings of the Isis cult, Plato, and the Hermetica. We are selective in this chapter. Other areas of investigation can certainly be pursued comparing FG with additional Greco-Roman mystery cults, as well as Greek and Roman Classics. Some allusion or reference will be made for further areas of investigation.

Isis

The cults of the Greco-Roman world were practiced around the ancient Mediterranean during the Hellenistic and Roman periods (i.e., late fourth century BCE–fifth century CE). These were periods of complex political and cultural change and syncretism in which first the Greeks and then the Romans provided the dominant political and cultural frameworks for life in the ancient Mediterranean world. Thus Greco-Roman religions include not only those public and private cults which had developed out of archaic

---

4. J. Z. Smith argues that the (*mostly* Protestant) preference for Jewish origins of the NT was often embraced as an insulating device against later syncretistic tendencies of Christendom beginning in the fourth century (suspected as a Roman Catholic tendency) *Drudgery Divine*, 46–48. See also Conzelmann, "Mother of Wisdom," 230–43. Conzelmann detects this syncretism in Hellenistic Judaism. For example, Sir 24:3–7: "I came forth from the mouth of the Most High and I covered the earth like a mist," employs the liturgical form of the Isis aretalogy.

5. Talbert, *Reading John*, 66.

6. From "kann nicht monocausal erklärt werden," in Schnelle, *Die Evangelium nach Johannes*, 40. ET quotation from Frey, "Between Torah and Stoa," 194. M. Becker strongly agrees with Schnelle's statement (above), see his "Zeichen," in Frey and Schnelle, *Kontexte*, 235–36.

VII. GRECO-ROMAN CULTS AND PHILOSOPHIES: ISIS, PLATO, HERMETICA 105

and classical Greek (e.g., Dionysus of Thrace) and Roman religious practices (Bacchus), but also the many native cults and mystery religions that had arisen on ancient Near Eastern soil (Isis of Egypt) and which had subsequently spread in hellenized form to the major urban areas of the Mediterranean world, coexisting with early Judaism and Christianity.[7] Because they were close-knit associations attempting to overcome fate and offer new hope, mystery cults, like Isis and Dionysus, spread throughout the Roman world.

Isis is well known from Egyptian pyramid texts (from 21st century BCE) as one of the "Great Ennead" or nine ruling gods of Egypt.[8] She is the sister-wife of Osiris and mother of Horus. After absorbing aspects of other cults, the fame of Isis reached beyond Egypt through Greek sea ports to many parts of the Mediterranean world (e.g., Cyrene, Colossae, Philippi, Cenchrae, Delos, Pompeii, Rome).[9] Mixed fortunes awaited the cult of Isis in Rome under Tiberius Caesar (Josephus, *Ant.* 18.79–80), but more hospitable treatment came from Gaius Caligula. The Roman poet Tibullus (ca. 25 BCE) was impressed with legends of her healing powers and mastery of the sea. In *Metamorphoses* 11, a devoted Lucius echoes many who revered Isis for her sensitivity, passion for uprightness (*dikaios, dikaiosunē*), and her many blessings on people. The "I am" formulas dominate several of her aretalogies cataloging her beneficence.[10]

---

7. N. C. Croy, "Religion, Personal," in Evans and Porter, *Dictionary*, 926–30. On the different mystery cults (e.g., Mithra, Cybele) with places of origin (e.g., Asia Minor, Persia), see also Puskas and Robbins, *Introduction*, 16–19. For some second century CE parallels with FG, see the following: on the healing power of the well in the Asclepius temple (cf. John 5), according to Aelius Aristides, *Speech* 39:14–15 (266–67); the wine flowing at the feast of Dionysus (cf. John 2) (248); and the "Mithras Liturgy" (cf. new birth, John 3:3–5) (256–58), in Boring et al. *Hellenistic Commentary*; see also Martin, *Narrative Parallels*, 215.

8. Mercer, *Pyramid Texts*. These and other texts relating to Isis are found in Pritchard, *Ancient Near Eastern Texts*, 3 (Great Ennead: Atum the creator, Shu, god of air, Tefnut, goddess of moisture, Geb, god of earth, Nut, god of sky, Osiris, Isis, Seth, Nephthys, sister of Isis), on Isis, see also 5, 12–17, pyramid texts from twenty-first century BCE, see 32.

9. Smith mentions that Herodotus (ca. 440 BCE), among others, had favored Egyptian influence over that of the more syncretistic Persians (*Histories* 1.135; 2.43–50, 57–58, 79) in his *Drudgery Divine*, 45–46.

10. Our citations are from Bergman, *Ich bin Isis*, especially the Greek text of the Isis aretalogy, a textual recension of the Cyme hymn and Memphis stele, noting the minor variants, 301–3; cited also in Horsley, *New Documents*, 1:18–20. We also consulted Apuleius, *Metamorphoses* 11 (LCL, Apuleius, *Golden Ass*, 538–95); Plutarch, *Isis and Osiris* (LCL, Plutarch's Moralia V, 3–191); Diodorus Siculus, *Library of History* I.25.1–7 and 27.3–4 (LCL, Diodorus Siculus I, 78–83, 87); inscription from Maroneia, Macedonia, second century BCE, from Y. Grandjean, *Une Nouvelle Aretalogie*, cited in Horsley, *New Documents*, 1:10–12. See also Grant, *Hellenistic Religions*, 131–33; Conzelmann, "Mother of Wisdom," 230–43; Burkert, *Ancient Mystery Cults*, 15–18, 41, 48–49; Kee,

A. Isis and the Fouth Gospel

1. Isis (Cyme-Memphis)	The Fourth Gospel
3a "I am (*egō eimi*) Isis, mistress of every land and I was taught by Hermes..."	"I am (*egō eimi*) the way, the truth, and the life," 14:6; "Before Abraham was, I am," 8:58. "I am the light of the world," 8:12.
4 "I gave and established laws for people that no one is able to change..."	
7 "I am (*egō eimi*) she who finds fruit for people."	"I am the vine, you are the branches. Those who abide in me bear much fruit," 15:5.
12-15 "I (*egō*) divided the earth from the heaven. I showed the paths of the stars. I ordered the course of the sun and the moon. I devised business in the sea."	"All things came into being through him, and without him not one thing came into being," 1:3; Jesus "walking on the sea and coming near the boat" saying "I am (*egō eimi*), fear not," 6:19-20. "Judge with right (*dikaios*) judgment," 7:24. Jesus blesses a wedding couple with his first sign (water into wine), 2:1-11.
17-18 "I made strong the right (*dikaios*). I brought together woman and man."	
24 "I taught to honor images of the gods. I consecrated the precincts of the gods."	"Stop making my Father's house a marketplace... destroy this temple and in three days I will raise it up," 2:16, 19. "I am the light of the world. Whoever follows me will not walk in darkness," 8:12.
28-29 "I made the right to be stronger than gold and silver. I ordained that the true should be thought good."	
34-36 "I have delivered the one who plots evil against others into the hands of those he plots against. I established penalties for those who practice injustice (*adikos*). I decreed mercy (*elean*) to the suppliants."	"The one who handed you over to me is guilty of a greater sin,"19:11b; cf. justice, judgment 3:19; 12:31; 16:11. "From his fullness we have all received, grace upon grace," 1:16.
38-41 "The right (*dikaios*) prevails with me. I am the Queen of rivers, winds, and sea. No one is held in honor without my knowing it. I stir up the sea and I calm it" (cf. Sir. 24:11-12).	"I speak these things as the Father instructs me... I always do what is pleasing to him," 8:28-29 (cf. 6:19-20, Jesus walking on the sea).

New Testament in Context, 149-51; Meyer, *Ancient Mysteries*, 155-96; Cotter, *Miracles*, 30, 35-37; Klauck, *Religious Context*, 128-38; Danker, "Isis," 3:95-96; Bremmer, *Initiation into the Mysteries*, 110-23; this form of self-predication recurs in gnostic writings that use a paradoxical "I Am" style to depict the cosmological and soteriological role of Wisdom/Eve. See Thund. (VI, 2) and the discussion of its paradoxical language of divine self-predication by B. Layton, "The Riddle of Thunder," in Hedrick and Hodgson, *Nag Hammadi, Gnosticism, and Early Christianity*, 37-54.

48 "I free (*luō*) the captives."

55–56 "I overcome Fate (*himarmenos nikos*). Fate listens (*akouō*) to me."

Inscription from Cyme, Asia Minor (second century BCE), in Meyer, *Ancient Mysteries*, 172–74.

2. Isis (Metmorphoses)

Lucius addressing the goddess: "Queen of heaven . . . illuminating the walls of all cities . . . dispensing abroad your dim radiance when the sun was abandoned . . . support my broken life and give me rest and peace . . . restore me to the sight of those that love me," 11:2.

The goddess to Lucius: "I, the natural mother of all life, the mistress of the elements, I, who govern by my nod the crests of light in the sky, the purifying wafts of the ocean . . . the uniform manifestation of all gods and goddesses . . . I whose single godhead is venerated all over the earth under manifold forms, varying rites, and changing names [Minerva, Venus, Juno] but my true name is Queen Isis . . . Behold I am come to you in your calamity. I am come with solace and aid. Away then with tears. Cease to moan . . . soon through my providence shall the sun of your salvation arise," 11.5.

"You will know the truth and the truth will make you free," 8:32.

"You would have no power over me unless it had been given you from above," 19:11 (cf. "will," *thelēma*, 4:34; 5:30; 6:38–40; 7:17; 9:31).

Fourth Gospel

"In him was life and the life was the light of all people. The light shines in the darkness and the darkness could not overcome it," 1:4–5. Greeks at Passover to Philip: "Sir, we wish to see Jesus," 12:20.

"I am the light of the world. Whoever follows me will never walk in darkness," 8:12.

"And the Word was with God and the Word was God," 1:1. "Before Abraham was, I am," 8:58. "The Father and I are one," 10:30. "I am the Good Shepherd . . . the Door, . . . the Bread of Life, . . . the Way, the Truth and the Life, . . . the Light of the world, . . . the Vine, I Am the Resurrection and the Life (6:35; 8:12; 10:9, 11: 11:25: 14:6); Son of God, Lamb of God, Son of Man, Messiah (1:18, 29, 34, 41, 51).

"Do not let your hearts be troubled. Believe in God, believe also in me. In my Father's house there are many dwelling places. I go to prepare a place for you," 14:1–2. "I came that they may have life, and have it abundantly," 10:10.

"Keep the remembrance fast in your heart's deep core, that all the remaining days of your life must be dedicate to me, and that nothing can release you from this service but death ... you should devote your life to her who redeems you back into humanity. You shall live blessed. You shall live glorious under my guidance ... if you are found to merit my love by your dedicated obedience, religious devotion, and constant chastity, you will discover that it is within my power to prolong your life beyond the limit set to it by Fate," 11.6 (second century CE).

"If you abide in me, and my words abide in you, ask for whatever you wish, and it will be done for you. My Father is glorified by this, that you bear much fruit and become my disciples," 15:7–8. "If you keep my commandments, you will abide in my love ... I have said these things to you so that my joy may be in you, and that your joy may be complete," 15:10–11. "I am the resurrection and the life. Those who believe in me even though they die, will live," 11:25. "'Lazarus, come out,' the dead man came out ... 'unbind him, and let him go,'" 11:43–44.

Apuleius, *Metamorphoses* 11.2, 5–6 (LCL, Apuleius, *Golden Ass*, 540–41, 544–51). On multiple names, see our tbls. in chs. 8.C. Dionysus, p. 135 and 10. E. Trimorphic Protennoia, pp. 176–77.

3. Isis (Diodorus Siculus)

"As for Isis ... now that she has attained immortality, she finds her greatest delight in the healing of people ... manifesting both her presence and her beneficence towards those who ask for help," 1.25.2–3.

"Numbers who have altogether lost the use of their eyes or of some other part of their body, wherever they turn for help to this goddess are restored to their previous condition," 25.5.

"She not only raised from the dead her son Horus ... but also made him immortal," 25.6

Diodorus Siculus, *Library of History* 1.25.2–3,5–6 (LCL, Diodorus Siculus, Book I, 80–83); late first century, BCE.

Fourth Gospel

"In him was life and the life was the light of all people," 1:4. "'Go, your son will live,'" Jesus heals the son of a royal official when he asked for help, 4:49–50, 52. "'Do you want to be made well?'" Jesus heals a lame man who had wanted to be healed, 5:6–9.

The man born blind recounting his healing to curious neighbors: "The man called Jesus made mud, spread it on my eyes and said to me, 'Go to Siloam and wash.' Then I went and washed and received my sight," 9:11.

"I am the resurrection and the life. Those who believe in me even though they die, will live," 11:25. "'Lazarus, come out,' the dead man came out ... 'unbind him, and let him go,'" 11:43–44.

In his "The Ego-Proclamation in Gnostic Sources," George W. MacRae, before discussing the relevant Nag Hammadi texts (e.g., Thund., VI, 2), provides an overview of the Deutero-Isaiah, Wisdom, and Johannine texts (204–11). He then mentions the development of the Isis aretalogy hymn from Egypt to the Roman world, citing the work of J. Bergman, *Ich bin Isis*, in MacRae's own *Studies in the New Testament and Gnosticism*, 212–13. He observes that the antiquity of the similar Isis "I am" sayings (fourth century BCE and earlier), might make some contribution, along with the Deutero-Isaiah and Wisdom literature, for an understanding of the "I am" sayings in both gnostic and NT writings.

As stated earlier in our introduction, important factors to consider when making any causal connections are: similar contexts, chronological proximity to FG, availability to author and readers, common viewpoints, and verbal/thematic coherence of FG and writings in question.[11] We will briefly reflect on each one.

B. Tests for Evaluating Alleged Parallels

1. **Similar Contexts**: Having determined earlier the *pervasive* influence of Hellenism upon Judaism, the evidence of *a break* with Torah-focused Judaism in FG, and the unknown identities of the author and final editor, FG's exposure to non-Jewish Greco-Roman influence (Heraclitus, Euripides, Plato) should not, therefore, be ruled out of consideration. J. Z. Smith argues that the (*mostly* Protestant) preference for Jewish origins of the NT was often embraced as an insulating device against later syncretistic tendencies of Christendom beginning in the fourth century (suspected as a Roman Catholic tendency), *Drudgery Divine*, 46–48. As we mentioned (Intro, p. 3n9) both Judaism and Christianity developed in the Hellenism of the Roman era and are even regarded as "Greco-Roman cults." In contrast to the mystery cults with their idol worship (*Protr.* 1–4), Clement of Alexandria presents Christianity as a religion with "truly sacred mysteries," (12.20). Shrines and temples for Isis were found throughout the Roman world (see point 4, p. 110, below) and exclusive devotion was not required. Professor George W. MacRae, SJ, suggested that the milieu of FG was varied deliberately so as to make the universality and transcendence of the divine son appealing to a wide audience.[12] Perhaps FG had employed similar cultic language to reach those readers influenced by the Greco-Roman mystery cults that were so prevalent in the Roman world.[13]

---

11. We cited earlier, Intro. n31, but see especially Smith, *Drudgery Divine*, 46–53; Hays, *Echoes in the Letters of Paul*, 29–33 and his *Echoes in the Gospels*, 7–14, 291–344; see also the four criteria of evaluating intertextual comparisons with compositions that *postdate* the NT period, in Evans, *Word of Glory*, 18–28. See also (Intro, p. 5n16) Davila, "Perils of Parallelism"; Sandmel, "Parallelomania," 1–13; and Ronning, *Jewish Targums and John's Logos Theology*, 261–69.

12. McRae, *Studies in the New Testament and Gnosticism*, 15–31, esp. 18, 30–31. On similar reflections, see Frey and Schnelle, *Kontexte*, 35–45. From another angle, Kysar raises the question "Is it likely that any of the four evangelists would have gone through the trouble (and expense) of writing a whole Gospel for only one specific church?" *The Maverick Gospel*, 26.

13. On patron deities influencing almost every club or association in the Roman world, see Ascough et al., *Associations in the Greco-Roman World*.

2. **Chronological proximity:** The Isis cult as a Hellenistic cult flourished from the fourth century BCE up to the fifth century CE, but its origins in Egypt go back much earlier (e.g., pyramid texts). If we can *already* find it (e.g., "I am" formula) in the LXX (2 Isa, Wis), what significance does a similar and earlier theme provide? Is it making any *distinct* contribution to an understanding of FG? If so, in what way?

3. **Contamination,** cited in C. A. Evans, *Word of Glory*, 19–20. Evans also includes the criterion of **contamination** (19) that concerns the question: to what extent has the NT or FG influenced the material with which it is compared? Both Justin Martyr (1 *Apol.* 66.4; *Dial.* 70.1) and Tertullian (*Praescr.* 40; *Bapt.* 5) argued that the mystery cults (e.g., Mithra, Isis), were demonic imitations of true Christianity. The Isis cult is certainly syncretistic adapting motifs from other cults of the Mediterranean world, however, no explicit NT terminology is detected in the sources for Isis. Our comparisons (ch. 7. A.) appear to reflect a common tradition or perhaps independent parallel traditions.

4. **Availability to FG and his readers:** The shrines and temples of Isis were almost everywhere that Jews and Christians gathered: Cyrene, Colossae, Philippi, Cenchrae/Corinth, Delos, Pompeii, and Rome. Availability is a given, receptivity is the issue. To what extent could or would FG borrow from the mystery cults? Many are the Jewish and Christian objections regarding the polytheism or henotheism of the mystery cults. What about Isis as the queen of all gods and goddesses? Or Isis with the God of Israel? (Deut 5:6–7; 6:4; 13:1–15; cf. Isa 42:8, 17). In the NT, Paul wrote "flee from idolatry" (1 Cor 10:14), "they sacrifice to demons, not to God" (v. 20; cf. Gal 4:8; 5:19–21). Justin Martyr and Tertullian would have agreed with Paul. In rabbinic thought idol worship is condemned (b. Shab. 2.6; 9.3; b. Yeb. 4.12) and "two powers in heaven" (e.g., God and Lady Wisdom) was considered heresy (b. Hag. 15a). See Segal, *Two Powers in Heaven*, 84–97; Dever, *Did God Have a Wife?*; Willis, *Idol Meat in Corinth*.

5. **Common viewpoints:** In a *general* sense, both FG's audience and the Isis cult appear to be close-knit communities, that center upon worship of the divine in sometimes similar language of salvation, hope, and devotion (as do most mystery cults of that day). This common milieu of cultic language cannot be as easily dismissed. Nevertheless, the different cultural and literary contexts, as we have stated, limit our understanding of a "common viewpoint." On early Christian distinctiveness (contra idolatry) in the Roman world, see Hurtado, *Destroyer of the Gods*, 82–94.

6. **Verbal and thematic coherence with FG:** The nature of the parallels as linguistic, verbal, and thematic has been noted earlier.[14] As one of the criterion for determining the authentic sayings of Jesus, it concerns what coheres or is consistent with what we already know about Jesus (e.g., he preached and taught about the kingdom of God),[15] here it includes the coherence of specific wording

---

14. See our ch. 6, p. 99n29 where we cite Davila, "Perils of Parallelism"; Smith, *Tannaitic Parallels*, chs. 1–5; and Smith, *Drudgery Divine*, chs. 2–5.

15. See Puskas and Robbins, *Introduction*, 179.

and similar perspective or emphasis that "point to a genuine and meaningful relationship of language and conceptuality."[16] Consulting the primary sources in Greek is important here. What is the "exegetical payoff"? What insight does it bring to our understanding of FG that we would not have previously had without it? This category is a challenging one to satisfy in our comparison of FG with Isis. If FG employed similar cultic language of devotion to a divinity in order to reach those influenced by the mystery cults, it was accomplished in a subtle and indirect manner.

Plato, Platonism

In a pragmatic age of anxiety and aspiration, the Hellenistic philosophies were popular quasi-religious movements of wandering preacher-philosophers and healers.[17] The influential ideas of **Plato** (d. 347 BCE) were continued in what is labeled Middle Platonism (ca. 80 BCE—220 CE).[18] These Platonists followed the three characteristic aspects of Plato's dualism. (1) A distinction was made between two levels of reality: the imperfect, temporal, changing, material world of particulars over against the perfect, eternal, unchanging, spiritual world of Forms. (2) True knowledge of the Forms can only be attained by reason, not sense experience. (3) The immortal soul is imprisoned by the mortal body (also Pythagorean). Plato's theological speculations were also developed by his disciples and the later Platonists. Plato's conception of the Good as the highest of Forms was identified as a supreme Deity (Middle Platonism). His **Demiurge** (Divine Craftsman in Plato's *Timaeus*) was equated with Aristotle's Unmoved Mover (Albinus of Smyrna), and his mention of intermediaries (*daimones*) between heaven and earth was delineated into good and evil demons (Xenocrates of Chalcedon).

Thomas Tobin, SJ, wrote of the pervasive influence of Platonism and Stoicism for our understanding of *Logos* in Middle Platonism and Philo:

---

16. On this "dictional and thematic coherence," see Chilton, *Galilean Rabbi*, cited in Evans, *Word of Glory*, 19–20. This criterion seeks to determine if the parallel is *more* than just a formal analogy or coincidental similarity.

17. For full discussion of the Greco-Roman era as an "age of anxiety and aspiration," see Puskas and Robbins, *Introduction*, 12–26.

18. A selection of sources for Plato and Middle Platonism are: Plato, *The Republic, Symposium, Timaeus, Parmenides*; Diogenes Laertius, *Lives*, Bk 3; Albinus of Smyrna (AD 150); Plutarch, *Platonic Essays* (120 CE; *Moralia* LCL XIII). All are available from LCL (Harvard University Press). Helpful secondary sources are: Dillon, *Middle Platonists*; Merlan, *From Platonism to Neoplatonism*; Shorey, *Platonism*. See also the survey in Puskas and Robbins, *Introduction*, 21–22.

Logos was used by the pre-Socratic philosopher Heraclitus (ca. 500 B.C.E.) . . . of proportion, account, and explanation. But he may also have used *Logos* in the sense of an underlying cosmic principle of order coextensive with the primary cosmic element of fire. For Plato (429–347 B.C.E.) *Logos* was associated with the rational or, in contrast to myth *(mythos)*, was a rational account *(Phaedrus* 61b). Aristotle (384–322 B.C.E.) often used the term *Logos* to refer to rational speech and rationality. Reason *(logos)* also distinguished human beings from lower animals *(Politica* 1332b) . . . For the Stoics, *Logos*, God, and nature were in reality one (Diogenes Laertius 7.135). *Logos* was the rational element that pervades and controls the universe *(SVF* 1:87) and was ultimately material. *Logos* was used in Middle Platonism (the Platonic tradition from ca. 80 B.C.E. to ca. 220 C.E.) in the sense of rational discourse and human rationality. At the level of cosmology, it also sometimes played an important role in relation to other concepts in Middle Platonism. Middle Platonism, unlike Stoicism, emphasized the reality of the immaterial, intelligible realm. One characteristic of Middle Platonism was its distinction between two aspects of the divine. The first was essentially transcendent and inner-directed. The second was an active power responsible for the ordering of everything else. Early Middle Platonists sometimes adopted the Stoic *Logos* into their systems as the term for this active force of the divine in the world. More often, however, they gave this aspect of the divine a different name (e.g., idea, mind). This view influenced Hellenistic Judaism and particularly Philo of Alexandria.[19]

Regarding some of the general themes common to FG and Platonism, Raymond E. Brown wrote,

In John there are contrasts between what is above and what is below (3:31), between spirit and flesh (3:6, 6:63), between eternal life and natural existence (11:25–26), between the real bread from heaven (6:32) and natural bread, between the water of eternal life (4:14) and natural water. These contrasts may be compared to a popular form of Platonism where there is a real

---

19. Tobin, "Logos," 894. *SVF* is the abbreviation for *Stoicorum Veterem Fragmenta*, 4 vols., ed. H. von Arnim. We have alluded to the writings of Heraclitus and the Stoics on *Logos* in our ch. 4 on Philo. On the blending of Stoic and Platonic ontological ideas, see T. Engberg-Pedersen, "Stoicism and Platonism," in Rasimus et al., *Stoicism*, 1–14. See comparisons of FG's Farewell Discourse (13:31—17:26) with the Roman Stoic Seneca's consolation writings (*Helv.; Marc.; Polyb.*) by M. Lang, "Johanneische Abschiedsreden und Senecas Konsolationsliteratur," in Frey and Schnelle, *Kontexte*, 365–412.

world, invisible and eternal, contrasted with the world of appearances here below.[20]

Professor Brown also pointed out that Platonism had already influenced Judaism, for example, in the writings of Philo (see our ch. 4, pp. 56, 59, 66) and also at Qumran (1QS IV, 20–22; cf. Isa 31:3) and that many of these similar themes "are quite explicable in light of Palestinian Judaism."[21]

On the "Last Supper" in John (13–16) and Plato's *Symposium*, Professor Harold W. Attridge writes,

> Plato's *Symposium* and the Gospel according to John, involve dialogues focused on love ... Both articulate a theory of what love is really about, Diotima's speech in the *Symposium*, and the Last Supper discourse in John. Both texts frame the dialogue with a narrative that exemplifies in a concrete way what the theory means in very human terms. For Plato that narrative is the account given by the drunken Alcibiades ... of his relationship with Socrates ... For the evangelist, the account of the passion and resurrection of Jesus gives a distinct shape to the command to love.[22]

On the trials of Socrates and Jesus, Brown continues,

> Educated Greco-Roman pagans would have been familiar with the death of Socrates described by Plato. Execution by self-administered poison was forced upon this philosopher of lofty principles who was innocent of crime. Without tears and without impassioned pleas to be spared, he accepted his fate, nobly encouraging his followers not to grieve since he was going to a world of perfect truth, beauty, and goodness, only the shadows of which were glimpsed here below.[23]

Brown adds,

> some hearers/readers imbued with Platonic/Socratic ideals might react disparagingly toward the Mark/Matt picture of a Jesus distraught and troubled, throwing himself prostrate to the earth and begging God to deliver him" (1:217).

The above comment might apply to the Synoptic portrait of Jesus at Gethsemane (Mark 14:32–37; Matt 26:36–40), but FG's portrait is much bolder

---

20. Brown, *Gospel according to John*, 1:lvii. See also Barrett, *John*, 28.
21. Brown, *Gospel according to John*, 1:lvii. On dualism, see our ch. 5, pp. 71–73.
22. Attridge, "Three Symposia on Love," 378. On ancient symposia and the spoken word, see Bakhtin, *Rabelais and His World*, 283–84.
23. Brown, *Death of the Messiah*, 1:217.

and resolute (as in Phaed. 117-18; John 12:23-24, 27-28; 19:8-11, 16-17, 28-30).[24]

The Syrian Stoic philosopher Mara bar Serapion from Antioch (late first or early second century CE) draws a comparison between the executions of Socrates, Pythagoras, and Jesus by their own people and the subsequent divine punishment that the people receive.

> What advantage did the Athenians gain by putting Socrates to death? Famine and plague came upon them as a judgment for their crime. What advantage did the men of Samos gain from burning Pythagoras? In a moment their land was covered with sand. What advantage did the Jews gain from executing their wise King? [Jn 19:19] It was just after that that their kingdom was abolished. [Jn 11:48]. God justly avenged these three wise men: the Athenians died of hunger; the Samians were overwhelmed by the sea; the Jews, ruined and driven from their land, live in complete dispersion. But Socrates did not die for good; he lived on in the teaching of Plato. Pythagoras did not die for good; he lived on in the statue of Hera. Nor did the wise King die for good; he lived on in the teaching which he had given. [John 20:21-23][25]

Let us look closer at these alleged parallels and evaluate them as we have done in other comparisons. We highlight some of the similarities in bold type. We will also note some similarities that we have already provided in our chapter 4 on Philo.

---

24. Thompson, refuting any naïve Docetism here, portrays the human Jesus bravely submitting to death, in obedience to the Father's will, in her *Humanity of Jesus*, 105-15. In Luke 22:41-45, vv. 43-44, are lacking in certain ancient authorities, see Metzger, *Textual Commentary*, 151.

25. The ms dates from the seventh century CE, located in the British Library. Trans. from Bruce, *Jesus and Early Christian Origins*, 31. We added [brackets]. Compare John 20:30-31 with what Iamblichus (ca. 300 CE) wrote of Pythagoras (ca. 300 BCE) who did many more "divine and admirable deeds" but these are written "to indicate his piety" in *Iamblichus' Life of Pythagoras* ch. 28 (trans. T. Taylor, 1818), 98-99. On Jesus and Socrates, see text and discussion in Van Kooten, "Last Days of Socrates and Christ," 219-21; see also in the same volume B. Lang, "Jesus among the Philosophers," 187-218.

C. The Fourth Gospel	Plato, Platonism
	Logos and truth
"In the beginning (*archē*) was the Word (*logos*) and the Word was with God (*ho theos*) and the Word was God (*theos*) He was (*ōn*) in the beginning with God," 1:1–2. "The true (*alēthinos*) light which enlightens everyone," v. 9. "Full of grace and **truth** (*alētheia*)," v. 14. "But the one who sent me is **true** (*alēthēs*), and I declare to the world what I have heard from him," 8:26.	And whereas the body of the Heaven is visible, the Soul [*tēn Psychēn*] is herself invisible but partakes in reasoning [*logismos*] and in harmony, [37] having come into existence by the agency of the best of things intelligible and ever-existing as the best of things generated [*Demiurge*] . . . And her announcement [*logos*], being identically **true** [*alēthēs*] concerning both the Other and the Same, is borne through the self-moved without speech or sound; and whenever it is concerned with the sensible, and the circle of the Other moving in straight course proclaims it to the whole of its Soul, opinions and beliefs arise which are firm and **true** [*alēthēs*]; and again, when it is concerned with the rational [*logistikos*], [C] and the circle of the Same, spinning truly, declares the facts, reason and knowledge of necessity result" (*Tim.* 36E–37C, LCL, 73–75).[26]
	The light that enlightens
"In him was life and the life was the light of all people. The light shines in the darkness, and the darkness did not overcome it," 1:4–5. "The true light (*to phōs to alēthinos*) which enlightens (*phōtizō*) everyone," 1:9; "the light has come into the world, and people loved darkness rather than light," 3:19. "**I am the light of the world**. Whoever follows me will never walk in darkness but will have the light of life," 8:12. "The light is with you for a little longer. Walk while you have the light, so that the darkness may not overtake you . . . **while you have the light, believe in the light**, so that you may become children of light," 12:35–36.	"Which one can you name of the divinities in heaven as **the author and cause of this, whose light makes our vision see best and visible things to be seen?**" (*Rep.* 508A Bk 6 ch. 10); "**The true light (*to phōs to alēthinon*)**" that Socrates hopes to see after death (*Phaed.* 109E–110A). The ascent from the cave with shadow images revealed by fire light to slowly **behold the brightness of the sun and eventually see things themselves** (515E–516A; Bk. 7) is then applied to **the soul's ascension to the intelligible reason** which finally perceives "**the idea of good** (*agathos idea*) . . . the cause for all things of all that is right and beautiful, **giving birth in the visible world to light, and the author of light** . . . being the authentic source of truth (*alētheia*) and reason (*nous*)," (517B–C). See Van Kooten, "'True Light' (John 1:9)," 149–94.

---

26. "Plato borrowed his statement that God, having altered matter which was shapeless, made the world, hear the very words spoken through Moses [Gen 1:1], who, as above shown, was the first prophet" (Justin, *1 Apol.* 59 [*ANF* 1:182]). See our ch. 4, pp. 66–67, for a similar claim made by Philo.

C. The Fourth Gospel	Plato, Platonism

God's eternal today

"Whoever believes in the Son **has** (*echei*, Pres. Indic. Active) **eternal life**; whoever disobeys will not see life, but must endure God's wrath" 3:36; cf. 5:24; 6:47, 54; 8:51. "I am the resurrection and the life. Those who believe in me, even though they die, will live" 11:25. "Father **the hour has come** to glorify your Son so that your Son may glorify you, since you have given him authority . . . to give (*dōsē*, Aor. Subj. Act.) eternal life (*zōe aiōnios*) to all whom you have given him. And this is (*estin*) eternal life, that you may know the only true God . . . I glorified you on earth . . . **now** (*nun*) **Father** glorify me in your own presence with the glory that I had in your presence **before the world existed**" (17:1–5, bold print added).	"And these are all portions of Time; even as 'Was' and 'Shall be' are generated forms of Time, although we apply them wrongly, without noticing, to Eternal Being. For we say that it 'is' or 'was' or 'will be,' whereas, in truth of speech, **'is' alone** [38] **is the appropriate term;** "was" and "will be," on the other hand, are terms properly applicable to the Becoming which proceeds in Time, since both of these are motions; but it belongs not to that which is ever changeless in its uniformity to become either older or younger through time, nor ever to have become so, **nor to be them so now,** nor to be about to be so hereafter, nor in general to be subject to any of the conditions which Becoming has attached to the things which move in the world of Sense, these being **generated** forms of Time, which **imitates** Eternity and circles round according to number," Plato, *Tim.* 37D–38A (LCL, 77). See also Philo, Philo, *Deus* 32. This is a life not measured by time, and has neither past nor future, but is lived in "God's eternal To-day," Dodd, *Interpretation*, 150.

Socratic irony

"Jesus answered him. 'Are you a teacher of Israel, and yet **you do not understand** these things?'" 3:9. "If I have told you about earthly things and you do not believe, how can you believe if I tell you about heavenly things?" 3:12. "Even if I testify on my own behalf, my testimony is valid; because I know where I have come from and where I am going, but **you do not know** where I come from or where I am going" (to the Pharisees, 8:14, bold print added).	Socrates: "As I perceive that **you are lazy** [Euthyphro], I will myself show you how you might instruct me in the nature of piety; and I hope that you will not grudge your labour" (*Euthyphr.* 11; B. Jowett, 2:87). "This I do declare, was my experience: those who had the most reputation to me to be almost **the most deficient** . . . and others who were of less repute seemed to be superior men in the matter of being sensible" (*phronimos*, *Apol.* 22A, bold print added).

New conception of deity

VII. GRECO-ROMAN CULTS AND PHILOSOPHIES: ISIS, PLATO, HERMETICA

C. The Fourth Gospel	Plato, Platonism
"For this reason the Jews were seeking all the more to kill him, because he was not only breaking the sabbath, but was also calling God his own Father, thereby **making himself** equal to God (*poieō theos*)," 5:18; The Jews answered, "It is not for a good work that we are going to stone you, but for blasphemy, because you, though only a human being, are **making yourself God**" (*poieō seautou theos*), 10:33; cf. 19:17.	Meletus of Pitthus (an opponent of Socrates) "says I am a **maker of gods** (*poieō theos*); and because I make new gods and do not believe in the old ones, he indicted me for the sake of these old ones, as he says," Plato, *Euthyphr.* 3B. See G. van Kooten, "Last Days of Socrates and Christ," in Petersen et al., *Religio-Philosophical Discourses*, 229–31.

Accused of having a demon

The Jews said to him, "Now we know that you have **a demon** (*daimonion*), 8:52; "Many of them were saying, 'He has a demon and is **out of his mind** (*mainomai*). Why listen to him?'" 10:20; cf. 7:20; 8:48.	Euthyphro, sympathizing with his teacher: "I understand, Socrates, it is because you say the *daimonion* keeps coming to you, so he [Meletus] brought the indictment against you for making innovations in religion" Plato, *Euthyphr.* 3B. The *hoi polloi* "even laugh at me and say **I am crazy** (*mainomenos*) when I say anything in the civic assembly about divine things," *Euthyphr.* 3B-C.

Appeal to a higher authority

"And the word that you hear is not mine, but is from the Father who sent me," 14:24; cf. 3:34; "**My teaching is not mine, but his who sent me,**" 7:16; 8:26; "The Father who has sent me has given me commandment about what to say and what to speak," 12:49.	Socrates: "**For the word which I will speak is not mine.** I will refer you to a witness who is worthy of credit; that witness shall be the God of Delphi [oracle]—he will tell you about my wisdom" (*Apol.* 20). "**At god's behest**" (*kata ton theon*, 22A). "The god gave me a station," (28E). "**I have been commanded by the god to do this**," (33C).

Speaking the truth openly

"For this I came into the world, to **testify to the truth.** Everyone who belongs to the truth listens to my voice" 18:37 (cf. 8:26). "I have spoken openly to the world . . . **I have said nothing in secret,**" (18:20).	"But think only of **the truth of my words**, and give heed to that: let the speaker speak truly and the judge decide justly" (*Apol.* 18). "But I must speak the truth to you" (22A). "There you have the truth . . . **I speak without hiding anything from you.** And yet I know pretty well that I am making myself hated by just that conduct; which is also proof that I am speaking the truth," (24A).

C. The Fourth Gospel	Plato, Platonism

Symposia on love

In the "last symposium" of Jesus (13:1—17:26),[27] they gathered for supper (*deipnon*, 13:2b, 14, 26) attended by "the disciple whom Jesus loved" who is mentioned here for the first time, reclining next to Jesus, at his bosom (13:23; cf. 19:26). Although wine is not mentioned, it is mentioned elsewhere (2:9–10; 4:46; 6:53–56) and is assumed to be present at the meal (cf. Luke 22:17–18, 20). Jesus speaks of love: "Just as I have loved you, you also should love one another," John 13:34; "Those who love me will keep my word, and my Father will love them," 14:23; **"No one has greater love (*agapē*) than this, to lay down one's life for one's friends (*philos*),"** 15:13; "so that the love with which you have loved me may be in them," 17:26.	"When Socrates had taken his place and dined (*deipneō*) with the rest" (*Symp.* 176A) Aristodemus of Cydathenaeum (173B–174E) "being one of the chief among Socrates' lovers at that time" (173B), reclining next to Eryximachus (175A). "What method of drinking will serve us best?" (176A). Eryximachus proposes the theme of love (*erōtos*, 177) and there follows various eulogies on love (*agapē*, 180B). **"Only such as are in love will consent to die for others"**(179B; cf. John 15:13). "Strong friendships (*philias*) and communions (*koinōnias*); all of which Love (*erōs*) is pre-eminently apt to create" (Pausanias, *Symp.* 182C). "Love is . . . the attraction of all creatures to a great variety of things . . . all growths upon the earth, and practically in everything that is . . . how mighty and wonderful and universal is this god [of love] over all affairs both human and divine," (Eryximachus in *Symp.* 186a).
In a similar manner, FG in John 4, gestures towards a scene with erotic overtones "to tell a tale how *eros* can be converted to *agapē* and apostolic mission."[28]	

---

27. On symposia, see also cf. Plutarch, *Amat.*; *Quaest. Conv.* (*Moralia* LCL IX); Xenophon, *Symp.*; Attridge, "Three Symposia on Love," 367–78; Steiner, "Two Suppers," 33–61; Smith, *From Symposium to Eucharist*; on banquet imagery in medieval and renaissance writings, see Bakhtin, *Rabelais and His World*, 278–303.

28. Attridge, "Three Symposia on Love," 372. George van Kooten sees in FG the theme of love in various symposia: e.g., primitive, John 4; 21; and luxurious, John 2; 13–17; "marital love in Cana; insatiable love at the Samaritan well; spiritual, abiding love at the table of the Last Symposium; or the mending of unfaithful, unrequited love at the shores of the Sea of Tiberius; with hints of erotic love—desires of which are then transformed and transcended . . . " (Van Kooten, "Last Days of Socrates and Christ," 224–25).

VII. GRECO-ROMAN CULTS AND PHILOSOPHIES: ISIS, PLATO, HERMETICA   119

C. The Fourth Gospel	Plato, Platonism
Facing death bravely	
"The hour (*hōra*) has come for the Son of Man to be glorified," 12:23; "It is for this reason that I have come to this hour," v. 27. "Then he handed him over to be crucified . . . and **carrying the cross by himself**, he went out to . . . Golgotha," 19:16–17. "When Jesus had received the wine, he said, 'it is finished.' Then he bowed his head and gave up his spirit," 19:30. See G. van Kooten, "Last Days of Socrates and Christ," in Petersen et al., *Religio-Philosophical Discourses*, 219–43.	"But now **the hour (*hōra*) has come** to go away. I go to die," *Apol.* 42A. "A man must not kill himself until god sends some necessity upon him, such has now come upon me," (*Phaed.* 62C). "'I understand,' said Socrates; 'but I may and must pray to the gods that my departure hence be a fortunate one; so I offer this prayer that it may be granted.' With these words he raised the cup to his lips and **very cheerfully and quietly** drained it. Up to that time most of us had been able to restrain our tears fairly well, but when we watched him drinking and saw that he had drunk the poison, we could do so no longer" (117C).

Let us evaluate our comparisons.

D. Tests for Evaluating Alleged Parallels

1. **Similar Contexts:** As we mentioned earlier both Judaism and Christianity developed in the Hellenism of the Roman era. FG's exposure to non-Jewish Greco-Roman influence (Heraclitus, Euripides, Plato) cannot be easily ignored. In our chapter 4, we noted that Philo of Alexandria (20 BCE to 50 CE) was a Greek-speaking Jew who lived in the Diaspora (outside Judea), so were—the apostle Paul (of Tarsus, Cilicia), the author of Hebrews (Alexandria or Ephesus), and perhaps FG (Syria-Palestine and Ephesus). Unlike FG, however, Philo displayed a keen knowledge of Greek philosophy throughout (*Congr.* 78–80; *Aet.* 15–19). Philo also agreed with Plato (429–347 BCE) that the world of ideas which we know through our mind's eye is the *real* world, of which the world of our senses only gives us a shadowy picture. Clement of Alexandria (ca. 200 CE) was greatly indebted to Middle Platonism, citing Plato, the Stoics, and Philo favorably (*Protr.* 6.61; *Strom.* 1.15; 2.4.5). In FG there are contrasts between *what is above* and what is below (3:31), between spirit and flesh (3:6, 6:63), between *eternal life* and natural existence (11:25–26), between *the real bread* from heaven (6:32) and natural bread, between *the water of eternal life* (4:14) and natural water. These contrasts may be compared to a *popular* form of Platonism where there is a *real* world, invisible and eternal, contrasted with the world of appearances here below (Brown, *John* 1:lvii). Philo, *Leg.* 1:108, even reflects upon the Platonic (non-Jewish) view that the soul is entombed in the body until death when it is released from its sepulchre (cf. Plato, *Gorg.* 493A; *Cratyl.* 400B); something not found in FG, see Schnelle, *Human Condition*, 114–44 (on FG). In both literary and cultural contexts, similar phrases and themes (e.g., divinity, love, soul, material world) are interpreted very differently in FG and Plato. See also Marrow, "Κόσμος in John," 90–102. Finally, the Word in FG can be viewed (in some way) as an intermediate "craftsman" (*Demiurge*), but at some remove from

Plato (Layton, *Gnostic Scriptures*, 16). In FG, Jesus is the divine Word of Revelation sent to bring light and life to a world of moral darkness.

2. **Chronological proximity:** Plato (429–347 BCE) and his writings occurred much earlier, but Middle Platonism (ca. 80 BCE–ca. 220 CE) would have been closer to FG, especially via Philo of Alexandria (20 BCE–50 CE). If we can *already* find some parallels with Philo, what significance does a comparison with even earlier writings by Plato provide?[29] Is it making any *distinct* contribution to an understanding of FG? If so, in what way?

3. **Contamination**, cited in Evans, *Word of Glory*, 19–20. Evans also includes the criterion of **contamination** (19) that concerns the question: to what extent has the NT or FG influenced the material with which it is compared? None found in Plato or Philo and little or no Christian influence is found in the Neo-Platonists Plotinus (204–70 CE) and his successors Porphyry (ca. 232–305) and Iamblichus (ca. 245–320). Our comparisons did not employ these last three sources.

4. **Availability to FG and his readers:** The author of Acts mentions "Epicurean and Stoic philosophers" debating with Paul in Athens (17:18), and betrays knowledge of Aratus (v. 28) and Euripides's *Bacchae* (26:14); 2 Peter has some acquaintance with Heraclitus (2 Pet 2:22; Heraclitus, Frg. B 13; NA[28] marginal note); and Paul seems to be familiar with Menander (1 Cor 15:33). FG appears to be acquainted with Wis (e.g., John 3:20; 8:44; 10:20; 14:15; 16:8; 17:15) a Jewish wisdom book influenced by Stoic and Platonic ideas. See also NA[28] (873–74, citations, allusions).

5. **Common viewpoints:** Regarding FG's more-educated Jewish and gentile readers, many would have been familiar with the death of Socrates described by Plato and noticed some similarities with the trial and death of Jesus in FG. The different contexts, however, of the word, phrase, concept (teacher, hero), directly effects our understanding of "common viewpoint." This basic difference alone qualifies or limits our understanding of "common viewpoint."

6. **Verbal and thematic coherence with FG:** The nature of the parallels as linguistic, verbal, and thematic has been noted earlier.[30] As one of the criterion for determining the authentic sayings of Jesus, it concerns what coheres or is consistent with what we already know about Jesus,[31] here it includes the coherence of specific wording and similar perspective or emphasis that "point to a genuine and meaningful relationship of language and conceptuality."[32] In our comparisons (ch. 7. C.) we have highlighted in bold where wording and perspective cohere to some degree. Consulting the primary sources in Greek is important here. What is the "exegetical payoff"? What insight does it bring to our understanding of FG that we would not have previously had without it? Many of the themes and related features

---

29. This question is best answered by examining first—education in antiquity and the learning of Greek (e.g. how to read, composition), see Marrou, *History of Education in Antiquity*; Hock and O'Neil, *Chreia*; MacDonald, *Mimesis and Intertextuality*; Kennedy, *Progymnasmata*.

30. See our ch. 7, p. 110n14 where we cite Davila, "Perils of Parallelism"; Smith, *Tannaitic Parallels*, chs. 1–5; and Smith, *Drudgery Divine*, chs. 2–5.

31. See Puskas and Robbins, *Introduction*, 179.

32. On this "dictional and thematic coherence," see Chilton, *Galilean Rabbi*, cited in Evans, *Word of Glory*, 19–20. This criterion seeks to determine if the parallel is *more* than just a formal analogy or coincidental similarity.

that we have explored in our comparisons with Platonism and Plato's Socrates have highlighted and exemplified significant aspects of FG's account of Jesus (e.g., enlightened, insightful, bold, provocative, trustworthy, resolute).

Hermetica

These writing from Egypt (second-third centuries CE) centered on Hermes Trismegistus ("Thrice-Greatest Hermes"), a legendary sage of ancient Egypt believed to have been deified as the god Toth (protector of knowledge), Hellenized as Hermes, the messenger god of Zeus. The thoughts expressed here are of Platonic and Stoic philosophy combined with ancient Near Eastern religion (written in Greek, Latin, and Coptic). Although the various books, largely independent of each other, were written after FG, some contain earlier traditions. Composed in the form of dialogues between Hermes and his pupils, these writings proclaim a lofty concept of God and human ethical obligations. On knowledge of God and salvation, for example, we learn the following. The perfect human possesses the knowledge of God and is reborn. Salvation is attained through this revealed knowledge (*gnōsis*; cf. John 17:3). Elements of pantheism and the dualism of gnostic thought are also found here.[33]

Acquaintance with Genesis 1–2 (LXX) is evident. Is this a Hellenistic Jewish mystical work? Its pantheism and henotheism (even polytheism) of the Mind, Logos, and Demiurge pervading the universe, makes it a difficult book to classify as Jewish (perhaps Jew-ish). Because it is profoundly influenced by Greco-Roman philosophy, we have located it in this chapter.

We will list the alleged parallels with FG, drawing mostly upon **Corpus Hermeticum 1**: *Poimandres* (Gk. "shepherd man," or Copt. "knowledge of the Sun-God [Ra]"), a Greco-Egyptian mystical revelation of the creation of the world (relying on Gen 1–2) and the ascent of the soul to God through seven spheres. Also, Corpus Hermeticum 13, "Concerning Rebirth," 1.2.

---

33. For text we used Nock and Festugiére, *Corpus Hermeticum*, vol. 1, Poimandrés, Traités 1–12; vol. 2, Traités 13–18, Asclépius (Paris, 1945); and Reitzenstein, *Poimandres*, Gk. text, 328–60; see also Brown, *Gospel according to John*, 1:lviii–lxiv; Dodd, *Interpretation of the Fourth Gospel*, 10–53 and his *Historical Tradition*, 319–22, 342, 361; Cartlidge and Dungan, *Documents*, 250–57; Jonas, *Gnostic Religion*, 147–73 (ET and commentary); Heinrici, *Die Hermes-Mystick*; Bultmann, *John*, numerous citations; Rudolph, *Gnosis*, 25–26, 86–87, 107–8, 120–21, 186–87; and Barrett, *New Testament Background*, 93–103. Umberto Eco understands the less-defined, unshaped symbols of the Hermetic tradition, which spread from the Renaissance and permeated romantic philosophy, as a new paradigm of interpretation, in his *Limits of Interpretation*, 18–20, 24–29.

E. Hermetic Writings	The Fourth Gospel

Creation

Poimandres to a disciple: "The cosmos is ordered and controlled by the Mind (Nous, i.e., God) whose reasoning order (Logos) gave structure to existence," 1.6–7. A secondary creator-god (Demiurge) begotten from God by the Logos, is the shaper of the world, with the Logos, who descends into creation, sets the planets in motion according to the Mind (God), 9–11, Nock and Festugiére, *Corpus Hermeticum*, 1:8–10. Note: e.g., ref., 1.6-7 is Gk. text.; and ref. to Nock et al., 1:8 (vol. 1, p. 8), is Eng. trans. used with permission.	"In the beginning was the Word (Logos) and the Word was God. He was in the beginning with God. All things came into being through him and without him not one thing came into being," 1:1–3. "And the Word became flesh and lived among us," 1:14. "No one has ascended into heaven except the one who descended from heaven, the Son of Man," 3:13. "for I have come down from heaven not to do my own will, but the will of him who sent me," 6:38.

Light and unity

Poimandres to a disciple: "That light . . . am I, Mind, your God, who is before the wet substance which appeared out of the darkness. The shining Logos coming from the Mind is the Son of God . . . The Logos of the Lord and the Mind is the Father, God. They are not to be distinguished from each other. Their union is life," 1.6, Nock and Festugiére, *Corpus Hermeticum*, 1:8.	"I am the light of the world," 8:12; "God is light," 1 John 1:5. "The light of all people," John 1:4b. "The true light which enlightens everyone," v. 9. "The Word (Logos) was with God and the Word was God," 1:1b. "I and the Father are one," 10:30.

Knowledge of God

"This is the good goal of those who have knowledge (*gnōsis*), to become God," 1.26.12–13, Nock and Festugiére, *Corpus Hermeticum*, 1:16. Knowledge (*gnōsis*) of God is the way of salvation," 10.15.8–9, Nock and Festugiére, *Corpus Hermeticum*, 1:120; The Mind (God) enters the pious soul and leads it to the light of knowledge, 10.21.25–26, Nock and Festugiére, *Corpus Hermeticum*, 1:123.	"And this is eternal life, that they may know (*ginōskō*) you, the only true God and Jesus Christ whom you sent," 17:3. For FG, God is known by believing and receiving his Son (1:10–12; 6:69; 14:9; 20:28, 31). Jesus knows God (7:29; 8:55; 17:20), he knows the Father as the Father knows him (10:15), and those who know Jesus know the Father (14:7).

VII. GRECO-ROMAN CULTS AND PHILOSOPHIES: ISIS, PLATO, HERMETICA

E. Hermetic Writings	The Fourth Gospel

Father and Son

"Mind, the Father of all, being life and light, generated a Man equal to himself, whom he loved as being his own offspring, for he was very beautiful since he bore the image of his Father. Truly therefore did God love his own form, and delivered over to him all his own creations . . . He came into the sphere of the Demiurge where he was to have all authority," 12.1–3 (Gen 1:28), Nock and Festugiére, *Corpus Hermeticum*, 1:174–75.

"The Father loves the Son and shows him all that he is doing," 5:20. "Knowing that the Father had given all things into his hands, and that he had come from God and was going to God," 13:3. "Since you have given him (the Son) authority over all people" 17:2.

Heavenly ascent

Disciple to Poimandres: "Tell me about the ascension which takes place," 1.24. Poimandres describes the ascent of the soul to God through seven different stages and spheres, 1.25–26, Nock and Festugiére, *Corpus Hermeticum*, 1:15–16. "Immortality consists in returning to the light and life that is the Father of the universe" (ch. 21).[34]

"The angels of God ascending and descending," 1:51. "No one has ascended into heaven except the one who descended from heaven, the Son of Man," 3:13. "Then what if you were to see the Son of Man ascending to where he was before?" 6:62. "I have not yet ascended to the Father. But go to my brothers and say to them, 'I am ascending to my Father and your Father, to my God and to your God," 20:17.

Rebirth (*palingenesis*)

"No one could be saved before rebirth." One is reborn by the seed of true Good provided by the will of God. "He who is begotten will be another person, God the child of God, the All in All, composed of all the Powers," 13.1–3, Nock and Festugiére, *Corpus Hermeticum*, 2:200–201.

"Verily I tell you, no one can enter the kingdom of God without being born from above" (*gennaō anōthen*; 3:3, 7). "But all who received him . . . he gave power to become children of God," 1:12. On FG and Hermetic dialogues, see Dodd, *Historical Tradition*, 319–22.

---

34. Quote from Perkins, *Gnosticism*, 120, who would agree with C. Colpe that there is no evidence here or in FG for a heavenly redeemer myth, Colpe, *Die religionsgeschichtliche Schule*, 16–17, 60–61.

E. Hermetic Writings	The Fourth Gospel
Holy Father	
"Holy is God and the Father of all. Holy is God whose will is fulfilled by his own powers. Holy is God who wishes to be known and is know by his own. Holy are you who established all by the Logos," 1.31, Nock and Festugiére, *Corpus Hermeticum*, 1:17–18.	"Holy Father, protect them in your name that you have given me," 17:11. "Sanctify them in your truth, your word (Logos) is truth," v. 17. "But you have been anointed by the Holy One and all of you have knowledge," 1 John 2:20. Creation by the Word (Logos), 1:1–3.
Prophet's mission	
Disciple leaving Poimandres: "Filled with power and instructed regarding the nature of the universe and the supreme vision . . . I began to preach to people the beauty of the piety and knowledge . . . why, O earth-bound people, have you given yourselves to death, when you have the right to partake of immortality? . . . And some of them mocked me . . . others begged me to teach them," 1.27–28, Nock and Festugiére, *Corpus Hermeticum*, 1:16–17.	"I have said this to you, so that in me yu may have peace. In the world you face persecution. But take courage; I have conquered the world," 16:33. "As you have sent me into the world, so I have sent them into the world," 17:18. "'As the Father has sent me, so I send you' . . . he (Jesus) breathed on them and said to them 'receive the Holy Spirit. If you forgive the sins of any, they are forgiven them; if you retain the sins of any, they are retained,'" 20:21–23.

F. Tests for Evaluating Alleged Parallels

1. **Similar Contexts:** As we mentioned (Intro. n9) both Judaism and Christianity developed in the Hellenism of the Roman era. FG's exposure to non-Jewish Greco-Roman influence (Heraclitus, Euripides, Plato) cannot be easily ignored. For example, "The Word leaves matter behind to join the demiurgic mind that will govern what has come into being (C.H. 1.4–11) . . . Life and light are the source of the soul and the mind respectively (1.17) . . . A drunken humanity must awaken from unreasoning sleep (ch.27)."[35] In both FG and the Hermetic dialogues, "we find the oracular utterance of the teacher, met by the pupil with incomprehension or misunderstanding, and as in John , this sometimes provokes a reprimand, but invariably leads to a further explication of the theme. The interlocutor plays an essentially passive part; his interpellations do no more than provide the teacher with an occasion to elaborate his thought" (C. H. Dodd, *Historical Tradition*, 319–20). We appeal again to the following works, distinguishing FG from dualistic cosmogony of seven spheres, Marrow, "Κόσμος in John," 90–102, and salvation by means of *gnōsis*, Schnelle, *Human Condition*, 114–44 (on FG).

35. Quotations from Perkins, *Gnosticism*, 119–20, citing Hermetic texts from Foerster, *Gnosis*, 1:326–36; Reitzenstein, *Poimandres*, esp. 328–60 (Gk. text).

VII. GRECO-ROMAN CULTS AND PHILOSOPHIES: ISIS, PLATO, HERMETICA 125

2. **Chronological proximity:** The Hermetic writings (second-third centuries CE) are later than FG (ca. 95 CE). Earlier traditions are difficult to detect as we have indicated, e.g., the five or six criteria used for determining the authentic sayings of Jesus, have produced tentative results at best. If we can *already* find some parallels with Gen 1–2, what significance does a comparison with later interpretations provide? Is it making any *distinct* contribution to an understanding of FG? If so, in what way? See Yamauchi, *Pre-Christian Gnosticism*, 71–72.

3. **Contamination,** cited in Evans, *Word of Glory*, 19–20. Evans also includes the criterion of **contamination** (19) that concerns the question: to what extent has the NT or FG influenced the material with which it is compared? Although the Hermetica are later than FG, LXX influence (Gen 1–2) is evident, but Christian influence appears to be minimal.

4. **Availability to FG and his readers:** As stated earlier, the author of Acts mentions "Epicurean and Stoic philosophers" debating with Paul in Athens (17:18), and betrays knowledge of Aratus (v. 28) and Euripides's *Bacchae* (26:14); 2 Peter has some acquaintance with Heraclitus (2 Pet 2:22); and Paul seems to be familiar with Menander (1 Cor 15:33). FG appears to be acquainted with Wis (e.g., John 3:20; 8:44; 10:20; 14:15; 16:8; 17:15) a Jewish wisdom book influenced by Stoic and Platonic ideas. See NA[28] (873–74, citations, allusions). It is plausible that FG, and some in his audience, would have some familiarity with concepts similar to those we find in the Hermetica.

5. **Common viewpoints:** Regarding FG's more-educated readers (Jewish and gentile), acquaintance with LXX Gen 1–2 is assumed. Although some might understand the Middle Platonic and Stoic speculations in the Hermetica, it is uncertain if they would have shared its view of cosmogony, divinity with Mind, Logos, and Demiurge, the seven spheres of heaven (but see "the third heaven," in 2 Cor 12:2), none of these concepts are similar *in detail* to what we find in FG.

6. **Verbal and thematic coherence with FG:** The nature of the parallels as linguistic, verbal, and thematic has been noted earlier. As one of the criteria for determining the authentic sayings of Jesus, it concerns what coheres or is consistent with what we already know about Jesus, here it includes the coherence of specific wording and similar perspective or emphasis that "point to a genuine and meaningful relationship of language and conceptuality." Consulting the primary sources in Greek is important here. Again, we ask the questions. What is the "exegetical payoff"? What insight does it bring to our understanding of FG that we would not have previously had without it? This category is a difficult one to satisfy in our comparison of FG with the Hermetica. The Hermetic themes compared with FG (above) nevertheless disclose for us some noteworthy kinship of ideas (e.g., knowledge of God, rebirth).

VIII. The Dionysian Gospel[1]

THE FOLLOWING QUOTATIONS PROVIDE for this chapter some reasons for writing it.

> ... it should be no surprise that the apostle who wrote the Gospel of John should be acquainted with Greek theater and that he should be influenced by it in his writing.[2]

> The most influential and most sublime portrayal of the Dionysian world comes only at the end of the fifth century with the *Bacchae* of Euripides, performed at about 400.[3]

> There can be no doubt that the story has been taken from heathen legend and ascribed to Jesus. In fact the motif of the story, the changing of water to wine, is a typical motif of the Dionysus legend.[4]

> ... at present there are two main approaches seeking a *Vorlage* for the production of this miracle story ... those who favor the story of the god Dionysus and those who favor an Old Testament background, such as the prophet Isaiah or the book of Esther with its early traces of the feast of Purim.[5]

> ... Dionysiac echoes have been noticed throughout centuries of fourth-gospel research.[6]

---

1. The title of this chapter is the title of a recent book by Dennis MacDonald: *The Dionysian Gospel*, the contents of which are a major subject of this chapter. Koester (*Symbolism in the Fourth Gospel*, 81) has suggested that the Dionysus traditions "help us understand how the story could communicate the significance of Jesus to Greeks as well as Jews."

2. Wead, *Literary Devices in John's Gospel*, 122. See our discussion of dramatic aspects of FG (Introduction, p. 8n25).

3. Burkert, *Greek Religion*, 163. The dating is BCE.

4. Bultmann, *John*, 118–19.

5. Claussen, "Turning Water to Wine," 80.

6. Stibbe, *John as Storyteller*, 112.

VIII. THE DIONYSIAN GOSPEL

Many Johannine scholars have noted similarities between the gospel's representation of Jesus and both Euripides's protagonist in the Bacchae and Greco-Roman traditions about Dionysus.[7]

[I am Dionysus, the son of Zeus, returned to Thebes revealed, a god to men.] But the men [of Thebes] blasphemed me. They slandered me; they said I came of mortal man, and not content with speaking blasphemies [they dared to threaten my person with violence.][8]

the 'moral' of the *Bacchae* is that we ignore at our peril the demand of the human spirit for Dionysiac experience.[9]

For us the Bacchae is a unique specimen of a Dionysiac passion-play; but for its first audience it was a rehandling of a theme already familiar to generations of Athenian play-goers.[10]

Introduction

In this chapter we will examine both some early Christian interaction with the *Bacchae* (specifically that which included some allusion or reference to the FG), and we will summarize and discuss a few modern scholarly theories about it, presenting their evidence for a relationship. The quotations above indicate how extensive is this field of study, especially related to Jesus as the dispenser of wine (John 2:1–11).[11]

We will begin by introducing briefly the pieces of this discussion: **the god Dionysus**, the mystery cult, the dramatist Euripides and the play *Bacchae*. Our review of some early Christian literature will begin with Justin Martyr, then proceed to Origen, to show the antiquity of the topic. We will then discuss in varying detail three modern contributing scholars: Mark Stibbe and David Wead, followed by Dennis MacDonald, whose recent book takes the topic much further. As we show in the notes, there have been many who have engaged in this discourse.

---

7. Jo-Ann A. Brant's review of Dennis R. MacDonald, *The Dionysian Gospel: The Fourth Gospel and Euripides*, in *Review of Biblical Literature* 3 (2018).

8. Arrowsmith, Appendix to *Bacchae*, 83.

9. Dodds, *Euripides Bacchae*, xlv.

10. Dodds, *Euripides Bacchae*, xxviii.

11. See for example, Bultmann, *John*, 118–20; Brant, *Greek Tragedy in the Fourth Gospel*; Pratt, "Gospel of John from the Standpoint of Greek Tragedy," 448–59; Claussen, "Turning Water to Wine," 78–97; Hoskyns, *Fourth Gospel*, 191–92; Thompson, *John: A Commentary*, 64.

Bacchae is a tragedy written by Euripides, who was born "between 485 and 480 BCE. He presented his first set of tragedies in 455, winning his first victory in 441."[12] The *Bacchae* was written shortly before his death (407–406 BCE), and was "posthumously presented along with *Iphigenia in Aulis* and *Alcmaeon in Corinth*,"[13] winning first prize. His style among tragedians was criticized by many as being below the standard set by Sophocles, by both technical analysts (Aristotle, *Poetics*), and by satirical writers (Aristophanes). But "after his death Euripides became the most admired of the tragic poets and his plays were often revived."[14] The enduring and pervasive influence of Euripides's subject matter—the Dionysian cult—in the Hellenistic world where Christianity was birthed should certainly capture the attention of New Testament scholars.[15] It was not a new subject or topic to the Greeks.[16]

---

12. Lattimore's introduction in Euripides, *Euripides I*, v.

13. Green and Lattimore, "Chronological Note on the Plays of Euripides," in *Euripides V*, 1.

14. Lucas, "Euripides," 421. "After the death of Alexander the Great, when Greek theaters and Greek culture spread over the world, Euripides was played everywhere" (Roche, *Three Plays of Euripides*, viiin1).

15. See Friesen, *Reading Dionysus*. And from the more chthonic world of archaeology, see V. J. Hutchinson, "The Cult of Dionysus/Bacchus in the Greco-Roman World" *JRA* 4 (1991) 222–30 (reference culled from Bell, *Exploring*, 147). And from the world of art, see Massa, *Tra la vigna e la croce* (reference culled from review by James Hume, *Bryn Mawr Classical Review* 10 [2015]). Hume writes, "The author's task is complicated, first, by the polyvalence of Dionysus' symbolism, in whose myths the vine is as likely to represent entanglement and destruction as fertility and joy; and, second, by the influence of another tradition (the biblical one) which was grafted by early Christian writers and artists onto that of Bacchus. In the OT and NT, after all, wine, the vine, and the vineyard have symbolic and sacramental meanings peculiar to their own cultural contexts." But "the complexity of the relationship between Dionysus and the Christian sources" (15) does not deter Massa. Indeed, that complexity is very much to his purpose, which is to trace the vicissitudes of this relationship "from opposition to cohabitation, and from religious competition to cultural mediation" (our translation). In Massa's account, early conflict (*scontro*) between the two sects gave way to a vigorous encounter (*incontro*), and though one of these sects eventually triumphed over the other, that outcome is best described as a case of *sovrapposizione* (which should, we think, be translated as "overlay" rather than "conquest," inasmuch as each sect could equally be said to have taken over the other). Similarly, the process that led to this triumph was, in Massa's preferred terminology, a matter of *reconfigurazione* (reshaping) and *resemantizzazione* (reinterpretation). Both cults, Christian and Dionysiac, were profoundly affected by this cultural exchange, but the book's principal focus is on the identity that the Church forged for itself out of this welter of influences." See also our discussion in ch. 7, "Greco-Roman Cults and Philosophies," p. 109.

16. "The *pathē* (πάθη) of Dionysus, the patron god of drama, may well be the oldest of all dramatic subjects. For us the *Bacchae* is a unique specimen of a Dionysiac passion-play; but for its first audience it was a rehandling of a theme already familiar to

1. Celsus and Origen

Although we do not have the original critical Discourse[17] written by Celsus, a Greek philosopher of the second century CE, we do have the response to the discourse that recalled "two generations prior"[18] by Origen "who was over 60 years old,"[19] titled *Contra Celsum (Cels.)* in which a full review with full collection of quotations is preserved. Martin Hengel, quoting from *Cels.* 2.34, 35, summarizes:

> "Celsus makes his Jewish informant quote Dionysius [sic], captured by Pentheus, in Euripides' *Bacchae* (498): 34: 'The God himself will set me free whenever I wish it.' 'But the one who condemned him [Pilate] does not even suffer any such fate as that of Pentheus by going mad or being torn to pieces.' 35: 'Why, if not before, does he [Jesus] not at any rate now show forth something divine, and deliver himself from this shame, and take his revenge on those who insult him and his Father?'"[20]

In this way, Celsus argues "Euripides' *Bacchae* and the Homeric Hymn to Dionysus[21] show how a real god in disguise deals with his opponents."[22] Of course the comment was made to criticize the divine sonship of Jesus. So continues a literary trail of FG being read within a Hellenistic environment, being specifically compared to *Bacchae*.[23] It is not the first time that Jesus and Dionysus were so connected in thought, for Justin Martyr in his *First Apology*, and in *Dialogue with Trypho* refers to the Greek traditions of "sons of god,"[24] including specific mention of Dionysus in both texts.[25]

---

generations of Athenian play-goers" (Dodds, *Euripides Bacchae*, xxvii).

17. The title of which was *True Word (Λογος Αληθης)*. It was written around 175 CE. Origen's response was written around 248 titled *Contra Celsum*. For the Greek text: numerous links are accessible, e.g., https://archive.org/details/contracelsumlibooselwgoog/page/n5; or see Migne, *Patrologiae Graeca* (Origen vols. 11–17). For a modern translation: Henry Chadwick, *Origen: Contra Celsum*, Cambridge University Press, 1980.

18. Cf. Hans von Campenhausen, "zwei Menschenalter zuvor" (*Griechische Kirchenväter*, 58).

19. Eusebius, *Hist. eccl.* 6.36.1.

20. Hengel, *Johannine Question*, 70, 191n86 (*Cels.* trans. H. Chadwick). Brackets are from us.

21. Hesiod, *Hesiod*, 286–88.

22. Hengel, *Johannine Question*, 70.

23. For a full discussion of Origen and Celsus, Dennis MacDonald recommends Friesen, *Reading Dionysus*, 149–73.

24. Justin, *Apol.* 21, 54.

25. Justin, *Apol.* 54; *Dial.* 69.

2. Clement of Alexandria (ca. 150–211 CE)

In Clement of Alexandria's *Exhortation to the Greeks* is the excerpt below (quotation taken from Dennis MacDonald [DM], *Dionysian Gospel*, 34–35). The *Exhortation* or *Protrepticus* was the first of Clement's popular trilogy (the other two being *Paedagogus* and *Stromata*, all being written perhaps between 189 and Clement's death [211 CE]; the *Stromata* is believed to be his last work). The text is notable for its focus upon the *Bacchae* (especially the Prologue speech of Dionysus) and its use of John's Gospel, (especially the Prologue).[26] Some Greek words are used or played upon from *Bacchae* (as noted by DM). The intertextuality within this short excerpt of FG and *Bacchae* is strong evidence of how the two would have been read by Greeks, at least someone with Clement's substantial aptitude. Dennis MacDonald's point was that Clement was inviting Dionysus to convert.

> "Come [ἥκε], O madman, not propped up by a thyrsus [25] not wreathed with ivy [25]! Throw off your headband! Throw off your fawnskin [24]! Get sober! I will show you the Logos and the mysteries of the Logos, and I will describe them with your own imagery. This mountain [33] is beloved of God and is not subject to tragedies, like Cithaeron [a bacchic mountain prominent in the *Bacchae*], but exalted by dramas of truth, a sober mountain and shaded by chaste woods [cf. 38]. Reveling here are no maenads [52], daughters of "thunder-stricken" Semele [6], initiates in the disgusting distribution of raw flesh [139]; instead, they are the daughters of God, the beautiful lambs [ἀμνάδες, a pun on μαινάδες], who utter the solemn rites [ὄργια ; 34] of the Logos and gather together a sober chorus. This chorus consists of the righteous, and their song is a hymn to the King of all. Young girls pluck their instruments [cf. 58–59], angels sing praises, prophets speak, the sound of music carries. Quickly they follow the thiasos [56]; those who were called scurry off, longing to welcome the Father. (*Protrepticus* 12.119.1–2)

3. Mark W. G. Stibbe, David W. Wead and Dennis MacDonald

We have chosen to discuss here three modern scholars contributing to this subject: the first two as a preface to the more-detailed presentation of the third (DM).

---

26. Further mention of Clement of Alexandria and FG, is also made in our chs. 4, 7–8, 10–12.

Mark Stibbe gives these eleven broad similarities between the *Bacchae* and the FG:[27]

A. The Fourth Gospel and the *Bacchae* (Mark Stibbe)

1. The Prologue of both stories concentrates upon the same theme: a divine being goes to his home but is rejected by members of his family.[28]
2. In both stories the protagaonist is an unrecognized deity, a stranger from heaven, who faces intense hostility and unbelief from the ruling part of the city.
3. In both stories the goal of the deity is basically philanthropic, for it is Dionysius's desire to share the wine that alleviates man's sufferings, whilst it is Jesus's desire that man should drink of his life-giving blood (John 2, where the wine has been seen as a dionysiac symbol, and John 6, where the blood of Jesus arguably points to the wine of the Eucharist).
4. In both stories, the tragic *hamartia* consists of the antagonist's failure to recognize one who is really a member of the same family.
5. In both stories the *pathos* consists of the victim being dressed up in humiliating garb (John 19:2-3), led out of the city to an accursed hill (19:17), hoisted up on to a 'tree' (19:18) and then killed.
6. In both stories, women fulfill the role of true worshipers of the visiting deity.
7. In both stories, the *theomachus*, the enemies of the deity, attempt to stone the god.
8. In both stories, the deity is ambiguous and elusive, often speaking and acting in such a way as to escape definition and capture.
9. In both stories, the place of the city is important as a symbol of institutionalized religion and the loss of the immediacy of belief.
10. In both stories the divine stranger has thaumaturgic powers.
11. In both stories, the tragic action is not centred upon one person. The *Bacchae* is not called *Dionysus*, nor is it called *Pentheus*, even though both titles would have been possible given the prominence of these protagonists. In John's story too, the tragic action centres not only on Jesus but also on the Jews and Pilate.

Of the "several scholars who have compared the FG with Euripides drama,"[29] "none have argued for any direct mimetic connection," which is most surprising to MacDonald, who quotes Stibbe at length:

27. Stibbe, *John as Storyteller*, 134-35.
28. Concerning the Prologue, DM quotes Parsenios, *Rhetoric and Drama in the Johannine Lawsuit Motif*, 47, that it "represents a creative union of Greek tragic elements and the theological and linguistic world of the Old Testament. It sounds like Genesis 1, but it operates like the prologue of a Greek play."
29. Cf. MacDonald, *Dionysian Gospel*, 25-27.

> I am not arguing that John necessarily knew the *Bacchae* by heart and that he consciously set up a number of literary echoes ... What I am arguing is that John unconsciously chose the *mythos* of tragedy when he set about rewriting his tradition about Jesus and that general echoes with Euripides' story of Dionysus are therefore, in a sense, inevitable ... It is important to repeat at this stage that I have nowhere put forward the argument for a direct literary dependence of John on Euripides. That, in fact, would be the simplest but the least likely solution.[30]

David Wead also stops short of saying that a reconstruction of the Gospel would "fit well" to a format of Greek play used by Aeschylus, Sophocles, or Euripides.[31] But he does say that "we should look at the basic structure to gain insights into the pattern John used to construct his Gospel."[32]

MacDonald's work both says that the author of the FG consciously set up literary echoes, and that one should and can look for "direct literary dependence" on the *Bacchae*. In his book he even proposes that if this trail is pursued, it offers answers to long recognized dilemmas in the FG. Our review of his work will look only at the echoes and evidence offered for literary dependence.

4. Dennis MacDonald (DM)

DM's primary proposal is that there was a *first* edition of the Gospel which was written in imitation or *mimesis* of Euripides's tragedy *Bacchae* with the goal of using Dionysus as a christological foil for explaining Jesus. Successive editions or "relectures" of the FG did not build upon this mimesis.[33] The

---

30. MacDonald, *Dionysian Gospel*, 26.

31. Wead, *Literary Devices*, 22. The conclusion of Pratt. After giving mention to the 1897 work of Thirlwall, and the 1907 work of Pratt ("Gospel of John from the Standpoint of Greek Tragedy") Wead eases back and says "we would not go this far."

32. Wead, *Literary Devices*, 122. The difference between "basic structure" that Wead proposes, and "the format used by" the three famous Greek tragedians, which Pratt proposed, is given some explanation in the seven-page epilogue, that is helpful reading. He defends, for example, the authenticity of John 21 stating that while it looks like a secondary ending, added by a later redactor, it was typical for Euripides to close in at least three different ways: *deus ex machina*, an aetiological reference, and the use of the chorus" (125), and "often more than one of these elements might be used." Thus he concludes "we find that they (John 20 and 21) are akin to the epilogue as Euripides used it" (127).

33. DM gives a conjectural reconstruction (in Greek) of this first edition with a 4-page introduction, *Dionysian Gospel*, 173–201 (Appendix 1). He states "the authors of the second and third editions add no further Dionysian elements" (25). An integral part of his thesis is an explanation of the order of production of our extant Johannine canonical literature. The chronological order he proposed is 2 John, 3 John, 1 John, then the first edition of FG. See discussion in our Introduction (n49, pp. 11–12) that FG may reflect at least two editions.

VIII. THE DIONYSIAN GOSPEL

List of Proposed Imitations are given on page xvii–xviii, which is provided in Table B. These are somewhat explained in Macdonald's substantive intertextual commentary in *Dionysian Gospel*, 28–123, briefly summarized in Table C below. The methodological basis for DM's mimesis proposal are summarized in 7 criteria, given in Table D (pp. 143–44) and in *Dionysian Gospel*, 110–23. DM explains how all of these criteria are satisfied in the first edition of FG.

B. List of Proposed Imitations[34]

FG	*Bacchae*
1:1–5. The Origin of the Logos	1–9
1:6–8. John, the faithful witness	10–12
1:9–11. The rejection of the Logos	13–34
1:14, 16. The Logos assumes a human body	43–63
1:18. The one in the lap of the Father	63–113
1:32–51. The Son of God with many names	64–113
2:1–11. Changing water into wine	266–85
2:13–17. Avenging the Father's house	35–42
3:1–4, 10, 16. An old man seeks rejuvenation	170–209
3:29–31. The Son of God must increase	170–209, esp. 181–83
4:4–29, 40–42. The donor of living water	114–66
4:46–54. The healing of the royal official's son	519–603
5:2–9. An old cripple walks again	170–209
6:35, 53–58. Eating the flesh of the Son of God	114–66
7:31–52. Jesus escapes arrest	657–777
8:2–19. Interrogating the Son of God	451–518
8:32–36. The true liberator	519–642
8.58–59. The escape artist	519–642
9:1–41. The blind seer	286–342
11:3–5, 35–36. The love God	210–65
11:37–46. The life-giver	519–642
11:47–57. The God-fighters	343–430, esp. 352–66
15:1–2, 4. The true grapevine	266–85
18:1–12. Arresting the Son of God	431–50
18:13—19:16. Interrogating the Son of God, again	451–518
19:25–30. Violent death and attending women	738–1167, esp. 1115–21
20:11–18. A woman's recognition	1168–329
20:19–23. Exit stage up	1330–87
20:30–31. Postscript	1388–92

---

34. From MacDonald, *Dionysian Gospel*, xvii–xviii.

C. Intertextual Commentary (*Dionysian Gospel*, 28–123)[35]

There is some variation between the "List of Proposed Imitations" in the Introduction and the "Intertextual Commentary." We have listed below what appears in the "Intertextual Commentary" with brief explanation of what seemed to us to be the points scored. As has been noticed by his reviewers, some points are strong, and they must carry the weaker points towards what DM hopes to be a compelling argument. The Conclusion of the Intertextual Commentary is a synopsis of how the data satisfy the "Seven Criteria of Mimesis Criticism."

Meeting the Criteria of Mimesis Criticism

FG	Bacchae
1:1–5 "The Origin of the Logos" protagonist identified as a god	1–9 begins with the god declaring his identity
1:6–8 "Join the Faithful Witness" attention shifted to the sole witness of the light; later the Baptist again plays the role of Cadmus	10–12 Cadmus, is singled out for praise
1:9–11 "The Logos and Dionysus both came to their own regions, and their own people did not receive them"	13–34
1:14,16 "The Logos Assumes a Human Body" Logos became flesh to offer grace and truth.	43–64 Dionysus says, in order to reveal power and punish Pentheus, "To these ends I have laid my deity aside and go disguised as a man."

35. Part C provides what MacDonald calls an "Intertextual Commentary." For eighty-two pages MacDonald takes us through a reading of the Fourth Gospel laying comparison passages from the Bacchae, as well as other relevant texts, showing where similarities in action, motifs, and wording appear. The gospel begins by identifying Jesus as God and the Bacchae begins with Dionysus identifying himself as the son of Zeus. Both prologues shift attention to predecessors of the protagonists, then continue to the story of a hero who comes to his own people but is rejected and then reveals himself in mortal flesh: the Greek god to punish and the biblical God to bring "gift after gift" (24–34). MacDonald's commentary proceeds to explore how FG imitates Euripides's play in order to present Jesus as a god bearing Dionysian gifts of wine, rejuvenation, springs of water, and life as well as Demeter's grain (40–66). MacDonald compares the Johannine discourse on eating Jesus's flesh and drinking his blood to the Dionysian rites of *sparagmos* (dismembering living beasts) and *omophagia* (eating raw flesh), the symbolic acts that bring joy and union with the god (64–67). John's blind man is Euripides's Tiresias, who though blind can see (73–75) (excerpt Brant, "Review").

FG	Bacchae

1:18 "The One in the Lap of the Father" Logos called *monogenēs* [μονογενής] to exclude other such offspring (such as Dionysus, who is twice in *Bacchae* called "Zeus's offspring [Διος γονος]" 603, 1038).

63–113
The story of Dionysus's birth after being sewn into into the thigh of Zeus[36] after the death of the pregnant Semele is well known.

DM translates *kolpos* [κόλπος] as "lap"—"the one in the lap of the Father"—it is normally translated "bosom" (cf. LSJ), but refers to "the region of the body extending from the breast to the legs, especially when a person is in the seated position" (DM quoting the Louw-Nida Greek-English Lexicon).

1:19–51 "The Son of God with many names" In the first chapter of the Gospel the reader learns that Jesus is "the Logos," "the light, "the one-of-a-kind God," "the chosen one of God" (34), "Messiah ... Christ" (41), "son of Joseph" (45), "rabbi, ... Son of God, ... king of Israel" (49,) and "Son of Man" (51).

"Dionysus was notorious for his multiple titles. In the *Bacchae* ... Dionysus, but also Bacchus, Bromios (Clamor), Iacchos, Dithyrambos, "the god," and the "Child of Zeus." On multiple names see also our tbls. in chs. 7.A.2, pp. 107–8. Isis, and 10. E. Trimorphic Protennoia, 176–77.

2:1–11 "Changing Water into Wine" "By making Jesus's first miracle the production of wine the Johannine Evangelist notifies the reader that Jesus will rival Dionysus" (42).

"The Changing of water into wine was Dionysus's signature miracle" (40).[37]

---

36. "Was taken by Zeus and sheltered
Deep within his thigh:
stitched with golden brackets
Secreted from Hera"
Bacchae 95–99 (Roche, *Three Plays of Euripides*, 82).

37. For the evidence DM refers the reader to Ingo Broer, "Das Weinwunder zu Kana," 91–308). He offers (Excursus 4, 43–45) the text in Achilles Tatius as an example of Dionysus turning water to wine. See his discussion there, using the work of Friesen, "Dionysus as Jesus," 222–40, who argues that the miracle of the FG informed Tatius's telling of the story, and isolates parallels or "similarities" between the romance and the Gospel texts, which DM says "are too strong to be accidental" and would "certainly not have gone unnoticed by a reader with a knowledge of Christianity" (44).

Whether Dionysus himself is ever said to have turned water into wine (as Jesus had done in John 2:7-10) is a debated issue in the literature. Textual evidence that Dionysus "made" wine, and that he gave it as a gift to humankind, and that empty jars were overnight mysteriously turned into wine, are abundant. For a collection of some sources (some post-Christian, several of which reflects hints or suggestions of water), see Meyer, *Ancient Mysteries*, 63–109. Those most suggestive for the presence/ transformation of water are *The Adventures of Leucippe and Clitophon*, Book 2.2-3

FG	Bacchae
2:13–17 "Avenging the Father's House"	"resembles Dionysus's intention to vindicate his mother in the place of his birth"
5:2–9; 2:23–24 "An Old Cripple Walks Again" "The man had been crippled for thirty-eight years ... an old man by ancient standards" (47).	"Early in the *Bacchae* two old men, Cadmus and Tiresias, gain the strength to dance ... " (47) (*Bacchae*, 180–90, 193, 195, 197–98, 204–9).
3:1–24 "Another Old Man Seeks Rejuvenation" Nicodemus, "like Cadmus a ruler" (48) and an old man (self-described as "being old" (γέρων ὤν) vs.4), thinking about youth, childhood, rebirth). "The word γέρων appears nowhere else in the New Testament and both here and in the *Bacch.* 189 it is followed by a present participle of the verb "to be." (49)	Cadmus and Nicodemus being paralleled (*Bacchae*, 187–89, 193). "Although Cadmus was old, the god made him dance; although Nicodemus was old, he could be born from above" (49). "Only Nicodemus among the Pharisees recognized Jesus's divine agency. In the *Bacchae* only Cadmus and Tiresias among the men of Thebes regarded Dionysus's miracles as evidence of his divinity" (49).

(Meyer, 93–94: "the herdsman ... said to the god: 'Where did you get this purple water, my friend? Wherever did you find blood so sweet? For it is not that water that flows on the ground ... This, said Dionysos, is harvest water, the blood of the grape'"); and Pausanias, *Description of Greece,* Book 6: Elis 2, 26.1–2 ("It was said, for instance, that a fountain of wine flowed by itself from the ground and that spring water from the temple of Liber (identified with Dionysos) had the flavor of wine on festival days"); Diodorus Siculus, *Library of History,* 3.66–12; Pliny the Elder, *Nat.* 2.106, 31.13; cp. "the springs of cool water and wine that comes forth when a Bacchante strikes the ground with her thyrsus in Euripides" (*Bacchae*, Meyer, *Ancient Mysteries*, 94–95).

But some interpreters are unconvinced. Meier (*Marginal Jew,* 2:949n255) says "I have not bothered to treat in detail the suggestion made by Bultmann (*Das Evangelium des Johannes*, p.83) and accepted by a number of British exegetes (E.g. Dodd, Lindars) that the first Cana miracle is connected with the Hellenistic cult of the wine god Dionysus. Simply as a matter of fact, many scholars have not been convinced by this position. Even the hardly credulous Haenchen points out the difficulties of the theory; see his *John 1,* 177–78 and the literature cited there. Haenchen depends especially on Noetzel, *Christus und Dionysos.* ... Specifically he shows that nowhere in the Dionysus myth or cult is Dionysus said to turn water into wine." See also the Roman Catholic scholar, Raymond F. Collins, who finds marriage (e.g., Ezek 16:8–13) and wine motifs (Amos 9:13; Isa 25:6; 2 Bar 29:5) from prophetic and apocalyptic traditions more helpful for understanding the wedding of Cana story, in his *These Things Have Been Written,* 158–82.

FG	Bacchae
3:25–30 "The Son of God must Increase" "it is necessary [δεῖ] that that he increase [αὐξάνειν] and that I decrease" (50).	"For it is now necessary [δεῖ]—with respect to the child of my daughter, / Dionysus, a god manifest to people—/to increase [αὐξάνειν μέγαν] him as much as we are able" (50; Bacchae, 181–83).
"This is the only instance of the verb αὐξάνω in the Johannine corpus." Particularly impressive is the use of the infinitive verb with "it is necessary" in both books" (50).	
4:1–42 "The Donor of Living Water" (51–56) "The scene modestly resembles Dionysus and the maenads" (51).	
4:46–54 "The Healing of the Royal Official's Son" (56–58) Jesus's arrival, on the other hand, brought life to the royal official's son and faith to his house: "he and his entire household [οἰκία] believed" (4:53).	
6:53b–66 "Eating the Flesh of the Son of God" (64–67) "The Johannine Evangelist creates a radically new soteriology, namely, that by eating Jesus' flesh (σάρξ) and drinking his blood (αἷμα) his followers will gain eternal life" (65).	"The cult of Dionysus famously involved two related rites, *sparagmos* and *omophagia* . . . specifically the eating of the flesh and blood of the god and the immortality that initiates gain by such activity" (65).[38]
"There is no Passover, no inner room, no ritual setting, no meal, no loaf of bread being broken for anyone, no cup to drink and no wine at all, no mention of a substitutionary death, no new covenant, and nothing to remember. The setting is outdoors during the day, before a large and mixed multitude of outsiders and disciples, in the midst of a difficult controversy in which Jesus seems to offend purposely as many people as possible."[39]	"This symbolic act brought union with Dionysus, Dionysus with the celebrant, who granted eternal life."[40]

---

38. Cf. Dodds, *Euripides: Bacchae*, xvi–xxii for a discussion of these rites.
39. Riley, *I Was Thought to Be What I Am Not*, 19–22.
40. Riley, *I Was Thought to Be What I Am Not*, 22.

FG	Bacchae
"my flesh is true [ἀληθής] food, and my blood is true [ἀληθής] drink. The one chewing [τρώγων] my flesh and drinking my blood abides in me and I in him" (John 6:55–56) (66).	"Such mystical union is not articulated in the *Bacchae*" but from other related sources (65).
7:31–52 "Jesus Escapes Arrest" (67–68) "No person ever [οὐδενὸς θεῶν] spoke like this man."	"Dionysus is inferior to none of the gods [οὐδεπότε . . . ἄνθρωπος]" (*Bacchae*, 777).
The Pharisees persisted in their murderous hostility.	Pentheus persisted in his murderous hostility.
8:12–19 "Interrogating the Son of God" (68–71) "Two passages in the first Johannine Gospel imitate Pentheus's interrogation of Dionysus. In the first it is the Pharisees who question Jesus; in the second it is Pilate. . . . The density of affinities with *Bacc.* 451–518, . . . requires mimesis of Euripides" (68).	451–518
	-Pentheus interrogates the priest / god in disguise.
-The Pharisees interrogate Jesus, who claims to be the light of the world. -The Pharisees do not know "from where [πόθεν]" Jesus came (14b). -Jesus states that he came from his Father (16b). -"you do not know [οὐκ οἴδατε] where I came from" (8:14).	-Pentheus asks "from where [πόθεν]" the stranger brought the new cult (465). -Dionysus states that the sacreed rites come from "the son of Zeus" (466–67). -"You do not know [οὐκ οἶσθ'] what life you live, or what you are doing, or what you are" (506).
-[Jesus:] "I am not alone—I and [with me] the Father who sent me." [Pharisees:] "Where is [ποῦ ἐστιν] your Father?" [Jesus:] "You know neither me nor the Father [οὔτε ἐμὲ οἴδατε οὔτε τὸν πατέρα]; if you had known [ᾔδειτε] me, you also would have known [ᾔδειτε] my Father" (8:19).	-[Dionysus:] Even now he is near and sees what I am suffering / [Pentheus:] where is [ποῦ ἐστιν] he? He is not visible to my eyes. / [Dionysus:] He is here with me; because you are impious, you do not see him (500–502).
The Pharisees remain defiant and try to stone Jesus.	Pentheus remains defiant and decides to kill the god by stoning or decapitation.

FG	Bacchae
8:32–37a, 58b–59a. "The True Liberator" (71–73) "If the Son liberates [ἐλευθερώσει] you, you really are liberated [ἐλεύυεροι] (8:36). "Of the Gospels, only John uses the root ελευθερ- of Jesus; he does so under the influence of Dionysian religion" (73).	519–642 In *Bacchae*, Dionysus was liberated or set free [λυσεῖν] (498, 641), thus becoming a liberator? Dionysus was "a liberator, as evidence in his various cult titles, such as Ἐλευθερεύς, Λύσιος, Λυαῖος, σωτήρ" (72).
9:1–41 "The Blind Seer" (73–75) Tragedians, like Gospel writers, play with the "blindness" of those that can see, and the clear vision of those that are blind.	286–342 "Clement of Alexandria contrasted the blindness of Tiresias in this section of the *Bacchae* with the sight that Christ offers the blind" (75, quoting from *Protr.* 12.119.3–4, but without explicit reference to FG by Clement).
10:39–42 "The Escape Artist" (75–76) "they sought to nab him again, and he left their grasp" (10:39). cf. 8:59 "They took stones to throw at him, but Jesus was hidden [ἐκρύβη] and left [ἐξῆλθεν]." This is more than a Johannine motif (cf. Luke 4:30 "Passing through their midst, He went his way").	Similarly "Dionysus quietly "left [ἐκβάς] / the house" thanks to a deceptive phantom and his invisibility (636–37) (76) (see 630ff).
11:1–5 "The Love God" (78–79) "Love in the Johannine Gospel is not sexual love" (78). DM uses the bride, bridegroom, and friend of the bridegroom (3:29) to describe how "it is reasonable to propose that the Evangelist presented his protagonist as a different kind of lover from Dionysus" (79).[41]	Though the sexuality of Dionysus's influence is "downplayed" (DM 78) in the *Bacchae*, the historical connection of the cult is strong. "In 186 BCE Rome was so overrun with Bacchic sex that the Roman Senate passed laws against it" (DM 79).
11:6–44 "The Life-Giver" (79–81) "In Jesus's presence, death is but sleep" (80).	"like Dionysus, he (Jesus) is a liberator from death" (81).

41. There are times when the Evangelist seems to be taking advantage of the typical sexual proclivitites of the culture. For example in the entire episode of conversation between Jesus, the Samaritan Woman, and the late-coming disciples, where eat and drink seem to carry sexual overtones. Jesus finally says to the disciples "I have food to eat that you do not know about" (4:32). See L. Schottroff, "Samaritan Woman . . . and Sexuality," in Segovia, *What is John?*, 157–81. If the foil for this non-sexual love was Dionysus, then it is another example of Jesus being presented as greater than Dionysus.

FG	Bacchae
11:47–50, 53–57 "God-Fighters" (81–82) Messengers to the Pharisees reported what Jesus had done, in raising Lazarus.	"Euripides similarly uses a messenger to notify Pentheus of the maenad miracles in the mountains (*Bacch.* 677–774)" (81).
12:12–15, 17–19 "The Triumphal Entry" (82–83) Jesus gets a mixed reception after the Lazarus miracle.	The mixed reception "resembles Euripides' depiction of the acceptance of Dionysus by the maenads, the chorus, Tiresias, Cadmus and the messenger, on the other hand and the violent rejection of his miracle working by the king, on the other" (83).
13:1a, 31–35; 14:4, 6, 31b; 15:1–2, 4 "The True Grapevine" (83–85) "I am the True Grapevine" [Ἐγώ εἰμι ἡ ἄμπελος ἡ ἀληθινή] "Jesus is the *true* grapevine [ἡ ἄμπελος ἡ ἀληθινή] and thus is superior to Dionysus; because of this his disciples ought to abide in him" (84).	"Grapes and grapevines were distinctive Dionysian markers in ancient art and literature" (84). Cf. [ἄμπελος] in *Homeric Hymn to Dionysus* 38–39.
18:1–13 "Arresting the Son of God" (85–87) "Then the cohort, the officer, and the subordinates of the Jews arrested Jesus, bound him [ἔδησαν], and brought [ἤγαγον] him to [the chief priest]."	434–46 "Laughing, he even told me to tie him up and to lead him away [δεῖν κἀπάγειν] / and was waiting for me to do so, making my job easy / And out of shame I said, 'O stranger, it is not gladly / that I lead you away [ἄγω].'"
18:19–27 "Defying the God-Fighters" (87–89)	
18:28—19:16 "Interrogating the Son of God, Again" [42] (89–96) "Surely the following parallels are mimetic" (90). [Pilate:] Your own people [ἔθνος] and the chief priests delivered you to me (18:35b).	[Pentheus:] So first tell me, who are your people [γένος]? (460).

---

42. DM (95) cites Stibbe: "In both, the one on trial is an unacknowledged deity ... Secondly, in both cases, the interrogator is a ruling figure in the city where the deity should be worshiped ... Thirdly, in both cases the one on trial is really the judge. Fourthly, in both interrogation scenes the deity proves extremely elusive, so that the interrogator finds him hard to understand ... In both scenes the deity uses language

VIII. THE DIONYSIAN GOSPEL

FG	Bacchae
[Jesus:] My kingdom . . . is not from here [οὐκ ἔστιν ἐντεῦθεν], [His true home is with the Father.] (18:36).	[Dionysus:] I am from here [ἐντεῦθέν εἰμι]: Lydia is my country. [His true home is Mount Olympus.] (464).
[Jesus:] For this reason I was born and came into the world: to witness to the truth.	[Dionysus:] They [the Dionysiac mysteries] are ineffable for the understanding of uninitiated mortals . . . /
Everyone who is of the truth hears [ἀκούει] my voice.	It is not permitted for you to hear [ἀκοῦσαι] them, but they are worth knowing . . . /
[Pilate:] What is truth? (18:37b–38)	Thee rites of the god are inimical to one who exercises impiety. (472, 474, 476).
**************	************
[Pilate:] From where [πόθεν] do you come?	[Pentheus:] From where [πόθεν] did you bring these rites to Greece? (465)
	[Pentheus:] You say nothing so very well! (479)
Jesus gave him no answer	
[Pilate:] Will you not speak to me? Do you not know [οὐκ οἶδας] that I have authority to release [ἀπολῦσαί σε] you and authority to crucify you?	[Pentheus:] I am more powerful than you—to tie you up.
[Jesus:] You have no authority over me whatsoever, except what was given to you from above.	[Dionysus:] You do not know [οὐκ οἶσθ'] what life you live, what you are doing, or what you are (505–6).
[God will free Jesus from death.]	[Dionysus:] The god himself shall free me [λύσει με] whenever I want (498).
[Pilate commands Jesus to be crucified, but he soon will escape the tomb.]	[Pentheus shuts Dionysus in his granary, but he soon will escape his prison.]

19:17–30 **"Violent Death and Attending Women"** (96–100)

19:38–40 **"Burial in a Garden"** (101–2)

---

evasively" (Stibbe, *John as Storyteller*, 143); and Brant, "Pentheus appears to prevail because he succeeds in arresting his opponent, but in the broader context of the play, Dionysus has baited Pentheus into performing the act of injury for which Dionysus can seek revenge. Jesus participates in a similar sort of baiting designed to goad the Jews into requesting the act, crucifixion, by which Jesus can demonstrate his glory" (Brant, *Dialogue and Drama*, 134).

FG	Bacchae
20:1, 11b–18 "A Woman's Recognition" (102–8) The jubilant recognition of Mary: "Mary's tears turn to jubilation when she recognizes the gardener to be her teacher" (107).	The tragic recognition of Agave: (1200–1285) "Agave's jubilation turns to tears when she recognizes the head of her son" (107).
20:19, 21b–23 "Exit Stage Up" (108–9)	1330–87 "After line 1351, the *machina* lifts the *deus* out of site. Exit stage up" (109).
20:30–31 "Postscript" (109–10)	1388–92

D. The Seven Criteria of Mimesis Criticism[43]

1. "The Criterion of *accessibility* pertains to the likelihood that the author of the later text had access to the proposed antetext" (110).

   FG proposed location of origin is Ephesus, which had a famous theatre. The *Bacchae* was often performed, and Dionysian religion was pervasive.

2. "*Analogy* likewise pertains to the popularity of the target. It seeks to know if other authors imitated the same mimetic model" (112).

   The *Bacchae* inspired lost plays on the same subject; DM then lists 12 other texts (two from the NT; 3 from NT Apocrypha) where influence and imitation of *Bacchae* is proposed.

3. "*Density*: simply stated, the more parallels one can posit between the two texts, the stronger the case that they issue from a literary connection" (114).

   "The density of possible correspondences . . . makes a conscious literary connection highly likely" (114).

4. "The criterion of *order* examines the relative sequencing of similarities in two works. If parallels appear in the same order, the case strengthens for a genetic connection" (114).

   Listing numerous likenesses in sequence in both texts, DM concludes "There is no more compelling explanation . . . than literary imitation" (115).

---

43. MacDonald's other publications apply these criteria to other Hellenistic texts, and his defense against criticisms can be found in "My Turn: A Critique of Critics of *Mimesis Criticism*." Some of these criteria are similar to those that we have already used elsewhere (Introduction, n31).

5. "A *distinctive trait* is anything unusual in the targeted antetext and the proposed borrower that links the two into a special relationship" (115). What in the antetext might have triggered its adaptation in the later text?

6. "*Interpretability* asks what might be gained by viewing one text as a debtor to another. As often as not, ancient authors emulated their antecedents to rival them, whether in style, philosophical adequacy, persuasiveness or religious perspective" (115).

7. "Often Greek readers prior to 1000 CE were aware of affinities between biblical narratives and their classical Greek models. Such *ancient and Byzantine recognitions* are useful for identifying mimesis in the original composition of the Gospels" (119).

Among other things mentioned, the beginning miracle—"water into wine"; and the last speech to the disciples—"I am the true grapevine" alert the reader to the connection. The Dionysian *omophagia* suggested by Jesus's words about eating his flesh.

1. "Mimetic indebtedness would largely explain why the Fourth Gospel differs so dramatically from the Synoptics. The differences issue not from deviating oral traditions of the life and teachings of Jesus but from imitation of Euripides" (115).

2. Jesus presented as a rival to Dionysus.

3. It may also explain the role of female characters in FG.

4. "Also sheds light on contemporary disputes about Docetism; can one find in the Gospel a denial that Jesus possessed a physical body?" (117f)

"A common criticism of Mimesis Criticism is the alleged failure of the history of interpretation to recognize the influence of the proposed antetext. This objection surely does not apply to the imitation of the *Bacchae* in the Fourth Gospel" (123).

Analysis and Assessment[44]

Some features of DM's study seem on the periphery of his mimetic analysis. But the book is a *tightly wrapped* package. For example, the effort in the FG to define Jewish words, rituals, and locations may reflect an interest in an audience who would read this text with a rather blank slate (most Greeks).[45] The study also reflects much consideration and a wide reading of secondary and primary literature.[46]

44. MacDonald, *Dionysian Gospel*. Reviewed by Tyler Smith: http://rblnewsletter.blogspot.com/2018/12/20181239-macdonald-dionysian-gospel.html. See the excellent reviews of DM's book by Jo-Ann Brant (*Review of Biblical Literature* 3 [2018]) and Tyler Smith (*Review of Biblical Literature* 12 [2018]).

45. See his discussion on *Dionyesian Gospel*, 111.

46. Of interest also is the discussion in Plutarch comparing a Jewish festival of Booths to a Bacchanalia (*Moralia* IV, 671D—672B). In the Jewish Virtual Library

Some problems may be felt by the reader. For example, by claiming that the first edition of FG was an imitation of the *Bacchae*, DM is also circumscribing the possible objectives of much of its contents, for as a literary piece its primary context is then the play by Euripides, or John's perception of it, or even his contemporaries' perception of it. Giving it this social location allows DM to highlight certain features, and subordinate, or even eliminate others (e.g., ecclesial).

DM's source-critical approach may lead to troublesome consequences. For example, Keener says "The primary significance of wine in this story seems to lie mainly in the changing of water into wine,"[47] a statement with which MacDonald could concur, but for different reasons. What MacDonald might say is that the comparison with Dionysus is thus effectually guaranteed; but what Keener probably means is that Jesus's challenge to Jewish rituals is thus textualized (as it was water for purification). Here is an example of the competing hermeneutical horizons: Jewish or Greek?[48] MacDonald prioritizes the Greek literary tradition.

Of course, scholars or interpreters who neglect or completely ignore the Greek literary tradition of the Hellenistic world, in which Christianity was birthed and grew, have been showing a similar bias in prioritizing *other* literary traditions . . . effectively abandoning the life-setting of the authors and texts. One may almost say that to NT students and scholars, the Jewish religious and literary tradition was a sacred cow, and everything else was unclean and has been avoided.[49]

Another cautionary note: While MacDonald marshals an impressive collection of parallels in defense of his theory of Johannine mimesis of the *Bacchae*, the collection must be surrounded and prefaced by an elaborate list of hypotheses for their weight to be felt. Thus he spends considerable time explaining his theory of editions, redactions, displacements, and community contexts. A comparable phenomenon has occurred in Q studies.

The discussion and exegesis of the hypothetical text Q has given rise to theories about layering, stratification, editions and redactions of the

---

under the cult of Dionysus (https://www.jewishvirtuallibrary.org/dionysus-cult-of) are discussed these supposed similarities to non-Jewish observers. The whole discussion is quite suggestive of what might take place when religious traditions (that come into contact) are viewed through a foreigner's eyes. And one may suppose that similar things would occur when a Greek heard of Jesus making wine, or calling himself "the True Vine." But it is often *tightly wrapped* with much hypothetical reconstruction, as is much of scholarship.

47. Keener, *John* 1:494. Keener also adds "hence both Jesus' benevolence and his lack of attachment to religious tradition" (are associated with his changing water into wine).

48. See the excellent discussion of this in Claussen, "Turning Water to Wine," 78–97.

49. See Smith, *Drudgery Divine*, 46–48, 80–81, and discussion in both our introduction and conclusion.

hypothetical Q itself. And with the emergence of these complicated imaginative theories of social locations and social origination comes an equally creative rewriting of the early Jesus Movement, based ultimately upon a restoration of the trimmed down first edition of Q (Q1), or around 80 verses of text ("minimal Q" is about 250 verses).

> Layering and stratification may explain one thing, but its more powerful advantage is the opportunity afforded of rewriting criteria of interpretation and relocating *Sitze im Leben*. The layers can be dated and imagined in a way that can conceivably dovetail with any historic event and serve to profile the community in any conceivable posture. It can be a very subjective artifice.[50]

We make a cautionary observation here. The fact is, we have never found *any* edition of Q (be it Q1, Q2 or Q3) just as we have never found any edition of MacDonald's first edition of FG, "the Dionysian Gospel."

In DM's defense, however, we notice in scholarship that important questions are generated by texts, and the best scholarship is done by those who read the clues well and fill in the gaps imaginatively. Often, and hopefully, new insights are gained from even wrongheaded hypotheses. And also, hopefully, hypotheses do not require the rewriting of more certain historical data. Craig Keener, who is well known for his wide reading and use of contemporary primary literature, is perhaps correct when he says,

> it is useful to produce parallels which shed light on their common milieu; pointing to these parallels as uniquely significant, however, indicates inadequate information concerning other ancient Mediterranean sources.[51]

Nevertheless, as a foil for the cross-cultural communication of Jesus as "Son of God" in the interest of showing his greater stature, the parallels may have been potent indeed.

Conclusions

In a world where Barnabas was seen as Zeus and Paul as Hermes by Greeks (Acts 14:12) who had only recently met them, how unlikely is the possibility that more such comparisons would be made, or that such comparisons could become a form of theological communication?[52] And how unlikely

---

50. Robbins, *Testing of Jesus in Q*, 116.

51. Keener, *John*, 1:161.

52. The creative use of stories and mythology that have shared elements in the multicultured Mediterranean world can be evidenced in another text from the Johannine school, the Apocalypse of John (cf. Puskas and Robbins, *Introduction*, 157). Mentioned

would it be that a Greek, upon hearing or reading that Jesus turned water into wine would begin to compare him to Dionysus? Or might not the same people reading or hearing that Jesus said "and the bread that I give for the life of the world is my flesh" (6:51) or

> Very truly, I tell you, unless you eat the flesh of the Son of Man and drink his blood, you have no life in you. Those who eat my flesh and drink my blood have eternal life, and I will raise them up on the last day; for my flesh is true food and my blood is true drink. Those who eat my flesh and drink my blood abide in me and I in them ... whoever eats me will live because of me (6:53–57)

or "I am the True Vine" (15:1) not again think of Dionysus?[53] In closing, the words of Jo-Ann Brant seem quite appropriate:

> At the least, MacDonald demonstrates that source and redaction criticism are still vital methodological tools for Johannine scholarship. The tendency to be concerned with only the textus receptus may obscure the theological and cultural diversity of Christian authors and readers and the speed with which successive editors adapted the text to suit their various purposes. MacDonald may not succeed in convincing many readers that John sat with texts of the Synoptic Gospels and the Bacchae resting next to his lap or residing in his memory. However, he does make it impossible to simply dismiss the possibility. Many of MacDonald's readers might shrug off many of the parallels as coincidental and concede only that MacDonald's methodology is necessary to the proof of mimesis but not sufficient for

---

there in reference to Rev 12 are the woman, child, and the dragon with international correlations such as Egypt's Isis, Horus, and Seth; Babylon's Demkina, Marduk, and Tiamat; Greece's Letho, Apollo, and Python; and Palestine's Israel, Messiah, and Satan (or Leviathan).

53. Cf. Hutchinson, "Cult of Dionysus/Bacchus in the Greco-Roman World," 222–30 (reference culled from Bell, *Exploring*, 147), and Massa, *Tra la vigna e la croce* (reference culled from review by James Hume, *Bryn Mawr Classical Review* 2015.10.29). Hume says "The author's task is complicated, first, by the polyvalence of Dionysus' symbolism, in whose myths the vine is as likely to represent entanglement and destruction as fertility and joy; and, second, by the influence of another tradition (the biblical one) which was grafted by early Christian writers and artists onto that of Bacchus. In the OT and NT, after all, wine, the vine, and the vineyard have symbolic and sacramental meanings peculiar to their own cultural contexts. But "the complexity of the relationship between Dionysus and the Christian sources" (15) does not deter Massa. Indeed, that complexity is very much to his purpose, which is to trace the vicissitudes of this relationship "from opposition to cohabitation, and from religious competition to cultural mediation" (my translation). Both cults, Christian and Dionysiac, were profoundly affected by this cultural exchange, but the book's principal focus is on the identity that the church forged for itself out of this welter of influences.

certitude. After reading this work, nevertheless, they ought to recognize the following: wherever the gospel asserts Jesus's capacity to provide divine gifts, given the broad familiarity of the Dionysian traditions within their milieu, contemporary readers would have been cognizant that the gospel's assertions about Jesus implicitly negated similar assertions about Dionysius.[54]

---

54. Jo-Ann A. Brant's review of Dennis MacDonald, *The Dionysian Gospel*, in *Review of Biblical Literature* 3 (2018).

IX. The Odes of Solomon, The Samaritans, and Mandaean Literature

IN THIS CHAPTER WE will examine the Odes of Solomon, the Samaritan writings, and the Mandaean literature. All have been compared in some manner to what we find in FG. The Odes are second century, but contain earlier material. External attestation for the Samaritans is early (2 Kings; Ezra; Nehemiah; NT; Josephus), but their own body of writing is late: ninth to eleventh centuries CE at the earliest. The Mandaean writings are dated from the third to sixth centuries CE, contain more esoteric and mystical ideas than what we find in the Odes or among the Samaritans, yet they afford some thought-provoking insights not too dissimilar from what we find in FG. It is intriguing to mention that today there are adherents to the Samaritan and Mandaean faith traditions, although small in number and having evolved, to some degree, in their beliefs and practices through the centuries.[1]

The Odes of Solomon

In 1785, the British Museum purchased a Coptic manuscript that was filed as *Pistis Sophia* (Manusript C). It was later noted (1812) that five odes found in the manuscript were attributed to Solomon. In 1904, J. Rendel Harris discovered a Syriac Psalter (obtained near the Tigris river, Iraq) containing the Psalms and **Odes of Solomon** (pseudonymously ascribed to the son of David). This latter discovery, now in the John Rylands Library (Codex Syr. 9; MS H) contains most of what we know to be the Odes of Solomon (with some missing sections). Although the work is still incomplete, additonal Odes (11; 17–42) have been recovered in subsequent manuscripts (Codex Nitriensis; Bodmer Papyrus XI, G).[2]

---

1. Most of our sources for the Samaritans and the Mandaeans, esp. *AYBD*, *NIDB*, contain information on both groups in our modern period.

2. Harris and Mingana, *Odes and Psalms of Solomon*. A more complete account of the discovery is found in Charlesworth, *Odes of Solomon*, 1–12.

IX. THE ODES OF SOLOMON, THE SAMARITANS, AND MANDAEAN LITERATURE

In his *Jesus as Mirrored in John*, James H. Charlesworth writes, "The Odes of Solomon are a neglected key for unlocking the historical and theological enigmas of John."[3] He blames this lack of interest in the Odes to the misleading views originally held by Adolf Harnack, who had argued for a Jewish *Grundschrift* with gnostic influence and dated it late.[4] Recent scholarship, Charlesworth notes, demonstrates that the Odes are neither gnostic nor late (ca. late first or early second century CE). To support these last two points, similarities to DSS and other second temple Jewish sources have been made (but they are not extensive).[5]

Before looking at the numerous thematic parallels, we should note some differences. The Odes were composed in Syriac and FG in Greek. The Odes form a poetic hymnbook and FG is a prose gospel. Both rework inherited traditions so that direct verbal parallels are lacking. We must seek to discern shared phraseology and concepts since both appear to be products of Syria-Palestine.[6]

A. The Odes of Solomon	The Fourth Gospel
The Preexistent Word	
"And light dawned from **the Word that was before time** in Him. The Messiah in truth is one. And He was known **before the foundations of the world**," 41:14–15. "And the Word from the truth who is self-originate," 32:2.[7]	"In the beginning was the Word, and the Word was with God" 1:1; "the glory that I had in your presence **before the world existed**," 17:5, "you loved me **before the foundation of the world**," v. 24.

---

3. Charlesworth, *Jesus as Mirrored in John*, 315. For those who made use of the Odes Sol., he cites commentaries by W. Bauer, G. Bert, R. Bultmann, and H. Odeberg. Among those who have ignored this source, he cites C. K. Barrett, R. E. Brown, J. Marsh, P. H. Menoud, J. N. Sanders, and A. Wikenhauser

4. Harnack, *Jüdisch-Christliches Psalmbuch* based on the Syriac version by J. Rendel Harris, 1909. W. Bauer argued for gnostic influence and a late date in his "Oden Salomos," in Hennecke and Schneemelcher, *Neutestamentliche Apokryphen*, 2:577; and also Rudolph, *Gnosis*, 29, 221–22.

5. Charlesworth, "Odes—Not Gnostic," 357–69; and his *John and the Dead Sea Scrolls*, 107–36; see also Lattke, *Odes of Solomon*.

6. Chapter and verse headings are from Charlesworth, *Odes of Solomon*. We also consulted Charlesworth, "Odes of Solomon," in *Old Testament Pseudepigrapha*, 2:725–71; Harris and Mingana, *Odes and Psalms of Solomon*; Sanders, "Hag Hammadi, Odes, and NT," 51–66; Burney, *Aramaic Origins of the Fourth Gospel*, 166–69.

7. See discussion of the Syriac masculine (*Mlt'*) and feminine (*Ptgm'*) forms of "Word" in J. T. Sanders, "Nag Hammadi, Odes, and NT," in Goehring et al., *Gnosticism*, 56–57.

A. The Odes of Solomon	The Fourth Gospel
\<td colspan="2" align="center"\>Creation by the Word\</td\>	

A. The Odes of Solomon	The Fourth Gospel
"And **the worlds were made by His Word**, and by the thought of His heart," 16:19. "And there is nothing outside of the Lord, because He was before anything came to be," 16:18.[8]	"**All things came into being through** him [the Word] and without him not one thing came into being," 1:3; "**the world came into being through him**," v. 10.

Light and life

"The Lord has directed my mouth by His Word and has opened my heart by His light," 10:1; "The Savior who gives life," 41:11; "And the light dawned from the Word . . . that He might give life to persons for ever," vv. 14–15; "I was named the Light, the Son of God," 36:3; "And his possession is immortal life, and those who receive it are incorruptible," 40:6.	"**In him was life and the life was the light of all people**," 1:4; "the true light which enlightens everyone, was coming into the world," 1:9; "I am the light of the world. Whoever follows me will never walk in darkness but **will have the light of life**," 8:12.

Life with the Son

"Indeed he who is joined to Him who is immortal truly shall be immortal," 3:8. "He who delights in the Life will become living," 3:9; cf. 9:4; 10:2; 28:7–8.	"because I live, you will live also," 14:19; cf. 3:16; 10:10. "I am the resurrection and the Life; he who believes on me, though he die, yet shall he live," 11:25; cf. 1:4; 5:26, 40; 10:28; 14:6.

Light and darkness

"And His light has dismissed all darkness," 15:2; "Let not light be conquered by darkness," 18:6; "And darkness dissipated before His [the Lord's] appearance," 31:1.	"The light shines in the darkness, and the darkness did not overcome it," 1:5; "Whoever follows me will never walk in darkness," 8:12; "Walk while you have the light, so that the darkness may not overtake you," 12:35.

Grace and truth

"For His glory will go before thee; and thou shalt receive of His kindness and of His grace; and thou shalt be anointed in truth with the praise of His holiness," 20:9; "He was gracious to me in **His abundant grace**," 7:10; "And His truth is love," 12:12.	"And we have seen his glory, the glory as of a father's only son, full of grace and truth," 1:14; "From his fullness we have all received, grace upon grace," v. 16.

---

8. "'Lord' refers to God and not to Jesus. Yet the Odist does *not* equate Jesus Christ with God (see Ode 36:4 'And the greatest among the great ones')," in Charlesworth, *Odes of Solomon*, 48.

IX. THE ODES OF SOLOMON, THE SAMARITANS, AND MANDAEAN LITERATURE

A. The Odes of Solomon	The Fourth Gospel
	He came to his own
"For **the dwelling place of the Word is man**," 12:12; "The Son of the Most Hight appeared in the perfection of His Father," 41:13; "He [the Lord] has generously shown Himself to me in His simplicity . . . **He became like me, that I might receive Him**," 7:3–4.	"He was in the world," 1:10; "He came to what was his own . . . but to all who received him," 1:11–12; "And the Word . . . dwelt among us," 1:14.
	Descent/ascent
"He who caused me to descend from on high, and to **ascend from regions below**," 22:1; "**His will descended from on high**," 23:5; "He caused me to ascend from the depths of Sheol," 29:4. C. Colpe doubts that these texts support the theme of the descent of a divine Redeemer to *release* human souls and *lead them back* to the realm of light, in his *Die religionsgeschichtliche Schule*, 180.	"No one has ascended into heaven except the one who descended from heaven, the Son of Man," 3:13; cf. 3:21; 6:38; 13:3; "but now I am going to him who sent me," 16:5; "I came from the Father and have come into the world; again, I am leaving the world and am going to the Father," v. 28 (cf. 42); "I am ascending to my Father and your Father," 20:17.
	Divine presence and help
"And His Word is with us in all our way," 41:11; "For **there is a Helper for me, the Lord**," 7:3; "For the right hand of the Lord is with you, and **He will be your Helper**," 8:6.	"I will not leave you orphaned; I am coming to you," 14:18; "But the Advocate [ESV Helper, *paraklētos*], the Holy Spirit, whom the Father sill send in my name, will teach you everything and remind you of all that I have said to you," v. 26.
	The Way
"**A way has been appointed for those who cross after him**," 39:7; "**the Way has been appointed for those who cross over after Him**," v. 13; Your hand leveled **the way for those who believe in you**," 22:7; "your way was without corruption," 22:11; "**His Word is our way**," 41:11 (cf. "I was the opening of everything," 17:11).	"Make straight the way of the Lord," 1:23/Isa 40:3; "I go to prepare a place for you,"; John 14:2; "And you know the way to the place where I am going," v. 4; "**I am the way, the truth, and the life**. No one comes to the Father except through me," v. 6 (cf., "I am the gate for the sheep,"10:7, 9).
	Gather the scattered
"And the Gentiles who had been dispersed were gathered together," 10:5.	"to gather into one the dispersed children of God," 11:52.

A. The Odes of Solomon	The Fourth Gospel
\multicolumn{2}{c}{Dwellings in Paradise}
"Indeed, there is much room in paradise," 11:23.	"In my Father's house there are many [ESV rooms, *monai*] dwelling places," 14:2.
\multicolumn{2}{c}{Father, Son, Holy Spirit}
"The Son is the cup [of sweet milk offered to me] and the Father is He who was milked; and the Holy Spirit is She who milked Him," 19:2; "**And the name of the Father was upon it; and of the Son and of the Holy Spirit,**" 23:22; cf. "union of the Lord Most High, the Beloved Son, and the Spirit of the Lord," 3:5–10. "This is **the Spirit of the Lord, which is not false,**" v. 10. "(The Spirit) brought me forth . . . the Son of God," 36:3.	"And I will ask the Father and he will give you another Advocate to be with you forever. This is **the Spirit of truth** . . . you know him because he abides with you and he will be in you," 14:16–17; "**But the Advocate, the Holy Spirit, whom the Father will send in my** [the Son's] **name** . . . " 14:26; "When the Advocate comes whom I will send to you from the Father, **the Spirit of truth** who comes from the Father," 15:26 (cf. divine nourishment from the Son of Man who was sent by the living Father, 6:53–57). He on whom the Spirit descends will baptize with the Holy Spirit, this is the Son of God (1:33–34/Mark 1:8).
\multicolumn{2}{c}{Abide in my love}
"And **abide in the love of the Lord**; and you who are loved in the Beloved, and you who are kept in Him who lives," 8:20–22; "keep my faith, you who are kept by it," v. 10; "And they are my own. And upon my right hand I have set my eternal ones," v. 18; "I love the Beloved and I myself love Him," 3:5.	"Abide in me and I abide in you," 15:4; "As the Father has loved me, so I have loved you; **abide in my love,**" v. 9; "If you keep my commandments, you will abide in my love, just as I have kept my Father's commandments and abide in his love," v. 10; "I protected [*phylassō*] them in your name that you have given me," 17:12.
\multicolumn{2}{c}{Living Water}
"Then all the thirsty upon the earth drank, and thirst was relieved and quenched; for from the Most High the drink was given. Blessed , therefore, are the ministers of that drink, who have been entrusted with His water," 6:11–13;	"If you knew the gift of God, and who it is that is saying to you, 'give me to drink,' you would have asked him and he would have given you **living water,**" 4:10; "those who drink of the water that I will give them will never be thirsty.

IX. THE ODES OF SOLOMON, THE SAMARITANS, AND MANDAEAN LITERATURE

A. The Odes of Solomon	The Fourth Gospel
"Because everyone recognized them as the Lord's and lived **by the living water of eternity,**" v. 18. "And I drank and became intoxicated, from the living water that does not die," 11:7. "Fill for yourselves water from **the living fountain of the Lord** . . . and come all of you thirsty and take a drink . . . because it is pleasing and sparkling, and perpetually refreshes the self. For much sweeter is its water than honey . . ." 30:1-4.[9]	The water that I will give will become in them **a spring of water gushing up to eternal life.**" The woman said to him [Jesus], 'Sir give me this this water, so that I may never be thirsty . . .'" vv. 14-15. "Let everyone who is thirsty come to me, and let the one who believes in me drink. As scripture has said, 'Out of the believer's heart shall flow rivers of living water,'" 7:37-38 (cf. Prov 18:4; Isa 55:1; Zech 14:8).
Son of God, Son of Man	
"Son of God," 36:3b; 42:15; "Son of the Most High," 41:13; "Son of Man," 36:3; "The Man who humbled Himself, but was exalted," 41:12; "our Lord Messiah," 24:1; 39:11; "His Messiah," 9:6; 41:3, "the Messiah," v. 15.	"Son of God," 1:34, 49; 3:18; 5:25; "Son of Man," 1:51; 3:13-14; 5:27; 6:27, 53; 8:28, "the Son of Man must be lifted up," 12:34; "the Messiah," 1:41; 4:25; *Christos*, 7:41; 9:22.
Praying for his followers	
"Then He lifted His voice towards the Most High, and offered to Him those that had become sons through Him," 31:3-4.	"After Jesus had spoken these words, he looked up to heaven and said, 'Father, the hour has come,'" 17:1; "I have made your name known to those whom you gave me . . . they have kept your word," v. 6.

From the above table, we can see that the parallels between the Odes and FG are numerous (although scattered). Both have a shared dualism, use similar imagery, and analogous key terms and phrases. Further research is needed to explain the similarities and differences in their distinct literary, theological, and social contexts. Below is a summary of major views concerning the relationship of the Odes with FG.[10]

B. Assessing the Literary Relationship

The Odes depend on the Fourth Gospel. A number of scholars have taken this position. Rudolf Schnackenburg in his *John* (Crossroad, 1990), 1:145, cites Ode 31:3-5 as reminiscent of John 17 and Ode 39:11-13 of John 14:2-6. In addition he compares Odes 10:3-4 and 22:1 with Eph 4:8-9;

---

9. On living water in Odes and FG, see Charlesworth, *Jesus as Mirrored in John*, 328.

10. The following points are derived from Charlesworth, *Jesus as Mirrored in John*, 329-32.

Odes 19:6-11 recalling the Synoptic Virgin Birth, Odes 27 and 42:1-2 alluding to the cross in the Gospels, 41:12 to Christ's humiliation and exaltation (Phil 2), and 42:11-20, Christ's descent into the underworld (1 Pet 3:18-22). The usage of the "Word" (Ode 12) and "the Way" (Ode 22:7-12; 33:7-13; 39:5-13) teem with gnostic interpretations. R. E. Brown supports this view in his *Gospel according to John*, 1:21. Their views are based on *a priori* judgments with no conclusive evidence, according to J. H. Charlesworth (*Jesus as Mirrored in John*, 330). Dating for the Odes range from the late first century (Charlesworth) to the early second century (Brown, Schnackenburg) as we mentioned. The other two views, however, are not without their problems. T. Nagel observes some influence of FG on the Odes (Ode 3:8/John 14:19b; Ode 8:20-22/John 15:4,9) in his *Die Rezeption des Johannesevangeliums*, 158-94, esp. 165-66, 190-92.

John Depended upon the tradition represented in the Odes. In 1910, Adolf Harnack argued that (a) the author of FG was a Jew from the same circle as the Odist and that (b) the Christian interpolator of the Jewish Odes probably knew FG.[11] Rudolf Bultmann, under Harnack's influence, argued, (a) from the Odes we learn of a Jewish circle from which FG piety and theology are derived and (b) we learn of a Christian editor of the Odes from which FG itself *originates*.[12] Later, Bultmann wrote that the Odes reflect gnostic and hymnic sources, e.g., a Savior myth, used by FG, in his *Gospel of John* (29-30). J. T. Sanders argued that the concept of "the Word" in the Odes as a personal agent of God (Hypostatization) developed independent of, and in some respects prior to, FG's use of Logos in his prologue.[13] If Sanders, we presume, has claimed that "the Word" in the Odes is earlier because the Odist does *not* equate Jesus Christ with God (Ode 36:4), whereas FG does (John 1:1; 5:18; 10:30), it is special pleading. Paul, writing as early as mid-first century CE, *equated* Jesus with God (e.g., 1 Thess 3:11; 5:9-10; 1 Cor 1:2; 16:22; 2 Cor 13:13; Rom 10:9-13; Phil 2:9-11). Devotion to Jesus as divine therefore appears in the *earliest* Christian stratum, and therefore makes the positing of a late date for a high Christology (without additional support), problematic.[14] Also, the Odes may contain earlier traditions, but source and redaction analyses require more than the presentation of images and terminology similar to the DSS for arguing that these "early" traditions in the Odes are a source for FG.[15] There are other Jewish sources (LXX) al-

---

11. Harnack, *Ein Jüdisch-Christliches Psalmbuch*, 110-11.
12. Bultmann, "Ein jüdisch-christliches Psalmbuch," 23-29, esp. 28.
13. Sanders, *New Testament Christological Hymns*, 119.
14. See Hurtado, *Lord Jesus Christ*, esp. ch. 2; and his *Honoring the Son*, ch. 5.
15. "The numerous and pervasive parallels between the Odes and John cannot be explained by literary dependence of the Odist upon John or vice versa, J. H. Charlesworth, "Qumran, John, and the Odes," in his *John and Dead Sea Scrolls*, 135.

ready available long before the DSS or the Odes to establish an influence on FG.[16] For these reasons, establishing the influence of early "Odes traditions" in FG is even more challenging than arguing for the use of Markan or Lukan traditions in FG!

John and the Odes come from the same religious environment. Harnack, we mentioned, claimed that the Christian interpolator of the Jewish Odes and FG belonged to the same circle. R. Harris found the community of ideas in the Odes and Johannine writings "most pronounced."[17] C. H. Dodd argued that the Odes and Epistles of Ignatius are "writings emanating from a circle whose thought certainly resembles that of the Fourth Gospel in some respects."[18] J. Carmignac argued that the Odist was so profoundly marked by the DSS and FG that he must have spent time in both communities to assimilate their rich spirituality.[19] Dodd's view is more cautious than that of Carmignac's and therefore appears to be less problematic. On a common religious environment, Hans Jonas interpreted Gnosis (broadly defined) as a characteristic of the "spirit of late antiquity."[20] The question arises: to what extent? J. W. Charlesworth, nevertheless, concludes that this hypothesis (carefully argued) best explains the data presented.[21]

3. The Samaritans

A number of studies of the last century focus on the relationship of FG to Samaria and the Samaritans.[22] These have included theories ranging from

---

16. Borrowing an insight from Bauckham, "Qumran Community and the Gospel of John," 115. D. E. Aune regards the case for Essene influence on FG and the Odes (J. H. Charlesworth) as astonishingly weak and that of indirect dependence (R. E. Brown; R. Schnackenburg) as a foggy conception, in "Dualism," in Aune, *Neotestamentia et Philonica*, 302-3.

17. Harris and Mingana, *Odes and Psalms of Solomon*, 1:74.

18. Dodd, *Interpretation*, 272.

19. Carmignac, "les affinités qumrâniennes de la ozième Ode de Salomon," 71-102.

20. Jonas, *Gnosis and spätaniker Geist*. E. R. Goodenough writes of a Mediterranean "lingua franca" of similar concepts and images in his *Jewish Symbols in the Greco-Roman Period*.

21. Charlesworth, *Jesus as Mirrored in John*, 332. Charlesworth has taken more space to explain the nature of the parallels than we have done (see his 315-29). See also "Qumran, John, and the Odes," in his *John and Dead Sea Scrolls*, 107-36, where he has concluded from his study that the Odes and FG may have had Essene influence (135-36). On this view, D. E. Aune is not convinced, see above (n16).

22. On the relation of FG to Samaria and the Samaritans, see Bowman, "Samaritan Studies," 298-308; Buchanan, "Samaritan Origin of John," 149-75; Crown, *Samaritans*;

proposals that FG was dependent on christological traditions that originated in northern Palestine (W. A. Meeks), to suggestions that FG was developed by Samaritan Christians (G. W. Buchanan), or that it was a missionizing tract to win over converts from the Samaritans (J. Bowman).

Despite their differences, all have agreed that traditions preserved in Samaritan literature are helpful in understanding the backdrop of FG or the audience it has addressed. James H. Charlesworth even suggests that the tensions between worship on Mt. Gerizim and on Mt. Zion (John 4:20-21) seem to antedate 70 CE because after that time, when the Jerusalem temple was destroyed, worship only continued on Mt. Gerizim.[23]

There are noteworthy references in FG that lend considerable support for some Samaritan connection.

C. The Fourth Gospel and the Samaritans

1. The Samaritans are mentioned in a favorable light (4:1-42).[24]

2. Jesus retreated to Ephraim (11:54), an exact location is uncertain, but it was probably within the tribal territory assigned to Ephraim, the region of Samaria.[25]

3. John the Baptist may have been active in Samaria, if "Aenon near Salim" (3:23) is a reference to a location in Samaria as argued by William F. Albright.[26]

4. The northern locations of Galilee and Samaria fulfill a symbolic function in FG.[27] Jerusalem is the place of judgment and rejection in FG. Jesus is welcomed in Galilee (4:45), as he was well-received in Samaria (4:39-42).[28]

Meeks, *Prophet-King*, 216-57, 286-319; Purvis, "Fourth Gospel and the Samaritans," 148-85 (with a survey of scholarship) and Purvis, *Samaritan Pentateuch*, esp. 98-118. For source material, see: Anderson and Giles, *Samaritan Pentateuch* and *Tradition Kept*; Montgomery, *Samaritans*; Tsedaka and Sullivan, *Israelite Samaritan Version of Torah*; Bowman, *Samaritan Documents*.

23. Charlesworth, *Jesus as Mirrored in John*, 54. See also Coggins, *Samaritans and Jews*; and Bóid, "Use, Authority and Exegesis," 595-633.

24. Samaritans are also mentioned favorably in Luke-Acts, e.g., Luke 9:52; 10:33-37; 17:16; Acts 1:8; 8:1-25.

25. Stauffer, *Jesus*, 104, cited in Keener, *John*, 2:858. See also Freed, "Samaritan Influence," 580-87.

26. See W. F. Albright, "Recent Discoveries," in Davies and Daube, *Background of the New Testament*, 159-60 as cited in J. D. Purvis, "Fourth Gospel and the Samaritans," 155.

27. Meeks, *Prophet-King*, 313-18.

28. Perhaps the reference to "a prophet has no honor in his own country" John 4:44-45, refers to those Judeans who "did not accept him [Jesus]" (1:11).

5. His Judean critics even called him a Samaritan and accuse him of having a demon (8:48–49).[29]

6. The Jews (*hoi 'Ioudaoi*) are represented as the opponents of Jesus (e.g., 5:18, 41, 52; 7:1, 11, 13; 8:48, 57; 9:18; 18:12, 38; 19:7, 12, 20) and are contrasted with believing Israelites or faithful Israel (*'Israēleitēs*, 1:47; cf. 1:31, 49; 3:10; 12:13). Israelite was the term used by Samaritan to distinguish themselves from the Jews.[30]

7. Jesus is described as a prophet (4:19; 6:14; 9:17), the Messiah (from the Samaritan woman, 4:25–26), Savior of the world (the Samaritans, v. 42), Son of God, but *not* "son of David"—similar to the non-Davidic Samaritan tradition.

8. An allusion to Deut 18:15 is made in John 5:46, a favorite text in the Samaritan Pentateuch (found also in SP Exod 20). In FG, however, Jesus is *greater* than Moses.

9. The role of Moses in Samaritan theology[31] is analogous to the role of Jesus in FG (1:17; 6:49–58; 9:24–40). In FG, Jesus fulfills the roles given to Moses by the Samaritans as "the supreme prophet, God's emissary and revealer, and the defender of truth in the heavenly court of the true Israelites who trusted him."[32]

10. Dissatisfaction with the Jerusalem temple (John 2:13–22; cf. Mark 11:15–19; Luke 9:52–53; Acts 7:47–48) was also espoused by the Samaritans (4:20; cf. Deut 11:29; 27:12) and the community of Qumran (CD VI, 11–16).

The best known account of Samaritan origins is from 2 Kings 17, supplemented by Josephus (*Ant.* 9.277–91).[33] According to these sources, the **Samaritans** are mostly immigrants brought into Samaria by the Assyrians after the fall of the Israelite (northern) kingdom, 722 BCE. Intermarriage

---

29. Justin Martyr reports that Meander, a Samaritan, and disciple of Simon [Magus, Acts 8:9] deceived many in Antioch with his magic that was "inspired by devils," *Apol.* 1:26. Perhaps the Judean critics (John 8:48) perceived the works of Jesus in this manner. Perhaps FG is suspicious of these magicians and portrays the work of Jesus in contrast to them (e.g., John 10:10–15). See discussion in Purvis, "FG and the Samaritans," 182–85.

30. Purvis, "FG and the Samaritans," 158. The Samaritans regarded themselves as descendants of the northern kingdom of Israel that fell in 722 BCE, Hoppe, "Monarchic Period," 3:562–66.

31. See, e.g., "Where is there any like Moses, apostle of the True One, faithful one of the House of God and His servant? . . . His mouth is like the Euphrates, rolling with living waters which quench the first of all who drink of them," Memar Marqah 6:3 cited in Boring et al. *Hellenistic Commentary*, 263. On Memar Marqah (fourth century CE) see Tal, "Samaritan Targum of the Pentateuch," 192–95. On analogous refs. to Jesus in John 4:14,19; 7:37–38, see Justin, *Dial*. 114.

32. Purvis, "FG and the Samaritans," 173 citing Mosaic titles in Meeks, *Prophet-King*, 295, and esp. Meeks on "Moses as king and prophet in Samaritan sources," 220–28.

33. See discussion of its mythic history in Purvis, *Samaritan Pentateuch*, 88–118; and Knoppers, *Judah and Samaria*, 16–35.

of the immigrants with the remnants of the northern tribes probably took place as declared later, with apparent disapproval by Judeans returning to rebuild the temple (fifth century BCE; Ezra 4:1–6; Neh 2:19; 4:2–3, 7–8). Even centuries later "Jews do not share things in common with the Samaritans" (John 4:9b; cf. Sir. 50:25–26; Josephus, *Ant.* 11.346–47).[34]

Samaritan traditions state that the Persians provided support for them to build a sanctuary at Mt. Gerizim near ancient Shechem and Josephus admits as much in his polemical account (*Ant.* 13.254–56). As did the Judeans, the Samaritans also experienced enforced Hellenization under Antiochus IV (175–164; 2 Macc 6:2). Tensions with the Judeans greatly increased when John Hyrcanus, Hasmonean governor and high priest, had the sanctuary at Mt. Gerizim destroyed (128 BCE; Josephus, *Ant.* 13.255–56; *J.W.* 1.63). Roman dominance and oppression had a negative impact on both Samaritans (*Ant.* 18.85–89) and Judeans.[35]

The Book of Acts describes Samaria as the earliest mission field for the followers of Jesus (Acts 1:8; 8:4–8). The speech of Stephen (Acts 7) reflects traditions and heroes of the Samaritan Pentateuch (e.g., Jerusalem temple polemics, Abraham, Jacob, Joseph, Moses).[36] In the first century CE, a split occurred between the priestly class and the lay-oriented Dositheans (Origen, *Cels.* 1.57; 6.11).[37] Some traditions identify, Simon Magus as a Samaritan. He practiced magic and "amazed the people of Samaria" (Acts 8:9) and fits the role of a lay-oriented Dosithean (cf. John 8:48–49; Justin Martyr, *Apol.* 1.26; Origen, *Comm. Jo.* 13.162).[38]

In the third and fourth centuries, social structure and polity were strengthened under the leadership of Bab Raba ("Great Gate"). Complementing the work of Bab Raba, Marqe, a theologian, wrote a treatise, *Tibat Marqe* (written in Aramaic; also called *Memar Marqe*) discussing the Exodus, ethics, Mt. Gerizim, and the death of Moses. The *Tibat Marqe* includes a fully-developed creed that epitomizes Samaritan beliefs:

---

34. See Purvis, *Samaritan Pentateuch*, 119–29; Coggins, *Samaritans and Jews*.

35. Josephus reports that the Roman prefect, Pilate, killed a multitude of Samaritans who followed a charismatic leader to Mt. Gerizim to see sacred Mosaic vessels that were believed to be hidden there, in his *Ant.* 18.85–89. See also Anderson, "Samaritans," 5:75–82.

36. On Samaritans and the gospel see Bowman, *Samaritan Problem*, ch. 3; and Plummer, "New Evidence for Samaritan Christianity?" 98–117.

37. See Isser, *Dositheans: A Samaritan Sect*; Crown, *Samaritans*.

38. Cited in Purvis, "Fourth Gospel and the Samaritans," 182–83. See also our n30, above.

IX. THE ODES OF SOLOMON, THE SAMARITANS, AND MANDAEAN LITERATURE

> We say: My faith is in thee, YHWH: and in Moses the son of Amram, thy servant; and in the Holy Law; and in Mt. Gerizim Bethel; and in the Day of Vengeance and Recompense.[39]

Marqe the theologian also wrote many hymns that became part of Samaritan liturgy. Other works are *Asatir* (twelfth century CE; an annotated chronicle from Adam to Moses), Samaritan Joshua (thirteenth century CE; from the time of Moses to Baba Rabba), the Annals of Abu'l Fath, 1355 (*Kitab al-Tarikh*; from Adam to Muhammad), and additional Samaritan Chronicles (1900; New Chronicle; Chronicle II). These traditions may include some early information about Samaritan beliefs and practices, but this "early data" is difficult to discern and to verify as we discover with the rabbinic and targumic traditions. We can compare what we know from Josephus, the NT, and the early church fathers with these later documents to confirm any early information from the Roman period.[40]

Their primary text was the Samaritan Pentateuch (SP Gen–Deut) written in Samaritan Hebrew with Greek (early third century; in Origen, *Hex.*) and Arabic translations, as well as Aramaic paraphrases (similar to Jewish targums).[41] More than one hundred hand-written copies of SP exist, the earliest date from the ninth to the eleventh centuries CE (similar to MT). The SP agrees with the LXX (third century BCE) against the MT (tenth century CE) in 1,900 readings, and that according to Gesenius this is best explained as a dependence upon an earlier common recension.[42] Emmaneul Tov observes,

> In its present form, the Sam. Pent. contains a clearly sectarian text. However, when its thin sectarian layer is removed, together with that of the Samaritan phonetic features, the resulting

---

39. From Macdonald, *Memar Marqah*, 1:34. Was the creed influenced by Islam or did it influence Islam? See Anderson and Giles, *Tradition Kept*, 265. The statement on day of vengeance may be a later addition (266).

40. See our ch. 6 Rabbinica and Targumim, where we apply the four criteria of evaluating intertextual comparisons with compositions that *postdate* the New Testament period, pp. 98–100, derived from Evans, *Word of Glory*, 18–28 and the responses to finding early data in later material, pp. 100–101, derived from Ronning, *Jewish Targums and John's Logos Theology*, 261–69.

41. Waltke, "Samaritan Pentateuch," 5:935. Similarities have been made with the priestly Sadducees who adhered only to the Pentateuch and not to the Law, Prophets, and Writings (TaNaK) as did the scribal Pharisees.

42. Waltke, "Samaritan Pentateuch," 5:934, citing F. H. W. Gesenius, *De pentateuchi samaritani origine* (Halle, 1815).

text probably did not differ much from the texts we now label "proto-Samaritan."[43]

Professor Judith Sanderson, concluded that SP is "a loose but common text tradition circulated that encompassed the Old Greek text (OG), the MT, the 4QExod, and SP."[44]

As a sectarian document, the Samaritan text, for example, adds to Exod 20:14 a commandment affirming Mt. Gerizim as the holy site of worship. Phrases from Deut 18:15–18 are also inserted into SP Exodus 20:18. Samaritan scribes, affirming divine transcendence, often made use of angels to represent God's presence (SP Num 22:20; 23:4–5, 16) and they sought to avoid many of the human (i.e., anthropomorphic) portrayals of God in the Hebrew Bible (e.g., Exod 4:24; 15:3; Deut 32:6).[45]

From the comparisons of Samaritan traditions with FG, Wayne Meeks, who does not support direct influence, finds evidence for "overlapping traditions and mutual influence" coming from a region of Palestine near Samaria, such as Galilee. Here in northern Palestine where prophetic-royal and priestly roles of Moses are so central in Samaritan tradition and survive in some rabbinic material, and where ambiguities in its relationship to Jerusalem and Judea exist.[46] Out of such a context some of FG's Christology may have emerged.

In FG, Jesus appears to fulfill the roles given to Moses by the Samaritans as supreme prophet and king, God's emissary and revealer, who ascended to heaven.

> "The law indeed was given through Moses; grace and truth came through Jesus Christ" (1:17). "We have found him about whom Moses in the law and also the prophets wrote" (v. 45).
>
> "And just as Moses lifted up the serpent in the wilderness, so must the Son of Man be lifted up, that whoever believes in him may have eternal life" (3:14–15). "If you believed Moses, you would have believed me, for he wrote about me" (5:46). "Verily truly, I tell you, it was not Moses who gave you the bread from heaven, but it is my Father who gives you the true bread from

---

43. Tov, "Textual Criticism," 6:399.

44. Sanderson, *Exodus Scroll from Qumran*, 311, cited in Anderson and Giles, *Tradition Kept*, 4.

45. Anderson, "Samaritans," 5:77–79; Anderson and Giles, *Tradition Kept*, 3–48 (SP), 265–358 (*Tibat Marqe*); Waltke, "Samaritan Pentateuch," 5:932–39.

46. Meeks, *Prophet King*, 257 (see Moses as prophet and king in rabbinic haggada, 176–215, and our ch. 6, Rabbinica and Targumim, pp. 87–89, 95–97).

heaven" (6:32). "I am the living bread that came down from heaven" (v. 51a).

Mandaean Literature

The **Mandaeans** are a gnostic baptizing sect that flourished in the third through the eighth centuries CE, although a small group of adherents still survive today.[47] They may have originated from Syria-Palestine in the second or even the first century CE based on the east Aramaic dialect of their writings.[48] They are thought to have been followers of John the Baptist, but in their writings he is hailed as a prophet or priest (*tarmida*). Although influenced by Israel's Scriptures, the sect was not sympathetic with early and rabbinic Judaisms. They were also critical regarding the followers of Jesus the "pseudo-messiah."

Their earliest self-designations are "elect of the righteous" (*bhirē zidga*) and "guardians" or "possessors" (*naṣuraiyī*) of secret rites and knowledge. The word "Mandaean," refers back to the ancient term for "knowledge," (*mandayī, gnōsis*). Their cosmology is marked by a strict (gnostic) dualism of the "world of light" (*alma dnhura*) and "world of darkness" (*alma dhṣuka*) The soul or "spirit" (*mana*) in humans must be rescued from the dark evil body of the world by heavenly beings of light. Their two chief rituals (continuing today) are baptism (*maṣabūta*) of initiates in flowing water along with their being anointed with oil (*sesam*) and mass for the dead conducted three days after death when the soul is released from the body and makes its heavenly ascent until it reaches the "home of Life."

The most important Mandaean works are the "Treasure" ("Ginza" or "Great Book," *sidra rabbā*) which consists of two parts: the larger "Right Ginza" and the smaller "Left Ginza." The "Right Ginza" is a collection of eighteen tractates with mostly cosmological, theological, and didactic material. The "Left Ginza" concerns the ascent of the soul to the realm of light. It is also called the "Book of Souls." The "Book of John" of the "Book

---

47. See Lupieri, *Mandaeans*; See also Rudolph, "Mandaeism," 4:500–502; his *Gnosis*; and his *Die Mandäer*.

48. On the exodus of Mandaeans from Palestine to Mesopotamia, see Drower, *Haran Gawaita and the Baptism of Hibili-Ziwa* and the attempts to reconstruct their first century CE migration from it, by R. Macuch and K. Rudolph as summarized in Haenchen, *John*, 123–24. See especially, Rudolph, *Die Mandäer*; and Schenke, "Die Gnosis," 1:396–98. Edwin Yamauchi argues that a "pre-Christian date remains hypothetical and speculative" (*Gnostic Ethics and Mandaean Origins*, 71).

of Angels" is a collection of mixed contents.[49] The main parts are "sermons" of John the Baptist, the discourses of *Sūm* (Shem), the appearance of *Anoš* (Enosh) in Jerusalem, and the story of the conversion of *Miryai* (Mary the Mother of Jesus). A series of other ritual texts are recently available: e.g., wedding ritual, ordination of priests, and purification rites. Some historical information is provided in the (fragmentary) "Diwan of the great Revelation," called *Haran Gawaita*. In a manner similar to the Jewish rabbinica, these texts contain traditions that were circulated orally centuries (second–fourth centuries, CE) before they were first put into writing (seventh–eighth centuries, CE).

Before making our comparisons, we will expound further some of the Mandaean teachings.[50] The sect believes not only in a "First Life" (world of light) but a second (*Ypshamiu*), third (*Abathus*), and fourth (*Ptahil*), all successively created. *Ptahil* created the material world (*Tibil*) with the aid of the evil Spirit (*Ruha*), the Seven (planets), and the Twelve (signs of the Zodiac). *Ptahil* also creates humans, dual beings, comprised of a physical Adam and a secret Adam. The primary emissary, *Manda d-Haiye*, "Gnosis of Life" or "The Messenger," descends into our world and reveals himself to humans as an incarnation of the three Uthras or "heavenly spirits." At death the soul of the Mandaean leaves behind his "stinking" body and ascends back to the world of light through seven hostile planetary spheres (a forty-five day sojourn).

D. Mandaean Writings	The Fourth Gospel
Creation	
The World of Light came into being through the power of the King of Life (Right Ginza 1; 3).[51]	1:1–3
The World of Darkness (material world) created by the Lord of Darkness, climaxed in the creation of Adam whose soul is from the World of Light (Right Ginza 3.100).	12:31 (25–26); 16:11

---

49. See Häberl and McGrath, *Mandaean Book of John*.

50. See Rudolph, *Gnosis*, 357–60. For our comparisons, we also consulted Drower, *Canonical Prayerbook of the Mandaeans* that we cite as Mandaean Prayerbook; Foerster, *Gnosis*, 2:125–319; Bultmann, *John*, see his Index under "Mandaeans," 739.

51. See "King and Prophet in Mandaean Sources," in Meeks, *Prophet-King*, 258–85.

IX. THE ODES OF SOLOMON, THE SAMARITANS, AND MANDAEAN LITERATURE

D. Mandaean Writings	The Fourth Gospel
Light	
"The Messenger of Light am I; the Light of Life" (*Manda d-Haiye*, Right Ginza 2.3).	1:9; 8:12
Heavenly Messenger	
A messenger of light, the "Gnosis of Life" comes to redeem people from the evil, material world of darkness and enable the soul/spirit to embark on its journey to the world of light (Right Ginza 2.3; Mandaean Prayerbook 8–9, 131–35, 181–86).[52]	1:4–5,9; 3:17; 6:38; 8:12; 12:35–36
The Evil One	
"I will kill the evil one and cast him into the end of the world."	12:31; 14:30; 16:11
Truth and lies	
The Messenger says to *Ruha* (the demonic spirit): Your eyes are eyes of lying, my eyes are eyes of truth. The eyes of lying grow dark and do not see the truth (Mandaean Prayerbook 133).	8:44; 16:10–11
	8:45–47 (cf. 1:14b)
I am the true Messenger in whom there is no lie (Right Ginza 2.3)	
Blindness	
"I put it before his eyes but he would not see, I showed him, but he would not see with his eyes" (Book of John; cited in Bultmann, *John*, 340).	3:19; 9:39; 12:40 (cf. Isa 6:10; Mark 4:12)

---

52. For criticism of FG and the heavenly redeemer myth, see Yamauchi, *Pre-Christian Gnosticism*, 30–34. See, however, the rejoinder by Stephen J. Patterson, "Prologue," in Fortna and Thatcher, *Jesus in Johannine Tradition*, 323–32, esp. 329–30.

D. Mandaean Writings	The Fourth Gospel
Those who believe	
"The faithful and believing Nazoreans will ascend and view the place of light. The faithful and believing Nazoreans, the excellent ones, will not be held back in this world. Not [in this world] will they be held back, and they will not be held accountable in the great judgment. Over them the judgment will not be spoken, that is to be spoken over all beings. They will not be found before the judgment court, and will not fall into the great Suf-lake..." (Treasure [Ginza] lines 13–22, cited in Boring et al., *Hellenistic Commentary*, 262. "Nazoreans" is a self-designation for the Mandaeans.	3:16,18, 21 5:24; 12:48
Divine authorization	
"The great life has created and commissioned me... The great life... has laid his wisdom upon me... He laid over me love... He laid over me gentle words" (Right Ginza 15.2, 10).	3:35; 5:21–23; 17:23–24
Living Water	
"Living waters (water of Life) from the House of Life shall burst forth" (Mandaean Prayerbook 54). The Messenger is told, "you are living water" (Bultmann, *John*, 185n1). Mandaeans immerse initiates in running/flowing (living) water giving them eternal life (with anointing of oil; Right Ginza 3; 11; 15.3; Mandaean Prayerbook, 18–21; 31).	4:10–14; 7:38
Eternal life now	
"The dead heard thee and lived" (Right Ginza 12.2); "In thy presence (Messenger) there will be restoration for our spirit and our souls" (Mandaean Prayerbook 75). See also the final eschatology, e.g., "on the day of deliverance" (Mandaean Prayerbook 76).	4:23; 5:25–26 5:28–29

D. Mandaean Writings	The Fourth Gospel
Divine Presence	
"Say not I am alone, we will be with you" (Right Gina 14). "I am not standing alone" (Book of John 39.15; cf. Bultmann, *John*, 354). "I will dwell in the hearts of my friends and disciples (Mandaean Prayerbook, 133). "You will dwell with me and in your heart we will settle" (Left Ginza 2.5).	8:16, 29 14:18, 21, 23
Heavenward ascent	
The "Left Ginza" concerns the ascent of the soul to the realm of light. It is also called the "Book of Souls."	3:13, 21; 6:38; 13:3; 16:28; 20:17
Paraclete (helper)	
The Mandaean *Yawar* (helper) is one of many heavenly revealers (Right Ginza 5.1).	14:16–17, 26 (*paraklētos*, "helper," ESV)
Shepherd	
The Messenger of Light loves his sheep, protects his sheep and provides for his sheep (Right Ginza 5.2; Book of John 11; cf. Bultmann, *John*, 367–69).	10:1–39

As a concluding summary to our study, see the table below.

E. Mandaean and Related Writings in Bultmann's *Gospel of John* Commentary

The prologue of John shows that the divine Logos was manifest in Christ who revealed the glory of God to people (John 1:14; Bultmann, *John*, 67–68).

As in the Mandaean literature, Christ comes as a "messenger" (10:36–37) and reveals himself to his own in the great gnostic revealer pronouncements: e.g., "I am the light of the world" (8:12; cf. "I am the true Messenger of Light," Right Ginza 2.3).

In the Gospel, there is an eschatological shift from the Jewish futuristic expectations to the present realization of the resurrection experience (John 5:24–25;11:25; 12:31).

The Johannine Shepherd discourse (10:1–18) is of proto-Mandaean origin based on parallels from the Right Ginza 5.2 (and other sources, e.g., Ezek 34; 1 En 89–90).

Based on additional parallels from the Odes of Solomon and the Hermetica, a Gnostic Revealer Discourse can also be detected with the following three basic elements:

The self-predication of the Revealer (e.g., "I am")

The invitation or call to decision (e.g., leave darkness, draw near to the light)

A promise to those who accept the invitation, often coupled with a warning to those who refuse (e.g., whoever hears me has eternal life, 5:24)

Because the Mandaean traditions were put into writing relatively late (seventh to eighth centuries CE; cf. rabbinica), it has become difficult to distinguish primitive pre-Christian source material from their later redactions.[53] The criticisms that we have applied to FG and the Nag Hammadi corpus (see our ch. 10, pp. 177–79) are also relevant here with FG and the Mandaean writings. The closest parallels appear to betray some knowledge of FG.

In 1929, Hugo Odeberg, whose work is cited by Rudolf Bultmann in his commentary,[54] makes this observation regarding the Mandaean Right Ginza 5.2-3 and its connection to FG

> This passage is important, since it shows familiarity with and dependence upon thoughts and expressions occurring in the Fourth Gospel. Thus there are allusions to Christ as the shepherd and his followers as the herd (John 10.11, 14), as the giver (or, at least, promiser) of "water" to the thirsty (John 4.10, 14; 7.31,38), as the one, who said: "all has been given into my hands" (John 3.35; 6.37) . . . The context in which these allusions occur shows, further, that the Fourth Gospel with which the Mandaeans were confronted belonged to the holy scriptures of the Christian circles to which they were in opposition.[55]

Rudolf Schnackenburg in his four-page review of FG and Mandaeanism, in his commentary,[56] concludes:

---

53. These chronological challenges are reviewed in Yamauchi, *Pre-Christian Gnosticism*, ch. 8. The Mandaic Evidence. Space does not permit us here to apply in detail the criteria, used earlier, of evaluating intertextual comparisons with compositions that *postdate* the NT period, in Evans, *Word of Glory*, 18–28, but they are relevant in our discussion here. See our use of them in ch. 7, pp. 109–11.

54. For example, see Bultmann, *John*, 55, 378.

55. Odeberg, *Fourth Gospel*, 163, as cited in Yamauchi, *Pre-Christian Gnosticism*, 31–32.

56. Schnackenburg, *John*, 1:142–43, who maintains that pre-Christian gnosis is possible only if the sources "are really ancient", see entire review 138–43. J. Frey writes that the existence of Bultmann's redeemer myth, has been deconstructed by authors

Mandaeanism, is therefore, an example of the Gnostic faith in redemption, with its own type of ideas about "envoys," and, if its origins are really ancient, offers valuable material for a pre-Christian and non-Christian Gnosis (it always remains anti-Christian). But it can hardly be regarded as the immediate background of John, since the many designations of the envoys from the heavenly world do not include the specific title which occurs in the Johannine statements about the descent and ascent of the revealer and redeemer, the "Son of Man." Attempts to find him behind the figure of Anosh or Enosh have broken down, because parts of Mandaean literature which come into question have been recognized as late.

---

such as Carsten Colpe, Roland Bergmeier, and others, as discussed in Frey, *Die johanneische Eschatologie* 1:133–37, and cited in Frey, "Between Torah and Stoa," 193n19. See also the arguments of Yamauchi, *Pre-Christian Gnosticism*, 30–34, 163–69, 177–78.

X. The Nag Hammadi Library

THE NAG HAMMADI LIBRARY (NHL), discovered in 1945, is a collection of thirteen codices (bound books) found buried in upper Egypt, probably mid-fourth century CE. There are fifty-two tractates and forty-six different texts (six are duplicates). Forty-one texts are not previously extant, although ten are fragmentary. The collection adds much to our knowledge of early Jewish and Christian, Neoplatonic, Hermetic, Sethian, and Valentinian thought (e.g., Apoc. Adam; 1 Ap. Jas.; Gos. Thom.; Three Forms; Disc. Seth; Gos. Truth; Paraph. Shem). Precise dates are uncertain for time of composition, from the second to the third centuries CE. All were written in Greek and translated into Sahidic Coptic (ca. 350 CE). The collection was hidden by monks (from the nearby Pachomian monastery) probably in response to the Easter Letter of Athanasius, 367 CE, calling on churches and monasteries to eliminate from their libraries all apocryphal writings that were outside the recognized canon of OT and NT books. In addition to the Nag Hammadi library are tractates from the Berlin Codex (BG 8502; fifth century CE), discovered in Egypt, 1896, containing four tractates (Gos. Mary; Act Pet.) and the recently discovered, Codex Tchacos (Egypt, 1978; fourth century CE) includes two new tractates (Gos. Jud.; Bk. Allog.).[1]

Those writings of the Nag Hammadi Library (NHL) that have been identified as gnostic (from Gk., *gnōsis*)[2] remythologize Genesis traditions

---

1. From the preface by J. M. Robinson in Meyer, *Nag Hammadi Scriptures*. Robinson, was the gen. ed. of The Facsimile Edition of the Nag Hammadi Codice (12 vols.; Brill, 1972–1984). See also Perkins, "Nag Hammadi Texts," 4:205–10. Time must be subtracted from ca. 350 CE date of NHL to allow for the prior translation from original Greek into Coptic, see Layton, *Gnostic Scriptures*, 20. The discovery of elaborate gnostic systems in NHL with no apparent Christian influence, e.g., *Paraph. Shem, Apoc. Adam*, seem to indicate that Gnosticism had an *earlier* and more independent development than most critics suppose. Despite problems of definition, e.g., King, *What is Gnosticism?*, 5–19, it seems unlikely, to us, that these writings have been "de-Christianized," see Yamauchi, *Pre-Christian Gnosticism*, 181–84, 248. See our discussion of Sethian Gnosticism, p. 169n4, in this ch.

2. None of the Nag Hammadi texts use "gnostic" as a self-designation. In Testim. Truth, gnostic leaders, Valentinus (56:2–5), Basilides (57:6–8), and the Simonians (58:2–3) are singled out for criticism, probably for differences over certain rituals and

(creation, Adam, Seth) and Jewish wisdom materials (knowledge, truth) or adapt Platonic themes from earlier astrological and magical texts. A basic conviction shared by what we call "gnostics" is: that although humankind exists in ignorance and illusion in the inferior, material world, one can, through *gnōsis* (special revealed knowledge), attain spiritual liberation, that is, recognition of one's own identity with the divine.[3]

At least four gnostic groups have been identified in NHL. Those associated with the Gospel of Thomas (Gos. Thom; Bk Thom.), those affiliated with Seth as a heavenly revealer (Apoc. Adam; Ap. John; Three Forms),[4] a third group reflect the teachings of Valentinus (Alexandria; Rome; ca. 150 CE; Gos. Truth),[5] the last group focuses on Neo-Platonic speculation (Zostr.) on the divine and also the soul's upward ascent to the divine.[6]

Birger A. Pearson comments on the use of Genesis and Wisdom traditions, along with Neo-Platonic speculation and Greco-Roman mythology in the NHL. He also reflects on the implied authors and readers.

> Intimate familiarity with specifically Jewish forms and traditions, an awareness of popular philosophy and pagan lore, a highly sophisticated and creative hermeneutical approach, a sensitivity for profound questions of human existence—such are the characteristics of the early Gnostic literature. We can readily posit as authors and avid readers of the Gnostic materials

---

practices (e.g., water baptism, marriage). Patristic authors, e.g., Irenaeus (180 CE) *Haer.* 1.11.1, called Valentinus a "gnostic" and his descriptions of the "pleroma," 2.7.4 matches up with what we find in NHL (Gos. Truth 16:35). Irenaeus also labels others as "gnostics," e.g., Barbelites (*Haer.* 1.29.1), See discussion in King, *What is Gnosticism?*, ch. 6; Marjanen, *Was There A Gnostic Religion?*; Williams, *Rethinking Gnosticism*. As mentioned above, not every NHL book can be identified as gnostic.

3. See Pagels, "Gnosticism," 364–67; Schenke, "Die Gnosis.," 1:371–415.
Novelist Vladimir Sorokin's *Ice* trilogy begins with a modern re-imagining of an esoteric group like the gnostics. In the novel, he creatively addresses many questions raised by those who have read these ancient esoteric and mystical texts: (1) Who are the enlightened few? (2) How are they identified and (3) how do they receive enlightenment? See Sorokin, *Ice*.

4. See Schenke, "Gnostic Sethianism" 2:588–616; J. D. Turner, "Sethian Gnosticism," in Hedrick and Hodgson, *Nag Hammadi, Gnosticism, and Early Christianity*, 55–86; Robinson, "Trimorphic Protennoia and the Prologue," 39–42.

5. See Mirecki, "Valentinus," 6:783–84, that includes discussion of Gos. Truth and Ap. John. Both Tertullian and Hippolytus called Valentinus a Platonist (Tertullian, *Praescr.* 7; 30; Hippolytus, *Haer.* 6.16, 24, 32; both early third century CE).

6. See Perkins, "Gnosticism," 2:581–84 (includes mention of four gnostic groups, 583). King reexamines these four classifications in *What is Gnosticism?*, 154–69. For a classic definition of gnostic thought, see Pagels, "Gnosticism," 364–67. For patristic sources on the gnostics, see Layton, *Gnostic Scriptures*, see, e.g., the gnostic teacher Basilides (ca. 135 CE, Alexandria), rarely mentioned in NHL (Testim. Truth 57:6–8), Layton, *Gnostic Scriptures*, 417–44. See also Puskas and Robbins, *Introduction to New Testament*, 19–21.

Jewish intellectuals who, estranged from "mainstream" of their own culture and dissatisfied with traditional answers, adopted a revolutionary stance vis-à-vis their religious traditions, not by rejecting them altogether but by applying to them a new interpretation.[7]

Certain authors of the NT, some of them Jewish, also made use of writings outside of second temple Jewish literature (e.g., Acts 17:28; cf. Aratus, *Phaemomena* 5; Acts 26:24; cf. Euripides, *Bacchae* 795; 2 Pet 2:22; cf. Heraclitus, Frg. B 13; 1 Cor 15:33; cf. Menader, *Thaïs* Frg. 165). Certain apologists of the later second century, CE, also cited Greek and Roman classics in their writings (Justin, *1 Apol.* 18 [Homer]; Minucius Felix (*Oct.* 191 [Homer and Virgil]).[8]

Noteworthy surveys of the NT and gnostic teachings are by Robert MacLachlan Wilson and Pheme Perkins.[9] In addition, are many essays of collected writings on a variety of texts and themes.[10] Individual essays from specific collections, will be cited as we focus on specific books of NHL and compare them with FG.

Before the discovery of the Nag Hammadi Codices, Rudolf Bultmann, following insights from Wilhelm Bousset, and Hans Jonas, argued for a pre-Christian gnostic mythology, and especially a revelation-discourse source, that best conveyed the characteristics of the Word and its activity as depicted in FG's prologue.[11] Bultmann made use of the Odes

---

7. B. A. Pearson, "The Problem of 'Jewish Gnostic' Literature," in Hedrick and Hodgson, *Nag Hammadi, Gnosticism, and Early Christianity*, 34–35. He cites as an example, Tiberius Alexander, a Jewish intellectual who departed from the torah to the dismay of Philo, his uncle and Jewish intellectual, who had observed torah, see Philo, *Virt.* 182; *Conf.* 2–3. We add that the unknown author of Let. Aris. compared the God of Israel to Zeus (16). In his essay, Pearson focused on the NHL Sethian writings Ap. John and Apoc. Adam.

8. See Citations and Allusions, in NA[28], 878 and Holladay, *Acts*, 340–46; Norden, *Agnostos Theos*. Acts 17:28a (Aratus quote) may be our context for understanding John 1:4.

9. Wilson, *Gnosis and the New Testament*; Perkins, *Gnosticism and the New Testament*, 1993, and, e.g., her "Johannine Traditions in Ap. Jas," 403–14.

10. For examples, see MacRae in his *Studies in the New Testament and Gnosticism*; Hedrick and Hodgson, *Nag Hammadi, Gnosticism, and Early Christianity*; Goehring and Hedrick, *Gnosticism and the Early Christian World*. For an index disclosing hundreds of intertextual connections between NHL and FG, see Evans et al., *Nag Hammadi Texts and the Bible*, 503–16.

11. Bultmann, *John*, 21–25. See also Bousset, *Hauptproblem der Gnosis*; and Jonas, *Gnosis und spätantiker Geist* (1:193) cited in Bultmann, *John*, 730–31. Bultmann's student gave further support for an early gnostic revelation-discourse, see Becker, *Die Reden des Johannesevangelums*. We will mention later, some criticism of the notion of a pre-Christian gnostic myth.

X. THE NAG HAMMADI LIBRARY

of Solomon, the Hermetic Corpus, and Mandaean writings to support his thesis for an early gnostic influence. We have already discussed these and their alleged connections to FG.

Why a comparison of FG with some titles from the *later* NHL collection? It must be noted that the discovery of elaborate gnostic systems in NHL with no apparent Christian influence, e.g., *Paraph. Shem, Apoc. Adam*, seem to indicate that Gnosticism had an *earlier* and more independent development than most critics suppose.[12] Also, NT studies is replete with chronological challenges, e.g., the sources for the historical Jesus, post-date his earthly life by thirty-five to sixty years, yet most scholars are convinced that his authentic sayings and deeds can be gleaned from them.[13]

In his commentary,[14] Rudolph Schnackenburg, reviewed the work of Bultmann along with the relationship of FG to the recent publications of NHL. He cites the Gospel of Truth (Gos. Truth; Valentinus) and Apocryphon of John (Ap. John; classic gnostic myth) as representatives of typical gnostic thought.

Although we cite from the page and line referencing of NHLE, edited by James M. Robinson, we retain some of phrasings here from the English translated edition of Schnackenburg's commentary (based on W. Till's, "Das Evangelium der Wahrheit," 1959; and S. Giversen's *Apocryphon Johannis*, 1963).

---

12. See John D. Turner's case for Jewish and pre-Christian strands of Gnosticism, in his "Sethian Gnosticism," in Hedrick and Hodgson, *Nag Hammadi, Gnosticism*, 55–86; see esp. Hans-Martin Schenke, "Das Sethiahische System," 165–73; and Hedrick, *Apocalypse of Adam*, 209–15. See survey of discussion in King, *What is Gnosticism?*, 175–81.

13. We have noted these challenges and assumptions in ch. 10. "The Historical Jesus," of Puskas and Robbins, *Introduction*, 169–80.

14. Schnackenburg, *John*, 1:135–52, on FG and NHL see 1:146–49 (we cite from NHLE). Regarding Gos. Truth, George W. MacRae wrote that it is a second-century composition "which does not yet actually know John but shares with it some tendencies in the reinterpreting of common tradition," in his *Studies in the New Testament and Gnosticism*, 181. Hengel cites several parallels in his *Johannine Question*, 146n46.

A. Gospel of Truth (Gos. Truth); Apocryphon of John (Ap. John) [15]	Fourth Gospel
	The Word who is from the Father
"The gospel of truth is joy for those who have received from the Father of truth the grace of knowing him through the power of the Word that came forth from the pleroma, the one who is in the thought and mind of the Father, that is, the one who is addressed as the Savior that is the name of the work he is doing for the redemption of those who were ignorant of the Father, while in the name (of) the gospel is the proclamation of hope, being discovery for those who search for him," Gos. Truth 16:31—17:4.	The Word who was with God was in the world to be a light to those in darkness to give them power to be children of God, receiving glory of a father's only son, full of grace and truth, from his fullness (*pleroma*) he dispenses grace upon grace. He is God's only Son who is close to the Father's bosom (*kolpos*) has made the Father known (to those who do not know him) John 1:1–5, 9–18.
	The whence and whither of life
"He has learned this, knows whence he is come and whither he goes," Gos. Truth 22:13–15. "But this is the Father, from whom the beginning proceeded, to whom all who proceeded from him shall return," Gos. Truth 37:38—38:4. "He has returned again to the place from which he came," Ap. John 1:12. "For this reason has he brought him forth (the Son), that he might speak of the place and of his (the Father's) place of repose, when he (the Son) has come . . . He (the Son) will speak of the place, whence every single one (each man) has proceeded, and he (each man) will hasten to return to the place from where he received his origin, and to be brought away from that place, the place where he has stood, since he has tasted of that place (the divine world of light) and received nourishment and growth from it" (Gos. Truth 40:30—41:12).	The "whence" and "whither" regarding the origin and mission of Jesus, John 7:27–28, 35; 8:14; 9:29–30; 19:19.

Seekers and disciples are included in the question of where their way leads, 7:34, 36; 8:21–22; 12:26; 13:33, 36; 14:3–4; 17:24.

The revealer and life-bringer who descended from heaven and who alone has ascended there again, will throw open the way of light and life to all who believe, 3:31–36, 13–21. See Schnackenburg, *John*, 1:147. |

---

15. See introduction of Gos. Truth by E. Thomassen in Meyer, *Nag Hammadi Scriptures*, 31–35. Unless noted otherwise, our NHLE citations are the Robinson ed. (1990). For helpful illustration and explanation of the "classic gnostic myth" in Ap. John, see Layton, *Gnostic Scriptures*, 12–17. For recent study on Ap. John and FG, see Nagel, "Zur Gnostisierung der Johanneischen Tradition," 675–93.

A. Gospel of Truth (Gos. Truth); Apocryphon of John (Ap. John)	Fourth Gospel

From above and from below

"If one has knowledge, he is from above," Gos. Truth 22:4; "the salvation which is coming from on high," 35:1; "those who possess (something) from above of the immeasurable greatness" (42:13).

"So, you do the will of the Father, for you are from him," (33:32); "Came from him (the Father)" (38:7).

We also add: "For he is an earthly man, but I am from above" (Disc. Seth. 51:34—52:3).[16]

"To be from above," 8:23; "to come from above," 3:31; cf., 3:3, 7; 19:11).

"I came from the Father," 16:28; cf. "I declare what I have seen in the Father's presence . . . you should do what you have heard from the Father," 8:38. Those who do the will of God, 6:38; 7:17.

"You are from below, I am from above," 8:23.

Appearance of the Son in human form

"for he had come out of it in fleshly likeness . . . speaking about what was in the Father's heart, for he had produced the Word . . . and light spoke forth from his mouth. And his voice gave birth to life," Gos. Truth 31.4-16; in Layton, *Gnostic Scriptures*, 259.

"And the Word became flesh and lived among us, and we have seen his glory, the glory as of a father's only son, full of grace and truth," 1:14. "In him was life, and the life was the light of all people," v. 4; "I speak just as the Father told me," 12:50.

One with the Father

"And the Father is in them and they are in the Father," Gos. Truth 42:27–28; cf. 43:9–10.

I in them and you in me, 14:11, 20; 15:4; 17:23.

Suffering and death of Jesus

"faithful Jesus became patient and accepted the sufferings . . . inasmuch as he knew that his death would mean life for many" (Gos. Truth 20.10-14), "Jesus appeared . . . was nailed to a piece of wood, and published his Father's edict upon the cross," (20.23-27).

"I lay down my life for the sheep," 10:15; cf. 15:13; "it is better for you to have one man die for the people than to have the whole nation destroyed," 11:50; cf. 18:14; "Now my soul is troubled. And what should I say—'Father, save me from this hour'? No, it is for this reason that I have come to this hour," 12:27; "**carrying the cross by himself, he went out to . . . Golgotha. There they crucified him** . . . Pilate also had an inscription written and put on the cross," 19:17-19.

---

16. Lakoff and Johnson call the images of "above" and "below" orientational metaphors, where "above" is good, and "below" is bad, as in John 8:23 and Disc. Seth 51:34—52:3 (*Metaphors We Live By*, 16-17).

A. Gospel of Truth (Gos. Truth); Apocryphon of John (Ap. John)	Fourth Gospel
Return to the heavenly realm of light	
"this is the Father ... to whom all will return who have come forth from him" (Gos. Truth 37:38–38:4); "He will hasten to return again to that place from which he stood, receiving nourishment and growth, his own resting place" (41:7–12). "And now I shall go up to the perfect aeon," (Ap. John 31:26–27).	"I go to my Father," John 14:12; 16:10, 28; 20:17.
The way of truth	
"He enlightened them; he showed them a way and the way is the truth which he taught them" (Gos. Truth 18:18–21; cf. Ap. John 5:32–34).	"I am the way, the truth and the life, no one comes to Father except through me," 14:6.
Light and life	
God (the Parent of Entirety) is praised as immeasureable light and the giver of life (Ap. John 3:17–18; 4:2–4); "He who comprehends himself in his own light which surrounds him, who indeed is the source of life, the light completely pure. The spring of the Spirit streamed from the living water of the light" (4:19–21, cf. 22–26).	"In him was life and the life was the light of all people," 1:4; "the truth light that enlightens everyone," 1:9; "the water that I will give will become in them a spring of water gushing up to eternal life," 4:14.

B. Gospel of Thomas (Gos. Thom)[17] and The Fourth Gospel

1. Jesus having appeared in the flesh (Gos. Thom, logion 28: John 1:14)
2. "When you seek me and do not find me," (logion 38; John 7:34, 36)
3. "If you become my disciples and listen to my words ... " (logion 19; John 8:31)
4. A vine not well established will be uprooted (logion 40: John 15:6)
5. "You shall find the Kingdom; because you come from it, (and) you shall go there again" (logion. 49; John 3:3–8)
6. "We have come from the Light, where the Light has originated through itself" (logion 50; John 3:19–21).

---

17. Plisch, *Thomas*. Schenke, "On the Compositional History of the Gospel of Thomas." We shall devote the next ch. 11 to Gos. Thom. To the above comparisons provided by Schnackenburg, *John*, 1:148, we have added a few others. See also Koester, *Ancient Christian Gospels*, 264n2.

C. Gospel of Philip (Gos. Phil.)[18] and The Fourth Gospel

1. The perfect man "has brought bread from heaven," (Gos. Phil., logion 11: John 6:31–32)

2. "Christ came to deliver some and to save others. He made strangers his own . . . he laid down his life" (logion 5; John 13:1; 10:17)

3. "He who does not eat my flesh and drink my blood does not have life within him" (logion 21; quotation of John 6:53)

4. "If you know the truth, the truth will set you free" (logion 104 [84:10]; John 8:32)

5. "He who has knowledge of the truth is free, but he who is free does not sin" (logion 93; John 8:32, 34).

6. "Therefore he became a murderer like his father, for he was the son of a snake" (logion 36; "He [your father] was a murderer from the beginning," John 8:44)

7. "Those who inherit the living are alive" (logion 2; John 11:25)

8. "The father existed in the son, and the son existed in the father" (logion 83; John 14:10)

9. "Mary, his mother, his sister, and the Magdalene" (logion 28; John 19:25)

Regarding the texts that he examined (above), Prof. Schnackenburg detected traits of Valetinian influence, deliberate exploitation of FG for gnostic speculations, and reveals a gnostic frame of mind that "was not wholly unknown to the fourth evangelist, and of which he took to it silent cognizance, to oppose it to the Christian message."[19]

As shown in the table below, Pheme Perkins presents her own gnostic reading of John's Prologue.[20] She begins with some allusions to both the Gospel of Truth and Apocryphon of John, but focuses her attention on the Trimorphic Protennoia (Three Forms of First Thought).[21]

18. We cite the logia from Layton, *Gnostic Scriptures*, 325–53, that includes both logia (2) as well as page and line divisions (52.1–13); Hengel cites several parallels in his *Johannine Question*, 146n46.

19. Schnackenburg, *John*, 1:149. Statments like "the Word became flesh" are viewed as reflecting FG's opposition to a docetic form of gnosticism. Citing mostly NT Apocrypha and patristic polemics, see Schnelle, *Antidocetic Christology*, 61–70, although he cautions us with reference to NHL "that gnosis and docetism [Jesus did not come "in the flesh"] are in no way identical and not necessarily mutually related," 65n151, citing Brox, "'Doketismus,'" 312–14. Our comments are in brackets (above). The following collection of essays seeks to reexamine the use of "docetic," in Verheyden et al., *Docetism in the Early Church*. See also p. 178n29 of this ch. and also our ch. 12, p. 215n16.

20. Perkins, *Gnosticism and the New Testament*, 112–21. See survey of parallels in S. J. Patterson, "Prologue" in Fortna and Thatcher, *Jesus in Johannine Tradition*, 323–32.

21. See also Evans, "On the Prologue and the Trimorphic Protennoia," 395–401; Y.

D. The Gospel of Truth,[22] The Apocryphon of John, and FG (Redux)

1. Monastic gnostic systems may assert that "all things came into being through him" (John 1:2): "This is the first thought, his image; she became the womb of everything for it is she who is prior to them all, the Mother Father" (Ap. John 5:4-7).

2. Wisdom's power passes to Adam when Yaltabaoth (crafty creator god) blows on him (Ap. John 19.15-33); Epinoia of the light (luminous afterthought) is hidden within Adam as his helper (20:14-16; 22:15-18; cf. John 20:20-22; also 14:26; 16:13).

3. Nothing happens without the Logos, that is, without the Father's will (Gos. Truth 37:21-24; cf. John 4:34; 5:30).

4. The Word pervades the Pleroma as God's creative activity so that those in the divine realm come to know the Father (Gos. Truth 23:33—24:24; John 1:18; 12:44-45; 14:9-10).

5. "Gospel of Truth begins with an evocation of the Johannine prologue (Gos. Truth 16:32-36). The Word here designates the perfect knowledge of the Father that comes through revelation (36:18—37:18). But the author's real interest is in the name of the Son as the proper revelation of the Father (38:5—41:3). The Johannine echoes in Gospel of Truth include extensive allusions to the life and crucifixion of Jesus."[23]

E. Trimorphic Protennoia (Three Forms) and the Fourth Gospel

Three Forms contain first person "I am" discourses of the perfect Protennoia or First Thought (Three Forms 35:1-32), who descends into the world of darkness as savior (35:32—36:27; 40:29—41:1).[24] She appears three times: as the hidden Voice, as the Speech of the First Thought (42:4-27; 45:2-12; 45:21—46:3), and finally as the Word who assumes a human appearance and restores her members into the light (46:5-6; 47:5-22; 49:15-22; 50:9-12, 18-20; cf. John 1:9; also 12:36).

Janssens, "Trimorphic Protennoia and the Fourth Gospel," in Logan and Wedderburn, *New Testament and Gnosis*, 229-44; Robinson, "Trimorphic Protennoia and the Prologue," 37-50. Robinson argues that the content of Three Forms reflects a Sethian type of gnostic thought (cf. Ap. John; Gos. Eg.; Steles Seth) (39-42).

22. See the denouncements of Irenaeus concerning the Valentinian "Gospel of Truth" (*Haer.* 3.11.8). Irenaeus may have referred to the same writing (above) found in NHL. For full Irenaeus quote, see our ch. 12, pp. 226-27.

23. Perkins, *Gnosticism and the New Testament*, 118. Perkins concludes here that the treatment of the Word in Gos. Truth has been derived from FG.

24. On the gnostic redeemer myth, see: descent (Mandaean Liturgies 196-97; Steles Seth 119:15-24; Apoc. Adam 77.27—82.19; Ascen. Isa. 10.17-30); appearance in the form of a human (Gos. Thom. 28; Gos. Truth 31.4-8; Ascen. Isa. 11:1-18; Treat. Res. 44, 14-20); suffering and death (Gos. Truth 20.10-14, 23-27; Ascen. Isa. 11.19-20); return to the Father and exaltation (Treat. Res. 45.15-39; Odes Sol. 41.12; Ascen. Isaiah 11:22-32; Ap. Jas 15.15-25). As mentioned earlier, the discovery of elaborate gnostic systems in NHL with no apparent Christian influence, e.g., Paraph. Shem, Apoc. Adam, seem to

1. Wisdom exists before all things and in all. She is light and life (35:1—36:3; 47:29–48:7; cf. John 1:1–5).²⁵

2. The Son reveals this heavenly Wisdom to those who originated from above (37:3–9; 38:16–18; 50:15–16; cf. John 1:9, 18; also 3:21; 13:1).

3. Only "children of light" (37:18–20) receive this revelation, but the others fail to perceive it (41:15–16; 47:10–11, 22–25; cf. John 1:10–13).

4. "I am the Word" (46:5); "I alone am the Word" (46:15); "bearing a Fruit of Life, pouring forth a Living Water from the . . . immeasurable Spring" (46:16–18; cf. John 7:37–39; 8:12).

5. On its third descent, the Word appears in human form wearing the "tent" or garment of the archons (47:13–16; cf. John 1:14).

6. The Word announces that "I am the Light that illumines the All," I came down to mortals to deliver and "gave to them from the Water [of Life] which strips them of the chaos of darkness" (47:29—48:14; cf. John 4:10–15; 8:12; 12:36).

7. I "established him in the dwelling places of the Father" (50:14–15; cf. John 14:2).

8. The revealer has come to abide in believers that they may abide in him (50:10–11; cf. John 15:4–5).

9. "Because Barbelo is a multiplicity, she can reveal herself as the triad of Proetnnoia, Voice, and Word, the 'unknowable Father' cannot do so. In some sense, the Son shares in multiplicity that the Father cannot do. Consequently, the Son can reveal God."²⁶ See John 10:27–30; 14:9–14, 20.

10. FG's prologue (1:5, 10–13) can be viewed as a comment on the elements of conflict between the rulers of the lower world and the Light (recalling ancient conflicts, Gen 3:14–18; 6:4; 1 En 6–10; Jub 3–7; John 12:31, 35–36; 14:30; Rev 12:1–6).²⁷

Although the NHL is translated from Sahidic Coptic and the NT from Hellenistic Greek, we find similar lexical constructions despite different

---

indicate that Gnosticism had an earlier and more independent development than most critics suppose. Nevertheless, the evidence for a so-called gnostic redeemer myth in the first century remains contestable, see Perkins, "Gnosticism," 2:581–84; and King, *What is Gnosticism?*, 109, 137–38; see esp. the criticism of Colpe, *Die religionsgeschichtliche Schule*, Yamauchi, *Pre-Christian Gnosticism*; we share some (dating problems), but not all of their conclusions (see, e.g., our p. 168n1, above).

25. In comparing the many scattered parallels to FG's prologue in wisdom literature (see our ch. 3, tbl. A, pp. 46–49), Three Forms appears to bring them together in a unique way, although not in the same order as the prologue, writes Robinson, citing Carsten Colpe, in her "Trimorphic Protennoia and the Prologue," 46; for the source cited, see C. Colpe, "Heidnische, Juedische und Christliche Ueberlieferung," 122, 124.

26. Perkins, *Gnosticism and the New Testament*, 117. She mentions here Clement of Alexandria who argued that the Son has a name and a face the Father cannot have.

27. Perkins, *Gnosticism and the New Testament*, 119, see also 15–18. For more support from biblical and extracanonical literature, see also Stuckenbruck, *Myth of Rebellious Angels*, 187–212.

meanings conveyed in their respective contexts. This conclusion makes the establishing of a genetic relationship difficult to maintain.[28] Three Forms of First Thought (Trimorphic Protennoia), for example, shares many of the images in FG's prologue, but the historicizing references to John the Baptist, to Moses, and the fleshly incarnation of Jesus are missing. The succinct words of "the Word became flesh and lived (*skēnoō*, "tabernacle") among us" (John 1:14) are contrasted with the elaborate explanation of the revealer wearing the garments of all the powers in order to bring revelation to his people (47:14–27).[29] Although FG and Three Forms presuppose a narrative of redemption, Three Forms consists of allusions to episodes in a gnostic mythologizing of Genesis with a Demiurge creator god (38:13—41:1),[30] a corrupting tree of life (44:20—45:24), and a baptism ritual of living waters for the children of light (46:33—50:12).[31] Nevertheless, FG and the gnostic authors of Three Forms have established a meaningful narrative framework within which their affirmations about the divine revealer are set.

Concerning parallels with the Gospel of Truth, FG's prologue ("the darkness did not overcome [*katalambanō*, "seize, attack"] it" (1:5; cf. Gos. Truth 18:4–6), "his own people did not accept him" (vv. 10–13; cf. Gos. Truth 18:16–23) can be viewed as a comment on the elements of opposition between the rulers of the lower world and the Light (recalling ancient conflicts, Gen 3:14–18; 6:4; 1 En 6–10; Jub 3:17–25; 5:1–11; John 8:44; 12:31, 35–36; 14:30; Rev 12:1–6).[32] Pheme Perkins again observes:

> Early gnostic dualism depicts the opposition between the rulers of the lower world and the Light as a mythological fact, not a dualism of abstract, cosmological principles (e.g., Philo). Wisdom personified in the spiritual Eve or in her various manifestations suffers the attack of the rapacious archons. As already noted, Jewish traditions about the lust of the "sons of God" for the "daughters of men played a formative role in gnostic accounts of humanity's

---

28. R. McL. Wilson states that "from a phenomenological point of view it may be perfectly legitimate to group religious movements together on the basis of common elements; but this does not necessarily mean that these movements stand in a genetic relationship, or that there is any direct connection between the earlier and the latter," in his *Gnosis and the New Testament*, 7.

29. Perkins, *Gnosticism and the New Testament*, 116. The Gnostic Redeemer appears on earth in a docetic body (Colpe, *Die religionsgeschichtliche Schule*, 198).

30. See points 1 and 10 in the last table (E.2. Three Forms, p. 177) above. On Demiurge, see our tbls. 7.C p. 115, and E., p. 122; ch. 12. E. p. 218.

31. On Mandaeans and "living water," see our tbl. 9.D. On our criteria for evaluating intertextual comparisons that postdate the NT period, see chs. and tbls.: 5.B; 6.C.; 7.B, D, F.

32. Perkins, *Gnosticism and the New Testament*, 15–18, 118–19. For more support from biblical and extracanonical literature, see also Stuckenbruck, *Myth of Rebellious Angels*, 187–212. See also our discussion in ch. 3, pp. 53–54.

plight. The lust of the archons has corrupted human life. Only the pure seed of Seth escapes this condition.[33]

Although FG lacks the elaborate gnostic cosmogony, it betrays some elements of a similar cosmic conflict that are implicit in the text (John 1:5, 10–13; 8:44; 12:31, 35–36; 14:30).

FG's concept of the world (*kosmos*) is often a negative spatial entity associated with death and darkness, resistance to Jesus, and believers must depart from it in order to be saved (1:9–10; 7:7; 8:23; 9:4–5; 12:31; 14:17; 16:11; 17:14; cf. Gos. Truth 18:16–22). It sometimes is used in a neutral sense (3:16–17; 4:42; 6:14, 33; 8;12; 12:47; even positive, cf. 1:1–5; Gen 1;), and of human habitants of the world (3:16–17; 4:42; 12:47; the public, 7:4; 8:26; 12:19).[34] The concept of an intermediate "craftsman" (*Demiurge*) can also be seen, at some remove from Plato's *Timaeus*[35] and NHL, in FG's "The Word . . . was in the beginning with God; all things were made through it" (John 1:1–3).[36] In FG, the Word, unlike the "craftsman," of Plato and NHL, is not morally ambiguous or incompetent, but the divine Word of Revelation sent to bring light and life to the world.

Gesine Robinson concludes with this observation regarding FG's prologue, Three Forms, and their common influences from Genesis and Wisdom traditions:

> Regarding the history-of-religious background, it has of course been uncontested that the Prologue, in its cosmological and salvation-historical speculations, is dependent on pre-Christian traditions that go back to Genesis. Most would also insist that this was mediated through Hellenistic-Jewish Wisdom or Logos speculation. But it should be clear, especially in view of the Nag Hammadi texts, that neither of these roots precluded gnostic orientation, in that Gnosticism itself appealed to Genesis and built on Wisdom speculation. On the fast-moving field of late antiquity, Wisdom speculation and gnostic myth influenced and accelerated each other mutually.[37]

---

33. Perkins, *Gnosticism and the New Testament*, 118–19. Hans Jonas maintains that these Jewish traditions are incorporated into a new speculative (gnostic) system, in ch. 8 of Hyatt, *Bible in Modern Scholarship*, 286–93.

34. See Reinhartz, *Word in the World*, 38–41, 79–80. See also our ch. 1, p. 19n17.

35. See our discussion of Plato in ch. 7, pp. 111, 115.

36. Layton, *Gnostic Scriptures*, 16.

37. Robinson, "Trimorphic Protennoia and the Prologue," 50. E. M. Yamauchi argues that the gnostic use of Genesis may often be a reaction to early Christian OT interpretations, in his *Pre-Christian Gnosticism*, 234–35, 243. M. Hengel contends that Three Forms knew FG, in his *Johannine Question*, 113.

XI. The Gospel of Thomas[1]

Over the years, the study of the Gospel of John has collided with research on the Gospel of Thomas.[2]

At the early stage of research in the *Gospel of Thomas*, the main question above all was how this document is related to the Synoptic Gospels. Only rather late did scholars recognize that the links between the *Gospel of Thomas* and the Gospel of John are even more complex.[3]

BOLD CLAIMS HAVE BEEN made about the historical Jesus and the beginnings of Christianity using **the Gospel of Thomas** (GTh) as a point of departure. It serves as an example of what happens when our understanding of historical events and historical categories is disrupted by the emergence or discovery of something new and unusual, for our understanding of history is filled with gaps. Even though some of the gaps are large and long, we get comfortable with them and our arrangement and understanding of them, often even forgetting they are there! Such a discovery as the GTh affords an opportunity for historians gifted at filling in the gaps to emerge and be noticed.[4]

---

1. For a convenient version of the Coptic text, with a parallel English translation, plus a 46-page introduction to GTh, see Kloppenborg et al., *Q-Thomas Reader*. The translation in the Reader is by Marvin Meyer. See also original text and commentary: Plisch, *Thomas*. Other English translations that can be consulted are in *NHLE* 126–38 by Bentley Layton (see also his *Gnostic Scriptures*, 380–99). For Coptic text and English trans., see Guillaumont et al. *Gospel according to Thomas*. See online http://www.early-christianwritings.com/thomas.html.

2. DeConick, *Voices of the Mystics*, 26.

3. Enno E. Popke, "About the Differing Approach to a Theological Heritage" in: Charlesworth, *Bible and the Dead Sea Scrolls*, 3:281–317, quotation is from 290.

4. We would gladly do without the gaps, just as communities of faith would gladly do without quarrels, dissension, and division. But Paul's comment is wise, and perhaps we can borrow it here: "For there must also be factions among you, in order that those who are approved may become evident" (1 Cor 11:19). The word translated here "approved" is a favorite word of Paul (δόκιμος), and suggests "approved after testing."

Some of the issues about it that are debated should pique the reader's interest and curiosity, since there are many likenesses to issues that swirl around FG. Debated, for example, are the text's (1) date and provenance,[5] (2) relation to Wisdom traditions,[6] (3) relation to Gnosis and gnosticism,[7] (4) connection to an apostolic tradition,[8] (5) relation to the Synoptic tradition,[9] (6) eschatology and resurrection motifs, (7) unique, high Christology,[10] (8) relation to Judaism and Temple traditions, (9) relation to Platonic traditions, (10) et al.[11]

General Introduction to GTh

As we mentioned in our last chapter, the text we possess was recovered in 1945. It is very close in time to the discovery of the DSS. There are in fact numerous comparisons that can be made between the two manuscript collections. James M. Robinson writes

> Both manuscript collections are libraries of off-beat monastic groups . . . One hid its library in jars in the caves . . . near the Dead Sea in Palestine as the Roman Tenth Legion attacked their monastery in 68 A.D. in a war leading to the fall of Jerusalem; the other hid its library in a jar . . . near the Nile in Upper Egypt

---

5. Fallon and Cameron, "Gospel of Thomas," 41-95; Desjardins, "Where was the Gospel of Thomas Written?" 121-33. It is clear to anyone reading the Coptic text that it is a translation of a Greek original. And soon after its discovery it was realized that we have had fragmentary Greek copies of some of the sayings since around the turn of the twentieth century. The Greek papyrus manuscripts were unearthed at Oxyrhynchus. See discussion with references and bibliography in Koester, *Ancient Christian Gospels*, 76-77. See also Brown, "Where Indeed Was the Gospel of Thomas Written?"

6. See the creative and acclaimed study by Davies, *Gospel of Thomas and Christian Wisdom*. Hans-Martin Schenke, sees the more pessimistic and speculative wisdom (Qoheleth) on a continuum toward Gnosticism, in his "Die Tenenz der Weisheit zur Gnosis," 351-72. See also our ch. 3 on wisdom and angelology, pp. 45-46.

7. Grobel, "How Gnostic is the Gospel of Thomas?" 367-73; Koester, *Ancient Christian Gospels*, 75-128; Robinson, "On Bridging the Gulf from Q to the Gospel of Thomas," 127-75; DeConick, *Seek to See Him*, 3-27; Hill, *Johannine Corpus*, esp. 270-80 in ch. 5, "John and the Gnostics"; Marjanen, "Is *Thomas* a Gnostic Gospel?"

8. Cameron, "Gospel of Thomas and Christian Origins."

9. Patterson, "Gospel of Thomas and the Synoptic Tradition."

10. One should be wary of attributing a low Christology to GTh simply because it makes sparse use of titles.

11. It has been said that "the two gospels share material which is not found in the Synoptics, or interpret material in a common manner but distinct from the Synoptics. One aspect of this situation is that it is possible to see John at points as a correction not of some lost Gnosis, but of ideas actually preserved in the Gospel of Thomas. Likewise, and to a significant extent, *Thomas* is in a reciprocal relationship with John" (Riley, *Resurrection Reconsidered*, 3).

... perhaps when Roman authorities, now in the name of orthodox Christianity, were stamping out Gnosticism in the region of the Pachomian monasteries around 400 A.D. One library was written primarily in Hebrew; the other originally composed in Greek ... but translated into the Egyptian language of the day, Coptic. One was written in the Second Century B.C. to the First Century A.D.; the other from the First to the Fourth Century A.D. One was written mainly on parchment scrolls; the other ... in papyrus codices ... One library contains the texts of heretical Jews expelled from the Jerusalem temple, part of a group called Essenes; the other contains the texts of heretical Christians perhaps expelled from the monasteries founded by Saint Pachomius, part of a group called Gnostics. The Essenes used the Hebrew Scriptures, but interpreted them in terms of dualism; the Gnostics used both the Old and New Testaments, but reinterpreted them radically in terms of cosmic dualism and a mythological gnostic redeemer.[12]

The texts discovered in Egypt, as we mentioned, are named the Nag Hammadi Library.[13] Each of the twelve codices contains several essays called tractates, plus there were eight loose leaves from a thirteenth codice, totaling 52 separate tractates. Among this collection, as a tractate in the second codice or book, was a text titled "The Gospel of Thomas."[14] It was a collection of 114 separate sayings of Jesus. Enumeration of the sayings were added by scholars studying the text. However, each saying was introduced by "Jesus said" or something similar.[15] From it we can learn a great deal about a group of early Christians, and what they thought about Jesus. What we can learn about "the historical Jesus" from this gospel is, of course,

---

12. Robinson, *Nag Hammadi Codices*. Robinson's critical account of the discovery can be found in "The Discovery of the Nag Hammadi Codices." More recently, Enno E. Popkes has compared the FG and GTh as "two quite different theological streams in early Christianity" which "had contact with each other or rivaled each other" (Charlesworth, *Bible and the Dead Sea Scrolls*, 3:282). Their theological profiles are then discussed using information gained by the pre-christian collection of the DSS and the later collection of the NHL which "offer an insight into the controversial phase of the search for a Christian identity of the early church, when the New Testament canon was still in the making" (281), in his "Theological Heritage" in Charlesworth, *Bible and the Dead Sea Scrolls*, 3:281–317.

13. See now Robinson et al., *Nag Hammadi Library*.

14. L. T. Johnson pays close attention to the positioning of GTh within NHL and FG within the NT, in his "John and *Thomas* in Context."

15. All of our references in this chapter to "sayings" in the Gospel of Thomas will look like this: Saying #1 = S1; Saying #100= S100, etc. And since some sayings contain complexes these are referred to as a subset, such as 1.1, 1.2, or 1.3. Some refer to saying/sayings as Logion/Logia.

debated. We knew of the existence of a text like this from other early Christian sources, but had never seen such a copy.

> The one incontrovertible testimonium to *Gos. Thom.* is found in Hippolytus of Rome (*Haer.* 5.7.20). Writing between the years 222-235 C.E., Hippolytus quotes a variant of saying 4 expressly stated to be taken from a text entitled *Gos. Thom.* Possible references to this gospel by its title alone abound in early Christianity (e.g. Eus. *Hist. Eccl.* 3.25.6). But such indirect attestations must be treated with care, since they might refer to the *Infancy Gospel of Thomas*. Parallels to certain sayings in *Gos. Thom.* are also abundant; some are found, according to Clement of Alexandria, in the *Gospel of the Hebrews* and the *Gospel of the Egyptians*. However, a direct dependence of *Gos. Thom.* upon another noncanonical gospel is problematic and extremely unlikely. The relationship of *Gos. Thom.* to the *Diatessaron* of Tatian is even more vexed, exacerbated by untold difficulties in reconstructing the textual basis of Tatian's tradition, and has not yet been resolved.[16]

So, even though we knew about this gospel from the writings of some of the church fathers it was not until December of 1945 that we were actually given a chance to read it ... or a version of it. In the first centuries of the Common Era it was one of the many early Christian texts caught in the cross-fire of heated theological debate and censorship, and it consequently (almost) perished.

The version of it that was "recovered" in 1945 at the base of a cliff along the Nile River near the modern town of Nag Hammadi, about 370 miles south of Cairo in Upper Egypt, had clearly been hidden carefully, for it was in a clay jar, with a lid on top sealed with pitch (tar) to keep out moisture. Here it lay until the middle of the twentieth century.[17] The collection together is known today as The Nag Hammadi Library. It was hidden sometime in the fourth century by some monks or desert ascetic cave dwellers (or possibly they lived in a desert community monastery close by, as Robinson suggests). Why they hid the books is not clear, though to protect them, as Robinson above suggests, is possible. The content of the Library is diverse, but it is clearly a collection of gnostic and mystical texts betraying a diverse heritage, some of Christian influence, some Platonic, some Jewish.

---

16. Cameron, "Thomas, Gospel of," 6:535.

17. For interesting, even dramatic discussion (with pictures) of the discovery of the Nag Hammadi texts see Robinson, *Nag Hammadi Codices*; "Introduction" (1-26) to Robinson et al., *Nag Hammadi Library*; also by Robinson, "Nag Hammadi."

A. FG and GTh: Assessing the Relationship[18]

The objective here is to provide a database which will help further students in imagining methods for recognizing parallels or other types of connectedness by sampling a pool of scholarly work already done. Some of these scholars have already provided historical and literary paradigms for reflecting further about the data. It is hoped that all of this will help the student understand the material, and think further in creative ways about it. Enno Popkes wrote in 2006, "The relationship between the Gospel of John and the Gospel of Thomas has only been discussed intently for less than ten years"[19] and there he lists "four basic types or schemes for relating these traditions."[20] These four, including the bibliography (nn. 19–22), are from his essay.

(1) The GTh was inspired by the FG "either directly or by means of a gnostically-oriented mediator."[21]

(2) The FG and GTh occurred independently from traditions that could derive either from Jewish-Christian encratite, or wisdom influences.[22]

---

18. For a review of research broader than what is done here see DeConick, *Voices of the Mystics*, 26–33.

19. Popkes, "Gospel of John, Gospel of Thomas, and Qumran," in Charlesworth, *Bible and the Dead Sea Scrolls*, 3:294–95.

20. Referring to Ismo Dunderberg "John and Thomas in Conflict," 381f. Cf. Popkes, "Ich bin das Licht,'" esp. 642. Popkes, "Gospel of John, Gospel of Thomas, and Qumran" in Charlesworth, *Bible and the Dead Sea Scrolls*, 3:295–97.

21. Cf. e.g., Sell, "Johannine Traditions in Logion 61 of the Gospel of Thomas," 4–37; Markovich, "Textual Criticism on the Gospel of Thomas," 53–74, esp. 73–74; or by means of a gnostically oriented mediator [n31]. Cf. e.g., Brown, "Gospel of Thomas and St. John's Gospel," 155–77, esp. 176–77; also similarly Dunderberg, "Thomas' I-Sayings and the Gospel of John," 33–64, esp. 63–64; Dunderberg, "Thomas and the Beloved Disciple," 65–88, esp. 73–76; Attridge, "'Seeking' and 'Asking,'" 295–302, esp. 300–302.

22. On a Jewish-Christian Encratite setting, see, e.g., Quispel, "'Gospel of Thomas' and the 'Gospel of the Hebrews,'" 371–82; Quispel, "Qumran, John and Jewish Christianity," 137–55, esp. 144–46. On a wisdom setting, see, e.g., Patterson, "Gospel of Thomas and the Synoptic Tradition," 45–97; Patterson, *Gospel of Thomas and Jesus*; Zöckler, *Jesu Lehren im Thomasevangelium*, 101–6, esp. 253–59; however, he does not undertake a uniform interpretation of the character of the Gospel of Thomas. The wisdom or early-gnostic characterizations also vary in Koester, *Ancient Christian Gospels*, 113–15, esp. 256–63; Koester, *History and Literature of Early Christianity*, 2:178–80; Koester, "Gnostic Writings as Witnesses for the Development of the Sayings Tradition," in Layton, *Rediscovery of Gnosticism*, 1:238–61; in both traditions different redaction levels should be distinguished

(3) FG and GTh both emerge from the same circles and rival each other.[23]

(4) FG and GTh rival each other but do not emerge from the same circles.[24]

We have chosen the following scholars to use as precis for presenting the data, and discussing methods: Raymond E. Brown,[25] Helmut Koester,[26] Gregory Riley,[27] April DeConick,[28] M. David Litwa,[29] and Christopher Skinner.[30]

It is apparent that Raymond Brown's method is a "whatever might be possible" approach. He was also concerned with determining whether or not GTh was dependent upon FG. His work assumes FG preceded GTh. Helmut Koester's list builds upon different assumptions, is not organized around words and phrases, but around themes. The table beneath his name will display these themes. Gregory Riley's work is yet another different variety of reflection, perhaps even a new paradigm. His study is specific in topic (resurrection), but broad in its reach. April DeConick's study shares features of Riley's work, for example, that there is reflected in the texts a conversation between communities, but her study centers around ascent mysticism and soteriology. Litwa does not build upon a conversation between communities, but he does identify a theological tradent common to both: deification. In FG, Jesus is deified, in GTh, his disciples are also. The work of Christopher Skinner is in some ways a response to Riley's thesis. It reflects upon portrayals in FG that Riley noticed, but Skinner reads it all quite differently, and the Doubting Thomas pericope (for Skinner) becomes just one of several other similar literary characterizations within FG.

---

23. Cf. e.g., Charlesworth, *Beloved Disciple*, 387–89; Davies, "Christology and Protology of the Gospel of Thomas," esp. 681–82; Davies, *Gospel of Thomas and Christian Wisdom*, 116.

24. DeConick, *Seek to See Him*, 72–73; DeConick, *Voices of the Mystics*, 68–70, 86–88; Pagels, *Das Geheimnis des fünften Evangeliums*, 36–79, esp. 45; similar approaches in Koester, *Ancient Christian Gospels*, 263; Onuki, "Traditionsgeschichte von Thomasevangelium," 399–415, 410–12.

25. Brown, "Gospel of Thomas and Saint John's Gospel," 155–77.

26. Koester, *Ancient Christian Gospels*, 113–28.

27. *Resurrection Reconsidered* is the title of Riley's published Harvard dissertation.

28. DeConick, *Voices of the Mystics*.

29. Litwa, "'I Will Become Him': Homology and deification in the Gospel of Thomas," 427–47.

30. Skinner, *John and Thomas—Gospels in Conflict?*

Raymond E. Brown (1962)

> In proposing parallels we shall concentrate on phrases or ideas that are found in John and not in the Synoptic Gospels... Some of the parallels that will be suggested will be honestly characterized as remote; we mention them only for the sake of completeness. After giving the parallels, we shall in the second part of the article attempt an evaluation of the evidence.[31]

Raymond Brown looks for some sort of lexical likeness, resulting in a broad range of suggested possible parallels. At the beginning of the study he notes that several scholars have previously looked at the two gospels, and provided short lists of possible parallels. Professor Brown tells his readers, for example, that Robert McLachlan Wilson states the "evidence for the use of John is comparatively slight, and indeed the similarities would seem to be more in the realm of ideas than of actual citation."[32] Brown says further, "He [Wilson] suggests the possibility that the author of *GTh* did not know John, or else reflected the mentality of a backwater locality reached only by Johannine 'ripples'"[33] and in a note reports that Wilson "points out that the possibility that the author of *GTh* did not know John but had Johannine ideas [and that this suggestion] might be an indication of the early character of *GTh*."[34]

Professor Brown, however, is "presuming that GTh is the later work,"[35] and would thus be dependent upon FG. This presumption emerges frequently throughout the article. Presumptions must always be made carefully, since they can easily predetermine outcome.

As the table shows, Brown has quarried a large collection of comparable texts. He includes in his essay an evaluation of the evidence[36] where he states that 55 out of the total 114 Sayings in GTh have some such sort of parallel in FG. Some of these are "tenuous,"[37] leaving the list of more probable parallels to 30 Sayings plus its Prologue, and covering all chapters of

---

31. Brown, "Gospel of Thomas and Saint John's Gospel," 158.
32. Wilson, *Studies in the Gospel of Thomas*, 87.
33. Brown, "Gospel of Thomas and Saint John's Gospel," 156.
34. Brown, "Gospel of Thomas and Saint John's Gospel," 156n9.
35. Brown, "Gospel of Thomas and Saint John's Gospel," 157.
36. Brown, "Gospel of Thomas and Saint John's Gospel," 174–77.
37. "So tenuous that they would be of significance only after a clear relationship between John and GTh had already been established." These are SS2, 4, 6, 10 11, 15, 21, 22–23, 29, 30, 40, 42, 49, 52, 55, 56, 64, 76, 90, 101, 104, 105, 110, 114, "or almost one half of the Sayings discussed" (Brown, "Gospel of Thomas and Saint John's Gospel," 174).

FG except 2, 18, and 19.[38] He also excludes the possibility of direct contact "because there is not a single verbatim citation of John."[39]

After looking at the "rather likely" parallels (table below), and observing the words and phrases upon which such a possible connection might be made, it is challenging not to be suspicious of the method, the procedure and the result. Nevertheless, some are very thought provoking, and Brown's article and notes are worth working through (though hard to organize as a table of data). We use translations as found in Professor Brown's article.

B. The Gospels of John and Thomas (Raymond E. Brown)

FG	Text	GTh	Text
1:1	In the beginning existed the Word and the Word existed with God	61	I am he who came into existence from that which is equal
1:10	light come into the world	28	I took my stand in the midst of the world
1:38	1:38, 41, 45, 49 contain attribution of titles given to Jesus by disciples in ascending order.	13	A similar attribution occurs in GTh 13.
1:41		13	
1:45		13	
1:49		13	
3:5	begetting in spirit	53	circumcision in spirit
3:6	flesh / spirit	29	flesh / spirit
3:19–21	the light is come into the world	28	I took my stand in the midst of the world
3:31	is above all	77	which is above them all
3:35	Father loves the Son and has placed all things in his hands.	61	to me was given from the things of my Father
4:14	whoever drinks of water I give	13	because you have drunk …
4:23	true worshipers … in spirit and truth	53	true circumcision in spirit
5:18	he called God his Father making himself equal to God	61	I am he who came into existence from that which is equal [or "undivided," NHLE]

38. Prologue, SS1, 3, 8, 12, 13, 17, 18, 19, 24, 25, 27, 28, 37, 38, 43, 44, 50, 51, 53, 59, 61, 69a, 77, 78, 79, 91, 92, 100, 108.

39. Brown, "Gospel of Thomas and Saint John's Gospel," 175.

FG	Text	GTh	Text
5:23	he who does not honor the Son does not honor the Father who sent him	44	Whoever blasphemes against the Father will be forgiven, whoever blasphemes against the Son will be forgiven
6:27	not for the food that will perish but for the food which will endure	76	the treasure which does not fail, which endures
6:30	that we may believe in you	91	that we may believe in you
6:35	How can he now say, "I have come down from heaven"	50	if they say to you, "From where have you originated?"
6:42	whose father and mother we know	105	whoever knows mother and father
6:57	the living Father	3	the living Father
7:27	we know where this man is from	50	... from where have you originated?
7:34	You will search for me ... and where I am, you cannot come.	24	show us the place where you are for we must seek it
7:34	you will seek me and not find me	38	you will seek me and not find me
7:37	Let anyone who is thirsty come to me	108	whoever drinks from my mouth
7:38–39	from his innermost being shall flow rivers of living water	13	the bubbling brook that I have measured out [NHLE, 35.6–7]
8:12	I am the light ... never walk in darkness.. shall have the light of life	24	there is light within a man of light [38:7–8]
8:12	I am the light	77	I am the light
8:14	where I came from ... where I am going	50	from where have you originated?
8:19	if you knew me you would know my Father also	69a	these are they who have known the Father in truth
8:21	you will search for me ... and where I am you cannot come	24	show us the place where you are for we must seek it
8:25	what I am telling you from the beginning	18	have you discovered the beginning that you inquire about the end

XI. THE GOSPEL OF THOMAS

FG	Text	GTh	Text
8:31	if you continue in my words you are my disciples	19	if you become my disciples and hear my words
8:32	to know the truth	78	to know the truth [NHLE, 47:2–3]
8:46	can any of you convict me of sin	104	what is the sin I have done?
8:47	the reason you do not hear them is you are not of God	19	if you become my disciples and hear my words
8:52	shall not see death	1	will not see death
8:52	shall not taste death	19	will not taste death
8:58	before Abraham came into being, I am	19	blessed is he who was before he came into being
8:58	before Abraham existed I exist	61	I am he who came into existence from that which is equal
9:4	night comes when no one can work . . . I am the light of the world	24	when he does not shine there is darkness [38.9–10]
9:5	I am the light of the world	77	I am the light
10:15	and I know the Father	69a	these are they who have known the Father [45:26–27]
10:25	I told you and you do not believe	43	you do not realize who I am from what I say to you
10:28–29	My Father, who has given *them* to Me	61	to me was given from the things of my Father [43:40]
10:32	for which of them are you stoning me?	104	what is the sin I have done?
11:10	the light is not in them	24	there is light within a man of light
11:16	Didymus	Prologue	Didymus
11:26	will not die forever	11	the living will not die
11:26, 32, 37	all have concerns for fear of death, life in Jesus	59	look upon the living one as long as you live, for fear that you die
12:25	love life/ lose it; hate life / keep it	42	become passers-by [regarding life]

FG	Text	GTh	Text
12:32	will draw all men to myself	77	the All came forth from me and the All has come to me
12:35	walk while you have the light . . . darkness	24	there is light within a man of light . . . dark
12:36	where I go you cannot follow	12	we know you'll go away from us [34:26]
13:3	had given all things into His hands	61	to me was given from the things of my Father
13:33	you will seek me . . . where I am going you cannot come	24	show us the place where you are for we must seek it
13:36	where I go you cannot follow	12	we know you'll go away from us
14:5	we don't know where you are going	12	we know you'll go away from us
14:7	you will know my Father also	69a	who have known the Father in truth
14:9	have I been with you so long and yet you do not know who I am?	43	you do not understand who I am
14:9	have I been with you so long and yet you do not know who I am?	51	what you expect has come but you do not know it
14:9	have I been with you so long and yet you do not know who I am?	91	you do not know how to test this time [48:25]
14:22	when will you be manifest?	37	how is it that you will manifest?
15:15	No longer do I call you servants	13	I am not your master [35:5]
16:3	they have not known the Father or me	43	you do not know who I am
16:3	they have not known the Father	69a	who have known the Father in truth
16:4–5	I did not say these things to you from the beginning	92	those things which you asked me in those days, I did not tell you then; now I desire to tell them, but you do not inquire after them

FG	Text	GTh	Text
16:12	I still have many things to say to you, but you cannot bear them now	92	those things which you asked me in those days, I did not tell you then; now I desire to tell them, but you do not inquire after them
16:15	all things the Father has are mine	100	give me what is mine
16:16	you will no longer behold Me	59	you will be unable to see
16:28	you will see me no longer	59	seek to see him and be unable to see
16:33	I have conquered the world!	104	in what have I been conquered?
17:9–10	those whom Thou hast given Me; for they are Thine and all things that are Mine are Thine, and Thine are Mine	100	give me that which is mine
20:24	Didymus	Prologue	Didymus
21:2	Didymus	Prologue	Didymus
21:11	he drew the net to shore full of large fish	8	drew it up from the sea full of small fish, among them he found a large fish
21:23	this disciple would not die	59	promise of not dying [cf. saying 111]

C. The Gospels of John and Thomas
(Helmut Koester, 1990)[40]

In his Introduction to the GTh in NHLE, Helmut Koester comments that the parallels between FG and GTh are "especially striking."[41] In his later

---

40. Koester, *Ancient Christian Gospels*, 113–24. This author (now deceased) has been accused of predatory actions towards certain of his female students according to Pagels, *Why Religion?*, 28–30. In reviewing this author's academic work, we do not intend it to be an implied endorsement of, or an effort to minimize, his alleged ethical misbehaviors.

41. Koester, "Introduction: The Gospel According to Thomas" (1990), 124–25.

analysis he analyzes the two gospels on the assumption that in the two texts, similar or related materials took on different forms. The reason for the change in form is that it went through another process of development and had a different "life situation" than a related saying in GTh. Discourses in FG are built up from sayings.

> The purpose of the discourses is to explore and discuss critically the meaning and interpretation of such sayings. This is accomplished through changes of the wording of such sayings as well as by placing the sayings into a particular context in the composition of a discourse so that the context becomes a critical commentary.[42]

Over against this particular composition technique is that of GTh, which creates variants in the saying "which thus illuminate particular aspects of understanding."[43] Hence, with these two texts we have two different methods being used of interpreting a saying. FG elaborates with discourse context, GTh elaborates with variant readings.

This "hypothesis" and method is clearly different than Brown's and will yield a set of "parallels" much different in character. Koester is getting us closer to the notion that FG and GTh are indebted to the same tradition but using and developing it rather differently. For this reason, Koester divides his sampling of texts thematically, since it may be difficult to discern behind the two traditions a parallel saying. This method involves the obvious difficulty of how we are to know what constitutes variants in GTh, unless we assume that from FG we can deduce the key components of a saying.[44]

---

42. Koester, *Ancient Christian Gospels*, 114.

43. Koester, *Ancient Christian Gospels*, 114.

44. Koester is aware of the difficulty. In a previous study ("Gnostic Sayings and Controversy Traditions in John 8:12–59," Koester says "The type of sayings tradition which confronts us here is fundamentally different from the one we are accustomed to in the Synoptic Gospels, because interpretations are not *added* to traditional sayings, rather, they are expressed in the transformation of the sayings themselves" (109). And, "Thus, original metaphors can disappear in favor of the new epexegetical equivalents." NT scholars have difficulty isolating these things for "the exegete's eyes are not sufficiently trained for this task" (109). On sayings and pronouncement stories in the Synoptic Gospels, see Aune, *Westminster Dictionary*, 378–79.

1. Sayings about Life-Giving Power.

FG	GTh
8.51	S1
8.52	S111
6.63	S18b
6.68–69	S19c

From these it is clear that according to GTh, not Jesus's words but their interpretation gives life . . . "Whoever finds the interpretation of these sayings will not experience death" (S1). FG, it seems from these examples (6:63, 68), either retains unaltered the adjective "eternal" before "life" (so Koester), or possibly adds "eternal." Hence, GTh is either guilty of subtracting "eternal" or just not adding it. For GTh, the one who has life simply does not experience death.

2. Abiding by and Ingesting Jesus' Words

8.31–2	S19b
4.14	S13 [NHLE, 35.5–7]
7.37–8	S108

3. Sayings about the Light

11.9–10	S24b
12.35f	S77a
8.12	

There is possibly a difference between FG and GTh here insofar as GTh would describe the identity of the disciples as light, while FG would say that they possess the light, or became "children of light." Koester also explains that although there appears to be a similarity between 8.12 and S77, they are in fact different predications. One (GTh) using "light" for the supremacy of the divine; the other (FG) using "light" in antithesis to darkness.

Enno Popkes calls the light metaphor the "clearest parallel between the Gospel of John and the Gospel of Thomas"[45] but argues that the chris-

---

45. E. E. Popkes, "Theological Heritage," in Charlesworth, *Bible and the Dead Sea Scrolls*, 3:296–97.

tological and soteriological functions of the metaphor are different. In FG, with its christological focus, the metaphor is "directed towards the audience acknowledging Jesus as the light of the world. Corresponding to this, the Gospel of John presents no anthropological motifs of an imminent light, the human capacity for knowledge (cf., e.g., Luke 11:33-36; par. Matt 6:22-23), and certainly no motifs of a saving spark of light in the disciples as they strive back to their place of origin."[46]

4. Sayings about "the all" and one's origin

3.31	S77a
8.58	S19a [NHLE, 36:18]
16.28	S49
8.14b	S50a
1.9	
13.3	
16.28	S49
16.23b-24	S92
16.4b-5	
16.12	
16.23a	
16.30	

"John consciously avoids this application of divine origin to all believers and restricts it to Jesus as the revealer" (*Ancient Christian Gospels*, 118).

5. Jesus as paradigm for the Gnostic; Salvation through Jesus

13.33 (7.34; 8.21)	S38b
14.3	S24a
14.7 (8.19)	S69a [45:26-27]
14.22	S37a

"Where I am going you cannot come" (13:33) is, according to Koester, a negation of using Jesus as a paradigm for the Gnostic, and "the concept of the discovery of one's own divine origin" (*Ancient Christian*

---

46. Popkes, "Theological Heritage," in Charlesworth, *Bible and the Dead Sea Scrolls*, 3:297. For a full presentation of the argument, see Popkes, "Ich bin das Licht," 641-74. See also Pagels, "Exegesis of Genesis 1," 477-96.

Gospels, 120). "The disciples are not united with Jesus by following him, but by keeping his new commandment of loving each other as Jesus has loved them (13.35)" (120).

6. Miscellaneous

8.25–26a	S43
5.18; 3.35	S61
11.26	S11
15.15	S13 [35:3–5]
3.6	S29

Koester's samplings above add to Brown's collection some Sayings from GTh to the list of likely parallels with texts of FG, and in some measure maintains some of the parallels.[47]

Dissimilarity

Rather than similar parallels, some scholars have focused on the opposite as a starting point for discussing a relationship.[48] Do differences in these two texts reflect a dialogue or debate going on between the communities of Thomas and John?

Gregory Riley (1995)

Gregory Riley's approach to and treatment of our subject was a new paradigm. We don't find in his study lists of comparative texts, as we have seen much of above. In *Resurrection Reconsidered* (1–5) he introduces his study, and the discussion of FG and GTh:

---

47. Sayings where Brown finds parallels: Prologue, 1, 3, 8, 11, 12, 13, 18, 19, 24, 28, 29, 37, 43, 42, 44, 50, 51, 53, 59, 61, 69a, 76, 77, 78, 91, 92, 100, 104, 105, 108. Koester's list: 1, 11, 13, 18, 19, 24, 29, 37, 38, 43, 49, 50, 61, 69, 77, 92, 108, 111. Charles Hill states, however, that "Koester identifies only six or eight out of the 114 sayings in the GTh which are specially close to John" (*Johannine Corpus*, 274). They are SS 13, 19, 24, 38, 49, 92 (from Koester's "Introduction to the Gospel of Thomas" 125); from *ACG* add SS 1, 108. Hill dispenses from the list SS 24b, 50a, 77a, 117 for preserving only metaphors "seeing" or "tasting death" (*Johannine Corpus*, 274n279).

48. See discussion by Hill, *Johannine Corpus* 276ff. The scholars he mentions are Gregory Riley, Elaine Pagels, April D. Deconick.

This study centers on a protracted debate within early Christianity concerning a foundational aspect of the *Gospel of Thomas* and its related literature: the concept of the body and resurrection. It traces the background of this idea in the Semitic and Greco-Roman world, and its expression in the Thomas literature as a whole: the *Gospel of Thomas, Book of Thomas,* and *Acts of Thomas.* But the inspiration for the study, and its main focus, is the controversy between the closely related Christian communities of Thomas and John, between the *Gospel of Thomas* and the Gospel of John, on the issue of resurrection, expressed in John most clearly in the story of Doubting Thomas.[49]

While most work on GTh had been comparing it to the Synoptics, Riley says that it is FG and GTh that have the more fundamental relationship . . . though it is not one of dependency of the latter on the former as Brown (pre)supposed.

> Instead, the two Gospels stand in a somewhat similar and parallel position relative to the traditions preserved in the Synoptics. Each expresses its own distinctive and at times opposing theology in part by manipulating this common inheritance, yet the two are much closer to each other in spirit than either is to the Synoptics. In addition, the two Gospels share material in a common manner but distinct from the Synoptics. One aspect of this situation is that it is possible to see John at points as a correction not of some lost Gnosis, but of ideas actually preserved in the *Gospel of Thomas.* Likewise and to a significant extent, *Thomas* is in reciprocal relationship with John. This reciprocity, as will be seen, is much in evidence in the pericope of Doubting Thomas.[50]

Riley then cites Rudolf Schnackenburg as a commentator who perceived the important role of Thomas in the FG, and even the existence of contact between the two communities.[51] Although Schnackenburg tried to envision a relationship between the "communities" of John and Thomas, he did so with the notion (mistaken according to Riley) that the "Syrian

---

49. Riley, *Resurrection Reconsidered*, 2. FG advocates for bodily resurrection, using the disciple Thomas as a foil. "All three of the major Thomas documents preserved, the *Gospel of Thomas,* the *Book of Thomas,* and the *Acts of Thomas,* are consistent in their denigration of the body, and their denial of physical resurrection" (178).

50. Riley, *Resurrection Reconsidered*, 3.

51. Some explanation for the role of the disciple Thomas seems necessary. See Riley's discussion in ch. 2 "Thomas and the Appearance Stories," 69–99. Cf. also Dunderberg, "Thomas and the Beloved Disciple," 65–88; and his "Beloved Disciple in John," 243–69; Pamplaniyil, "Beloved Disciple and Thomas," 560–78; Popkes, "Theological Heritage," in Charlesworth, *Bible and the Dead Sea Scrolls*, 3:292f.

Thomas tradition developed in dependence upon the Gospel of John in 'Gnostic circles' of a post-Johannine era."[52] According to Riley,

> It is far more consonant with the evidence to view Thomas Christianity in Syria as a continuum, founded in the early decades of the Christian movement, which developed in its own linguistic and cultural environment according to its own lights. The character "Thomas" in John is a literary portrayal of the dominant figure in somebody else's community and is meant to convey a message to that community. The picture of Thomas in John, far from being the original source of Thomas tradition, is an attempt to influence a Thomas Christianity already in existence. The earlier stage is the living Syrian Thomas tradition that John is at pains to counter.[53]

This broadening of the landscape to include not just "texts" (with the limitations of source and form criticism) but actual leaders and communities with dialogue between them is a new posture in which to view the data and imagine literary issues. Riley's study emerged from his examination of the Temple Saying and the "doubting Thomas" pericope in FG.[54]

Riley argues that the reason for such sustained and programmatic reference to Thomas in FG is that it "is an attempt to influence a Thomas Christianity already in existence."[55] The study is a masterful review and analysis of the subject of resurrection and the afterlife in the multi-cultural/multi-lingual world of the Mediterranean basin in the period of Jesus and the early church. But it is also an elegantly conceived and written application

---

52. Riley, *Resurrection Reconsidered*, 4. On Schnackenberg and GTh, see our ch. 10, tbl. B, p. 174.

53. Riley, *Resurrection Reconsidered*, 4. Among Riley's conclusions are: "These communities arose," according to the position taken here, "in conversation with each other, that is, in a circumstance of reciprocal development and debate over, among other ideas, the issue of bodily resurrection. The creation of the Doubting Thomas pericope by the author of John is one side of this debate; the version of the Temple Saying ("Destroy this temple and in three days I will raise it up") in the Gospel of Thomas is another" (177).

54. Christopher Skinner refers to this as "the community-conflict hypothesis." In his review of it, he focuses on Greg Riley's work, but adds two other scholars who have embraced it and added new topics to the conflict. April DeConick ("'Blessed are Those Who Have Not Seen,'" 381–98), and also Pagels, "Exegesis of Genesis 1 in the Gospels of Thomas and John," 477–96. DeConick's essay argues that there was a dispute between the two communities over a salvation issue—for FG "believing without seeing," for GTh disciples seeking visions through ecstatic ascent. Elaine Pagels's essay, as the title suggests, is about "a Johannine polemic against Thomasine Christianity rooted in competing views of the creation narrative" (Skinner, *John and Thomas—Gospels in Conflict?* 14).

55. Riley, *Resurrection Reconsidered*, 4.

of the data to, and creative reading of, two primary ancient texts. If Riley is correct, it represents an argument that "the *Gospel of Thomas* itself was already at some stage of completion, either written or oral, and that its contents were known to the author of John, probably through verbal contact with members of this rival community."[56]

April D. DeConick, *Voices of the Mystics* (2001)[57]

DeConick also proposes a dialogue taking place (begun by Riley). It is a textualized conversation taking place between the Johannine and the Thomasine communities over soteriology (vision mysticism in GTh—"what you see you shall become" vs. faith mysticism in FG—"Blessed are those who have not seen and yet believe"). This textualized conversation in FG and GTh (as well as the Acts of Thomas) pulls in religious tradents, some centuries old,[58] spanning Jewish, Greek, and other Mediterranean cultures. FG uses the character of Thomas as a foil to embody the error of their community, and the words of Jesus as the correct teaching of FG's own community.[59]

The book is an engaging introduction to and discussion of a pervasive presence of vision mysticism and ascent to heaven in the multicultural Hellenistic world (ch. 2), beginning with the ancient mystery religions, then Hermeticism, and strands of Judaism (Qumran, Philo, Jewish and Christian apocalyptic literature). It is the claim of DeConick that our two texts (FG and GTh) use language couched in these mystic traditions to dialogue with each other, FG representing a polemic against vision mysticism, GTh in support of it. The third, fourth, and fifth chapters represent the bulk of her evidence.[60]

---

56. Riley, *Resurrection Reconsidered*, 178.

57. DeConick, *Voices of the Mystics*. For brief, readable and informative discussions of Jewish mysticism during the Second Temple period, see these various articles (with bibliographies) in Collins and Harlow, *Early Judaism*: Segal, "Mysticism"; Harlow, "Ascent to Heaven"; Boustan, "Hekhalot Literature"; Hurtado, "Mediator Figures"; Orlov, "Metatron."

58. Her second chapter (34–67) introduces texts, ideas, and religious traditions both Jewish and gentile.

59. Alluding to John 20:29, the Danish philosopher, Søren Kierkegaard, writing in 1844, states "The believer (and only he, after all, is a follower) continually has the *autopsy* of faith; he does not see with the eyes of others and sees only the same as every believer sees—with the eyes of faith" in his *Philosophical Fragments, Johannes Climacus*, 101–2.

60. Ch. 3, "Johannine Polemic Against Vision Mysticism: The Traditio-Religious Horizon and the Point of Discourse"; ch. 4, "Thomasine Support for Vision Mysticism:

The tables below represents a few of the ways the dialogue takes place, often with the relevant lexemes in the two texts being in opposition, all connecting to the horizon of ascent mysticism.

D. The Gospels of John and Thomas on Mystical Themes

1. Ascent

"No one has ascended into heaven except the one who descended from heaven" (3:13).	see below.

2. Vision

"No one has ever seen God. It is God the only Son, who is close to the Father's heart, who has made him known" (1:18).	Look for the Living One while you are alive, lest you die and then seek to see him and you will be unable to see him (S59).

3. Way

"I am the way, and the truth, and the life" (14:6).[61]	see below.

4. Agent

"No one comes to the Father except through me" (14:6).	see below.

The blank cells in the first, third, and fourth tables above on the GTh side can be commented on here. The evidence for and development within the Thomasine tradition of Thomas and Jesus being "twins" is used by April DeConick to argue for a very high anthropology for Thomasine Christians. Being equal to Jesus in many ways diminishes Jesus's uniqueness as a mediator. In GTh 13 Thomas is the only disciple who answers Jesus's question about his identity correctly, resulting in Jesus telling him that he is no longer Thomas's teacher.[62] What Thomas has received from Jesus (three visionary sayings?) is too much for the other disciples to comprehend or withstand (GTh 13b [35:10–15]).

The Traditio-Religious Horizon of John's Opponents"; ch. 5, "Faith Mysticism in the Gospel of John: The Interpretative Trajectory and Synthetic End Point."

61. In this passage, Thomas is presented as the "false hero"—" Thomas said to him, "Lord, we do not know where you are going. How can we know the way?" (14:5).

62. That Thomas can be described in the *Acts of Thomas* 39 as "Twin of the Messiah, and Apostle of the Most High, and sharer of the hidden word of the Life-giver, and receiver of the secret mysteries of the Son of God" further elaborate on the heroic quality of Thomas.

These samples, and DeConick's discussion, offer some evidence to strengthen the notion that FG was on a (polemical) continuum with the mysticism tradents of visionary experience, "seeing" God, ascending to heaven and mediator figures. The evidence that GTh was offering support for "vision mysticism" as a polemical dialogue partner against FG seems less certain.

M. David Litwa (2015)[63]

Litwa's essay develops ideas already suggested above about the high anthropology of GTh. He seeks to present an early form of Christian deification parallel to those also found in FG (428). For Litwa, deification is manifest in political, mythological, Orphic, Hermetic, Christian, and philosophical contexts, a distinct category from mysticism (430). He writes:

> In short, both the Johannine Jesus and the Thomasine Christian share many of the same divine predicates and prerogatives. The application of such divine prerogatives constitutes in both documents a discursive form of deification. In essence, John presents a picture of what a deified human looks like (Jesus), and thus a roughly contemporary early Christian model for understanding the divinity of other human beings. The comparison is executed in two parts: the first focusing on the divine nature of Jesus and Thomasine Christians, and the second on their divine destiny. (431).

> By using the Johannine Christ as a means of comparison, I do not wish to imply that John's Christ was directly in mind when the composer(s) of Thomas depicted the true nature of Christians. Thomasine Christians identify with Jesus by identifying with Thomas, Jesus's spiritual twin (431n15).

The last excerpt makes clear that this essay is not a development of the community dialogue paradigm proposed by Riley. But Litwa does take an example of a theological tradent (deification)[64] illustrated supremely in the Christology of the FG, and uses it as an example of what takes place, or seems to be taking place, in GTh's depiction of "the ideal Christian."

---

63. Litwa, "'I Will Become Him.'"

64. It is a subject on which he has written more: Litwa, *We Are Being Transformed*; *Becoming Divine*. See also Koester, "Divine Human Being"; Robbins, *Testing of Jesus*, 95–101; Keener, *John* 1:298–99.

Therefore, it certainly belongs in any discussion of the "Conceptual Worlds" of the FG.

His comparisons are illustrated in the following charts.

E. The Gospels of John and Thomas (M. David Litwa)

1. Divine Nature

FG	GTh
Preexistent light (431–32)	
"In Johannine literature, both God and the Logos are directly called 'light' (1 John 1:5, John 1:9)."	77 "It is I who am the light that is above them all" [Litwa's translation]
Sonship (433)	
"In John, the 'sonship' relation is reduced to one man. Members of the Johannine community become 'children' (τέκνα) of God, apparently a meaningful but secondary kind of kinship (John 1:12, 1 John 3:1)."	"In GTh Jesus (as the child of God) and Christians (as the children of God) are not equally ranked (e.g., log. 13: 'I am not your master'; cf. John 15:15)."
Knowledge (433–34)	
In John 8:14, Jesus directly claims that he knows "from where I came and where I am going" (cf. 13:3, 16:28).	"such knowledge is also the privilege of Thomasine Christians; they are from the kingdom (of light) and to it they return" (logion 49–50).
Light within (434–35)	
In John 8:12, Jesus declares, "I am the light of the world" (cf. 9:5; 12:35). By making this remark, Jesus positions himself as God's unique revelation. Humans do not have the light. Instead, Jesus the true Light enlightens every human coming into the world (1:9).	In log. 24, Jesus says that "there is light existing within a person of light and it enlightens the whole world. If he does not shine, it is dark." This saying indicates that divine light exists within other humans as well as Jesus. Its divine nature is signified in that it enlightens the entire world.
Primal unity (435–36)	
"the divine human union that John envisions for the future, Thomas places in the past. But the past oneness of Thomasine Christians makes them appear all the more like the Johannine Christ who, as Logos, was eternally with the Father."	"Log. 50 says that the sign of the Father within is 'motion and repose'. The words are mysterious but can helpfully be explained in light of ancient philosophy. Platonists told a story of salvation wherein the soul, first resting in the

FG	GTh
	divine, wandered and fell. The destiny of the soul was to rediscover its repose by returning to the light." See also Saying 11, where a primal unity or "repose" is "hinted at."

2. Divine Destiny

Return to the light (436–37)

This egressus-regressus pattern is reminiscent of the Johannine Christ, who was "in the beginning" with God (John 1:1). In time, he descended in flesh to reveal the Father (1:14). When his mission was complete, he hastened to return above (16:28). The Johannine Jesus evidently envisioned some kind of ascent for believers, "that where I am you may be also" (14:3). Nevertheless this ascent does not occur until after death. Jesus firmly states: "No one has ascended into heaven except the one who descended from heaven—the Son of the Human" (3:13).	Thomasine soteriology involves a return to the primal state of light. In Thomas, Jesus assumes that a return to the light is the fate of his followers: "When you come to be in the light . . . " (log. 11). Miroslav Marcovich (p. 40) pointed out that the language of "coming to be in the light" may have been inspired by 1 John 1:7, where Jesus is "in the light" (2:9; cf. John 12:36). The (temporal particle) in log. 11 makes clear that arriving in the light is not a matter of "if" but "when." Thomasine Christians came from the light (log. 50), and to it they will return "For where the beginning is, there will the end be. Blessed is the one who will take his place in the beginning" (log. 18).

Assimilation (437–440)

John never calls Jesus the image of God, but the idea is at the heart of the Fourth Gospel. "He who has seen me has seen the Father" (John 14:9). For John, Jesus is the eternal image of God. Yet when he comes in flesh, he does not cease to be the image. His glory (or divinity) can be seen through the flesh (as vividly illustrated in the story of "doubting" Thomas, John 20:19–28; cf. 1:14).	Logia 11, 22, 77, 83, 84 The return to the light also involves assimilation to it. The view that there were archetypes or ideas (logia 83–84) was a common Platonic notion. The idea that an image could conform to the archetype was the presupposition of Platonic "assimilation to God" (ὁμοίωσις θεῷ) (Plato, *Theaet.* 176b).

It would seem, then, that Jesus alone is the image. Believers are never invited to become "the same image" as Christ. For Thomas, however, Christians and Christ do end up as the same image.

Such assimilation seems to be appealed to in a central statement of Thomasine soteriology: "Jesus said to them [his disciples], 'When you make the two one, and when you make the inside like the outside and the outside like the inside, and the above like the below . . . and an image in place of an image, then you will come into [the kingdom]'" (log. 22).

Again, we see that what in John is reserved for Jesus alone (identity as the light and image of God) becomes the prerogative of all Christians.

Equality (440–41)

John 5:18: "So on this account the Jews all the more were seeking to kill him [Jesus], . . . [because] he was calling God his own Father, making himself equal with God [ἴσον ἑαυτὸν ποιῶν τῷ θεῷ]" (cf. 10:33).

Thomasine Christians become conscious of their equality when they realize their own internal light. In Thomas, this realization does not necessarily occur through the mediation of Jesus. At best, Jesus and the elect share a similar nature and destiny. Those who are equal to God are also equal to each other.

In the end, the one fully conformed to the archetype becomes equal to it. Logion 61 offers a profound statement about equality: "Salome said, 'Who are you, man? As being from One, you have come up on my couch and eaten from my table.' Jesus said to her, 'I am he who exists from he who is equal. I was given some of the things of my father.' [Salome said,] 'I am Your disciple.' [Jesus said to her,] 'Therefore I say, if one is equal, that one will be filled with light, but if one is divided, that one will be filled with darkness.'" [trans. by Litwa]

Identification (441–43)

The union envisioned with Jesus has some similarity to the union portrayed in John 17:21: "may they also be one in us" [see discussion of this verse in Brown, *Gospel according to John* 2:769]

In Thomas, the union seems more radical, and more mutual than: Jesus will become like the disciple just as the disciple becomes like Jesus.

Radical conformation to the archetype (Jesus) leads to equality with it. Radical equality with Jesus, in turn, leads to identification. No saying more starkly expresses identification with the divine Jesus than log. 108: "Jesus said, 'He who will drink from my mouth will become as I am. I myself shall become he, and the things that are hidden will be revealed to him.'"

> "This *communicatio idiomatum* (sharing of properties) between Jesus and Thomasine Christians becomes especially pronounced when we compare Thomas with John's Gospel. Over and over again we have seen that what Thomas claims for Christians, John reserves for Christ."[65]

Christopher W. Skinner (2009)

> One of the more calculating and artistically deft aspects of John's Gospel is its creation and manipulation of characters.[66]

This statement by Riley is amply demonstrated by him, and by Christopher Skinner.[67] But Skinner's aim was to demonstrate that the Thomas character sketch in FG was typical, not programmatic.

> The focus of this study has been intentionally narrow, seeking to challenge one key element of the theory that the Fourth Gospel contains a theological response to the Gospel of Thomas or the traditions contained therein.[68]

And Skinner continues,

> It has been my aim to show that Thomas is merely one stitch in a wider literary pattern where uncomprehending characters serve as foils for Jesus' words and deeds.[69]

This comment by Skinner is a noteworthy observation. He shows how FG's characters function in this manner throughout the narrative. From a narrative-critical perspective, Skinner challenges the scholarly construct of traditions in conflict.[70]

The characters are Thomas (42–77), Peter (78–138), Andrew, Philip, Judas [not Iscariot] (139–64), Nicodemus (165–88), the Samaritan Woman (189–210), Martha and Mary (210–26). So the discussion in the first chapter reviewing recent work on the relation between FG and GTh is not a prelude

---

65. Litwa, "'I Will Become Him,'" 443. On communicatio idiomatum, see Muller, *Latin and Greek Theological Terms*, 69–71.

66. Riley, *Resurrection Reconsidered*, 73.

67. Skinner, *John and Thomas—Gospels in Conflict?*

68. Skinner, *John and Thomas*, 227.

69. Skinner, *John and Thomas*, 227. See also his edited vol.: *Characters and Characterization in the Gospel of John*.

70. We are reminded here of "period pieces" like Weeden, *Mark*, where the Gospel of Mark, with its portrait of the suffering Son of Man, seeks to combat the wonder-working divine man Christology attributed to some early Christ followers.

to a study of Thomas, but rather to locate and describe in the recent history of scholarship what he believes to be a misreading of John (especially the community conflict hypothesis). As a study of Johannine characterization in its literary context it is a very worthwhile study.

Summation

With the lexeme based listings of Raymond E. Brown we have a start at noticing and thinking about likenesses and differences between the two texts. With the form-critical observations of Helmut Koester, we have an insight or hypothesis as to what literary transformations of the tradition may have taken place within communities of faith. With the help of Greg Riley's study, we have an example of a theory about theological tendencies of the communities manifested in their literature. His examination of resurrection motifs as a point of discussion gives us a test-case to observe living traditions, theological positions, and communities in debate. The studies by DeConick and Litwa are both further examples of observable living traditions and theological positions, possibly textualized by the two communities in debate. With the study of Christopher Skinner, we have a critique of this "community—conflict hypothesis." Skinner's book is less a study of the possible relationship between FG and GTh, and more an exploration of literary characterization within the FG narrative. His critique asserts that the "community—conflict hypothesis" depends upon the questionable characterization of Thomas in FG as "a theological response to the *Gospel of Thomas* or the traditions contained therein" (the position of Riley).[71]

---

71. Skinner, *John and Thomas*, 227.

XII. The Early Reception of the Fourth Gospel

As we mentioned in our introduction (n8), the concerns of our book are related to:

(1) the religio-historical method or history of religions (Ger. *Religionsgeschichte*), "tradition history" (Ger. *Traditionsgeschichte*), "theological worldview" (*theologische Weltanschauung*), and "comparative religious studies";[1] (2) a "common word field" or a "shared stream of linguistic tradition" that provides a thesaurus of terms and images, for each set of comparisons;[2] and finally (3) "history of interpretation" (*Auslegungsgeschichte*), and "history of effects" (*Wirkungsgeschichte*) of the earlier work upon the later.[3] This last concern (3), the early history of FG's effects, is the focus of this chapter.[4]

On the importance of the reception history of FG, Jörg Frey observes,

> Their reading can point us to some aspects of the intellectual world in which the gospel was originally written and heard.

Commenting on the extent of FG's early influences, Professor Frey adds,

> The early reception of the Fourth Gospel was by no means limited to gnostics ... The influence of the Johannine tradition can be traced from Papias down to Irenaeus: the gospel is widely

---

1. See Frey, "Between Torah and Stoa," 190–95; Frey and Schnelle, *Kontexte*, 3–4, 35n156; Seelig, *Religionsgeschichte Methode*, 260–335.

2. See Fishbane, *Biblical Interpretation*, 288; Middleton, *Liberating Image*, 62–64.

3. For this ch., see Brooke, *Fragments of Heracleon*; J. C. Elowsky, *John 1–10* and *John 11–21*; R. Evans, *Reception History, Tradition*, 1–50; M. Edwards, *John*, 1–14; Frey, "Between Torah and Stoa," 197–201; Hill, *Johannine Corpus*; Nagel, *Die Rezeption des Johannesevangeliums*; Pagels, *Johannine Gospel in Gnostic Exegesis*; Pollard, *Johannine Christology and Early Church*; Rasimus, *Legacy of John*; Wiles, *Spiritual Gospel*; A. Wucherpfennig, *Heracleon Philologus*.

4. It does not mean that earlier comparisons (e.g., FG and Odes or Gos. Truth) in this book are excluded from a reception-history interpretation, we have, in this ch., focused on some of the most obvious examples.

attested among the apologists and some fathers before Irenaeus, such as Tatian, Melito, and Theophilus, in a number of apocryphal gospels from Papyrus Egerton 2 to the Gospel of Peter and also to some Nag Hammadi texts.[5]

We will briefly examine the influence of FG in the works of Ignatius of Antioch (ca. 110), Justin Martyr (ca. 160), Heracleon (ca. 170; cited in Origen, *Comm. Jo.*, ca. 240), Melito of Sardis (ca. 180), the so-called Epistle of the Apostles (ca. 180; Asia?), Papyrus Egerton (ca. 180), and Hippolytus of Rome (ca. 225; *Haer.*).[6] We will concentrate on those plausible citations of, quotations from, embedded allusions to, and loud echoes of FG in these post-first century works.[7]

We conclude this chapter with some attention to the so-called Johannine controversy in the second and third centuries, focusing on references in Irenaeus of Lyons (*Haer.*; ca. 180), Eusebius (*Hist. eccl.*; ca. 330), and Epiphanius (*Pan.*; ca. 390). This section might be regarded as the negative influence of FG in the second and third centuries.

The Reception History of the Fourth Gospel in the Second and Third Centuries.

Ignatius of Antioch is known to us from seven letters which he wrote early in the early second century (ca. 110 CE) as a Roman prisoner on his way to Rome from Antioch (awaiting a death sentence). Given permission to meet other Christians along the way, he was well received in Smyrna by Polycarp, and visited by representatives from Ephesus, Magnesia, and Tralles. In return, Ignatius wrote a letter to each of these communities. Ignatius links his self-understanding as a martyr and his theology at one crucial point: He asks how his impending death can have any meaning if the Lord did not truly die (*Trall.* 10; *Smyrn.* 4.2). Anti-docetic themes (Christ came "in the

---

5. Both quotes are from Frey, "Between Torah and Stoa," 197; cf. Frey and Schnelle, *Kontexte*, 197–98. See also the debate on the possible connection between the high amount of Egyptian papyri on FG and its reception in (Egyptian) gnostic circles (W. Bauer, K. Aland), challenged by R. A. Kearsley, "Fragment of John," in S. R. Llewelyn et al., *New Documents*, 7:244–48.

6. We have noted earlier that certain similarities of FG with, e.g., Hermetica, Odes, and (certainly, some) NHL can be attributed to the influence of FG. Mention will be made of these influences as they relate to our discussion in this chapter. On Odes in reception history, see Nagel, *Die Rezeption des Johannesevangeliums*, 158–94.

7. On allusions and echoes, see Hays, *Echoes in the Letters of Paul*, 29–33 and his *Echoes in the Gospels*, 7–14, 291–344; see also Evans, *Word of Glory*, 18–28; Köstenberger and Patterson, *Invitation to Biblical Interpretation*, 538–48, esp. 543.

flesh" and truly died) are common in Ignatius and are found especially in the letters to Tralles (ch. 9) and Smyrna (ch. 3). Ignatius probably responds also to a distinct Judaizing form of Christianity in his letters to Magnesia and Philadelphia (*Magn.* 8-10; *Phld.* 5-9). Ignatius saw a connection between the reality of the incarnation and passion of the Lord, his divine presence in the sacred meal, and a genuine commitment to concrete deeds of faith and love (*Smyrn.* 6.2—8.2), to be found in a community united under its bishop.[8] In addition to FG, Ignatius betrays some knowledge of Paul's writings (1 Corinthians; Romans; Galatians; Philippians; 1 Thessalonians; Deutero-Pauline: Col.; Ephesians; 1-2 Timothy), the Gospels of Matthew (*Smyrn.* 1.1) and Luke (*Smyrn.* 3.2).[9]

A. The Fourth Gospel	Ignatius of Antioch
"In the beginning was the Word [*logos*], and **the Word was with God**, and the Word was God," 1:1; "And **the one who sent [*pempō*] me is with me**; he has not left me alone, for I always do what is **pleasing** [*arestos*] to him," 8:29.	"There is one God who revealed [*phaneroō*] himself through **Jesus Christ his Son, who is his Word** [*logos*] that came forth from silence, who in everything **pleased** [*euarestos*] **the one who sent** [*pempō*] him," Ignatius, *Magn.* 8.2.
"And **the Word became flesh** [*sarx egeneto*] and lived among us," 1:14a.	"There is one physician, who is both flesh and spirit, born and unborn, **God in man** [*en anthōpō theou*],* true life in death, both from Mary and from God, first subject to suffering and then beyond it, Jesus Christ our Lord." Ignatius, *Eph.* 7.2. *Greek text of Ussher (1644) based on the Latin version by Grosseteste (1250 CE) reads **"God come in flesh,"** (*en sarki genomenos theos*). Cf. Christ "became flesh," [*egeneto sarx*], 2 Clem 9.5 (ca. 120 CE). See Holmes, *Apostolic Fathers*, 188-89.
"The wind blows where it chooses, and you hear the sound of it, but you do not know where it comes from or where it goes [*pothen erchetai kai pou hypagei*]. So it is with everyone who is born of the Spirit [*pneuma*]," 3:8.	"For it [the Spirit, *pneuma*] **knows from where it came and where it is going** [*pothen erchetai kai pou hypagei*] and it exposes the hidden things," Ignatius, *Phld.* 7.1. Classified as a probable allusion to FG here in Nagel, *Die Rezeption des Johannesevangeliums*, 238-43.

8. Schoedel, "Ignatius, Epistles of," 3:384-85. For texts and translations, we used Brannan, *Apostolic Fathers in English*; Holmes, *Apostolic Fathers*; and Lake, *Apostolic Fathers*. Nagel, *Die Rezeption des Johannesevangeliums*, 207-51.

9. Holmes, *Apostolic Fathers*, 174-75.

XII. THE EARLY RECEPTION OF THE FOURTH GOSPEL

A. The Fourth Gospel	Ignatius of Antioch
"If you knew the gift of God, and who it is that is saying to you, 'Give me a drink,' you would have asked him, and he would have given you **living water** [*hydōr zōn*]." The woman said to him, "Sir, you have no bucket, and the well is deep. Where do you get that living water [*hydōr to zōn*]?" 4:10–11; cf. 7:38 [*hydōr zōn*].	My passion has been crucified and there is no fire of love for material things in me, but **water living** [*hydōr de zōn*] and speaking in me, saying within me, "Come to the Father," Ignatius, *Rom.* 7.2b.
"For **the bread of God** [*artos tou theou*] is that which comes down from heaven and gives life to the world," 6:33.	"I desire **the bread of God** [*arton theou*, John 6:33–35], which is the flesh [*sarx*] of Jesus Christ, who *is* from the seed of David; and for drink I desire his blood, which is imperishable love," Ignatius, *Rom.* 7.3; cf. "the bread of God" [*arton tou theou*], Ignatius, *Eph.* 5.2.
"The Son can do nothing on his own [*poieō, ouden*], **but only what he sees the Father doing**," 5:19; "I can do nothing [*poieō, ouden*] on my own," 5:30a. "That I do nothing on my own [*poieō ouden*]," 8:28.	Therefore, just as **the Lord did nothing** [*ouden poieō*] without the Father [being united *with him*],* Ignatius, *Magn.* 7.1. **hēnōmenos ōn* from Greek text of Ussher based on the Latin version by Grosseteste.
"I am **the gate** [*hē thura*] for the sheep. I am the gate [*hē thura*]. Whoever enters by me will be saved," 10:7, 9.	"He alone is **the door** of the Father [*thura to patros*] through which Abraham and Isaac and Jacob and the prophets and apostles and the church enter. All of these *are brought* into the unity of God." Ignatius, *Phld.* 9.1–2; cf. "the gate (*pylē*) of the Lord," Ps 117:20 LXX; 1 Clem 48:2-4 "the gate (*pylē*) of righteousness." Cf. "I am **a door** to you ... I am a way to you," Acts John 95 (third century).

A. The Fourth Gospel	Ignatius of Antioch
"If you keep **my commandments** [*entolē*], you will abide in my love, just as I have kept my Father's commandments and **abide** in his love. I have said these things to you so that my joy may be in you, and that **your joy** may be complete," 15:10-11 (cf. 14:15, 21).	"Having been adorned [*kosmeō*] in every way with **the commandments** [*entolē*] **of Jesus Christ**, in whom also I rejoice greatly," Ignatius, *Eph.* 9.2; "Let the one who has love in Christ fulfill the commandments [*paraggelō*] of Christ. Who can describe the bond of God's love? 1 Clem 49:1-2; (second century) Did. 4.3; Bar. 10.12 (second to third centuries); Herm. *Mand.* 7.1; Herm. *Simil.* 8.7.6 (only a selection provided). Note: We use the older, tripartite numbering for the Shepherd of Hermas corpus.
"'Look at my hands and my feet; see that it is I myself. **Touch me and see** [*psēlaphēsate me kai idete*]; for a ghost does not have flesh and bones as you see that I have,'" Luke 24:39. To Thomas: "Then he said to Thomas, 'Put your finger here and see my hands. Reach out your hand and put it in my side. Do not doubt but believe [*pisteuō*],'" John 20:27.	To Peter (and the others): "'Take hold. **Touch me and see** [*psēlaphēsate me kai idete*]; that I am not a bodiless demon.' And immediately they touched him and they believed [*pisteuō*]," Ignatius, *Smyrn.* 3.2. Same phraseology as in Luke 24:39, but some thematic similarities with John 20:27 (touch, see, believe); cf. To Peter, Thomas, and Andrew, touch, see, know, *Ep. Apos.* 11-12 (ca. 180).

In his comparisons, Titus Nagel concludes that Ignatius knew FG, and his use of FG in his letters to churches of Asia implies that it was known to these churches also (ca. 110).[10] We agree here with Prof. Nagel's conclusions.

Justin Martyr was the most significant of the second-century apologists for Christianity. He was born in Samaria, lived for a time at Ephesus, and finally conducted a training school for Christians at Rome until his martyrdom about 165 CE.[11] His most famous pupil was the Syrian Tatian, who wrote a four-gospel harmony (ca. 172; *Diatessaron*). Tatian later modified his teaching and organized an ascetic sect (perhaps the Encratites).[12] In addition to FG, Justin seems acquainted with traditions

---

10. Nagel, *Die Rezeption des Johannesevangeliums*, 473-74. Nagel also mentions here the familiarity of Papias, bishop of Hierapolis (ca. 130), with FG (as cited in Irenaeus, *Haer.* 5.33.4; Frag. of Papias 14; Eusebius, *Hist. eccl.* 3.24; 3.39). On the Fragments of Papias, esp. 3.5-6; 4.4-11; 7.5; 18:19; 23, see Holmes, *Apostolic Fathers*, 722-67.

11. Grant, "Justin Martyr (Person)," 3:1133; Edwards, "Tatian," 6:335-36, 424. For sources, we used Roberts and Donaldson, *Ante-Nicene Fathers*, and Nagel, *Die Rezeption des Johannesevangeliums*, 94-116 (which includes the Greek text).

12. In Tatian's *Diatessaron* (ca. 160 CE) the first and last paragraphs of the Johannine

found in Mark (e.g., christological interpretation of Ps 22 LXX) and perhaps Luke (*Dial.* 99–107).

B. The Fourth Gospel	Justin Martyr
"In the beginning was the Word [*logos*], and the Word was with God" 1:1; "And the Word became flesh [*sarx egeneto*] and lived among us," 1:14a; "Who were born, not of blood (*ouk eks haimatōn*) nor of the will of the flesh or of the will of man, but of God (*oude ek thelēmatos andras all' ek theou*), 1:13.	"And the first power after God the Father and Lord of all is the Word [*logos*], who is also the Son; and of Him we will, in what follows, relate how He took flesh (*sarx*) and became man. For as man did not make the blood of the vine but God, so it was hereby intimated that the blood [*tou haimatos*] should not be of human seed, but of divine power," Justin, 1 *Apol.* 32.9; "As his blood is not from human seed, but from the will of God ['*all' ek thelēmatos theou*]," Justin, *Dial.* 63.2; "The Word (*logos*), who is also the first-born of God," Justin, 1 *Apol.* 33.
"He confessed and did not deny it, but confessed, 'I am not the Messiah [*ouk eimi ho Christos*].' And they asked him, 'What then? Are you Elijah?' He said, 'I am not.' 'Are you the prophet?' He answered, 'No.'" He said, 'I am the voice of one crying out [*phōnē boōntos*] in the wilderness, 'Make straight the way of the Lord,' as the prophet Isaiah said,'" 1:20, 23.	"But he [John the Baptist] cried to them, 'I am not the Christ [*ouk eimi ho Christos*], but the voice of one crying [*alla phōnē boōntos*]," Justin, *Dial.* 88.7
"Jesus answered him, 'Very truly, I tell you, no one can see the kingdom of God without being born from above [*gennaō anōthen*].' Nicodemus said to him, 'How can anyone be born after having grown old? Can one enter a second time into the mother's womb [*koilia mētēr*] and be born?'" 3:3–4.	"For Christ also said, 'Except you are born again [*anagennaō*], you shall not enter into the kingdom of heaven.' Now, that it is impossible for those who have once been born to enter into their mothers' wombs, [*mētēr, tiktō*, pl.] is manifest to all," Justin, 1 *Apol.* 61.4–5. Also noted in Bruce, *Gospel and Epistles of John*, 83, 98.
"I have received this command from my Father [*lambanō patēr*]," 10:18b.	"This [mandate] He has obtained from the Father [*lambanō patēr*]," Justin, *Dial.* 100.1.

Gospel form the opening and closing statements in this gospel-narrative anthology. Likewise, Jesus's interactions with Mary, Martha, Lazarus, and Nicodemus are all reported extensively, as well as the Johannine renderings of Jesus's healings in Jerusalem and engagements with leaders in Jerusalem. See Edwards, "Tatian," 6:335–36, 424, and his "Diatessaron or Diatessara?" 88–92.

B. The Fourth Gospel	Justin Martyr
"They will look on [*horaō*]the one whom they have pierced [*ekkenteō*]," 19:37b; following a Greek rendering of MT Zech. 12:10b "pierce through," [Heb. *daqar*], not found in LXX.	"And then they shall look on [*horaō*] Him whom they have pierced [*ekkenteō*]," Justin, *1 Apol.* 52.12; "The one in which He was pierced [*ekkenteō*] by you; a second, when you shall know Him whom you have pierced [*ekkenteō*]," *Dial.* 32.2. Justin follows John 19:37 ("pierced"), not LXX Zech. 12:10 rendering.
"And now I have told you this before it occurs, so that when it does occur, you may believe [*pisteuō*]," 14:29; "Do not doubt but believe [*apistos 'alla pistos*]," 20:27b.	"For things which were incredible [*apista*] and seemed impossible with men, these God predicted by the Spirit of prophecy as about to come to pass, in order that, when they came to pass, there might be no unbelief, but faith [*mē apisteuō 'alla, pisteuō*], because of their prediction," Justin, *1 Apol.* 33.2. Cf. "John, do not be faithless, but believing," Acts John 90:15–17 (third century); Ep. Apos. 11 (ca. 180).

F. F. Bruce comments on the use of FG in Justin Martyr:

> Justin's identification of Christ with the *logos* ('Word') is probably dependent on Jn. 1:1–14, although Justin develops it along lines of his own (*First Apology*, 46.1–6); again, the words, 'Christ also said, "Unless you are born again, you will not enter into the kingdom of heaven"' (*First Apology*, 61.4), can scarcely be anything other than a quotation from memory of John 3:3, 5.[13]

The ***Epistle* to *the Apostles*** (or *Epistula Apostolorum*) is an early apocryphal Christian work of unknown authorship. Originally written in Greek, it (*Ep. Apos.*) survives only in Ethiopic (Eth., complete text), Coptic (Copt., approx. two thirds), and Latin (Lat., fragments). The title has been inferred from the opening sentence, "What Jesus Christ revealed to his disciples as a letter . . . the letter of the council of the apostles" (1.1). The

---

13. Bruce, *Canon of Scripture*, 129n43. For more parallels, see Hengel, *Johannine Question*, 12–14, 150n72.

work is dated around 170–180 CE from the province of Asia or Syria.[14] Titus Nagel[15] outlined the book showing Johannine influence:

Letter-like Opening   Ep. Apos. 1–2 (1 John 1:1–4)

Text Opening   Ep. Apos. 3; John 1:1–18

The Work of the Revealer in the World   Ep. Apos. 4–6; John 1:19—2:50

Revelation before the Disciples   Ep. Apos.; John 13:1—17:26

Passion, Resurrection and Apparitions/Appearances   Ep. Apos. 13–50; John 18:1—20:29

Resurrecting the Risen One   Ep. Apos. 51

Letter-like Conclusion—(1 John)

C. The Fourth Gospel; 1 John	Epistle to the Apostles
"We declare to you what was from the beginning, what we have heard, what we have seen with our eyes, what we have looked at and touched with our hands, concerning **the word of life**, this life was **revealed, and we have seen it and testify to it, and declare to you** the eternal life that was with the Father and was revealed to us—we declare to you what we have seen and heard so that you also may have fellowship with us; and truly our fellowship is with **the Father and with his Son Jesus Christ. We are writing these things** so that **our joy** may be complete," 1 John 1:1–4.	"What Jesus Christ revealed to his disciples in a letter, and how Jesus Christ **revealed** the letter . . . that you be established and not waver, not be shaken and not turn away from **the word of the** Gospel that you have heard. **As we have heard** [it], **kept** [it], **and have written** [it] **for the whole world, so we entrust** it to you . . . in joy and in the name of **God the Father** . . . **and in Jesus Christ**. May Grace increase in you," Ep. Apos. 1 (Eth.). Note: we added **bold** print.

---

14. Hills, "Apostles, Epistle of," 1:311–12 and his *Tradition and Composition in the Epistula Apostolorum*; Lake, "Epistola Apostolorum," 14:15–29. Text from C. D. G. Muller and H. Deunsing, "Epistula Apostolorum," in Schneemelcher, *New Testament Apocrypha*, 1:249–84.

15. Nagel, *Die Rezeption des Johannesevangeliums*, 156 (our trans. from the Ger.).

C. The Fourth Gospel; 1 John	Epistle to the Apostles
"Who were born, **not of blood or of the will of the flesh** or of the will of man, but of God. And **the Word became flesh** and lived among us, and we have seen his glory, the glory as of a father's only son, full of grace and truth," John 1:13–14.	"We believe: **the word became flesh** . . . and was born **not by the lust of the flesh but by the will of God**," Ep. Apos. 3 (Eth.); cf. 14 (Eth.).
"On the third day there was **a wedding in Cana of Galilee, and the mother of Jesus was there**," 2:1.	"Then there was **a marriage in Cana of Galilee. And he was invited with his mother and his brothers. And he made water into wine**," Ep. Apos. 5 (Eth.).
"He [Jesus] said to them, 'Now draw some out, and take it to the chief steward.' So they took it. When the steward tasted **the water that had become wine**, and did not know where it came from," 2:8–9a.	
After this he went down to Capernaum with **his mother, his brothers**, and his disciples; and they remained there a few days," 2:12.	
"Indeed, just as the Father raises the dead and gives them life, so also the Son gives life to whomever he wishes," 5:21.	"I am the hope of the hopeless . . . **the resurrection of the dead**," Ep. Apos. 21 (Eth.).
"Very truly, I tell you, anyone who hears my word and **believes him who sent me** has eternal life, and does not come under judgment, but has passed from death to life," v. 24.	"In regeneration you obtain **the resurrection in your flesh** . . . believe in him **who sent me**; for my Father has found pleasure in you," Ep. Apos. 21 (Eth.). cf. 28 (Eth.).
"**I give you a new commandment, that you love one another**," 13:34; cf. "anyone who loves me **obeys my commandments**," 14:23; cf. 15:10.	"**I give you a new commandment; love one another**," Ep. Apos. 17 (Eth.; Copt.); cf. "those who love me and . . . have **done my commandment**," 26 (Eth.)
"Do you not believe that **I am in the Father and the Father is in me**? The words that I say to you I do not speak on my own; but **the Father who dwells in me** does his works. Believe me that I am in the Father and **the Father is in me**; but if you do not, then believe me because of the works themselves," 14:10–11; cf. 10:38; 17:21.	"**I am wholly in the Father and the Father in me**," Ep. Apos. 17 (Eth.; Copt.).

XII. THE EARLY RECEPTION OF THE FOURTH GOSPEL

C. The Fourth Gospel; 1 John	Epistle to the Apostles
"Then he said to Thomas, 'Put your finger here and see my hands. Reach out your hand and put it in my side. Do not doubt but **believe**,'" John 20:27; cf. 1 John 1:1.	"John and Thomas and Peter [and the other Apostles] . . . recounting to you concerning our Lord Jesus Christ, as we have written; and we have heard and felt him after he had risen from the dead; and how he has revealed to us things great, astonishing, real," Ep. Apos. 2 (Eth.); "**lay your hand**, Peter [and your finger, Eth.], in the nail prints of my hands, and you, Thomas, **put your finger in the spear wounds of my side**," 11 (Copt.; Eth.); cf. "But we touched him that we might truly know whether he had risen," 12 (Copt.).
"Blessed are those who have **not seen** and yet have come to believe," 20:29.	"**Blessed will they be who do not see me and [yet] believe in me**," 29 (Eth.; Copt.).
"When she had said this, she turned around and saw Jesus standing there, but she did not know that it was Jesus. **Jesus said to her, 'Woman, why are you weeping? Whom are you looking for?'** . . . Jesus said to her, 'Mary!' She turned and said to him in Hebrew, 'Rabbouni!' (which means Teacher)," 20:14-16. "**Go to my brothers and say to them,** 'I am ascending to my father . . . " v. 17.	"And as they [Mary and Martha, Mary Magdalene] were mourning and weeping, **the Lord** appeared to them and said to them: [Copt. 'For whom **are you weeping**? Now] do not weep. I am he whom you seek. But let one of you **go to your brothers and say to them**. Come, our Master has risen from the dead," Ep. Apos. 10 (Eth.).

Charles E. Hill identifies the use of FG in the Epistle to the Apostles with the work of Irenaeus of Lyons (ca. 180), because both avoided or resisted docetic and gnostic interpretations of FG.[16]

Hippolytus (ca. 170-236), was an important third-century theologian of the Roman Church, little is known of his life. His writings were almost forgotten in the western church by reason of his schismatic activities and because he wrote in Greek (not Latin). He was a prominent Roman presbyter in the first decades of the third century. When Origen came to Rome (ca. 212) he attended one of his sermons. Soon afterwards Hippolytus attacked Sabellius for his modalism that obscures the Son and Spirit as

---

16. Hill, *Johannine Corpus*, 472-73. Hill also avoids here the conclusion that 1 John (as a midrash on FG), along with Ep. Apos. and Irenaeus, *rescued* FG from gnostic interpretation by showing that there is a "right way" for the church to read FG, suggested in Brown, *Community of the Beloved Disciple*, 149-50. On the problematic use of "docetic," see the essays in Verheyden et al., *Docetism in the Early Church*.

distinct persons of the triune Godhead. He was also embroiled in theological disputes with Pope Zephyrinus (198–217), and his successor, Callistus (217–222).[17]

D. The Fourth Gospel	Hippolytus of Rome
"The true light which enlightens everyone, was coming into the world," 1:9.	And this, he [Basilides] says, is that which has been stated in the Gospels: "He was the true light, which enlightens every one that cometh into the world," [John 1:9] Hippolytus, *Haer.* 7.10.22.[18]
"Very truly, I tell you, no one can [*ou dynamai*] enter [*eiselthein*] the kingdom of [*theou*] God without being **born of water and Spirit**," 3:5.	"Unless one is **born of water and of Spirit**, he will not **enter into the kingdom** of heaven," Hippolytus, *Haer.* 8.10.8. Verbatum in Greek except for usage here of "will not enter," (*ouk eiseleusetai*) and "kingdom of heaven" [*tōn ouranōn*].
"If you knew the gift of God, and who it is that is saying to you, 'Give me a drink,' you would have asked him, and he would have given you **living water** [*hydōr zōn*]." The woman said to him, "Sir, you have no bucket, and the well is deep. Where do you get that **living water** [*hydōr to zōn*]?" 4:10–11; [*hydōr zōn*]. The water that I will give will become in them a spring of water **gushing up** [*hallomai*] to eternal life," 4:14b; cf. 7:38.	"And when he has sworn this oath, he goes on to the Good One, and beholds 'whatever things eye hath not seen, and ear hath not heard, and which have not entered into the heart of man;' and he drinks from **life-giving water**, which is to them, as they suppose, a bath, a fountain of **life-giving** [*hydōr zōn*], **bubbling** [*hallomai*] water," Hippolytus, *Haer.* 5.9.18–19 (from his report on Naasene sect).
"No one can come to me unless **drawn by the Father** who sent me"[*oudeis dunatai elthein pros mē ean mē ho pempsas me elkysē auton*], 6:44.	"No one can come unto me, except my heavenly **Father draw some** one unto me" [*oudeis dunatai elthein pros mē ean mē tina elkysē ho patēr mou ho ouranios*], Hippolytus, *Haer.* 5.3.

---

17. "Hippolytus expresses his own trinitarian theology in a form of Logos doctrine calculated to answer the charge of ditheism which Callistus had levelled against him," Cross, *ODCC*, 778. See also Foerster, *Gnosis*, 1:261–82; Nagel, *Die Rezeption des Johannesevangeliums*, 209–315.

18. Hippolytus cites John 1:9 in the context of his discussion about the gnostic-like cosmogony of Basilides of Alexandria (active, ca. 130–140); see also Irenaeus, *Haer.* 1.24.1; Layton, *Gnostic Scriptures*, 417–44 (his life and writings).

XII. THE EARLY RECEPTION OF THE FOURTH GOSPEL

D. The Fourth Gospel	Hippolytus of Rome
"As he walked along, he saw a man **blind from birth** [*typhlon ek genetēs*]," 9:1; "The true light, which **enlightens everyone** [*to phōs to alēthinon, ho phōtizei panta anthōpon erkomenon eis ton kosmon*], was coming into the world," 1:9.	"But if any one, he says, is **blind from birth** [*typhlos ek genetēs*], and has never beheld the true light," "which **enlightens every man** that cometh into the world [*to phōs to alēthinon, ho phōtizei panta anthōpon erkomenon eis ton kosmon*]," "by us let him recover his sight, and behold, as it were, through some paradise planted with every description of tree [cf. I see people like trees walking, Mark 8:24], and supplied with abundance of fruits," Hippolytus, *Haer.* 5.4.9-10 (report on the Naasenes).

From our comparisons of FG with Ignatius of Antioch, Justin Martyr, Epistle to the Apostles, and Hippolytus, it appears that FG satisfies and even surpasses (in some cases) their expectation of FG as an apostolic writing (see reception history in our Introduction, p. 10).

Heracleon (ca. 145–80), a Hellenistic teacher with gnostic leanings, was a disciple of Valentinus of Rome (ca. 160). Heracleon wrote an allegorizing commentary (Ὑπομνήματα) on FG, but only fragments have survived, mainly in quotations in Origen's commentary on FG.[19] Because it is evident that both Heracleon and Origen are reading from a copy of FG (and Origen's commentary ends at John 13:33),[20] only a selection will be provided. Origen apparently believed that the intentions of FG and its author(s) would only disappoint and refute Heracleon's expectations of it.

---

19. Cross, *ODCC*, 760. For primary texts: Brooke, *Fragments of Heracleon*; Foerster, *Gnosis*, 1:162–83; Origen, *Origenes Johannes Commentar*, 3–480; Nagel, *Die Rezeption des Johannesevangeliums*, 315–41; see also Attridge, "Heracleon and John," in his *Essays*, 193–207; Pagels, *Johannine Gospel in Gnostic Exegesis*, see especially 123–24 for index of technical Greek terms, e.g., aeon, demiurge, pleroma, pneumatic. For Heracleon as a more independent Hellenistic thinker, see Wucherpfennig, *Heracleon Philologus*.

20. Origen, *Commentary on John*, 7.

E. The Fourth Gospel	Heracleon (in Origen's Commentary)
"In the beginning was the Word, and the Word was with God, and the Word was God. He was in the beginning with God. **All things came into being through him** [*panta di auto egeneto*], and without him not one thing came into being. What has come into being," John 1:1–3.	"Without evidence, in my opinion, has Heracleon... in interpreting the [saying] '**All things came into being through him**,' [*panta di auto egeneto*] expounded 'all things' as meaning the world and what is in it, and excluded from that 'all,' to suit his own view... for he says: 'Neither the aeon nor what was in the aeon came into being through the Logos'—for that, he believes, came into being *before* the Logos...' Frag. 1 on John 1:3 in Origen, *Comm. Jo.* 2.14 (Logos inspired the *Demiurge* to create, according to Heracleon).[21] Note: **bold** and *italics* are from us.
"**In him was life** [*en autō zōē ēn*], and the life was the light of all people," 1:4.	"In the saying, '**What was made in him was life**' [*ho gegonen en autō zōē ēn*] he [Heracleon] understood 'in him' as meaning 'for spiritual men'[pneumatics]. ... And he says, 'For he [Logos] provided for them the first formation according to their generation in that what had been sown by *another* [Demiurge] he brought to form, illumination, and to an individual delineation, and set it forth.' Frag. 2 on John 1:4 in Origen, *Comm. Jo.* 2.21.
"He said, 'I am **the voice** of one crying out **in the wilderness**, 'Make straight the way of the Lord,'" as the prophet Isaiah said," 1:23 (Isa 40:3 LXX).	"Heracleon... says: 'The Logos is the Savior, **the voice in the wilderness** [*phōnē en tē erēmō*] is that symbolized by John, and the echo is the entire prophetic order,' Frag. 5 on John 1:23 in Origen, *Comm. Jo.* 6.20–21; cf. "The Lord's voice (*phōnē*), the Word (*logos*), without shape, the power of the Word (*logos*), the luminous word of the Lord, the truth from heaven" (Clement of Alexandria, *Strom.*VI, 3, 34).

21. See critical comments of Irenaeus concerning the Demiurge, the lesser creator god (as employed by the Valentinians) in his *Haer. 1.5.3*. On Demiurge first used by Plato as the world's craftsman in *Timaeus*, see Layton, *Gnostic Scriptures*, 15n4. Irenaeus (ca. 180) cites John 1:1–3 "all things were created by him" (i.e., the Word) without any qualification (*Haer.* 3.11.8).

E. The Fourth Gospel	Heracleon (in Origen's Commentary)
"The next day he [John] saw Jesus coming toward him and declared, 'Here is the Lamb of God who takes away the sin of the world!' [*ide ho Amnos tou theou ho airōn tēn hamartian tou kosmou*]" 1:29.	"Here again **John the Baptist** plays a double role: as prophet, he says, 'This is the Lamb of God,' [*Ide ho Amnos tou theou*] which is taken to refer to the [physical] body of Christ, which is psychic; as more than a prophet he says, **'which takes away the sins of the world'** [*ho airōn tēn hamartian tou kosmou*] and that must refer to the pneumatic realm. There is, however, no talk of forgiveness of sins among the pneumatics," Frag. 10 on John 1:29 in Origen, *Comm. Jo.* 6.60.
"The Passover of the Jews was near, and Jesus went up to Jerusalem. **In the temple** [temple precincts, *hieron*] **he found** people selling cattle, sheep, and doves, and the money changers seated at their tables. Making a whip of cords, he drove all of them out of the temple, both the sheep and the cattle. He also poured out the coins of the money changers and overturned their tables. He told those who were selling the doves, 'Take these things out of here! Stop making my Father's house a marketplace!'" 2:13–16; "temple building/body of Jesus," *naos*, 2:19–21.	"The statement '**He** [Jesus] **found** them in the **sanctuary**' [*hieron*] and not 'in the temple' [*naos*] he [Heracleon] thinks, 'so that it may not be thought to be the mere *calling*, apart from the Spirit, which elicits help from the Lord.' For he claims that 'the sanctuary' is the Holy of Holies, into which only the High Priest enters, in which'—I think he says—'the pneumatics go. The **temple** forecourt, where the Levites also are, is a symbol of the psychics who attain a salvation outside the Pleroma,'" Frag. 13 on John 2:13–16 in Origen, *Comm. Jo.* 10.33.
"'Are you greater than our ancestor Jacob, who gave us **the well**, and with his sons and his **flocks** drank from it?' Jesus said to her, 'Everyone who drinks of this water will be thirsty again, but those who drink of the water that I will give them **will never be thirsty**. **The water that I will give** will become in them a spring of water gushing up to **eternal life**.' The woman said to him, 'Sir, give me this water, so that I may never be thirsty or have to keep coming here to draw water,'" 4:12–15.	"Let us look at Heracleon's [commentary] on these verses: 'the cattle of Jacob drank from it [the well] . . . but **the water which the Savior gives** is from his spirit and power'...And the words 'he **will never thirst again**' [John 4:14] he literally renders: '**For this life is eternal** and never perishes, as does the first [life which] the well [provides], but rather is lasting. For the grace and gift of the Savior cannot be taken away, and is not consumed or destroyed . . . the first life is perishable," Frag. 17 on John 4:12–15 in Origen, *Comm. Jo.* 13.10.

E. The Fourth Gospel	Heracleon (in Origen's Commentary)
"God is spirit [*Pneuma ha theos*], and those who worship him must worship in spirit and truth" [*Kai tous prosynountas auton en pneumatic kai alētheia dei proskunein*], 4:24.	"On 'God is spirit' [*Pneuma ha theos*] Heracleon says, 'Undefiled, pure, and invisible is his divine nature' [*aoratos hē theia physis autou*]. On the phrase 'those who worship him must worship him in spirit and in truth' [*Tous prosynountas en pneumati kai alētheia dei proskunein*] he says: "Worthily of him who is worshipped, in a spiritual, not a fleshly fashion [*pneumatikōs, ou sarkikōs*]. For those who have the same nature as the Father are themselves **spirit**, and they worship in **truth** and not in error,'" Frag. 24 on John 4:24 in Origen, *Comm. Jo.* 13.25.
"Jesus said to them, 'My food [*emon brōma*] is to do the will of him who sent me and to complete his work' [*hina poiēsōto thelēma tou pempsanatos me*]" 4:34.	"Heracleon says that 'with the words **My meat** [*emon brōma*] **is to do the will of him who sent me** [*hina poiēsōto thelēma tou pempsanatos me*] the Savior explains to the disciples that this was what he had discussed with the woman, calling the will of the Father his **meat**. For this was his **food**, rest, and power. **The will of the Father**,' he goes on, 'is that men should know the Father and be saved. This was the work of the Savior, on account of which he was sent to Samaria, that is, into the world [*ton kosmon*],'" Frag. 31 on John 4:34 in Origen, *Comm. Jo.* 13.38.
"You are from your father **the devil** [*tou diabolou*], and you choose to do your father's **desires** [*epithumias tou Patros hymōn*]. He was a murderer from the beginning and does not stand in the truth, because there is no truth in him. When he lies, he speaks according to his own nature, for he is a liar and the father of lies," 8:44.	"Heracleon says: 'This was said not to those who are by nature children of **the Devil** [*tou diabolou hious*], the choics [*tous khoikous*], but to the psychics [*tous psychikous*] who have become sons of **the Devil** by intent; some who are of this nature may also be called sons of God *by intent.*' And he adds: 'Because they have loved **the desires** of **the Devil** [*epithumias tou diabolou*] and performed them, they become children of the Devil, though they were not such by nature,'" Frag. 46 on John 8:44 in Origen, *Comm. Jo.* 20.24.

In places indicated by Origen, Heracleon appears to be using FG as a sounding board for his specific views on the creation of the world by a

Demiurge, antipathy to the flesh and the material world, the pneumatics and psychic peoples. Although Origen endorsed some of Heracleon's speculations in his great commentary, "he domesticated the allegorical method by submitting it to a statement of belief which he believed to be held by all churches . . . His Christ is divine, yet also man in body, soul and spirit."[22] Origen made use of all four Gospels and when FG appeared to conflict with the others, he would interpret it as a "spiritual gospel" (from Clement of Alexandria in Eusebius, *Hist. eccl.* 6.14.7).[23]

FG may have been Heracleon's favorite Gospel, but he also betrays a fondness for Matthew, Luke, and the writings of Paul (cf. Origen, *Comm. Jo.* 6.60; 13.32, 60).[24] Although Heracleon can be identified with Valentinian teachings, which is only part of what we find in the Nag Hammadi Library, the following data is noteworthy. In their index of allusions and echoes to the NT, Craig Evans and his co-editors have supplied us with approximately 864 allusions to Matthew's Gospel, ca. 1056 regarding Paul's writings (disputed and undisputed), and about 1248 for FG. There were about 480 allusions or echoes to Genesis.[25] What we find in the Nag Hammadi is not unlike what we would find in Heracleon, Ptolemy (Letter to Flora),[26] and the Naasenes: ample use of *different* NT writings that were being circulated among the congregations associated with Paul, FG, and Ignatius. The writings of Origen, Hippolytus, and Irenaeus sought to correct what they saw as misinterpretations of their authoritative writings.[27]

---

22. Edwards, *John*, 3. Edwards also adds (24) that Origen had a keener grasp of the incarnation than did Ignatius of Antioch (Ignatius, *Magn.* 8.3), arguing that "the flesh of the incarnation has been retranslated into the word of Scripture" (citing Origen, *Cels.* 4.15). See also Origen, *Cels.* 5.39 and *Princ.* 1.2.13.

23. Reflecting on Clement's "spiritual gospel" designation, Sir Edwyn Hoskyns writes that FG has so presented the history of Jesus that his readers are confronted with what is beyond time and beyond visible occurrence—with the Word of God and life of eternity, in his *Fourth Gospel*, 17. We note also that Jesus is called "The Word of God" in Rev 19:13 and the "word of life" in 1 John 1:1.

24. See also Pagels, *Gnostic Exegesis*, 75-78, 84-85, 92-93; and Clement, *Strom.* 4.9 citing Heracleon on Luke 12:11-12.

25. Evans et al., *Nag Hammadi Texts and the Bible*, 468-73 (Gen), 482-91 (Matt), 518-29 (Paul). Some are in bold type indicating a citation and probable influence (e.g., ca. 30 percent are in bold type in John 1). M. Hengel makes a similar conclusion: "So we cannot say that the Fourth Gospel was particularly the Gospel of the Gnostics" (*Johannine Question*, 9-10).

26. For text of Ptolemy's Letter to Flora, see Layton, *Gnostic Scriptures*, 306-15; for discussion, see Pagels, *Gnostic Exegesis*, 28-32 and Hengel, *Johannine Question*, 8, 145.

27. For lists and catalogues of OT and NT writings received as authoritative by Irenaeus, Origen, and others, see McDonald and Sanders, *Canon Debate*, 585-95.

Melito of Sardis made a visit to Palestine to visit the Holy Places (ca. 190). He was described by Polycrates (in Eusebius, *Hist eccl.* 5.24.5) as one of the great lights of Asia who observed Easter on the fourth day of Nisan (as a Christian Passover, i.e., Quartodeciman practice). He was a prolific writer, but only fragments of his works were known until 1940, when C. Bonner published a work preserved in a papyrus shared between the Chester Beatty collection and the University of Michigan. The work bore no title in this papyrus, but other texts found among the Bodmer papyri (pub. 1960) and also the Coptic and Georgian versions provide the title "On the Pascha" (Περὶ Πάσχα, *Peri Pascha*). A Latin epitome also survives among the sermons of both Augustine and Leo I. Its main theme is the new Passover inaugurated by Christ. Melito's theology probably influenced Irenaeus and Tertullian.[28]

F. Fourth Gospel	Melito, *On the Pascha*
"He was **in the beginning** [*en archē*] with God. **All things came into being through him** [*panta di' autou egeneto*] and without him not one thing came into being. What has come into being," John 1:2-3;	"God, in the beginning [*en archē*], having made [*poiēsas*] the heaven and the earth and all in them [*panta to en autois*] through the Word [*dia tou logou*]," 47.
"We have found him about whom Moses **in the law and also the prophets** wrote," 1:45.	"He it is **who made** [*ho epoiēsen*] **the heaven and the earth**, and formed humanity **in the beginning**, [*ta ap' archēs*] who was proclaimed through the law and the prophets," 104.
"Here is **the Lamb** [*ho amnos*] **of God who takes away the sin of the world!**" 1:29; "I am the good shepherd. The good shepherd **lays down his life** for the sheep," 10:11; cf. 13:1 (Jesus as Passover lamb). "And I myself have seen and have testified that this is **the Son** of God,"1:34; cf. 20:19-29 (appearance of the risen Jesus).	"For he was born **a son, and led as a lamb** [*ho amnos*], **and slaughtered as a sheep**, and buried as a man, and rose from the dead as God, being God by his nature and a man," 8.

---

28. Cross, *ODCC*, 1075. Critical edition by Othmar Perler, *Sur la Pâqe et fragments* (Paris, 1966) with Eng. trans. by Hall, *Melito of Sardis*. Chester Beatty—Michigan papyrus of the *Peri Pascha*, ed. C. Bonner (Studies and Documents 12; Philadelphia and London, 1940); the Bodmer text by M. Testuz (Papyrus Bodmer 13; Cologny and Geneva, 1960); and the Georgian version, with Eng. trans. by J. N. Birdsall, *Muséon* 130 (1967) 121–38. See Chadwick, "A Latin Epitome of Melito's Homily," 76–82; we cite from Stewart, *Melito of Sardis* (see 45–49 for complete bibliography).

F. Fourth Gospel	Melito, *On the Pascha*
"he saw a man blind from birth [*typlos ek genetēs*]," 9:1; "[Jesus] saying to him, 'Go, wash in the pool of Siloam' (which means Sent). Then he went and washed and came back able to see," v. 7.	"Give me a price on those blind from birth [*ek genetēs typlous*] whom he illumined by a voice," 89.
"I am the way, the truth, and the life [*egō eimi . . . hē zōē*]," 14:6.	"I am your life [*egō hē zōē*],
"I am the light [*egō eimi to phōs*] of the world," 8:12.	I am your light [*egō to phōs*]
"I am the good shepherd. The good shepherd lays down his life for the sheep," 10:11.	I am your salvation,
"I am the resurrection [*egō eimi anastasis*] and the life," 11:25.	I am your resurrection, [*egō hymas anastēsō*]" 103. cf. "resurrection . . . Son . . . life," Acts John 98.
"When Jesus arrived, he found that Lazarus had already been in the tomb [*en tō mnēmeiō*] four days [*tessaros, hēmeras*]," 11:17; "he [Jesus] cried with a loud voice, 'Lazarus, come out!' The dead man came out . . . Jesus said to them, 'Unbind him, and let him go,'" 11:43–44; "So the chief priests and the Pharisees called a meeting . . . and said, 'What are we to do? This man is performing many signs' [*sēmeia*]" 11:47.	"Nor did you regard the strangest of signs [*sēmeia*] a corpse four days dead called alive from a tomb [*ek mnēmeiou*]," 78; "who, four days [*tessaron hēmeron*] later, were raised from the tomb," 89; cf. "because of the crowd standing here" [John 11:42] "with a loud voice," [v. 43] Acts John 24.
"And if I go and prepare a place for you, I will come again and will take you to myself, so that where I am, there you may be also. And you know the way to the place where I am going." "I am the way, and the truth, and the life. No one comes to the Father except through me. If you know me, you will know my Father also. From now on you do know him and have seen him," 14:3–4, 6–7. "Philip said to him, 'Lord, show us the Father' [*deikson hemin ton patera*],'" v. 8.	"I shall raise you up by my right hand, I will lead you to the heights of heaven, there shall I show you [*hymin deiksō*] the everlasting Father [*ton . . . patera*]," 103.

Egerton Papyrus 2[29] consists of a group of five fragments from one of the oldest known sayings collections of Jesus (200 CE). Some fragments *appear to* echo the following texts: e.g., Mark 1:40–45 (cleansing of leper) and 12:13–17 (taxes to Caesar) along with the parallel accounts found in Matthew and Luke. One miracle story along the banks of the Jordan River (miraculous seed growth?) has no equivalent in the Canonical Gospels (frag. 2 lines 60–75). Fragments 1–4 are in the British Museum and fragment 5 is in Köln, Germany. Fragment 4 is only a scrap with one letter. There also appear to be some parallels to controversy stories in John's Gospel (John 3:2a; 5:39, 45–46; 7:30, 44; 9:29; 10:25b, 31). We find no evidence to support the claim that Egerton Papyrus 2 is a "gnostic" writing. For this document and that of Melito, FG appears to have satisfied and even surpassed their expectations of it as an apostolic writing.

G. The Fourth Gospel	Egerton Papyrus 2
"Rabbi, we know that you are a teacher who has come from God [*oidamen hoti apo theou elēluthas didaskalos*]; for no one can do these signs that you do [*ha sou poieis*] apart from the presence of God," 3:2. "The works that I do [*ha egō poiō*] in my Father's name testify [*marturei*] to me," 10:25b.	"Teacher [*didaskale*], Jesus, **we know that you are come from God** [*oidamen hot apo theou elēluthas*] for what you do [*ha gar poieis*] bears a testimony [*marturei*]."
"You search the scriptures because [*hoti*] you think that in them you have eternal life [*zōēn aiōnion*]; and it is they that testify [*marturousai*] on my behalf," 5:39.	"You search the scriptures in which [*en ais*] you think that in them you have [eternal] life [*zōēn*]; these are they [*ekeinai eisin*] that testify [*marturousai*] on my behalf," Frag. 1, lines 7b–10a.
"Do not think that I will accuse you you [*egō katēgoresai hymōn*] before the Father; your accuser is Moses, on whom you have set your hope," 5:45.	"Do you think that I came to accuse you [*egō ēlthon katēgoresai hymōn*] to my Father! There is one that accuses you, even Moses on whom you have set your hope," Frag. 1, lines 10b–14.
"If you believed Moses, you would believe me, for he wrote about me," 5:46.	If you **had believed** [*episteusate*] Moses you would **have believed** [*episteusate*] me for concerning me [*peri emou*] he wrote to your fathers," Frag. 1, lines 20–23.

---

29. Benefactor: Francis Henry Egerton, Eighth Earl of Bridgewater (1756–1859). For text and translation, see: J. Jeremias and W. Schneemelcher, "Papyrus Egerton 2," in Schneemelcher, *New Testament Apocrypha*, 1:96–99; Llewelyn and Kearnsley, *New Documents*, 9:99–101; Nagel, *Die Rezeption des Johannesevangeliums*, 194–207; see also http://www.kchanson.com/ANCDOCS/greek/egerton.html.

G. The Fourth Gospel	Egerton Papyrus 2
"Then they tried **to arrest him**, but no one laid hands on him, because his hour **had not yet come** [*hotu oupō elēluthei hē hōra autou*]," 7:30; cf. v.44.	"But they were not able **to arrest him** because the hour of his betrayal [*tēs paradoseōs*] **was not yet come** [*hotu oupō elēluthei autou hē hōra*]," Frag. 1, lines 30–32.
"We know [*hēmeis oidamen*] that God has spoken to Moses, but as for this man, we do not know where he comes from," 9:29.	"We know [*oidamen*] that God has spoken to Moses, but as for you, we know not from where you are [*oidamen pothen ei*]," Frag. 1, lines 15–17.
"Then they tried to arrest him again, but he escaped from their hands [*eksēlthen ek tēs cheiros autōn*]," 10:39; cf. 7:44.	"But he himself, the Lord, escaped from their hands [*eksēlthōn ek tōn cheirōn*] and turned away from them," Frag. 1, lines 30–33.

The Johannine Controversy of the Second and Third Centuries

A prominent theory of scholarship in the twentieth century has been challenged recently in the works of Charles Hill and Allen Brent.[30] The quotation below by Ernst Haenchen is a convenient summary of this prominent view:

> In *Adv. Haer.* 3.11.9, Irenaeus fought a group that went so far in their antithesis to Montanism (and Gnosticism) that they rejected the Gospel of John and the Apocalypse as works of the heretic Cerinthus. Epiphanius gave these people a name of opprobrium, *Alogoi* ("without reason, without logos"). The Roman bishop, Gaius, whose orthodoxy is beyond dispute, also rejects the Fourth Gospel and the Apocalypse as gnostic-Montanist writings, as Eusebius reports.[31]

The quotation from Irenaeus (*Haer* 3.11.9) is not self-evident, nor is its connection to the Epiphanius reference and the mention of Gaius. The above citation from Professor Haenchen, presupposes an intricate piecing of diverse data that requires some unpacking.

---

30. Hill, *Johannine Corpus*; and Brent, *Hippolytus and the Roman Church*, 131–84. See, however, Hill's critical review of Brent's "Degrees of Docetism?" in his review of Verheyden et al, eds., *Docetism in the Early Church* in RBL 09 (2019): https://www.bookreviews.org/pdf/12232_13633.pdf.

31. The citation is from Haenchen, *John*, 1:23–24, but the theory goes back to Bauer, *Orthodoxy and Heresy in Earliest Christianity* (1st Ger. ed. 1934) and later Sanders, *Fourth Gospel in Early Church*. See also Roloff, *Revelation*, 2.

The references that we will cite are from **Irenaeus** (ca. 130–200), Bishop of Lyons, who made many allusions to FG.[32] Unlike Clement of Alexandria, who wrote about his own version of Christian gnosis, Irenaeus seems to oppose all types of Gnosticism and docetism, emphasizing church rule under a bishop, Scripture (OT and NT), and the rule of truth/faith.[33] His opposition to Gnosticism also led to an emphasis on Christian Monotheism, on the unity of Father and Son in the work of Revelation and Redemption, and on the reality of the Incarnation of Christ, the Word "enfleshed" (Gk. *sesarkōsthai*).[34] He developed a doctrine of the "recapitulation" (ἀνακεφαλαίωσις; Lat. *recapitulatio*), or summary, of human development in the Incarnate Christ, and thereby gave a positive value to the humanity of Christ. He also laid great stress on the co-ordinate authority of all four Gospels.[35]

> Those, moreover, who follow Valentinus, making copious use of that according to John, to illustrate their conjunctions, shall be proved to be totally in error by means of this very Gospel (*Haer.* 3.11.7) . . . Indeed their audacity has gone so far that they entitle

---

32. Irenaeus (ca. 180) first made the association of John 1:3 and Ps 32:6 LXX (Ps 33:6 MT), "by the Word (*logos*) of the Lord the heavens were made firm," in his *Haer.* 3.8.3. For more of his many FG allusions, see *Haer.* 3.11.1 (John 1:1-4), 2 (John 1:10-11), 8 (John 1:1); 3.16.2 (John 1:13-14),5 (John 20:31), 7 (John 2:4; 17:30); 4.2.3 (John 5:46-47), 7 (John 4:41); see also 4.10.1; 4.13.4; 4.14.1; 4.37.5; 5.1.3; 5.7.1; 5.18.1-3.

33. "Rule of truth" (*kanōn tēs alētheias*) in Irenaeus, *Haer.* 1.22.1; 1.9.4; 2.28.1; church as a receptable of truth 3.4.1-2. "Rule of faith" is more common in Irenaeus, *Epid.* (extant in a seventh-eighth cent. Armenian trans.). See D. W. Jorgensen, "Irenaeus of Lyons," in Iricinschi, *Beyond the Gnostic Gospels*, 128-29. See reconstruction of FG traditions from Ptolemy, Polycarp, and Papias to Irenaeus in Mutschler, "Was weiß Irenäus vom Johannesevangelium?" 714-16. Irenaeus cites an opponent, the Valentinian teacher, Ptolemy, to argue that both, despite their differences, ascribe John 1 to "John the disciple of the Lord."

34. Irenaeus, *Haer.* 3.16.2. According to Irenaeus, "Gnostics like Cerinthus and also the Valentinians transgress the text [of FG], reading it as if it pointed to a Father beyond YHWH and multiple Sons" (Irenaeus, *Haer.* 1.9.1), citation from A. D. DeConick, "Gnostic Spirituality," in Iricinschi, *Beyond the Gnostic Gospels*, 157. The Father beyond YHWH probably refers to the "Ineffable, unengendered parent" and multiple Sons may refer to Christ and "the Craftsman" (Demiurge), in the Valentinian cosmogony (Irenaeus, *Haer.* 1.11.1), see Layton, *Gnostic Scriptures*, 223-24.

35. Cross, *ODCC*, 851-52. The *Adv. Haer.* was edited by Erasmus (Basle, 1526). Later ed. was by W. W. Harvey (Cambridge, 1857). Crit. text by A. Rousseau, OSB, and others (SC 100, 152 f., 210 f., 263 f., and 293 f.; 1965-1982). Eng. trans. of *Adv. Haer.* by J. Keble in LF (posthumous, 1872) and by A. Roberts and W. H. Rambaut in ANCL (2 vols., 1868-1869); of chief passages in *Adv. Haer.* by F. R. M. Hitchcock ("Early Christian Classics," 1916) and by R. M. Grant ("Early Church Fathers," 1997); of "Demonstration" by J. A. Robinson, with good notes ("Translations of Christian Literature," 1920) and J. P. Smith (ACW 16; 1953).

their recent composition the Gospel of Truth, though it agrees in nothing with the Gospels of the apostles (*Haer.* 3.11.8).

Irenaeus might be opposing here the Valentinian teaching of the same Gospel of Truth (I, 3 and XII, 2, ca. 150 CE) that is found in the Nag Hammadi Library (ca. 350).[36]

> Others, again (the Montanists), that they may set at nought the gift of the Spirit, which in the latter times has been, by the good pleasure of the Father, poured out upon the human race, do not admit that *aspect* [of the evangelical dispensation] presented by John's Gospel, in which the Lord promised that He would send the Paraclete; but set aside at once both the Gospel and the prophetic Spirit [claiming that their prophets alone received the first installment of the Spirit/Paraclete]. Wretched men indeed! (*Haer.* 3.11.9)

Both quotations from Irenaeus reflect some concern as to how FG is interpreted by Valentinian gnostics and the Montanists. Valentinus and his followers (e.g., Heracleon) made use of the Gospel of John, as did Cerinthus, but they were not the first. Echoes of FG are found in the letters of Ignatius and the writings of Polycarp and Papias, and nowhere are they disagreed with or disparaged. The discovery of Papyrus 457 (P52), Bodmer Papyri II and XV (P66 and P75), and Papyrus Egerton 2 show that FG was used and disseminated broadly in the first or second quarter of the second century CE as far away as Egypt.[37] There is no indication here that people that share the faith of Irenaeus have rejected FG because of its use by the controversial (heretical) Valentinians and the Montanists.

Eusebius (ca. 260–340), bishop of Caesarea, is known as the "Father of Church History." He was a pupil of Pamphilus, who trained him in the tradition of Origen and inspired him to oppose Sabellianism (e.g., Father, Son, and Spirit are three modes of One God). By 315 he was bishop of Caesarea. During the Arian controversy he supported Arius (Jesus is a subordinate deity) and was condemned by the Council of Antioch (324/5). At the Council of Nicaea he was reinstated by the Emperor Constantine when he produced the baptismal creed of Caesarea as evidence of his orthodoxy. In 335 he attended the Council of Tyre and the dedication of the Church of the Resurrection at Jerusalem, and was afterwards summoned by Constantine to advise on the case of Athanasius (with whom Eusebius was in conflict). He delivered the

---

36. See our comparsions of Gos. Truth and Ap. John with FG in our ch. 10, tbls. A, p. 174, D, 176.

37. Salmon, *Fourth Gospel*. For reminiscences of FG in the Letters of Ignatius (Greek parallels), see Burney, *Aramaic Origin of the Fourth Gospel*, 153–59.

Tricennial Oration in honor of the thirtieth anniversary of Constantine's accession to power in 336 and was active until the emperor died.

Of Eusebius's many writings the most celebrated is his *Ecclesiastical History*, the principal source for the history of Christianity from the Apostolic Age up to his own day. It contains a wide range of material on the Eastern church (he has little to say about the Western), mostly in the form of long extracts taken over from earlier writers. The *History* originally ended before 303 with book 7, and that the later books were added in successive editions, the final edition with book 10 was revised ca. 325. Besides the original Greek, it survives in Latin, Syriac, and Armenian versions.[38]

> We have received the tradition that at the time under discussion Cerinthus founded another heresy. Gaius, whose words I have quoted before, in the inquiry attributed to him writes as follows about Cerinthus. "Moreover, Cerinthus, who through revelations attributed to the writing of a great apostle, lyingly introduces portents to us as though shown him by angels, and says that after the resurrection the kingdom of Christ will be on earth and that humanity living in Jerusalem will again be the slave of lust and pleasure He is the enemy of the scriptures of God and in his desire to deceive says that the marriage feast will last a thousand years" (reports Gaius, in Eusebius, *Hist. eccl.* 3.28.1-2).[39]

The reference above concerns the NT Book of Revelation, Cerinthus, and his views of a literal millennial reign of peace and pleasure, at the consummation of Christ's kingdom. It is evident that Cerinthus interprets Revelation for articulating his millennial views, but the authorship of that NT book is not ascribed to him here. Our knowledge of Gaius (the alleged source of this reference) is fragmentary, Eusebius mentions elsewhere that Gaius a "learned person" wrote a *Dialogue with Proclus* the Montanist (in his *Hist. eccl.* 6.20.1-3). Elsewhere, Gaius is called a "church man" (*Hist. eccl.* 2.25.6).[40]

> Then, in due course, lower down he speaks thus, with reference to the Apocalypse of John: "Some indeed of those before our time rejected and altogether impugned the book, examining it chapter by chapter and declaring it to be unintelligible and illogical, [2] and its title false. For they say that it is not John's, nor yet an apocalypse (unveiling), since it is veiled by its heavy, thick

---

38. Cross, *ODCC*, 577-78. Eng. trans. of *Hist. eccl.* by K. Lake and J. E. L. Oulton (2 vols., Loeb, 1926-1932); H. J. Lawlor and J. E. L. Oulton (2 vols., London, 1927-1928); J. P. Migne, PG 19-24. Attridge and Hata, *Eusebius, Christianity, and Judaism*.

39. Lake and Oulton, *Ecclesiastical History*, 1:263-65.

40. References from Hill, *Johannine Corpus*, 174.

XII. THE EARLY RECEPTION OF THE FOURTH GOSPEL

> curtain of un-intelligibility; and that the author of this book was not only not one of the apostles, nor even one of the saints or those belonging to the Church, but Cerinthus, the same who created the sect called "Cerinthian" after him, since he desired to affix to his own forgery a name worthy of credit (Dionysius of Alexandria, in Eusebius, *Hist. eccl.* 7.25.1-2).[41]

The second reference again refers to Revelation and those who reject it because of its "unintelligible" contents, that John the apostle did not compose the book, and that some ascribe its authorship to Cerinthus. The source of this comment, Dionysius of Alexandria (Eusebius, *Hist. eccl.* 7.24.3) did not reject Revelation nor ascribe its authorship to Cerinthus, although he is uncertain regarding the authorship of Revelation.

Epiphanius, St (ca. 315-403), was the bishop of Salamis, Cyprus. A native of Palestine, he became an enthusiastic supporter of the monastic movement and founded (ca. 335) a monastery in Judaea. He continued throughout his life an ardent upholder of the faith of Nicaea, and was intolerant of all suspicion of heresy. Of his writings in defence of orthodox belief, the most important was his *Panarion*, commonly known as the *Refutation of all the Heresies*, in which he described and attacked every heresy known to him from the beginning of the church. In his later life he took an active part in the Apollinarian controversy, and after meeting Jerome in Rome in 382, joined forces with him in his attack on Origenism (e.g., the soul's preexistence).[42]

> Now these Alogi say — this is what I call them. They shall be so called from now on, and let us give this name, beloved, "Alogi." (2) For they believed in the heresy for which that name was a good one, since it rejects the books by John. As they do not accept the Word which John preaches, they shall be called Dumb (*Alogoi*). (3) As the complete strangers to the truth's message they deny its purity, and accept neither John's Gospel nor his Revelation. (4) And if they accepted the Gospel, but rejected the Revelation, I would say they might be doing it from scrupulousness, and refusing to accept an "apocryphon" because of

---

41. Lake and Oulton, *Ecclesiastical History*, 2:197.

42. Cross, *ODCC*, 556-57. Greek text: J. Oporinus, Basle, 1544 with much improved text ed. D. Petavius, SJ, 2 vols., Paris, 1622; repr. in J. P. Migne, *PG* 41-43. Eng. trans. of "Panarion," by F. Williams (Leiden, 1987, 1994); Eng. trans. of selected passages by P. R. Amidon, SJ (New York and Oxford, 1990). See also A. Pourkier, *L'hérésiologie chez Épiphane de Salamine* (Christianisme Antique, 4 [1992]). *CPG* 2 (1974) 324-41 (nos. 3744-807), and Suppl. (1998), 207-19. For Engl. trans., we use F. Williams, *Panarion of Epiphanius* as cited in Hill, *Johannine Corpus*, 175-77.

the deep and difficult sayings in the Revelation. But since they do not accept books in which St. John actually proclaimed his Gospel, it must be plain to everyone that they and their kind are the ones of whom St. John said in his General Epistles [1 John 2:18]: "it is the last hour and you have heard the Antichrist comes; even now behold, there are many Antichrists." (6) For they offer excuses [for their behavior]. Knowing, as they do, that St. John was an apostle and the Lord's beloved, that the Lord rightly revealed the mysteries to him, and that he learned upon his breast, they are ashamed to contradict him and try to object to these mysteries for a different reason. For they say that they are not John's composition but of Cerinthus and have no right to a place in the church (*Pan.* 51.3.1-6).

Epiphanius cites a group that he labels the "Alogoi" ("senseless). The Alogoi reject both FG ("they do not accept the Word') and Revelation (for its "deep and difficult sayings"). Their extreme views qualify them, according to Epiphanius, to be identified as "antichrists" (cf. 1 John 2:18). This group knows that John the beloved disciple is the author of FG and Revelation, but falsely ascribe their authorship to Cerinthus (writes Epiphanius). Both FG and Revelation disappointed their expectations as authoritative writings.

Concerning the Epiphanius reference, Charles Hill observes:

> It is notable, however, that for the first time in our sources [recalling Irenaeus and Eusebius] a single group is mentioned who is said to have opposed both the Gospel and the Apocalypse. It will be noticed that Epiphanius never names any members of this group of "Alogoi," and we cannot tell if he connected the name of Gaius with the predecessors Dionysius mentioned [according to Eusebius] who had assigned the Apocalypse of John to Cerinthus. Also though Epiphanius charges that this group rejected both the Gospel and Apocalypse and assigned them both to Cerinthus, neither Cerinthus nor his view are mentioned in their specific objections to the Johannine books.[43]

Epiphanius appears to be a summary of earlier views expressed by Irenaeus and Eusebius, but the specific identity of the so-called Alogoi is unclear. This Alogoi group is not identified here as Valentinian or the Montanist (Irenaeus). There is no connection made to Gaius the learned church man (Eusebius). Epiphanius, however, does maintain the view (predominant in

---

43. Hill, *Johannine Corpus*, 177.

his church) that John the Beloved Disciple was the author of FG, Revelation, and First John (where he cites 1 John 2:18 in his *Pan.* 51.3.5).[44]

Paul N. Anderson,[45] draws a similar conclusion as that of Charles Hill:

> Indeed, the Johannine interests of Montanus and his followers were motivated by the belief that John's presentation of a spirit-based ecclesiology was closer to the primitive church than its more institutional developments in the second century. They embraced John's story of Jesus *because* they felt it was apostolic in its origin and character. Further, those later disparaged by Epiphanius as the "alogoi" were held to be problematic because in their aversion to the Montanists with their egalitarian and pneumatic interpretations, so they sought to diminish the Johannine basis for their advances. The Alogoi also held an adoptionistic Christology rooted in synoptic readings of Jesus's ministry, and in their aversion to apocalyptic interpretations of Revelation, they are accused of rejecting the *Logos*-centered authority of the Johannine Prologue. Thus, being labeled as mindless "Alogoi" posed a challenge to their heretical leanings, in that they were not Johannine enough to be considered orthodox.

In conclusion, we have looked at the impact of FG on later writings. It has changed the horizons of its early readers. It has satisfied, surpassed, disappointed, and even refuted some of their expectations. In significant ways, the early reception of FG has influenced our own understanding of the text. Umberto Eco also reminds us that with this interaction of author, text, and reader, "the aesthetics of reception maintains that a literary work is enriched by the various interpretations it underwent along the centuries."[46] We hope also that our understanding of FG has been enriched by this study of its early reception.

---

44. The following work cites numerous traditions from the ancient church on the authorship questions of FG, see Schnackenburg, *John*, 1:77–91, for example: the testimonies of Polycarp and Papias according to Irenaeus, the witness of Polycrates from Ephesus according to Eusebius, *Eccl. hist.* 5.24, and the list of the Muratorian Fragment that includes FG. See our discussion regarding the contents and date of the Muratorian Fragment (late second or fourth century CE?) in Puskas and Robbins, *Introduction*, 265–66. Regardless of its date, the Muratorian Fragment may still reflect a late second-century viewpoint.

45. Paul N. Anderson, "The Son of Zebedee and the Fourth Gospel: Some Clues to John's Authorship and the State of the Johannine Question" is the final draft of a paper presented at the SNTS pre-conference on "The Johannine Question": https://www.academia.edu/28253466/_The_Son_of_Zebedee_and_the_Fourth_Gospel_Some_Clues_to_Johns_Authorship_and_the_State_of_the_Johannine_Question_.

46. Quotations from Eco, *Limits of Interpretation*, 52. See also our Introduction, p. 12n51.

Conclusion

As we stated in our introduction, over, under, and through John's story of Jesus are unforgettable ideas and concepts, profoundly simple and simply profound, for his own audience and beyond. The conceptual or thought worlds of the Fourth Gospel (FG), are also the product of diverse and complex Hellenistic and Jewish intertextual relationships. It is a cross-cultural achievement. It is so diverse and complex that Robert Kysar, on the history of FG research, wrote "nearly every conceivable religious and/or philosophical movement in the Roman world has been proposed as the intellectual setting of the Fourth Gospel" and concluded that "there has never been (in recent years) anything like a consensus of scholars on the history of religions background of the gospel."[1] Nevertheless, as a corollary of reading FG as narrative theology, Charles H. Talbert, states "It is inappropriate to focus on only one background for understanding the narrative (e.g., Qumran, rabbinic Judaism, mystical Judaism, Hellenistic Judaism, Greco-Roman philosophy, Hermetica, Gnosticism, etc.) since it will likely take knowledge of most or all to comprehend a tradition that developed not only through time but also moved geographically."[2] Udo Schnelle programmatically states that any one-sided explanation of FG (e.g., within an inner-Jewish context) is insufficient.[3] Hans-Josef Klauck adds that "understanding a text only reaches its goal when the whole circle of its context has been measured off."[4]

---

1. Kysar, "Fourth Gospel: Report on Recent Research," 2413 (see also 2389–480).

2. Talbert, *Reading John*, 66.

3. From "kann nicht monocausal erklärt werden," in Schnelle, *Das Evangelium nach Johannes*, 40. ET quotation from Frey, "Between Torah and Stoa," 194. M. Becker strongly agrees with Schnelle's statement (above), see his "Zeichen," in Frey and Schnelle, *Kontexte*, 235–36.

4. Our translation of "Das Verstehen eines Textes gelangt erst zu seinem Ziel, wenn der ganze Zirkel seiner Kontexte abgeschritten ist" in Klauck, *Herrenmahl und hellenistischer Kult*, 4. Klauck's definition of context is also noteworthy here "in a broad sense the entire spiritual or intellectual space of an expression, taking into account its history" (our trans.). "Kontext im wietesten Sinn ist der gesamte geistige Raum, in dem eine Äußerung steht, unter Einbezug seiner Geschichte" (Klauck, *Herrenmahl und hellenistischer Kult*, 4).

Much of our understanding of the conceptual worlds of FG has been derived from "parallels" that involve similar or analogous vocabulary, phrases, and sentences (linguistic and verbal), as well as parallel themes, concepts, images, forms, structural patterns, or social and cultural contexts. Such parallels have helped to determine the meaning of a word or expression, the translation of a particular language, direct literary influence (e.g., quotations), the influence of ideas (whether a body of work, specific teaching, shared context, or similar historical trajectory), shared membership in a social group (sectarian, missional), or cross-cultural type (e.g., prophet, king), or phenomenological pattern (agent, intermediary).[5]

The many generic similarities that John's Gospel (FG) shares with different writings of late antiquity, however, may point to a common type of intellectual milieu that had developed then: a complex, Greco-Roman, universalizing Jewish, and mystical ("gnostic-like") context. On a common religious environment, Hans Jonas interpreted Gnosis (broadly defined) as a characteristic of the "spirit of late antiquity and E. R. Goodenough wrote of a Mediterranean "lingua franca" with similar concepts and images.[6]

George W. MacRae, SJ observed that "the process of Johannine theology according to John's intention corresponds to a process of 'Hellenization' that is paralleled elsewhere in the history of ancient religion" (e.g., Isis aretalogy).[7] Robert Kysar ironically adds "It is the accomplishment of current Johannine scholarship that the evidence for the syncretistic, heterodox Jewish milieu of the gospel has become irresistible."[8] Pursuing these observations, we hope, have opened up more interpretive possibilities that have been forgotten or overlooked in Johannine research today.

Despite all of the suggested tests of verifiable relations that we have presented, along with the cautionary notations,[9] our most important efforts have been to supply you the reader with parallel tables of the comparisons. We have briefly introduced the material to be compared (e.g., date, location, literary focus), focusing on particular books in a collection (e.g., GThom in NHL)

---

5. Derived from Davila, "Perils of Parallelism." Prof. Davila (a DSS scholar) also cites the works of Sandmel, "Parallelomania"; and Smith, *Drudgery Divine*, esp. 51–52. On the ongoing importance of comparative studies in a suspicious post-modern era, see the essays in Patton and Ray, *Magic Still Dwells*.

6. Jonas, *Gnosis and spätaniker Geist*. Goodenough, *Jewish Symbols in the Greco-Roman Period*.

7. MacRae, *Studies in the New Testament and Gnosticism*, 29–30 (from "The Fourth Gospel and Religionsgeschichte," *CBQ* 32 [1970] 13–24).

8. Kysar, *Fourth Evangelist*, 270 (heading C).

9. See the five or six criteria, used earlier, of evaluating intertextual comparisons with compositions that *postdate* the NT period, in our ch. 6. C, pp. 98–100; ch. 7. F, pp. 124–25.

when space permitted it, we commented on the differing literary and cultural contexts with FG, but these efforts have only functioned as a starting point for you, the reader, to further analyze and draw conclusions about the relationship of FG and the given document or tradition to be compared.

Professor George W. MacRae, SJ, observed that the milieu of FG was varied deliberately so as to make the universality and transcendence of the divine son appealing to a wide audience.[10] Our study supports this observation, we have not only learned something about the conceptual worlds of FG, but also discovered the broad readership that FG envisioned and sought to address by its universal and transcendent Christologies. As Gregory of Nazianzus,[11] Cappadocia (ca. 330–390 CE) wrote,

> Matthew wrote the marvels of the Christ for the Jews ['*Ebraiois*], Mark for Italy, Luke for Greece [*Achaidi*], but John, the great herald, the heaven-haunting [*ouranophoitēs*], wrote for all.

We summarize this portrayal of the universal and transcendent son with the following words:

> Jesus of Nazareth is the spoken Word of God at creation, the source of all that came into being. He enjoys a unique relationship with God from the beginning as a son to his father. He is the Revealer of God's wisdom and knowledge from above. Although he was with God, at the beginning, he came in human flesh to bring truth and life to the world. He was enmeshed in the feasts and customs of his people. He embodied the way to God and his discourses astounded those who believed and confounded those who would not. He lived boldly and died bravely for the sake of others. He fulfilled the prophetic writings in obedience to his Father's divine will. Those who trust in the Son will abide forever in God's love just as the Son now abides with God forever.

Given the diverse verbal and thematic associations posited as contexts for understanding the conceptual worlds of FG, our research has raised some noteworthy questions that we have attempted to answer in our study:

---

10. MacRae, *Studies in the New Testament and Gnosticism*, 18, 30–31, and 216–17. On similar reflections, see Frey and Schnelle, *Kontexte*, 35–45; on the broad FG readership, not simply written for the specific needs of a particular Johannine community, see Bauckham, *Gospel for All Christians*; Frey and Schnelle, *Kontexte*, Frey's citing Bauckham on audience, 39n178 and 132n68; and the following work, with essays supporting, qualifying, or contesting Bauckham's position, Klink, *Audience of the Gospels*.

11. His poem on the books of Scripture, St. Gregory of Nazianzus, *Poems of Scripture* (trans. B. Dinkle; St. Vladimir's Press, 2012), 39, from Migne, *Patrologia Graeca*, 37:474. The word *ouranophoitēs* allludes to John's experience in his Patmos vision (cf. Rev 4:1–2).

1. What kind of **audience** was FG addressing? How broad and diverse was it? Was the author responding only to the request of fellow believers with no interest in the general circulation of his gospel?[12] Did the author conceive of himself as the member of a hetero-orthodox sect, separate from the mainstream? Does his writing, instead, reflect a missionizing effort to outsiders?[13] Did the author envision *other* communities reading his work, aside from his own immediate readership? Our study has supported Professor MacRae's contention that the context of FG was varied deliberately so as to make the universality and transcendence of the divine son appealing to a wide audience. Nothing in our study detracts from this idea that FG envisioned a broad audience in the province of Asia and elsewhere in the Roman world.[14]

2. Is it necessary for us to draw sharp distinctions regarding the conceptual worlds of FG? If it is primarily Jewish (*'Ioudaios*), does it necessarily rule out any influence from a non-Jewish (gentile) source? If we have broadly defined our understanding of "Hellenistic Jewish," can we not also define FG's audience as **Jewish and gentile**, from "pagan" as well as Jewish backgrounds? Our study supports the view of a Jewish- and gentile-Christian audience for FG. We cannot exclude one group in favor of the other.

3. How does our study relate to the so-called "**nature vs. nurture**" debate of cultural anthropology?[15] If FG is by "nature" a Jewish document, how much did this writing develop by way of its interaction with the environment that nurtured it? Is FG's identity innate or culturally and socially constructed? How pertinent are these questions based on our assumption (pt. 2, above) of an assimilated Hellenistic Jewish culture where the widespread use of Greek language and contacts between

---

12. John who "was urged by his disciples" wrote a "spiritual gospel," quotation of Clement of Alexandria found in Eusebius, *Eccl. hist.* 6.14.7. The question concerns the debate between Mitchell, "Patristic Counter-Evidence," 36–79, and R. Bauckham, "Is there Patristic Counter-Evidence?" in Klink, *Audience of the Gospels*, 68–110, regarding a specific readership or general audience for the four gospels.

13. See Gorman, *Abide and Go*, esp. ch. 2.

14. See esp. in FG: the universalisms (John 1:3–4) and worldwide mission field (1:9–10, 29; 3:16–17; 4:42; 6:33; 8:12; 12:46–47), the specific appeal of Jesus to the Pharisee Nicodemus (3:1–21), the Samaritans (4:1–45), the "royal official" (4:46–54), "the Greeks" (12:20–21), and his having "other sheep who do not belong to this fold" (10:16). Some of FG's universal and missionizing concerns may be the work of a final editor, although our focus has not been on FG's redaction history.

15. The nature vs. nurture question is raised much earlier in Shakespeare's *Tempest* 4.1 and Chretien de Tryoe's *Perceval*, see Ceci and Williams, *Nature-Nurture Debate*.

Greeks and non-Greeks were not unusual in the Roman world?[16] FG was written for and belongs to Jewish and non-Jewish Christ followers.

4. Is the argument with the most bullet points, the most plausible one? See D. R. MacDonald's **criterion of density** (ch. 8, tbl. D., p. 142, pt. 3). Is NT studies more scientific than aesthetic? Is it more of a learned art of theorizing and reflecting, than it is a scientific enterprise of organizing data? How much consideration has been given regarding our own presuppositions and ideology in such a comparative study? We have left the reader to draw his or her own conclusions on the data that we have presented.

5. The focus of narrative- and reader-response criticisms on the world of the text "before us" is an important area of study, but what prevents these approaches from making the text communicate only what the final reader wants it to communicate? Is not the world "of the text" and **the world "behind the text"** just as important when reading an ancient document? Can we afford to read the text in "splendid isolation" from other related documents of antiquity? Despite our careful analysis of the "text before us," what do we bring to the text aside from our own modern conceptions? This study has attempted to fill some lacuna regarding the conceptual worlds that are closest to that of FG.

6. What is more important: scholarly consensus or **renewed interpretive possibilities?** Does our long familiarity with a book like FG cause us to be more "set in our ways" regarding its interpretation or more open to different ways of viewing it? For example, Chris Skinner, by means of narrative criticism, has challenged certain scholarly notions of traditions in conflict (regarding GThom and FG). We hope that returning to these comparisons of FG with other relevant literature has opened more contextualized interpretative possibilities.

7. What is the most meaningful **"so what" factor** when we look at verbal and thematic parallels? What are we attempting to accomplish in our comparisons? How does "the *intention* behind the comparison determines its outcome?" Do our comparisons contribute to a *better* interpretation of FG?[17] We hope that our readers can draw their own conclusions here.

---

16. S. E. Porter prefers "Judaism within Hellenism," in his "The Context of Jesus," in Holmén and Porter, *Handbook for the Study of the Historical Jesus*, 2:1456, 1461.

17. Our trans. of the first quote "die hinter dem Vergleich stehende Intention sein Ergebnis bestimmt," in Seelig, *Religionsgeschichtliche*, 262, and our trans. of Seelig's concluding remark: "alles, was er tut, um einer sachgemäßen Auslegung des Neuen Testaments willen tut: Alle Wege und notwendigen Umwege bekommen erst dann

8. Because LXX OT influences in FG are determinative, must we stop there in our search for parallels and comparisons? Do these LXX writings alone provide compelling parallels to FG? Did FG draw *only* on these sources for its composition, and no others? It appears to many that FG has made creative and distinctive use of these sources (oral and written). Was FG's *selection and use* of the LXX, for example, influenced, in some way, by the DSS, Philo, and other ancient writings? How or why did FG interpret the LXX in this *particular* way? Were there any **other influences on FG**, direct or indirect, to *explain* its creative and distinctive approach to the OT (broadly defined) and especially the life and teachings of Jesus? If so, how and why? What can explain FG's *particular* tendencies, views, and nuances of expression (if explanations can be found). We hope our study has answered some of these questions.

9. Greek Lexical research, e.g., is replete with **parallel language examples** from LXX, Greek classical and Hellenistic sources, and Greek patristics. What criteria do we employ, aside from what the lexicographer recommends, to determine the best rendering of a word? If we are eclectic in our lexical choices, why are we usually not that way in our study of FG's conceptual worlds? Some of the criteria of evaluation that we have used will be helpful here (see our ch. 6. C, pp. 98–100; ch. 7. F, 124–25).

10. In our comparisons, how much is presupposed regarding introductory matters (date, place of writing, authorship, purpose)? Introductory questions are more easily answered with sufficient data that best fit the culture, history, and ideology of the book in question. How much weight should be given to the type of data employed (lexical, verbal, thematic), how it is used, and the forcefulness of the stated argumentation. **What makes the comparisons compelling?** We have favored a more comprehensive and inclusive approach in our study. What part does the reader play in the mix? Jean Zumstein[18] concludes

> Reading FG as an intertext puts a premium on the competence of the readers. The text's meaning is not a set, immanent element to be discovered and worked out through exegesis, but emerges through a dialect interplay between what Umberto Eco calls the *intention operis* and *intentio lectoris* (1992, 19–47).

---

einen Sinne, wenn er davon etwas mitbringen kann, das zu diesem Ziel beiträgt," 335.

18. Zumstein, "Intratextuality and Intertextuality," 135. The citation regarding the intention of the work and intention of the reader is from Eco, *Limits of Interpretation*, 35–52, see esp. 50–54.

FG's ideal narrative and authorial audience both share a common culture, history, and ideology.[19] In our comparisons of FG with similar and analogous conceptions of late antiquity, it is our hope that we, as contemporary readers, have broadened the context of interpretation for FG and made some progress toward learning and adopting the perspective of FG's ideal author and audience for a better understanding of this NT text.

---

19. On what can be assumed of FG's ideal narrative and authorial audience, see Culpepper, *Anatomy of the Fourth Gospel*, 208. We hope that we have shown that *more* than a general understanding of first-century Jewish customs, the gospel story, and the LXX can be assumed. Also, despite the chronological challenges, later works of antiquity (e.g., rabbinica, Hag Hammadi) are able to capture some first-century understandings of FG and its audience that may not be found in second temple sources (e.g., LXX, Philo, DSS).

Bibliography

Abbreviations for journals (*JBL*, *NTS*), periodicals (BA), major reference works (*NIDB*), and series (LCL, NIGTC) follow those of *The SBL Handbook of Style: for Biblical Studies and Related Disciplines*, 2nd ed., B. J. Collins et al.; Atlanta, GA: SBL Press, 2014; and also *The Chicago Manual of Style*, 15th ed; Chicago: University of Chicago Press, 2003. On the use of particles before Ger. and Dutch names (e.g., von, Van), we follow *CMOS*, 8.12–13.

Aageson, James W. "Lectionary." In *AYBD* 4:270–71.
Abegg, Martin, Jr., et al., trans. and eds. *The Dead Sea Scrolls*. San Francisco: HarperSanFrancisco, 2005.
Abegg, Martin, Jr., et al., trans. and eds. *The Dead Sea Scrolls Bible*. New York: Harper Collins, 1999.
Aland, Barbara, et al., eds. *The Greek New Testament*. 4th rev. ed. Stuttgart: Deutsche Bibelgesellschaft, 1994.
———. *Novum Testamentum Graece*. 28th rev. ed. Stuttgart: Bibelgesellschaft, 2012.
Aland, Kurt, ed. *Synopsis Quattuor Evangeliorum*. 12th ed. Stuttgart: German Bible Society, 1983.
———. *Synopsis of the Four Gospels. A Greek-English Ed. of the Synopsis Quattuor Evangeliorum*. 6th rev. ed. New York: United Bible Societies, 1983.
Aland, Kurt, et al., eds. *The Greek New Testament*. 4th rev. ed. Peabody, MA: Hendrickson, 2011.
Albl, Martin C. *"And Scripture Cannot Be Broken": The Form and Function of the Early Christian Testimonia Collections*. NovT Suppl. Series 96. Boston and Leiden: Brill, 1999.
Alexander, P. S. "Targum, Targumim." In *AYBD* 6:320–21.
Alter, Robert, and Frank Kermode, eds. *The Literary Guide to the Bible*. Cambridge: Belknap Press at Harvard University Press, 1990.
Amidon, Philip R., trans. *The Panarion of Epiphanius Bishop of Salamis: Selected Passages*. New York: Oxford University Press, 1990.
Amir, Yehoshua. "Authority and Interpretation of Scripture in the Writing of Philo." In *Mikra: Text, Tranlsation, Reading and Interpretation of the Hebrew Bible in Ancient Judaism and Early Christianity*, edited by Martin Jan Mulder and Harry Sysling, 421–53. Assen: Van Gorcum, 1988.
Anderson, Paul N. "Bakhtin's Dialogism and the Corrective Rhetoric of the Johannine Misunderstanding Dialogue: Exposing Seven Crises in the Johannine Situation." In *Bakhtin and Genre in Biblical Studies*, edited by Roland Boer, 133–59. Semeia 63. Atlanta: SBL, 2007.

———. *Christology of the Fourth Gospel: Its Unity and Disunity in the Light of John 6.* Repr. Eugene, OR: Cascade, 2010.

———. *The Fourth Gospel and the Quest for Jesus: Modern Foundations Reconsidered.* London: T. & T. Clark, 2006.

———. "The Johannine Logos-Hymn: A Cross-Cultural Celebration of God's Creative-Redemptive Work." In *Creation Stories in Dialogue: The Bible, Science, and Folk Traditions: Radboud Prestige Lectures by R. Alan Culpepper*, edited by R. Alan Culpepper and Jan van der Watt, 219–42. Leiden: Brill Academic, 2015.

———. "John and Qumran: Discovery and Interpretation over Sixty Years." In *John, Qumran, and the Dead Sea Scrolls: Sixty Years of Discovery and Debate*, edited by Mary Coloe and Tom Thatcher, 15–50. Atlanta: SBL, 2011.

———. *The Riddles of the Fourth Gospel: An Introduction to the Gospel of John.* Minneapolis: Fortress, 2011.

———. "The Son of Zebedee and the Fourth Gospel: Some Clues to John's Authorship and the State of the Johannine Question." https://www.academia.edu/28253466/_The_Son_of_Zebedee_and_the_Fourth_Gospel_Some_Clues_to_Johns_Authorship_and_the_State_of_the_Johannine_Question_.

Anderson, Paul N., et al., eds. *John, Jesus, and History, Volume 2: Aspects of Historicity in the Fourth Gospel.* SBL Symposium Series 44. Atlanta: SBL, 2009.

Anderson, R. Dean, Jr. *Glossary of Greek Rhetorical Terms Connected to Methods of Argumentation, Figures and Tropes from the Anximenes to Quintillian.* CBET 24. Leuven: Peters, 2000.

Anderson, Robert T. "Samaritans." In *NIDB* 5:75–82.

Anderson, Robert T., and Terry Giles. *The Samaritan Pentateuch: An Introduction to Its Origin, History, and Significance for Biblical Studies.* Resources for Biblical Study. Atlanta: SBL, 2012.

———. *Tradition Kept: The Literature of The Samaritans.* Peabody, MA: Hendrickson, 2005.

Archer, Gleason L., and Chirichigno, Gregory. *Old Testament Quotations in the New Testament.* Eugene, OR: Wipf & Stock, 2005.

Arnim, Hans von. *Stoicorum Veterum Fragmenta.* 4 vols. Leipzig: Teubner, 1902–1904. Repr. Eugene, OR: Wipf and Stock, 2016.

Arrowsmith, William, trans. *The Bacchae.* In *Euripides V: Electra, The Phoenician Women, The Bacchae. The Complete Greek Tragedies*, edited by David Grene and Richard Lattimore, 11–84. Chicago: University of Chicago Press, 1959.

Ascough, Richard S., et al. *Associations in the Greco-Roman World: A Sourcebook.* Waco, TX: Baylor University Press, 2012.

Asgeirsson, Jon Ma, et al., eds. *From Quest to Q: Festschrift James M. Robinson.* BETL 147. Leuven: Leuven University Press, 2000.

Ashton, John. *Discovering John: Essays by John Ashton.* Edited by C. Rowland and K. H. Williams. Eugene, OR: Cascade, 2020.

———. *The Gospel of John and Christian Origins.* Minneapolis: Fortress, 2014.

———. *The Interpretation of John.* Issues in Religion and Theology 9. Philadelphia: Fortress, 1986.

———. *Understanding the Fourth Gospel.* 2nd ed. Oxford: Oxford University Press, 2009.

Attridge, Harold W. "An Emotional Jesus and Stoic Traditions." In *Stoicism in Early Christianity*, edited by Tuomas Rasimus et al., 77–92. Peabody, MA: Hendrickson, 2010.

———. *Essays on John and Hebrews*. Grand Rapids: Baker, 2012.
———. *First-Century Cynicism in the Epistles of Heraclitus*. Introduction, Greek Text and Translation by the author. Harvard Theological Studies 29. Missoula, MT: Scholars, 1976.
———. "Genre Bending in the Fourth Gospel." *JBL* 121/1 (2002) 3–21.
———. *History, Theology, and Narrative Rhetoric in the Fourth Gospel*. The Père Marquette Lecture Series. Mikwaukee: Marquette University Press, 2019.
———. "Plato, Plutarch, and John: Three Symposia on Love." In *Beyond the Gnostic Gospels: Studies Building on the Work of Elaine Pagels*, edited by Eduard Iricinschi et al., 367–78. STAC 82. Tübingen: Mohr Siebeck, 2013.
———."'Seeking' and 'Asking,' in Q, Thomas, and John." In *From Quest to Q: Festschrift James M. Robinson*, edited by Jon Ma Asgeirsson et al., 295–302. BETL 147. Leuven: Leuven University Press, 2000.
———."Three Symposia on Love." In *Beyond Gnostic Gospels*, edited by E. Iriscinschi et al., 367–78. Mohr Siebeck, 2013.
Attridge, Harold W., and Gohei Hata, eds. *Eusebius, Christianity, and Judaism*. Detroit: Wayne State University Press, 1992.
Audi, Robert, ed. *Cambridge Dictionary of Philosophy*. 2nd ed. Cambridge: Cambridge University Press, 1999.
Aune, David E. "Dualism in the Fourth Gospel and the Dead Sea Scrolls: A Reassessment of the Problem." In *Neotestamentica et Philonica: Studies in Honor of Peder Borgen*, edited by David E. Aune et al., 281–303. NovTSup 106. Leiden: Brill, 2003.
———. *The New Testament in its Literary Environment*. Philadelphia: Westminster, 1987.
———. *Revelation*. 3 vols. WBC 52. Nashville: Thomas Nelson; Grand Rapids: Zondervan, 1997—1998.
———. *The Westminster Dictionary of New Testament and Early Christian Literature and Rhetoric*. Louisville: Westminster John Knox, 2003.
Bailey, James L., and Lyle D. Vander Broek. *Literary Forms in the New Testament: A Handbook*. Louisville: Westminster John Knox, 1992.
Baird, William. *History of New Testament Research, Vol. 1. From Deism to Tübingen*. Minneapolis: Fortress, 1992.
———. *History of New Testament Research, Vol. 2. From Jonathan Edwards to Rudolf Bultmann*. Minneapolis: Fortress, 2002.
———. *History of New Testament Research, Vo. 3, From C. H. Dodd to Hans Dieter Betz*. Minneapolis: Fortress, Press, 2013.
Bakhtin, Mikhail M. *The Dialogic Imagination: Four Essays*. University of Texas Slavic Series. Translated by Michael Holmquist and Caryl Emerson. Austin: University of Texas, 1981.
———. *Rabelais and His World*. Translated by Helen Iswolsky. Bloomington: Indiana University Press, 1984.
Barclay, John M. G., and Benjamin G. White, eds. *The New Testament in Comparison: Validity, Method, and Purpose in Comparing Traditions*. LNTS 600. London: T. & T. Clark, 2020.
Barclay, John, and John Sweet, eds. *Early Christian Thought in its Jewish Context*. Festschrift in Honour of Morna Hooker's 65th Birthday. Cambridge: Cambridge University Press, 1996.
Barr, James. *Biblical Words for Time*. London: SCM, 1962.

———. "Common Sense and Biblical Language." *Biblica* 49 (1968) 377–87.
———. *Semantics of Biblical Language*. Oxford: Oxford University Press, 1961.
Barrett, Charles K. *Essays on John*. Louisville: Westminster John Knox, 1982.
———. *The Gospel According to St. John*. 2nd ed. London: SPCK, 1978.
———. *New Testament Background: Selected Documents: Revised and Expanded Edition*. New York: HarperOne, 1989.
———. "The Old Testament in the Fourth Gospel." *JTS* 48 (1947) 155–69.
Bartlett, John. *Bartlett's Familiar Quotations*. 14th ed. Boston: Little, Brown, 1968.
Bauckham, Richard. *Gospel of Glory: Major Themes in Johannine Theology*. Grand Rapids: Baker, 2015.
———. *Jesus and the Eyewitnesses: The Gospels as Eyewitness Testimony*. 2nd ed. Grand Rapids: Eerdmans, 2017.
———. "The Qumran Community and the Gospel of John." In *Dead Sea Scrolls Fifty Years after Their Discovery*, edited by L. H. Schiffman et al., 105–15. Jerusalem: Israel Exploration Society/Shrine of the Book, Israel Museum, 2000.
———. *The Testimony of the Beloved Disciple: Narrative, History, and Theology in the Gospel of John*. Grand Rapids: Baker Academic, 2007.
———, ed. *The Gospels for All Christians: Rethinking the Gospel Audiences*. NT Studies. Grand Rapids: Eerdmans, 1997.
Bauckham, Richard, and Carl Mosser, eds. *The Gospel of John and Christian Theology*. Grand Rapids: Eerdmans, 2008.
Bauer, Walter. *Orthodoxy and Heresy in Earliest Christianity*. Translated by Robert A. Kraft and Gerhard Krodel. Philadelphia: Fortress, 1971.
———, et al., eds. *A Greek-English Lexicon of the New Testament and Other Early Christian Literature*. Rev. and ed. by W. F. Danker. 3rd ed. Chicago: University of Chicago Press, 2000.
Beale, G. K. *The Book of Revelation*. The New International Greek Testament Commentary. Grand Rapids: Eerdmans, 1999.
Beale, G. K., and D. A. Carson, eds. *Commentary on the New Testament Use of the Old Testament*. Grand Rapids: Baker Academic, 2007.
Beasley-Murray, George R. *John*. WBC 36. 2nd ed. Grand Rapids: Zondervan Academic, 1999.
Becker, Heinz. *Die Reden des Johannesevangelums und der Stil der gnostischen Offenbarungsrede*. Göttingen: Vandenhoeck & Ruprecht, 1956.
Becker, Michael. "Zeichen: Die johanneische Wunderterminologie und die frürabbinische Tradition." In *Kontexte des Johannesevangeliums: Das vierte Evangelium in religions-und traditionsgeschichtlicher Perspective*, edited by Jörg Frey and Udo Schnelle, 233–76. WUNT 175. Tübingen: Mohr Siebeck, 2004.
Bell, Albert A., Jr. *Exploring the New Testament World*. Nashville: Thomas Nelson, 1998.
Bergman, Jan. *Ich bin Isis. Studien zum mephtitischen Hintergrund der griechischen Isisaretalogien*. Uppsala: Almqvist and Wiksell, 1968.
Betz, Hans Dieter. *The Greek Magical Papyri in Translation, including the Demotic Spells*, Vol. 1. 2nd ed. Chicago: University of Chicago Press, 1992.
Beutler, Johannes. "The Use of 'Scripture' in the Gospel of John." In *Exploring the Gospel of John: In Honor of D. Moody Smith*, edited by R. Alan Culpepper and C. Clifton Black, 147–62. Louisville: Westminster John Knox, 1996.
Beutler, Johannes, and Robert T. Fortna, eds. *The Shepherd Discourse of John 10 and Its Context*. SNTSMS 67. Cambridge: Cambridge University Press, 1991.

Bianchi, Ugo, ed. *The Origins of Gnosticism / Le origini dello gnosticismo: Colloquium of Messina, 13–18 April 1966*. Texts and Discussions. Numen Book 12. Leiden: Brill Academic, 1970, 1997.

Bieringer, Didier Pollefeyt, and F. Vandcasteele-Vanneuville, eds. *Anti-Judaism and the Fourth Gospel*. Louisville: Westminster John Knox, 2001.

Birnbaum, Ellen. "Philo of Alexandria." In *NIDB* 4:512–13.

Bishop, Eric F. F. "Angelology in Judaism, Christianity and Islam." *ATR* 46 (1964) 142–54.

Black, Matthew. *An Aramaic Approach to Gospels and Acts*. 3rd ed. Repr. Peabody, MA: Hendrickson, 1998.

Blackman, Philip. *Mishnayoth: Pointed Hebrew Text, English Translation, Introductions, Notes, Supplement*. 7 Vols. New York: Judaica, 1964.

Blackwell, Ben C., ed. *Reading Revelation in Context: John's Apocalypse and Second Temple Judaism*. Grand Rapids: Zondervan, 2019.

Blass, Friedrich W., and Albert Debrunner. *A Greek Grammar of the New Testament and Other Early Christian Literature*. Trans. and rev. by Robert. W. Funk with supplementary notes of A. Debrunner. Chicago: University of Chicago Press, 1961.

Boers, Hendrikus. "Religionsgeschichtliche Schule." Pages 383–87 in *Dictionary of Biblical Interpretation*. Vol. 2. John H. Hayes, ed. Nashville: Abingdon, 1999.

Bóid, Ruairidh (M. N. Saraf). "Use, Authority and Exegesis of Mikra in the Samaritan Tradition." In *Mikra: Texts, Translations, Reading and Interpretation of the Hebrew Bible in Ancient Judaism and Early Christianity*, edited by Martin Jan Mulder, and Harry Sysling, 595–633. Repr. Peabody, MA: Hendrickson, 2004.

Bonner, Campbell. *The Homily on the Passion by Melito Bishop of Sardis and Some Fragments of the Apocryphal Ezekiel*. London: Christophers, 1940.

Borgen, Peder. *Bread from Heaven: An Exegetical Study of the Concept of Manna in the Gospel of John and the Writings of Philo*. Johannine Monograph Series. Repr. Eugene, OR: Wipf and Stock, 2017.

———. "God's Agent in the Fourth Gospel." In *The Interpretation of John*, edited by John Ashton, 67–78. Issues in Religion and Theology 9. Philadelphia: Fortress, 1986.

———. *The Gospel of John: More Light from Philo, Paul and Archaeology. The Scriptures, Tradition, Exposition, Settings, Meaning*. NovTSup 154. Leiden and Boston: Brill, 2014.

———. "Logos Was the True Light." In *Composition of John's Gospel*, edited by D. E. Orton, 107–22. Leiden: Brill, 1999.

———. "Philo of Alexandria." In *AYBD* 5:533–42.

———. *Philo of Alexandria: An Exegete For His Time*. NovTSup 86. Leiden: Brill, 1997.

———, et al. *The Philo Index: A Complete Greek Word Index to the Writings of Philo of Alexandria*. Grand Rapids: Eerdmans, 2000.

Boring, M. Eugene, et al., eds. *Hellenistic Commentary to the New Testament*. Nashville: Abingdon, 1995.

Boustan, Ra'anan. "Hekhalot Literature." In Collins and Harlow, *Early Judaism*, 719–21.

Bousset, Wilhelm. *Hauptprobleme der Gnosis*. Göttingen: Vandenhoeck & Ruprecht, 1907.

Bowman, John, trans. and ed. *Samaritan Documents: Relating to their History, Religion, and Life*. Pittsburgh Original Tests and Translations. Repr. Eugene, OR: Pickwick, 2009.

———. *The Samaritan Problem: Studies in the Relationships of Samaritanism, Judaism, and Early Christianity.* Translated by Alfred M. Johnson Jr. Pittsburgh Theological Monograph Series 4. Repr. Eugene, OR: Pickwick, 2008.

———. "Samaritan Studies." *BJRL* 40 (March, 1958) 298–327.

Boyarin, Daniel. *Border Lines: The Partition of Judaeo-Christianity. Divinations: Rereading Late Ancient Religion.* Philadelphia: University of Pennsylvania, 2004.

———. "The Gospel of the Memra: Jewish Binitarianism and the Prologue to John." *HTR* 94 (2001) 243–84.

———. *Intertextuality and the Reading of the Midrash.* Repr. Eugene, OR: Wipf & Stock, 2001.

———. "Logos, A Jewish Word: John's Prologue as Midrash." In *The Jewish Annotated New Testament: NRSV*, edited by Amy-Jill Levine and Marc Zvi Brettler, 546–49. New York: Oxford University Press, 2011.

Bradshaw, Paul F., et al. *The Apostolic Tradition: A Commentary.* Hermeneia. Minneapolis: Fortress, 2002.

Brakke, David. *The Gnostics: Myth, Ritual, and Diversity in Early Christianity.* Cambridge, MA: Harvard University Press, 2010.

Brannan, Rick, trans. *Apostolic Fathers in English: A New Translation.* Bellingham, WA: Lexham, 2012.

Brant, Jo-Ann. *Dialogue and Drama: Elements of Greek Tragedy in the Fourth Gospel.* Peabody, MA: Hendrickson, 2004.

———. *John.* Paideia: Commentaries on the NT. Grand Rapids: Baker Academic, 2011.

———. Review of *The Dionysian Gospel* by Dennis R. MacDonald. *SBL Review of Biblical Literature* 3 (2018). https://www.bookreviews.org/pdf/11778_13140.pdf.

Bratcher, Robert G. ed. *Old Testament Quotations in the New Testament.* Helps for Translators 3. London: United Bible Societies, 1961.

Braun, Herbert. *Qumran und das Neue Testament.* 2 vols. Tübingen: Mohr Siebeck, 1966.

Bremmer, J. N. *Initiation into the Mysteries.* Berlin: de Gruyter, 2014.

Brent, Allen. *Hippolytus and the Roman Church.* Leiden: Brill, 1995.

Breytenbach, C., and H. Paulsen, eds. *Anfänge der Christologie: Festschrift für Ferdinand Hahn zum 65. Geburtstag* Göttingen: Vandenhoeck & Ruprecht, 1991.

Brodie, Thomas L. *The Gospel according to John: A Literary and Theological Commentary.* Oxford: Oxford University Press, 1993.

———. *Quest for Origins.* Oxford: Oxford University Press, 1993.

Broer, Ingo. "Das Weinwunder zu Kana (John 2.1–11) und die Weinwunder der Antike." In *Das Urchristentum in seiner literarischen Geschichte*, edited by Ulrich Mell and Ulrich B. Müller, 91–308. BZNW 100. Berlin: deGruyter, 1999.

Brooke, A. E. *The Commentary of Origen on St. John's Gospel. Texts Revised with Critical Notes and Indices.* 2 vols. Cambridge: Cambridge University Press, 1896.

———. *The Fragments of Heracleon.* Texts and Studies 1.4. Cambridge: Cambridge University Press, 1891.

Brooke, George J. "Dead Sea Scrolls." *NIDB* 2:52–63.

———. *The Dead Sea Scrolls and the New Testament.* Minneapolis: Fortress, 2005.

———. "Isaiah 40:3 and the Wilderness Community." In *New Qumran Texts and Studies*, edited by George Brooke and Florentino García Martínez, 117–32. Leiden: Brill, 1994.

Brown, Ian Phillip. "Where Indeed Was the Gospel of Thomas Written? Thomas in Alexandria." *JBL* 138 (2019) 451–72.

Brown, Raymond E. *The Community of the Beloved Disciple: The Life, Loves and Hates of an Individual Church in New Testament Times.* New York: Paulist, 1979.

———. "The Date of the Last Supper." *TBT* 11 (1964) 727–33.

———. *Death of the Messiah. From Gethsemane to the Grave, Volume 1: A Commentary on the Passion Narratives in the Four Gospels.* AYB Reference Library. New Haven, CT: Yale University Press, 1994.

———. *The Epistles of John. A New Translation with Introduction and Commentary* AYB 30. New Haven, CT: Yale University Press, 1982.

———. *The Gospel according to John I–XII. A New Translation with Introduction and Commentary.* AYB 29. New Haven, CT: Yale University Press, 1970.

———. *The Gospel according to John XIII–XXI. A New Translation with Introduction and Commentary.* AYB 29. New Haven, CT: Yale University Press, 1966.

———. "The Gospel of Thomas and Saint John's Gospel." *NTS* 9 (1962–1963) 155–77.

———. *New Testament Essays.* New York: Doubleday, 1965.

Brown, Raymond E., et al., eds. *The New Jerome Biblical Commentary.* Englewood, Cliffs, NJ: Prentice Hall, 1990.

Brown, Raymond E., and Francis J. Moloney. *An Introduction to the Gospel of John.* Anchor Yale Bible Reference Library. New Haven, CT: Yale, 2003.

Brox, Norbert. "'Doketismus—eine Problemanzeige.'" *ZKG* 95 (1984) 301–14.

Bruce, F. F. *The Canon of Scripture.* Downers Grove, IL: IVP Academic, 1988.

———. *The Gospel and Epistles of John.* Grand Rapids: Eerdmans, 1983.

———. *Jesus and Early Christian Origins.* Grand Rapids: Eerdmans, 1974.

Buchanan, George W. "Samaritan Origin of John." In *Religions in Antiquity: Essays in Memory of Erwin Ramsdell Goodenough,* edited by Jacob Neusner, 149–75. Leiden: Brill, 1968.

Bultmann, Rudolf. "Ein jüdisch-christliches Psalmbuch aus dem ersten Jahrhundert." *Monatsschrift für Pastoraltheologie* 7 (1910) 23–29.

———. *Exegetica: Aufsatze Zur Erforschung Des Neuen Testaments.* Edited by Erich Dinkler. Tübingen: Mohr Siebeck, 1967.

———. *The Gospel of John: A Commentary.* Translated by George Beasley-Murray et al. Translated from the 1964 printing of *Das Evangelium des Johannes* (with the Supplement of 1966). Göttingen: Vandenhoeck & Ruprecht. Philadelphia: Westminster, 1971.

———. "The History of the Religious Background of the Prologue of the Gospel of John." In *The Interpretation of John,* translated by John Ashton, 18–35. Issues in Religion and Theology 9. Philadelphia: Fortress, 1986.

———. *The History of the Synoptic Tradition.* Translated by John Marsh. Repr. Peabody, MA: Hendrickson, 1994.

———. *Primitive Christianity in Its Contemporary Setting.* Translated by R. H. Fuller. Cleveland: World Publishing, 1956.

Burkert, Walter. *Ancient Mystery Cults.* Cambridge, MA: Harvard University Press, 1987.

———. *Greek Religion.* Translated by Johon Raffan. Cambridge, MA: Harvard University Press, 1985.

Burnett, D. Clint. *Studying the New Testament through Inscriptions: An Introduction.* Peabody, MA: Hendrickson, 2020.

Burney, C. F. *The Aramaic Origin of the Fourth Gospel.* Oxford: Clarendon, 1922. Repr. India: Pranava.

Burridge, Richard A. *Four Gospels, One Jesus? A Symbolic Reading*. 3rd ed. Grand Rapids: Eerdmans, 2014.

———. *Imitating Jesus: An Inclusive Approach to New Testament Ethics*. Grand Rapids: Eerdmans, 2007.

———. *What Are the Gospels? A Comparison with Graeco-Roman Biography*. A Twenty-fifth Anniversary Edition. Waco, TX: Baylor University Press, 2018.

Buttrick, George A., ed. *The Interpreter's Dictionary of the Bible*. Nashville: Abingdon, 1962.

Bynum, William. R. *The Fourth Gospel and the Scriptures: Illuminating the Form and Meaning of Scriptural Citation In John 19:37*. Leiden and Boston: Brill, 2012.

———. "Quotations of Zechariah." In *Abiding Words: The Use of Scripture in the Gospel of John*, edited by Alicia D. Myers and B. G. Schuchard, 47–74. Atlanta: SBL, 2015.

Cameron, Ron. "The Gospel of Thomas and Christian Origins." In *The Future of Early Christianity: Essays in honor of Helmut Koester*, edited by Birger Pearson, 381–92. Minneapolis: Fortress, 1991.

———. "Thomas, Gospel of." In *AYBD* 6:535.

Campenhausen, Hans von. *Griechische Kirchenväter*. Stuttgart: Kohlhammer, 1955.

Caragounis, Chrys C. *The Development of Greek and the New Testament: Morphology, Syntax, Phonology, and Textual Transmission*. WUNT 167. Tübingen: Mohr Siebeck, 2004.

———. "The *Weltanschauung* of the New Testament Authors." In *The Press of the Text: Biblical Studies in Honor of James W. Voelz*, edited by Andrew H. Bartelt et al., 46–66. Eugene, OR: Pickwick, 2017.

Carmignac, Jean. "Les affinités qumrâniennes de la onzième Ode de Salomon." *RevQ* 3 (1961) 71–102.

Carson, D. A. *The Gospel According to John*. PNTC. Grand Rapids: Eerdmans, 1991.

Carter, Warren. *John: Storyteller, Interpreter, Evangelist*. Peabody, MA: Hendrickson, 2006.

Cartlidge, David R., and David L. Dungan, eds. *Documents for the Study of the Gospels*. 3rd ed. Minneapolis: Fortress, 2015.

Cassidy, Richard J. *John's Gospel in New Perspective*. Maryknoll, NY: Orbis, 1992.

Ceci, Stephen J., and Wendy M. Williams, eds. *The Nature-Nurture Debate: The Essential Readings*. Essential Readings in Developmental Psychology. Oxford: Blackwell, 1999.

Celsus. *Celsus on the True Doctrine: A Discourse against the Christians*. Translated by R. Joseph Hoffmann. Oxford: Oxford University Press, 1987.

Chadwick, H. "A Latin Epitome of Melito's Homily on the Pascha." *JTS* NS 11 (1960) 76–82.

Charlesworth, James H. *The Beloved Disciple: Whose Witness Validates the Gospel of John?* Philadelphia: TPI, 1995.

———. *The Bible and the Dead Sea Scrolls, Vol. 2: The Dead Sea Scrolls and the Qumran Community*. The Second Princeton Symposium on Judaism and Christian Origins. Waco, TX: Baylor University Press, 2006.

———. *The Bible and the Dead Sea Scrolls, Vol. 3: The Scrolls and Christian Origins*. The Second Princeton Symposium on Judaism and Christian Origins. Waco, TX: Baylor University Press, 2006.

———. *The Dead Sea Scrolls: Hebrew, Aramaic, and Greek Texts with English Translations*. Westminster Knox, 1994.

———. *Graphic Concordance to the Dead Sea Scrolls*. Tübingen: Mohr Siebeck, 1991.
———. "A History of Pseudepigrapha Research: The Re-Emerging Importance of the Pseudepigrapha." *ANRW* II 19 (1979) 54–88.
———. *Jesus as Mirrored in John: The Genius in the New Testament*. London: Bloomsbury Academic, 2019.
———. "Odes—Not Gnostic." *CBQ* 31 (1969) 357–69.
———, ed. *The Bible and the Dead Sea Scrolls, Vol. 1: Scripture and the Scrolls*. The Second Princeton Symposium on Judaism and Christian Origins. Waco, TX: Baylor University Press, 2006.
———, ed. *John and the Dead Sea Scrolls*. Christian Origins Library. New York: Crossroad, 1990.
———, ed. *The Messiah: Developments in Earliest Judaism and Christianity*. First Princeton Symposium on Judaism and Christian Origins. Minneapolis: Fortress, 1992.
———, ed. *The Odes of Solomon*. Pseudepigrapha 7. Missoula, MT: Scholars, 1978.
———, ed. *The Old Testament Pseudepigrapha, Vol. 1: Apocalyptic Literature and Testaments* Repr. Peabody, MA: Hendrickson, 2010.
———, ed. *The Old Testament Pseudepigrapha, Vol. 2: Expansions of the Old Testament and Legends, Wisdom and Philosophical Literature, Prayers, Psalms, and Odes, Fragments of Lost Judeo-Hellenistic works*. Repr. Peabody, MA: Hendrickson, 2010.
Charlesworth, James H., et al. *Qumran Messianism: Studies in the Messianic Expectations in the Dead Sea Scrolls*. Tübingen: Mohr Siebeck, 1998.
Charlesworth, James H., and Peter Pokorný, ed. *Jesus Research: An International Perspective. The First Princeton Prague Symposium on Jesus Research. Prague 2005*. Grand Rapids: Eerdmans, 2009.
Chatman, Semour. *Story and Discourse* Ithaca, NY: Cornell University Press, 1978.
Chester, Andrew. *Divine Revelation and Divine Titles in the Pentateuchal Targumim*. Tübingen: J. C. B. Mohr [Paul Siebeck], 1986.
Chilton, Bruce D. *A Galilean Rabbi and His Bible: Jesus Use of the Interpreted Scriptures of His Time*. Repr. Eugene, OR: Wipf & Stock, 2013.
———. *The Glory of Israel: The Theology and Provenance of the Isaiah Targum*. JSOT. Sheffield: Sheffield Academic, 1983.
Chilton, Bruce D., and Craig A. Evans. *Studying the Historical Jesus: Evaluations of the State of Current Research*. NTTS 19. Leiden: Brill 1994.
Cicero. *Cicero: De Senectute, De Amicitia, De Divinatione*. Translated by William A. Falconer. Cambridge, MA: Harvard University Press, 1946.
Claasens, J. "Biblical Theology as Dialogue." *JBL* 122 (2003) 127–44.
Clark, K., and M. Holquist. *Mikhail Bakhtin*. Cambridge, MA: Harvard University Press, 1984.
Claussen, Carsten. "Turning Water to Wine: Re-reading the Miracle of the Wedding at Cana." In *Jesus Research: An International Perspective: The First Princeton Prague Symposium on Jesus Research. Prague 2005*, edited by James H. Charlesworth and Petr Pokorný, 78–97. Grand Rapids: Eerdmans, 2009.
Clement of Alexandria. *Clement of Alexandria: Exhortation to the Greeks, The Rich Man's Salvation, and To the Newly Baptized*. Translated by G. W. Butterworth. LCL. Cambridge, MA: Harvard University Press, 1953.
Coggins, Richard J. *Samaritans and Jews: Origins of Samaritanism Reconsidered*. Growing Points in Theology. Atlanta: John Knox, 1975.

Coggins, Richard J., and J. L. Houlden, eds. *Dictionary of Biblical Interpretation.* London: SCM, 1990.

Cohen, Shaye J. D. *From the Maccabees to the Mishnah.* Library of Early Christianity 7. Louisville: Westminster John Knox, 1988.

———. "The Significance of Yavneh: Pharisees, Rabbis, and the End of Jewish Sectarianism." *HUCA (Hebrew Union College Annual)* 55 (1984) 27–53.

Collins, B. J., et al., eds. *SBL Handbook of Style.* Atlanta: SBL, 2014.

Collins, John J. *Between Athens and Jerusalem: Jewish Identity in the Hellenistic Diaspora.* The Biblical Resource Series. 2nd ed. Grand Rapids: Eerdmans, 2000.

———. *Beyond the Qumran Community: The Sectarian Movement of the Dead Sea Scrolls.* Grand Rapids: Eerdmans, 2010.

———. *Jewish Cult and Hellenistic Culture: Essays on the Jewish Encounter with Hellenism and Roman Rule.* Leiden: Brill, 2005.

———. *Jewish Wisdom in the Hellenistic Age.* OT Library. Louisville: Westminster John Knox, 1997.

Collins, John J., Craig A. Evans, and Lee Martin McDonald, *Ancient Jewish and Christian Scriptures: New Developments in Canon Controversy.* Louisville: WJK, 2020.

Collins, John J., and Daniel C. Harlow, eds. *Dictionary of Early Judaism.* Grand Rapids: Eerdmans, 2010.

Collins, Raymond F. *These Things Have Been Written: Studies on the Fourth Gospel.* Louvain Theological & Pastoral Monographs 2. Grand Rapids: Eerdmans, 1990.

Coloe, Margaret. *God Dwells with Us: Temple Symbolism in the Fourth Gospel.* Collegeville, MN: Liturgical, 2001.

Coloe, Margaret, and Tom Thatcher, eds. *John, Qumran, and the Dead Sea Scrolls: Sixty Years of Discovery and Debate.* Atlanta: SBL Press 2011.

Colpe, Carsten. *Die religionsgeschichtliche Schule.* Göttingen: Vandenhoeck & Ruprecht, 1961.

———. "Heidnische, Juedische und Christliche Ueberlieferung." *JAC* 17 (1974) 109–25.

Colwell, E. C. "A Definite Rule for the Use of the Article in the Greek new Testament." *JBL* 52 (1933) 12–21.

Comfort, Philip. *Encountering the Manuscripts: An Introduction to New Testament Paleography and Textual Criticism.* Nashville: Broadman & Holman, 2005.

Comfort, Philip, and David P. Barrett, ed. *The Complete Text of the Earliest New Testament Manuscripts.* Grand Rapids: Baker, 1999.

Conzelmann, Hans. "The Mother of Wisdom." In *The Future of Our Religious Past: Essays in Honour of Rudolf Bultmann,* edited by James M. Robinson, 230–43. London: SCM, 1971.

Cotter, Wendy. *Miracles in Greco-Roman Antiquity: A Sourcebook for the Study of New Testament Miracle Stories.* The Context of Early Christianity 1. New York: Routledge, 2012.

Cox, Roger L. "Tragedy and the Gospel Narratives." In *The Bible in its Literary Milieu,* edited by Vincent L. Tollers and John Maier, 298–317. Grand Rapids: Eerdmans, 1979.

Crim, Keith, ed. *The Interpreter's Dictionary of the Bible Supplementary Volume.* Nashville: Abingdon, 1976.

Cross, F. L. Gen., ed. *Oxford Dictionary of the Christian Church.* 3rd rev. ed. Oxford: Oxford University Press, 2005.

Cross, Frank M. *The Ancient Library of Qumran.* 3rd rev. ed. Minneapolis: Fortress, 1995.
Crown, Alan D. *The Samaritans.* Tübingen: Mohr-Siebeck, 1989.
Crum, Walter E. *A Coptic Dictionary.* Repr. Ancient Language Resources. Eugene, OR: Wipf & Stock, 2005.
Cryer, Frederick H., and Thomas L. Thompson, eds. *Qumran between the Old and New Testaments.* The Library of Hebrew Bible/Old Testament Studies 290. Sheffield: Sheffield Academic, 1998.
Culpepper, R. Alan. *The Anatomy of the Fourth Gospel: A Study in Literary Design.* Philadelphia: Fortress, 1983.
———. *The Johannine School: An Examination of the Johannine-School Hypothesis Based on the Investigation of the Nature of Ancient Schools.* SBLDS 26. Missoula, MO: Scholars, 1975.
Culpepper, R. Alan, and Paul N. Anderson, eds. *Communities in Dispute: Current Scholarship on the Johannine Epistles.* ECL 13. Atlanta: SBL, 2014.
Daly-Denton, Margaret. *David in the Fourth Gospel: The Johannine Reception of the Psalms.* Leiden: Brill, 2000.
Danby, Herbert. *The Mishnah: Tranlated from the Hebrew with Introduction and Brief Explanatory Notes.* Oxford: Oxford University Press, 1933.
Daniélou, Jean. *The Theology of Jewish Christianity, Vol. 1: History of Early Christian Doctrine before the Council of Nicaea.* Translated and edited by John Baker. Philadelphia: Westminster, 1977.
Danker, F. W. "Isis." In *NIDB* 3:95–96.
Daube, David. *Ancient Jewish Law: Three Inaugural Lectures.* Leiden: Brill, 1988.
———. *The New Testament and Rabbinic Judaism.* Repr. Eugene, OR: Wipf & Stock, 2011.
Davies, Stevan. "The Christology and Protology of the Gospel of Thomas." *JBL* 111 (1992) 663–82.
———. *The Gospel of Thomas and Christian Wisdom.* 2nd ed. Oregon House, CA: Bardic, 2004.
Davies, W. D. *Introduction to Pharisaism.* Philadelphia: Fortress, 1967.
———. *Paul and Rabbinic Judaism: Some Rabbinic Elements in Pauline Theology.* 4th ed. Philadelphia: Fortress, 1980.
Davies, W. D., and David Daube, eds. *The Background of the New Testament and its Eschatology.* Cambridge: Cambridge University Press, 1956.
Davila, J. R. "The Perils of Parallelism." https://www.st-andrews.ac.uk/divinity/rt/dss/abstracts/parallels/.
Day, Adam W. *Jesus the Isaianic Servant.* Piscataway, NJ: Gorgias, 2018.
DeConick, April. "'Blessed are Those Who Have Not Seen' (John 20:29): Johannine Dramatization of an Early Christian Discourse." In *The Nag Hammadi Library after Fifty Years: Proceedings of the 1995 Society of Biblical Literature Commemoration*, edited by John Turner and Anne McGuire, 381–98. NHMS 44. Leiden: Brill, 1997.
———. *Seek to See Him: Ascent and Vision Mysticism in the Gospel of Thomas.* Leiden: Brill, 1996.
———. *Voices of the Mystics. Early Christian Discourse in The Gospels of John and Thomas and Other Ancient Christian Literature.* Edinburgh: T. & T. Clark, 2001.
Deissmann, Adolf. *Light from the Ancient East: The New Testament Illustrated by Recently Discovered Texts of the Graeco-Roman World.* Translated by Lionel R. M. Strachan. Grand Rapids: Baker, 1978.

Delobel, Joël, et al., eds. *Logia: les paroles de Jésus: memorial Joseph Coppens*. Leuven: Peeters and Leuven University Press, 1982.

Desjardins, Michael. "Where was the Gospel of Thomas Written?" *TJT* 8 (1992) 121–33.

Dever, W. G. *Did God Have a Wife? Archaeology and Folk Religion in Ancient Israel*. Grand Rapids: Eerdmans, 2008.

Di Tomasso, Lorenzo. *A Bibliography of Pseudepigrapha Research 1850–1999*. JSPSup 39. Sheffield: Sheffield Academic, 2001.

Dillon, John. *The Middle Platonists, 80 BC to AD 220*. Ithaca, NY: Cornell University Press, 1977.

Dines, Jennifer. *The Septuagint*. UBW. New York: Continuum, 2004

Dodd, C. H. *According to the Scriptures*. London: Nisbet, 1952.

———. *The Apostolic Preaching and Its Development*. New York: Harper & Row, 1964.

———. *Historical Tradition in the Fourth Gospel*. London: Cambridge University Press, 1963.

———. *The Interpretation of the Fourth Gospel*. London: Cambridge University Press, 1968.

Dodds, E. R. *Euripides Bacchae*. 2nd ed. Oxford: Clarendon, 1960.

———. *The Greeks and the Irrational*. Berkeley: University of California Press, 1951.

———. *Pagan and Christian in an Age of Anxiety*. London: Cambridge University Press, 1965.

Drower, E. S. *The Canonical Prayerbook of the Mandaeans*. Leiden: Brill, 1957.

———. *The Haran Gawaita, and The Baptism of Hibil-Ziwa*. Vatican City: Biblioteca Apostolica Vaticana, 1953.

Duke, Paul D. *Irony in the Fourth Gospel*. Atlanta: John Knox, 1985.

Dunderberg, Ismo. "The Beloved Disciple in John: Ideal Figure in an Early Christian Controversy." In *Fair Play: Diversity and Conflicts in Early Christianity; Essays in Honour of Heikki Räisänen*, edited by I. Dunderberg et al., 243–69. NovTSup 103. Leiden: Brill, 2001.

———. "How Far Can We Go? Jesus, John, the Synoptics, and Other Texts." In *Beyond the Gnostic Gospels: Studies Building on the Work of Elaine Pagels*, edited by Eduard Iricinschi et al., 347–66. Tübingen: Mohr Siebeck, 2013.

———. "John and Thomas in Conflict." In *The Nag Hammadi Library after Fifty Years*, edited by John D. Turner and Aime M. McGuire, 361–80. Leiden: Brill, 1997.

———. "Thomas and the Beloved Disciple." In *Thomas at the Crossroads: Essays on the Gospel of Thomas*, edited by Risto Uro, 65–88. Studies of the New Testament and Its World. Edinburgh: T. & T. Clark, 1998.

———. "'Thomas' I-Sayings and the Gospel of John." In *Thomas at the Crossroads: Essays on the Gospel of Thomas*, edited by Risto Uro, 33–64. Studies of the New Testament and Its World. Edinburgh: T. & T. Clark, 1998.

Dunn, James D. G. *Beginnings from Jerusalem: Christianity in the Making, Vol. 2*. Grand Rapids: Eerdmans, 2009.

———. *Christology in the Making: An Inquiry into the Origins of the Doctrine of Incarnation*. 2nd ed. London: SCM, 1989.

———. *Jesus Remembered. Christianity in the Making, Vol. 1*. Grand Rapids: Eerdmans, 2003.

———. *Jews and Christians: The Parting of the Ways, AD 70 to 135*. Grand Rapids: Eerdmans, 1999.

Dupont-Sommer, A. *Essene Writings from Qumran*. Translated by Geza Vermes. Repr. Cleveland: World, 1973.

Dyer, Bryan R. "Rudolf Bultmann and the Johannine Literature." In *The Gospel of John in Modern Interpretation*, edited by Stanley E. Porter and Ron C. Fay, 119–40. Milestones in NT Scholarship. Grand Rapids: Kregel Academic, 2018.

Easton, Burton Scott, trans. and ed. *The Apostolic Tradition of Hippolytus*. Repr. Ann Arbor, MI: Archon, 1962.

Eco, Umberto. *The Limits of Interpretation*. Advances in Semiotics. Bloomington: Indiana University Press, 1990.

———. *Les limites de l'interprétation*. Fr. trans. of 1990 Ital. ed. Paris: Grasset, 1992.

Edwards, O. C. "Diatessaron or Diatessara?" *StPatr* 16 (1985) 88–92.

———. "Tatian." In *AYBD* 6:335–36.

Edwards, M. *John through the Centuries*. Oxford: Blackwell, 2004.

Edwards, James R. *The Hebrew Gospel and the Development of the Synoptic Tradition*. Grand Rapids: Eerdmans, 2009.

Ehrman, Bart D. *The Orthodox Corruption of Scripture: The Effect of Early Christological Controversies on the Text of the New Testament*. Oxford: Oxford University Press, 1993.

Ehrman, Bart D., and Michael W. Holmes. *The Text of the New Testament in Contemporary Research: Essays on the Status Quaestionis*. SD 46. Grand Rapids: Eerdmans, 1995.

Elliott, John H. "A Catholic Gospel: Reflections on 'Early Catholicism' in the NT." *CBQ* 31 (1969) 213–23.

———. *What is Social-Science Criticism?* GBS NT. Minneapolis: Fortress, 1993.

Ellis, E. Earle. *The Old Testament in Early Christianity: Canon and Interpretation in the Light of Modern Research*. Grand Rapids: Baker, 1992.

Elowsky, Joel C. *John 1–10*. Ancient Christian Commentary on Scripture. Downers Grove, IL: IVP Academic, 2006.

———. *John 11–21*. Ancient Christian Commentary on Scripture. Downers Grove, IL: IVP Academic, 2007.

Elwell, Walter A., and Robert W. Yarbrough. *Readings from the First-Century World*. EBS. Grand Rapids: Baker, 1998.

Emerton, John A. "Problem of Vernacular Hebrew in the First Century AD and the Language of Jesus." *JTS* 24 (1973) 1–23.

Engberg-Pedersen, Troels. *John and Philosophy*. Oxford: Oxford University Press, 2017.

Epstein, Isidore, trans. and ed. *Babylonian Talmud*. 35 vols. New York: Soncino, 1935–1952.

Esler, Philip F. *Modeling Early Christianity: Social Scientific Studies of the NT in Its Context*. London: Routledge, 1995.

Euripides. *Euripides: Bacchanals, Madness of Hercules*. Translated by Arthur S. Way. LCL. Cambridge, MA: Harvard University Press, 1988.

———. *Euripides I: Alcestis, The Medea, The Heracleidae, Hippolytus*. In *The Complete Greek Tragedies*, edited by David Grene and Richard Lattimore. Chicago: University of Chicago Press, 1955.

Eusebius. *Eusebius: The Preparation of the Gospel*. Translated by E. H. Gifford. Repr. Grand Rapids: Baker, 1981.

———. *Ecclesiastical History, Books 1–5*. Translated by Kirsopp Lake. LCL 153. Cambridge, MA: Harvard University Press, 1926.

———. *Ecclesiastical History, Books 6–10*. Translated by J. E. L. Houlton. LCL 265. Cambridge, MA: Harvard University Press, 1932.
Evans, Craig A. *Ancient Texts for New Testament Studies: A Guide to Background Literature*. Peabody, MA: Hendrickson, 2005.
———. "Introduction: An Aramaic Approach Thirty Years Later." In *An Aramaic Approach to the Gospels and Acts* by Matthew Black, v–xxv. 3rd ed. repr. Peabody, MA: Hendrickson, 1998.
———. "On the Prologue and the Trimorphic Protennoia," *NTS* 27 (1981) 395–401.
———. *Word of Glory: On the Exegetical and Theological Background of John's Prologue*. London: Bloomsbury Academic, 1993.
Evans, Craig A., et al., eds., *Nag Hammadi Texts and the Bible: A Synopsis and Index*. NT Tools and Studies 18. Leiden: Brill, 1993.
Evans, Craig A., and James A. Sanders. *Early Christian Interpretation of the Scriptures of Israel: Investigations and Proposals*. Sheffield: Sheffield Academic, 1997.
Evans, Craig A., and Stanley E. Porter Jr, eds. *Dictionary of New Testament Background*. The IVP Bible Dictionary Series. Downers Grove, IL: IVP Academic, 2000.
Evans, Robert. *Reception History, Tradition and Biblical Interpretation: Gadamer and Jauss in Current Practice*. London: Bloomsbury, 2014.
Falk, Z. W. "Binding and Loosing." *JJS* 25 (1974) 92–100.
Fallon, F. T., and Ron Cameron. "The Gospel of Thomas: A Forschungsbericht and Analysis." In *Aufstieg und Niedergang der Römischen Welt*, edited by W. Haase and H. Temporini, 41–95. New York: Walther De Gruyter, 1988.
Farmer, William R. *Maccabees, Zealots and Josephus*. New York: Columbia University Press, 1956.
Feldman, Louis H. "Diaspora Synagogues: New Light from Inscriptions and Papuri." In *Sacred Realm: The Emergence of the Synagogue in the Ancient World*, edited by Steven Fine, 48–67. New York: Oxford University Press and Yeshiva University Museum, 1996.
Ferguson, Everett. *Backgrounds of Early Christianity*. 3rd ed. Grand Rapids: Eerdmans, 2003.
Ferguson, John, ed. *Greek and Roman Religion A Source Book*. Park Ridge, NJ: Noyes, 1980.
———. *The Religions of the Roman Empire*. Ithaca, NY: Cornell University Press, 1970.
Finegan, Jack. *Handbook of Biblical Chronology: Principles of Time Reckoning in the Ancient World and Problems of Chronology in the Bible*. 2nd ed. rev. and exp. Peabody, MA: Hendrickson, 1998.
———. *Myth and Mystery. An Introduction to the Pagan Religions of the Biblical World*. Grand Rapids: Baker Academic, 1989.
Finkelstein, Louis. *The Pharisees: The Sociological Background of Their Faith*. 2 vols. 3rd ed. Philadelphia: Jewish Publication Society, 1963.
Fiorenza, Elizabeth Schussler. "Apokalypsis and Propheteia: The Book of Revelation in the Context of Early Christian Prophecy." In *L'Apocalypse johannique et l' Apocalyptic dans le Nouveau Testament*, edited by J. Lambrecht Leuven, 106–28. Leuven: University of Leuven Press, 1980.
———. *The Book of Revelation: Justice and Judgment*. Philadelphia: Fortress, 1985.
———. "The Followers of the Lamb: Visionary Rhetoric and Social-Political Situation." *Semeia* 36 (1986) 123–46.
Fishbane, Michael. *Biblical Interpretation in Ancient Israel*. Oxford: Oxford University Press, 1988.

———. "Use, Authority and Interpretation of Mikra at Qumran." In *Mikra: Text, Translation, Reading and Interpretation of the Hebrew Bible in Ancient Judaism and Early Christianity*, edited by M. J. Mulder, 339–77. Assen, NL: Van Gorcum, 1988.

Fitzmyer, Joseph A. *The Dead Sea Scrolls and Christian Origins. Studies in the DSS and Related Literature*. Grand Rapids: Eerdmans, 2000.

———. *The Gospel According to Luke I-IX*. Vol 1. AYB 28. New Haven, CT: Yale University Press, 1981.

———. *A Guide to the Dead Sea Scrolls and Related Literature*. Rev. and Exp. Grand Rapids: Eerdmans, 2008.

———. *The Impact of the Dead Sea Scrolls*. Mahwah, NJ: Paulist, 2009.

———. "The Languages of Palestine in the First Century." *CBQ* 32 (1970) 501–31.

———. *The Semitic Background of the New Testament*. Biblical Resources Series. Grand Rapids: Eerdmans, 1997.

Flesher, Paul V. M., and Bruce D. Chilton, eds. *The Targums: A Critical Introduction*. Waco, TX: Baylor University Press, 2011.

Flusser, David. *Judaism of the Second Temple Period, Volume 2: The Jewish Sages and Their Literature*. Grand Rapids: Eerdmans, 2009.

———. *Judaism of the Second Temple Period, Volume 1: Qumran and Apocalypticism*. Translated by Azzan Yadin. Jerusalem: Hebrew University Magnes Press, 2007.

Flusser, David, and R. Steven Notley. *The Sage from Galilee: Rediscovering Jesus' Genius*. Grand Rapids: Eerdmans, 2007.

Foerster, Werner. *Gnosis: A Selection of Gnostic Texts*. 2 vols. Translated by R. McL. Wilson. Oxford: Clarendon, 1972–1974.

Fortna, Robert T. *The Fourth Gospel and its Predecessor*. London: T. & T. Clark, 2004.

Fortna, Robert T., and Tom Thatcher, eds. *Jesus in the Johannine Tradition*. Louisville: Westminster John Knox, 2001.

Freed, Edwin D. *Old Testament Quotations in the Gospel of John*. Supplements to NovT XI. Leiden: Brill, 1965.

———. "Samaritan influence in the Gospel of John." *CBQ* 30 (1968) 580–87.

Freedman, David Noel, ed. *The Anchor Yale Bible Dictionary*. 6 vols. New Haven, CT: Yale University Press, 1992.

Freedman, David Noel, and Pam Fox Kuhlken. *What Are the Dead Sea Scrolls and Why Do They Matter?* Grand Rapids: Eerdmans, 2007.

Freedman, Harry, and Maurice Simon, trans. and eds. *Midrash Rabbah*. 10 vols. New York: Soncino, 1939.

Frei, H. W. *Eclipse of Biblical Narrative*. New Haven, CT: Yale University Press, 1974.

Frey, Jörg. "Between Torah and Stoa." In *Prologue of the Gospel of John*, edited by Jan G. van Der Watt et al., 189–234. Tübingen: Mohr Siebeck, 2016.

———. *Die johanneische Eschatologie*. Vol. 3, *Die eschatologische Verkündigung in den johanneischen Texten*. WUNT 117. Tübingen: Mohr Siebeck, 2000.

———. *The Glory of the Crucified One: Christology and Theology in the Gospel of John*. Translated by Wayne Coppins and Christoph Heilig. Baylor-Mohr Siebeck Studies in Early Christianity. Waco, TX: Baylor University Press, 2018.

———. "The Impact of the Dead Sea Scrolls on New Testament Interpretation: Proposals, Problems, and Further Perspectives." In *The Bible and the Dead Sea Scrolls, Volume Three: The Scrolls and Christian Origins: The Second Princeton Symposium on Judaism and Christian Origins*, edited by James H. Charlesworth, 407–62. Waco, TX: Baylor University Press, 2006.

———. *Qumran, Early Judaism, and New Testament Interpretation: Kleine Schriften III.* Edited by Jacob Cerone. WUNT 424. Tübingen: Mohr Siebeck, 2019.

———. *Theology and History in the Fourth Gospel: Tradition and Narration.* Waco, TX: Baylor University Press, 2018.

Frey, Jörg, et al., eds. *Imagery in the Gospel of John: Terms, Forms, Themes, and Theology of Johannine Figurative Language.* WUNT. Tübingen: Mohr Siebeck, 2006.

———. *Pseudepigraphie und Verfassserfiktion in frühchristlichen Briefen. Pseudepigraphy and Author Fiction in Early Christian Letters.* Tübingen: Mohr Siebeck, 2009.

Frey, Jörg, and Udo Schnelle, eds. *Kontexte des Johannesevangeliums: Das vierte Evangelium in religions-und traditionsgeschichtlicher Perspective.* WUNT 175. Tübingen: Mohr Siebeck, 2004.

Friesen, Courtney. "Dionysus as Jesus: The Incongruity of a Love Feast in Achilles Tatius' *Leucippe and Clitophon*." HTR 107 (2014) 222–40.

———. *Reading Dionysus: Euripides' Bacchae and the Cultural Contestations of Greeks, Jews, Romans, and Christians.* Studien und Texte zu Antike und Christentum 95. Tübingen: Mohr Siebeck, 2015

Fuglseth, Kåre Sigvald. *Johannine Sectarianism in Perspective: A Sociological, Historical, and Comparative Analysis of the Temple and Social Relationships in the Gospel of John, Philo, and Qumran.* NovtSup 119. Leiden: Brill, 2005.

Funk, Robert W., and the Jesus Seminar. *The Five Gospels: The Search for the Authentic Words of Jesus.* New York: Polebridge and Macmillan, 1993.

Furnish, Victor Paul. *Love Command in the New Testament.* NT Library. Nashville: Abingdon, 1972.

Gadamer, Hans-Georg. *Truth and Method.* 2nd rev. ed. Translated by Joel Weinsheimer and Donald G. Marshall. New York: Continuum, 1994.

Gamble, Harry Y. *Books and Readers in the Early Church: A History of Early Christian Texts.* New Haven, CT: Yale University Press, 1995.

———. *The New Testament Canon: Its Making and Meaning.* Eugene, OR: Wipf & Stock, 2002.

Garcia Martinez, Florentino. *The Dead Sea Scrolls Translated. The Qumran Texts in English.* Grand Rapids: Eerdmans, 1996.

———. *Qumran and Apocalyptic: Studies on the Aramaic Texts from Qumran.* STDJ 9. Leiden: Brill, 1992.

———, ed. *Wisdom and Apocalypticism in the Dead Sea Scrolls and in the Biblical Tradition.* BETL 168. Leuven: Peeters, 2003.

Garcia Martinez, Florentino, and Eibert J. C. Tigchelaar, eds. *The Dead Sea Scrolls: Study Edition.* 2 vols. 2nd ed. Grand Rapids: Eerdmans, 1999.

Garrett, Susan R. *No Ordinary Angel: Celestial Spirits and Christian Claims about Jesus.* London: Yale University Press, 2008.

Gaster, Theodore H. *The Dead-Sea Scriptures.* 3rd rev. ed. Garden City, NY: Anchor, 1976.

Gaventa, Beverly Roberts, and Richard B. Hays, eds. *Seeking The Identity of Jesus: A Pilgrimage.* Grand Rapids: Eerdmans, 2008.

Geden, Alfred Shenington, et al., eds. *A Concordance to the Greek New Testament.* T. & T. Clark Biblical Languages. Edinburgh: T. & T. Clark, 2004.

Genette, Gerard. *Narrative Discourse: An Essay in Method.* Ithaca, NY: Cornell University Press, 1980.

Georg, Larry Darnell. *Reading the Tapestry: A Literary-Rhetorical Analysis of the Johannine Resurrection Narrative (John 20–21)*. StBibLit 14. New York: Peter Lang, 2000.
Gerhardsson, Birger. *Memory and Manuscript: Oral Tradition and Written Transmission in Rabbinic Judaism and Early Christianity with Tradition and Transmission in Early Christianity*. Translated by Eric Sharpe. 2nd ed. BRS. Grand Rapids: Eerdmans, 1998.
Gieschen, Charles A. *Angelomorphic Christology: Antecedents and Early Evidence*. Library of Early Christology. Waco, TX: Baylor University Press, 2017.
Gillingham, Susan. *Psalms through the Centuries: A Reception Commentary on Psalms 1–72*. Wiley Blackwell Bible Commentaries 2. Hoboken, NJ: Wiley-Blackwell, 2018.
Giversen, Søren. *Apocryphon Johannis*. Acta Theologica Danica 5. Copenhagen: Munksgaard, 1963.
Goehring, James E., et al., eds. *Gospel Origins and Christian Beginnings. In Honor of James M. Robinson*. Sonoma, CA: Polebridge, 1990.
Goehring, James E., and Charles W. Hedrick et al., eds. *Gnosticism and the Early Christian World: In Honor of James M. Robinson*. Sonoma, CA: Polebridge, 1990.
Goldin, Judah. *The Fathers According to Rabbi Nathan*. Yale Judaica Series. New Haven, CT: Yale University Press, 1955.
Goodenough, E. R. *Jewish Symbols in the Greco-Roman Period*. 13 vols. New York: Pantheon, 1953–1968.
Goodman, Robert F., and Walter R. Fisher, eds. *Rethinking Knowledge: Reflections Across the Disciples*. SUNY Series in the Philosophy of the Social Sciences. Albany, NY: State University of New York Press, 1995.
Gorman, Michael J. *Abide and Go: Missional Theosis in the Gospel of John*. The Didsbury Lecture. Eugene, OR: Cascade, 2018.
Gramcord for Windows/Bible Companion. Gramcord Institute/White Harvest. http://www.gramcord.org/windows.htm.
Grandjean, Yves. *Une Nouvelle Aretalogie D'Isis a Maronee*. Études Préliminaires Aux Religions Orientales Dans l'Empire 49. Leiden: Brill Academic, 1997.
Grant, Frederick C. *Hellenistic Religions: The Age Of Syncretism*. Indianapolis: Bobbs-Merrill, 1953.
Grant, Robert M. *Irenaeus of Lyons*. The Early Church Fathers. London: Routledge, 1997.
———. "Justin Martyr (Person)." In *AYBD* 3:1133.
Graves, Robert. *The Greek Myths: 1*. Aylesbury, UK: Hazell Watson & Viney Ltd., 1960.
Green, David, and Richard Lattimore, eds. *The Complete Greek Tragedies Euripides V: Electra, The Phoenician Women, The Bacchae. With a Chronological Note by Richard Lattimore*. Chicago: University Press of Chicago, 1959.
Green, Joel B., et al. *A Dictionary of Jesus and the Gospels*. A Compendium of Biblical Scholarship. 2nd Ed. Downers Grove, IL: IVP Academic, 2013.
———, ed. *Hearing the New Testament: Strategies for Interpretation*. 2nd ed. Grand Rapids: Eerdmans, 2010.
Greenspoon, L. "Septuagint." In *NIDB* 5:170–77.
Gregory of Nazianzus. *Saint Gregory of Nazianzus, Poems on Scripture*. Edited by Brian Dunkle and John Behr. Popular Patristics 46. Yonkers, NY: St Vladimir's Seminary Press, 2013.

Grenfell, Bernard P., and Arthur S. Hunt, eds. *New Classical Fragments and Other Greek and Latin Papyri*. Oxford: Oxford University Press, 1897.

Grobel, Kendrick. "How Gnostic is the Gospel of Thomas?" *NTS* 8 (1961–1962) 367–73.

Gruen, Erich S. *Heritage and Hellenism*. Berkeley: University of California, 1989.

Guggenheimer, Heinrich W., ed. *The Jerusalem Talmud. First Order: Zeraim Tractate Berakhot*. Studia Judaica 18. Berlin: Walter de Gruyter, 2000.

"Guide to Resources in Rabbinic Literature." State University of New York at Albany. http://library.albany.edu/subject/guides/Guide_to_Resources_in_Rabbinic_Literature.html

Guilding, Aileen. *The Fourth Gospel and Jewish Worship*. Oxford: Oxford University Press, 1960.

Guillaumont, A., Henri Charles Puech, et al., trans. and eds. *The Gospel According to Thomas: Coptic Text Established and Translated*. Leiden: Brill, 1954.

Guinan, M. D. "Aramaic, Aramaism." In *NIBD* 1:228–31.

Guirard, Felix, ed. *New Larousse Encyclopedia of Mythology*. New ed. Translated by D. Ames and R. Aldington. London: Hamlyn, 1968.

Guthrie, W. K. C. *The Greeks and their Gods*. Boston, 1951.

Haase, W., and H. Temporini. *Aufstieg und Niedergang der Römischen Welt*. Berlin and New York: Walther De Gruyter, 1988.

Häberl, Charles G., and James F. McGrath, eds. *The Mandaean Book of John: Critical Edition, Translation, and Commentary*. Berlin: De Gruyter, 2020.

Hadas, Moses, and Morton Smith. *Heroes and Gods: Spiritual Biographies in Antiquity*. New York: Harper & Row, 1965.

Haenchen, Ernst. *John 1: A Commentary on the Gospel of John, Chapters 1–6*. Translated by Robert W. Funk and Ulrich Busse. Hermeneia. Philadelphia: Fortress, 1984.

———. *John 2: A Commentary on the Gospel of John, Chapters 7–21*. Translated by Robert W. Funk and Ulrich Busse. Hermeneia. Philadelphia: Fortress, 1984.

Hahneman, G. M. T. *Muratorian Fragment and the Development of the Canon*. Oxford: Oxford University Press, 1992.

———. "The Muratorian Fragment and the Origins of the New Testament Canon." In *The Canon Debate*, edited by Lee Martin McDonald and James A. Sanders, 405–15. Peabody, MA: Hendrickson, 2002.

Häkkinen, Sakari. "Ebionites." In *A Companion to Second-Century Christian 'Heretics,'* edited by Antti Marjanen and Petri Luomanen, 247–78. Leiden: Brill, 2008.

Hall, S. G., trans. *Melito of Sardis*. Original title *Sur la Pâqe et fragments*, edited by Othmar Perler. Oxford: Oxford University Press, 1979.

Halliday, Michael A. K. "Anti-languages." *American Anthropologist* 78 (1976) 570–84.

———. *Language as social semiotic: The social interpretation of language and meaning*. London: Edward Arnold, 1978.

Hammond, N. G. L., and H. H. Scullard, eds. *The Oxford Classical Dictionary*. 2nd ed. Oxford: Clarendon, 1970.

Hanson, K. C. "Home page." http://www.kchanson.com/.

Harlow, D. C. "Ascent to Heaven." In *Dictionary of Early Judaism*, edited by John J. Collins and Daniel C. Harlow, 387–90. Grand Rapids: Eerdmans, 2010.

Harnack, Karl Gustav Adolf von., ed. *Ein Jüdisch-Christliches Psalmbuch aus dem Ersten Jahrundert. The Odes of Solomon*. Translated from the Syriac by Johannes Flemming. Leipzig: J. C. Hinrichs, 1910.

---. *The Mission and Expansion of Christianity in the First Three Centuries*. Translated by James Moffatt. Repr., New York: Harper & Row, 1962. http://www.ccel.org/ccel/harnack/mission.i.html.

---. *Sokrates und die Alte Kirche*. Giessen: Alfred Töpelmann, 1901.

Harris, J. Rendel, and Alphonse Mingana, trans. and eds. *The Odes and Psalms of Solomon*. 2 vols. London: Longmans, Green & Co., 1916–1920.

Hase, Karl von. *Geschichte Jesu: Nach akademische Vorlesungen*. 2nd ed. Leipzig: Breitkopf & Hartel, 1876.

Hayes, John H. *New Testament History of Interpretation*. Foreword by Edgar Krentz. Nashville: Abingdon, 2004.

---, ed. *Dictionary of Biblical Interpretation*. 2 Vols. Nashsville: Abingdon, 1999.

Hays, Richard B. *The Conversion of Imagination: Paul as Interpreter of Israel's Scripture*. Grand Rapids: Eerdmans, 2005.

---. *Echoes of Scripture in the Gospels*. Waco, TX: Baylor University Press, 2016.

---. *Echoes of Scripture in the Letters of Paul*. New Haven, CT: Yale University Press, 1989.

Hayward, Robert. *Divine Name*. Montclair, NJ: Allanheld, Osmun, 1981.

Hedrick, Charles W. *The Apocalypse of Adam: A Literary and Source Analysis*. SBL Dissertation Series 46. Repr. Eugene, OR: Wipf & Stock, 2005.

---. "Authorial Presence and Narrator in John: Commentary and Story." In *Gospel Origins and Christian Beginnings: In Honor of James M. Robinson*, by James E. Goehring, et al., 74–93. Sonoma, CA: Polebridge, 1990.

---. "Narrative Asides in the Gospel of John." In *1900th Anniversary of St. John's Apocalypse: Proceedings of the International and Interdisciplinary Symposium*, 650–53. Athens: Holy Monastery of St. John, 1999.

Hedrick, Charles W., and Robert Hodgson, Jr., eds. *Nag Hammadi, Gnosticism, and Early Christianity*. Peabody, MA: Hendrickson, 1986.

---. *Unlocking the Secrets of the Gospel according to Thomas: A Radical Faith for a New Age*. Eugene, OR: Cascade Books 2010.

Hegel, George W. F. *Hegel's Philosophy of Right*. Translated by Samuel W. Dyde. Repr. Mineola, NY: Dover, 2005.

Heilig, Christoph. *Hidden Criticism?: The Methodology and Plausibility of the Search for a Counter-imperial Subtext in Paul*. Minneapolis: Fortress, 2017.

Heil, J. P. *1–3 John*. Eugene, OR: Cascade, 2015.

Heinrici, Carl F. G. *Die Hermes-Mystick und das Neue Testament*. Edited by Ernst von Dobschütz. Leipzig: J. C. Hinrichs, 1918.

Helmer, Christine, and Steven L. McKenzie, et al., eds. *The Encyclopedia of the Bible and Its Reception, Vol. 14: Jesus—Kairos*. Berlin: De Gruyter, 2017.

Hemer, Colin J. *The Letters to the Seven Churches of Asia in their Local Setting*. The Biblical Resource Series. Grand Rapids: Eerdmans, 2001.

---. "Towards a New Moulton and Milligan." *NovT* 24 (1982) 97–123.

Hengel, Martin. "The Dionysian Messiah." In *Studies in Early Christology*, 293–331. Edinburgh: T. & T. Clark, 1995.

---. *The Four Gospels and the One Gospel of Jesus Christ*. Translated by John Bowden. Harrisburg, PA: Trinity, 2000.

---. *Hellenization of Judaea in the First Century After Christ*. London: SCM, 1990.

---. *The Johannine Question*. Translated by John Bowden. Philadelphia: Trinity, 1989.

---. *Judaism and Hellenism: Studies in Their Encounter in Palestine during the Early Hellenistic Period*. Translated by John Bowden. Philadelphia: Fortress, 1974.

---. *Judentum und Hellenismus: Studien zu ihrer Begegnung unter besonderer Berücksichtigung Palästinas bis zur Mitte des 2.Jh.s v.Chr*. WUNT 10. Tübingen: Mohr Siebeck, 1973.

---. "The Old Testament in the Fourth Gospel." In *The Gospel and the Scriptures of Israel*, edited by Craig A. Evans and W. Richard Stegner, 380–95. JSNTSup 104. Sheffield: Sheffield Academic, 1994.

---. "The Prologue of the Gospel of John as the Gateway to Christological Truth." In *The Gospel of John in Christian Theology*, edited by Richard Bauckham and Carl Mosser, 265–94. Grand Rapids: Eerdman, 2008.

---. *The Septuagint as Christian Scripture: Its Prehistory and the Problem of Its Canon*. Translated by Mark E. Biddle. Grand Rapids: Baker, 2004.

---. *The Zealots: Investigations into the Jewish Freedmen Movement in the Period from Herod I until 70 AD*. Edinburgh: T. & T. Clark, 1989.

Hennecke, E. and W. Schneemelcher, eds. *Neutestamentliche Apokryphen*. 2 vols. Tübingen: Mohr, 1964.

Henze, Matthias, ed. *Biblical Interpretation at Qumran*. Studies in the Dead Sea Scrolls and Related Literature. Grand Rapids: Eerdmans, 2005.

Heraclitus. *Fragments: The Collected Wisdom of Heraclitus*. Translated by Brooks Haxton, with foreword by James Hillman. New York: Viking Penguin, 2001.

Hesiod. *Hesiod: The Homeric Hymns and Homerica*. Translated by Hugh G. Evelyn-White. LCL. Cambridge, MA: Harvard University Press, 1974.

Hewett, James Allen. *New Testament Greek: A Beginning and Intermediate Grammar*. Rev. ed. with CD by C. Michael Robbins and Steven R. Johnson. Peabody, MA: Hendrickson, 2009.

Hicks, Robert D. *Stoic and Epicurean*. New York: Russell & Russell, 1962.

Hill, Charles. *The Johannine Corpus in the Early Church*. New York and Oxford: Oxford University Press, 2006.

---. Review of Verheyden, Joseph, Reimund Bieringer et al., eds. *Docetism in the Early Church: The Quest for an Elusive Phenomenon*. Tübingen: Mohr Siebeck, 2018 in RBL 09 (2019): https://www.bookreviews.org/pdf/12232_13633.pdf.

Hills, Julian V. "Apostles, Epistle of." In *AYBD*, 1:311–12.

---. *Tradition and Composition in the Epistula Apostolorum*. HDR 24. 1990. Expanded ed. HTS 57. Minneapolis: Fortress, 2008.

Hirsch, E. D. *Validity in Interpretation*. New Haven, CT: Yale University Press, 1967.

Hock, Ronald F. and Edward N. O'Neil, eds. *Chreia and Ancient Rhetoric: Classroom Exercises*. Writings from the Greco-Roman World 2. Leiden: Brill Academic, 2003.

Holladay, Carl R. *Acts: A Commentary*. NT Library. Louisville: Westminster John Knox, 2016.

Hollander, John. *The Figure of Echo: A Mode of Allusion in Milton and After*. Quantum Book. Berkeley, CA: Univeristy of California, 1981.

Holmén, Tom, and Stanley E. Porter, eds. *Handbook for the Study of the Historical Jesus*. 4 vols. Leiden: Brill, 2011.

Holmes, Michael W., ed. *The Apostolic Fathers: Greek Texts and English Translations*. 3rd ed. Grand Rapids: Baker, 2007.

Hoppe, L. J. "Monarchic Period." In *AYBD* 3:562–66.

Horbury, William. "Benediction of the *Minim* and Early Jewish-Christian Controversy." *JTS* 33 (1982) 19–61.

Horgan, Maurya P. *Pesharim: Qumran Interpretations of Biblical Books.* The CBQ Monograph Series 8. Washington, DC: Catholic University of America Press, 1979.

Hornblower, Simon, and Anthony Spawforth, ed. *The Oxford Classical Dictionary.* 3rd ed. Oxford: Oxford University Press, 1996.

Horsley, G. H. R., et al., eds. *New Documents Illustrating Early Christianity.* Vols. 1–9. A Review of the Greek Inscriptions and Papyri published in 1976–87. Grand Rapids: Eerdmans, 1998–2002.

Hoskyns, Edwin C. *The Fourth Gospel.* Edited by F. N. Davey. London: Faber & Faber, 1947.

Howe, Bonnie. *Because You Bear This Name: Conceptual Metaphor and the Moral Meaning of 1 Peter.* Atlanta: SBL, 2008.

Hume, James. Review of *Tra la vigna e la croce: Dioniso nei discorsi letterari e figurativi cristiani (II-IV secolo)*, by Francesco Massa. *Bryn Mawr Classical Review* 10 (2015). https://bmcr.brynmawr.edu/2015/2015.10.29.

Hunt, Arthur S., and C. C. Edgar. *Select Papyri*, 2 vols. LCL. Cambridge, MA: Harvard University Press, 1932.

Hurtado, Larry W. *Destroyer of the Gods: Early Christian Distinctiveness in the Roman World.* Waco, TX: Baylor University Press, 2016.

———. *The Earliest Christian Artifacts: Manuscripts and Christian Origins.* Grand Rapids: Eerdmans, 2006.

———. *Honoring the Son: Jesus in Earliest Christian Devotional Practice.* Edited by Michael F. Bird. Bellingham, WA: Lexham, 2018.

———. *Lord Jesus Christ: Devotion to Jesus in Earliest Christianity.* Grand Rapids: Eerdmans, 2003.

———. "Mediator Figures." In *Dictionary of Early Judaism*, edited by John J. Collins and Daniel C. Harlow, 926–29. Grand Rapids: Eerdmans, 2010.

———. *One God, One Lord.* New York: T. & T. Clark, 1998.

Hutchinson, V. J. "The Cult of Dionysos-Bacchus in the Graeco-Roman World: New Light from Archaeological Studies." *JRA* 4 (1991) 222–30.

Hyatt, J. Philip., ed. *Bible in Modern Scholarship: Papers Read at the 100th Meeting of the SBL December 1964.* Nashville: Abingdon, 1965.

Iamblichus. *Iamblichus' Life of Pythagoras accompanied by fragments of The Ethical Writings and a collection of Pythagoric Sentences.* Translated by Thomas Taylor. London: A. J. Valpy, 1818.

Irenaeus of Lyons. *St. Irenaeus of Lyons: Agains Heresies. Books 1–3.* Translated by Dominic J. Unger et al. Ancient Christian Writers. New York: Paulist, 1992–2012.

Iricinschi, Eduard, et al., eds. *Beyond the Gnostic Gospels: Studies Building on the Work of Elaine Pagels.* Tübingen: Mohr Siebeck, 2013.

Iser, Wolfgang. *The Implied Reader: patterns of communication in prose fiction from Bunyan to Beckett.* Baltimore, MD: John Hopkins University Press, 1974.

Isser, Stanley Jerome. *The Dositheans: A Samaritan Sect in Late Antiquity.* Studies in Judaism in Late Antiquity 17. Leiden: Brill, 1976.

Jastrow, Marcus. *Dictionary of the Targumim, the Talmud Babli and Yerushalmi, and the Midrashic Literature.* New York: Judaica, 1996.

Jaubert, Annie. *The Date of the Last Supper.* Translated by Isaac Rafferty. Staten Island, NY: Alba House, 1965.

———. "Le calendrier des Jubilés et de la secte de Qumrân. Ses origines bibliques." *VT* 3 (1953) 250–64.

Jauss, Hans Robert. *Towards an Aesthetic of Literary Reception*. Translated by Timothy Bahti. Theory & History of Literature 2. Minneapolis: University of Minnesota, 1982.

Jewish Encyclopedia. http://www.jewishencyclopedia.com/view.jsp?artid=543&letter=J.

Jewish Virtual Library. https://www.jewishvirtuallibrary.org.

Jipp, Joshua. "Raymond E. Brown and the Fourth Gospel: Composition and Community." In *The Gospel of John in Modern Interpretation*, edited by Stanley E. Porter and Ron C. Fay, 173–96. Milestones in NT Scholarship. Grand Rapids: Kregel Academic, 2018.

Jobes, Karen, and Moises Silva. *Invitation to the Septuagint*. Grand Rapids: Baker, 2005.

Johnson, Luke Timothy. "John and *Thomas* in Context: An Exercise in Canonical Criticism." In *The Word Leaps the Gap: Essays on Scripture and Theology in Honor of Richard B. Hays*, edited by J. Ross Wagner et al., 284–309. Grand Rapids: Eerdmans, 2008.

Johnston, George. *The Spirit-Paraclete in the Gospel of John*. SNTSMS 12. Cambridge: Cambridge University Press, 1970.

Jonas, Hans. *Gnosis und Spätantiker Geist. Vol. 1: Die mythologische Gnosis. Mit einer Einletiung zur Geschichte und Methodologie der Forschung*. FRLANT 51. 2nd ed. Göttingen: Vandenhoek & Ruprecht, 1954.

———. *Gnosis und Spätantiker Geist. Vol. 2: Von der Mythologie zur mystischen Philosophie, Erste und zweite Hälfte*. FRLANT 159. 2nd ed. Göttingen: Vandenhoek & Ruprecht, 1993.

———. *The Gnostic Religion: The Message of the Alien God and the Beginnings of Christianity*. 2nd ed. Boston: Beacon, 1963.

Jones, Larry Paul. *The Symbol of Water in the Gospel of John*. JSNT Suppl. Series 145. Sheffield: Sheffield Academic, 1997.

Josipovici, Gabriel. *The Book of God: A Response to the Bible*. New Haven, CT: Yale University Press, 1988.

Just, Felix, and Tom Thatcher, eds. *John, Jesus, and History, Volume 1: Critical Appraisals of Critical Views*. SBL Symposium Series 44. Atlanta: SBL, 2007.

———. *John, Jesus, and History, Volume 2: Aspects of Historicity in the Fourth Gospel*. SBL Symposium Series 44. Atlanta: SBL, 2009.

Kampen, John. *Hasideans and the Origin of Pharisaism*. SBLCSC. Atlanta: SBL, 1989.

Käsemann, Ernst. "The Structure and Purpose of the Prologue to John's Gospel." In *New Testament Questions of Today*, 138–67. Philadelphia: Fortress, 1969.

———. *The Testament of Jesus according to John 17*. Translated by Gerhard Krodel. Philadelphia: Fortress, 1968.

Katz, Steven T. "Issues in the Separation of Judaism and Christianity after 70 CE: A Reconsideration," *JBL* 103 (1984) 43–76.

Kaufman, S. A. "Targums." In *NIDB* 5:471–73.

Kee, Howard Clark. *The New Testament in Context: Sources and Documents*. Englewood Cliffs, NJ: Prentice Hall, 1984.

Keener, Craig S. *The Gospel of John: A Commentary. Volume 1*. Peabody, MA: Hendrickson, 2003.

———. *The Gospel of John: A Commentary. Volume 2*. Peabody, MA: Hendrickson, 2003.

———. "'We Beheld His Glory' (John 1:14)." In *John, Jesus, and History, Volume 2: Aspects of Historicity in the Fourth Gospel*, edited by Paul N. Anderson et al., 15–26. SBL Symposium Series 44. Atlanta: SBL, 2009.

Keith, Chris, and Anthony Le Donne, eds. *Jesus, Criteria, and the Demise of Authenticity*. London: T. & T. Clark, 2012.

Kennedy, George A. *Progymnasmata: Greek Textbooks of Prose Composition and Rhetoric*. Writings from the Greco-Roman World 10. Atlanta: SBL, 2003.

Kerenyi, Carl. *Dionysus: Archetypal Image of Indestructible Life*. Translated by Ralph Manheim Princeton: Princeton University Press, 1976.

Kerr, Alan R. *The Temple of Jesus' Body: The Temple Theme in the Gospel of John*. LNTS. Sheffield: Sheffield Academic, 2002.

Kierkegaard, Søren. *Philosophical Fragments, Johannes Climacus*. Edited and translated by Howard V. Hong and Edna H. Hong. Princeton, NJ: Princeton University Press, 1985.

King, Karen L. *What is Gnosticism?* Cambridge, MA: Harvard University Press, 2003.

Kimelman, Reuven. "*Birkat ha-minim* and the Lack of Evidence for an Anti-Christian Jewish Prayer in Late Antiquity." In *Jewish and Christian Self-Definition Vol. 2: Aspects of Judaism in the Greco-Roman Period*, edited by E. P. Sanders, 226–44. Philadelphia: Fortress, 1981.

Kirk, Alan. Review of M. David Litwa. *How the Gospels Became History*. SBL *RBL* 8 (2020), https://www.bookreviews.org/pdf/13171_14689.pdf.

Kirk, G. S. *Heraclitus: The Cosmic Fragments*. A Critical Study with Introduction, Text and Translation. Cambridge: Cambridge University Press, 1954.

Kirk, J. R. Daniel. *A Man Attested by God: The Human Jesus of the Synoptic Gospels*. Grand Rapids: Eerdmans, 2016.

Kittel, Gerhard and Gerhard Friedrich, eds. *Theological Dictionary of the New Testament*. 10 vols. Translated by Geoffrey W. Bromiley. Grand Rapids: Eerdmans, 1977.

Kittel, Rudolf, et al., eds. *Torah, Neviim u-Khetuvim. Biblia Hebraica Stuttgartensia*. 5th ed. Stuttgart: Deutsche Bibelstiftung, 1997.

Klauck, Hans-Josef. *Herrenmahl und hellenistischer Kult: Eine religionsgeschichtliche Untersuchung zum ersten Korintherbrief*. Neutestamentliche Abhandlungen/Neue Folge. Münster: Aschendorff, 1986.

———. *The Religious Context of Early Christianity: A Guide to Graeco-Roman Religions*. Translated by Brian McNeil. Minneapolis: Fortress, 2003.

Kleinknecht, Hermann. "The λόγος Concept in the Greek World." In *TDNT* 4:81–85.

———. "Logos in the Greek and Hellenistic World." In *TDNT* 4:77–91.

Klink, Edward W., ed. *The Audience of the Gospels: The Origin and Function of the Gospels in Early Christianity*. London: Bloomsbury, 2019.

———. *John*. Zondervan Exegetical Commentary on the New Testament. Grand Rapids: Zondervan Academic, 2016.

———. *The Sheep of the Fold: The Audience and Origin of the Gospel of John*. Cambridge: Cambridge University Press, 2007.

Kloppenborg, J. S. *Q Parallels. Synopsis, Critical Notes, and Concordance*. Sonoma, CA: Polebridge, 1988.

Kloppenborg, J. S., et al. *Q-Thomas Reader* Sonoma, CA: Polebridge, 1990.

Knoppers, Gary N. *Judah and Samaria in Post-Monarchic Times: Essays on Their Histories and Literature.* Forschungen zum Alten Testament 129. Tübingen: Mohr Siebeck, 2019.

Koehler, Ludwig, et al., eds. *The Hebrew and Aramaic Lexicon of the Old Testament.* Brill, 2001.

Koester, Craig R. *The Dwelling of God: The Tabernacle in the Old Testament, Intertestamental Jewish Literature, and the New Testament.* CBQMS 22. Washington, DC: Catholic University Press, 1989.

———. "'Spirit' (Pneuma) in the Greco-Roman Philosophy of John." Pages 235–50 in *The Prologue of the Gospel of John: It's Literary, Theological, and Philosophical Contexts.* Papers read at the Colloquium Ioanneum 2013. Edited by Jan G. van der Watt, R. Alan Culpepper, and Udo Schnelle. WUNT 359. Tübingen: Mohr Siebeck, 2016.

———. *Revelation: A New Translation with Introduction and Commentary.* AYB. New Haven, CT: Yale University Press, 2015.

———. *Symbolism in the Fourth Gospel: Meaning, Mystery, Community.* 2nd ed. Minneapolis: Fortress, 2003.

———. *The Word of Life: A Theology of John's Gospel.* Grand Rapids: Eerdmans, 2008.

Koester, Craig, and Reimund Bieringer, eds. *The Resurrection of Jesus in the Gospel of John.* WUNT 222. Tübingen: Mohr Siebeck, 2008.

Koester, Helmut. *Ancient Christian Gospels: Their History and Development.* Philadelphia: TPI, 1990.

———. "The Divine Human Being." HTR 78 (1985) 243–52.

———. "Gnostic Sayings and Controversy Traditions in John 8:12–59." In *Nag Hammadi, Gnosticism, and Early Christianity,* edited by Charles W. Hedrick and Robert Hodgson Jr., 97–110. Peabody, MA: Hendrickson, 1986.

———. "Introduction: The Gospel According to Thomas." In *Nag Hammadi Codex II,* edited by Bentley Layton, 38–49. Nag Hammadi Studies 20. Leiden: Brill, 1989.

———. "Introduction: The Gospel According to Thomas." In *The Nag Hammadi Library,* edited by J. M. Robinson, 124–26. Rev. ed. New York: Harper Collins, 1990.

———. *Introduction to the New Testament: History, Literature, and Religion of the Hellenistic Age.* Vol. 1. 2nd ed. New York: Walter de Gruyter, 2002.

———. *Introduction to the New Testament: History and Literature of Early Christianity.* Vol. 2. 2nd ed. New York: Walter de Gruyter, 2000.

Kok, Michael J. *The Beloved Apostle? The Transformation of the Apostle John into the Fourth Gospel.* Eugene, OR: Cascade, 2017.

Köstenberger, Andreas J. "The Glory of God in John's Gospel." In *The Glory of God,* edited by Christopher W. Morgan and Robert A. Peterson, 107–26. Theology in Community 2. Wheaton: Crossway, 2010.

———. *A Theology of John's Gospel and Letters: The Word, the Christ, the Son of God.* Biblical Theology of the NT Series. Grand Rapids: Zondervan Academic, 2009.

Köstenberger, Andreas J., and Richard B. Patterson. *Invitation to Biblical Interpretation: Exploring the Hermeneutical Triad of History, Literature, and Theology.* Invitation to Theological Studies Series. Grand Rapids: Kregel Academic & Professional, 2011.

Krell, D. F., ed. *Martin Heidegger: Basic Writings.* Rev. ed. New York: HarperCollins, 1993.

Kristeva, Julia. *Desire and Language: A Semeiotic Approach to Language and Art.* Translated by Leon S. Roudiez et al. European Perspectives Series. Rev. ed. New York: Columbia University Press, 1980.

———. *Tales of Love.* Trans. Leon S. Roudiez. European Perspectives Series. New York: University of Columbia Press, 1987.

Kurz, William S. "The Johannine Word as Revealing the Father." *PRSt* 28 (2001) 67–84.

Kysar, Robert. "The Background of the Prologue of the Fourth Gospel." *CJT* 16 (1970) 250–55.

———. *The Fourth Evangelist and the Gospel: An Examination of Contemporary Scholarship.* Minneapolis: Augsburg, 1975.

———. "The Fourth Gospel. A Report on Recent Research." *ANRW* II 25 (1985) 2389–480.

———. *John.* ACNT. Minneapolis: Augsburg, 1986.

———. *John, The Maverick Gospel.* John Knox, 1976. 3rd ed. Louisville: Westminster John Knox, 2007.

———. "The Whence and Whither of The Johannine Community." In *Life in Abundance: Studies of John's Gospel In Tribute To Raymond E. Brown*, edited by John R. Donahue, 65–81. Collegeville, MN: Liturgical Press, 2005.

Lake, Kirsopp, trans. *The Apostolic Fathers. Vol. 1: 1 Clement, 2 Clement, Ignaitus, Polycarp, Didache, Barnabas.* LCL 24. Cambridge, MA: Harvard University Press, 1949.

———. *The Apostolic Fathers. Vol. 2: The Shepherd of Hermas, The Martyrdom of Polycarp, The Epistle to the Diognetus.* LCL 25. Cambridge, MA: Harvard University Press, 1950.

———. "Epistola Apostolorum." *HTR* 14 (1920) 15–29.

Lake, Kirsopp, and J. E. L. Oulton, trans. *Ecclesiastical History.* LCL. Cambridge, MA: Harvard University Press, 1926–1932.

Lakoff, George, and Mark Johnson. *Metaphors We Live By.* Chicago: University of Chicago Press, 2003.

Lakoff, George, and Mark Turner. *More Than Cool Reason: A Field Guide to Poetic Metaphor.* Chicago: University of Chicago Press, 1989.

Lamb, David A. *Text, Context and the Johannine Community: A Sociolinguistic Analysis of the Johannine Writings.* Library of NT Studies 447. London: T. & T. Clark, 2014.

Lampe, G. W. H. *A Patristic Greek Lexicon.* Oxford: Oxford University Press, 1969.

Lanham, Richard A. *A Handlist of Rhetorical Terms.* 2nd ed. Berkeley: University of California Press, 1991.

Lattke, Matthew. *The Odes of Solomon.* Hermeneia. Minneapolis: Fortress, 2009.

Lauterbach, Jacob Z., trans. and ed. *Mekhilta de-Rabbi de-Ishmael.* Repr. Philadelphia: Jewish Publication Society, 2004.

Layton, Bentley. *The Gnostic Scriptures: A New Translation with Annotations and Introductions.* The Anchor Yale Bible Reference Library. New Haven, CT: Yale University Press, 1995.

———, ed. *The Rediscovery of Gnosticism.* 2 Vols. Proceedings of the Conference at Yale March 1978. Leiden: E.J. Brill, 1981.

Lee, John A. L. *A History of New Testament Lexicography.* Studies in Biblical Greek. Berlin: Peter Lang, 2003.

Leipoldt, Johannes and Walter Grundman, eds. *Umwelt de Christentums.* 2 vols. Berlin: Evangelische Verlagsanstalt, 1965–1967.

Leon Levy Dead Sea Scrolls Digital Library. www.deadseascrolls.org.il.

Levey, Samson H. *The Targum of Ezekiel*. Collegeville, MN: Liturgical, 1987.
Levine, Etan. *Aramaic Version of the Bible*. Berlin: de Gruyter, 1988.
Lewis, Frank Grant. *The Irenaeus Testimony to the Fourth Gospel: Its Extent, Meaning and Value*. Repr. Eugene, OR: Wipf & Stock, 2008.
Lewis, Jack P. "What Do We Mean By Jabneh?" *JBR* 32 (1964) 125–32.
Liddell, George Henry, and Robert Scott, eds. *A Greek-English Lexicon*. Rev. and augmented by H. S. Jones, et al. Oxford: Clarendon, 1996.
Lidzbarski, M. *Das Johannesbuch Der Mandäer*. Repr. Wentworth Press, 2018.
Lieu, Judith and Martinus de Boer. *The Oxford Handbook of Johannine Studies*. Oxford: Oxford University Press, 2018.
Lightfoot, John. *A Commentary on the New Testament from the Talmud and Hebraica; Matthew–I Corinthians*. 4 vols. Repr. of 1859 ed. Grand Rapids: Baker, 1979.
Lincoln, Andrew T. *The Gospel According to Saint John*. Black's NT Commentary. London: Continuum, 2005.
———. *Truth on Trial: The Lawsuit Motif in the Fourth Gospel*. Repr. Eugene, OR: Wipf & Stock, 2019.
Lindars, Barnabas. *Behind the Fourth Gospel*. Studies in Creative Criticism. Repr. Eugene, OR: Wipf & Stock, 2010.
———. *The Gospel of John*. NCB. Grand Rapids: Eerdmans, 1972.
———. "John and the Synoptic Gospels: A Test Case." *NTS* 27 (1980–1981) 287–94.
Litwa, M. David. *Becoming Divine: An Introduction to Deification in Western Culture*. Eugene, OR: Cascade, 2013.
———. *How the Gospels Became History: Jesus and the Mediterranean Myths*. New Haven: Yale University Press, 2019.
———. "'I Will Become Him': Homology and deification in the Gospel of Thomas." *JBL* 133 (2015) 427–47.
Llewelyn, Stephen R., and R. A. Kearnsley, eds. *New Documents Illustrating Early Christianity, Vol. 7: A Review of the Greek Inscriptions and Papyri published in 1982–83*. North Hyde, NSW: The Ancient History Documentary Research Centre of Macquire University, 1994.
———. *New Documents Illustrating Early Christianity, Vol. 9: A Review of the Greek Inscriptions and Papyri published in 1986–87*. Grand Rapids: Eerdmans, 2002.
Loader W. *Jesus in John's Gospel*. Grand Rapids: Eerdmans, 2017.
———. *We Are Being Transformed: Deification in Paul's Soteriology*. BZNW 187. Berlin: de Gruyter, 2012.
Logan, Alastair, and Alexander J. M. Wedderburn, eds. *The New Testament and Gnosis: Essays in Honour of Robert McL. Wilson*. Bloomsbury Academic Collections: Biblical Studies. Edinburgh: T. & T. Clark, 1983.
Logos Bible Study Software. http://www.logos.com/.
Longenecker, Richard N. *Biblical Exegesis in the Apostolic Period*. 2nd ed. Grand Rapids: Eerdmans, 1999.
Longman, Tremper, and Peter Enns, eds. *Dictionary of the Old Testament: Wisdom, Poetry and Writings*. Downers Grove, IL: IVP Academic, 2008.
Louw, J. P., and Eugene A. Nida. *Greek-English Lexicon of the New Testament: Based on Semantic Domains*. 2nd ed. New York: United Bible Societies, 1996.
Lucas, David William. "Euripides." In *The Oxford Classical Dictionary*, edited by Hammond, N.G.L. and H.H. Scullard, 420–21. 2nd ed. Oxford: Clarendon, 1970.

Lüdemann, Gerd, and Martin Schröder. *Die religionsgeschichtliche Schule in Göttingen.* Göttingen: Vandenhoeck & Ruprecht, 1987.
Lupieri, Edmondo. *The Mandaeans: The Last Gnostics.* Translated by Charles Hindley. Italian Texts and Studies on Religion and Society. Grand Rapids: Eerdmans, 2002.
Luz, Ulrich. *Matthew 1-7: A Commentary.* Translated by James E. Crouch from the German EKK series. Rev. ed. Hermeneia. Minneapolis: Fortress, 2007.
MacDonald, Dennis R. *The Dionysian Gospel: The Fourth Gospel and Euripides.* Minneapolis: Fortress, 2017.
———. "My Turn: A Critique of Critics of *Mimesis Criticism*." Claremont, CA: Institute for Antiquity and Christianity, 2009. http://docplayer.net/43600625-My-turn-a-critique-of-critics-of-mimesis-criticism.html.
———, ed. *Mimesis and Intertextuality in Antiquity and Christianity.* Harrisburg, PA: TPI, 2001.
MacDonald, John, trans. and ed. *Memar Marqah: The Teaching of Marqah.* 2 vols. BZAW 84. Berlin: Töpelmann, 1963.
Mack, Burton L. *Logos und Sophia: Untersuchungen zur Weisheitstheologie im Hellenistischen Judentum.* Göttingen: Vandenhoeck & Ruprecht, 1973.
MacRae, George W. *Studies in the New Testament and Gnosticism.* Edited by D. J. Harrington and S. B. Marrow. Repr. Eugene, OR: Wipf & Stock, 2007.
Magness, Jodi. *The Archaeology of Qumran and the Dead Sea Scrolls.* Studies in the Dead Sea Scrolls and Related Literature. Grand Rapids: Eerdmans, 2002.
———. "Qumran." In *NIDB* 4:708.
Malherbe, Abraham J. *The Cynic Epistles: A Study Edition.* SBLSBS 12. Missoula: Scholars, 1977.
———. *Moral Exhortation: A Greco-Roman Sourcebook.* LEC. Philadelphia: Westminster, 1986.
Malina, Bruce J., and Richard L. Rohrbaugh. *Social Science Commentary on the Gospel of John.* Minneapolis: Fortress, 1998.
———. "Jesus as Charismatic Leader." *BTB* 14 (1984) 55-62.
Manning, G. T. *Echoes of a Prophet: The Use of Ezekiel in the Gospel of John and in Literature of the Second Temple Period.* JSNTS 270. New York: T. & T. Clark, 2004.
Marcos, Natalio Fernandez. *The Septuagint in Context.* Translated by W.G.E. Watson. Leiden: Brill, 1998.
Maritz, Petrus, and Gilbert van Belle. "The Imagery of Eating and Drinking in John 6:35." In *Imagery in the Gospel of John,* edited by J. Frey et al., 333-52. Tübingen: Mohr Siebeck, 2006.
Marjanen, Antti. "Is *Thomas* a Gnostic Gospel?" In *Thomas at the Crossroads: Essays on the Gospel of Thomas,* edited by Risto Uro, 107-39. Edinburgh: T. & T. Clark, 1998.
———. ed. *Was There a Gnostic Religon?* Finnish Exegetical Society. Göttingen: Vandenhoeck & Ruprecht, 2005.
Marjanen, Antti, and Petri Luomanen, eds. *A Companion to Second-Century Christian 'Heretics.'* Leiden: Brill Academic, 2008.
Markovich, Miroslav. "Textual Criticism on the Gospel of Thomas." *JTS* 20 (1969) 53-74.
Marlowe, Michael D., ed. *Bible Research Internet Resources for Students of Scripture.* http://www.bible-researcher.com/index.html.
Marrou, Henri I. *The History of Education in Antiquity.* Wisconsin Studies in Classics. Translated by George Lamb. Repr. Madison: University of Wisconsin Press, 1982.
Marrow, Stanley B. "Κόσμος in John." *CBQ* 64 (2002) 90-102.

Marshall, I. Howard. *New Testament Interpretation: Essays on Principles and Method.* Paternoster, 1977. Repr. Eugene, OR: Wipf & Stock, 2006.
Martin, Francis, ed. *Narrative Parallels to the New Testament.* Resources for Biblical Study 22. Atlanta: SBL, 1988.
Martin, Luther H. *Hellenistic Religions. An Introduction.* Oxford: Oxford University Press, 1987.
Martin, Ralph P., and David H. Edwards, eds. *Dictionary of the Later New Testament and Its Developments.* IVP Bible Dictionary Series. Downers Grove, IL: InterVarsity, 1997.
Martyn, J. Louis. *The Gospel of John: Essays for Interpreters.* New York: Paulist, 1978.
———. *The Gospel of John in Christian History: Seven Glimpses into the Johannine Community.* Johannine Monograph Series 8. Eugene, OR: Wipf & Stock, 2019.
———. *History and Theology in the Fourth Gospel.* Rev. and exp. 3rd ed. Louisville: Westminster John Knox, 2003.
———. "Source Criticism and Religionsgeschichte in the Fourth Gospel." In *The Interpretation of John,* edited by John Ashton, 99–121. Issues in Religion and Theology 9. Philadelphia: Fortress, 1986.
Mason, Steve. *Flavius Josephus on the Pharisees.* Leiden: Brill, 1991.
———. *Josephus and the New Testament.* Peabody, MA: Hendrickson, 1992.
Massa, Francesco. *Tra la vigna e la croce: Dioniso nei discorsi letterari e figurativi cristiani (II–IV secolo). Potsdamer Altertumswissenschaftliche Beiträge, Bd 47.* Stuttgart: Franz Steiner Verlag, 2014.
Mburu, E. W. *Qumran and Johannine Language.* Jewish and Christian Texts 8. London: T. & T. Clark, 2010.
McDonald, Lee Martin, and James A. Sanders, eds. *The Canon Debate.* Peabody, MA: Hendrickson, 2002.
McKim, Donald K., ed. *Dictionary of Major Biblical Interpreters.* Downers Grove, IL: InterVarsity, 2007.
McKnight, Scot, and Grant R. Osborne, eds. *The Face of New Testament Studies: A Survey of Recent Research.* Grand Rapids: Baker, 2004.
McLay, R. Timothy. *The Use of the Septuagint in New Testament Research.* Grand Rapids: Eerdmans, 2003.
McNamara, Martin J. *Targum and Testament Revisited.* 2nd ed. Grand Rapids: Eerdmans, 2011.
McNamara, Martin J., et al., trans. and eds. *The Aramaic Bible Series.* 22 vols. Collegeville, MN: Liturgical, 1990–2007.
Meeks, Wayne. "The Man from Heaven in Johannine Sectarianism." *JBL* 91 (1972) 44–72.
———. *The Prophet-King: Moses Traditions and the Johannine Christology.* Johannine Monograph. Repr. Eugene, OR: Wipf & Stock, 2017.
Meier, John P. *Jesus the Marginal Jew: Rethinking the Historical Jesus.* 4 vols. AYB Ref. Library. New Haven, CT: Yale University Press, 1991–2009.
Menken, M. J. J. *Old Testament Quotations: Studies in Textual Form.* CBET 15. Kampen: Kok, 1996.
Mercer, Samuel A. B. *The Pyramid Texts in Translation and Commentary.* 4 vols. New York: Longmans, Green & Co, 1952.
Merlan, Philip. *From Platonism to Neoplatonism.* 3rd rev ed. The Hague: Martinus Nijhoff, 1975.

Metzger, Bruce M. *The Bible in Translation: Ancient and English Versions*. Grand Rapids: Baker, 2001.
———. *A Textual Commentary on the Greek New Testament*. 2nd ed. Stuttgart: Deutsche Bibelgesellschaft, 1994.
Metzger, Bruce M., and Bart D. Ehrman. *The Text of the New Testament: Its Transmission, Corruption, and Restoration*. 4th ed. New York: Oxford University Press, 2005.
Meyer, Marvin W. *The Ancient Mysteries: A Sourcebook of Sacred Texts*. New York: HarperCollins, 1999.
———, ed. *The Gospel of Thomas: The Hidden Sayings of Jesus*. New York: Harper Collins, 1992.
———, et al., eds. *The Nag Hammadi Scriptures: The Revised and Updated Translation of Sacred Gnostic Texts Complete in One Volume*. New York: Harper Collins, 2007.
Michaels, J. Ramsey. *The Gospel of John*. NICNT. Grand Rapids: Eerdmans, 2010.
Middleton, J. Richard. *The Liberating Image: The Imago Dei in Genesis 1*. Grand Rapids: Brazos, 2005.
Migne, J.-P., ed. *Patrologia Graeca*. 162 vols. Paris, 1857–1886.
———. *Patrologia Latina*. 217 vols. Paris, 1844–1864.
Mihalios, Stefanos. *The Danielic Eschatological Hour in the Johannine Literature*. Library of NT Studies 436. London: Bloomsbury Academic, 2011.
Mirecki, P. A. "Valentinus." In *AYBD* 6:783–84.
Mitchell, Margaret. "Patristic Counter-Evidence to the Claim that 'The Gospels Were Written for All Christians.'" *NTS* 51 (2005) 36–79.
Moloney, Francis J. *Belief in the Word: Reading John 1–4*. Minneapolis: Fortress, 1993.
———. *Glory Not Dishonor: Reading John 13–21*. Minneapolis: Fortress, 1998.
———. *The Gospel of John*. SP 4. Collegeville, MN: Liturgical, 1998.
———. *Signs and Shadows: Reading 5–12*. Minneapolis: Fortress, 1996.
Montgomery, James Alan. *The Samaritans, the Earliest Jewish Sect: Their History, Theology and Literature*. The Bohlen Lectures for 1906. Philadelphia: John C. Winston, 1907.
Moore, George Foote. "Intermediaries in Jewish Thought." *HTR* 15 (1922) 41–85.
Morgan, Christopher W., and Robert A. Peterson. *The Glory of God*. Theology in Community. Wheaton, IL: Crossway, 2010.
Morris, Leon. *The Gospel According to John*. Rev. ed. NICNT. Grand Rapids: Eerdmans, 1995.
Moule, C. F. D. *An Idiom Book of NT Greek*. 2nd ed. Cambridge: Cambridge University Press, 1971.
Moulton, James Hope, and George Milligan. *The Vocabulary of the Greek Testament*. Repr. Grand Rapids: Eerdmans, 1980.
Moulton, James Hope, and Nigel Turner. *A Grammar of New Testament Greek*. Edinburgh: T. & T. Clark, 1976.
Moyise, Steve. "Intertextuality and the Study of the OT in the NT." In *The Old Testament in the New Testament: Essays in Honour of J. L. North*, edited by Steve Moyise, 14–41. Sheffield: Sheffield Academic, 2000.
———. *The Old Testament in the New: An Introduction*. T. & T. Clark Approaches to Biblical Studies. 2nd ed. rev. and exp. London: Bloomsbury, 2015.
Mulder, Martin Jan, and Harry Sysling, eds. *Mikra: Texts, Translations, Reading and Interpretation of the Hebrew Bible in Ancient Judaism and Early Christianity*. Compendia Rerum Iudaicarum ad NovT. Repr. Peabody, MA: Hendrickson, 2004.

Müller, M. *First Bible of Church*. Sheffield: Sheffield Academic, 1996.
Muller, Richard A. *Dictionary of Latin and Greek Theological Terms: Drawn Principally from Protestant Scholastic Theology*. 2nd ed. Grand Rapids: Baker Academic, 2017.
Murphy, Roland E. *Proverbs*. WBC 22. Grand Rapids: Zondervan, 1998
———. *The Tree of Life: The Exploration of Biblical Wisdom Literature*. 3rd ed. Millennium Suppl. Grand Rapids: Eerdmans, 2002.
Mutschler, Bernard. "Was weiß Irenäus vom Johannesevangelium? Der historische Kontext des Johannesevangelium aus der Perpektive seiner Rezeption bei Irenäus von Lyon." In *Kontexte des Johannesevangeliums: Das vierte Evangelium in religions-und traditionsgeschichtlicher Perspective*, edited by Jörg Frey and Udo Schnelle, 695–742. Tübingen: Mohr Siebeck, 2004.
Myers, Alicia D., and Bruce G. Schuchard. *Abiding Words: The Use of Scripture in the Gospel of John*. Resources for Biblical Study 81. Atlanta: SBL, 2015.
Nagel, Titus. *Die Rezeption des Johannesevangeliums im 2. Jahrhundert: Studien zur vorirenäischen Aneignung und Auslegung des vierten Evangeliums in christlicher und christlich-gnostischer Literatur*. ABG 2. Leipzig: Evangelische Verlagsanstalt, 2000.
———. "Zur Gnostisierung der johanneischen Tradition: Das 'Geheime Evangelium nach Johannes' (Apokryphon Johannis) als gnostische Zusatzoffenbarung zum vierten Evangelium." In *Kontexte des Johannesevangeliums: Das vierte Evangelium in religions-und traditionsgeschichtlicher Perspective*, edited by Jörg Frey and Udo Schnelle, 675–94. Tübingen: Mohr Siebeck, 2004.
Nelson, W. David, trans. and ed. *Mekhilta de-Rabbi Shimon bar Yoḥai*. Philadelphia: Jewish Publication Society, 2006.
Nestle, Eberhard, et al., eds. *Novum Testamentum Graece*. 27th ed. Stuttgart: Bibelgesellschaft, 1993.
Neusner, Jacob. *Development of a Legend: Studies on the Traditions Concerning Yohanan Ben-Zakkai*. Studia Post Biblica. Leiden: Brill, 1970.
———. *Early Rabbinic Judaism*. Leiden: Brill, 1975.
———. "The Formation of Rabbinic Judaism: Yavneh (Jamnia) from A.D. 70–100." ANRW 2.19.2 (1979) 3–42.
———. *Genesis Rabbah*. 3 vols. Brown Judaic Studies. Atlanta: SBL, 1985.
———. *Introduction to Rabbinic Literature*. New Haven, CT: Yale University Press, 1994.
———. *Midrash Reader*. Philadelphia: Fortress, 1990.
———. *The Mishnah: A New Translation*. New Haven, CT: Yale University Press, 1988.
———. *Rabbinic Judaism: The Documentary History of its Formative Age, 70–600 C.E.* Bethesda: CDL, 1994.
———. *Rabbinic Literature: An Essential Guide*. Nashville: Abingdon, 2005.
———. *Rabbinic Literature and the New Testament*. Philadelphia: TPI, 1994.
———. *Rabbinic Judaism: The Theological System*. Leiden: Brill Academic, 2003.
———. *The Rabbinic Traditions About the Pharisees Before 70*. 3 vols. Eugene, OR: Wipf & Stock, 2005.
———, trans. *Babylonian and Jerusalem Collection*. 50 vols. Peabody, MA: Hendrickson, 2008–2011.
———, trans. *The Babylonian Talmud: Translation and Commentary*. 50 vols. Peabody, MA: Hendrickson, 2008–2011.

———, trans. *The Jerusalem Talmud: Translation and Commentary.* Peabody, MA: Hendrickson, 2008.

———, trans. and ed. *The Tosefta: Translated from the Hebrew with a New Introduction.* 2 vols. Repr. Peabody, MA: Hendrickson Publishers, 2002.

Neusner, Jacob, et al., eds. *The Encyclopedia of Judaism.* 2nd ed. Leiden: Brill, 2005.

Neusner, Jacob, and William Scott, eds. *Dictionary of Judaism in the Biblical Period: 450 B.C.E to 600 C.E.* New York: Macmillan, 1996. Peabody, MA: Hendrickson, 1999.

Newsom, Carol A. "Angels: Old Testament." In *AYBD* 1:248–53.

Neyrey, Jerome. H. *Gospel of John.* Cambridge: Cambridge University Press, 2009.

Nickelsburg, George W. *Ancient Judaism and Christian Origins: Diversity, Continuity, and Transformation.* Minneapolis: Fortress, 2003.

Nickelsburg, G. W. E. "Enoch." In *IDBSup,* 265–68.

———. *Enoch 1.* Hermeneia. Minneapolis: Fortress, 2001.

———. *Jewish Literature between the Bible and the Mishnah: A Historical and Literary Introduction.* Minneapolis: Fortress, 2005.

Nilsson, Martin P. *The Dionysiac Mysteries of the Hellenistic and Roman Age.* Lund, SE: C.W.K. Gleerup, 1957.

Nissen, Johannes, and Sigfred Pedersen. *New Readings in John: Literary and Theological Perspectives. Essays from the Scandinavian Conference on the Fourth Gospel, Århus, 1997.* New York: T. & T. Clark, 2004.

Nock, A. D., and A. J. Festugière. *Corpus Hermeticum.* 4 vols. Collection des Universités de France. Repr. Paris: Les Belles Lettres, 1972–1974.

Norden, Eduard. *Agnostos Theos: Untersuchungen zur Formengeschichte religiöser Rede.* Leipzig-Berlin: Teubner, 1913.

North, W. E. S. *Journey Round John: Tradition, Interpretation and Context in the Fourth Gospel.* London: Bloomsbury T. & T. Clark, 2015.

Nussbaum, Martha C. "Heraclitus." In *OCD,* 687.

O'Day, Gail R. "The Gospel of John." In *NIB,* 9:491–865. Nashville: Abingdon, 1995.

———. *Revelation in the Fourth Gospel: Narrative Mode and Theological Claim.* Philadelphia: Fortress, 1986.

Odeberg, Hugo. *The Fourth Gospel, Interpreted in Its Relation to Contemporaneous Religious Currents in Palestine and the Hellenistic-Oriental World.* 1929 ed. Repr. Amsterdam: B. R. Grüner, 1968.

Olson, Dennis T. "Biblical Theology." In *NIDB* 1:461–65.

Ong, Walter J. "A Writer's Audience is Always a Fiction." In *Interfaces of the Word: Studies in the Evolution of Consciousness and Culture,* 53–81. Ithaca, NY: Cornell University Press, 1977.

Onuki, Takashi. "Traditionsgeschichte von Thomasevangelium 17 und ihre christologische Relevanz." In *Anfänge der Christologie: Festschrift für Ferdinand Hahn zum 65. Geburtstag,* edited by C. Breytenbach and H. Paulsen, 399–415. Göttingen: Vandenhoeck & Ruprecht, 1991.

Origen. *Commentary on the Gospel according to John Books 1–10.* Translated By Ronald E. Heine. Washington, DC: Catholic University of America Press, 1989.

———. *Origen: Contra Celsum.* Translated by Henry Chadwick. Cambridge University Press, 1980.

———. *Origenes Johannes Commentar.* In *Origenes,* edited by Erwin Preuschen, 4:3–480. Die Griechischen Christlicher Schriftsteller der Ersten drei Jahrunderte. Leipzig: J. C. Hinrich, 1903.

Orlov, Andrei A. "Metatron." In *Dictionary of Early Judaism*, edited by John J. Collins and Daniel C. Harlow, 942–43. Grand Rapids: Eerdmans, 2010.

Oropeza, B. J., and Steve Moyise. *Exploring Intertextuality: Diverse Strategies for NT Interpretation of Texts*. Eugene, OR: Wipf & Stock, 2016.

Orton, David E., ed. *The Composition of John's Gospel: Selected Studies from Novum Testamentum*. Leiden and Boston: Brill, 1999.

Osborne, Grant R. *John, Verse by Verse*. Bellingham, WA: Lexham, 2018.

Pagels, Elaine. *Das Geheimnis des fünften Evangeliums*. Munich: C. H. Beck, 2004.

———. "Exegesis of Genesis 1 in the Gospels of Thomas and John." *JBL* 118 (1999) 477–96.

———. *The Gnostic Gospels*. New York: Random, 1979.

———. "Gnosticism." In *IDBS* 364–67.

———. *The Johannine Gospel in Gnostic Exegesis: Heracleon's Commentary on John*. SBLMS 17. Repr. Atlanta: SBL, 1989.

———. *Why Religion? A Personal Story*. New York: HarperCollins, 2018.

Paget, James Carleton. "The Definition of the Terms *Jewish Christian* and *Jewish Christianity* in the History of Research." In *Jewish Believers in Jesus: The Early Centuries*, edited by Oskar Skarsaune and Reidar Hvalvik, 22–52. Peabody, MA: Hendrickson, 2007.

Painter, John. *The Quest for the Messiah: The History, Literature and Theology of the Johannine Community*. 2nd ed. Nashville: Abingdon, 1993.

———. *1, 2, and 3 John*. SP 18. Collegeville, MN: Liturgical, 2002.

Painter, John, et al., eds. *Word, Theology, and Community in John*. St. Louis: Chalice Press, 2002.

Palmer, Micheal. "A Comprehensive Bibliography of Hellenistic Greek Linguistics." http://www.greek-language.com/Palmer-bibiography.html.

Pamplaniyil, Joseph. "The Beloved Disciple and Thomas: The Literary Didymoi of the Fourth Gospel." *Vid* 68 (2004) 560–78.

Parry, Donald W., and Emanuel Tov, eds. *The Dead Sea Scrolls Reader*. 6 vols. Leiden: Brill, 2004.

Parsenios, George L. *First, Second, and Third John*. Paidea. Grand Rapids: Baker Academic, 2014.

———. *Rhetoric and Drama in the Johannine Lawsuit Motif*. WUNT 258. Tübingen: Mohr Siebeck, 2010.

Patterson, Stephen J. *The Gospel of Thomas and Jesus*. Foundations & Facets Reference Series. Sonoma, CA: Polebridge, 1993.

———. "The Gospel of Thomas and the Synoptic Tradition: A *Forschungsbericht* and Critique." *Foundations and Facets Forum* 8 (1992) 45–97.

———. "The Prologue to the Fourth Gospel and the World Speculative Jewish Theology." Pages 323–332 in Robert T. Fortna and Tom Thatcher, eds. *Jesus in Johannine Tradition*. Louisville: Westminster John Knox, 2001.

Patton, K. C., and B. C. Rav. *A Magic Still Dwells: Comparative Religion in the Postmodern Age*. Berkeley: University of California Press, 2000.

Pazdan, Mary Margaret. *The Son of Man: A Metaphor for Jesus in the Fourth Gospel*. Zacchaeus Studies. Collegeville, MN: Liturgical, 1991.

Pearson, Birger. "Basilides the Gnostic." In *A Companion to Second-Century Christian 'Heretics,'* edited by Antti Marjanen and Petri Luomanen, 1–31. Leiden: Brill Academic, 2008.

———. "The Problem of 'Jewish Gnostic' Literature." In *Nag Hammadi, Gnosticism, and Early Christianity*, edited by Charles W. Hedrick and Robert Hodgson, Jr., 15-35. Peabody, MA: Hendrickson, 1986.

———. ed., *The Future of Early Christianity: Essays in honor of Helmut Koester*. Minneapolis: Fortress, 1991.

Pearson, Birger, and James E. Goehring, eds. *The Roots of Egyptian Christianity*. Studies in Antiquity and Christianity. Minneapolis: Fortress, 1986.

Penchansky, David. *Twilight of the Gods: Polytheism in the Hebrew Bible*. Louisville: Westminster John Knox, 2003.

Perkins, Pheme. "Gnosticism." *NIDB* 2:581-84.

———. *Gnosticism and the New Testament*. Minneapolis: Fortress, 1993.

———. "Johannine Traditions in Ap. Jas. (NHC I,2)." *JBL* 101 (1982) 403-14.

———. *Love Commands in the New Testament*. New York: Paulist, 1982.

———. "Nag Hammadi Texts." In *NIDB* 4:205-10.

Petersen, Anders Klostergaard, and George H. van Kooten, eds. *Religio-philosophical Discourses in the Mediterranean World: From Plato, Through Jesus, to Late Antiquity*. Ancient Philosophy and Religion. Leiden: Brill Academic, 2017.

Petersen, Norman R. *The Gospel of John and The Sociology of Light*. Repr. Eugene, OR: Wipf & Stock, 2008.

Petersen, Walter L. *Tatian's Diatessaron: Its Creation, Dissemination, Significance and History in Scholarship*. Leiden: Brill, 1994.

Petronius. *Satyricon; Seneca: Apocyntosis*. Translated by Michael Heseltine and W. H. D. Rouse. LCL. Cambridge, MA: Harvard University Press, 1925.

Philo. *Philo, with an English Translation*. Edited by F. H. Colson et al. 10 vols and 2 suppl. vols. LCL. Cambridge, MA: Harvard University Press: 1929-1962.

———. *Works of*. Translated by C. D. Yonge. Foreword by David M. Scholer. New updated version. Peabody, MA: Hendrickson, 1993.

Pilch, John. *The Cultural Dictionary of the Bible*. Collegeville, MN: Liturgical, 1999.

Pietersma, Albert, and Benjamin G. Wright, eds. *A New English Translation of the Septuagint and the Other Greek Translations Traditionally Included under That Title*. Oxford: Oxford University Press, 2007.

Plato. *Euthyphro, Apology, Crito, Phaedo*. Translated by Harold North Fowler. LCL. Cambridge, MA: Harvard University Press, 2005.

———. *Lysis, Symposium, Gorgias*. Translated by W. R. M. Lamb. LCL. Cambridge, MA: Harvard University Press, 1983.

———. *Timaeus, Critias, Cleitophon, Menexenus, Epistles*. Translated by R. G. Bury. LCL. Cambridge, MA: Harvard University Press, 1961.

Plisch, Uwe-Karsten. *The Gospel of Thomas: Original Text with Commentary*. Translated by Gesine Schenke Robinson. Stuttgart: Deutsche Bibelgesellschaft, 2008.

Plummer, Reinhard. "New Evidence for Samaritan Christianity?" *CBQ* 41 (1979) 98-117.

Pollard, T. E. *Johannine Christology and the Early Church*. Cambridge: Cambridge University Press, 1970.

Popkes, Enno E. "About the Differing Approach to a Theological Heritage: Comments on the Relationship between the Gospel of John, The Gospel of Thomas, and Qumran." In *The Bible and the Dead Sea Scrolls, Vol. III: Qumran and Christian Origins*, edited by J. H. Charlesworth, 281-317. Waco, TX: Baylor University Press, 2006.

———. "Ich bin das Licht"—Erwägungen zur Verhältnisbestimmung des Thomasevangelium und der johanneischen Schriften anhand der Lichtmetaphoric." In *Kontexte des Johannesevangeliums: Das vierte Evangelium in religions-und traditionsgeschichtlicher Perspektive*, Jörg Frey und Udo Schnelle, 641–74. Mohr Siebeck, 2004.

Porter, James I. "Stoic Interpretation." In *The Homer Encyclopedia*, edited by Margalit Finkelberg, 3:823–26. London: Wiley-Blackwell, 2011.

Porter, Stanley E. "The Context of Jesus: Jewish and/or Hellenistic." In *Handbook for the Study of the Historical Jesus*, edited by Tom Holmén and Stanley E. Porter, 2:1441–63. Leiden: Brill, 2011.

———. "The Use of the Old Testament in the New Testament: A Brief Comment on Method and Terminology." In *Early Christian Interpretation of the Scriptures of Israel*, edited by C. A. Evans and J. A. Sanders, 79–96. Sheffield: Sheffield Academic, 1997.

———, ed. *The Criteria for Authenticity in Historical-Jesus Research: Previous Discussions and New Proposals.* JSNTSup 91; Sheffield: Sheffield Academic, 2000.

———, ed. *Handbook to the Exegesis of the New Testament.* Leiden: Brill, 1997.

———, ed. *Hearing the Old Testament in the New Testament.* Grand Rapids: Eerdmans, 2006.

———, ed. *The Language of the New Testament: Classic Essays.* Sheffield: Sheffield Academic, 1991.

Porter, Stanley E., and Craig A. Evans. *The Scrolls and the Scriptures: Qumran Fifty Years After.* London: Bloomsbury Academic, 1997.

Porter, Stanley E., and Dennis L. Stamps, eds. *Rhetorical Criticism and the Bible.* London: Sheffield Academic, 2002.

Porter, Stanley E., and Ron C. Fay, eds. *The Gospel of John in Modern Interpretation.* Milestones in NT Scholarship. Grand Rapids: Kregel Academic, 2018.

Pourkier, Aline. *L'hérésiologie chez Épiphane de Salamine.* Christianisme antique 4. Paris: Beauchesne, 1992.

Powell, Mark Allan, and David R. Bauer, eds. *Who Do You Say That I Am? Essays on Christology in Honor of Jack Dean Kingsbury.* Louisville: Westminster John Knox, 1999.

Pratt, D. Butler. "The Gospel of John from the Standpoint of Greek Tragedy." *Biblical World* 30 (1907) 448–59.

Price, H. H. *Thinking and Experience.* 2nd ed. London: Hutchinson, 1969.

Pritchard, James B. *Ancient Near Eastern Texts Relating to the Old Testament with Supplement.* 3rd rev. ed. Princeton: Princeton University Press, 1969.

Procksch, O. "Divine Word of Creation." In *TDNT* 4:99–100.

Purvis, James D. "The Fourth Gospel and the Samaritans." In *The Composition of John's Gospel: Selected Studies from Novum Testamentum*, edited by David E. Orton, 148–85. Leiden and Boston: Brill, 1999.

———. *The Samaritan Pentateuch and the Origins.* Harvard Semitic Monographs 2. Cambridge, MA: Harvard University Press, 1968.

Puskas, Charles B. *Hebrews, the General Letters, and Revelation: An Introduction.* Eugene, OR: Cascade, 2016.

Puskas, Charles B., and C. Michael Robbins. *An Introduction to the New Testament.* 2nd ed. Eugene, OR: Cascade, 2011.

Puskas, Charles B., and David Crump. *An Introduction to the Gospels and Acts.* Grand Rapids: Eerdmans, 2008.

Puskas, Charles B., and Mark Reasoner. *The Letters of Paul: An Introduction*. 2nd ed, Collegeville, MN: Liturgical, 2013.
Quispel, Gilles. "'The Gospel of Thomas' and the 'Gospel of the Hebrews.'" *NTS* 12 (1965–1966) 371–82.
———. "Qumran, John and Jewish Christianity." In *John and the Dead Sea Scrolls*, edited by J. H. Charlesworth et al., 137–55. Crossroad Christian Origins Library. New York: Crossroad, 2013.
Rad, Gerhard von. *Wisdom in Israel*. Nashville: Abingdon, 1972.
Rahlfs, Alfred, ed. *Septuaginta: id est vetus testamentum graece juxta LXX interpretes*. Rev. ed. 2 vols. in one. Stuttgart: Deutsche Bibelgesellschaft, 2006.
Rankin, O. S. *Israel's Wisdom Literature: Its Bearing on Theology and the History of Religion*. New York: Schocken Books, 1969.
Rasimus, Tuomas, ed. *The Legacy of John*. Supplements to NovT 132. Leiden: Brill Academic, 2009.
Rasimus, Tuomas, et al., eds. *Stoicism in Early Christianity*. Grand Rapids: Baker Academic, 2010.
Regev, Eyal. "Were the Early Christians Sectarian?" *JBL* 130:4 (2011) 771–93.
Rendsburg, Gary A. "The Hazon Gabriel Inscription." *DSD* 16 (2009) 107–16.
Reinhartz, Adele. *Befriending the Beloved Disciple: A Jewish Reading of the Gospel of John*. New York: Continuum, 2001.
———. "Building Skyscrapers on Toothpicks: The Literary-Critical Challenge to Historical Criticism." In *Anatomies of Narrative Criticism: The Past, Present, and Future of the Fourth Gospel as Literature*, edited by Tom Thatcher and Stephen D. Moore, 55–76. Leiden and Boston: Brill, 2008.
———. *Cast Out of the Covenant: Jews and Anti-Judaism in the Gospel of John*. Lanham, MD: Lexington Fortress Academic, 2018.
———. *The Word in the World: The Cosmological Tale in the Fourth Gospel*. SBLMS 45. Atlanta: Scholars, 1992.
Reitzenstein, Richard. *Hellenistic Mystery Religions: Their Basic Ideas and Significance*. Translated by John E. Steely. Pittsburgh: Pickwick, 1978.
———. *Poimandres: Studien zur Grieschisch-Ägyptischen und Frühchristlichen Literatur*. Repr. Darmstadt: Wissenschaftliche Buchgesellschaft, 1966.
Rhea, Robert. *The Johannine Son of Man*. Reprint with new preface. Eugene, OR: Wipf & Stock, 2017.
Rhoads, D. "Narrative Criticism," In *NIDB* 4:222–23.
Rice, David G., and John E. Stambaugh. *Sources for the Study of Greek Religion*. Sources for the Study of Greek Religion 14. Atlanta: SBL, 2009.
Ricken, Friedo. *Philosophy of the Ancients*. Translated by Eric Watkins. Notre Dame: University of Notre Dame, 1991.
Ricœur, Paul. *Interpretation Theory: Discourse and the Surplus of Meaning*. Fort Worth: Texas Christian University Press, 1976.
———. *Rule of Metaphor*. Toronto: University of Toronto Press: 1981.
Riley, Gregory. *I Was Thought to Be What I Am Not: Tradition and the Johannine Jesus. Docetic Jesus and the Johannine tradition*. Claremont, CA: Institute for Antiquity and Christianity, 1994.
———. *One Jesus, Many Christs. How Jesus Inspired Not One True Christianity, But Many*. New York: Harper SanFrancisco, 1997.

———. *Resurrection Reconsidered. Thomas and John in Controversy.* Minneapolis: Augsburg Fortress, 1995.

———. *The River of God: A New History of Christian Origins.* New York: HarperSanFrancisco, 2001.

Ringe, Sharon H. *Wisdom's Friends: Community and Christology in the Fourth Gospel.* Louisville: Westminster John Knox, 1999.

Rist, J. M. *Stoic Philosophy.* Cambridge: Cambridge University Press, 1969.

Rist, Martin. "Pseudepigraphy and the Early Christians." In *Studies in NT and Early Christian Literature,* edited by David Aune, 3–24. Leiden: Brill, 1972.

Roberts, Alexander, and James Donaldson, et al., trans. and eds. *The Ante-Nicene Fathers. The Writings of the Fathers Down to A.D. 325.* ANCL. 10 vols. Rev. ed. Peabody, MA: Hendrickson, 1994.

Robbins, C. Michael. *The Testing of Jesus in Q.* Berlin: Peter Lang, 2007.

Robinson, Gesine. "The Trimorphic Protennoia and the Prologue of the Fourth Gospel." In *Gnosticism and the Early Christian World: In Honor of James M. Robinson,* edited by James E. Goehring et al., 37–50. Sonoma, CA: Polebridge, 1990.

Robinson, H. Wheeler. *The Religious Ideas of the Old Testament.* 2nd ed. rev. London: Gerald Duckworth & Co., 1956.

Robinson, James M. "The Discovery of the Nag Hammadi Codices." *BA* 42 (1979) 206–24.

———. "Nag Hammadi: The First Fifty Years." A Plenary Address given at the Annual Meeting of the SBL, 1995, published as *Occasional Papers #34* by the Institute for Antiquity and Christianity.

———. *The Nag Hammadi Codices: A General Introduction to the Nature and Significance of the Coptic Gnostic Library from Nag Hammadi.* 2nd rev. ed. Official Catalogue of the Nag Hammadi Exhibit. Claremont, CA: Institute for Antiquity and Christianity, 1977.

———. "On Bridging the Gulf from Q to the Gospel of Thomas" In *Nag Hammadi Gnosticism and Early Christianity,* edited by Charles W. Hedrick and Robert Hodgson Jr, 127–75. Peabody, MA: Hendrickson, 1986.

———, ed. *The Future of Our Religious Past: Essays in Honour of Rudolf Bultmann.* London: SCM, 1971.

Robinson, James M., et al., eds. *The Nag Hammadi Library.* Rev. ed. New York: Harper Collins, 1990.

Roche, Paul, trans. *Three Plays of Euripides: Alcestis, Medea, The Bacchae.* New York: W. W. Norton, 1974.

Roloff, Jürgen. *Revelation.* CCS. Translated by John E. Alsup. Minneapolis: Fortress, 1993.

Ronning, John. *The Jewish Targums and John's Logos Theology.* Grand Rapids: Baker Academic, 2011.

———. "The Targum of Isaiah and Johannine Literature." *WJT* 69 (2007) 274–77.

Rudolph, Kurt. *Die Mandäer 1. Prolegomena:Das Mandäerproblem* FRLANT 74. Edited by Rudolf Bultmann. Göttingen: Vandenhoeck & Ruprecht, 1960.

———. *Gnosis: The Nature and History of Gnosticism.* Translated by Robert McLachlan Wilson et al. New York: HarperCollins, 1987.

———. "Mandaeism." In *AYBD* 4:500–502.

Runia, David T. *Philo in Early Christian Literature: A Survey.* Compendia Rerum Iudaicarum ad Novum Testamentum. Minneapolis: Fortress, 1993.

Ryle, H. S., and M. R. James. *Psalmoi Solomontos: Psalms of the Pharisees.* Cambridge: Cambridge University Press, 1891.
Sabbe, Maurits. "Can Mt 11,25–27 and Lc 10, 22 Be Called a Johannine Logion?" In *LOGIA: les paroles de Jésus: memorial Joseph Coppens*, edited by Joël Delobel, Tjitze Baarda et al., 263–71. Leuven: Peeters and Leuven University Press, 1982.
Sáenz-Badillos, Angel. *History of Hebrew Language.* Translated by John Elwolde. Cambridge: Cambridge University Press, 1993.
Safrai, Shmuel, ed. *The Literature of the Sages: First Part, 3a: Oral Tora, Halakha, Mishna, Tosefta, Talmud, External Tractates.* Rerum Iudaicarum Ad NovT. Section 2: Literature of the Jewish People in the Period of the Second Temple and the Talmud. Leiden: Brill, 1987.
———, et al., eds. *The Literature of the Sages. Second Part, 3b. Midrash, and Targum; Liturgy, Poetry, Mysticism; Contracts, Inscriptions, Ancient Science and the Languages of Rabbinic Literature.* Rerum Iudaicarum Ad NovT. Section 2: Literature of the Jewish People in the Period of the Second Temple and the Talmud. Minneapolis: Fortress, 2006.
Sakenfeld, Katharine Doob, ed. *The New Interpreter's Dictionary of the Bible.* 5 vols. Nashville: Abingdon, 2006–2009.
Saldarini, A. J. "Rabbinic Literature and the NT." In *AYBD* 5:602–4.
Salmon, Victor. *Fourth Gospel: A History of the Textual Tradition.* Translated by M. J. O'Connell; Collegeville: Liturgical, 1976.
Sanders, E. P. *The Historical Figure of Jesus.* New York: Penguin, 1995.
———. *Jesus and Judaism.* London and Philadelphia, 1985.
———. *Jewish Law from Jesus to the Mishnah: Five Studies.* Harrisburg, PA: Trinity, 1990.
———. *Paul and Palestinian Judaism: A Comparison of Patterns of Religions.* Philadelphia: Fortress, 1977.
———, ed. *Jewish and Christian Self-Definition, Vol. 2: Aspects of Judaism in the Greco-Roman Period.* Philadelphia: Fortress, 1981.
Sanders, J. N. *The Fourth Gospel in the Early Church.* Cambridge: Cambridge University Press, 1943.
Sanders, Jack T. "Nag Hammadi, Odes, and the New Testament." In *Gnosticism and the early Christian World: in honor of James M Robinson*, edited by James E. Goehring et al., 51–66. Sonoma, CA: Polebridge, 1990.
———. *The New Testament Christological Hymns. Their Historical Religious Background.* SNTSMS 15. Cambridge: Cambridge University Press, 1971.
Sanderson, Judith E. *An Exodus Scroll from Qumran: 4QpaleoExod and the Samaritan Tradition.* Harvard Semitic Studies 30. Atlanta: Scholars, 1986.
Sandmel, Samuel. *Herod: Profile of a Tyrant.* Philadelphia: J. B. Lippincott, 1987.
———. *Judaism and Christian Beginnings.* New York: Oxford University Press, 1978.
———. "Parallelomania." *JBL* 81 (1962) 1–13.
Saunders, Jason L. *Greek and Roman Philosophy after Aristotle.* 1966. New York: Free Press, 1994.
Saylor, Gwendolyn B. *Have The Promises Failed? A Literary Analysis of 2 Baruch.* SBLDS 72. Chico, CA: Scholars, 1984.
Schaps, David. *Handbook for Classical Research.* New York: Routledge, 2009.
Schechter, Solomon, trans. *Fragments of a Zadokite Work. Documents of Jewish Sectaries.* Edited by Harry M. Orlinsky from Hebrew Manuscripts in the Cairo Genizah Collection. Repr. New York: Ktav Publishers, 1970.

Schenck, Kenneth. *Philo of Alexandria: Introduction to Life and Work*. Louisville: Westminster John Knox, 2005.

Schenke, Hans-Martin. "Das sethianische System nach Nag-Hammadi-Handschriften." In *Studia Coptica*, edited by Peter Nagel, 165–73. Berlin: Akademie Verlag, 1974.

———. "Die Gnosis." In *Umwelt des Christentums*, edited by Johannes Leipoldt and Walter Grundman, 1:371–415. 6th ed. Berlin: Evangelische Verlaganstalt, 1982.

———. "Die Tendenz der Weisheit zur Gnosis." In *Gnosis: Festschrift für Hans Jonas*, edited by Barbara Aland, 351–72. Göttingen: Vandenhoeck & Ruprecht, 1978.

———. "Gnostic Sethianism." In *Rediscovery of Gnosticism*, edited by Bentley Layton, 2:588–616. Leiden: Brill, 1981.

———. "On the Compositional History of the Gospel of Thomas." Occasional Papers of the Institute for Antiquity and Christianity 40. Claremont, CA: Institute for Antiquity and Christianity, 1998.

Schiffman, Lawrence. *Qumran and Jerusalem*. Grand Rapids: Eerdmans, 2010.

———. *Reclaiming the Dead Sea Scrolls*. Philadelphia: Jewish Publication Society, 1994.

———. *Texts and Traditions. A Source Reader for the Study of Second Temple and Rabbinic Judaism*. Hoboken: KTAV, 1998.

Schiffman, Lawrence, et al. *The Dead Sea Scrolls Fifty Years After Their Discovery Proceedings of the Jerusalem Congress, July 20-25, 1997*. Jerusalem: Israel Exploration Society, 2000.

Schiffman, Lawrence, and James C. VanderKam, eds. *Encyclopedia of the Dead Sea Scrolls*. Oxford: Oxford University Press, 2000.

Schlatter, Adolf. *Der Evangelist Johannes*. 2nd ed. Stuttgart: Calwer Verlag, 1948.

———. *Die Sprache und Heimat des vierten Evangelißten*. Gütersloh: C. Bertelsmann Verlag, 1902.

Schmeller, Thomas. "Stoics, Stoicism." In *AYBD* 6:210–14.

Schnackenburg, Rudolf. *The Gospel according to St. John*. Vol. 1. Trans. Kevin Smyth. Eds., J. Massingberde Ford and K. Smyth. New York: Herder & Herder, 1968. Vol. 2. New York: Seabury, 1980. Vol. 3. New York: Crossroad, 1982.

———. *The Johannine Epistles: A Commentary*. New York: Crossroad, 1992.

Schneemelcher, Wilhelm, ed. *New Testament Apocrypha*. 2 vols. Translated by R. McL. Wilson. Rev. ed. Louisville: Westminster John Knox, 2003.

Schnelle, Udo. *Antidocetic Christology in the Gospel of John*. Translated by Linda M. Maloney. Minneapolis: Fortress, 1992.

———. *Das Evangelium nach Johannes*. THKNT 4. Leipzig: Evangelische Verlgsanstalt, 2004.

———. *Die Johannesbrief*. THKNT 17. Leipzig: Evangelische Verlagsanstalt, 2010.

———. *The Human Condition: Anthropology in the Teachings of Jesus, Paul, and John*. Translated by O. C. Dean Jr. Minneapolis: Fortress, 1996.

———. *Theology of the New Testament*. Translated by M. Eugene Boring. Grand Rapids: Baker Academic, 2009.

Schoedel, William R. *Ignatius of Antioch*. Hermeneia. Philadelphia: Fortress, 1985.

———. "Ignatius, Epistles of." In *AYBD* 3:384–85.

Schoeps, Hans Joachim. *Jewish Christianity: Factional Disputes in the Early Church*. Translated by Douglas R. A. Hare. Philadelphia: Fortress, 1969.

Scholtissek, Klaus. "The Johannine Gospel in Recent Research." In *The Face of New Testament Studies: A Survey of Recent Research*, edited by Scot McKnight and Grant R. Osborne, 444–72. Grand Rapids: Baker, 2004.

Schuchard, Bruce G. *Scripture within Scripture: The Interrelationship of Form and Function in the Explicit Old Testament Citations in the Gospel of John.* SBLDS 133. Atlanta: Scholars, 1992.

Scott, Martin. *Sophia and Johannine Jesus.* Sheffield: Sheffield Academic, 1992.

Sedley, David, ed. *Cambridge Companion to Greek and Roman Philosophy.* Cambridge Companions. Cambridge: Cambridge University Press, 2003.

Seelig, Gerald. *Religionsgeschichtliche Methode in Vergangenheit und Gegenwart: Studien zur Geschichte und Methode des religionsgeschichtlichen Vergleichs in der neutestamentlichen Wissenschaft.* Arbeiten zur Bibel und ihrer Geschichte 7. Leipzig: Evangelische Verlagsanstalt, 2001.

Segal, Alan. "Mysticism." In Collins and Harlow, *Early Judaism*, 982–86.

———. *Two Powers in Heaven: Early Rabbinic Reports About Christianity and Gnosticism.* Leiden: Brill, 2002

Segal, M. H. *Grammar of Mishnaic Hebrew.* Repr. Wipf & Stock, 2001.

Segovia, Fernando F. *The Farewell of the Word: The Johannine Call to Abide.* Minneapolis: Fortress, 1995.

———, ed. *"What is John?"* Vol. 2: *Literary and Social Readings of the Fourth Gospel.* Symposium Series 7. Atlanta: SBL, 1998.

Sell, Jesse. "Johannine Traditions in Logion 61 of the Gospel of Thomas." *PRSt* 7 (1980) 24–37.

Seneca. *Seneca: Moral Essays I: De Providentia, De Constantia, De Ira, De Clementia.* Translated by John W. Basore. LCL. Cambridge, MA: Harvard University Press, 1928.

Shanks, Hershel, ed. *Christianity and Rabbinic Judaism: A Parallel History of Their Origins and Early Development.* Washington, DC: Biblical Archaeology Society, 1992.

Sheridan, Ruth. "They Shall Look Upon the One They Have Pierced: Intertextuality, Intratextuality and Anti-Judaism in John 19:37." In *Searching the Scriptures: Studies in Context and Intertextuality,* edited by Craig A. Evans and Jeremiah J. Johnston, 191–210. London: Bloomsbury T. & T. Clark, 2015.

Shorey, Paul. *Platonism, Ancient and Modern.* Sather Classical Lectures. 14th ed. Berkeley: University of California Press, 1938.

Siliezar, Carlos Raúl Sosa, *Creation Imagery in the Gospel of John.* London: Bloomsbury, T & T Clark, 2015, 2018.

Silva, Moises. *Biblical Words and Their Meaning.* Grand Rapids: Zondervan, 1991.

Skarsaune, Oskar, and Reidar Hvalvik, eds. *Jewish Believers in Jesus: The Early Centuries.* Peabody, MA: Hendrickson, 2007.

Skehan, Patrick W., and Alexander A. Di Lella. *The Wisdom of Ben Sira.* AYB 39. New Haven, CT: Yale University Press, 1987.

Skinner, Christopher W., ed. *Characters and Characterization in the Gospel of John.* LNTS 461. London: T. & T. Clark, 2013.

———. *John and Thomas—Gospels in Conflict? Johannine Characterization and the Thomas Question.* Princeton Theological Monograph Series 115. Eugene: Pickwick, 2009.

———. *Reading John.* A Cascade Companion. Eugene, OR: Cascade, 2015.

Smalley, Stephen S. *1, 2, and 3 John.* WBC 51. Grand Rapids: Zondervan, 2008.

Smith, Dennis E. *From Symposium to Eucharist: The Banquet in the Early Christian World.* Minneapolis: Fortress, 2003.

Smith, D. Moody. *The Composition and Order of the Fourth Gospel: Bultmann's Literary Theory*. Yale, 1965. Reprint. Foreword by R. Alan Culpepper. Johannine Monograph Series. Eugene, OR: Wipf & Stock, 2015.
———. *First, Second, and Third John*. Interpretation. Louisville: John Knox, 1991.
———. *The Fourth Gospel in Four Dimensions: Judaism and Jesus, The Gospels and Scripture*. Columbia, SC: University of South Carolina, 2008.
———. *Johannine Christianity*. Columbia: University of South Carolina Press, 1984.
———. *John among the Gospels*. 2nd ed. Columbia, SC: University of South Carolina Press, 2001.
———. "John," Pages 96–111 in John Barclay and John Sweet, eds. *Early Christian Thought in its Jewish Context*. Festschrift in Honour of Morna Hooker's 65th Birthday. Cambridge: Cambridge University Press, 1996.
———. *The Theology of the Gospel of John*. NT Theology. Cambridge: Cambridge University Press, 1995.
Smith, Eric C. *Jewish Glass and Christian Stone: A Materialist Mapping of the "Parting of the Ways."* Routledge Studies in the Early Christian World. London: Routledge, 2018.
Smith, Jonathan Z. *Drudgery Divine: On the Comparison of Early Christianities and the Religions of Late Antiquity*. Jordan Lectures on Comparative Religion 14. Chicago: University of Chicago, 1990.
———. *Map is Not Territory: Studies in the History of Religions*. Chicago: University of Chicago, 1993.
Smith, Morton. *Tannaitic Parallels to the Gospels*. JBL Monograph Series 7. Repr. Philadelphia: SBL, 1968.
Smith, Robert H. "Exodus Typology in the Fourth Gospel." *JBL* 81 (1962) 329–42.
Smith, Tyler. Review of *The Dionysian Gospel* by Dennis R. MacDonald. *SBL Review of Biblical Literature* 12 (2018). https://www.bookreviews.org/pdf/11778_14227.pdf
Sorokin, Vladimir. *Ice Trilogy*. Translated by James Gambrell. New York: NYRB, 2007.
Soulen, Richard N., and R. Kendall Soulen. *Handbook of Biblical Criticism*. 3rd ed. rev. and expanded. Louisville: Westminster John Knox, 2001.
Stauffer, Ethelbert. *Jesus and His Story*. Translated by Richard and Clara Winston. New York: Alfred A. Knopf, 1960.
Stegemann, Hartmut, ed. *The Library of Qumran: On the Essenes, Qumran, John the Baptist, and Jesus*. Grand Rapids: Eerdmans, 1998.
Steiner, George. "Two Suppers." *Salmagundi* 108 (1995) 33–61.
Steinsaltz, Adin, ed. *Reference Guide to the Talmud*. 2nd rev. ed. Jerusalem: Koren, 2014.
Sterling, Gregory E. "Philo." In Collins and Harlow, *Early Judaism*, 1063–70.
Stewart, A. C. trans. *Melito of Sardis*. New York: St Vladimir's Seminary Press, 2016.
Stibbe, Mark W. G. *John's Gospel*. NT Readings. Edited by John Court. London: Routledge, 1994.
———. *John as Storyteller: Narrative Criticism and the Fourth Gospel*. SNTSMS 73. Cambridge: Cambridge University Press, 1992.
———. "Magnificent but Flawed: The Breaking of Form in the Fourth Gospel." Pages 149–66 in Anatomies of Narrative Criticism, edited by Tom Thatcher and S. D. Moore. Leiden: Brill, 2008.
Stock, Brian. *Listening for the Text: On the Uses of the Past*. The Middle Ages Series. Philadelphia: University of Pennsylvania Press, 1997.
Strack, Hermann L. and G. Stemberg. *Introduction to the Talmud and Midrash*. Translated by Markus Bockmuehl. Edinburgh: T. & T. Clark, 1991. Minneapolis: Fortress, 1992.

Strack, Hermann L., and Paul Billerbeck. *Kommentar zum Neuen Testament aus Talmud und Midrasch*. 6 vols. Munich: Beck, 1922–1961.

Stuckenbruck, Loren T. *Angel Veneration and Christology: A Study in Early Judaism and in the Christology of the Apocalypse of John*. Wissenschaftliche Untersuchungen zum Neuen Testament Second Series 70. Tübingen: Mohr, 1995.

———. "An Approach to the New Testament through Aramaic Sources: The Recent Methodological Debate." *JSP* 8 (1991) 3–29.

———. *The Myth of Rebellious Angels: Studies in Second Temple Judaism and New Testament Texts*. Grand Rapids: Eerdmans, 2014.

Tal, Abraham. "The Samaritan Targum of the Pentateuch." In *Mikra: Texts, Translations, Reading and Interpretation of the Hebrew Bible in Ancient Judaism and Early Christianity*, edited by Martin Jan Mulder and Harry Sysling, 189–216. Compendia Rerum Iudaicarum ad NovT. Repr. Peabody, MA: Hendrickson, 2004.

Talbert, Charles H. "The Concept of Immortals in Mediterranean Antiquity." *JBL* 94 (1975) 419–36.

———. *Reading John: A Literary and Theological Commentary on the Fourth Gospel and the Johannine Epistles*. Rev. ed. Reading the NT Series. Macon, GA: Smyth & Helwys, 2005.

Talbert, Richard J. A., ed. *The Barrington Atlas of the Greek and Roman World*. Princeton: Princeton University Press, 2000.

Talmon, Shemaryahu. *The Importance of the Qumran Calendar in Early Judaism*. The Dead Sea Scrolls and Christian Origins Library. Repr. North Richland Hills, TX: D. & F. Scott, 2002.

Tate, W. Randolph. *Handbook for Biblical Interpretation*. 3rd ed. Grand Rapids: Baker, 2012.

———. *Interpreting the Bible: A Handbook of Terms and Methods*. Peabody, MA: Hendrickson, 2006.

Taylor, Bernard A., et al., eds. *Analytical Lexicon to the Septuagint*. Peabody, MA: Hendrickson, 2009.

Testuz, M., ed. *Papyrus Bodmer XIII, Méliton de Sardes Homélie sur la Pâque*. Geneva: Bodmer, 1960.

Thatcher, Tom. "Remembering Jesus." In *Messiah in the Old Testament and the New Testament*, edited by S. E. Porter, 165–89. Grand Rapids: Eerdmans, 2007.

———, ed. *What We Have Heard from the Beginning: The Past, Present, and Future of Johannine Studies*. Waco, TX: Baylor University Press, 2007.

Thatcher, Tom, and Stephen D. Moore, eds. *Anatomies of the Narrative Criticism: The Past, Present, and Futures of The Fourth Gospel of Literature*. RBS 55. Atlanta: SBL, 2008.

Thayer, Joseph Henry. *Thayer's Greek-English Lexicon of the New Testament*. Repr. Peabody, MA: Hendrickson, 1996.

Theobald, Michael. *Die Fleischwerdung des Logos: Studien zum Verhältnis des Johannesprologs zum Corpus des Evangeliums und zu 1 Joh*. Münster: Aschendorffsche, 1988.

Thesaurus Linguae Graecae: A Digital Library of Greek Literature. University of California, Irvine. http://www.tlg.uci.edu/.

Thesaurus Linguae Latinae. Bayerische Akademie. http://www.thesaurus.badw.de/english/index.htm.

Thiselton, Anthony C. *Hermeneutics: An Introduction*. Grand Rapids: Eerdmans, 2009.

———. *Thiselton on Hermeneutics. Collected Works with New Essays*. Eerdmans, 2006.

Thompson, Marianne Meye. *The God of the Gospel of John*. Grand Rapids: Eerdmans, 2001.
———. *The Humanity of Jesus in the Fourth Gospel*. Philadelphia: Fortress, 1988.
———. *John: A Commentary*. NTL. Louisville: Westminster John Knox, 2015.
———. "'They Bear Witness of Me': The Psalms in the Passion Narrative of the Gospel of John." In *The Word Leaps the Gap: Essays on Scripture and Theology in Honor of Richard B. Hays*, edited by J. Ross Wagner et al., 267-83. Grand Rapids: Eerdmans, 2008.
———. "Word of God, Messiah of Israel, Savior of the World: Learning the Identity of Jesus from the Gospel of John." Pages 166-179 in Gaventa, Beverly Roberts, and Richard B. Hays, eds. *Seeking The Identity of Jesus: A Pilgrimage*. Grand Rapids: Eerdmans, 2008.
Till, W. C. "Das Evangelium der Wahrheit: Neue Übersetzung des vollständigen Textes," ZNW 50 (1959), 165-85.
Tobin, T. H. "Logos." In Collins and Harlow, *Early Judaism*, 894.
Tov, Emanuel. *The Greek and Hebrew Bible: Collected Essays on the Septuagint*. Vetus Testamentum Suppl. 72. Leiden: Brill Academic, 1999.
———. *Hebrew Bible, Greek Bible, and Qumran: Collected Essays*. Texts and Studies in Ancient Judaism 121.Tübingen: Mohr Siebeck, 2008.
———. "The Septuagint." In *Mikra: Text, Tranlsation, Reading and Interpretation of the Hebrew Bible in Ancient Judaism and Early Christianity*, edited by Martin Jan Mulder and Harry Sysling, 161–88. Assen: Van Gorcum, 1988.
———. *Textual Criticism of the Hebrew Bible*. 3rd ed. rev. and expanded. Minneapolis: Fortress, 2012.
———. "Textual Criticism: OT." In *AYBD* 6:393–411.
Townsend, John T., trans. and ed. *Midrash Tanḥuma*. 2 vols. New York: Ktav, 1997.
Trebolle, J. "Canon of the OT." In *NIDB* 1:548–63.
Tsedaka, Benyamin, and Sharon Sullivan, trans. and ed. *The Israelite Samaritan Version of the Torah: First English Translation Compared with the Masoretic Version*. Grand Rapids: Eerdmans, 2013.
Turner, John D. "The History of Religions Background of John 10." In *The Shepherd Discourse of John 10 and Its Contex*t, edited by Johannes Beutler and Robert T. Fortna, 33–52. SNTSMS 67. Cambridge: Cambridge University Press, 1991.
Turner, John, and Anne McGuire, eds., *The Nag Hammadi Library after Fifty Years: Proceedings of the 1995 Society of Biblical Literature Commemoration*. NHMS 44. Leiden: Brill, 1997.
Utzschneider, Helmut. "Text—Reader—Author Towards a Theory of Exegesis: Some European Viewpoints." *JHebS* 1 (1996) 1–22.
Van den Broek, Roelof. "Jewish and Platonic Speculations in Early Alexandrian Theology: Eugnostus, Philo, Valentinus, and Origen." In *The Roots of Egyptian Christianity* edited by Birger A. Pearson and J. E. Goehring, 190–203. Minneapolis: Fortress, 1986.
Van den Broek, Roelof, and Peter W. Flint. *The Meaning of the Dead Sea Scrolls: Their Significance for Understanding the Bible, Judaism, Jesus, and Christianity*. New York: HarperSanFrancisco, 2002.
Van der Toorn, Karel, et al. *Dictionary of Deities and Demons in the Bible*. Leiden: Brill Academic, 1995.
Van der Watt, Jan G. *Family of the King: Dynamics of Metaphor in the Gospel According to John*. Biblical Interpretation Series. Leiden: Brill Academic, 2000.

Van der Watt, Jan G., and George H. van Kooten, eds. *The Prologue of the Gospel of John.* Tübingen: Mohr Siebeck, 2016.

Van Kooten, George H. "The Last Days of Socrates and Christ: *Euthyphro, Apology, Crito,* and *Phaedo* Read in Counterpoint with John's Gospel." In *Religio-Philosophical Discourses in the Mediterranean World: From Plato, through Jesus to Late Antiquity,* edited by Anders Klostergaard Petersen and George van Kooten, 219-43. Leiden: Brill, 2017

———. "The 'True Light' (John 1:9) and Plato's Allegory of the Cave." In *Creation of Heaven and Earth,* 149-94. Leiden: Brill, 2005.

———. , ed. *The Creation of Heaven and Earth: Re-Interpretations of Genesis I in the Context of Judaism, Ancient Philosophy, Christianity, and Modern Physics.* Themes in Biblical Narrative 8. Leiden: Brill Academic, 2005.

VanderKam, James C. *The Dead Sea Scrolls Today.* 2nd ed. Grand Rapids: Eerdmans, 2010.

———. "Essenes." In *NIDB* 2:315-16.

Vanhoozer, Kevin J. *Is There a Meaning in This Text? The Bible, the Reader, and the Morality of Literary Knowledge.* Grand Rapids: Zondervan, 1998.

Verheyden, Joseph, et al., eds. *Docetism in the Early Church: The Quest for an Elusive Phenomenon.* Tübingen: Mohr Siebeck, 2018

Vermes, Geza. *The Complete Dead Sea Scrolls in English.* 7th ed. New York: Penguin Putnam, 2004.

———. *An Introduction to the Complete Dead Sea Scrolls.* Philadelphia: Fortress, 1999.

———. "Rule of War (4Q285)." *JJS* 43 (1992) 85-90.

Visotzky, Burton L. "Rabbi, Rabbinic Interpretation and Rabbinic Literature." In *NIDB* 4:718-23.

Wahlde, Urban C. von. *Gnosticism, Docetism, and the Judaisms of the First Century: The Search for the Wider Context of the Johannine Literature and Why It Matters.* LNTS. London: Bloomsbury T. & T. Clark, 2015.

———. *The Gospel and Letters of John, Vol. 1: Introduction, Analysis, and Reference.* Grand Rapids: Eerdmans, 2010.

———. *The Gospel and Letters of John, Vol. 2: The Gospel of John.* Grand Rapids: Eerdmans, 2010.

———. *The Gospel and Letters of John, Vol. 3: The Three Johannine Letters.* Grand Rapids: Eerdmans, 2010.

Waltke, B. K. "Samaritan Pentateuch." In *AYBD* 5:932-40.

Wassertein, Abraham, and David Wasserstein. *The Legend of the Septuagint. From Classical Antiquity to Today.* Cambridge: Cambridge University Press, 2006.

Watson, Duane F. "Angels: New Testament." In *AYBD* 1:253-55.

Wead, David W. *The Literary Devices in John's Gospel.* Edited by Paul N. Anderson and R. Alan Culpepper. Johannine Monograph Series. Eugene, OR: Wipf and Stock, 2018.

Weeden, Theodore W. *Mark: Traditions in Conflict.* Philadelphia: Fortress, 1971.

Welker, Michael. "Angels in the Biblical Traditions." *Theology Today* 51 (1994) 367-80.

Westcott, B. F. *The Gospel According to St. John.* London: John Murray, 1908.

Wevers, John William, and Detlef Fraenkel, et al. *Göttingen Septuagint.* 67 vols. Göttingen: Vandenhoeck & Ruprecht, 1967-2008.

Wheaton, Gerry. *The Role of Jewish Feasts in John's Gospel.* SNTSMS 162. Cambridge: Cambridge University Press, 2015.

Whybray, R. N. *Wisdom in Proverbs: The Concept of Wisdom in Proverbs 19*. SBT 45. London: SCM, 1965.
Wiles, Maurice F. *Spiritual Gospel. The Interpretation of the Fourth Gospel in the Early Church*. Cambridge: Cambridge University Press, 1970.
Willett, Michael E. *Wisdom Christology in the Fourth Gospel*. Distinguished Dissertations. Lewiston, NY: Edwin Mellon, 1992.
Williams, Frank, trans. *The Panarion of Epiphanius of Salamis: Book I (sects 1–46)*. Nag Hammadi Studies 35. Leiden: Brill, 1987.
———. *The Panarion of Epiphanius of Salamis: Books II and III (sects 47–80)*. Nag Hammadi Studies 36. Leiden, Brill, 1994.
Williams, M. H. "The Expulsion of the Jews from Rome in A.D. 19." *Latomus* 48 (1989) 765–84.
Williams, Michael Allen. *Rethinking Gnosticism: An Argument for Dismantling A Dubious Category*. Princeton: Princeton University Press, 1996.
Williamson, Ronald. *Jews in the Hellenistic World: Philo*. Cambridge Commentaries on the Writings of the Jewish & Christian World 200 BC to AD 200. Cambridge: Cambridge University Press, 1989.
Willis, W. L. *Idol Meat in Corinth*. Atlanta: SBL, 1985.
Wilson, J. M. "Angel." In *International Standard Bible Enclyclopedia*, 1:124–27. Rev. ed. Grand Rapids: Eerdmans, 1979–1988.
Wilson, Robert McLachlan. *Gnosis and the New Testament*. Oxford: Blackwell, 1968.
———. *Studies in the Gospel of Thomas*. London: A. R. Mowbray 1960.
Windisch, Hans. *Spirit-Paraclete in the Fourth Gospel*. Translated by James W. Cox. Philadelphia: Fortress, 1968.
Winston, David. *Logos and Mystical Theology in Philo of Alexandria*, Cincinnati: Hebrew Union College Press, 1985.
———. "Philo and Rabbinic Literature." In *The Cambridge Companion to Philo*, edited by Adam Kamesar, 231–53. Cambridge: Cambridge University Press, 2009.
———. *Philo of Alexandria*. The Contemplative Life. Giants and Selections: Classics of Western Spirituality. New York: Paulist, 1980.
———. "Philo's Mysticism." *SPhilo* 8 (1996) 74–82.
———. "Was Philo A Mystic?" In *SBL Seminar Papers*, edited by Paul J. Achtemeier, 161–80. Missoula, MT: Scholars, 1978.
———. *The Wisdom of Solomon*. AYB 43. New Haven, CT: Yale University Press, 1979.
Winter, Bruce W. *Philo and Paul among the Sophists: Alexandrian and Corinthian Responses to a Julio-Claudian Movement*. Grand Rapids; Eerdmans, 2002.
Wise, Michael Owen. *Language and Literacy in Roman Judaea: A Study of the Bar Kokhba Documents*. AYB Reference Library. New Haven, CT: Yale University Press, 2015.
———, et al., trans. and eds. *The Dead Sea Scrolls: A New Translation*. New York: HarperCollins, 1996.
Witherington, Ben, III. *Jesus the Sage*. Philadelphia: Fortress, 1994.
———. *John's Wisdom: A Commentary on the Fourth Gospel*. Westminster John Knox, 1995.
Wucherpfennig, Ansgar. *Heracleon Philologus: Gnostische Johannesexegese im zweiten Jahrhundert*. WUNT 142. Tübingen: Mohr Siebeck, 2002.
Yamauchi, Edwin M. *Gnostic Ethics and Mandaean Origins*. Harvard Theological Studies 24. Cambridge, MA: Harvard University Press, 1970.

———. *Mandaean Incantation Texts.* AOS 49. New Haven, CT: Yale University Press, 1967.

———. *Pre-Christian Gnosticism: A Survey of the Proposed Evidences.* 2nd ed. Repr. Eugene, OR: Wipf and Stock, 2003.

Yee, Gale. *Jewish Feasts and The Gospel of John.* Repr. Eugene, OR: Wipf & Stock, 2007.

Zimmerman, Ruben. *Christologie der Bilder im Johannesevangelium: Die Christopoetik des vierten Evangeliums unter besonderer Berucksichtigung von Joh 10.* WUNT 171. Tübingen: Mohr Siebeck, 2004.

Zöckler, Thomas. *Jesu Lehren Im Thomasevangelium.* Nag Hammadi and Manichaean Studies 47. Leiden: Brill Academic, 1999.

Zumstein, Jean. "Intratextuality and Intertextuality in the Gospel of John." In *Anatomies of Narrative Criticism: The Past, Present, and Future of the Fourth Gospel as Literature,* edited by Tom Thatcher and Stephen D. Moore, 121–35. Leiden and Boston: Brill, 2008.

Index

Page numbers on noteworthy discussion or comparisons are in **bold**

abide,
   and bear fruit (John 15:5) 106
   in FG and 1 John, **3**
   if you keep my commandments, 210
   in-group language? 2n5
   intimacy, mystical union, 61, 108, 138, 140
   John 6:56 and the Dionysiac rites, 146
   in the love of the Lord (John 15:9; Odes 8:20), **152**
   of the redeemer with the believer, 177
   as the Son with the Father (John 15:10), 234
Abraham
   Believed God, 61
   Friend of God, 63
   I was before, 92, **96**, 106–7, 189
   in Genesis interpretation, 77
   Patriarch, 41, 158, 209
   Testament of, 52
   your father (Tg. Isa), 96
Acts of the Apostles
   1:8; 8:1–25, mission to Samaritans, 156n24, 15
   1:16, the betrayer (John 18:2), 38
   7:2, 8, 22, heroes of SP: Abraham, Jacob, Moses, 158
   7:47–50, Jerusalem temple polemics, 157
   8:9, Simon the magician, 157–58
   10:36–43, apostolic preaching, 24
   14:12, Barnabas and Paul as Zeus and Hermes, **145**
   14:19–20; 18:6–7; 19:8–9, expulsion from the community, 76
   17:8, Epicureans and Stoics, v. 28, Aratus quote, 120, 125, **170**
   18:24—19:7, JBap followers, 18n13
   26:14 "kick against the goads" (*Bacchae* 794), 120, 125, **170**
   28:27, on Isa 6:10, **38**
   (Book of Acts), missional network, 16
Acts of John, 209, 212, 223
Acts of Thomas, 196, 198, 199n62
agent,
   commissioned, **87**
   of creation, 46–47
   of divine power, 64, 66, 80
   God's, **49–50**, 51n20, 53
   intermediary, 5, 233
   mediator, 57–58
   personal, 154, 199. *See also* Mediator.
agapaō agapē, 20, 61, 118. *See* Love.
alogoi, 18n12, **230–31**
Alexandria, Egypt, 35n1, 56–57, 119, 169. *See also* Clement of Alexandria; Philo.
allegorical, allegorizing, 52;
   DSS, 71n16
   Heracleon, 217, 221. *See also* Heracleon.
   of Homer, Hesiod, Stoics, **56**
   of Philo, 60, 66. *See also* Philo

INDEX

Anderson, Paul N., 28, 42n29, 231
  "Bakhtin's Dialogism," **9n33**
  "John and Qumran," **68n3**, 69n5, 71n15, 72n20, 78n27, 79n31
  "Logos-Hymn," 17n8, 21n28
  "Naming Stars," FG's theology, 20n25, 22n32, 30n55
  "Passion Narrative," 25n40
  Riddles of FG, FG and Synoptics, 17n5, 25n40
Anderson, Robert T., and Terry Giles, 156n22, 158n35, 159n39, 160nn44–45
angel(s), angelology,
  archangel, 54, 59
  ascending and descending, **39n14**
  mediator, 53, 123
  Book of, Mandaean, 161–62
  in cosmic conflict, 71n17
  of darkness, 73–74
  evil, **52n23**
  of the Lord, **51**, 54, 57
  represent God, 160
  reveal future/divine wisdom, 50, 54, 228
  sent by/from God, 51, 53
  wisdom and 7, 35, 45,
anointed, anointing
  anointed (one), 75, **78n25** (Christ)
  by the Holy One (1 John 2:20), 124
  of Jesus, 23–25, 27–28
  of oil, 161, 164
  in truth, 150
antichrist, 230
Apocalypse of Adam, 13, **171n12**
  Apocalypse of John. *See* Revelation, Book of
apocalyptic
  genre, 48n9; pre-apocalyptic, 43n34
  themes, **42–43**
  texts, 45
  traditions, 21n31, 30n55, 136
Apocrypha, NT, 142, 175n19, 213n14, 224n29
Apocrypha, OT, 35
  deutero-canonical (NRSV), 45n1
  and Pseudepigrapha, 7, 36n4, 39n14, 103

Apocryphon of John, 13, 171–76
Apostles, Epistle to, 207, 212–15, 217
Apuleius, *Metamorphoses*, 105n10, 108
Aramaic, 40n21, 45n2, 52n24, 159, 161
  and FG's author, 35n2, 98
  in DSS, 69; of Palestine, 80n33
  Targums, 83, **91**, 92–98
archetype in Philo
  Somn. 1.75 "God is light (*phōs*, Ps 26:1 LXX) archetype of every other light," **59**
  Deus 32 "For God's life is not a time, but eternity, which is the archetype and pattern of time, in eternity there is no past or future, but only present existence," 59
argument
  of Philo, 67, 68n4
  rabbinic, **88–90**
Aristobulus of Alexandria, 57n6, 67n19
Aristotle
  and *Logos*, 64n8, 112
  Poetics, 128;
  Rhetoric, 88
Arnim, Hans von, 112n19
ascetic
  in DSS, 71, 77
  monks and NHL, 183
  Tatian, 210
Ashton, John,
  author of FG and Qumran, 68, 81n34
  FG's world is 1st cent. Judaism, aversion to FG's non-Jewish context, e.g., Isis-FG analogy, **7n29**, 103n3
  Jewish wisdom context, 46n5;
Attridge, Harold W., xxiii
  "Cubist Principle," on Philo and symbolic interpretation, 65n15
  Essays on John, on Philo and FG, 65n14;
  Eusebius, Christianity, and Judaism (with Hata), 228n38
  "Heracleon and John," 217n19, 228n38
  "Jesus and Stoic Tradition," 26n42

"John and DSS," 82n38
"Philo and John," 64n9, 65n14, **67**
"Resurrection Motifs," 30n55
"Seeking and Asking," 184n21
"Three Symposia," **113**, 118nn27–28
audience of *Bacchae*, 127–28
audience of FG
   authorial, 238
   broad, 2, **14**, 100, 212, 234
   close-knit, 110
   Greek-speaking, **37**, 125, 143
   implied, 50
   intended, 6, 156, 194, 235
Augustine of Hippo, **39n14**, 99, 222
Aune, David E.,
   "Dualism," *Neotestamentia et
     Philonica*, critical of Essene or
     Odes influences in FG, 78n27,
     155n16
   NT in Its Literary Environment,
     Jewish and Hellenistic, 6n21;
     two-level perspective, **12n49**
   Westminster Dictionary, ed., parable,
     2n3; sayings, pronouncement
     stories, 192n44
author,
   of 1 John, 31n61, 34, 231
   of Acts, 120, 125
   of Aristeas, Letter of, 170n7
   of FG, xxiii, 8, 11, **16n3**, 27, 29, 31,
     34, 43, 67–68, 79, 98, 104, 109,
     132, 142, 154, 197–98, 217,
     230–31, 235, 238
   of GTh, knew FG? 186
   of Hebrews, 55, 57, 119
   implied, 50, 231; authors, 169–70
   of Revelation, 229–31
authority (divine)
   of Aaron's sons until Messianic era
     (DSS), 75
   of all four gospels, 226
   appeal of Socrates to, 117
   over the Demiurge, 123
   given to the Son of Man, 43
   to grant eternal life now (Philo), 59
   John 5:26–27, rabbinic argument,
     89–90

Logos-centered, 231
   of ruling officials 141
authorship, 34, 237
   of 1–3 John, 37n67
   Epistle of the Apostles, 22
   of FG, **11n48**, 79n30, 231nn44–45
   of Revelation, 228–30. *See also*
     Beloved Disciple (BD)

Babylon
   Talmud of (ca. 600CE), 35n1, 84.
     See also Talmud.
Bacchae, The
   Acts 26:14 "kick against the goads,"
     (Euripides, *Bacchae* 794), 120,
     125, **170**
   analysis and assessment of
     Dionysian gospel (DM), 143–45
   authorship of play and date, **128**
   Christianity superior to Dionysian
     cult (Clement of Alex., *Protr.*
     12.119), 130
   Dionysus avenges like a true god,
     not Jesus (Origen *Cels.* 2.34–35),
     129
   FG and *Bacchae* parallels (Stibbe),
     131
   imitations, intertextual commentary,
     criteria (DM), 133–43
   most influential portrayal of the
     Dionysian world, 126. *See also*
     Dionysus; Euripides.
Bakhtin, Mikhail M.
   Dialogic Imagination, intertextuality,
     9; material grounding of
     utterance, 9n33
   Rabelais and His World, ancient
     symposia, spoken word,
     113n22; on banquet imagery in
     medieval-renaissance writings,
     118n27
baptism,
   of John and Jesus, 18, 22
   rituals of gnostics, 169n2, 178
   ritual of Mandaeans, 161
Bar Kokhba (Simon ben Kosiba), 79, 91,
   80n33

INDEX

Barrett, C. K., xxiii;
    Essays, evaluating comparisons, 8n30, 98n26; FG's date, location, 11n45; FG and Platonism, 113n20
    John, FG's use of Mark, 28n50; on epilogue, 22n33
    "OT in FG," 36n8
    NT Backgrounds, Hermetica, **121n33**; on Odes and FG, 149n3
Baruch (LXX), 45–48, 51, 210
2 Baruch (apocalyptic), 71n17, 136
Basilides of Alexandria, 168n2, 169n6, 216
Bauckham, Richard,
    Audience of the Gospels (ed., E. W. Klink), 235n12
    Gospel for All Christians, **12n50, 14n56,** 16n3; "Patristic Counter-Evidence?" 234n10
    Gospel of Glory, FG's theology, 78n27
    Gospel of John and Theology (with C. Mosser), 6n24, 20n25, 22n32, 30n55, 34n67
    Jesus and Eyewitnesses, Testimony of BD, FG's authorship, **11n48,** 34n67
    "Qumran Community," dualism? 71n19, on FG and DSS, **78,** 155n16
BDAG (Bauer et al.), **40nn21–22, 41n25,** 43n35
belief, believe,
    in FG, e.g., John 3:12–18; 6:29; 11:25–26
    ca. 98 times, 21
    in Philo (e.g., *Abr.* 268) **61**
    in Targums, 93, 97
    in Justin Martyr, 212
    John 4:53 "he and his household believed," (official's household), 137
    worthy of, cf. John 1:14 and "arise which are firm and true," (Plato, *Tim.* 37B), **115.** See also Faith; Unbelief

beliefs and practices of a group,
    Epiphanius, 229
    Mandaeans, 148
    Origen, 221
    Samaritans, **158–59**
beloved,
    friends, 49
    of God, 130
    Israel, 85–86
    Son, **152**
Beloved Disciple (BD),
    author of FG and Revelation, **230–31**
    BD and Thomas, 196n51
    John the Elder, not BD, author of FG, 34n67
    John 13:23–25; 19:26–27, 35; 20:2–8; 21:24–25, sources, 11
    John 13:23; 19:26; 20:2, 8; 21:7, 20, identified by name, 20
    John 21:24, "who has written these things," 22
Bergman, Jan, *Ich bin Isis*, 105n10, 109
Birkat ha-minim, 14n56
    Kimelman critique, 76
    meaning, influence, **84.** See also Expel(led); Martyn, J. Louis
Borgen, Peder,
    Bread from Heaven, 41n26, **63,** 87
    "God's Agents," 46n4, 51n20, **53**
    "Logos Was the True Light," 86
    "Philo of Alexandria," **56nn2–3,** 86–87
Boring, M. Eugene,
    belief in Mandaean *Ginza*, 164
    Greco-Roman cults, 3n9
    John 4:24 and Stoics, 64n8
    new birth in Mithra, Isis cults, **105n7**
    Samaritans on Moses, 157n31
born,
    anew/from above/again, **19, 123,** 136, 211–12
    blind, 22, 54, 108
    born and unborn, 141, 208, 222
    of water and Spirit, 18n11, 208, 216
    of the will of God, 32, 211, 214

INDEX

Bousset, Wilhelm, *Hauptprobleme der Gnosis*, 4n10, primal gnostic myth, 170
Boyarin, Daniel,
"Logos, A Jewish Word" *JANT*, 58
Borderlines, FG and Targumim, 91n18, 92n23, Jewish influence on FG, 102n35
Brooke, A. E., *Fragments of Heracleon*, 206n3, 217n19
Brooke, George J.,
"Dead Sea Scrolls," *NIDB*, 39n17, 68n1, contents, **69n9**, categories, 70n10
"Biblical Interpretation," *Bible and DSS* (J. Charlesworth), 72n20, scriptural interpretation, **77**
Brown, Raymond E., xxiii-xiv, 5n18, 8n29; 12n50 (J. Jipp essay), 27 (quote); Odes, 78n27, 149n3; Essene influence? 155n16
Community of Beloved, 11n46, 33; 1 John as midrash of FG, 215n16
Death of the Messiah, Jesus-Socrates, 113n23
Epistles of John, and FG, 30n57; order of composition, 31n62; midrash of FG, 31n61, **33n66**
Gospel according to John, religious thought of FG, 3n8; intratextuality, 9n34; metaphorical comparisons, **18n15**; epilogue, Luke 5 and John 21, **22n33**, passion narratives, FG and Synoptics, 24–26, Num 11 in FG, 41n27; wisdom motifs, 46n5; *theos* with no article, 64n11; modified dualism, 71n19, Plato-FG, Jesus-Socrates, **112–13**, 119; FG and Hermetica, 121n33, Odes as semi-gnostic, 154, 203
and GTh, *NTS* essay, 184n21, 185–87, 195n47; contrast with Riley, 196

Introduction, 3-stage development, 12n49, FG and JBap followers, 18n13; FG and Synoptics, 27n47; *NT Essays*, FG and Qumran calendar, 71n14
Bultmann, Rudolf, xxiii,
apophthegmata, 10n37
Dionysus legend, 126n4, 127n11, 136n37
epilogue, 22n33
FG and Odes, 149n3
Gospel of John, metaphorical language, 18n15
Greek philosophical tradition, 64n8
Hermetica, 121n33
history of religion studies, 4n10
Mandaeans, 162n50, **163–65**
pre-Christian gnostic myth, 166n54, 170n11
primal gnostic myth, **170**
primal pagan myth, 102n35
"Prologue," wisdom motifs, 46n5
"Psalmbuch," FG, Odes, and common Jewish origins, 154n12
redeemer myth, 166n56
source theory, 27n46
and Synoptic tradition, 28n47
Bynum, William,
FG's acquaintance with Hebrew and Aramaic, 39n15, 79n32

Cana, wedding of,
Dionysian and OT allusions, 136n37
in Ep. Apos.. 214
symposia, marital love, 118n28
not in Synoptics, 18n12, 22
canon,
Jewish (OT), 35, 36n4, 45–46, 51n19, 69
NT, 182n12
OT and NT, 168, 221n27
canonical
Gospels, 224
Johannine literature, 132n33
Charlesworth, James H.
Beloved Disciple, FG and GTh as rival traditions, 185n23

INDEX

Charlesworth, James H. *(continued)*
   Bible & DSS, Brooke, "Biblical Interpretation," 72n20; Popke, "FG, GTh, and Qumran," 180n3, parallel traditions, 182n12; 4 basic schemes, 184nn19–20; light metaphor, **193n45**; FG and GTh on light, 194n46; the disciple Thomas, 196n51
   on FG and Odes (Aune essay), 78n27, 155n16;
   Graphic Concordance, 68n1
   Jesus Mirrored in John, FG authorship, 11n48; date of 1st ed., 12n49; Enoch traditions, **21–22n31**, 30n55, 47n7; Greek equivalents of Heb., 80n32; *Birkat ha-minim*, 84n5, 149n3; Odes and FG, **153nn9–10**, 154, 155n21; Mt. Gerizim and Mt. Zion, 156n23
   John and the DSS, dualisms, 71n18; spirit, flesh, 73, 80n32, 154n15; *Odes of Sol*, the discovery, 148n2; early date, 149nn5–6; Jesus and Lord God, 150n8; common origins, 155
   OT Pseudepigrapha, 1 Enoch texts, 45n2; T. Abraham, T. Levi, et al,. 52n24; Aristobulus, **67n19**; Odes and FG, 149n6
children (*tekna, teknia*)
   little children (*teknia*), 32, 49
   of the Devil, 220
   of God (*tekna*), **32**, 48, **61–62**, 76, 85, 93, 123, 151, 172
   of Israel, 41, 95, 97
   of light, 47n7, 115, 177–78, 193
Chilton, Bruce,
   Galilean Rabbi, **99n31**, 111n16, 120n32
   Glory of Israel, 92n21
   Targums with Flesher, 83n3, 91n15
Christ, 33, 42, 75, **78n25**
   became flesh, 208
   and Demiurge, 226n34
   and Dionysos, 136n37
   divinity of, 89, 221
   humanity of, 226
   hymn of Colossians, 21n28
   incarnate, 226
   Jesus, **29n53**, 33, 122, passim
   for Jews, 234
   and the law, 82, 89
   and Logos, 212
   love commandment of, 210
   Messiah, 33, **42**, 75, **78n25**, 153
   and new Passover, 222
   and Odes of Sol, 150n8
   pre-incarnate, 51
   reveals God, 165, 208
   and Scripture, 88
   as shepherd, 166
   and Socrates, 66n17, 114n25, 117–19
   symbols and menorah (E. Smith), 76n23. *See also* Jesus; Logos.
christological
   foil to explain Jesus, 132
   hymn, 17n8
   interpretation of Ps 22 LXX, 211
   overtones, 29
   titles, **42n32**
   traditions of N. Palestine, 156
christology, 50–51
   adoptionistic, 231
   divine man, 204n70
   docetic, **175n19**, 207–8
   in FG, 21n28, 29, 67, 99, 194, 200–202 passim, 204
   in GThom, 181n10, 185n23, 203
   in Johannine Letters, 30n55
   pre-existent, **21n28**
   transcendent, 234
church, churches
   of Asia, 20n26, 210
   and DSS, 81–82
   and the door, 209
   Eastern, 228
   epilogue for, 22n33
   expulsion from, **76**
   identity and culture, **128n15**, 182n12
   Jesus and, 197
   large, world-oriented, 2, 12n50, 109n12

primitive, 231
reading FG, 33n66, 215n16, 231
reception, **221**, 230
Roman, 215
rule, 226
and synagogue, 5, 51n17
1 Clement, 209–210
Clement of Alexandria,
  and *Bacchae*, 130; on Christian gnosis, 226
  on FG, 11n45; as spiritual gospel (Eusebius, *Eccl. hist.* 6.14.7) 17, 221, **235n12**
  on Heracleon and Luke 12, 221n24
  the Lord's voice, 218
  on Plato and Philo, 57n4, 67n21, 119
  on the Son and the Father, 177n26
  on true, sacred mysteries, 109
coherence,
  DSS, **80**
  of FG with Synoptics and 1 John, 16, LXX, 36
  Hermetica, 125
  Isis, 110–11
  with other criteria, 42
  Plato, Platonism, 120
  rabbinica, **99**
  verbal and thematic, **8**
collection,
  "Book of John," Mandaean, **162**
  Chester Beatty, 222
  of Celsus quotations, 129
  DSS, 68–69
  of parallels for FG and *Bacchae*, 144
  for FG and GTh comparison, 186, 195
  of pesher texts, 71n6
  "Right Ginza," Mandaean, 161
  of Scripture, *Testimonia*, **39**
  of texts on ancient mysteries, 135n37
Collins, Billie Jean, ed., *SBL Handbook*
  abbreviations, xiv
  bibliography, 239
  Hebrew/Greek versification, **36n5**
  Philo abbreviations, 56n3
  rabbinic abbreviations, 84n8

Collins, John J.
  Between Athens and Jerusalem, on Philo, 56n3, wisdom, 46n3
  Dictionary of Early Judaism (with D. Harlow), "Apocrypha, et al." 36n4, 46n3, 52n4; "Bar Kokhba," 80n33; "dualism," 71n8; "Enoch," 45n2, LXX, 35n1; "mysticism, et al.," 198n57; "Pharisees," **88n9**; "rabbi," **83n3**; "Jews, Greeks, Romans," 3n9,103n1
  Jewish Wisdom, 46n3, 51n20
Collins, Raymond F., *These Things Have Been Written*, "to seek," 29n52; on John 1:14, 41n25; on John 2:1–11, **136n37**
Colossae, temple of Isis, 110.
Colossians, Letter of, xxiv, 208
  1:15–20, Christ hymn, 21n28
  Philonic characteristics, 57n5
Colpe, Carsten.
  Die religionsgeschichtliche Schule,
    critical assessment, 3n8;
    heavenly redeemer, 123n34, **151**, 167n56, 177n24; docetic body, 178n29
  JAC essay on Three Forms, 177n25
common
  authorship of 1–3 John, 34n67
  criticism of mimesis criticism, 143
  cultural milieu, 99, 101–2
  cycle of tradition, FG and Synoptics, **25**
  dialect of Palestine, Aramaic, 91
  eyewitness tradition within Johannine community, 25
  images (living water, shepherd), 7
  Jewish midrash tradition, 91n18
  Jewish texts (Gen 1, wisdom), 102n35
  manner of interpretation in FG and GTh, 181n11
  milieu of language and expression, 92, 145
  religious environment, **155**
  script of textual communities, 11n46
  source (OT, wisdom), 7, **179**

common *(continued)*
    themes in John 13–17 and 1 John, 30n56; John 1 and Exod 33–34, **41n24**; with Synoptics, 25; FG and Rev, 43n33
    type of intellectual milieu, 10
    word field, xxiv, **3n8**
communicatio idiomatum, 204
community, communities
    Alexandrian Jewish, 56
    of *Bacchae* and FG, 144–45
    DSS
        authority over, love of, 75
        Essene? 70, 79
        expulsion from, 76
        how sectarian? **68–69**
        Sadducean remnant? 70n13
        Teacher of, 73
        temple, entry prohibited **74**; criticisms of (with NT and Samaritan literature), 157
    diverse views of, e.g., textual, **11n46**
    ecclesiastical reconstructions, 5n18, 12n50, 50, 51n17
    FG response to Thomasine, 197–98
    FG's
        BD as founder of, 11
        conflict hypothesis, 197n54, 205
        cultic not sectarian? 71n15
        rivals, 198
        world-oriented not sectarian? 2n5, **14n56**, 16n3, 234n10
    Ignatius, united under its bishop, 208
    Johannine, 1 John and FG, 30–31, 33–34, 201
    of Odes and FG, **155**
    NHL, 183
comparison(s),
    compelling **7**
    for conceptual understanding, **2**
    on dualisms, 71n18
    FG and
        Bacchae, 134n35, 144
        Hermetica, 125
        Isis, 111
        NHL, 100n31, 171, 200
        Plato, 120
        Socrates, Pythagoras, Jesus, **114**
    Synoptics, 21
    of Hebrew/Greek versification, 36n5
    intention behind, **34**, 236
    Jesus and
        angelology, 51n17
        Judaism, 78
        wisdom, 50
    limitations of, 14
    Nathanael as true Israelite, 41
    parabolic and metaphoric, 18n5
    according to J. Z. Smith, 5n17
conceive,
    author's self-conception, 235
    definition **3n8**
    difficult to conceive of, 24
    elegantly conceived, 197
    preconceived, 5
    texts broadly conceived, 9
concept,
    of the body and resurrection, 196
    of cognition, **2n2**
    of Demiurge, 179,
    of dialectic history, 21n29
    different contexts of words and, 99, 120
    of the discovery of one's divine origins, 194,
    of intertextuality, **9**
    is lofty of God and human ethics, 121
    of Logos in Greek world, 64n8
    of post-catastrophic utopia, 71
    of *Mēmra*, 100,
    of Word in the Odes, 154
conception(s),
    of death as departure, **53n25**,
    foggy on direct dependence, 78n27, 155n16,
    modern, 236
    New conception of deity, **116–17**
    Plato's conception of the Good, 111
    similar and analogous, 238
    Stoic conception of God, 64n8,
conceptual,
    cognition, 1
    echoes and allusions, 33
    system metaphorically structured, 2

or thought worlds of FG, 3, 7,
13n54, 201
understanding by means of analogy,
2, 4
viewpoints and similar contexts, 46
worlds and transcendent
Christologies, 14.
conclude,
that FG and Philo are riffs on a
common theme (Attridge), 67
that non-Jewish influence not be
excluded, 7n29, 103–4, 144n49,
235–36
with the so-called Johannine
controversy in 2nd and 3rd
cents., 207, 231
conclusion,
of *Conceptual Worlds of the FG*,
232–38
of DM's "Intertextual Commentary,"
134
doubts that FG was rescued from
gnostic abuse, 215n16
that FG could be reconstructed as a
Greek play, 132
of Hengel on FG as a gnostic
favorite? 221n25
letter-like (1 John, Ep. Apos.), 213
NHL and FG have a problematic
genetic relationship, 178
conflict,
communities/traditions in, **197n54**,
204–5, 236
cosmic, **71n17**, 177, 179. *See* angel,
angels.
of early Christian and Dionysiac
sects, 128n15
Eusebius and Athanasius, 227
of FG and GTh, 184n20, 185n30,
204n67,
of FG and Synoptic accounts
(literary), 221
with Jewish leaders in FG, 102
context(s)
coherence, 99
common viewpoints as FG, 8
Synoptics, 16
LXX, 36

wisdom, 46
community, FG and
Dionysic, 144
GThom, 197–98
comparing, criteria, 9, 99n29
distinct/differing literary and
cultural, **3n8**, 13, 39, 99, 110,
120
entire spiritual and intellectual
space, **4n13, 232n4**
evaluations of FG and
GTh, 182n14, 192
Hermetica, 124–25
Isis, **109–10**
Mandaeans, 160
Odes, 153–55
Plato, Platonism, 119–20
Rabbinica, **98–100**
generic, 233
historical and literary, 90, 98, 205,
importance, 98n26,
of "I am" statements (Philo), 65
inner-Jewish, 103–4, 232
mystical, gnostic-like, **10, 233**
non-Jewish, 103
original, 42n30, OT, 42
prophetic, 43n34
Sandmel quote on, 77,
similar, and different, 5. *See also*
criteria (or tests) of evaluation.
social and cultural, 2, 5, 11n6
of "Spirit of truth," in FG and DSS,
71n19, 78
Coptic,
Ep. Apos. extant ms, 212
Hermetic text, 121
Odes ms, 148
Sahidic dialect of NHL, 168, 177
text in *Q-Thomas Reader*, 180n1
transl. of Greek, NHL, **168n1,
181n5**, 182
version of Melito, *On the Pascha*,
222
1 Corinthians,
1–4, Philonic features, **57n5**
1:2, Jesus equated with God, 154
10:3, spiritual food, 37
10:14, "flee from idolatry," 110

1 Corinthians *(continued)*,
  10:20 "they sacrifice to demons," 110
  11:19, on factions, 180
  15:3–17 apostolic preaching summary, **24**
2 Corinthians,
  12:2, "third heaven," **125**
  13:13, Jesus equated with God, 154
cosmic,
  conflict, **179**. See also conflict, cosmic
  dualism, 21, 182
  element of fire (Heraclitus), 112
  ethical dualism of FG and DSS, 71n18
  principle of order (Heraclitus), 112
cosmology
  of Mandaean dualism, 161
  of Middle Platonism, 112
cosmological,
  dualism of DSS and FG, 71
  principles of abstract dualism (gnostic), 178
  and salvation-historical speculation (FG), 179
  and soteriological role of Wisdom, 106n10
  tales in FG (Reinhartz), **5**–7, 44, 50–51
  theological, and didactic material (Right Ginza), 161
cosmos in Hermetica, 122
covenant,
  with Abraham, Targumim, 96
  with David, DSS, 75
  members
    DSS, 74
    FG, 102n35
  new, absent in *Bacchae*, 137
  obedience, DSS, 75
creation. *See* Genesis
credibility
  of historical-critical answers, 34
  of hypotheses on NT and DSS, 68
criteria (or tests) of evaluation, 5n16, 8–9, 16, 36, **78**–**81**, 98–99, 109–11, 124–25, 159n40, 178n31, 233n9, 237

availability to FG and readers, **79**, 99, 110, 120, 125
chronological proximity, **99**, 110, 120, 125
common viewpoints, 99, 110, 120, 125
contamination (by NT), **110**, 120, 125
interpretability asks what might be gained by viewing one text as a debtor to another (DM), 143
similar contexts, 99, 110, 120, 125
verbal and thematic coherence, 99, 110, 120, 125
criticism
  of comparative methodology, **5n17**, 8n30
  composition, 12n51
  of FG's mission to JBap followers, 18n13
  of FG as sectarian, **2n5**, 18n56
  hidden criticism (Baye's theorem), **8n31**, 79n29, 81n35, 98n26
  historical methods of, 83, 99
  mimesis (DM), 134, 142–43
  narrative, **6n23**, 9n34, 12n49, 14n56, 50, 236
  of parallels with FG, 166, 178. *See also* Criteria (tests) of evaluation.
  pre-Christian redeemer myth (Yamauchi), 163n52
  reader-response, 12n51, 236
  redaction, 12n53, 146
  of Simonians in NHL, 168n2
  source, 8n30, 33, 98n26
  textual, of OT, 35n3, of SP, **159**–**60**
crucifixion
  demonstrates his glory, 141
  in Mark and FG, 26
  on or before Passover, **20**
Culpepper, R. Alan,
  Anatomy of FG
    FG narrative, 6n25
    implied author and reader, **50n16**
    ideal narrative, 238n19

"Christology," essay, FG's
  Christology, 21n28
Johannine School
  diverse views of community,
    11n46
  house of Hillel, 101n32
  "Realized Eschatology," essay, 30n55

Damascus Document (CD-A, CD-B)
  CD II, 14–15 (works of God), 73
  CD III, 20 (eternal life), 74
  CD VI, 12–13, 16 (wealth of
    temple), 74, 154
  CD X, 14–23 (legal interpretation),
    77
  CD-A II, 11 (remnant), **76**
  CD-A VI, 18–20, (solar calendar),
    70n14
  CD-A VI, 20–21, (love your
    brother), 75
  CD-B XX, 1, (messiah), 75. *See also*
    Dead Sea Scrolls (DSS).
  discovery in Cairo Genizah, **69n7**,
Daniel, Book of,
  2:4 "interpretation" (Aramaic),
    71n16
  9:25 "anointed prince," messianic
    expectation, **75**
  10:5–6; 12:6 "man in linen," 54
  12:2 "everlasting life," 74; "man in
    linen" (Gabriel? 10:5–6; 12:6), 54
  Middle Aramaic in, 91
  prophetic and apocalyptic themes
    (e.g., 7:13–14; 8:17,19; 12:1–4),
    42–3
  a source of angel speculation, 52
date
  of DSS, 69, 79
  for a high Christology, 154
  of FG, **11–12**, 31n59
  Last Supper (Jaubert), 70n14
  Mandaean literature, 161
  Muratorian fragment, 231n44
  NHL, 168
  Odes, 149
  SP, 159

David, King of Israel
  appeals to (DSS), 77,
  in FG, 36n8, 40n8; seed of, town of
    (7:42), **37**, 42n32;
  Ignatius, 209,
  Messiah, branch of, DSS, 71, **75**,
    78n25,
  Odes ascribed to son of, 148; not in
    Samaritan tradition, 157
  the shepherd, FG, 42n31; DSS, 75
Davies, Stevan
  "Christology and Protology," *JBL*,
    185n23
  GThom and Christian Wisdom,
    181n6
Davila, James R.,
  "Perils of Parallelsim," definition,
    criteria of evaluation, **4–5**, 8n31,
    12n53, 98n26, 99n29, 109n11,
    110n14, 120n30, 233n5
Dead Sea Scrolls
  the collection, its significance,
    68–69,
  compared with the NHL collection,
    181–82; date of, 69,
  differences and similarities with FG,
    70–71,
  Essenes, Zadokites, Qumran, 70;
    and Odes, 149, 154–55,
  parallels with FG, **72–77**
  similarities with rabbinic
    hermeneutics, 88n10,
  tests for evaluating parallels with
    FG, 79–81.
  See also Damascus Document,
    Essenes, Pesher Habakkuk
    (1QpHab), Qumran, Rule of
    Community (1QS).
DeConick, April,
  "Blessed Are Those," community-
    conflict, 197n54,
  Seek to See Him, 181n7
  Vision of the Mystics, 180n2
    FG and GTh, **184**
    vison mysticism (GTh) vs. faith
      mysticism (FG), 198–200

INDEX

Deissmann, Adolf, *Light from the Ancient East*, analogy or genealogy? 7n28, 103n2

Demiurge,
- according to Heracleon, inspired to create by the Logos, 218
- general comments, 178n30, 217n19, 220–21
- in FG, the Word, unlike Demiurge, not morally ambiguous or incompetent, but the divine Word of Rev. sent to bring light, life to the world, 119–20, **179**
- in Hermetica, creator god begotten from God by the Logos, **122**;
- Irenaeus: the Word created all without *any* qualification, 218n21
- in Plato, an intermediate divine craftsman (*Timaeus*), 111, 115, 119
- shares divinity with Mind-Logos, 121; but a Man generated by the Mind has authority over, 123
- Three forms portrays it in a mythologizing of Gen, 178
- For Valentinus: one of the sons of the ineffable parent, 226n33

demon (*daimonion*)
- "I am not a bodiless demon" (Ignatius of the risen Christ), 210,
- Jesus accused of having one (John 8:52), **52**, 157,
- mystery cults as demonic imitations (Tertullian), 110,
- Plato's *daimones* become good and evil demons (Xenocrates), 111,
- protection from demonic power in DSS, 74n22,
- *Ruha* the demonic spirit (Mandaean Prayerbook), 163,
- "they sacrifice to demons" (1 Cor 10:20), 110
- Socrates accused of having a *daimonion* (by Meletus), 117

Tobias protected from Asmodeus, 54. *See also* Angel(s); evil; Devil; Satan.

descent
- and ascent of angels (John 1:51; Gen 28:12), **31**
- in cosmological tale, 6
- as key FG themes, 3
- as metaphors of death, 53n25;
- of Spirit on Jesus as seen by John (John 1:32–33), 95
- of chief angel (Jos. Asen. 14–15; 17:8–10), **53**; of heavenly redeemer (Odes 22:1; 23:5), 151;
- of Christ to underworld (1 Pet 3:18–22), 154
- from heaven of Son of Man who has ascended (John 3:13), **53**, 167;
- of perfect Protennoia into the world of darkness as savior (Three Forms 35:32—36:29), 176
- of Spirit and vision of God connected with *Dibbera* (Targumim), 92, 95
- Wisdom's descent from heaven to dwell with people (Sir 24:8; Wis 9:10), 48
- as the Word in human form, on its third descent she appears (Three Forms 47:13–16), 177

Deuteronomy (LXX)
- 4:4, "you are alive today," (Philo), 59
- 5:6-7; 6:4; 13:1–15, "no other gods before me" (contra Isis), 110
- 5:16; 6:2; 30:16–20, live a long *life*, 40
- 8:3 He fed you with manna (John 6:31–32), 41
- 8:7 a promised land of flowing waters (Philo), 60
- 11:11 drink water from the rain (Philo), 60
- 11:29; 27:12 a blessing on Mt. Gerizim (SP), **157**
- 14:1 they are called children of God (m. Abot 3:15), 85

15:2; 17:2; 32:47 in legal
interpretation (CD X, 14–23), 77
16:13–14 feast of Booths/Sukkoth, 42
18:15–22 to raise up a prophet like
Moses, **41**, DSS, 75, SP, 157
19:5 take refuge in Him and life
(Philo), 59
21:22–23 take down the body (cf.
John 19:31), 38
30:1–2 obey YHWH, appealing to
Moses (DSS), 77
30:20 to love the living God (Philo), 61
32:6 avoids human portrayals of
God (e.g., Exod. 15:3 SP), 160
32:39 "I am the Lord, there is no god
except me" (LXX), 42–43
34:4–5 the offspring of servant
Moses enter the land (Philo), 63
deuterocanonical (e.g., 1–4 Macc, Sir,
Wis LXX), 35
Deutero-Isaiah
Isa 41:4:; 43:10; 45:3 I am the Lord
God, LXX, 39n13, **43n33**. See
also Isaiah
Deutero-Pauline: Col, Eph, 1–2 Tim, 208
devil (*diabolos*)
Asmodeus the demon (Tob 3:16–17)
children of the devil who love his
desires (Heracleon), 220
incites Judas to betray Jesus (John
13:2, 27), **19n21**
incites men to sin (1 Chr 21;1; Wis
2:24; LXX), **52**
Jesus prays that his disciples be
protected from evil one (John
17:15), 19n21
Judas described as a devil (John
6:70), 19n21
Meander, disciple of Simon Magus,
inspired by devils (*Apol.* 1:26), 157n29
You are from your father the (John
8:44), 220
See also Angel(s); evil; Demon;
Satan.

Dibbera
in an absolute sense in some early
texts (Tg. Neof), 100
Aramaic of "Word" related to
Hebrew *dabar*, 40n21
"I will remove the word of my glory
& you will perceive that which
is behind me" (Tg. Onq. Exod
33:20–33), 95
in texts of seeing God and descent
of the Spirit, 92 *See also Mēmra, Mēmer*
the word speaking with Moses (Tg.
Ps-J. Num 7:89), 95
diachronic
combine(s) with synchronic
Hays and Reinhartz, 44n39, 50n16
Stibbe, 12n49
work, reader, author, 12n51
and synchronic approaches
(Moloney quote), 6n29
dialogue(s)
concise Synoptic aphorisms become
in FG extended discourses of
dialogues and monologues, 18
FG and Mark reflect independent
dialogue with parallel traditions, 28n50
FG and GTh reflect a dialogue
or debate between their
communities, 195–200
Logos as speech, dialogue, oracle,
matter or thing, 40n21
Symposium and FG involve
dialogues focused on love, **113**
Tests and criteria to be used in
intertextual dialogue, 42n30.
Dionysius of Alexandria, 229–30
Dionysius of Halicarnassus, 5n16
Dionysus (Bacchus)
christological foil for explaining
Jesus, 132, 147
criteria for evaluating parallels with
FG (DM), 142–43
Did the god himself turn water into
wine? **135n37**

INDEX

Dionysus (Bacchus) *(continued)*
    eating the flesh and blood of the god (John 5:53–66, *Bacchae*), 137
    escape artist (John 10:30, *Bacchae*), 139
    first ed. of FG is the Dionysian Gospel, 132n33
    how a real god in disguise deals with opponents, 129
    interrogation before Pentheus (cf. John 18:28—19:16), 140
    Jesus rivals Dionysus at Cana, 126, 135
    multiple titles of Jesus and Dionysus, 135. See also *Bacchae, The*.
disciple(s)
    GTh 13, Thomas, the only one who answers the questions correctly, 199
    GTh 61, "I am your disciple" [Jesus said to her], 203
    Heracleon was a disciple of Valentinus, 217
    Jesus will become like the disciple, disciple becomes like Jesus, 203
    John the disciple of the Lord, author of 1 John, 226
    Poimandres to a disciple (Hermetica), 122
    "This disciple would not die" (John 21:23), 191
    Thomas as foil for FG advocates on bodily resurrection, 196n49
    Wisdom instructs and forms them (Wis 9:11; Sir 4;11, 17), **44**
discourse(s)
    on bread (John 6:22–51), 24–25, 28
    Diotima's speech in *Symposium* and FG's Last Supper, 113
    Does it illuminate the surrounding discourse? 81
    early gnostic revealer discourse (Bultmann), 166, 170
    on eating flesh, drinking blood (John 6), 20, 23; with Dionysiac rites, **134n35**
    Farewell Discourse of the resolute Jesus, **20**, 22; with Seneca's consolation writings, 112n19
    FG elaborates with discourse context, GTh with variant readings, 192
    FG's Shepherd Discourse (10) of proto-Mandaean origin (Bultmann), 165
docetism,
    anti-docetic themes in Ignatius, 207
    contra Docetism (1 John 1:1–4; 4:2–3; 5:6; 2 John 7), **31**
    denial that Jesus possesses physical body in FG, 143
    FG epithets of Jesus misrepresented in a docetic manner, 30n53
    gnosis and docetism, not identical (Schnelle), **175n19**
    gnostic Redeemer appears in a docetic body, 178n29
    Irenaeus and Ep. Apos. resist docetic, gnostic interpretations of FG, 215
    Irenaeus opposes all types of Gnosticism, docetism, 226
    on problematic use of docetic (Verheyden), 215n16, 225n30
    refuting view of naïve Docetism in FG (Thompson), 114n24
Dodd, C. H.,
    According to the Scriptures, 39n16
    Apostolic Preaching and Its Development, 24n39
    Historical Tradition in FG, FG and Hermetic dialogues, **123–24**
    Interpretation of FG, FG and Hermetica, 121, "God's eternal To-day," 58; Philo and FG, 56n3, 65; Wisdom and the Word, 46; Odes and Ignatius from a similar context as FG, 155
Dodds, E. R., ed., Euripides, *Bacchae*, a Dionysiac passion play, 127–28; rites of *sparagmos* and *omophagia* (cf. John 6), 137.
Drower, E. S.,

Canonical Prayerbook of the Mandaeans, 162n50
Haran Gawaita and the Baptism of Hibil-Ziwa, on exodus of the Mandaeans from Palestine to Mesopotamia, 161n48
dualism
  Aune, noteworthy essay by, 155n16
  in Essene interpretation of Scripture, in gnostic cosmology, 182
  in Hermetica with pantheism, gnosis, 121
  modified cosmological in DSS and FG, **71–72**, 78
  between the rulers of lower world vs. the light, 178
  suggests some contact of FG author with Qumran (Ashton), 68n4
  of similar imagery in Odes and FG, 153
  Plato's two-levels of reality, 111
  in Qumran, Philo, apocalyptic, Hermetica, Neoplatonism, FG, 10n42
Dunderberg, Ismo
  FG and GTh in conflict, 184n20
  GTh inspired by FG, **184n21**
  "Lord's Supper" omission, 20n24
  the disciple Thomas and BD, 196n51
Dunn, James D. G.,
  Christology in the Making, on the Logos, 50, *theos* without the article (John 1:1; Philo), 64n11

early
  Christian/Christianity,
    distinctivenss (contra idolatry), 110
    interpretive conventions, **55**, 82
    mission-minded, 16
    preservation of Philonica, 56
    references to Thomas books, 183
    support for FG's dating, 20
    and 1st century Judaism, 82
    use of different Jesus titles, 50
    conflict between Bacchus and Christ cults, **128n15**
    edition of FG from Palestine, 80n32

    FG reception, 7, **10**, **12**, 103, 206, 231
  Gnostic, dualism, 178
    influence, 171
    literature, 169
    revelation discourse, 170n11
  Judaism, Christianity, and mystery cults, 105
    in scholarship, 99n27
    rabbinic stories, 84n7
    and targums, 101
    traditions in later documents, 83
  Odes, 154–55
  Samaritans, **159**
Eco, Umberto
  aesthetics of reception with interaction of author, text, reader, 231
  intentio operis and *intentio lectoris*, 237
  less-defined symbols of Hermetica, paradigm of interpretation, 121n33
  three levels of intention (work, reader, author), **12n51**
edition(s)
  FG, first and second, 11–12
  first ed. of FG and *Bacchae*, 132–33, 144–45
  John 21 as later, 22
  of *Hist. eccl.*, 228
education, in antiquity and learning Greek, 120n29
Egerton Papyrus 2
  date and contents, 224
  early reception of FG, 207, **224–25**
1 Enoch,
  1:3 a parable (cf. 45:1; 58:1), 18n15
  6–10 ancient conflict (cf. Gen 6:4), 55, 177
  19:3; 71:14; 103:2, Enoch exalted as the Son of Man, 21n31, 30n55
  42:1–2; 48:4; 104:2–3 e.g., light of God to the nations, 45, **47–48**, 62
  58:5 sun overcomes darkness, 47
  71:7 angelic appearances, 54
  89–90 Lord of the sheep, 165

INDEX

1 Enoch *(continued)*,
   99:3 angels bring judgment on sinners, 54
   a composite of different genres, 45n2; and also FG, **48n9**
   date of collection, extant mss, 45n2
   Grk. Trans. of 1 En from cave 7 (7Q4–10, 15), 68n2
   Parallels with FG: light, heavenly matters, gnosis, Lord of sheep/shepherd, Son of Man,
   peace unto you, **47n7**
2 Enoch 2:42, pre-existence of the divine creator, 46
Ephesians,
   1:1—3:13 with John 17:20–26, **21n27**
   2:2 ruler of this world (cf. John 12:31; 14:30; 16:11), 52
   3:14–21 with John 17:1–5, 21n27
   4:8–9 with Odes 10:3–4; 22:1 descent and ascent, 153
   5–6 with John 17:20–26, 21n27
Ephesus
   location of FG, 11, 31n59, 104, 119
   and Dionyian cult, 142
   Heraclitus, 21n29
   Ignatius, 207
   Justin Martyr, 51, 210
   Philo and Hebrews, 57, 119
   Polycrates, 231n44
Epictetus
   Disc. 2.8.1 and John 4;27, God is mind, reason, gnosis, Logos, 64n8
   Disc. 4.5.33 and John 2:4 *kai ti pros eme*; 43n36
Epicureans and Stoics debating with Paul in Athens (Acts 17:8), 120, 125
epilogue
   of Euripides is akin to John 21 (Wead), 132n32
   John 21 introduces the narrative into the church (Zumstein), **22n33**. See also Prologue.
Epiphanius, *Panarion*
   21.15–16, Alogoi reject FG because, e.g., it omits Synoptic material, 18n12 *(Panarion)*
   51.3.1–6, reject FG and Rev and ascribe them to Cerinthus, 18n12, **230**
   51.18.6, FG and Rev are not recognized by the Alogoi, 18n21
   closing comments by Hill and Anderson, 230–32
   his life and time of writing, 207, 229
   Irenaeus (*Adv. Haer*, 3.11.9) cites Epiphanius on the Alogoi, 225
epistle(s). *See* letter(s)
Epistle to the Apostles
   book outline showing Johannine influence, 213
   date, extant ms, contents, 212–13
   early reception of (1 John 1; John 1–2; 5; 13–14; 20), **213–15**
   Ep. Apos. 11–12, Mary, risen Lord before disciples, 210
eschatology
   in FG: shift from future to present realization (John 5:24; 11:25; 12:31), 165
   future day of deliverance (Mandaean Prayerbook 76), 164
   future expectation in 1 John (2:28; 3:2), 30
   Gos. Phil. 2 "those who inherit the living are alive," 175
   G. Thom. 51 "what you expect has come, you do not know it," 190
   present and future tension, 20n25, 22
   a present possession (John 3:36; 6:47), **21–22**
   realized (John 3:15–16, 36; 5:23–24; 11:25–26), 21, 29–30
   relationship of present to future in FG, 30n55
   some future eschatology in FG (John 5:28–29; 6:39–40; 12:25,48), 29
   some realized future hope in 1 John (2:5, 8, 13–14; 5:4), 30n55
2 Esdras

7:113 day of judgment, end of this age, 21
8:46, 52 eternal life, the age to come, 21

Essenes
connection to temple (Jos. *Ant.* 18.19), 74
and DSS community, 70
"dwell in every city" (Jos. *J.W.* 2.124)
FG and Essene contact, 81
and interpretation of Scripture, 182
in Philo, Pliny the Elder, and Josephus, **70**, 81
and Qumran community. 81, 182

Euripides, *Bacchae*
DM, 132–47
the dramatist and his play (400 BCE), 128
example (with Heraclitus, Plato) of non-Jewish influence, 8, **103–4**, 109, 119, 124, 170
Origen (*Cels.*2.34,35), cited by, **129**
Stibbe, M., comparisons of his *Bacchae* by, 131. *See also* *Bacchae*; Dionysus.

Eusebius of Caesarea
the author and *Hist. eccl.*, 227–28
Hill, C.: Eusebius on FG and Rev, 230
Historia ecclesiastica (*Hist. eccl.*):
2.16–18 Philo's report on the Therapeutae, 57n4
2.18.1 quote on Philo's elevated views, 67
2.25.6 Rev ascribed to Cerinthus, **228–29**
3.23.1–4 Apostle John in Ephesus, 11n45
3.24.11–12 Jesus' ministry before John, 18n14
3.28.6 Apostle John meets Cerinthus, 11n45
3.39.1–4 Apostle John, John the Elder, 11n47, 210n10
5.8.4 John BD wrote FG in Ephesus, 11n44
5.23–25 Easter observed on 14 Nisan, 20n26, 222
5.24 John BD buried in Ephesus, 231n44
6.14.7 John wrote a spiritual gospel, **17**, 221, 235
7.24.3 Dionysius of Alexandria and Rev, 229
7.25 authorship of FG, Rev, and 1 John, 11n47

Preparation of the Gospel (*Praep. Ev.*):
13.12.1 Plato, Pythagoras borrowed from Torah (Aristobulus), 67n19
13.12.3–4 God's voice at creation (Aristobulus), 57n6

Evans, Craig
"On the Prologue and Trimorphic Protennoia," 175n21
and S. E. Porter, *Dictionary of NT Backgrounds*, 105n7
and J. A. Sanders, *Early Christian Interpretation*, 40n18
and R. L. Webb et al., *Nag Hammadi Texts and the Bible*, 170n10; index of NHL and NT, 221
Word of Glory, 4
criteria of evaluating comparisons, 16n2, 26n6, 92n23, **109–110**,120, 125
criterion of contamination, 110, 125
dictional and thematic coherence, 99n31, 11n16

Evans, Robert, *Reception History*, 3n8, 10n37, 206n3

evil,
all who do/plot hate the light (John 3:20), 73
delivered to the offended (Isis), 106
protect them from evil one (John 17:15), 19n21
overcome (1 John 2:13–14), 32
protection from the power of (5:18–19), 32; Wis 7:30 does not prevail, 47; rescue/redeem from (Mandaean), 161, 163. Spirit (Mandaean), 162, demons (Xenocrates), 111

evil *(continued)*,
   tree of good and (Gen 2:9), 66n16. *See* angel(s); Devil; Demons; Satan.
execution
   of Jesus (John 11:50, *Qal vahomer*), **89**
   of Socrates, 113
exhortation
   Exhortation to the Greeks (Protrepticus), 130
   in scriptural interpretation (Deut 30; DSS), 77
Exodus (LXX)
   1–4 compared with John 4 (Brodie), 39n12
   3:7–8 "I came down to deliver them," (descent), 53
   3:14 "I am the Lord who is," **42**, 57, 61; Philo, 65; Targumim, 92
   4:8–9, 28–31 Moses performed signs before Israel, 41
   4:24; 15:3 SP avoids human portrayals of God, 160
   6:2–3 "I am the Lord who appeared to Abraham," 85
   7:1 "I have given you as a god to Pharaoh," **89**
   12:1–20 Passover/Pesach (John 2:13, 23), 42
   12:10 no bone broken (John 19:36), 38
   14:19 angel of the Lord, pre-incarnate Christ, 51, 54
   15:17–21 your dwelling place, Lord (rabbinica), 85
   16:2, 4, 8 Israel complained to Moses (John 6:61), 41
   16:4 bread from heaven (cf. John 6:31), **37, 39, 41**; Philo, 63; rabbinica, 86
   16:16–27 instruction on gathering manna, 87
   16:25 manna on sabbath, 87; v. 31 manna described, 87
   16:28–36 provision of manna on sabbath (rabbinics), 86
   20:2 "I am the Lord who brought you out," 85
   20:18 "the people saw the voice" (Philo), 58
   23:20–21 "I am sending my angel," 53–54
   24:16–17 God's glory on the Mt., 40
   25:8; 40:34 tent of witness for people, 41n25
   25:19 cherubim on the ark (Philo), 65n15
   32:34 "my angel will go before you," 54
   33–34 shares themes with John 1:14–18 (presence, glory), 41n24
   33:18–19 show me your glory, 40
   34:29 Moses was charged with glory, 41
expel(led), expulsion,
   as *Birkat ha-minim*, with John 9:22; 12:42; 16:2 (Martyn), **84**
   Kimelman critique, 76
   Reinhartz criticism of it, 14n56
   from Jerusalem temple with (DSS) texts (Robinson), 182
   from Jewish synagogues (ecclesiastical tale), 50n14
   from Pachomian monasteries (NHL texts), 182. *See also* Birkat ha-minim.

faith. *See also* belief, believe.
   or belief (*pistis*) in FG, 21
   eyes of faith, autopsy of what believers have (Kierkegaard; John 20:29), 198n59
   "keep my faith you who are kept by it (Odes 8:10; cf, John 15), **152**
   mysticism of FG vs. vision mysticism of GTh, **198**, 199n60
   and rule of truth (Irenaeus, *Haer* 1.22.1), 226, cf. Ignatius, 208; Epiphanius, 229
   and the spirit of prophecy (John 14:29; Justin, *1 Apol.* 33.2), **212**
   what sustained Jesus at Gethsemane (Mark 14:34–36), 29.

in YHWH and in Moses his servant
(Samaritans), 159
faithful
impress of divine image in the
heavenly man (Philo), 62
Israel(ites) in FG and SP, **157**
John 1:6–8 witness of John (cf.
Cadmus, *Bacchae* 10–12),
133–34
lead by the Teacher of Righteousness
(DSS), 73
members of FG and Qumran
communities, 80
one is Moses the servant
(Samaritans), 157n31
Shepherd, John 10:14–16 and DSS,
75; patterned after Moses, 42n31
and true witness of Word (John
8:14, 16; Tg. Jer. 42:5) **96**
false
hero is Thomas in John 14:5–6, "I
am the way," 199n61
is not the Spirit of the Lord (Odes
3:10; John 14:17), 152
title is the Apocalypse of John,
Cerinthus is author, 228
Farewell Discourse. *See* Discourse,
Farewell
Father (divine)
ascent to, 6
children of (Philo; John 1:12), 62
drink the cup given by (John 18;11),
26
dwelling place of (Three Forms
50:14–15; John 14:2), 177
"going to" (John 16;28), 19
"lifted up," (John 12:32), **41n29**;
to whom all return (Gos. Truth
37:38), 174
return to (Treat. Res; Odes; Ap. Jas;
Ascen. Isa.), 176n24
do the will of (John 6:37–38; Gos.
Truth 33:32), 173, 234
glorified by, glorify (John 17:1), 19;
he has God as his Father (Philo;
John 14:23), 62
Holy is God and Father of us all
(John 17:11; Corp. herm.), 124

the hour has come, cf. Philo, 59;
Plato, 116;
I have made known to you
everything from the Father
(John 15:15; Philo), 63
John 5:26–27 and 20:21 as rabbinic
arguments, **89–90**
John 20:17 and Corp. herm., 123
Logos and Lord, no distinction
(Corp. herm.; John 10:30), 122
mandate from the (John 10:18;
Justin Martyr), 211
in me and I in the Father (John
10:38b; Philo), 61
in Ep. Apos. 214
Father and Son (e.g., John 5:20;
13:3; Corp. herm.), 123
in GThom, 175
to me was given . . . from (GThom
61: John 3:35), 187
no one knows except Son (Luke
10:22; John 1:18), **28**
nothing happens without Father's
will (Gos. Truth 37:21–24), 176
in the perfection of, the son
appeared (Odes 41:13; John
1:14)
same nature of Father who is spirit
(John 4:24; Heracleon), 220
Son, and Holy Spirit (Odes 23:22;
John 14:26), 152
Son came to speak of Father's repose
(Gos. Truth 40:30);
Son can do nothing without (John
5:19; Ign. *Magn*. 7.1), 209;
special prerogative given to Word by
(Philo; John 12:49), 59;
they are in (Gos. Truth 42:27–28;
GThom 83; John 14:20), 175
whoever blasphemes (GThom 44;
John 5:23), 188
whoever has seen me has seen (John
14:9), 42n31
Word given in the Thought-Mind of
the Father (Gos. Truth 16:31–35;
John 1:1–5), 172, 176
beyond YHWH, ineffable,
unengendered parent
(Valentinus), 226n34

Fathers
  Early (reception of FG), 7, 206–31 passim
  Greek and Latin, 105, 159, 183
feasts, Jewish
  actions permitted on, 88
  in FG with OT background, 42–43
  Jesus in FG, 234
  observant Philo and FG, 65
  rabbinica and FG, 84, 98, 102
  in solar calendar of Qumran, 70
figure(s)
  divine figure of Hokmah, 46
  of Enoch (Mandaean), 167
  Figure of Echo (1981) by Hollander, 42n30
  of speech, or "veiled saying" (*paroima*, John 10:6), 18n15
  of reconciliation/mediation, 51
  messianic 71n17, mediator(s), 55, 198n57, 200
  Thomas, dominant in someone else's community, 197
Fishbane, Michael
  Biblical Interpretation
    "common wordfield," xxiv
    "shared stream of linguistic tradtion," 3n8, 8n31, 206n2
  "Use, Authority and Interpretation," essay, 72n20
Fitzmyer, Joseph A.
  DSS and Christian Origins, limited relevance, 82
  Impact of the DSS, 8n30, 68–69, 71; on dualism in DSS, 78, 98
  "Languages of Palestine," essay, 69n9, 80n33
  Semitic Background of the NT (1997), 3n9, 91
form(s),
  ancient biography in dramatic, 6n25
  discourses in form of dramatic dialogues (FG), 18
  early form of deification (GThom), 200
  familiarity with Jewish forms, traditions in NHL, 169
  FG's opposition to a docetic form, **175n19**
  FG and GThom: related material in different forms, 192
  "Form vs. Function," essay by B. Schuchard, 35n2, 79n32
  form-critical observations, 205
  God loved his own form (Man equal to himself, Corp. herm. 12), 123
  Hellenistic myth as form of theol. Communication (Rev 12), 145
  intertext at various levels, in various forms (R. Barthes), **2**
  Isis
    "I am" self-predication, **106n10**
    liturgical form of Isis aretalogy, 104n4
    native cult in hellenized form, 105
  limits of source and form criticism, 197
  literary forms of parallels, 99n29; parallel themes, images, forms, 5, 12, 233
  Logos brought to illumination what Demiurge began (Heracleon), **218**
  masculine, feminine forms of "Word" in the Syriac Odes, 149n7
  Odes form a poetic handbook, 149
  Plato
    generated forms of Time that imitate Eternity (*Timaeus*), 116
    Good as the highest of the, 111
    knowledge of the Forms through reason, 111
    perfect spiritual world of, 111
    popular form of Platonism, 112, 119
  rabbinic forms of argumentation, 98; also in FG, 101
  of the redeemer (GThom 28), 176n23
  Son in human form, 173
  sources and forms of FG's reference to Scripture (LXX), 40

SP in present form, sectarian, 159
Three Forms (Trimophic
    Protennoia), 50n12, 168–69,
    175–79
Trinitarian theology in the form of
    Logos doctrine (Hippolytus),
    216n17
    versus Judaizing form of
        Christianity (Ignatius), 208
    Wisdom tests her disciples, forms
        them (Sir 41:17–18), 49
    of the Word (Three Forms 47:13–
        16), 176
Fourth Gospel (FG), Gospel of John
    for audience, date, key themes, etc.:
        See authorship, of FG; date, of
        FG; Logos, in FG
free
    disciples go free at Jesus's arrest
        (John 18:8), 20
    "God will set me free whenever I
        wish" (Bacchae 498), 129, **139**,
        141
    "I free the captives" (Isis), **107**
    predestination and free will in
        tension, 22
    "the truth will make you free" (John
        8:32), 61; Gos. Phil. 93, 104;
        "truth, free," **175**
Frey, Jörg
    "Between Torah and Stoa"
        Bultmann's redeemer myth,
            166n56
        comparative studies, 3n8
        early reception of FG, 10
        one-sided explanation of FG's
            context is insufficient
            (Schnelle), **4n12**, 104, 232
        Philo and FG's audience, 67
        theology of God's names, 92n19
    Die johanneische Eschatologie
        realized and future, 30n54
        redeemer myth discussed,
            167n56
    Glory of the Crucified One
        doxa, 19n20
        gradual separation from
            synagogue, 76n23

John 1:14 and wisdom motifs,
    48n8, 58
Imagery in the Gospel of John
    Anderson essay, 25n40
    Attridge essay, 65n15
    FG's metaphors, 6n23
    Nielsen essay, 40n18
"Impact of the DSS on NT
    Interpretation," essay
    Christianity on Jewish mother
        soil, 82
    description and classification of
        parallels, 16n4, 36n7
    four patterns of development, **68**
Kontexte des Johannesevangeliums,
    with Udo Schnelle, 3n8
    Becker essay, 97, 104n6
    diverse milieu of FG, broad
        audience, 14n55, 109n12,
        234n10
    dualism in FG and DSS, 71n18,
        78n27
    FG's context, 4n12
    Lang essay on FG and Seneca,
        112n19; 206n1
    reception of FG from Papias to
        Irenaeus, 206–7
    Steigert essay, 64n10
    Zimmerman essay, 42n31
function
    corrective function of reception
        history, **10n40**
    of divine agency (Borgen), 51n20
    form and function of dualisms in
        FG and DSS, 71n18
    "Form vs. Function" essay by B.
        Schuchard, 35n2, 79n32
    how FG's characters function in the
        narrative, 204
    language has a social function, 7n5
    light metaphors in DSS and FG have
        different functions, 193–94
    of signs in FG, **97**
    symbolic functions of Galilee and
        Samaria, 156

INDEX

Gaius
- Roman bishop who rejected FG and Rev (Haenchen), 225
- reported on the millennial views of Cerinthus, 228

Galatians
- 3:13 "everyone who hangs on a tree (Deut 21:23; John 19:3), 38
- 4:8 "those who by nature are not gods," 110
- 5:19–21 idolatry and sorcery denounced, 110
- Ignatius had known of it, 208

Galilee
- FG moved from Judea-Galilee to Ephesus, 4n11
- John 2:1, Cana of Galilee, 214
- John 21 and Luke 5, Sea of Galilee (Tiberius), 22
- Mark 1:16 and John 1:43, departure to Galilee, 24
- Northern Palestine: Galilee, Samaria, 156, 160

Garcia Martinez, Florentino, *DSS:SE*, Heb. Text, 68n1, 72, 73, 75–77

Garrett, Susan R., *Celestial Spirits*, 55

Genesis
- 1–2
  - creation, God's work, 72
  - God's creative agent, 57
  - and Hermetica, 121, 125
  - life and light (Philo), 59–60
  - and wisdom, 40;
- 1:1 and 8:22
  - creation and permanence (Plato, Philo), 67
  - Plato knew Moses, 115
- 1:1 and John 1:1–5
  - "in the beginning" 37, 49
  - positive view of *kosmos*, **19n17**, 179
- 1:3
  - "and God said" (Heb.*'amar*), 40n21
  - "let there be light" (Philo, *Somn.*1), 59
- 1:26–27 creation of heavenly man in God's image (Philo), **62**
- 1:28 Father of all generated Man equal to himself (Corp. herm. 1:174–75), 123
- 2:1 and John 19:30 "it is finished," 43n38
- 2:7
  - creation of earthly man from dust of earth (Philo), **62**
  - and John 1:4 on "life," 40
  - and John 20:12 breath of life (LXX), 43
- 2:9 and 3:3 two trees in Eden (Philo), 66
- 2:10–4 four branches of rivers from Eden (Philo), 66
- 3:14–18 and 6:4 cosmic conflicts, **55**, 177
- 4:8 and 1 John 3:12 Cain murdered his brother, 30n56
- 14:17–24 Abraham and Melchizedek (DSS), 77
- 15:5–6 and John 8:39–57 children of Abraham, 77
- 17:1 and John 8:12 "I am" with pred. nom., 42
- 17:10–11 a precedent for new legislation (DSS), 77
- 18:1–3 and 19:1, 15 angels sent by God, 53–54
- 18:17–19 Abraham, child/servant of God (Philo), 63
- 18:23 Abraham "came near" to God (Philo), 61
- 22:11; Exod 14:19 angel of the Lord (Justin, *Dial.*56), 51
- 22:11–18 angels act on behalf of God
- 27:37 and John 1:47 "deceit" of Jacob/Israel, 41
- 28:12 and John 1:51 angels ascending, descending, **37**, 39n14, 41, 53
- 31:13 "I am *the God* who appeared to you" (Philo), 57, 64
- 32:28–30 and John 1:49 Jacob named "Israel," 41, 53
- 35:18 Rachel was giving up her soul (2:7; Philo, *Leg.* 1:108), 66n19

INDEX

allusions and echoes to Gen in NHL, **221n25**
FG's rereading of Gen, 37n11
FG and sequence of Gen to Deut, 39n12
genre
  composite
    of both FG and 1 En, 48n9
    of FG, **6n25**
    of 1 En, 45n2
  differences of FG and 1 John, 29
  survey of FG genre considerations, 6n25
gentiles (non-Jewish, "pagans")
  dispersed gathered together (Ode 10:5; John 11:52), **157**
  FG
    author: gentile god-fearer (Teeple), 79n30
    readers, Jewish and gentile, 120, 125, **235**
    written to dissuade gentiles sympathetic with Judaism, 102n35
  and Jewish religious traditions, 198n58
  lore, philosophy and pagan, 169; non-Jewish contexts, 103
  preference for Jewish origins over pagan, **8n29**
glory (Gk. *doxa*; Aram. *yegara*)
  all Adam's will be theirs (gen. Rab. 1:4), 74
  crucifixion demonstrates God's in FG (Brant), 141n42
  divine Logos, manifest in Christ, revealed glory of the Lord (Bultmann), 165
  divine power-presence conveyed by angels, the Word, glory, wisdom, power, spirit, the name (LXX), **54**
  eternal life as crown of glory with garment of honor in eternal light (1QS IV, 6–8), 74
  favorite FG theme, along with light, life, Spirit, 3
  "For His glory will go before thee; thou shalt receive of His kindness, of His grace" (Odes 7:10; John 1:14), 150
  glory (*Yegara*) of whose *Shekinah* is in midst of people (Tg. Neof. Onq. Num 14:14), 95
  God's agent of creation sharing God's glory as light in darkness (Wisdom), 50
  God glorifies Son, Son glorifies the Father in death, resurrection and return to Father, **19**
  Jesus has Father's glory that he manifests to people (John 1:14, 18; 8:50; 11:4; 17:5, 22, 24), 47
  John 1:14–15 shares with Exod 33–34 themes of glory, 41n24
  Moses "charged with glory" descending from Mt. Sinai (Exod 34:29 LXX), 41
  occurrences in FG: noun 19 times verb 23, **30n54**
  OT roots (e.g., Exod 24:16–17; 33:18–19; Isa 40:5), 40
  pure emanation of the glory of Almighty (Wis 7:25–26), 41
  receiving the glory of Father's only Son (John 1:14), 172–73, 202, 214
  signs in FG reveal God's glory in mission of Jesus, 19
  targumic Word (*Memra*) with Shekinah glory (cf. John 1:14), 92
  Torah and throne of glory (Gen. Rab. 1:4), 85
  Word of God reveals God's glory, 30
gnosticism
  Bultmann, Bousset and Jonas on pre-Christian gnostic mythology, 170–71
  complex Greco-Roman, universalizing Jewish, mystic (gnostic-like) context of FG, 10, 233
  content of NHL: mystical, gnostic, Jewish, Platonic, Christian, 183

308   INDEX

gnosticism *(continued)*
   cosmic conflict in Gos. Truth and
      FG (e.g., Gen 3;14–18; 6:4), 178
   definition of gnostics (Pagels), **169**
   divine self-predication, "I am," in
      Gnosticism, 106n10, 108–9
   dualism, pantheism, with gnostic
      concepts (Hermetica), 121
   early reception of FG, not limited to
      gnostics, 206, 221, **226–27**
   elaborate systems in NHL (e.g.,
      Apoc. Adam) an earlier history,
      168n1, 171n12
   Ep. Apos. and Irenaeus resist gnostic
      readings of FG, 215
   four groups in NHL: Thomasine,
      Sethian, Valentinian, Neo-
      Platonic, 169
   four views of GThom and FG, e.g.,
      from common circles, rivals, 184
   FG and Rev rejected as gnostic-
      Montanist writings, 225–26
   Genesis in NHL, 480 echoes and
      allusions, **221n25**
   Gnosis and docetism are not
      identical (Schnelle), **175n19**
   gnostic interpretation of OT, NT
      with cosmic dualism, redeemer
      myth, 182
   Heracleon betrays knowledge of
      Matt, Luke, Paul, FG, 221
   Irenaeus critical of gnostic readings
      of FG, 226–27
   Jesus, paradigm for gnostic salvation
      (table by Koester), 194
   Mandaean gnostic revealer
      discourses, recall Odes,
      Hermetica, 166–67
   parallels with FG: Gos. Truth, GTh;
      Ap. John, Gos. Phil., Three
      Forms, 172–77
   Prologue's context informed by
      Genesis, wisdom, gnostic myth
      (G. Robinson), 179
   See also Heracleon; Nag Hammadi
      Library; Valentinus; Thomas,
      Gospel of

God,
   1 John, **29**
   angels of God in FG, 39, 41, **53–54**,
      71
   in *Bacchae*, 126–29
   belief in, **61**, 77, 93
   born of, 32, 123
   bread of, 60
   breath of, 60
   children of, 32, 62, 76, 85, 151, 202
   creator, 49–51, 72, 85, 115n26, 222
   dwelling of, 41
   equal to, 117, 123, 187, 189, 199, 203
   eternal, 65
   (pre)exist with, 47, 49–50, 85, 92,
      149, 172, 187, 222, 234
   friends of, 49, 63
   glory of, **30**, 42n28, 165
   in GTh 187–88, 199, 203
   Hermetica, 121, 124
   image of, 62, 202–3
   in Isis, 105
   knowledge of, 28n49, 56n1, 59,
      61, 121–2, 125
   lamb of, 17, 219, 222
   love, 61, 133, 139
   as light, 32, 47, 59, 150
   name of, 53, 57, 92, 100
   in NHL, 174–78
   Odes, 154
   only one, 64, 66, 96, 110, 208
   in SP, 160
   as spirit, 64n8, 220
   transcendent, 51, 64n8, 66
   vision of, 53, 58, 92, 95, 199, 200
   will of, 173, 211, 214
   Wisdom of 46, 58
   Word of, 17, 53, 58, 60, 63, 91, 100,
      221n23, 234
   See also Father (divine)
Gospel of John. *See* Fourth Gospel (FG);
   authorship, FG; Logos, FG.
Gospels, Synoptic
   agree that crucifixion occurred on
      Passover (Nisan 15) shortly after
      Last Supper, 20
   Anderson, *Riddles of FG*, FG and
      Synoptics, 17n5, 25n40

Brown, *John*, passion narratives, FG and Synoptics, 24–26,
commom cycle of tradition, FG and Synoptics (tbl.1.B), **25**
concise Synoptic aphorisms become in FG extended discourses of dialogues and monologues, **18**
editions and redactions of Q (Synoptic Sayings Source), 144–45
FG
    agrees with Synoptics on a "Last Supper" with prophecy of betrayal (John 13:1–11), 23–24
    comparisons with Synoptics, 21–22
    differences with Synoptics explained by mimetic indebtedness to *Bacchae*, 143
    and GTh interpret distinct from Synoptics, 181n11
    omits teaching and stories crucial to all 3 Synoptics, 22
    parallels to Synoptics dominated by Johannine literary style and themes, 24
Lindars, "John and the Synoptic Gospels," John 3:3–5 an expansion of Synoptic saying (Mark 10:15, par.), **19n18**
Origen used all four Gospels, when FG appeared to conflict with the others, he would interpret it as a "spiritual gospel" (cf. Clement of Alex.in Eusebius, *Hist. eccl.* 6.14.7), 221
Puskas and Crump, *Gospels and Acts*, FG and Synoptics, 24n38; FG's (Synoptic-like) sources, 27n46; tbl. on FG and Mark, 25n40
Smith, D. M.
    John among the Gospels, FG and Synoptics, 17; similar, parallel traditions, 28n50
Theology of the Gospel of John, FG themes, 6n24; FG in agreement with Synoptics, 23
See also Luke, Gospel of; Mark, Gospel of; Matthew, Gospel of; Q
grace (*charis*)
    1QS IV, 4 "God's abundant mercy (*hesed*)," 73
    Ep. Apos. 1 "May Grace increase in you," 213
    Gos. Truth 16:31 grace of knowing him through power of Word, 172
    John 1:14 "full of grace (*charis*) and truth," **58**, 94, 100, 115, 134, 150, 172, 214
    John 1:16 "grace upon grace," 73, 106, 150, 172
    John 1:17 "grace and truth came through Jesus Christ," 160
    Ode 7:10 "he was gracious to me in his abundant grace," 150
    Ode 20:9 "thou shalt receive his kindness and his grace," 150
    Origen, Comm. Jo. 13.10 grace and gift of the Savior cannot be taken away, 219
    Tg. Ps.-J. Exod. 34:6 the Lord, full of kindness (*hesed*) and truth," 94
Greco-Roman
    and ancient near east, 42n31, 63
    anxiety and aspiration, 111n17
    backgrounds, 6
    complex, multi-cultural **10**, 233
    cults, both Judaism and Christianity, **3n9**
    cults and philosophies, 101, 104, 109
    culture and thought, 82
    educated pagans, 117
    milieu, xxiii, world, 9, 17n6, 104, 128n15
    mythology in NHL, 169
    non-Jewish influence, 8n29, 109, 119
    philosophy, 4, 121, 232
    religions, 104

Greco-Roman *(continued)*
    and Semitic, 196
    traditions about Dionysus, 127
Greek. *See* Koine Greek

Habakkuk, pesher on
    1QpHab pesher on, and 1 John with FG, 31n61
    1QpHab VII, 4 Teacher of Righteousness, **71**
    1QpHab VII, 1,11–12 who will not abandon the service of the truth, 73
Haenchen, Ernst, *John*
    John 1:1–18, Mandaeans east of Jordan, 161n48
    John 2:1–10, allusions to Dionysus, 136n37
    John 11:50, rabbinic parallels to, 89n13
    orthodox rejection of FG, 225
Haggadah
    stories and maxims of Midrash and Talmud, 84. *See also* Genesis, Gen. Rab.; Deuteronomy, Sipre Deut.
Hays, Richard B.
    Echoes in the Letters of Paul
        echoes explained **9**
        FG and DSS, **79–81**
        FG and Greco-Roman texts, 109–11
        FG and rabbinics, 98–99
        reception history, 207n7
        tests for discerning scriptural echoes 8n31
    Echoes in the Gospels
        on metalepsis, 42n30
        narrative criticism, 50n16
        scriptural references in FG, 36n6
        themes, images in FG, 40n18
    Seeking the Identity of Jesus (with Gaventa), on Christology, 21n28
Hebrew,
    740 MSS in DSS, 69
    75% of DSS, 79
    AT from Heb. text, 68n1
    Bar 1:1—5:9 and Sir, 45n3
    Barr on Heb. and Gk. thought, 8n30
    dabar, 'amar "word," **40n21**, 92
    earlier trans. of Heb. before LXX, 67n19
    FG knew Aram. and Heb., 35n2, 79, 98
    halakah, haggadah, 84
    Heb. in Roman Judea, 80
    imrah (Ps 105:19), 91n18
    John 19:37 and Zech 12:10 (MT), 39n15
    LAB, Jub., Tob. in DSS, 52n24
    OT versification, MT, LXX, 36
    Protestant OT canon, MT, 35, **37**, 46
    Samaritan Heb. in SP, 159
    shakan, "dwell," 41n25, 92
    tirgēm, "translate," targum derivation, 91
    See also Greek; Masoretic text (MT)
Hebrews, Letter to the
    Heb 1:1–4, high Christology, 21n28
    Hebrews. General Letters, and Rev (Puskas), Heb and Philo, **57n5**
Hedrick, Charles W.
    Apocalypse of Adam, Sethian gnostics, 171n12
    Gnosticism and EC World (with Goehring), various NHL essays, 170n10
    and Hodgson, *Nag Hammadi, Gnosticism, and EC*
    "I am" in Isis, NHL, 106n10
    Jewish intellectuals, **170n7**
    Sethian gnostics, 169n4, 171n12, 170n7
Hegel, George W. Friedrich, influence of Heraclitus on his dialectic, 21n29
Heidegger, Martin, *What is Called Thinking?* Krell Intro., 2n2
Hellenism
    FG and DSS, 82
    and Judaism, interconnected, **3n9**, 7n982n39, 119, 124, 236n16
    of non-Jewish, Gentile contexts, 103. pervasive, 103, 109
    See also Greco-Roman; Hengel, Martin

INDEX

Hengel, Martin
  Hellenization of Judea, 3n9
  Johannine Question
    FG and gnostics, 221
    gnosis broad def., **10n42**
    on Gos. Truth, 171n14
    John the Elder, FG author, 11n48, 34n67
    Justin and FG, 212n13
    quoting *Cels.* 2.34–35 on Dionysus, 129
    spiritual climate in 1st cent. Palestine, 4
    Three Forms knew FG, 179n37
  Judaism and Hellenism, **3n9**; 51n20, 103n1
  "OT in FG," essay, OT allusions and motifs, 40
  "Prologue," essay, FG, LXX, MT, 37n10
  "Septuagint as Scripture," 36n9
Heracleon
  commentary on FG, Valentinian and gnostic, 31n61
  date, place of writing, 217
  parallels with FG and anlysis, **218–21**
  sources, 217
Heraclitus of Ephesus
  with Euripides and Plato as non-Jewish influence, 8n29
  Logos as universal, structured principle, **64n8**
  pairs of opposites: day/night, life/death, 21n29
Hermetica
  acquaintance with Gen 1—2 LXX is evident, 121
  comparison with Odes to support early gnostic redeemer myth (Bultmann), 166
  Corp. herm. in form of dialogues between Hermes and pupils, 121
  Corp. herm. 1: *Poimandres* (Gk. "shepherd man," Copt. "knowledge of the Sun-God [Ra]"), originally sage of ancient Egypt, deified as Toth (protector of knowledge), Hellenized as Hermes, son of Zeus, 121
    Greco-Egyptian mystical rev. of the creation (relied on Gen 1–2 LXX) and the ascent of the soul to God through seven spheres, 121
    Nock and Festugiére, *Corpus Hermeticum*, vol. 1, Poimandrés, 121
    table of comparisons with FG: e.g., creation, light, knowledge, rebirth, **122–24**
    tests for evaluating parallels, 124–25
    thoughts expressed in Stoic, Platonic, ancient near eastern myth, written in Gk., Lat., and Coptic, 121
    written after FG, contain early traditions, 121
Hill, Charles, *Johannine Corpus in EC*
  FG and GTh, 181n7, 195n47
  FG, Synoptics, and Alogoi, 18n12
  FG's rescue from gnostics, 215n16
  orthodox rejection of FG, **230**
  reception history, 3n8, **10**, 206n3
Hillel the Elder
  Middoth of, 84, 88
  House of, 101n32
Hippolytus of Rome, *Refutation of All Heresies (Haer.)*
  and FG parallels, 216–17
  quotes variant of GTh 4 (Cameron), 183
  and Tertullian both called Valentinus a Platonist, 169n5
Holy Spirit
  1Q IV, 21 "Spirit of holiness," 72
  1QHa IV, 26 "your Holy Spirit," 73.
  John 1:32–33 and Luke 3:16, "the Spirit descending . . . the one who baptizes with," 23, 26
  John 14:16, 26; 15:26; 16:7,. as Paraclete, **32**, 151–52
  Odes 19:2 and 23:22 "Holy Spirit," 152
  See also Paraclete; Father, holy; Spirit.

312

INDEX

Homer
  allegorical interpretations of, used by Stoics, **56n2**
  cited by Justin and Minucius Felix, 170
hour (*hōra*)
  appropriate time (e.g., John 12:23; 13:1; Dan 12:1–4), 43
  of his betrayal had not yet come (Egerton Papyrus; John 7:30), 225
  "it is the last hour" 1 John 2:18 applied by Epiphanius to the Alogoi, 230
  point in time as the occasion for an event (BDAG), 43n35
  Milhalios, *Danielic Eschatological Hour*, (Dan 8:17, 19; 10:14; 11:14; 12:1–4), 43n35
  now is the appropriate time (Plato, *Tim.* 37E-38A; John 17:1–5), 116
  "now the time has come to go away. I go to die" (Plato, *Apol.* 42A; John 13:1), 119
  the time is now (Philo, *Deus* 32; John 17:1–5), 59
human(s), humanity
  appearance of Word and angels of God, **53**
  demands of human spirit (*Bacchae*), 127
  descent of Messenger to reveal himself to (Mandaeans), 162
  drunken humanity must awake (Corp. herm. 27), 124
  god of love over all human and divine affairs (Plato), 118
  Gos. Truth 31.4–16 (John 1:14) appearance of Son in human form, 173;
  Gos.Thom 28 "I appeared to them in flesh," 176n24;
  Word assumes human form (Three Forms), 176
  Human Condition (Schnelle), soul not entombed in body for FG, 119

Humanity of Jesus (Thompson)
  full humanity, 23n36
  Jesus bravely submits to death, **114n24**.
  humankind exists in ignorance before gnosis, 169
  inhabitants of the world (John 3:16–17; 4:42), 19n17, 179
  Jesus is what deified human looks like according to FG, 200
  John 10:35 some humans as gods (i.e., Moses, certain judges), 89
  knowledge of God best of human goals (Philo), 61
  lust of archons corrupts humanity (cf. Gen 6:4), 178–79
  perfect human possesses divine knowledge (Hermetica), 121
  Spirit of truth as power within (DSS), 80
  who redeems you back to humanity (Isis), 108
  Wis 9:1–2 humans formed by your Wisdom, 47
  See also Docetism
Hurtado, Larry W.
  Destroyer of the Gods, early Christian distinctives (contra idolatry), 110
  "Mediator Figures," essay on divine agents, 198n57
  One God, One Lord,
    personified attributes of God, principle agents, 46
    devotion to divine Jesus in early Christianity, **154**
hymn(s)
  Anderson, "Johannine Logos-Hymn," John 1 as Christ hymn opening FG, **17n8**, 40
  Christ hymn (Col 1:15–20), **21n28**
  Cyme hymn (Isis), 105n10
  development of Isis aretalogy hymn, 108–9
  Homeric hymn to Dionysus (Hesiod), 129, 140
  hymn to the King of all (Clement, *Protr.* 12), 130

hymns of Marqe the theologian
(Samaritan), 159
Odes reflect gnostic and hymnic
sources (Bultmann), 154
Sanders, *NT Christological Hymns*,
154n13

"I am" (*egō eimi*)
GTh 61, "I am your disciple" [Jesus said to her], 203
Ign. *Smyrn*. 3.2 "I am not a bodiless demon" (the risen Christ), 210
in Isis and NH (Thunder VI,2), **106n10**
John 14:5-6, "I am the way" (Jesus *not* Thomas), 199n61
Philo, *Somn*.1.229 and Gen 31:13 I am *God* who appeared to you, 57, 65
with, without pred. nom. in FG, LXX exemplars, **42-43**
Rev 1:8, 17 I am the Alpha and Omega, first, last (21:16; 22:13), 43n33
Ignatius of Antioch
congregations associated with Paul, FG, Ignatius, 221
Epistles and the Odes from same circle as FG (Dodd), 155
life and writings, 207
parallels with FG, **208-10**; in Gk. (Burney), 227n37
immortal, immortality
of Aseneth (Jos. Asen. 16), 54
in Corp. herm.
partake of it (not death), 124
a returning to the Father, 123
by eating flesh, blood of the god (*Bacchae*), 137
of Isis and her son, Horus, 108
in Odes, God offers it to those joined to him, **150**
in Philo
of eternal Father, 62
for those who drink everlasting fountain, 60
for those who take refuge in God, 59

soul imprisoned in the mortal body (Plato), 111
Wisdom to lead people to, 48
interpretation
1 John to refute the secessionist int. of FG? 33
DSS, pesher (Heb.) contemporizing, 71n16
figural of Israel's Scripture (Hays), **43-44**, 49n39, 50n16
GTh 1 "whoever finds the int. of these sayings will not experience death," **193**
history of, 3n8, 206
legal, exhortatory, narrative, and scriptural, **77**
prophetic of unfulfilled prophecies, 78, 80
Philo
allegorical, 52, **56n2**, 66
symbolic interpr. of temple, 65n15
Rabbinic methods of, **88-89**
rescue of FG from gnostic interpretation? 215n16
Targumim trans. and interpr. of Scriptures from Heb. into Aram., 91
intertextual
FG, product of diverse, complex relationships, 3, 232
Israel's Scriptures, engagement with, 44
with Johannine Letters, 29;
MD's commentary (*Bacchae*), 134-42
and metalepsis, **42n30**
tests for evaluating, **8n1**, 36n3, 98n26, 109n11, 159n40
Irenaeus of Lyons
Adversus haereses
identified Valentinus as gnostic; his censored Gos. Truth (3.11.18) may be same as NHL title, **169n2**, 176n22
criticism of Demiurge creator god, 218n21

Irenaeus of Lyons *(continued)*
   Adversus haereses
      information on John the Apostle, John the Elder, 11
      some of his many allusions to FG, **226n32**
   bishop who opposed gnosticism and docetism, 226
   irony, Socratic
      "those who had the most reputation to me are the most deficient" (Plato, *Euthyphr.* 11; cf. John 3:9), **116**
Isaiah, book of
   1QpIsa, pesher on Isaiah (DSS), 31n61
   6:10 (John 12:40–41) on the unbelief of the Judeans, **38**
   Tg. Isa. 30:11 on the disobedient of Judah, 92. *See also* Deutero-Isaiah
Isis
   comparisons of Isis texts with FG, **106–8**
   critique by Ashton, 7n29; 105, 109
   example (with Jesus) of how a local cult became a Hellenistic religion (MacRae) 11n43
   "I am Isis, mistress of every land" (Bergman 3a), 106
   I am sayings in Isis, Deutero-Isa., Wisdom, and FG (MacRae), 109
   "I free the captives" (Bergman, 48; John 8:32), 107
   Isis and the God of Israel, 110
Isocrates,
   To Demonicus 34
   letters written from two-level perspective, 12n49
   To Nicoles 35
Israel
   believing or faithful (John 1:47), 157
   beloved for they are called children of God (m. 'Abot. 3:15), 85
   disobedience in the wilderness (John 6:49), 77
   faithful shepherd to sit on the throne of (4Q504), 75
   feasts of, **42**, 65
   God's "tenting" with Israel (BDAG), 41n25
   Isis mismatched with the God of, 110
   Israelites were saved from death by (Tg. Ps.-J. Num 21; cf. John 3:14–15), **101**
   John 1:49 King of Israel (cf. Gen 32:28–30), 17, **41**, 57
   John 3:9 Are you a teacher and not yet understand? 116
   Lord brought bread down from heaven for Beloved (Mek.), 86
   Messiah of Aaron and of (DSS), 71, 75
   Moses defender of truth in the heavenly court of, 157
   through Moses, God gave Torah to (Sipre Deut.), 87
   Samaritans from northern kingdom of, 157
   scriptural heritage of, 9, 44
   Son of God with many names, e.g. King of, 135
   Talmuds of (Jerusalem and Babylon), 84
   targumic Word and YHWH of, 120
   used exclusively as inner Jewish speech (Talmud), **102**
   when Israel saw the signs (Tg. Ps.-J. Exod), 97
   Word, "he who sees" Israel (Philo), 53
   Word of Holy one of (Tg. Isa. 30:11), 97
   Word and Shekinah within (Tg. Ps.-J. Exod.), 94–95
   See also Jews; Judaism.

Jacob (patriarch)
   4QpIsaa remnant of Jacob shall return, 76
   Heracleon, 219
   hero in the SP (Samaritans), 158
   John 1:47, 49 (Gen 27:35; 32:28–30), Jacob-Israel, 41

John 1:51 (Gen 28:12) Jacob's dream, **41**
John 4:4–6 Jacob's well, 41
Somn. 1.229 to Jacob, "I am the God who was seen by you," 57
See also Israel
James, Apocryphon of, 15.15–25 ascension to heaven, 176n24
Jaubert, Annie, Qumran solar calendar, date of Last Supper, 70n14
Jauss, Hans Robert, history of effects, new horizons, 10
Jesus (of Nazareth)
    accused of having a demon (John 7:20; 8:48), 52
    Bultmann: the story (of Cana) taken from heathen legend and ascribed to, 126
    called Word of God and word of life, 17n10, 221n23
    conception of chief heavenly mediator used to portray him, 55
    confident resolve of FG's (John 12:27–28; 18:11), **29**, 113–14
    Dionysus as Christological foil for, 132
    and DSS community, **68**, 79, 81–82
    epithets used of him, misinterpreted by opponents of 1 John, 29n53
    execution of Socrates, Pythagoras, and, 114
    experiencing him, not imitating him, 17
    FG
        ascribes to Jesus what is ascribed to God in 1 John, 29, 32
        chose tragedy to write about him, 132;
        outline of ministry of, **24**
        own story of, 2, 17, 19–20, 22, 44, 232, 237
    food and drink, employs symbols of 49
    future promises in the present with coming of, 30n55
    Gos. Truth 20:10–14 accepts suffering, death to bring life, 173
    GTh 28 (cf. John 1:14) appeared in the flesh, 174
    "I am" sayings of, **42n33**, 65
    manifests Father's glory to people, 47
    Messiah, Son of God, not son of David (Samaritans), 152, 157
    Odes 16:8; 36:4 "Lord" refers to God, not Jesus, 150n8, 154
    as Sophia, the feminine face of God, **50**.
    truth and characterized by truth, 73
    whatever said of God is said of (John 5:26–27), 89
    See also Christ; Christological
Jews, Jewish people
    conflicts with leaders of the, in FG, 102, 117, 140–41, 157, 203
    contrasted with Israelites, 157
    diverse use in, e.g., Judeans, people, leaders, 31n58, **102n35**
    gnosis, a fascination with by intellectuals of the, **169–70**
    John 4:9 no association with Samaritans, 158
    John 18:33–39 Jesus, King of the 17, 26
    Jew-ish, not Jewish, 102n35
    and rabbinic arguments, **87**, 90
    and synagogue expulsion, 76
    Hellenistic in the Roman world, **3n9**, 7n29, 103
    non-Jewish Hellenistic (Gentile), **7n29**, 103, 110
    in Talmud, used in stories with "non-Jews," 102. *See also* Israel, Judeans
Jipp, Joshua, "R. E. Brown and FG" issues with two-level perspective, 5n18, 12n50
Job
    1–2 adversary in heavenly council, 52, 71
    9:8; 38:16 God walks on the sea, **90**
    11:6–7 power of wisdom disclosed, 48
    19:26 LXX (cf. John 19:30) "these were accomplished," **43**

Job *(continued)*
   28:12–28 preexistent wisdom revealed 46, 97
   28:21 (cf. John 1:10) wisdom escapes human notice, 48
   T. Job 2—5 angel imparts salvation and foresight, 54
Jonas, Hans
   Gnosis und spataniker Geist,
      Greco-Roman universalizing Jewish, mystical ("gnostic-like") context, **10**
      Philo's gnosis, 56n1
      pre-Christian gnostic myth, 170
      "spirit of late antiquity," **155**, 233
   Gnostic Religion, ET and commentary on Hermetica, 121n33
   "Gnosticism and NT," Jewish impact on gnostic thought, 179n33
John, Gospel of. *See* Fourth Gospel.
John (the Baptist)
   Bultmann on JBap and Synoptics, 28n47
   concurrent ministries of Jesus and, 18
   and DSS, 68
   FG
      as Beloved Disciple in? 11, 20
      not called "the Baptist" in, **18n3**
   followers of, 31
   John 1:20, 23 not Messiah, voice crying (Justin, *Dial.* 88), 211
   John 1:29 psychic-pneumatic interpretation of Heracleon, 219
   John 1:32 saw Spirit descend on Jesus, 18
   John 1:33 baptism of water and Spirit (cf. John 3:5), 18n11
   John 3:23 John active in Samaria? 156
   Luke 3 and JBap, 26
   and Mandaeans (true prophet), 161–62
   plays role of Cadmus (*Bacchae*), 134
   and Synoptics on Jesus and, 23
John, Letters/Epistles of (1–3 John)
   Brown, *Epistles of John*, 30n57, 33n66
   and FG, differences and similarities, 29–31
   Köstenberger, *John's Gospel and Letters*, 30n57
   Puskas, *Hebrews and General Letters*, **31**, 34n67, 57n5
   table of parallels, **32–33**
Johnson, B. D. "Jewish Feasts," 42n29
Johnson, Luke Timothy, GTh within NHL, FG within NT, 182n14
Johnson, Mark, with G. Lakoff, *Metaphors*, **2n3**, 8n23, 173n16
Josephus, Titus Flavius
   Antiquities
      9.277–91 Samaritan origins, 157
      13.254–56 Mt. Gerizim sanctuary built under Persians, 158
      13.255–56 Hyrcanus destroys it
      11.346–47 Jewish disdain for Samaritans, 158
      18.19 Essene connection to temple, **74**
      18.79–80 fate of Isis temple in Rome, 105
      18.85–89 Pilate kills many Samaritans at Mt. Gerizim, 158n35
   Jewish War
      2.119–61, Essenes, 70
      2.124 Essenes "dwell in every city," **79**
Jubilees, Book of
   3–7 (cf. Gen 3—6) ancient conflicts recalled, 55, 177
   3:1, by Word of the Lord animals brought to Adam, 47
   3:17–25, cf. Gen 3 Garden offense, **178**
   5:1–11, cf. Gen 6:1–4, defying boundaries, 178
   10:3–6 (cf. John 17:15) protection from evil spirits for Noah's sons, 54, 55n26

12:19–20 (John 17:15) protection from evil spirits (Abram, his seed), 54, 55n26
17:11–14 angel sent to Hagar, 53
27:21–23 in Jacob's dream (Gen 28:12–14), 53

Judaism
Christianity, and Hellenism, 3n9
different strands of (e.g. Qumran, Philo, apocalyptic), 198
Early Judaism by Collins and Harlow (eds.), **35n1**, 45n2, 71n18, 83n3
FG's break with Torah-focused, 7n29, 103, 109
Frey quote, **82**; 103. 105, 109, 119
gentiles sympathetic with, 102n35
Hellenistic Judaism, 4, 104, 112, 232
Judaism and Hellenism by Hengel, 9n3, 51n20
Neusner on the study of, **99n27**
and *other* background influences on FG, 4, 7n29104, 232
Philo's impact on, 56, 113
Rabbinic Judaism, 83n1, 83n2
Targums in early, 101.
See also Israel; Jews.

Judea
ambiguities regarding region of (in FG and SP), 160
diaspora outside of, 57, 119
DSS from there, 35n1, 79, 82
geographical movement (of FG) to Ephesus from, 4
Heb was used in Roman Judea, 80
Hellenization of Judea by Hengel, 3n9
Jewish leaders in, 5
Luke 4:44 synagogues of, 19n22
2 Macc from there, 52n24

Judeans
John 1:11; 7:1 those who did not receive him, 156n28
John 4:43–45 who did not honor prophets, 156n28
John 7:1; 10:22–24; 11:54; 18:31 of southern territory residing near Jerusalem, **102n35**

John 7:14–15 amazed by teaching of Jesus of *Galilee*
not well-received by northern inhabitants (Ezra, Neh), 158
and Samaritans suffer under Hasmoneans of, 158.
See also Judaism; Israel.

judgment, justice (*dikaios krisis*),
Isis: I made the strong right (*dikaios*); penalties for those who practice injustice (*adikaios*), **106**
John 7:24 judging (*krisis*) with right (*dikaios*) judgment, 106
John 12:31; 16:11 ruler of world to be driven out, 106
one of four cardinal virtues symbolized by one branch of rivers (Philo on Gen 2:10–14), 66

Keener, Craig S. xxiii–xxiv
Gospel of John
ancient parallels: promise, precaution,**145**
ancient precedent on use of sources, 31n62
authorship of FG, 11n48
comparing different authors, locating strongest, weakest points, 4n15
composite genre of FG, 48n9
diverse views on origins of FG's Logos, **3n7**, 17n6
FG's discourse and ancient speeches, 19n16
FG's genre, survey of views, 6n25
Greek divination, 200n64
John 2:6–10, Cana, 144
John 10:35 "gods," **89n12**
John 11:50, one for many, 89n13
John 11:54, Ephraim,156n25
multiple meanings of Son of Man "lifted up," 45n28
rabbinic exegesis, 88n10
source criticism of FG, 27n46

Keener, Craig S. *(continued)*
    "We Beheld His Glory," John 1:14–18 and Exod 33–34, common themes, 21n24
Kierkegaard, Søren, John 20:29, seeing "with the eyes of faith," 198n59
Klauck, Hans-Josef
    Herrenmahl und hellenistischer Kult, whole circle of context, 4, 232
    Religious Context, cult of Isis texts, 106n10
Klink, Edward W., *Audience of the Gospels*
    Bauckham vs. Mitchell on Patristic evidence, 235n12
    Bird on broad circulation of apocr. gospels, 16n3
    essays supporting, qualifying, contesting Bauckham's position, **14n56**, 234n10
    See also Audience of FG, broad; Bauckham, Richard; Missional
knowledge (Gk. *gnōsis*)
    1 En 103:2 k. of what is written on holy tablets (cf. John 5:47), 47n7
    1QS
        III, 15 "from God of knowledge comes all that there is," 72
        IX, 18 "the Instructor shall lead the faithful with knowledge" (cf. John 16:13), 73.
        XI, 11 "all things are accomplished by his knowledge," **72**
    Corp. herm.
        to become God, 121
        Hermes deified as Toth, protector of, 121
        of God, way of salvation, 122
        mind enters pious soul and leads it to light of, 122;
        salvation attained through revealed (cf. John 17:3), 122
        "Poimandres," knowledge of Ra, sun god (Coptic); **121–22**
    Epictetus, *Disc.* 2.8.1 God is mind, knowledge, right reason, 64n8
    Gos. Phil. 93 he who has knowledge of truth is free (John 8:32), **175**
    Gos. Truth
        22:4 "If one has knowledge he is from above," 173; Gos. 36:38—37:14 perfect knowledge of Father comes by rev., 176
    Jesus Revealer of God's wisdom and knowledge from above, **234**
    John 3:13, polemic against Enoch Son of Man who ascends to Heaven, receives divine knowledge (1 En 19:3), 21n31
    John 8:14 knowledge of one's origins (cf. GTh 50), 201; Luke 11:33–36;
    on knowledge of God in FG (Thompson), 28n49
    "Mandaean" and "knowledge" (*manda, madda*), elect are possessors of secret rites and knowledge, 161
    Matt 6:22–23 imminent light, capacity for human knowledge (in GTh, not FG), 194
    Philo: *Decal.* 81 knowledge of Him is best of human goals; *Deus* 143 end of reason's road is knowledge of God; *Conf.* 145 they who live in knowledge of the One are sons of God, **61–62**
    Plato
        Tim. 37C reason and knowledge obtained by soul, 115
        true knowledge of Forms obtained by reason, 111
    Rethinking Knowledge by Goodman and Fisher, eds., 2n2, 48n10
    Wis 10:10 Wisdom guided, showed, gave him knowledge of, 48
    See also Logos, wisdom
Koester, Craig R.
any compelling reasons for the comparison? 7n27
Dwelling of God
    FG, replete with OT echoes and allusions, 44n40

INDEX

John 1:14 "dwelt among us,"
  41n25
Resurrection of Jesus, ed. with
  Bieringer, Culpepper essay on
  realized eschatology, 30n55
Revelation, "I am" sayings in Rev
  closer to 2 Isa than FG, parallels
  here are independent, **41n33**
"'Spirit' (*Pneuma*) in Greco-Roman
  Philosophy and FG," essay, 64
Symbolism in FG
  Dionysian traditions in John 2
    relate to Greeks and Jews,
    126n1
  symbols with multiple meanings
    for a spectrum of readers,
    14n55
  themes, images derived from
    LXX, 40n18
  unpacking FG's images,
    metaphors, 6n22
Word of Life
  on roles, functions of Spirit,
    21n30
  theological message of FG, 6n24
Koester, Helmut
  Ancient Christian Gospels
    form-critical study of sayings
      traditions, 205
    Gk. fragments of GTh, 181n5
    independent use of similar
      traditions in FG and GTh,
      192n44
    parallels of FG and GTh
      arranged thematically, e.g.,
      life-giving power, light,
      193–95
    varied wisdom and gnostic
      motifs in GTh, 184n22
  "Divine Human Being," *HTR*,
    exploring deification, 200n64
  "Gnostic Sayings and Controversy
    Traditions," in Hedrick and
    Hodgson, *Nag Hammadi*,
    different sayings traditions in
    GTh and FG, 192n44
  "Gnostic Writing, Sayings Tradition"
    in Layton, *Rediscovering*, 184n22
  "GTh, intro." NHLE

striking parallels with FG, 191
Saying 13, 19, 24, 38, 49, 92 with
  FG, **195n47**
History and Literature of EC,
  encratite and wisdom influences,
  184n22
Koine Greek
  all of FG, DSS in Heb., 77–78, **79**
  of both FG and LXX, 36
Köstenberger, Andreas J.
  "Glory of God" in Morgan and
    Peterson, *Glory of God*, John
    1:14; 2:11, *doxa*, 30n54
  Invitation to Biblical Interpretation,
    with Patterson
    direct allusions, embedded
      echoes, **9n32**, 10n36
    intentional allusions, embedded
      echoes, 79n29, 207n7
    scale of allusion probability,
      33n65
  "John" in Beale and Carson,
    Commentary on NT Use of OT
    OT refs. in FG, **36n8**
    OT themes and images, 40n18
  Theology of John's Gospel
    FG and 1 John parallels, 31n63
    FG's theological message, 5n24
    FG's worldview and use of OT,
    30n57
Kristeva, Julia
  Desire and Language, a dialogical
    relationship between texts as a
    system of codes or signs, 9
  Tales of Love, 1 John 4:16 and
    notions of *agapē*, 20n23
Kysar, Robert
  "Fourth Gospel" *ANRW* nearly
    every religious/philosophical
    movement proposed for
    intellectual setting of FG, 3–4,
    234
  Fourth Evangelist (1975)
    intellectual milieu of the
      Evangelist, 3n8
    irresistible syncretistic,
      heterodox Jewish milieu,
      11, 233

Kysar, Robert *(continued)*
:   *John the Maverick Gospel* (1976), "John, the Universal Gospel," 14n55
    John the Maverick Gospel (2007), faith and experience with little ethical teaching, 17n9;
    why would all four go through all the trouble and expense to write for *only* one specific church? **109n12**

Lakoff, George
:   and M. Johnson, *Metaphors We Live By*
    insights for unpacking FG's metaphors, 6n23
    "most concepts are understood in terms of other concepts, 2
    and M. Turner, *More Than Cool Reason*
    death as departure on a journey, 53n25
    orientation metaphors: above is good, below is bad, 173n16
    walk as ethical metaphor, life as a journey, 84n6

Last Supper
:   FG agrees with Synoptics on a "Last Supper" with prophecy of betrayal (John 13:1–11), 23–24
    Jaubert, *Date of the Last Supper*, uses Qumran solar calendar to argue that Jesus ate Last Supper on Tuesday evening (Brown and Meier dissent), 70n14
    and Plato's *Symposium*, 113, **118**
    Synoptic words of institution (Mark 14:22–25) *not* in FG, **20**, 22–23
    Synoptics agree that crucifixion occurred on Passover (Nisan 15) shortly after Last Supper, 20

Latin
:   Corp. herm. written in Gk., Lat., and Coptic, 121
    Ep. Apos. survives in Ethiopic with Copt., Lat. fragments, 212
    Eusebius, *Hist. eccl.* survives in orig. Gk. with Lat., Syriac, Armen. Versions, 228
    Hippolytus wrote in Gk, not Lat., 215
    Ignatius, *Eph.*, Gk. text of Ussher based on Lat. version by Grossete
    epitome of Melito's homily, 232n28
    epitome of sermons of Augustine and Leo, 212. *See also* Koine Greek

law
:   *Bacchae*: in 186 BCE Roman laws against Bacchic cult, 139
    Isis: "I gave and established laws (*nomoi*) for people that no one is able to change" (Bergman text, 4), **106**
    John 1:17; 7:19, 23 references to Moses and the law are similar to rabbinic language (cf. Sipre on Deut 31:4), **87–88**
    John 1:17, 45; 3:14–15 Jesus fulfills supreme roles given to Moses the Law giver, 160
    John 15:25 to fulfill word that was written in law (*nomos*) citing Ps 34:19 LXX, 38
    Melito: He who made heaven and earth was proclaimed by law and prophets (cf. John 1:2–3, 45), 222

Philo
:   *Agri.* 51 on Ps 23:1, "this hallowed flock [of the world] He [God] leads in accord with right & law," 63
    Deus 69 All exhortations to piety in law refer either to our loving or our fearing the Existent," 61
    before Philo, Aristobulus claimed that Plato and Pythagoras knew Jewish law and borrowed from it, 67n19

INDEX

Samaritans: faith in YHWH, Moses,
Holy Law, Mt. Gerizim, Day of
Recompense (*Tibat Marqe*), 159
Sanders, *Jewish Law*, 83n1.
See also Pentateuch; Torah
Layton, Bentley
FG's Word similar to
"craftsman"(*Demiurge*), but
at some remove from Plato's
Timaeus, 119–20; 179, 218n21
Gnostic Scriptures, on Three Forms,
where heavenly redeemer,
Barbelos, identified as Father,
Mother, Word, Wisdom, 50n12
gnostic teachers, like Basilides,
rarely cited in NHL (Testim.
Truth 57:6–8), but found in
patristic sources, 169n6
Gos. Phil. text has logia refs. *as well
as* NHLE page, line divisions,
175
illustration & explanation of "classic
gnostic myth" in Ap. John,
172n15
Irenaeus, *Haer.*, texts and discussion
of gnostic sources in, 216n18
Ptolemy's Letter to Flora, text of,
221n26
Rediscovery of Gnosticism, ed.,
Koester, "Gnostic Writings as
Witnesses for the Development
of the Sayings Tradition,"
184n22
"The Riddle of Thunder," in Hedrick
and Hodgson, *Nag Hammadi*,
on gnostic use "I am" style
to depict cosmological and
soteriological role of Wisdom/
Eve (Thund. VI, 2), **106n10**. *See
also* Gnosticism.
the Son came in fleshly likeness
to speak of what was on the
Father's heart (Gos. Truth
31.14–16), 173
time must be subtracted from 350
CE NHL date to allow for prior
trans. from original Gk. into
Coptic, 168n1

on Valentinus in Irenaeus (*Haer*
1.11.1), 226n34
Lazarus
candidate for BD? 11, 20
John 11:43–44 parallels the power of
Isis to raise the dead, **108**
Melito on raising of Lazarus (cf.
John 11:17, 43–44, 47), 223
messengers reporting to Pharisees
on sign/miracle of Jesus similar
to messenger notifying Pentheus
of maenad miracles (*Bacchae*),
140
raising of as one of FG's seven signs
(John 11:1–54), **19**;
Synoptics, not found in, 22
Tatian's *Diatesseron* includes
interactions of Jesus with Mary,
Martha, Lazarus, 211n12
letter(s), epistle(s)
Easter Letter of Athanasius (367
CE), **168**
Egerton Papyrus, 229
Ep. Apos. *See* Epistle of Apostles
of Ignatius of Antioch, 207–8, 210,
227
of John. *See* John, Letters/Epistles of
of Paul
1 Cor, divisions,180n4
1 Cor, Gal, on idols, 110
1Thess, Rom, 1–2 Cor, Phil,
Christology, **154**
and Heracleon, NHL, 221
Ignatius and Paul's letters, 208
their wide circulation, 16
Ptolemy to Flora, 221n26
of Seneca, a Stoic on Plato, 64n8
of Simon bar Kokhba, **79–80**
use of Heb. in, **91**
life,
1 John 3:14, passed from death to
life, 33
1QS III, 7 light of life and 1QS IV,
6–8 perpetual life, life eternal, 72
Ap. John 3:17–18 God is
immeasurable light and giver of
life, 174

life *(continued)*,
  Bacchae
    as Jesus is the life-giver (John 11:37–46) so Dionysus is the liberator from death (DM), 146
    John 6:53, eating flesh and drinking blood of the god grants life to celebrants, **137**
  Corp. herm.
    12.1 Mind the Father of all being light, life, 123
    1.17 life and light are the source of soul and mind, 124
  in FG, about 35 times, **21–22**
  Gos. Truth 31:16 "his voice gives birth to life," 173
  Heracleon on John 4:12–15, first life perishes, second life is eternal (Origen), 219
  Isis
    devote your life to Isis and she will prolong your life (*Metam.* 11.6), 108
    the Mother of all life (Apuleius), 107
  John 1:4; 3:15–16; 4:14; 10:10; 11:25; realized, 29–30
  John 5:24; "I am the bread of," 42n33
  John 5:26–27; 14:19 in rabbinic argument, 89–90
  Mandaeans
    Messenger of Light is light and life with gnosis of life, 163
    living water from house of life, giving eternal life (Right Ginza), 164
  Melito: "I am your life" (cf. John 14:6), 223
  Ode 3:18 He who is joined to the Immortal shall be immortal (cf. John 14:19b), 150
  OT roots (Gen 2:7; Ps 16:10–11; Isa 44:3), **40–41**
  in Philo (e.g., *Fug.* 77–78), **58–60**; life as God's eternal today (Dodd), 58–59, 116
  Torah
    gives life to those who do it (m. 'Abot 6:7), 86
    life for world (Deut. Rab. 7:3; Sipre Deut.11:22), 86
  Three Forms 46:16–18 the Word bearing fruit of life, pouring out living water, 177; Heracleon on John 1:14, life in pneumatics (Origen, *Comm. Jo.*), 218
light,
  1 John 1:5, of God, 32
  1QS III, 7; John 8:12 in light of life, 72, 78
  1QS III, 13: John 12:36 sons of light, 72, 78
  Ap. John
    4:19–21 He who comprehends himself in his own light surrounding him, the light completely pure. The spring of Spirit streamed from living water of light, 174
    20:14–16; 22:15–18 Epinoia of the light (luminous afterthought) is hidden within Adam as his helper, 176
  Basilides on John 1:9 according to Hippolytus, 216–17
  b. Ketub. 111a, b "Whoever makes use of the light of Torah will revive (after death)," 86
  Corp. herm. 1:8 That light am I, Mind, your God, who is before wet substance which appeared out of darkness, shining Logos coming from Mind, 122
  Deut Rab. 7.3 words of Torah light for the world," 86
  in FG, about 24 times, **23**
  Frag. Tg. Gen 1:3 "Word of Lord said 'Let there be light.' & there was light in his Word," 93
  Gospel of Thomas
    logion 11; 22 return to light, 202

logion 24 "there is light within a man of light," 202
logion 50 "We have come from the Light, where the Light has originated through itself" (cf. John 3:19-21), 174;
logion 77 "I am the light" (cf. John 9:5), **189**, 201
"I am the light of the world," 42n33
John 1:4-5, 9; 3:19; 8:12; John 8:12, of Jesus, 32;
John 12:35; 1 John 1:7, walk in the light, 32
Melito: "I am your light" (cf. John 8:12), 223
Odes of Solomon
   10:1 "The Lord has opened my heart by His light," 150
   10:14 "And the light dawned from the Word," 150'
   36:3 "I was named the Light, the Son of God," 150
OT roots (Ps 27:11;119:105; Isa 49:6 LXX, **40**;
Philo, *Somn.* 1.75 "God is light (*phōs*, Ps 26:1 LXX) archetype of every other light" 59
Plato
   Phaed. 109E–110A "The true light that Socrates hopes to see after death," **115**
   Rep. 508A "Which one can you name of divinities in heaven as author and cause of this, whose light makes our vision see best and visible things to be seen?" 115
Right Ginza
   1.3 The World of Light came into being through King of Life, 162
   3.100 World of Darkness created by Lord of Darkness, climaxed in creation of Adam whose soul is from World of Light, 162;
   2.3 messenger of light, comes to redeem people from the evil, material world of darkness and enable soul to embark on its journey to the world of light, **163**, 165
Tg. Neof. Exod 12:42 there was void and darkness "And Word of the Lord was light and it shone," 93
Three Forms 47:29 "I am the Light that illumines the All," 188
Wis 7:10, 29, more radiant than light, and never ceases, 47
Wis 7:26, reflection of eternal light of God, 47
Lincoln, Andrew, *Truth on Trial*, FG allusions to Isa 40–55, esp. lawsuit motif, 39n13
liturgy
   Aramaic targums from the liturgy of the synagogue, **83**, 91
   DSS, 200 MSS of liturgy (prayers, worship calendar, poetry), 69
   Hellenistic development of Mithra liturgy (e.g., new birth), 100n7
   Hymns of Samaritan liturgy, 159
Litwa, M. David
   Becoming Divine, deification in FG's Christology and GTh's depiction of the Ideal Christian, 200
   How the Gospels Became History, impact of Greek myths on formation of gospels, 104
   "'I Will Become Him': Homology and deification in GTh" deification, theological trident common to FG and GTh, 185
   divine nature, divine destiny: comparisons of FG and GTh, **201–4**
Logos (Word)
   Aram.: *mēmra mēmer* "word," often substituted for "God." "*Memra* of the Lord" not only as substitute for YHWH, implies more thorough theo. of name of God, 91–92

Logos (Word) *(continued)*
- Clement of Alexandria: "The Lord's voice (*phonē*), the Word (*logos*), without shape, the power of the Word (*logos*), the luminous word of the Lord, the truth from heaven" (*Strom.*VI, 3, 34), **218**
- combination of targumic Word with Shekinah glory (*Yegara*), glory of *Shekinah* (cf. John 1:14). related to *Mēmra* (as Divine Creator) is *Dibbera* fem. of Heb. *dabar*, "word," **92**
- cosmological tale of the Word in the world confronting the forces that oppose his divine mission (Reinhartz), 5–6, **50–51**
- on the diverse views regarding origins of FG's *Logos*, 3n7
- Ep. Apos.: "We believe: the word became flesh and was born not by the lust of the flesh but by the will of God," (3; Eth.), 214
- FG's high Christology: preexistent Word, who descended from heaven, 21
- FG's readers confronted with what is beyond time and beyond visible occurrence, with the Word of God and life of eternity (Hoskyns), 12
- of God made flesh reveals God's glory, 30
- Gos. Truth
  - 16:31–36: "grace of knowing him through the power of the Word that came forth from the pleroma, **172**
  - 23:32–35: the Word of the Father goes forth in totality, 176
  - 37:1–18: the Word is the perfect knowledge of the Father that comes through, 176
- Heracleon: Logos inspired the *Demiurge* to create (Frag.1 on John 1:3 in Origen, *Comm. Jo.* 2.14), 218
- Hermetica: "The Word leaves matter behind to join the demiurgic mind that will govern what has come into being" (Corpus herm. 1.4–11), 124
- Ignatius: "his Son who is his Word [*logos*] that came forth from silence, who in everything pleased the one who sent him," (*Magn.* 8.2), 208
- intermediary beings include angels, the spirit, Word, Wisdom, 51, 53
- Irenaeus, *Haer.*
  - 3.16.2, incarnation of Christ, the Word enfleshed, 226
  - 3.83 by Word (*logos*) of Lord the heavens were made firm, 226n32
- Jesus of Nazareth is the spoken Word of God at creation, the source of all that came into being, **234**.
- Justin Martyr: "the Word [*logos*], who is also the Son . . . took flesh and became man" (*1 Apol.* 32), 211–12
- Later Stoics (300 BCE) followed notion of Heraclitus (Logos as a universal, structuring principle), regarded it as active divine principle that pervades the world, **64n8**
- in the LXX, *logos* is a trans. of the Heb. *dabar*. Both have wide range of meanings: speech, dialogue, narrative, oracle, matter, thing, **40n21**
- Melito, 47: "God, in the beginning, having made the heaven and the earth and all in them through the Word [*dia tou logou*]," 222
- Odes of Solomon
  - 16:18–19 creation by the Word, **150**

32:2, 7: "the Word from the truth who is self-originate," 149

41:14–15: "And light dawned from the Word that was before time in Him. The Messiah in truth is one. And He was known before the foundations of the world," 150

more comparisons (Odes 12:12; 41:11), 151, 154

Philo
  Conf. 146
  logos (300 refs.) an agent of divine power having its own existence, development beyond, Prov, Sir, and Wis, brings us closer to FG's understanding of *logos*, **61**
  Opif. 20 divine Word made the world, **57–58**

preexistent Word (*logos*), who "pitched his tent among us," 17, 41

rabbis applied to Torah what FG applied to Jesus the Word, 87

Tg. Onq. Exod.33:20–23
  When my glory (*Yegara*) passes by, I will shield you with my Word until I have passed by. Then I will remove the word (*Dibbera*) of my glory," you will perceive what's in front of me, but not what's behind me, 95
  more comparisons 96–97
  responses to critics, **100–101**

Three Forms
  35:1–32: Protennoia or First Thought, she appears 3 times: as hidden Voice as Speech of the First Thought, finally as the Word who assumes a human appearance & restores her members into the light (46:5–6; 47:5–22); cf. John 1:9; 12:36), 176

46:5, 15 "I am the Word"; "I alone am the Word," 177

in Wisdom texts are examples of personified attributes of God portrayed as his principal agent, God's Wisdom, and God's Word (*Logos*), 46–47

in the Word Become Flesh, we perceive the carnate, material grounding of the utterance," (Bakhtin), **8n33**

Word (*Mēmra*) of Lord revealed as "I am who is" (Tg. Ps.-J. Deut 32:39), 92

"By word of the Lord heavens were made" (Ps 33:6) in Mek. Shirata 10 (Exod 15:17–21), 85

See also Dibbera; *Mēmra*; Prologue; Word

Lord's Supper. *See* Last Supper.

love (*agapē, agapaō*)
  Corp. herm. 12.1 "Mind, the Father of all, being life and light, generated a Man equal to himself, whom he loved as being his own offspring," 123,
  although FG writes of God's love, Jesus's love for the Father, and Jesus's commandment to his disciples to "love one another" (*agapō agapē* 45 times), nowhere in FG does Jesus tell them to "love your enemies" (Matt 5:44; Luke 6:35), **20**
  John 3:35 "The Father loves the Son, and has given all things into his hand," 59
  John 8:42 "If God were your father, you would love me," **61**
  John 14:15 "If you love me you will keep my commandments," 61
  John 15:9 "As the father has loved me, so I love you, abide in my love," 61

love (*agapē, agapaō*) *(continued)*
   Plato, *Symp.*: Eryximachus proposes the theme of love (*eros*, 177) there follows various eulogies on love (180B). "Only such as are in love will consent to die for others" (179B; cf. John 15:13); FG in John 4, gestures towards a scene with erotic overtones "to tell a tale how *eros* can be converted to *agapē* and apostolic mission" (Attridge), **118**

Luke, Gospel of
   1:79; 2:32 light for people (cf. John 1:9), 23
   2:4 city of David (John 7:42), 42n32
   3:4 voice in the desert (John 1:23), 37
   3:16 Jesus will baptize with HSp (John 1:33), 23, 26
   3:22 Sp descended on him as a dove (John 1:32), 18, 23, 26
   4:30 escape artist (John 8:59b), 139
   4:44 the synagogues of Judea, 19
   5:1–11 call of disciples (John 1:35, 51), 23; John 21 recalls it, 22
   5:10 "fear not" (John 6:20), 27
   6:22 "when they exlcude you" (John 9:22), 76
   6:35 "love your enemies" (Q), 20
   7:1–10 healing in official's household (John 4:46–53), 23
   7:36–50 anointing of Jesus (John12:3–8), **27**
   9:52; 10:33–37; 17:16 Samaritans (John 4), 156n24
   10:16 the sender and the sent (John 12:44–45), 87
   10:22 Father-Son kinship (John 10:15), **28**
   10:38–42 Mary and Martha (John 11:1–44; 12:1–8), 27
   11:33–36 eye is lamp of body (Q), 194
   12:11–12 Heracleon knew it (Clement, *Strom.* 4.9), 221n24
   14:7–24 invitations to eat, drink (John 6:35), 49
   17:12–13 healing of lepers, not in FG, 19
   19:45–46 cleansing temple, final week (contr John 2:13–22), 20
   21:8 "I am," saying, 29
   22:3 Satan enters Judas (John 13:27), 26
   22:17–18 wine at Last Supper, 118
   22:43–44 lacking in certain ancient authorities, 114n24
   23:4, 14–15, 22; John 18:38; 19:4, 6, thrice declared innocent, **27**
   24:4, 23 angelic appearances (John 20:12), 54
   24:36, 40 risen Jesus before disciples (John 20:19–20), 27
   24:39 cited by Ignatius (*Smyrna* 3.2), 210
   differences with FG, **18**
   with Matthew follows Markan outline, 24n38
   OT references, direct allusions, 36
   refs. to "angels," 52n22; "demons, devil, Satan," 52n23

Maccabees
   1 Macc1:14 pagan influence on Hellenistic Judaism, 103
   2 Macc 6:2 Samaritans experienced enforced Hellenization under Antiochus IV (175–64), 158
MacDonald, Dennis R.
   The Dionysian Gospel, review of book, 126–47
   analysis and assessment, 143–45
   conclusions, 145–47
   Intertextual Commentary, **134–42**
   list of proposed imitations, 133
   The Seven Criteria of Mimesis Criticism, 142
   Mimesis and Intertextuality in Antiquity, 9n35, 120n29
   "My Turn: A Critique of Critics of *Mimesis Criticism*" 142n43
MacRae, George W., *Studies in NT and Gnosticism*

INDEX

"FG and Religionsgeschichte," Isis-FG analogy, **11**, 233
  appeal of universal, transcendent divine son to a wide audience, **14**, 109, 170n10, 234
"Ego proclamation in Gnostic Sources," on FG and Gos. Truth, 171n14
Mandaean(s)
  Book of John, 161–62
  Bultmann and, 165–66
  dating, origins, **161**;
  Gnostic baptizing sect, 161
  meaning of name, 161
  Odeberg and Mandaeans, 166
  parallels with FG, e.g., creation, light, Messenger, living, water, shepherd, **162–65**; problematic identity, 13
  Schnackenberg and, 166–67
  Treasure: Right and Left Ginza, 161
Mark, Gospel of
  1:3/John 1:23 voice in the wilderness, 31
  1:4 John "the Baptist," 18
  1:7–8 /John 1:26–27 John and Jesus, 23
  1:8/John 1:33 he on whom the Sp. descends, 152
  1:9–13 baptism, temptation (not in FG), 18, 22
  1:14 ministry begins with John imprisoned, 18
  1:16–20/John 1:35–51 call of disciples, 23
  1:21–28; 3:11 exorcisms (not in FG), 18
  1:34; 3:11–12 messianic secret (not in FG), 18
  1:40 healing of leper (not in FG), 18
  1:40–45 echoes in Egerton Papyrus, 224
  2:19–20/John 3:29 Jesus, bridegroom, 23
  4:12/John 12:13 (Isa 6:10), spiritual blindness, 38, 161
  4:13–20 explanation of parable, 18n5
  5:7/John 2:4 "what have I to do with you?" 43
  6:37—7:43/John 6:1–51 double-cycle tradition (tbl.1.B), 23–25, 28
  6:50; 13:6; 14:62 "I am" statements, **29**
  8:24/Hippolytus, *Haer* 5.4 "I see people like trees walking," 217
  9:2–8 transfiguration (not in FG), 22
  9:35/John 13:1–17, role of servant, 22
  10:15/John 3:3–5 receiving Kingdom of God as child, 19n18
  10:29–20 eternal life in age to come, 21, 64
  11:11 only one Jerusalem visit (contra FG), 19
  11:9–10/John 12:13 blessed is he who comes, 38
  11:15–19/John 2:13–22, temple cleansing differences, 20, similarity, 157
  11:17 den of robbers (at temple), 74
  13:14–23 warnings of Jerusalem's fall (not in FG), 22
  14—15/John 18—10 events of final week, 24
  14:3–9/John 12:3–8 anointing of Jesus, **27**
  14:18/John 13:18 the betrayer, 38
  14:22–25 words of institution (not in FG), 20, 22
  14:32–42 cry of agony in garden (not in FG), 20, 29, 113
  14:62/John 1:51 Son of Man, 28–29
  15:20–21 Simon bears the cross (not in FG), 20
  15:34/Ps 22:1/Justin, *Dial*. 98, christology, 211
  differences with FG, **18**
  lexical/thematic parallels with FG (tbl. 1.C.), 25–26
  OT references, direct allusions, 36
  refs. to "angels, 52n22; "demons, devil, Satan," 52n23

Mark, Gospel of *(continued)*
  similar sequence in FG (tbl. 1.A.), **24**, **28**
  suffering Messiah vs. divine man, 204n70
  verbal parallels with FG, 26
Marriage of Cana. *See* Cana, wedding of
Martyn, J. Louis, *History and Theology, Birkat ha-minim*, **84n5**. *See also* Birkat ha-minim.
  source theories, two-level drama, 27n46
Martyr, Justin
  1 Apol. 19/Homer, *Od.* 11.25, "pit of Homer" allusion 170
  1 Apol. 21 gospel more credible than Bacchus myth, 129n24
  1 Apol. 26 Samaritan Simon practiced magic (Acts 8:9), 158; his disciple, Meander, deceived many, **157n29**
  1 Apol. 32.9 "the Word, who is also the Son . . . took flesh and became man," 211–12
  1 Apol. 33.2; John 14:29 the spirit of prophecy, 212
  1 Apol. 54; *Dial.* 69 influence of Gen 49 on Bacchus cult, 129n25
  1 Apol. 59 Plato borrowed from Moses (cf. Philo), 67n20, 115n26
  1 Apol. 66.4 Mithra rite derived from Eucharist, 110
  comments on FG (tbl. 12.B.), **211–12**
  Dial. 32.2 "Him whom you pierced" (Zech 12:10), **39n15**, 212
  Dial. 56 Christ is angel of the Lord, 51
  Dial. 70 Mithra priests distort Dan and Isa prophecies, 110
  Dial. 88/John 1:20, 23 not Messiah, voice crying, 211
  Dial. 98/Ps 22 prophecy of Christ, 211
  Dial. 114 water of life (John 4:14) living fountain (Jer 2:13), 157n31
  in F. F. Bruce, *Canon of Scripture*, 212
  life and influence, 210
Matthew, Gospel of
  1:20; 2:1 son of David, Bethlehem, 42n32
  3:3/John 1:23 voice in the wilderness, **37**
  3:13—4:11 baptism and temptation scenes (not in FG), 17
  4:5 the devil took him to holy city, 19
  4:16/John 1:9 people have seen a great light, 23
  5:14/John 8:12 light of the world, 23
  5:44 love your enemies (not in FG), 20
  6:22–23 eye is lamp of the body (not in FG), 194
  10:24 servant not above master, 87
  10:39/John 12:25 losing life, finding it, 28
  11:27/John 10:15; 17:25 Father-Son relationship, **28**
  13:15/John 12:40–41 spiritual blindness, 38
  14:27 "I am" statement, 29
  16:19; 18:18/John 20:23 remit and pardon, **97**
  16:24–28, imitating Jesus (rare in FG), 17
  21:5/John 12:15 fear not, behold, 38
  21:9/John 12:13 blessed is he who comes, 38
  21:10 only one visit to Jerusalem (contra FG), 17
  21:12–13 temple cleansed in final week (contra FG), 19
  22:1–4 invitation to wedding feast/banquet, 49
  24:30 coming of Son of Man, 38
  26:23/John 13:18 the betrayer, 38
  26:36–40 sustaining faith, Gethsemane (not in FG), 113
  27:46 cry of agony on cross (not in FG), 38
  allusions to Matt in NHL, 221
  OT refs. and direct allusions, 36

INDEX

refs. to "angel(s)," 52n22, refs. to
    "demons, devil, Satan," 52n23
McNamara, Martin J.
    Aramaic Bible, 91n15
    Targum and Testament, 91n18,
        92n19
Mediterranean world
    ancient 104–5, 110
    cultures, 198
    eastern, 36
    lingua franca (Goodenough),
        155n20, 233;
    multi-cultured/cultural, 145n52, 197
Meeks, Wayne
    "Man from Heaven," FG as
        sectarian; John 3:31; 8:23 man
        from above, 62
    Prophet-King
        signs wrought in Egypt (Exod 4/
            John 4:48; 6:30), **41**
        Moses and David, shepherds,
            42n31
        OT themes in FG, 44n40
Mēmra, Mēmer, Dibbera, Yegara
    combination of targumic Word
        with Shekinah glory (*Yegara*),
        glory of *Shekinah* (cf. John 1:14).
        Related to *Mēmra* (as Divine
        Creator) is *Dibbera* (fem. Of
        Heb. *dabar*, "word," **92**
    substituted for "God." "*Memra* of
        the Lord" not only as substitute
        for YHWH, but implies more
        thorough theology of name of
        God, **91–92**
    targumic Word (*Memra*) with
        Shekinah glory (cf. John 1:14),
        92
    Tg. Ps.-J. Deut 5:24 the Lord's *Memer*
        has shown us the Shekinah, 94
    Tg. Ps.-J. Deut 32:39 the Lord's
        Memra is the I am who is, 92
    Tg. Onq. Deut 33:27 *Memra* is used
        for creation 100
    which my glory (*Yegara*) passes by,
        I will shield you with my Word
        until I have passed by. Then I
        will remove the word (*Dibbera*)

of my glory," you will perceive
    what's in front of me, but not
    what's behind me (Tg. Onq.
    Exod.33:20–23), 95
more comparisons 96–97
responses to critics by Ronning,
    100–101
Word (*Mēmra*) of Lord revealed
    as the "I am who is" (Tg. Ps.-J.
    Deut 32:39), 92
See also Logos (Word)
Messiah. *See* Christ; Jesus
Metzger, Bruce M. *Textual Commentary*
    on John 1:18 *monogenēs*, 17n7
    John 5:4 as a later gloss, **52n22**
    Luke 4:44 "synagogues of Judea,"
        19n22
    Luke 24:40 "hands and feet" (cf.
        John 20:20), **27n45**
    Luke 22:43–44 lacking in certain
        ancient authorities, 114n24
Meyer, Marvin W.
    Ancient Mysteries
        Greek mysteries of Dionysus,
            135n37
        Isis aretalogy from Cyme,
            106n10, **107**
        water into wine myths, **135n37**
    Kloppenborg's *Q-Thomas Reader*,
        Meyer's GTh trans., 180n1
    Nag Hammadi Scriptures, 168n1;
        intro. to Gos. Truth, 172n15
Masoretic Text (MT),
    Eccl. 8:1 MT "interpretation" Heb.
        pesher, 71n16.
    Exod 40:34 MT "tabernacle" Heb.
        mishkan, 41
    Deut 16:13 MT "Feast of
        Tabernacles" Heb. *ḥag sukkōth*,
        42
    Jewish and Protestant canon based
        on, 35
    Judg 11:34 "his only child" Heb.
        yaḥid (LXX in John 1:18), 17n7
    Isa 40:8 MT "word" Heb. *dabar*,
        40n21
    NRSV versification follows, 36

Masoretic Text (MT) *(continued)*,
  occasional NT departures from LXX favor MT text type, **35n2**, 37n10
  Ps 34:20 MT bone not broken (cf. John 9:36), **38**, 77
  Ps 41:9 MT "ate my bread ... lifted heel against," in John 13:18 not LXX, 38
  Ps 119:160 MT "the sum of your words is truth"(LXX in John 17:17), 43
  SP agrees with LXX against MT in 1900 readings, 159
  Zech 12:10 MT "on the one who whom they pierced," in John 19:37 not LXX, **38–39**; Justin Martyr, on Zech 12:10 favors MT over LXX, 212
  See also Septuagint (LXX)
mediator
  being equal with Jesus (Thomas in GTh) diminishes his uniqueness as a mediator, 184
  chief heavenly mediator identified with Jesus, **55**
  FG's faith mysticism vs. vision mysticism of mediator figures, 200
  Hurtado, "Mediator Figures," in Collins and Harlow, eds., 198n57.
  of the vision (John 1:14: 6:46; Philo, *Conf.* 146), **53**
  See also agent
Melito of Sardis,
  FG and *On the Pascha* (tbl. 12.F.), **222–23**
  in Frey quote, 207
  life and works, 222
mimesis, imitiation
  FG's mimetic indebtedness to *Bacchae* explains its differences with Synoptics, 143
  interrogations of Jesus by Pharisees (John 8:12-19) & Pilate (18:28—19:16) requires List of Proposed Imitations (tbl.8. B.), 133
  MacDonald, Dennis

  FG's 1st ed. an imitation/*mimesis* of Euripides, *Bacchae*, **132**
  meeting the criteria of Mimesis Criticism, **134–42**
  mimesis of Euripides, **138**, 140
  Mimesis and Intertextuality in Antiquity, 9n35, 120n29.
  "My Turn: A Critique of Critics of *Mimesis Criticism,*" 142n43
  See also MacDonald, Dennis.
  Seven Criteria of Mimesis Criticism (tbl. 8. D.), 142–43.
ministry of Jesus (MJ)
  adoptionist misreading of MJ in Synoptics (Alogoi), **231**
  begins when John is imprisoned (Mark 1:14) contra FG, 18
  FG's emphasis on Judean MJ (2:13; 5:1; 7:10), 19
  FG's focus on God's glory in the life and MJ (1:14; 2:1), **19**
  FG supplies info. on MJ *before* John's arrest (Esuebius, *Eccl. hist.* 3.24.11–12), 18n14
  healing MJ as further fulfillment of Word become flesh, 101
  length of MJ in FG, ca. 3 years, 21
  Matt and Luke follow Mark's outline of MJ, 24n18
  for Synoptics (not FG), temple cleansing at close of MJ, 20
  wisdom motifs help interpret human responses to MJ, 49
missional
  activities of mission-minded early Christian communities in the Roman world, **16**
  Audience of the Gospels (ed., E. W. Klink), 235n12
  Bauckham, *Gospel for All Christians*, **12n50**, 14n56
  Gorman, *Abide and Go: Missional Theosis* in FG, 235n13
  shared membership in a social group, sectarian or missional, 233. *See also* Audience of FG, broad; Bauckham, Richard; Klink, Edward W.

monologues, FG's extended dialogues and, 18
monotheism, What is Hokmah doing in OT, if monotheism won out? 46
Montanists, Montanism,
  aversion to their reading of FG caused Alogoi to diminish FG (Anderson), 231
  denounced in Irenaeus, *Haer.* 3.11.9 for misreading FG, 227
Moses
  Deut 18:15 cited in John 5:46, a favorite text in the SP (e.g., SP Exod 20), 157
  entered the tent of meeting and the Spirit descended on the mercy seat and from there the Word spoke to him (Tg. Ps.-J. Num 7:89; John 1:32–33), 95, 101
  exhortatory use of Scripture (Deut 30:1–2) appealing to M. (4QMMT), 77
  Exodus and the death of M. are mentioned in the Samaritan *Memar Marqe*, 158
  "My faith is in thee, YHWH: and in M. the son of Amram, thy servant" (Samaritan *Tibat Marqe*), 158–59
  as a "friend of God," (Philo, *Cher.* 49; cf. John 15:14–15), 63
  Heraclitus, certain ideas on life and death in are derived from M. (Philo, *Leg.*1:108), 66
  historicizing references in FG to John the Baptist, to M., and the fleshly incarnation of Jesus are missing in, e.g., Three Forms, 178
  as Israel saw his face charged with glory when he descended Mt. Sinai (Exod 34:29 LXX), "we beheld his glory" (John 1:14), 41
  Jesus is compared to (John 1:17; 5:46–47; Deut 34:10–11), **41**
  Jesus the good shepherd (John 10:11), recalls M. the shepherd (Exod 3:1), 42n13
  Jesus is often portrayed as "the prophet" (John 6:14) of whom M. wrote (Deut 18:15–22), 41
  John 1:45 "We have found him about whom M. in the law and also the prophets wrote" (cf. Melito), 222
  the Lord said to M. say to the people that in the morning you shall be filled with bread and shall know that I am he, the Lord your God (*Tg. Neof.* Exod 16:12; John 6:49–51), 96, 160–61
  Miriam in a dream sees a "man in linen" who foretells of the life and mission of (LAB 9:10; cf. John 20:12), 54
  the particular is embedded in an individual, Jesus, not in the Torah of Moses, in FG but not Philo, (Attridge), 65n14
  permanence of the created world stated years before Plato or Hesiod
    Justin Martyr, 115n26
    Philo (*Aet.* 19; Gen 1:1; 8:22), 67
  as prophet and king in the midrashim (Meeks, *Prophet-King*), 89n11, 157n32, 160
  recognizes as alive (Deut 4:4) those who take refuge in God (Philo, *Fug.* 57; cf. John 17:1–2), 59
  refs. to relationship to the law (John 7:19, 23), characteristic of rabbinic language (Sipre on Deut 31:4), 87–88
  revelation of God to in Exod 34: in the Pal. Tgs. Exod 33:23 is described beforehand as a rev. of the *Dibbera* that includes God's self-description as "full of grace and truth," 100, 160
  role of M. in Samaritan theology is analogous to the role of Jesus in FG (John 9:28–19), but Jesus is greater than M. (1:17), 157

Moses *(continued)*
- says to Israel "your life is to love the living God," (Deut 30:20; Philo, *Post.* 69), 61
- signs in FG recall those wrought in Egypt by (Exod 4:8–9/John 4:48; 6:30), **41**
- Son of Man must be lifted up (John 3:14) just as M. lifted up the serpent in the wilderness" (Num 21:8–9), 41, 44, 160
- Stephen's speech (Acts 7) and SP, M. is one of the heroes in, 158
- struck the rock: the first time it dripped blood; the second time, abundant water flowed forth, (Tg. Ps.-J.Num. 20:11; John 19:34), **97**
- There is one that accuses you, even M. on whom you have set your hope, if you had believed M. you would have believed me (John 5:45–46; Egerton Papyrus), 224
- "though he believed God, nevertheless he tried to avoid the office to which God was appointing him," (*Mos.* 1.83; cf. John 14:1), 61
- Torah of Moses, anyone who disobeys shall be expelled (1QS VIII, 22–23), 76
- "We know that God has spoken to M., but as for you, we know not from where you are" (John 9:29; Egerton Papyrus), 225.
- where is there any like M., apostle of the True One, faithful one of the House of God and His servant? (Memar Marqah 6:3), 157n31
- "the Word of the Lord said to M.: 'The One who said to the world in the beginning: come into being! And it came into being,'" (Frag. Tg. Exod 3:14), 92
- *See also* Law, of Moses.

Muratorian Fragment (Canon), 231n44

Myers, Alicia J.
- and Menken, 79n32
- and Schuchard, *Abiding Words: The Use of Scripture* in FG
- FG knew some Heb. and Aram. (Schuchard), **35n2**
- survey of scholarship, 40n20

Mystery cults (MC)
- Christianity as true MC (Clement of Alex., *Protr.* 12.20), 109
- close-knit, overcame fate, offered hope, 105, and salvation, **110**
- DeConick, *Voice of Mystics*, survey of MC, 198
- demonic imitations of Christianity (Justin Martyr, Tertullian), 110
- different MC listed with places of origin noted, 105n7
- Dionysus Isis, background info., 105
- Dionysus as a MC, 127. *See also Bacchae*
- and idol worship (Deut 5:6–7; 1 Cor 10:14), 110
- Isis-FG analogy, **11**, 233 (MacRae). *See also* Isis
- Isis parallels with FG (tbl. 7.C.1–3), 106–9
- public and private, developed from Greek classics, oriental myths and hellenized in the Roman world, 104–5

myth
- classic gnostic myth in Ap. John, 171, 172n15
- in Dionysus myth, no water into wine miracle (Haenchen), 136n37
- gnostic, pre-Christian myth in FG, 170n11
  - Robinson, 179
  - deconstructed (Frey), 166n56
- gnostic, primal, 170
- gnostic redeemer, in antiquity, **176n24**
- Greco-Roman mythology in NHL, 169
- heavenly redeemer, in FG
  - challenged by Colpe, 123n34
  - challenged by Yamauchi, 163n52, 177n24

Hellenistic myth as form of theol.
communication (Rev 12), 145
for Plato, Logos was associated with
the rational, not myth, 112
Rev. and multi-cultured myths,
145n52
Savior m. from Odes and gnosis
used by FG (Bultmann), 154
Stuckenbruck, *Myth of Rebellious
Angels*
ancient cosmic conflict (Gen
6:4; 1 En 6), **55**, 177n27,
178n32
on demons, devil, Satan, 52n23
DSS, 74n22
save/protect from evil 54
Three forms portrays demiurge in a
mythologizing of Gen, **178**
See also Bultmann, Rudolf;
Gnosticism; Nag Hammadi

NA[28] (ed., Aland et al.)
citations and allusions
FG echoes of LXX texts *outside*
the Jewish canon, 35n2,
45n1
FG has 23 refs. to LXX (Jewish
canon), 36n8
marginal notes: Aratus (Acts 17:28)
Bacchae (26:14); Heraclitus (2
Pet 2:22); Menander (1 Cor
15:33); Wis (John 10:20; 14:15),
120, **125**, **170**
Nag Hammadi Library (NHL)
citations/allusions to FG, in Evans,
NH Texts & the Bible, 170n10
and comparisons with FG (tbls. 10.
A—E), 172–77
discovery, texts, contents, **168**
elaborate gnostic systems
presuppose earlier history,
168n1, 171n12, 176n24
four groups identified in, 169
GTh and FG (tbls. 11.B—E),
187–203
its authors, avid readers, **169–70**
patristic allusions to, 168n2, 176n22

redeemer myth, heavenly, 176n24.
See also Gnosticism
Nagel, Titus,
*Die Rezeption des
Johannesevangeliums*
Egerton Papyrus 2, 224n29
on Heracleon, 217n19
on Hippolytus, 216n17
Ignatius knew FG (*Phld.* 7.1),
208, 210
includes Gk. text of Justin
Martyr with FG, 210n11
Odes, FG influence on (e.g.,
Ode 3:8/John 14:19b; Ode
8:20–22/John 15:4,9), **154**
Odes, Hermetica, and NHL, FG
influences on, 207n6
outline of Ep. Apos. with
Johannine parallels, **213**
Papias knew of FG, 210n10
reception history, 10n41, 206n3
"Zur Gnostisierung der
Johanneischen Tradition," on
Ap. John and FG, 172n15
narrative
affinities between biblical and
classical n. models before 1000
CE, 143
both FG and Three forms
established a meaningful n.
framework, 178
both *Symp.* and John 13—16 frame
the dialogue on love with a n.
that exemplifies the theory in a
concrete way (Attridge), **113**
by means of n. criticism traditions
in conflict are challenged
(Skinner), 236
cosmological tale coincides with and
is informed by n. criticism, 50
Culpepper, *Anatomy of the FG*,
foundational, 6n25
festival of Dionysus, 105n7
FG as a dramatic gospel of
biographical n., 6
FG's ideal n. and authorial audience
share a common culture, history,
ideology, **238**

narrative *(continued)*
- FG's n. is a unified, coherent utterance (Moloney, Synchronic), 6n26
- focus of n.- and reader-response criticisms on the world of the text before us, **236**
- Frei, *Eclipse of Biblical Narrative*, diachronic and synchronic, 7n26
- Genette, *Narrative Discourse*, theory and techniques, 50n16
- John 1–20 intros. Christ into the n., John 21 intros. The n. into the church, 22n33
- Martin, *Narrative Parallels*, rabbinic stories, 84n7
- Martin, *Tg. Neof.* (Num 21:4–9), 101n34
- more than one background necessary for understanding the FG n., 4, 104, 232
- Thatcher and Moore, *Anatomies of Narrative Criticism*, synchronic essays, 6n25

Neoplatonism. *See* Plato, Platonism,
Neusner, Jacob
- dates for Mishnah (200 CE), b. Talmud (600), Midrash (250—1200), **83n3**
- *Development of a Legend*, escape of ben Zakkai from Roman-held Jerusalem in a coffin (Lam. Rab. 1, 5) late legend, **39n15**
- *Midrash Reader*, 83n3
- *Rabbinic Judaism*, 83n1
- *Rabbinic Literature and NT*
  - historical-critical study of rabbinic, 83n4
  - promise and perils, 12n52
- *Rabbinic Traditions and the Pharisees*, 83n4
- relation to rabbinica, **88n9**
- translations
  - *Genesis Rabbah*, 84n8 89
  - *Mishnah* and *Babylonian and Jerusalem Collections*, 84n8
  - *Tosefta*, 84n8

"What We Cannot Show We Do Not Know," compares modern use of the rabbinic corpus by scholars to the study Christianity from 200–500 CE—treating it as one *seamless* body of work! **99**

new birth,
- Apuleius, *Metam.* 11.2 "restore me to the sight of those that love me," 107;
- Gos. Truth 31:16 "his voice gives birth to life," 173
- Isis "who redeems you back into humanity,"(11.6; cf. John 1:4), 108
- John 3:5 recalls 1:33 baptism of water and Spirit (cf. Ezek 36:25–27), **18n11**
- Lindars, "John and the Synoptic Gospels," John 3:3–5 an expansion of Synoptic saying (Mark 10:15, par.), **19n18**
- "No one could be saved before rebirth." One is reborn by the seed of true Good provided by the will of God. "He who is begotten will be another person, God the child of God, the All in All, composed of all the Powers," (*Corp. herm.* 13.1–3), **123**
- Wead, *Literary Devices*, on double meanings in FG (*anōthen*), 19n18
- *See also* born, anew/from above/again

Nicodemus
- appeal to fellow elites for a hearing (John 7:51), 87
- compared to Cadmus in *Bacchae*, **136**
- example of an uncomprehending character that serves as a foil for Jesus (Skinner), 204
- but FG is comprehensible for its readers, 2n4
- illustrates Jesus' appeal (in FG) to a variety of *different* characters, 235n14

Nock, A. D. and A. J. Festugière, *Corpus Hermeticum*
creation theme, light and life, knowledge of God 122
father and son, rebirth, **123**
heavenly father, 124

Odeberg, Hugo, *Fourth Gospel* (1929)
Odes cited when relevant, 149n3
quote on Right Ginza cited in his commentary, **166**
rabbinic sources cited, 83n1

Odes of Solomon
6:18 living water of eternity (John 4:14), 153
7:3 for there is a helper for me (14:18), 151
7:10 He was gracious to me in His abundant grace (John 1:16), 150
8:20 abide in the love of the Lord (John 15:4, 9), 152
11:23 there is much room in paradise (14:2), 152
12:12 dwelling place of the Word (1:14), 151
15:2 his light diminishes the darkness (John 1:5), 150
16:18 creation by the Word (John 1:5), 150
23:22 Father, Son, Holy Spirit (John 14:26), 152
31:3 lifted his voice to God and prayed for (John 17:1–5), 153
41:11 His Word is with us all the way (John 14:6), 151
41:14–15 light dawned from the Word (John 1:4), 150
assessing the literary relationship with FG, dependency, similar environment, 153–55
Aune challenges Essene influence on Odes and FG and even indirect dependence, 78n27
Charlesworth, *Odes of Solomon*, 148n2
comparisons of Odes with FG (tbl. 9.A), **149–53**
differences with FG: language and genre, 149
discoveries and extant mss, 148
early 2nd cent. dating, non-gnostic, 149
interchangeable names in Odes and FG (Word, Wisdom) and Three Forms (Mother, Father, Son), 50n12
Lattke, *Odes of Solomon*, 16n1

opponents
Alogoi who reject FG and Rev opposed by Epiphanius, 230
Celsus argues that Bacchae shows how a real god in disguise deals with opponents, **129**
FG's faith mysticism vs. GTh's vision mysticism (DeConick), 198
FG has Jewish critics and 1 John has docetic secessionists as, 31
FG misinterpreted in a docetic manner by opponents of 1 John? (Brown), **30n53**
fiercest opponents of Jesus in FG are Judeans who reside in or near Jerusalem (7:1; 11:55–57), 102n35
Jewish opponents of Jesus (7:1) are contrasted with faithful Israelites (1:47, 49), 157

Origen of Alexandria, *Celsus*
background info., 129n17
Bacchae shows how a real god responds to opponents says Celsus (2.34–35), 129
reports on a split (priests vs. laity) among Samaritans (*Cels.* 1.57; 6.11), 158
Comm. Jo., seeks to expose Heracleon's reading of FG, 217
Comparison of FG and Heracleon (tbl. 12. E.), **218–20**
Heracleon, Valentinian and gnostic, 31n61
SP text in Heb. with Gk. in his *Hex.*, 159

Pagels, Elaine
- *Das Geheimnis des fünften Evangeliums*, FG and GTh rival each other but do not emerge from the same circles, 185
- "Exegesis of Genesis 1," different views of FG and GTh, 194n46
- "Gnosticism," definition of Gnosticism, **169**
- *Why Religion?* accused H. Koester, her prof., of inappropriate behavior with female students, 191n40

Paraclete
- the gift and pneumatic instruction of (chs.14–16), **21**
- Jesus as the Paraclete, 1 John 2:1 refers to, 32n64
- Johnston, *Spirit-Paraclete*; Windisch, *Spirit-Paraclete*, 21n30
- in John 14:16 Jesus refers to the Holy Spirit as "another Paraclete" (14:16, 26; 15:26; 16:7), **32**
- Mandaean *Yawar* (helper) is one of many heavenly revealers (Right Ginza 5.1; John 14:16–17, 26), 165
- Montanists disregard FG's claim that the Lord promised the Paraclete to his church (Irenaeus, *Haer.* 3.11.9; John 14:16), 227
- *See also* Holy Spirit.

paradoxical language of divine self-predication in Thunder, e.g., I am the bride and bridegroom, slave and ruler, discussed in Layton, "Riddle of Thunder," in Hedrick and Hodgson, *Nag Hammadi*, 106n10

parallel(s)
- 55 of 114 GTh sayings have some sort of p. in FG (Brown), 186
- Davila, "Perils of Parallelism," **5n16**, 8n33, 110n14, 233n5
- definition of (Davila), **4–5**, 233
- each will need to be examined separately, 33
- early reception or parallel tradition? 7
- formal analogy or coincidental similarity? (Isis), 111n16; Plato, **120**
- FG and GTh in similar p. position relative to Synoptics (Riley), 196
- of FG's Logos and divine name trans. device of Targums, 91
- FG's *own* parallel scenes, intratextuality, 9n34
- Gk. lexica replete with p. words from LXX, classical, Hellenistic, 237
- independent p. tradition, of OT in Rev and FG and rev, 43n33; rabbinica, 98;
- influenced by or influencer of, 7
- involve the comparative method, 5
- light metaphor, clearest parallel of FG and GTh (Popkes), 193
- Sandmel, "Parallelomania," 8n30, 68n3, 69n6, **77**, 78n28
- theol. assumption behind Plutarch's *Lives* (*Dem.* 3.2), 4n15

pathos, paired with gnosis as one of the points of tension in FG, explored in Anderson's "Naming Stars," e.g., humanity and divinity, present and future eschatology, 20n25

Patterson, Richard B., *See* Köstenberger, Andreas J.

Patterson, Stephen J.
- *GTh and Jesus*, FG and GTh from a common tradition, 184n22
- "GTh and Synoptic Tradition," 181n9, 184n22
- "Prologue," finds early strands in Jewish speculative theology and Sethian hymns (contra Yamauchi), **163n52**

Paul and his Letters
- allusions in NHL to Paul's letters, **221**
- Barnabas seen as Zeus and Paul as Hermes by Greeks (Acts 14:12), 145

Corinthians approved by testing through "dissensions," (1 Cor 11:19), 180n4
Epicurean and Stoic philosophers debate with him (Acts 17:18), 120, 125
"Flee idolatry!" (1 Cor 10:14), 110
Heilig, *Hidden Criticism?* counter-cultural imperial subtexts in, 79n29
from Jewish diaspora like Philo, 57, 119
"They sacrifice to demons, not to God (1 Cor 10: 20; cf. Gal 4:8), 110
wide circulation of his writings in congregations, 221
Winter, *Philo and Paul*, 67n20
writing ca. 55 CE, equated Jesus with God (1 Thess 3:11; 2 Cor 13:13), 154
See also Hays, Richard B.

Pentateuch
about 5 refs. to it in FG, **39**
FG follows general sequence of it, 39n12
Samaritan (SP), extant mss, redactions, 157–60
Samaritan Targum of the, 157n31. *See also* Law

perfect(ion)
and eternal, unchanging, spiritual realm (Plato), **111**
going to a world of perfect truth, beauty, goodness (Socrates), 113
"I am" discourse of the Perfect Protennoia (Three Forms 35), 176
"I shall go to the perfect aeon" (Ap. John 31:26–27), 174
the perfect human possesses the knowledge of God and is reborn (Hermetica), 121
the perfect man has brought bread from heaven (Gos. Phil. 11), 175
the perfection in thought of the Father, the revelation of his Word (Gos. Truth 37:1–7), 176

Pericope (Gk. "section, passage")
of Doubting Thomas, 185, 196–97

Perkins, Pheme
Gnosticism and the New Testament, awaken from sleep, 124
Corp. herm: return to light 123n34
cosmic conflict (Gen 6:4), 55n26, 177n27
quote, **178–79**
"Gnosticism," four groups in NHL, 169n6
Love Commands, love in FG and NT, 20n23
"Nag Hammadi Texts" on NHL contents, 168n1
survey, 170n9;
tbls. 10.D-E, **176–77**

Pesher. *See* Interpretation, DSS

Peter, Simon
Ep. Apos. 11–12 risen Christ appears to Peter, Thomas, Andrew, 210
function of e.g., Thomas, Peter in narrative context (Skinner), **204**
Ignatius, *Smyrna* 3.2; risen Christ appears to Peter and others, 210
John 18:10, 27 impulsive, betraying Peter (cf. Synoptics), 23
John 21 his commissioning, foretelling his death, 22
Luke 5; John 21, featured in both, **22n33**
2 Peter 2:22 allusion to Heraclitus text 120, 125

Pharisees
adhered to Law, Prophets, Writings, 159n41
example of an uncomprehending group that serves as a foil for Jesus but FG is comprehensible for its readers, **2n4**
John 7:51 appeal of Nicodemus to Pharisees and other elites, **87**
John 8:14 Pharisees do not know Jesus, irony, 116
John 11:47 and chief priests call a meeting regarding Jesus, 223

Pharisees *(continued)*
    laws in 4QMMT not those of Pharisees, 70n13
    Neusner, *Rabbinic Traditions about the Pharisees*, 83n4, **88n9**
    only Nicodemus among them recognizes Jesus (cf. Cadmus in *Bacchae*), **136**
    oppose Jesus, Pentheus opposes Dionysus, 138
Philip, Gospel of
    e.g., logia (2) from Layton, *Gnostic Scriptures*, cited, but also include page, line divisions (e.g., 52.1–13), 175n14
    logion 5 Christ came to deliver some and save others. He made strangers his own he laid down his life (cf. John 10:15; 13:1), 175
    nine parallels with FG (tbl. 10.C), **175**. *See also* Nag Hammadi
Philo of Alexandria,
    allegoricalization, 52, **56**, 60, 66, 71n16. *See also* Allegorical
    although Philo valued the literal keeping of Jewish festivals, both he and John saw their *ultimate* significance in the symbolic (Schenck), 65
    Attridge, "Philo and John," 64n9, 65n14, **67**
    background info., 52n24, 56; Borgen, *Philo of Alexandria*, 56n3
    "belief" in Philo (e.g., *Abr.* 268), **61**
    cites Plato's *Timaeus* and Hesiod, but argues that Moses wrote on the constancy of creation years before, 67
    Conf. 146 For he is called the Beginning and the Name of God and His Word (*logos*), 57
    Deus 32 "For God's life is not a time, but eternity, which is the archetype & pattern of time; & in eternity there is no past or future, but only present existence," 59
    differences between FG and Philo (worldview), 66
    FG's selection and use of LXX influenced by Philo? 44
    FG's use of eternal life has Platonic sense, life not measured by month and years, life neither past nor future, but lived in God's eternal To-day (Dodd), 65
    Fug. 97 "The highest word (*logos*) of God, who is the fountain of wisdom, in order that by drinking of that stream he may find everlasting life," 60
    and Greek philosophy, Stoic, Middle-Platonic, Neo-Pythagorean, 56;
    Her. 79, 191 "The one who extends his vision to look steadfastly for the manna, which is the word of God, the heavenly incorruptible food of the soul, which delights in the vision," 63
    and Jewish Scriptures (Gen 1–2; Exod 3:14), 57–63
    Gen 1:3 "let there be light" (*Somn.*1), 59
    Gen 1:26–27 creation of heavenly man in God's image, **62**
    Gen 2:7 creation of earthly man from dust of earth, 62
    Gen 2:9; 3:3 two trees in Eden, 66
    Gen 2:10–4 four branches of rivers from Eden, 66
    Exod 3:14 "I am the Lord who is," 61, 65
    Exodus seeks common ground for Jewish tradition, Hellenistic philosophy, 56
    Leg. 1:108 Plato recalls Moses, 66
    and *Logos*, e.g., with God, on creation, 57–58, **64n8**
    loving or fearing the Existent, 61
    philosophy is handmaiden of wisdom (*Congr.* 79), 66
    Parallels of FG and Philo, **57–63**

Philo (10 vols. LCL), 56n3; *Works of Philo* (trans.Yonge), 56n3
Piety: Philo, *Abr.* 268 knowledge of and possession of happiness, 61; *Deus* 69
Schenck, *Philo of Alexandria*, 57, 64–65
use of the divine name (from Exod 3:14 LXX) provides a helpful context for understanding some of the "I am" statements of Jesus in FG, **65**
Winston, *Logos and Mystical Theology in Philo*, 56n1
Winter, *Philo and Paul*, 67n20.
word and wisdom are personifications of God & distinct powers or (divine) agents of God (Schenck), 57
See also Hellenism; Jews; Plato, Platonism
philosophy
2 Peter 2:22 allusion to Heraclitus text 120, 125
Acts 17:18 Epicurean and Stoic philosophers debate with Paul, 120, 125
backgrounds for understanding FG, one of several plausible, 4, 104, 232
Cambridge Dictionary of Philosophy, conceptualism, 2n2
Clement Alex. *Protr.* 6.61; *Strom.* 1.15, Plato, Stoics, and Philo, 119
Engberg-Pedersen, *John and Philosophy*, FG comprehensible to its readers, 2n4
Epictetus, *Disc.* 2.8.1, God is mind, right reason, *logos*; cf. Clement, *Strom.* 5.14, Stoics and God, 64n8
GTh 50 "repose" in Platonic thought, 201–2
Hegel, *Philosophy of Right*, dialectic, 21n29
Jewish tradition, Hellenistic philosophy (Philo), 56
Logos and Heraclitus, Stoics, **64n8**
Philo, *Leg.* 1:108 recalls Moses, 66
Ricken, *Philosophy of the Ancients*, pairs of opposites in Heraclitus, **21n29**
Sedley, *Greek and Roman Philosophy*, Stoics, 64n8
wisdom, as the handmaiden of (*Congr.* 79), 66
piety
disciple of Poimandres preaching the beauty of, 124
Hellenistic Jewish, rich sp. climate of 1st cent. Palestine (Hengel), **4**
Iamblichus: admirable deeds of Pythagoras indicate his, 114n25
loving or fearing the Existent, 61
Odes and FG derive it and their theol. from same Jewish circle (Bultmann), 154
Philo
Abr. 268 knowledge of and possession of happiness, 61
Deus 69
Plato, *Euthyphr.* 11 Socrates on piety, 116
Plato, Platonism
Clement of Alex. on Plato, other philosophers 57n4, 67n21, 119
comparisons of Plato-FG, Jesus-Socrates (Brown), **112–13**, 119
contexts of FG and Plato, Platonism, 119–20
cosmology of Middle Platonism, 112
Demiurge, an intermediate divine craftsman (*Timaeus*), **111**, **115**, 119
dualism in Qumran, Philo, apocalyptic, Hermetica, Neoplatonism, FG, 10n42
Eusebius, *Hist. eccl.* 13.12.1 Plato, Pythagoras borrowed from Torah (Aristobulus), 67n19
FG and Platonism, 113n20
FG's Word *similar to* Demiurge but at some remove from Plato's *Timaeus*, **119–20**

Plato, Platonism *(continued)*
  Forms
    generated forms of Time that imitate Eternity (*Timaeus*), 116
    Good as the highest of the, 111
    knowledge of through reason, 111
    perfect spiritual world of, 111
  four groups in NHL: Thomasine, Sethian, Valentinian, Neo-Platonic, 169
  Gen 1:1; 8:22, creation and permanence (Plato, Philo), 67; Plato knew Moses (Justin, *1 Apol.* 59), 115
  god of love over human, divine affairs (Plato), 118
  Hermetica: Gen 1–2, Platonism, Stoicism, gnosis, Mind, Logos, **121**
  Hippolytus and Tertullian called Valentinus a Platonist, 169n5
  John 1:14 and "beliefs arise which are firm and true," (Plato, *Tim.* 37B), 115
  Last Supper and Plato's *Symposium*, 113, **118**
  Light
    Phaed. 109E–110A "The true light that Socrates hopes to see after death," **115**
    Rep. 508A which of divinities in heaven is author & cause of this, "whose light makes our vision see best and visible things to be seen?" 115
  Love
    FG in John 4, gestures towards a scene with erotic overtones "to tell a tale how *eros* can be converted to *agapē* and apostolic mission" (Attridge) **118**
    "Only such as are in love will consent to die for others" (179B; cf. John 15:13), 118
    Symp.: Eryximachus proposes the theme of love (*eros*, 177) there follows various eulogies on love (180B), 118
  memorable deaths of Socrates, Pythagoras, Jesus, **114**
  for Plato, Logos was associated with the rational, not myth, 112
  now is the appropriate time (Plato, *Tim.* 37E-38A; John 17:1–5), 116
  Plato's *daimones* become good and evil demons (Xenocrates), 111
  popular form of Platonism, 112, 119
  Seneca, a Stoic on Plato, 64n8
  Socrates: "those who had the most reputation to me are the most deficient" (Plato, *Euthyphr.* 11; cf. John 3:9), **116**
  soul imprisoned in the mortal body (Plato), 111
  thematic coherence of FG and Plato, Platonism, 120
  Tim. 37C reason and knowledge obtained by soul, 115
  true knowledge of Forms obtained by reason, 111
  two-levels of reality (material-spiritual), 111
Pleroma
  Gos. Truth 16:31–36: "the grace of knowing him through the power of the Word that came forth from the pleroma, 172
  Irenaeus *Haer.* 2.7.4 descriptions of the "pleroma," match up with NHL (e.g., Gos. Truth), 169n3, 172
  John 1:16 "from his fullness (*pleroma*) he dispenses grace upon grace," 172
  temple forecourt, where the Levites are, is a symbol of the psychics who attain salvation outside the Pleroma," (Heracleon, in Origen), 219
  The Word pervades the Pleroma as God's creative activity so that

those in the divine realm come to know the Father (Gos. Truth), **176**

Plutarch
Isis and Osiris (*Moralia* LCL V, 3–191), 105n10
Jewish Feast of Booths compared to a Bacchanalian festival (*Moralia* IV,671—672), 143n46
Platonic Essays (*Moralia* LCL XIII), source for Platonism, 111n18
on symposia, see his *Amat.* (Love Stories), *Quaest. Conv.* (Symposium Qs), *Moralia* LCL IX, **118n27**
theol. assumption behind Plutarch's (*Dem.* 3.2; *Lives* LCL VII), 4n15
two-level perspective (back then and now) assumed in his *Lives* (*Aem.* 1.1; LCL VI), 12n49

Pneuma
gift and pneumatic instruction of the Paraclete (chs.14–16), **21**
"'Spirit' (*Pneuma*) in Greco-Roman Philosophy and FG," (C. Koester), **64**
See also Holy Spirit; Parclete; Spirit

pneumatic(s) in Heracleon
the flesh and the material world, the pneumatics and psychic peoples, 221
on John 1:29; John speaks as prophet and more than prophet to the pneumatic, **219**
life for pneumatics (Origen, *Comm. Jo.*), 218

Poems of Scripture, St. Gregory of Nazianzus, 234n11

Poimandres
Corp. herm. 1: Poimandres, a Greco-Egyptian mystical revelation of creation of the world (relying on Gen 1–2) and the ascent of the soul to God through seven spheres, 121
disciple of Poimandres preaching the beauty of piety, 124
discourses of Poimandres to a disciple (Hermetica), 122
Nock and Festugiére, *Corpus Hermeticum*, vol. 1, Poimandrés, 121–24
Poimandres (Gk. "shepherd man," or Copt. "knowledge of the Sun-God [Ra]"), **121**
Reitzenstein, *Poimandres*, Gk. text, 121–24. *See also* Hermetica

Polycarp of Smyrna
echoes of FG found in the writings of Ignatius, Polycarp, Papias, not disparaged, **227**
John BD, author of FG, Rev, 1 John in testimonies of Polycarp, Papias according to Irenaeus (*Haer*.3.1.1), 231
received Ignatius of Antioch on a visit, 207
reconstruction of FG traditions from Ptolemy, Polycarp, Papias to Irenaeus in Mutschler, "Was weiß Irenäus vom Johannesevangelium?" 226n33

Popkes, Enno E.
"Gospel of John, Gospel of Thomas, and Qumran," 4 ways to view FG and GTh, 184–85, 196n51
"Ich bin das Licht," in FG, "no motifs of saving spark of light in disciples as they strive back to their place of origin," **194**
"Theological Heritage," light metaphor the "clearest parallel" between FG and GTh, 193n45

Porter, James I., "Stoic Interpretation," allegorical interpretations of Homer and Hesiod also practiced by Stoics and philosophical schools on Pergamum, years earlier, **56n2**

Porter, Stanley E.
"Context of Jesus," *Handbook*, "Judaism within Hellenism," 3n9, 236n16

Porter, Stanley E. *(continued)*
    "Religion, Personal" essay in Evans and Porter, *Dictionary of NT Backgrounds*, 105n7
    "Use of the OT in the NT," echoes, intertextuality, 9n35

power
    Bacchae 43–64 Dionysus appears as a man to reveal his power and punish Pentheus,134
    Cain to the Lord: "before you there is power to remit and pardon," (Tg. Neof. Gen.4:13), 97
    in DSS, "spirit of truth," a power within humans to do good (contra "spirit of deceit"), 80
    disciple leaving Poimandres is "filled with power" to make known the divine vision to earth-bound people (Corp. herm. 1.27–28), **124**
    "the first power after God the Father and Lord of all is the Word [*logos*], who is also the Son" (Justin *1 Apol.* 32.9), 211
    "the grace of knowing him through the power of the Word that came forth from the pleroma (Gos. Truth 16:33–35), 172
    healing power of the well in the Asclepius temple (Aelius Aristides), 105
    Isis: it is within my power to prolong your life beyond the limit set to it by Fate,"(*Metam.* 11.6), **108**
    Jesus to Pilate: "You would have no power over me unless it had been given you from above," (John 19:11), 107
    John 1:12 *dynamis* "to become children of God" (John 1:12), 48, 62, 85, 123, 172
    Middle Platonism's two aspects of divine: (1) transcendent, inner-directed (2) active power (Logos) responsible for ordering everything, appealing to Philo, **112**
    the one begotten by God will be another person, the child of God "composed of all the Powers" (Corp. herm.13.1–3), 123
    Philo's on *logos* as an agent of divine power, 64
    "the power of the Word, the luminous word of the Lord" (Clement Alex., *Strom.*VI, 3, 34), 218
    On protection from demonic power in DSS relevant to FG (e.g., John 17), Stuckenbruck,
    Myth of Rebellious Angels, 74n22
    the water which the Savior gives is from his spirit and power (Frag. 17 on John 4:12–15 in Origen, *Comm. Jo.* 13.10.), 219
    the will of the Father, his food, rest, and power. The will of the Father, (Frag. 31 on John 4:34 in Origen, *Comm. Jo.* 13.38), **220**
    Wisdom's power passes to Adam when Yaltabaoth blows on him (Ap. John 19.15–33), 176
    World of Light came into being through the power of the King of Life (Right Ginza 1; 3), 162

Prologue(s)
    and 1 John (tbl. 3.E), **32**
    of *Bacchus* and FG, Stibbe, 131
    Bultmann
        "History of the Religious Background of the Prologue," 46n5
    John, early gnosis in Prologue, 170n11
    and cosmic conflict (Gen 6:4), 54–55, 177, **178–79**
    of the Dionysus speech and John 1 in Clement Alex., *Protr.* quote, 130
    Dunn, *Christology in the Making*, 50n13
    Evans, *Word of Glory*, background of FG's Prologue. See Evans, Craig and "Gospel of Truth (16:32–36), 176, 178–79

INDEX

Hengel, "Prologue," of FG as gateway to truth, 37n10
"an introduction to Jesus as Sophia, the feminine face of God" (Scott), **50**
Logos in Christ revealed divine glory (Bultmann), 165
and LXX (John 1:1–5; Gen 1:1–5; wisd), **37, 40**
Melito of Sardis, **222**
and NHL, Perkins, *Gnosticism and NT*, (tbls. 10.D-E),175–76
O'Grady, "Prologue and John 17," 17n8
Origen on Heracleon, 218
and Patristics: Ep. Apos. 214; Hippolytus (John 1:9), 216–17
Patterson
  FG Prologue and "World Speculative Jewish Theology," early gnosis, 163n52
  survey of parallels, 175n20
philosophical questions for FG's readership (Frey), 67
Philo
  the beginning (*Conf.* 146), 57
  creation (*Opif.* 20–25), 58
Robinson, G.,
  early gnosis quote, **179**
  "Trimorphic Protennoia and the Prologue," 169n4, 176–78;
Van der Watt et al, *Prologue of the Gospel of John*, **64n8**
  Philo, 67n22
wisdom
  parallels in wisdom lit. (tbl. 3.A), **48–49**, 177n25
  uses Word (*logos*) instead of Wisdom (*sophia*), while retaining wisdom motifs, 49
"Word" in Odes independent development, in some respects prior to it (J. Sanders), 154.
See also Life; Light; Logos
prophet(s)
  cross-cultural type of parallel (e.g., king), 5, 233
  fulfills the roles of Moses (John 1:17, 45), **160**
Jesus the prophet (John 4:19; 7:40), 41–42, **157**
John 4:44–45 expl., 156n28
John the Baptist
  John 1:20, 23 text, 211
  and pneumatic (Heracleon), 219
  and priest (Mandaeans), 161
  "until the prophet comes," (1QS IX, 7; John 1:19–23), **75**
  and king in Mandaean sources (Meeks), 162n51
Manning, *Echoes of a Prophet*, 9n34; OT allusions, 44n40
Moses: Meeks, *Prophet-King*, recalls Moses, 41n23, 89n11; king and prophet, 151n32
Moses as supreme prophet among Samaritans, 156–57
  in rabbinica, 160n46
Moses the first prophet, Justin Martyr (1 *Apol.* 59), 115n26
Proverbs
  1:20–21; 8:1–4 seeking people, 49
  1:20–24, 28–30 rejected people, 48
  3:16–18; 8:35 source of life, 47; Sophia, 46n25
  3:19 and creation, 47; Gen. Rab.1.4, Torah, 85
  4:10; 8:32–35 lead people to life, 48
  4:10–19 two ways, 71
  4:22 (Midr. Ps 1,18), life, 86
  8:1–8, 22–31; 9:1–6 and FG's prologue, **40**
  8:6–9 revealer of truth, 48; personified, 57
  8:12 and m. 'Abot 6:10, creation, **85**
  8:17 disciple formation (cf. John 15:15), 49
  8:22 and b. Pesaḥ 54a, creation, **85**
  8:29–30 and creation, 47
  8:30 with God, 47
  8:31; 30:4 wisdom among people, 48
  8:32; 13:33 wisdom's children, 49
  9:2–5 food and drink (John 6), 49; cf. rabbinca, 87
  18:4 and living water, 40–41; cf. rabbinics, 154

Psalms
- 21:19 LXX parted my garments (John 19:24), 38
- 32:6 LXX "by the word of the Lord the heavens were made firm" (Gen 1:1–5; John1:1–5), 37
- 33:21 LXX no bones crushed (Exod 12: John 19:36), 38
- 34:19 LXX "hate me without cause" (John 15:25), 38
- 34:20 MT bone not broken (cf. John 9:36), 38, 77
- 41:9 MT "ate my bread . . . lifted heel against," in John 13:18 not LXX, 38
- 68:10 LXX "zeal for your house" (John 2:17), 37
- 68:22 LXX "vinegar to drink" (John 19:28–29), 38
- 77:24 LXX bread from heaven (John 6:31), 37
- 81:6 :XX "you are gods" (John 10:34), 38
- 88:45 LXX offspring of David (Mic 5:2; John 7:42), 37
- 105:19 "Word (Heb. *imrah*) of the Lord," 91n18
- 117:25–26 LXX Blessed is the one who comes" (John 12:13), 38
- 119:160 MT "the sum of your words is truth" (LXX in John 17:17), 43
- christological interpretation of Ps 22 LXX, 211
- life, OT roots (Gen 2:7; Ps 16:10–11; Isa 44:3), **40–41**
- light, OT roots (Ps 27:11; 119:105; Isa 49:6LXX, **40**
- Midr. Ps 1,18 alluding to Prov 4:22 on life, 86
- Philo *Agri.* 51 on Ps 23:1, "this hallowed flock [of the world] He [God] leads in accord with right and law," 63
- "Psalmbuch," FG, Odes, and common Jewish origins, 154n12

Pseudepigrapha
- Charlesworth, *OT Pseudepigrapha*
- 1 En, **45n2**
- Aristobulus, 67n19
- Odes, 149n6
- T. 12 Patr., **52n24**;
- influence on FG, 71, 103
- no FG quotations from, 39n14
- Stuckenbruck, "Apocrypha and Pseudepigrapha," on OT canon, 36n4

Purvis, James D.
- "FG and Samaritans," 156–58
- *Samaritan Pentateuch*, **156–58**

Puskas, Charles B.,
- and Crump, *Gospels and Acts*
  - FG signs, 19n19
  - FG and Synoptics, 24n38
  - FG sources, 27n46
  - tbl. on FG and Mark, **25n40**
- *Hebrews, General Letters, Rev*
  - 1 John, date, location, 31n59
  - 1 John, midrash 31n61
  - 1–3 John, author, 34n67
  - FG and 1 John, 31n63
  - Heb and Philo, **57n5**
- and Robbins, *Intro to the NT*
  - coherence criterion, 99n30, 110n15, 120n31
  - FG, ancient drama, **6n25**
  - FG and Matt, discourses, 19n16
  - Gnosticism, 169n6
  - historical Jesus, 171n13
  - mystery cults, **105n7**
  - Muratorian, 231n44
  - pathos of Roman era, 111n7
  - Platonism, 111n18
  - Rev, mythic view, 145n52.
- See also Robbins, C. Michael

Pyramid texts,
- of Egypt, date and contents, 105, 110
- Mercer, *Pyramid Texts*, 105n8

Q (Synoptic Sayings Source)
- editions and redactions, 144–45
- Kloppenborg et al., *Q-Thomas Reader*, Copt-Eng text of GTh, 180n1
- Robbins, *Testing of Jesus in Q*, 145n50, 200n64

INDEX

Robinson, "On Bridging the Gulf from Q to the GTh," 181n7
Qohelelth (Ecclesiastes)
  example of speculative wisdom that gave birth to apocalyptic (von Rad), 45n2
  Midr. Qoh. 9.18; John 11:50, one for the many, 89
  speculative wisdom on a continuum to Gnosticism (Schenke), 181n7
Qumran, Khirbet
  900 MSS found in 11 caves near Khirbet Qumran, 69
  Anderson, "John and Qumran," 68n3, 69n5, 71n15, 72n20, 78, 79
  author of FG visited there (Ashton), 68, 81
  Bauckham, "Qumran Community," dualism, 71n19
  Charlesworth, "Qumran, John, and the Odes," 154–55
  dissatisfaction with Jerusalem temple (NT, Qumran, Samaritans), 157
  dualism in Qumran, Philo, Hermetica, Neoplatonism, FG, 10n42
  and the Essenes, 81, 182
  FG and Qumran communities, 80
  and gnosis broadly defined, 10n43, 13
  Kloppenborg et al., *Q-Thomas Reader*, Copt-Eng text of GTh, 180n1
  Magnes, *Archaeology of Qumran*, community and scrolls, 70–72
  Mburu, *Qumran and Johannine Language*, 72–73
  parallel traditions, 182n12
  Platonism at (1QS X, 23, 32), 113
  Popke, "FG, GTh, and Qumran," 180n3
  pre- and non-sectarian texts in caves of the sect, 70n10
  Quispel, "Qumran, FG, and Jewish Christianity," Encratites, 184n22
  and relationship with DSS, 70
  Ringgren, "Qumran and Gnosticism," context, 8n30, 98n27
  Schiffman, *Qumran and Jerusalem*, 69n7, 70n13, 71, **82**
  solar calendar of Qumran, 70–71
  Stegmann, *Library of Qumran*, 68n3
  Teeple, "Qumran and FG," 78–79
  See also Essenes, Dead Sea Scrolls

rabbinica
  'Abot 6:7 Torah gives life to those who do it, 86
  argumentation in FG, **87–90**
  Danby, *Mishnah*, 84n8
  Deut. Rab. 7:3 as oil is life and light so also in Torah, 86
  Epstein, *Babylonian Talmud*, 84n8
  evaluations of FG and Rabbinica, **98–100**
  Exodus 16:28–36 provision of manna on sabbath, 86
  and FG on the Feasts, 84, 98, 102
  Freedman and Simon, *Midrash Rabbah* and FG (tbl. 6.A), **85–87**
  Gen. Rab. 1:4 "God created world for the sake of Torah," 85
  Gen. Rab. 3:1–2 thy words give life (Ps 119:130), 86
  Gen. R. Ber. 5:5 "God created the world by Torah," 85
  Gen, Rab. 8:2 (Gen 1:26) Torah preceded creation, **85**
  Gen. Rab. 43:6 Torah, bread, wine (Melchizedek), 87
  Gen. Rab. 78:1 sender is greater than sent (John 13:16), 87
  Gen. Rab. 91:9; 94:9 better one die than many (John 11:50), 89
  Middot of Hillel, 88
  Midr. Ps 1,18 alluding to Prov 4:22 on life, 86
  and Moses (Meeks), 160n46
  Neusner
    Midrash Reader, 83n3
    Rabbinic Judaism, 83n1

rabbinica *(continued)*
  Neusner
    Rabbinic Literature and NT,
      promise, perils, 12n52;
      historical-critical study,
      83n4
    Rabbinic Traditions & the
      Pharisees, 83n4
    relation to rabbinica, 88n9;
    trans. of *Genesis Rabbah,* 84n8;
      89
    trans. of *Mishnah* and
      Babylonian and Jerusalem
      Collections, 84n8
    trans. *Tosefta,* 84n8;
    Sipre Deut. 11:22 as water is life so
      also is Torah, 86)
    Sipre Deut 31:4 Blessed be God who
      gave Torah to Israel, 87
    and Targumim, 83
    See also Law; Moses; Targumim;
      Torah
reader(s)
  aesthetics of reception with
    interaction of author, text,
    reader (Eco), 231
  authors, avid readers of NHL,
    169–70
  availability to FG and readers
    criterion, **79**, 99, 110, 120, 125
  Culpepper, *Anatomy of FG,* implied
    author and reader, 50n16
  Eco: three levels of intention (work,
    reader, author), **12n51**
  FG is comprehensible for its readers
    (Engberg-Pedersen), 2n4
  FG's Jewish and gentile readers, 120,
    125, **235**; FG
  FG's readers confronted with
    what is beyond time, beyond
    visible occurrence, with the
    Word of God & life of eternity
    (Hoskyns), 12
  focus on the world of the text before
    us, 236
  reader-response criticism, 12n51

  symbols with multiple meanings
    for a spectrum of readers (C.
    Koester), **14n55**
  work, reader, author combine it
    with synchronic, 12n51. *See also*
    author, narrative
reception
  Alogoi who reject FG and Rev
    opposed by Epiphanius, 229–30
  aesthetics of reception with
    interaction of author, text,
    reader (Eco), **231**
  corrective function of reception
    history, 10n40
  early FG reception, 7, **10**, **12**, 103,
    206, 231
  early reception of FG, not limited to
    gnostics, 206, 221, **226–27**
  Egerton Papyrus 2 and reception of
    FG, 207, **224–25**
  Evans, *Reception History,* 3n8,
    10n37, 206n3
  FG reception in NHL, **221**
  Frey on early reception of FG, 10
  Hill, *Johannine Corpus in EC*
    FG's rescue from gnostics,
      215n16
    orthodox rejection of FG, **230**
    reception history, 3n8, **10**,
      206n3
  Jauss *Aesthetic of Reception,* history
    of effects on subsequent readers,
    10
  Nagel, *Die Rezeption des*
    Johannesevangeliums
    Ep. Apos., 213
    FG influences on: on Heracleon,
      217n19; on Hippolytus,
      216n17; Odes, Hermetica,
      NHL, 207n6
    reception history, 10n41
Reinhartz, Adele
  cosmological tales in FG, **5–7**, 44
  criticism of *Birkat ha minim* and FG
    as sectarian, 14n56
  FG as Jew-ish, but not Jewish,
    102n35

use of synchronic and diachronic
    analyses, 44n39, 50n16
word and wisdom, 50–51
religion(s),
    analogy of two different religions,
        7n28, 103n2
    of Christianity as "truly, sacred
        mystery" (Clement Alex.), **109**
    comparative study of, 5n17
    Ephesus where Dionysian religion
        was pervasive, 142
    Greco-Roman (mystery) religions
        (Isis, Dionysus), 104–5
    Jonas, *Gnostic Religion*, 121n33,
        169n2
    mystic, survey of (DeConick), 198
    Near Eastern religion with Stoic and
        Platonic elements (Hermetica),
        121
    process of Hellenization in the
        history of religion, 11, 233
    religio-historical method/history
        of religions approach, 3n8, 4,
        206, 232
    Seelig, *Religionsgeschichte Methode*,
        3n8, 5n17, **34**, 236n17
    Socrates and innovations of religion,
        117
Religionsgeschichtliche Schule
    analogy of two different religions,
        7n28, 103n2
    Colpe, *Die religionsgeschichtliche
        Schule*, critical assessment, 3n8,
        123n8, 151
    comparative study of, 5n17
    religio-historical method or history
        of religions approach, 3n8, 4,
        206, 232
    Seelig, *Religionsgeschichte Methode*,
        3n8, 5n17, **34**, 236n17
resurrection
    Koester, C., and R. Bieringer,
        Resurrection of Jesus, 30n55
    Son glorifies the Father in death,
        resurrection and return to
        Father, **19**
    Thomas as foil for FG advocates on
        bodily resurrection, 196n49

Revelation, Book of
    and Alogoi, 225, **228–30**
    authorship of, 228–30
    Dionysius of Alexandria and Rev,
        229
    falsely ascribed to Cerinthus,
        228–29
    FG and Rev, 43n33
    Gaius who rejected FG and Rev
        (Haenchen), 225
    "I am" sayings in Rev closer to
        2 Isa than FG, parallels are
        independent (Koester), **41n33**
    use of MT text type, 37n10
    and multi-cultured myths (Rev 12),
        145n52
    rejected as gnostic-Montanist,
        225–26
    Rev 1:8, 17 I am the Alpha &
        Omega, first, last (21:16; 22:13),
        43n33
    See also apocalyptic
Reveal(er)
    angels reveal future/divine wisdom,
        50, 54, 228
    Christ reveals God, 165, 208
    Corp. herm.: salvation attained
        through revealed knowledge (cf.
        John 17:3), 121
    descent of Messenger to reveal
        himself to people (Mandaeans),
        162
    the divine Logos, manifest in Christ,
        revealed glory of the Lord
        (Bultmann), 165
    in FG, the divine Word of rev. sent
        to bring light, life to the world,
        119–20, **179**
    both FG and Three forms
        established a meaningful
        framework where their
        affirmations about a divine
        revealer are set, 178
    Gos. Truth 37:1–18 perfect
        knowledge of the Father comes
        through rev., 176
    Jesus Revealer of God's wisdom and
        knowledge from above, **234**

Reveal(er) *(continued)*
- Mandaean gnostic revealer discourses, recall Odes, & Hermetica, 166–67
- Mandaean *Yawar* (helper) is one of many heavenly revealers (Right Ginza 5.1; John 14:16–17, 26), 165
- Poimandres (Gk. "shepherd man," Copt. "knowledge of the Sun-God [Ra]"), Greco-Egyptian mystical rev. of the creation, 121
- the rev. of God to Moses in Exod 34, in the Pal. Tgs. Exod 33:23 is described beforehand as a rev. of the *Dibbera* that includes God's self-description as "full of grace and truth," 100, 160
- Tg. Neof. Exod 20:24 "I will be revealed in my Word," 94
- Tg. Neof. Exod 33:23 God's revelation to Moses, 100
- the Word of God reveals God's glory, 30
- Word (*Mēmra*) of Lord revealed as the "I am who is" (Tg. Ps.-J. Deut 32:39), 92

Riley, Gregory J.
- FG and GTh in similar parallel position relative to Synoptics, 196
- *Resurrection Reconsidered*, focus on controversy between 2 closely related communities of GTh & FG, on the issue of resurrection, expressed in FG most clearly in Doubting Thomas story, **196–97**

Robbins, C. Michael, *Testing of Jesus in Q*, editions and redactions, 144–45, 200n64. *See also* Puskas, Charles B.

Robinson, Gesine,
- quote on early gnostic myth, **179**
- "Trimorphic Protennoia and the Prologue," 169n4, 176–78

Robinson, James M.
- "On Bridging the Gulf from Q to the GTh," 181n7
- "Discovery of the Nag Hammadi Codices" **181–82**
- *Nag Hammadi Codices*; "Introduction," 182–83
- *Nag Hammadi Library*, 171–72, 182n13
- preface in Meyer, *Nag Hammadi Scriptures*, **168n1**

Roman
- Catholic, Bible, deuterocanonical, 35–36
- Protestant suspicion of emerging Roman Catholicism (J. Z. Smith), 8n29, 104n4, 109
- Church, of Hippolytus, 215
- Gaius, a bishop of Roman Church (Haenchen) 225
- classics (e.g., Virgil), 104, 170
- destruction
  - of Alexandria, **56**
  - of Jerusalem, **70**
  - of Qumran, 181
- dominance and suppression of Judea and Samaria (Josephus), 158
- era (200 BCE—200CE), 3n9
  - before, 103
  - Hellenism of, 103, 119, 124
  - period, Roman, 104, 159
  - world, Roman, 4, 16, 105, 109–10, 232, 235–36
- Roman Judea, Heb. used there, 80
- Tibullus (ca. 25 BCE), poet, 105
- Roman religions, 104–5, 109–10
- Stoic, Seneca, **64n8, 112n19**

Ronning, John
- *Jewish Targums & John's Logos Theology*
  - comparisons with FG (tbl. 6. B), **92–97**
  - early data in later material, 109n11, 159n40
  - intro, 83n2
  - John 17 parallels, 90n14
  - *Mēmra*, 91n18
  - response to objections, **100–101**
  - Shekinah, 92n21
- "Targum of Isaiah and Johannine Literature"

early data in later material,
  99n28
  Shekinah, 92n21
rule
  church (Ignatius), 226
  community (1QS), 68n1, 75
  of truth/faith, **226n33**
  of War (4 Q285), 69n5

Sabbath
  crucifixion, eve of Passover and
    before (b.Sanh. 43a), 20
  FG and Philo on (John 5:17; *Leg.*
    1.5–6), **65**
  FG and Qumran, differences, 70;
    legal interpretation of, 77
  FG and Rabbinica on, 84
  John 5:18 breaking sabbath, 117
  John 5:26–27 argument, 89–90
  John 7:23 and qal vahomer, 88
  Targums and worship on, 101. *See
    also* Exodus; Law
salvation, soteriology
  angel imparts salvation and foresight
    to Job (T. Job 2—5), 54
  Christ: "I am your salvation"
    (Melito; cf. John 10:11), 223
  cosmological tale (Reinhartz)
    makes room for implied reader
    in the history of salvation,
    50
  Son sent by God into the world
    to bring salvation, 44n39
  debate in FG and GTh communities,
    believing vs "seeing," 197n54
  FG and Isis, similar language of
    salvation, 110
  FG new soteriology: gain eternal life
    by eating flesh of and drinking
    blood of the Son of Man (John
    6:54–55; cf. *Bacchae*), 137
  GTh 22, central statement of
    soteriology is assimilation to
    God, 203
  "I am" style to depict the
    cosmological and soteriological
    role of Jesus/Wisdom/Isis/
    Thunder/Perfect Mind, **106n10**

Isis: "soon through my providence
    shall the sun of your salvation
    arise," (*Metam.* 11.5; John 14:2),
    107
  "Knowledge of God is the way of
    salvation" (Corp. Herm.10.15.8–
    9; John 17:3), **122**; differences
    with FG, 124
  knowledge of the father, salvation
    for persecuted (GTh 69; John
    14:7), 194
  light metaphor parallel in GTh and
    FG have different soteriologies,
    194
  no salvation theology in wisdom
    literature, 51n19
  Platonist salvation story of soul
    seeking to regain its lost place
    of repose (cf. GTh 50; Litwa),
    201–2
  psychics attain a salvation "outside"
    the Pleroma (Heracleon on John
    2:13–16 in Origen, *Comm. Jo.*),
    219
  "the salvation which is coming from
    on high" (Gos. Truth 35:1; John
    3:3), **173**
  salvation-historical speculations on
    Gen in FG's prologue, 179
Samaritans
  Anderson and Giles, *Tradition Kept:
    Literature of Samaritans*, 156n22
  beliefs and practices of, **158–59**
  David not in Samaritan tradition,
    157
  early traditions in late docs., **159**
  faith in YHWH and in Moses his
    servant, 159
  faithful servant Moses, 157n31
  hymns of Marqe the theologian, 159
  Josephus, *Antiquities*
    9.277–91 Samaritan origins, 157
    13.254–56 Mt. Gerizim
      sanctuary built under
      Persians, 158
    13.255–56 Hyrcanus destroys
      the sanctuary, 158

Samaritans *(continued)*
  Josephus, *Antiquities*
    11.346–47 Jewish disdain for
      Samaritans (cf. John 4:9),
      158
    18.85–89 Pilate kills many
      Samaritans at Mt. Gerizim,
      158n35
  Justin, 1 *Apol.* 26 Meander, disciple
    of Simon Magus, deceived many,
    157n29
  Knoppers, *Judah and Samaria*,
    mythic history, 157n33
  from northern kingdom, 157
  Purvis, "FG and Samaritans,"
    156–58
  Simon practiced magic in Samaria
    (Acts 8:9), 158
Samaritan Pentateuch (SP)
  allusions to Deut 18:15, "the
    Prophet," in Exod 20 SP, 157
  Anderson and Giles, *Samaritan
    Pentateuch*, 156n22
  extant mss, and redactions, **157–60**
  Purvis, *Samaritan Pentateuch*,
    156–58
  Samaritan Heb., Gk (Origen, *Hex.*),
    Arabic trans., 159
  Tal, "Samaritan Targum of the
    Pentateuch," on Moses in *Memar
    Marqah* (4th cent.), 157n31
  Tsedaka and Sullivan, *Israelite
    Samaritan Version of Torah*,
    156n22
Sanders, E. P.
  ed., *Jewish, Christian Self-Definition
    2*, Kimelman *Birkat ha-minim*
    essay, 76, 84n5.
  Jewish Law, 83n1. *See also* Law,
    Jewish
Sanders, J. N., *FG in the Early Church*,
  on *Alogoi*, 225n31
Sanders, Jack T.
  NT Christological Hymns, 154n13
  "Nag Hammadi, Odes, and NT,"
    149n6, **154**
Sanders, James A.

  Canon Debate (with L. McDonald),
    221n27
  Early Christian Interpretation (with
    C. Evans), 40n18
Sandmel, Samuel
  "Parallelomania," *JBL* (1962),
    compare *context*s not just
    excerpts, **8n30**; 68n3
  significance of parallels? 69n6; quote
    77, 78n28. *See also* Parallels
Schenck, Kenneth, *Philo of Alexandria*
  feasts, **65**
  God's children, 62
  God and Logos, 64
  three-story world of Middle
    Platonism, 66
  word and wisdom, **57**
Schenke, Hans-Martin
  "On the Compositional History
    of the Gospel of Thomas,"
    background, 174n17
  "Die Gnosis," *Umwelt des
    Christentums*
    def. of Gnosticism, 169n3
    Mandaean origins in Palestine,
      161n48
  "Gnostic Sethianism," *Rediscovery
    of Gnosticism*, Seth as heavenly
    revealer, 169n4
  "Das sethianische System nach Nag-
    Hammadi-Handschriften," early
    Sethians, **171n12**
  "Die Tenenz der Weisheit zur
    Gnosis" pessimistic wisdom
    (Qoh) on a continuum toward
    Gnosticism, 45n2, **181n6**
Schiffman, Lawrence
  Qumran and Jerusalem
    4QMMT as Sadducean, 70n13
    Damascus Doc. (CD), 69n7
    no messiahs in 1QM, 71n17
    no NT mss at Qumran, 68n2
    no pierced messiah (4Q285),
      69n5
    pesher and Teacher, 71n16
    quote on DSS and NT, **82**

INDEX

and J. VanderKam, eds.,
   Encyclopedia of the DSS, essay
   Kuhn, "Jesus," 69n6
Schlatter, Adolf
   Der Evangelist Johannes, Lam. Rab.
      1, 5 "piercing" (Zech 12:10; John
      19:37), **39n15**
   rabbinic insights, 83n1
   Die Sprache und Heimat des vierten
      Evangelisten, 11n45
Schnackenburg, Rudolf, *Gospel*
   according to St. John
   communities of FG and GTh,
      196–97
   FG authorship, 231n44
   FG's signs, 97
   Mandaeans and FG, 167
   NHL and FG: tbl. 10. A. Gos. Truth,
      Ap. John, **172–74**; tbl. 10. B.
      GosTh, 174; tbl. 10.C. Gos. Phil,
      175
   Odes follows FG, 153
Schnelle, Udo
   Antidocetic Christology
      Gnosis and Docetism, *not*
         identical in NHL, 175n19
      historical criticism (Moloney),
         6n26
      Mark and FG, 25n40
   Das Evangelium nach Johannes,
      one-sided expl. of FG's context,
      insufficient, 4, **104**, 232
   The Human Condition, FG's
      anthropology, 119; FG's dualism,
      124
   Die Johannesbrief, order of
      composition: 2 Jn, 3 Jn, 1 Jn, FG,
      31n62, 34
   Kontexte des Johannesevangeliums,
      relevant essays (with J. Frey),
      3–4, 14, 42, 64, 71, 78, 104, 109,
      112, 206–7, 232, 234. *See also*
      Frey, Jörg
Schuchard, Bruce G.
   Abiding Words: Use of Scripture
      (with A. Myers)
      FG knew Heb. but cited LXX,
         35n2

survey of scholarship, 40n20; FG
   knew Aram., Heb (Menken),
   79n32
Scripture within Scripture: OT
   Citations
   13 OT refs. in FG, 36n8
   OT themes/images, 40n18. *See*
      also Myers, Alicia J.
scripture(s), Jewish (OT). *See also*
   Septuagint.
   1 John has less OT refs. than FG and
      his ideal audience, 30
   Bynum, *FG and Scriptures*
      Zech 12:10; John 19:37 citation,
         39n15
      FG knew Aram. and Heb., 79
   Cerinthus, enemy of God's Scripture
      (Eusebius), 228
   Dodd, *According to Scriptures*,
      testimonia hypothesis, 39n16
   Gaster, *Dead Sea Scriptures*, 68n1
   Gk. philosophy inspired by Jewish
      Scriptures (Philo *Leg.*. 1:108), 66
   John 5:39 "you search the Scriptures
      . . ." (cf. Egerton Papyrus 2), 224
   Layton, *Gnostic Scriptures*, 50n12,
      120, 168–69, 173
   Mandaeans were confronted by FG
      which belonged to the Scriptures
      of the Church they opposed
      (Odeberg), **166**
   Meyer, *Nag Hammadi Scriptures*,
      168n1, 172n15
   three parallels of FG and DSS not
      found in OT (Teeple), 78
   Zumstein: FG text presumes other
      texts (LXX), 44n21
sect(s), sectarian
   Cerinthus created the Cerinthian
      sect (Eusebius), 229
   challenged by Bauckham and Klink
      for FG, **14n56**
   FG not reclusive and insular as
      Qumran sect, 71
   FG not sectarian, part of world-
      oriented community (Brodie),
      16n3

sect(s), sectarian *(continued)*
   Fuglseth: FG is cultic, not sectarian, 71n15
   Isser, *Dositheans: A Samaritan Sect*, 158n37
   Mandaeans, gnostic baptizing sect flourished, 3rd to 8th cents., 161
   Massa: Christian sect triumphed over Dionysian, 128n15
   mss of DSS are sectarian (only 200 of 900), 69
   Qumran sect and the Essenes, 70
   report of Hippolytus on Naasene sect, 216
   Tatian organized an ascetic sect (perhaps Encratites), 210
   Tov: sectarian redaction of SP text, 159–60
   view of FG with its "in group" language, 2n5
   was FG author, member of a hetero-orthodox sect separate from the mainstream?, 235
Seelig, Gerald, *Religionsgeschichte Methode*
   Do our comparisons contribute to a *better* interpretation of FG?, 236
   intention behind the comparison determines its outcome, 34
   review and assessment of comparative methodology, 3n8, 5n17
Seneca, Lucius Annaeus,
   Lang, M., "Johanneische Abschiedsreden und Senecas Konsolationsliteratur," comparisons of FG's Farewell Discourse with Seneca's consolation writings, 112n19
   rabbinic argument resembles rhetoric of his Disputes, 88
   reflected on spirit and reason (Helv. 8:3) and Platonism (Ep. 58:65; 102:22), 64n8
Septuagint (LXX)
   date (3rd cent. BCE), other Gk. versions (Theodotion), 35n1
   FG fluent in LXX but knowing some Heb. and Aram., 98
   Gottingen Septuagint, Wevers and Fraenkel, eds., 36n9, 45n1
   Hengel, *Septuagint as Christian Scripture*, 36n9
   includes books outside Jewish canon (1–4 Macc, Sir, Wis), 35
   NETS, Pietersma and Benjamin, eds., 36n9
   OT chs. and vv. of NRSV based on MT, *not* LXX, 36
   Rahlfs, *Septuaginta*, rev. ed. R. Hanhart, 36n9, 45n1
Seth, Sethian
   gnostics, 169n4, 170n7
   Hedrick, *Apocalypse of Adam*, Sethian gnostics, 171n12
   Jewish, pre-Christian strands of Gnosticism: Turner, "Sethian Gnosticism," 171n12
   NHL adds much to our knowledge of early Jewish and Christian, Neoplatonic, Hermetic, Sethian, and Valentinian thought, 168
   One of the four groups in NHL: Thomasine, Sethian, Valentinian, Neo-Platonic, 169
   Patterson, "Prologue," finds early strands in Jewish speculative theology and Sethian hymns (contra Yamauchi), 163n52
   Schenke, H.-M., "Gnostic Sethianism," *Rediscovery of Gnosticism*, Seth as heavenly revealer, 169n4
   "Das sethianische System nach Nag-Hammadi-Handschriften," early Sethians, 171n12
Shekinah (Eng. "dwelling")
   Heb. *shakan* Hiphil: God's "pitching a tent" (MT Ps 78:60) or "tabernacling" (Exod 25:8; 40:34; cf. John 1:14), 41n25
   Ronning "Targum of Isaiah & Johannine Literature" like *Memra*, *Shekinah* acquires a resemblance of personality

by its being a circumlocution for God in contexts where personal states or actions are attributed to him, 100
Shekinah, 92n21
- Tg. Ezek 43:7b-8 "I will make my Shekinah dwell there, in the midst of the children of Israel forever," 95
- Tg. Neof. Onq. Num 14:14 glory (*Yegara*) of whose *Shekinah* is in the midst of this people," 94
- Tg. Onq. Exod. 33:20-23, "You will not be able to see the face of my Shekinah; for no man may see me and live," 95
- Tg. Ps-J. Deut 5:24 the Lord's *Memer* has shown us the Shekinah, 94
- Tg. Ps.-J. Exod. 29:42b-45, "my Shekinah shall dwell in the midst of the sons of Israel, and I shall be their God," 94
- *Yegara* (Aram. "glory") often linked with it in Targums, **92**, 95

Shepherd of Hermas
- Herm. *Mand.* 7.1
- Herm. *Simil.* 8.7.6 keep the commandments, 210
- older, tripartite numbering for, 210

sign(s)
- the ancients had miracles done for them because they hallowed God's Name (b. Bera. 20a). If similar thinking prevailed in Jesus' time, the signs that he performed might have raised concerns that Jesus was a pious man of God, 88
- in FG, symbolically-loaded enactments, that reveal God's glory in the mission of Jesus and vindicate him as God's son and emissary (2:11; 4:54), **19**
- intertextuality: dialogical relationship between texts as a system of codes or signs (Kristeva), 9
- Israel's feasts "encode numerous latent signs and symbols of Jesus (Hays), 43
- of Jesus recall those that Moses did in Egypt (e.g., John 4:48; 6:30; Exod 4:8-9, 28-31), 41
- John 1:19—12:50 build around the theme of signs (2:11; 4:54; 12:37), 21
- Mandaeans: *Ptahil* created the material world (*Tibil*) with the aid of the evil Spirit (*Ruha*), the Seven (planets), and the Twelve (signs of the Zodiac), 162
- Melito: "Nor did you regard the strangest of signs a corpse four days dead called alive from a tomb (cf. John 11:17), 223
- rabbinic argument: the signs that God does (Job 38:16; Ps 77:19) are also granted to Jesus (John 6:19) because they are equals in divine power, **90**
- sign source (Fortna), 27n46
- Tg. Neof. Exod 8:20-22, "Thus says the Word of the Lord, I will do signs and wonders so that you may *know that I am he*, the Lord, whose Word dwells within the land," (cf. John 20:30-31), **97**
- Tg. Neof. Num 14:11 "How long will they not believe in the name of my Word in spite of all the *signs of my miracles* which I have performed among them?" (cf. John 12:37), 97

sin, sinners
- 1 Chr 21:1; Wis 2:24 LXX: devil incites men to sin, 52
- 1 En 99:3 angels bring judgment on sinners, 54
- 1 John 1:8; cf. Johnn 9:41, have no sin (tbl. 1.E), 32
- GTh 93, "He who has knowledge of the truth is free, but he who is free does not sin"(cf. John 8:32, 34), 175

sin, sinners *(continued)*
- GTh 104 what is the sin I have done? (cf. John 8:4610:32; tbl 11.B), **189**
- Isis: "I have delivered the one who plots evil against others into the hands of those he plots against. I established penalties for those who practice injustice (*adikos*). I decreed mercy to the suppliants," 106
- John 1:29 God's Lamb who removes the sin of the world, 17
- Origen on Heracleon: *as prophet*, JBap says, "This is the Lamb of God," which pertains to the [physical] body of Christ, which is psychic; as *more than a prophet* JBap says, "that takes away the sins of the world" and that refers to the pneumatic realm, but there is no talk of forgiveness of sins among the pneumatics, (on John 1:29; tbl 12.E), **219**
- Tg.Isa. 53:5 "he will rebuild the sanctuary which was profaned by our sins" (John 2:16), 95

Sirach
- 24:8 Wisdom's descent from heaven to dwell with people (cf. Wis 9:10), 48
- 4:11, 17 Wisdom instructs and forms them (cf. Wis 9:11), **44**
- 41:17–18 Wisdom tests her disciples, & forms them, 49
- originally written in Heb (ca. 175 BCE) and trans. into Greek, after 132 BCE, **45n3**
- outside post-70 Jewish canon (e.g., 1–4 Macc, Wis), 35

Skinner, Christopher W.
- *John and Thomas—Gospels in Conflict?*
  - Doubting Thomas pericope (contra Riley) is one of several other similar literary characterizations within FG, 185
  - examines the community-conflict hypothesis of Riley, DeConick, Pagels, 197n54
  - creation and manipulation of characters, 204
  - in FG, uncomprehending characters, like Thomas, serve as foils for Jesus' words, deeds, **204–5**
- *Reading John*
  - 2-level drama, for all Christians? FG's community, 12n50
  - 2-level drama, 3-stage gospel development, 27n46
  - Jews, Judeans, Jewish leaders, critics, 31n58

Smith, D. Moody,
- *Composition and Order of FG*, Bultmann source theory, 27n46
- *John among the Gospels*
  - FG and Synoptics, 17
  - similar, parallel traditions, 28n50
- "John," in Barclay and Sweet title, Jewish context for FG, 7n29,103n3
- *Theology of the Gospel of John*
  - FG in general agreement with Synoptics, **23**
  - FG themes, 6n24

Smith, Dennis E., *From Symposium to Eucharist*, Greco-Roman, philosophical, Jewish, 118n27

Smith, Eric C., *Jewish Glass and Christian Stone*, boundaries were porous and easily crossed among nonelite groups, 76n23

Smith, Huston, "Methodology, Comparisons, and Truth," defense of comparative study of religion, 5n17, 233n5

Smith, Jonathan Z.
- *Drudgery Divine*
  - analogical, genealogical comparisons, 5n16, 7n27, 8n30

INDEX

Herodotus, Egyptians, Persians, 105n9
Jewish origins of the NT
  embraced as insulating devices, **8n29**, 109
  nature & limits of comparative studies, 98n26
"In Comparison, A Magic Dwells," faulty methodological assumptions, 5n17
Smith, Morton, *Tannaitic Parallels*, verbal, idiomatic, literary, 83n1, 99n20
Smith, Robert H., "Exodus Typology in the Fourth Gospel," Moses imagery, 41n23
Smith, Tyler, Review of *Dionysian Gospel*, 143n44
Socrates
  accused of having a *daimonion* (by Meletus), **117**,
  appeal of Socrates to higher authority, 117
  Brown quote on Jesus-Socrates, 113n23
  deaths of Socrates, Pythagoras, Jesus, **114**;
  going to a world of perfect truth, beauty, goodness, 113
  Jesus-Socrates, 66n17, 113–14, 117–19
  Phaed. 109E–110A "The true light that Socrates hopes to see after death," 115
  on piety, 116
  and religious innovations of, 117
  Socrates: "those who had the most reputation to me are the most deficient" (Plato, *Euthyphr.* 11; cf. John 3:9), **116**
Son of God
  1 John 2:28; 3:2 future judgment and final revelation of the Son of God, 30
  Acts of Thomas 39 Thomas "receiver of the secret mysteries of the Son of God" 199n62
  John 1:19–51 the Son of God with many names (cf. *Bacchus*, tbl. 8.C.), **135**
  John 1:34 "And I myself have seen and have testified that this is the Son of God," 152, 222
  John 6:53b–66 "Eating the Flesh of the Son of God" (cf. Bacchus 64–67), 137
  John 20:31 these are written so that may come to believe that Jesus is the Messiah, the Son of God, and that through believing you may have life in his name." 97
  MacRae: appeal of universal, transcendent divine Son to a wide audience, **14**, 109, 170n10, 234
  Messiah, Son of God, not son of David (FG, Samaritans), 157
  on multiple names, e.g., Word, Son, Savior, tbl. 7.A.2. Isis, 108; 8.C., Dionysus, 135; and 10. E., 178.
  Ode 23:22 Father, Son, and Holy Spirit (cf. John 14:26), 152
  Ode 36:3 "I was named the Light, the Son of God," 150
  Son of God with many names, e.g. King of, 135
  Son of God, Son of Man (tbl. 9.A., FG, Odes), **153**
  See also Christ; Jesus.
Sophia. *See* Wisdom.
Sophocles
  compared with Euripides, 128
  format of Greek play used by Aeschylus, Euripides, or Soph., 132
spirit
  born of water and Spirit, **18n11**, 208, 216
  descent of Spirit on Jesus as seen by John (John 1:32–33), 95
  descent of Spirit and vision of God connected with *Dibbera*, 92, **95**
  divine power-presence conveyed by angels, the Word, glory,

spirit *(continued)*
  Father, Son, and Holy Spirit (Odes 23:22; John 14:26), 152
  God as spirit, 64n8
  "perfect spiritual world of Forms (Plato), 111
  spirit-flesh dualism 73, 80n32, 154n15
  spirit of prophecy (Justin, *1 Apol.* 33.2; cf. John 16:13), 212
  "spirit of truth," in FG and DSS, 71n19, 78
  Spirit of the Lord, not false (Odes 3:10; John 14:17), **152**
  those who have the same nature as the Father are spirit," (Heracleon on John 4:24 in Origen, *Comm. Jo.* 13.25), 220
  wisdom, power, spirit, the name (LXX), 54
  See also Holy Spirit; Paraclete
spirit of late antiquity
  Hengel, *Johannine Question*
    gnosis broadly defined., **10n42**
    Hellenistic Jewish, rich, spiritual climate of 1st c. Palestine, 4
  Jonas, *Gnosis und spataniker Geist*
    Greco-Roman, universalizing Jewish, mystical ("gnostic-like") context, **10**
    Philo's gnosis, 56n1
  "spirit of late antiquity," **155**, 233
  MacRae, *Studies in NT and Gnosticism*, appeal of universal, transcendent divine son to a wide audience, **14**, 109, 170n10, 234
spiritual gospel, FG as (Clement Alex. in Eusebius, *Eccl. hist.* 6.14.7), **17**, 221, **235n12**
Stoics, Stoicism
  Acts 17:8 Epicureans and Stoics, v. 28, Aratus quote, **120**, **125**, 170
  allegorical interpretations of Homer, Hesiod, and Stoics, 56
  Clement Aex. on Plato, Stoics, and Philo, 119

  Jewish wisdom with Stoic, Platonic ideas, 120, 125
  John 4:24 and Stoics on God, 64n8
  Middle Platonic and Stoic speculations in the Hermetica, 125
Strack, Herman L.
  and Billerbeck, *Kommentar zum NT aus Talmud und Midrasch*, 83n1
  on John 11:50 one for many, 89n13
  "Sometimes it's God Himself, sometimes it's His Memra who intervenes in the earthly events," **91n18**
  and Stemberger, *Talmud and Midrash*, 83n3
  history of rabbinic hermeneutics, 88n10
Stuckenbruck, Loren T.
  Angel Veneration, angelic and heavenly figures, 52n24
  "Apocrypha and Pseudepigrapha," in Collins and Harlow, *Early Judaism*, 83n1
  Myth of Rebellious Angels
    protection from evil one in FG, 52n23, **54**
    demonic conflict (Jub, DSS, 1En), 55n26, 74n22, 177n27, 178n32
  "Semitic Influence on Greek," in Keith & Donne, *Jesus, Criteria*, FG, 1 John, and Rev, closer to Heb., **37n10**
structure
  Corp. herm 1.6–7, God, whose Logos gave structure to the universe, 122
  in FG and 1 John: complication, crisis, denouement, **31n60**
  of FG, 1 John, and Ep. Apos. (Nagel), **213**
  of FG and Gk. tragedy (prologue, epilogue), **132n32**
  FG and Mark's sequence/structure, 24

Samaritan social structure & polity strengthened by Bab Raba ("Great Gate"), 158
study house (*beth midrash*), from where rabbinic writings mostly derived, 83
style
- of Euripides criticized by Aristotle, and Aristophanes, 128
- FG parallels to Synoptics dominated by Johannine literary style & themes, 24;
- "I Am" style in FG, Isis, and NHL, **106**
- *SBL Handbook of Style*, Eng/Heb/Gk versification, 36n5

symbol, symbolism
- FG and Philo saw significance of Jewish feasts in the symbolic (Schenck), 65
- FG's symbols have a range of meanings accessible to a "spectrum of readers" (C. Koester), **14n55**
- Galilee and Samaria fulfill symbolic functions (Meeks), 156
- Jesus and Sophia employ symbols of food and drink, **49**
- Heracleon: temple forecourt, where the Levites are, is a symbol of the psychics who attain salvation outside the Pleroma," (on John 2:13–16 in Origen), 219
- Israel's feasts "encode numerous latent signs and symbols of Jesus (Hays), 43
- less-defined symbols of Hermetica, a paradigm of interpretation (Eco), 121n33
- Philo: 4 branches of rivers from Eden (Gen 2:10–14), symbolize 4 cardinal Virtues, 66
- proximity of menorah and Christ symbols, inter-relations of Jews and Christians (E. Smith), 76n23
- signs: symbolically-loaded enactments, reveal God's glory in the mission of Jesus and vindicate him as God's son and emissary (2:11; 4:54), **19**
- symbolic interpretation using temple imagery in both FG, Philo (*Cher.*; Exod 25:19), **65n15**

symposium, symposia
- both *Symposium* and FG involve dialogues focused on love, 113
- Diotima's speech in *Symposium* and FG's Last Supper, 113
- Greco-Roman, philosophical, Jewish (Smith, *From Symposium to Eucharist*), 118n27
- Last Supper and Plato's *Symposium*, 113, **118**
- on symposia, see Plutarch's *Amat.* (Love Stories), *Quaest. Conv.* (Symposium Qs), *Moralia* LCL IX, **118n27**.
- *See also* Last Supper

synagogue(s)
- Aramaic targums from the liturgy of the synagogue, 83, 91
- *Birkat ha-minim*, with John 9:22; 12:42; 16:2 (Martyn), **84**
- and church, 5, 51n17
- expelled from Jewish synagogues, 50n14, 76
- gradual, not sudden, separation from synagogue (Frey), 76n23
- of Judea (Luke 4:44), 19n22

Syria, Syria-Palestine
- Ep. Apos. 170–80 CE from the province of Asia or Syria (J. Hills), 213
- FG's location in Syria-Palestine, and eventually, Ephesus (90–100 CE), 11, 31n59, 57, 119
- GTh in Syria, early decades of Christianity (Riley), 197
- Ignatius of Antioch, Syria, known wrote letters to churches of Asia in (ca. 110 CE), 207
- Justin Martyr was born in Samaria (Palestine), 210

Syria, Syria-Palestine *(continued)*
   Odes also seems to originate from Syria-Palestine (Charlesworth), **149**
   Mandaeans may have originated from Syria-Palestine (2nd—3rd cents. CE) based on east Aramaic dialect of their writings, 161
   Tatian of Syria, student of Justin Martyr, compiled *Diatessaron*, 210

Talbert, Charles H., *Reading John*
   interchangeability of names in Odes (41:9,11–5) is in line with other early Christian usage (John 1:1; Phil 2:6–9), **50n12**
   "multiple life situations, past and present, likely have their echoes in the text," 11n49
   Qumran, rabbinic Judaism, mystical Judaism, Hellenistic Judaism, Greco-Roman philosophy, Hermetica, Gnosticism, etc—all needed to comprehend FG tradition through time and geographically, 4, 104, 232

Talmud
   Epstein, *Babylonian Talmud*, 84n8
   Haggadah, stories and maxims of Midrash and Talmud, 84
   Neusner, *Mishnah* and *Babylonian and Jerusalem Collections*, 84n8
   Palestinian Talmud, third to fifth centuries CE) and Babylon (Babylonian Talmud, seventh century CE, **35n1**
   Strack and Billerbeck, *Kommentar zum NT aus Talmud und Midrasch*, 83n1.
   See also Babylon, Talmud of

Tanḥuma
   "But when you stood at Mount Sinai and accepted my Torah, you were called MY PEOPLE," (Midr. Tanḥum Exod. II Wa-ʾera 2.1), 85
   "There is no beginning but Torah (Prov 8:22). In the beginning (i.e., in Torah) God created" (Gen 1:1–2; Midr. Tanḥ. Ber. 1:5), 85. *See also* Genesis, Exodus, Rabbinica

Targumim
   Aramaic Targums, 83, **91**, 92–98
   belief, believe in Targums, 93, 97
   Boyarin, FG and Targumim, 91n18, 92n23
   covenant with Abraham, 96
   descent of Spirit and vision of God connected with *Dibbera*, 92, 95
   Flesher and Chilton, *The Targums*
   Frg. Tg. Gen. 1:3 "there was light in his Word," 93
   Frg, Tg. Gen. 40:23 Blessed is he who trusts in the Word, **93**
   Frg. Tgs. Exod 15:26 "my Word who heals you," 101
   from the liturgy of the synagogue, 83, 91
   Gen. Rab. 1:4 "God created world for the sake of Torah," 85
   Gen. Rab. 3:1–2 thy words give life (Ps 119:130), 86
   McNamara, *Aramaic Bible*, 91n15; *Targum and Testament*, 91n18, 92n19
   Neof. Gen. 1:3 the Word of the Lord was light, 93
   parallels of FG's Logos & divine name trans. device of Targums, 91
   Ronning, *Jewish Targums & John's Logos Theology*, comparisons with FG (tbl. 6. B), **92–97**
   response to objections, **100–101**
   Tal, "Samaritan Targum of the Pentateuch," on Moses in *Memar Marqah* (4th cent.), 157n31
   "Targum of Isaiah and Johannine Literature," Shekinah, 92n21
   Tg. Ezek 43:7b–8 "I will make my Shekinah dwell there, in the midst of the children of Israel forever," 95.

Tg. Neof. Exod 8:20–22 I will do signs and wonders, **97**
Tg. Neof. Exod 12:42 Word was light and shone, 93
Tg. Neof. Exod 14:31; Tg Ps-J. Exod 14:31 they believed the Word, 93
Tg. Neof. Exod 16:12 "you will be filled with bread," 96
Tg. Neof. Exod 20:24 "I will be revealed in my Word," 94
Tg. Neof. Exod 29:42–45 Shekinah in their midst
Tg. Neof. Exod 33:23 God's revelation to Moses, 100
Tg. Neof. Gen. 1:1 with wisdom the Word created, **92**
Tg. Neof. Gen. 3:24 Torah is the tree of life, 93
Tg. Neof. Gen 28:15 "my Word will not leave you," 94
Tg. Onq. Exod 33:20–23 seeing God, 95
Tg. Onq. Deut 33:27 *Memra* is used for creation 100
Tg. Ps-J. Deut 5:24 the Lord's *Memer* has shown us the Shekinah, 94
Tg. Ps-J. Deut 32:39 the Lord's *Memra* is the I am who is, 92
Tg. Ps-J. Exod 15:18 Israel saw signs and wonders, 97
Tg. Ps-J. Exod 34:5–6 the Lord's Shekinah , 94
Tg. Ps.-J. Gen 1:3 "light to lighten the world," 93
Tg. Ps.-J. Gen. 26:3, 24, 28 my Word will be at your assistance, 94
Tg. Ps.-J. Num 21 he would live "if his heart was directed towards the name of the Word of the Lord" (cf. John 3:14–15)
See also *Mēmra, Mēmer, Dibbera, Yegara*; Law; Torah; Rabbinica
Tatian of Syria
  his *Diatessaron*, difficult to determine any textual relationship with GTh (Cameron), 183
  later founded an ascetic sect (perhaps Encratites), 210
  student of Justin Martyr who compiled *Diatessaron*, 210
teaching
  FG's life and teachings of Jesus
  contact with DSS teaching, not improbable, esp. if there's connection to Essenes (Fuglseth), 79
  focus on faith and experience with little ethical teaching (Kysar), 17n9
  God's agent of creation, sharing divine glory, alight shining in the dark, teaching & revealing wisdom to people who would receive it (Reinhartz), 50
  Jesus employs symbols of food and drink in his teaching, 49
  "My teaching is not mine, but his who sent me," (John 7:16; cf. Plato, *Apol*. 20), **117**
  narrates life and teaching of Jesus, 1 John, expounds Johannine teaching, 29
  omits teaching & stories crucial to all 3 Synoptics, 22
  OT plus *other* influences, 44, 237, (DM), **143**
  uses the Thomas character as foil to embody the error of the GTh community & the words of Jesus as the correct teaching of FG's own community, 198
Haggadah, midrash of biblical stories & ethical teaching from homilies, maxims, 84
Mandaean teachings: four life changes, Ptahil created world with the help of evil spirit, humans are created as dual beings, 162
parallels include the influence of ideas, whether a body of work, teaching, or shared context (Davila), 5, 233

teaching *(continued)*
  Philo
    "love God and keep his commandments," (1John 5:2) reflects OT teaching also found in, 61
    teaching on *logos* as agent of divine power having its own existence, is a development beyond what we find in, e.g., Prov, Sir, and Wis, and may bring us closer to FG's understanding of *logos*, **64**
  Socrates, Pythagoras, and Jesus did not die for good, their teachings survive with their students (Serapion), 114
  of Valentinus are reflected in some of NHL (e.g.Gos.Truth), 169, 221
    Irenaeus might be opposing here (Haer. 3.11.9) the Valentinian teaching of the same Gos. Truth that is found in NHL, 227
temple(s)
  cleansing by Jesus
    final week (Luke 19:45–46, par.), 20
    start of ministry (John 2:13–22), 20
  entry prohibited in DSS (CD VI), **74**
  expelled from temple? 182
  forecourt, where the Levites are, is a symbol of the psychics who attain salvation outside the Pleroma," (Heracleon on John 2:13–16 in Origen), 219
  of Isis
    at Colossae, Philippi, Corinth, Rome, 110
  fate of Isis temple in Rome, 105
  Mark 11:17 den of robbers (at temple), **74**
  NT and Samaritan criticisms of the temple (cf. Acts 7:47–50), 157
  some Essenes retained connection to temple (Jos. *Ant.* 18.19), 74

Tertullian of Carthage
  Both Justin Martyr and Tertullian (*Praescr.* 40; *Bapt.*5) argued that the mystery cults (e.g., Mithra, Isis), were demonic imitations of Christianity, 110
  Both Tertullian and Hippolytus called Valentinus a Platonist (Tertullian, *Praescr.* 7; 30), 169
  Melito's theology probably influenced Irenaeus and Tertullian (Cross), 222
Testament of the Twelve Patriarchs, T.12 Patr., dates. locations: e.g., T. Abraham, T. Levi, T. Job, Egypt, 1st cent. CE (Charlesworth), **52n24**
T. Job 2—5 angel imparts salvation and foresight, 54
Testimonia of Scripture, Albl, "*Scripture Cannot Be Broken*" (*Testimonia*); Dodd, *According to Scriptures,* **39**
tests of evaluation. *See* criteria of evaluation.
Thatcher, Tom
  FG narrative, essays in Thatcher and Moore, *Anatomies of Narrative Criticism,* 6n25
  FG's 3-stage development, Stibbe, "Magnificent but Flawed," **12n49**
  Qs on FG sect, relevance of *Birkat ha-minim,* Reinhartz, "Skyscrapers on Toothpicks,"14n56
  Zumstein, "Intratextuality and Intertextuality," 9n34, 12n45
  Jesus in Johannine Tradition (with Fortna)
    Anderson, "John and Mark," 28n50; early gnosis, Patterson, "Prologue," 163n15
    diachronic and synchronic Qs, 7n26;
    survey of parallels, 175n20

INDEX   361

on Christology, "Remembering
Jesus." in Porter, *Messiah in OT
and NT*, 21n28
What We Heard from Beginning,
essay O'Grady, "Prologue & John
17," prologue,17n8
theism
ditheism (Father, Logos), Hippolytus
is accused of, 216n17
henotheism or pantheism of
mystery cults, 110, Hermetica,
121
monotheism (Christian) of Irenaeus
in opposition to Gnosticism, 226
themes, topics
common cycle of tradition Mark
and FG (tbl. 1.B), 25
mystical, GTh and FG (tbl.11.D),
199
OT themes, images, and phrases in
FG (e.g., signs, glory, shepherd,
hour) 4
parallels involve similar or
analogous vocabulary phrases,
sentences (linguistic, verbal),
parallel themes, concepts,
images, forms, structural
patterns, or social & cultural
contexts (Davila), 4–5
See List of Tables, **xi–xiii**, for
comparisons of similar themes
and language
theology
anti-docetic, incarnational theology
of Ignatius, 206–7
diversity of Jewish and Greco-
Roman backgrounds as as a
corollary of reading FG as
narrative theology (Talbert), 4,
104
of FG: Köstenberger, *Theology of
John's Gospel*; Bauckham &
Mosser, *Gospel of John and
Christian Theology*; Smith,
Theology of the Gospel of John,
6n24
FG and GTh

each expresses its own
distinctive and at times
opposing theology (Riley),
196
FG elaborates with discourse
context, GTh with variant
readings (H. Koester), 192
"FG, GTh, and Qumran,"
(Charlesworth), 180n3
GTh inspired by FG
(Dunderberg), 184n21
GTh location within NHL,
FG within NT (Johnson),
182n14
interpret distinct from
Synoptics, 181n11
reflect a dialogue or debate
between their communities,
195–200
rival traditions from same
circles (Charlesworth et al.),
185n23
similar light motif, 194n46
MacRae: process of Johannine
theology according to FG's
intention corresponds to a
process of Hellenization, 11
role of Moses in Samaritan theology,
analogous to that of Jesus in
FG, 157
Ronning, *Jewish Targums and John's
Logos Theology*, 90n14, 100
trinitarian theology of Hippolytus as
Logos doctrine, 216n17
Winston, "*Logos & Mystical
Theology in Philo*, 56
1 Thessalonians 3:14; 5:9–10 Paul
writing (ca. 55 CE) *equated* Jesus
with God, 154
Thomas, Gospel of,
55 out of the total 114 Sayings in
GTh have some such sort of
parallel in FG (Brown), 186
BD and disciple Thomas, 196n51
Brown: tbl. 11.B. FG and GTh
comparisosns, **187–91**
christology in GThom, 181n10,
185n23, 203

Thomas, Gospel of, *(continued)*
  collection for FG and GTh comparison, 186, 195
  community hypothesis, Pagels, *Das Geheimnis des funften Evangeliums*, 185
  conflict of FG and GTh communities, 184n20, 185n30, 204n67
  contexts of FG and GThom communities (Riley), 197–98
  Davies, *GThom and Christian Wisdom*, 181n6
  DeConick, *Vision of the Mystics*
    Thomas character as foil to embody the error of the GTh community, and the words of Jesus as the correct teaching of FG's own community, 198
    vison mysticism (GTh) vs. faith mysticism (FG), **198–200**
  evaluations of comparisons of FG and GTh, 182n14, 192
  four views of GTh and FG, e.g., from common circles, rivals, 184
  GTh 93, "He who has knowledge of the truth is free, but he who is free does not sin" (cf. John 8:32, 34), 175
  GTh 104 what is the sin I have done? (cf. John 8:4610:32; tbl 11.B), **189**
  Litwa, *Becoming Divine*, deification in FG's Christology and GTh's epiction of the Ideal Christian, 200
  location in Syria, early decades of Christianity (Riley), 197
  logion 1 "whoever finds the interpretation of these sayings will not experience death," **193**
  logion 4 Hippolytus, *Haer.* 5.7.20 quotes a variant of it (Cameron), 183
  logion 13, Thomas, the only one who answers the questions correctly, **199**
  logion 22, central saying of soteriology: assimilation to God (Litwa), 203
  logion 28 "I appeared to them in the flesh" (cf. John 1:14), 174
  logion 44; whoever blasphemes Father/the Son (cf. honor John 5:23), 188
  logion 50 "where did *you* come from?" Disciples: "the light," (cf. only Jesus, John 8:14), 201; cf. John 3:20 *disciples* know light (logion 50), 174
  logion 61, "I am your disciple" [Jesus said to her], 203
  logion 83 "The father existed in the son, and the son existed in the father" (cf. John 14:10), 175
  Kloppenborg's *Q-Thomas Reader*, 180n1; Robinson, "On Bridging the Gulf from Q to the GTh," 181n7
  Popkes
    "Gospel of John, Gospel of Thomas, and Qumran," 184–85, 196n51
    light metaphor, best parallels of FG and GTh, with differences, 193
  "repose" in Platonic thought (Litwa), 201–2
  parallels of FG and GTh arranged thematically, e.g., life-giving power, light, (H. Koester) **193–95**
  tbls. of FG and GTh comparisons, 10.B., **174**, and 11. B.—E., **187**–203
Thompson, Marianne Meye
  God of the Gospel of John, on knowledge of God in FG, 28n49
  Humanity of Jesus
    full humanity, 23n36
    Jesus bravely submits to death, **114n24**
  John: A Commentary
    hoi 'Ioudaioi, 31n58

"I am" sayings, 43n33
intratextuality in FG (parallel scenes in FG, framing devices), 9n34
Jesus surpasses Dionysus, 127n11
John 21, epilogue, 22n33
life, eternal, 41n22
Philo's use of divine name helpful context for FG's "I am" sayings, **65**
seven signs, 19n19
and Synoptics, 25n40
"Learning the Identity of Jesus," Word of God, Messiah, Savior in FG, 21n28
"'They Bear Witness of Me,'" Pss in FG's passion narrative, 44n40
thought world. *See* Conceptual, or thought worlds
Three Forms (Trimorphic Protennoia), 35:1–32 "I am" discourse of the Perfect Protennoia, **176**
47:13–16 on its third descent Three Forms appears as the Word in human form, 177
47:29 I am the Light that illumines the All," 188
50:14–15 dwelling place of the Father (cf. John 14:2), **177**
both FG and Three forms established a meaningful framework where their affirmations about a divine revealer are set, 178
interchangeability of names in Three Forms as Father, Mother, Son, Word, Wisdom parallels with FG's Word, Messiah, Savior (see also Odes), 50n12
knew FG (Hengel), 179n37
portrays Demiurge in a mythologizing of Gen, 178
1 Timothy 3:16 "revealed in the flesh," divine & preexistent Christology, 21n28

Tobit, Book of
12:17 "peace be with you" (cf. Luke 24:36; John 20:21), 27n45
3:8, 17; 6:8,16–18; 8:3 demon (*daimonion*, cf. John 10:20–21), 52
3:16–17; 5:21–22; 8:3; 11–12 Tobias, Tobit's son, who is protected from the demon Asmodeus (cf. John 17:15; 18:8–9), **54**
written ca. 200 BCE complete in Gk. with Heb. & Aram. fragments at Qumran, 50n24
Torah
anyone who disobeys the Torah of M. shall be expelled (1QS VIII, 22–23), 76
Deut. Rab. 7:3; Sipre Deut.11:22, Torah is life for world, 86; Deut Rab. 7.3 words of Torah light for the world;" b. Ketub. 111a, b "Whoever makes use of the light of Torah will revive (after death)," **86**
FG's break with Torah-focused, 7n29, 103, 109
Gen. Rab. 1:4 Torah and throne of glory, 85
m. 'Abot 6:7 Torah gives life to those who do it, 86
through Moses, God gave Torah to (Sipre Deut.), 87
Tg. Neof. Gen. 3:24 Torah is the tree of life, 93
What rabbis applied to Torah, FG applied to Jesus the Word, 87. *See also* Law; Rabbinica
Tov, Emanuel
Greek and Hebrew Bible, Greek equivalents of the Hebrew Bible, 35n2, **80n32**
"The Septuagint." in *Mikra*, date, trans., Hebraisms, 35n2
Textual Criticism of the Hebrew Bible, centrality of the MT (ca. 10th cent. CE) in the development of the Hebrew Bible, 35n3

Tov, Emanuel *(continued)*
"Textual Criticism: OT," LXX text, 35n1; SP sectarian redaction, **159–60**

tradition, traditions
all Jewish and Hellentistic contexts needed to comprehend FG traditions through time and geographically (Talbert), 4, 104, 232;
Anderson and Giles, *Tradition Kept: Lit. of Samaritans*, 156n22
common cycle of tradition Mark and FG (tbl. 1.B), **25**
FG and GTh, rival traditions from same circles (Charlesworth et al.), 185n23
Neusner, *Rabbinic Traditions & the Pharisees*, 83n4, 88n9
Samaritans: early traditions in late docs., **159**. *See also* Parallels

transcendent
appeal of universal, transcendent divine son to a wide audience (MacRae, *Studies in NT & Gnosticism*), 14, 109, 170n10, 234
conceptual worlds of FG, may disclose broad readership that FG sought to address with its universal & transcendent Christologies, 14
"Logos" is used to present Jesus as "the immanent Son who makes the transcendent Father visible (Scott), **50**
Middle Platonism: (1) Uncreated, transcendent God, (2) *Logos*, and (created) Dyad (3) world of senses, 66
Philo's Middle Platonism, *Praem.* 46 to discern the Uncreated (transcendent God) from the Creator, the monad (Logos, the Creator) from the dyad (the thing made), 66n16
summary of the universal and transcendent son, 234
two aspects of the divine: (1) essentially transcendent and inner-directed. (2) active power (Logos/Monad) responsible for the for the ordering of everything else (Tobin), 112
Wisdom served also as a figure of mediation between transcendent God and the world God created, 51

truth
1QpHab VII, 1,11–12 who will not abandon the service of the truth, 73
Clement of Alexandria: "the luminous word of the Lord, the truth from heaven" (*Strom.*VI, 3, 34), **218**
Gos. Phil. 93 he who has knowledge of truth is free (John 8:32), **175**
GTh 93, "He who has knowledge of truth is free, he who is free does not sin" (cf. John 8:32, 34), 175
Hengel, "Prologue," of FG as gateway to truth, 37n10
Jesus is truth and characterized by truth, 73
John 1:14 "full of grace (*charis*) and truth," **58**, 94, 100, 115, 134, 150, 172, 214
John 1:17 "grace and truth came through Jesus Christ," 160
Lincoln, *Truth on Trial*, FG allusions to Isa 40–55, lawsuit motif, 39n13
Moses defender of truth in the heavenly court of true Israelites, 157
Odes: "The Messiah in truth is one (41:15) "the Word from the truth who is self-originate,"(32:2), **149**
Prov 8:6–9 revealer of truth, 48
Ps 119:160 MT "the sum of your words is truth" (LXX in John 17:17), 43
rule of truth/faith (Irenaeus, *Haer* 1.22.1), 226

Socrates going to a world of perfect truth, beauty, goodness, **113**
Smith, H., "Methodology, Comparisons, and Truth," defense of comparative study of religion, 5n17, 233n5
spirit of truth
    as power within humans (DSS), 80
    "of truth," in FG and DSS, 71n19, 78
Tg. Ps.-J. Exod. 34:6 the Lord, full of kindness (*hesed*) and truth," 94
"the truth will make you free" John 8:32, 61
Gos. Phil. 93, 104; "truth, free," **175**
Turner, John D.
    explores the rich shepherd imagery in the ancient Near Eastern and Greco-Roman worlds, in Beutler and Fortna, *Shepherd Discourse*, 42n31, 63
    "Sethian Gnosticism," in Hedrick and Hodgson, *Nag Hammadi, Gnosticism*, Jewish & pre-Christian strands of Gnosticism, **171n12**
    one of four groups in NHL, 169n4
typology: R. H. Smith. "Exodus Typology in the Fourth Gospel," Moses imagery, 41n23

universal
    appeal of universal, transcendent divine son to a wide audience, **14, 109, 170n10, 234**;
    Kysar, *John the Maverick Gospel* (1976), "John, the Universal Gospel," 14n55
    Logos as universal, structured principle (Heraclitus), **64n8**
    MacRae: how a local, near eastern cult (Isis) was transformed into a universal symbol of worship, as a result of Hellenization, 11n43
    similarities of FG with other contemporary traditions may indicate a common intellectual milieu: a complex Greco-Roman, universalizing Jewish, mystic (gnostic-like) context, **10, 233**
    summary of the universal and transcendent son, 234
unity
    1 John 1:3; 2:24; 2 John 9; John 5:20; 10:30, 38; 14:10 unity of Father and Son, **32**
    Corp. herm. 1:8 Logos of the Lord and the Mind is the Father, God are not to be distinguished from each other. Their union is life," (John 10:30), **122**
    experience encompasses human beings and their world and combines them into a unity" (Ricken), 21n29
    Ignatius, *Phld.* 9.1–2 Abraham, Isaac, Jacob, the prophets, apostles and the Church enter the door (John 10:9). All of these *are brought* into the unity of God," **209**
    "the oneness of the GTh Christians makes them appear more like FG's Christ who was eternally with the Father" (Litwa), 201
    opposition of Irenaeus to Gnosticism also led to an emphasis on the unity of Father and Son in the work of Revelation and Redemption, 226

Valentinus, Valentinian
    commentary on FG by Valentinian gnostic Heracleon may parallel 1 John, both seek to update and apply the FG to their own situation (Brown), 31n61

Valentinus, Valentinian *(continued)*
  Haer. 1.5.3 critical comments concerning the Demiurge, the lesser creator god (as employed by the Valentinians), 218n21
  Heracleon a Hellenistic teacher with gnostic leanings, was a disciple of Valentinus of Rome, 217, 221
  Irenaeus *Haer.* 1.11.1, called Valentinus a "gnostic" and his descriptions of the pleroma matches with what we find in NHL (Gos. Truth 16:35),169n2
  denouncements of Irenaeus concerning the Valentinians and "Gospel of Truth" (*Haer.* 3.11.8) may refer to the same title in NHL, 176n22, **226–27**
  NHL adds much to our knowledge of early Jewish and Christian, Neoplatonic, Hermetic, Sethian, and Valentinian thought, 168; In Testim. Truth, gnostic leader, Valentinus (56:2–5) is identified, 168n3
  one of four groups represented in NHL (e.g., Gos. Truth), 169
  Tertullian (*Praescr.* 7; 30) and Hippolytus (*Haer.* 6.16, 24, 32) called Valentinus a Platonist, 169n5

Van Kooten, George H.
  Jesus/Socrates facing death bravely, 119
  "The Last Days of Socrates and Christ," 66n17, 114n25
  new conception of deity, 117
  theme of love in various symposia, e.g. marital in Cana, insatiable love at Samaritan well, **118n28**
  "The 'True Light' (John 1:9) and Plato's Allegory of the Cave," the true light that Socrates longed to see after death, 155

Vanderkam, James C.
  The Dead Sea Scrolls Today, John and perhaps Jesus had some acquaintance with Qumran community, 68n3
  on the discoveries, 69n7
  DSS categories: biblical, apocryphal/ pseudepigraphical, others (mostly sectarian), **70n10**
  Encyclopedia of the Dead Sea Scrolls (with Schiffman, eds.), "Jesus" essay by Kuhn, 69n6
  Essenes and DSS sect, 70n11
  "Essenes," *NIDB*, 70n11

vocabulary
  along with similar vocabulary (LXX), FG shares analogous conceptual viewpoints and reflects similar contexts with Wisdom (Brown), 46
  anointing of Jesus for burial, with similar vocabulary (Mark 14:3–9; John 12:3–8), 25
  FG tells its own story, having distinct literary style and thematic concerns (with a vocabulary of about 540 words), 17
  FG's intertextual relationships, e.g., interpretations of Word" (John 1) and favorite vocabulary: e.g., light and darkness, life, Spirit, glory, descent and ascent, 3
  Parallels involve similar or analogous vocabulary, phrases, and sentences (linguistic and verbal), as well as parallel themes, concepts (Davila), **4–5**, 233
  "Theological Vocabulary of the FG and Gos. Truth," in Barrett, *Essays on John*, in context, 8n30, 98n26

wisdom (Sophia, Hokmah)
  along with similar vocabulary, FG shares analogous conceptual viewpoints and reflects similar contexts with Wisdom (Brown, *John*), 46

angels reveal future/divine wisdom, 50, 54, 228
Boyari, *Borderlines*, use of common Jewish texts (Gen 1; Wisdom) and midrashic tradition behind FG's Logos and the targumic *Mēmra*, **102n35**
Bultmann, "History of the Religious Background of the Prologue," wisdom, 46n5
Collins, *Jewish Wisdom in the Hellenistic Age*, 46n3, 51n20
Davies, S., *GThom and Christian Wisdom*, 181n6
descent from heaven to dwell with people (Sir 24:8; Wis 9:10), 48
divine power-presence conveyed by angels, the Word, glory, wisdom, power, spirit, the name (LXX), **54**
Dodd, *Interpretation of FG*, Wisdom and the Word, 46
FG's Prologue "an intro. to Jesus as Sophia, the feminine face of God" (Scott, *Sophia and the Johannine Jesus*), 50
The Fourth Gospel and Jewish Wisdom (LXX), tbl.3. A., **46–49**
gives the righteous knowledge of holy (Wis 10:10), 48
humans formed by your Wisdom (Wis 9:1–2), 47
"I am" sayings in Isis, Deutero-Isa., Wisdom, and FG (MacRae), 109;
"I am" style to depict the cosmological and soteriological role of Jesus/Wisdom/Isis/Thunder/Perfect Mind, **106n10**
instructs and forms them (Wis 9:11; Sir 4;11, 17), **44**
interchangeable names in Odes and FG (Word, Wisdom) and Three Forms has more diverse (Mother, Father, Son, etc.), 50n12
Jesus as God's agent of creation, sharing divine glory, a light shining in the dark,teaching and revealing wisdom to people who would receive it (Reinhartz), **50**
Jesus Revealer of God's wisdom and knowledge from above, **234**
Jewish wisdom context for FG (Ashton, *Interpretation of John*), 46n5
Job
power of wisdom disclosed (11:6–7), 48
preexistent wisdom revealed (28:12–28), 46, 97
wisdom escapes human notice (28:21; cf. John 1:10), 48
Mack, *Logos und Sophia*, 46n5
Philo, *Fug.* 97 "The highest word (*logos*) of God, who is the fountain of wisdom (*sophia*), in order that by drinking of that stream he may find everlasting life," 60
for Philo word and wisdom are personifications of God and distinct powers or (divine) agents of God (Schenck), 57
power passes to Adam when Yaltabaoth blows on him (Ap. John 19.15–33), 176
Prologue's context informed by Genesis, wisdom, gnostic myth (G. Robinson), 179
Ringe, *Wisdom's Friends*, 46n5
Schenke, Die Tenenz der Weisheit zur Gnosis" pessimistic wisdom (Qoh) on a continuum toward Gnosticism, 45n2, **181n6**
tests her disciples, forms them (Sir 41:17–18), 49
texts are examples of personified attributes of God portrayed as his principal agent, God's Wisdom, and God's Word, 46–47
Tg. Neof. Gen. 1:1 with wisdom the Word created, **92**
Willett, Michael E. *Wisdom Christology in the Fourth Gospel*; Witherington,. *Jesus the Sage*, 46n5

Wisdom of Solomon (Wis)
- 9:10 Wisdom's descent from heaven to dwell with people (Wis 9:10), 48
- 9:11 Wisdom instructs & forms them (Wis 9:11), **44**
- 10:10 Wisdom gives the righteous knowledge of holy (Wis 10:10), 48
- is Jewish wisdom with Stoic, Platonic ideas, 120, 125
- written in Greek, between 100 to 50 BCE. Both Sir and Wis probably from Egypt, 45
- See also Wisdom (Sophia, Hokmah)

word (Gk. *logos*, Heb. *dabar*, Aram. *mēmra*)
- Aram.: *mēmra*, *mēmer* "word," often substituted for "God." "*Mēmra* of the Lord" not only as substitute for YHWH implies more thorough theol. of God's name, 91–92
- combination of targumic Word with Shekinah glory (*Yegara*), glory of *Shekinah* (cf. John 1:14). Related to *Mēmra* (as Divine Creator) is *Dibbera* (fem. of Heb. *dabar*, "word," **92**
- in LXX, *logos* is a trans. of the Heb. *dabar*. Both have wide range of meanings: speech, dialogue, narrative, oracle, matter, thing, **40n21**
- what rabbis applied to Torah, FG applied to Jesus the Word, 87
- when my glory (*Yegara*) passes by, I will shield you with my Word until I have passed by. Then I will remove the word (*Dibbera*) of my glory," you will perceive what's in front of me, but not what's behind me (Tg. Onq. Exod. 33:20–23), **95**
- "by word of the Lord heavens were made" (Ps 33:6) in Mek. Shirata 10 (Exod 15:17–21), **85**

Word (*Memra* of Lord revealed as the "I am who is"(Tg. Ps.-J. Deut 32:39), 92
See also Logos; Targumim

world (*kosmos*), the
- FG's concept of the world (*kosmos*): negative (John 1:10; 7:7; 8:23), neutral sense (3:16–17; 6:14), positive (1:1–4; Gen 1), human habitation (4:42; 12:47), the public (7:4; 8:26), 19n17, **179**
- John 1:10 "He was in the world," Philo, *Conf.* 97, "Logos was in world (*kosmos*), 57
- Marrow, "Κόσμος in John." *CBQ*, different views of "world" in antiquity, 119

works
- Aristobulus wrote of the voice of God at creation "not as words spoken but as construction of works/things, the whole *creation* of the world as words (Eusebius, *Praep. Ev.* 13.12.3–4), **57n6**
- "believe me that I am in the Father and the Father in me, but if you do not believe, then believe because of the works (*erga*) themselves" (John 14:11), 214
- God determined all that he created to his design when they came into being, at their appointed time, they will fulfill all their works according to his glorious design (1QS III, 15–16), 72
- Jesus, called a Samaritan & accused of having a demon (8:48–49), perhaps his Judean critics here perceived his works similar to Simon the magician in Samaria (Acts 8:9). FG, suspicious of such magicians, portrays the work of Jesus in contrast to them (John 10:10–15), 157n29
- Works of God (Gk. *erga*, John 6:28; 9:3; Heb. *ma'aseh*, 1 QS IV, 4; CD II, 14–15); evil works of men (John 3:19; 1 QS IV, 10, 20), **73**

"the works I do in my Father's name testify of me" (John 10:25b; Egerton Papyrus on John 3:2), 224

worship

Charlesworth suggests tensions between worship on Mt. Gerizim and on Mt. Zion (John 4:20–21) seem to antedate 70 CE because *after* that time, the Jerusalem temple was destroyed, and worship *only* continued on Gerizim, **156**

in contrast to the mystery cults with their idol worship (*Protr.* 1–4), Clement of Alex. presents Christianity as religion with "truly sacred mysteries," (12.20), **109**

in FG, Jesus and his followers did not completely detach from Jerusalem temple worship, as Qumran sect had, 70

in *general* sense, both FG's audience and the Isis cult seem to be close-knit communities, that center upon worship of the divine in similar language of salvation, hope, devotion, 110

"the hour is coming when true worshipers will worship the Father in spirit and truth" (John 4:23; cf. new temple worship, Tg. Isa 53:5), 95

on the Jewish lectionary for possible FG backdrop, see Guilding, *FG and Jewish Worship*, 91n16

Justin Martyr and Tertullian would have agreed with Paul (1 Cor 10:14, 20). in rabbinic thought idol worship is condemned (b. Shab. 2.6; 9.3; b. Yeb. 4.12), 110

MacRae notes how a local, near eastern cult (Isis) was transformed into a universal symbol of worship, as a result of Hellenization, **11n43**

only 200 MSS of the DSS are sectarian, dealing with liturgy (prayers, worship calendar, poetry, pesher commentaries), 69

SP adds to Exod 20:14 a commandment affirming Mt. Gerizim as the holy site of worship, 160

Yamauchi, Edwin,

Gnostic Ethics & Mandaean Origins, "pre-Christian date remains hypothetical and speculative," **161n48**

Pre-Christian Gnosticism

criticism of FG and heavenly redeemer myth, 163n52, **166n56**, 177n24

de-Christianized NHL texts?, 168n1

differing contexts, accessibility, and thematic coherence, 8n30; challenge of working with later docs, 125

Gnostic use of Gen a reaction to Christian use? 179n37

late Mandaean texts, 166n53

Mandaean dependence on FG, 166n55

Zebedee, son of. *See* Authorship, of FG

Zimmerman, Ruben,

Christologie der Bilder, explores "Messiah" and other Christological titles, 42n32

"Jesus im Bild Gottes," in Frey and Schnelle, *Kontexte*, compares FG with the OT shepherd imagery to substantiate the claim of Jesus in John 14:9, "whoever has seen me has seen the Father" (cf. John 12:45), 42n31

Zumstein, Jean, "Intratextuality and Intertextuality," Thatcher and Moore, *Anatomies of Narrative Criticism*
- diachronic and synchronic approaches, 12n49
- FG's use of OT the "paradigmatic example" of FG as a "networked text" or intertext that "presumes the existence of *other* writings" **44n41**
- framing devices and repeated themes within FG, not our *central* focus, 9n34
- John 1 provides hermeneutical framework for interpreting FG, 17n8
- John 1–20 "introduces Christ into the narrative, epilogue introduces the narrative into the church," 22n33
- reading FG as an intertext puts a premium on the competence of the readers. The text's meaning is not a set element to be discovered & worked out through exegesis, but emerges through a dialect interplay between the *intention operis* and *intentio lectoris*, **237**
- views 1 John as reception text (or hypotext) of FG that provides correct understanding of FG the reference text (or hypertext) according to the *relecture* model, **34n66**
- use of Scripture (hypotext A) in John 6 (hypertext B) generates new horizons of meaning for both texts (A & B), 41n26
- *See also* Eco, Umberto; Narrative Criticism

www.ingramcontent.com/pod-product-compliance
Lightning Source LLC
Chambersburg PA
CBHW051250300426
44114CB00011B/962